Crisis Management in Acute C

Michael St.Pierre • Gesine Hofinger
Robert Simon

Crisis Management in Acute Care Settings

Human Factors and Team Psychology in a High-Stakes Environment

Third Edition

Springer

Michael St.Pierre
Universitätsklinikum Erlangen
Klinik für Anästhesiologie
Erlangen
Germany

Robert Simon
Harvard University
Boston, MA
USA

Gesine Hofinger
Team HF Hofinger Künzer & Mähler PartG
Remseck
Baden-Württemberg
Germany

ISBN 978-3-319-82351-5 ISBN 978-3-319-41427-0 (eBook)
DOI 10.1007/978-3-319-41427-0

Softcover reprint of the hardcover 3rd edition 2016

Printed on acid-free paper

This Springer imprint is published by Springer Nature
The registered company is Springer International Publishing AG Switzerland

As authors we would like to dedicate this book to very special people

… to Ulrike who is the love of my life, and to three wonderful adult children: Marie-Catherine, Yannis Christoph, and Julian David

… Michael

… to my family, Michael, Daniel, and Julius, with gratefulness and love

… Gesine

… to my dear wife, Diane, and our children and in-law children: Bartholomew, Katie, Peter, Molly, Gabriel, Juliet, Xander, Kai, HueLinh and Hai. And to the 12 lights of our lives, the grandchildren: Oskar, Sadie, Henry, Malcolm, Desmond, Elena, Lewis, Lucie, Aquinnah, Larson, Kenny and Larissa

… Robert

… and to all our clinician colleagues who helped us shape this book by generously sharing their personal experiences caring for critically ill or injured patients when the stakes are high and time is limited. The dedication, skills and intelligence they apply every day to the sick and injured is awesome.

Foreword

The most significant exclusion from the third edition of *Crisis Management in Acute Care Settings* is any mention of Murphy's Law: *Anything that can go wrong, will go wrong*. Perhaps, Michael St.Pierre, Gesine Hofinger, and Robert Simon were uncomfortable about including a pseudoscientific law of nature that does not really exist? Or were they aware of the controversies surrounding the origin of this eponym? Whatever the case, this new edition of their now classic book does everything possible to explain the drivers of Murphy's Law in acute care settings.

Well covered is the notion that when people are under stress, time pressure, fatigue, or working within poorly designed structures many things can go wrong. This book discusses how these organizational, psychological, cognitive, social, or environmental systems can unravel. Importantly, the authors also reveal how to prevent or interrupt their progression to disaster in clinical practice.

With practical case examples and admirable parsimony, this book covers complex and diverse fields in easy-to-read prose. This book is a one-stop shop for those of us teaching or attempting to practice crisis management in acute care settings.

For those just needing a thumbnail sketch of topics such as cognition or communication under stress, the "in a nutshell" sections provide elegant one-page summaries synthesizing extensive research. The "quick tips" sections show clinicians and educators how to adapt their clinical management and teamwork to best crisis resource management practices. For those running blogs or journal clubs on teamwork or high reliability, each chapter can be read and discussed in depth; for those designing teamwork or CRM experiences, the extensive bibliography of each chapter provides a trove of evidence to explain the rationale behind learning objectives.

It is hard for all of us healthcare educators and quality and safety professionals to accept what Charles Perrow argued in his visionary book *Normal Accidents: Living with High-Risk Technologies*: that neither constant vigilance nor system design can prevent error and accidents in complex systems. Accidents and errors should not surprise us; rather, they are a normal part of what happens when humans interact with each other in complex technologies and complex organizations. But *Crisis Management in Acute Care Settings* gives us a fighting chance to reduce error and improve performance even when the odds are against us.

Jenny Rudolph
Harvard Medical School and Center for Medical Simulation
Boston, MA, USA

Daniel B. Raemer
Harvard Medical School and Center for Medical Simulation
Boston, MA, USA

Preface

Alone we can do so little; together we can do so much.

Helen Keller

Providing safe patient care in an acute care setting has always been and still is one of the great challenges of health care. On a regular basis, healthcare professionals are faced with problems that are unexpected and threaten the lives and well-being of our patients. During these events we don't have time for in-depth reflection, yet these high risk, time-constrained situations call for swift and correct decisions.

There are research traditions that focus on the clinical aspects of high acuity, emergent medical crises, e.g., multi-trauma, heart attacks, etc. Equally, there are rich and informative lines of research on psychology, teamwork, and organizational behavior. Until the advent of this book, there has been no single source in the field of healthcare that provided ways to think about and act on the combination of those disciplines: medicine, the psychology of human behavior under stress, teamwork for high-performance teams, and modern organizational behavior. The intent of this book is not only to organize and provide an overview of those disciplines as they apply to healthcare, but to make the fundamental concepts accessible, understandable, and actionable by interested clinicians – all in one place. After reading this book, those who want to pursue advanced or specific understandings and applications are encouraged to take advantage of the burgeoning literature on the subject of performing patient care in high acuity, time-stressed, high risk situations. The journals cited in chapter reference sections are a good place to start and your own discipline's journals may well contain enlightening information. We encourage you to use journals that you might not normally use because many useful findings are quite likely to come from disciplines outside of healthcare.

A set of skills is needed to enable healthcare professionals to reliably translate knowledge into safe patient care despite varying and often hindering circumstances. These skills are what the following pages are about. You will not encounter any information concerning the clinical management of critical situations throughout the entire book. Instead, the book at hand focuses on people: on healthcare providers from various specialties and professions who are expected to manage the unexpected: nurses, physicians, paramedics, and technicians. All of them have a set of clinical *and* human factors-related skills that enables or constrains their ability to manage critical situations. All of these practitioners can improve their performance by thoughtful application of the concepts, theories, and practical advice presented in Parts II, III, and IV of this book.

The first part of the book addresses basic principles of errors, complexity, and human behavior. It is designed to provide an overview of the problems that humans face in complex organizations in general and healthcare in particular. Data on human error and accidents are presented and an argument is made about why the characteristics of acute clinical care intensify the possibility for errors. The part presents a modern view of errors in healthcare, a view that the authors of this book subscribe to: Errors in healthcare are predominantly caused by people who are smart, capable, care about doing their best, and who are committed to improving their practice – but the human condition, poor teamwork, and organizational weaknesses combine to create circumstances that lead to poor performance or errors.

Parts II, III, and IV focus on three areas of importance regarding how we function within healthcare organizations when there is an emergent, high risk, temporally bound crisis: individual, team, and organizational. Part II focuses on the psychology of our shared human condition. Despite the best of intentions and superior clinical training, healthcare providers have inescapable cognitive limitations that contribute to errors and hinder successful crisis management. To help healthcare providers better understand their natural strengths and weaknesses as human decision makers and action takers, this part provides an outline of the way the human mind operates when the stakes are high and time is limited. Humans think and act the way they do because natural underlying psychological mechanisms provide an approach to cope with environmental demands. Given that healthcare providers are normally trying their best to help their patients, we present why errors are not the product of irrational psychological mechanisms, but instead are rational and originate from otherwise useful mental and psychological processes – most of which stem from and are common to all humans. Some of them, like communication patterns, can be changed. Other mechanisms have absolute limits or are very difficult to change or reorient – our perception, attention, motivations, feelings, and thoughts are not entirely subject to our will.

The third part of the book attends to teamwork considerations in healthcare.[1] Acute medical care, in fact all of modern healthcare, is not delivered by one person; instead it is provided through the combined efforts of professionals from various disciplines and specialties cooperating for a patient's sake. In emergent, acute situations, a team is all in one place at the same time and must share information and coordinate actions when it is highly likely that no one has all the needed information and no one can take all the needed actions. Performance-limiting factors that result in less than optimal care or errors are very often the result of applying weak, uninformed, or faulty teamwork practices. Many weaknesses in teamwork are amenable to training with feedback complemented by periodic reinforcement. Thus, knowledge of successful strategies for improving team performance and having opportu-

[1] Thanks to Walter Eppich, M.D., from the Feinberg School of Medicine, Northwestern University for contributions made to this book's 2nd Edition's teamwork section.

nities for practice and reinforcement will most certainly create a safer and more effective clinical environment.

The fourth part of the book focuses on human behavior in organizations. Organizations and their systems are deeply embedded in the culture of every healthcare organization and resistant to change. Changing the culture and putting effective systems in place is especially hard work. It is our firm belief, however, that raising human factors to a higher level of importance in organizational design and daily work habits will have a high payoff in terms of effectiveness and safety. There are many successful organizations around the world that place these considerations high among their priorities, e.g., aviation, nuclear power, and a number of other businesses that seek to be high reliability organizations.

There are two ways you may want to read the book. You may follow through the text according to its inner logic, chapter by chapter. Or you may prefer to read selected chapters. The book has a modular character in which every chapter stands alone and can be read without knowledge of previous ones. To avoid excessive redundancy, basic concepts are explained only once and then cross-referenced.

Every chapter follows the same pattern: A case study from an acute care situation illustrates central aspects of the subject matter and is then used as the reference point for the topic.[2] Every chapter provides answers to the same questions: "What is the relevance of the subject? What problems can be explained by this particular human factor? What can we transfer to our clinical environment? How can we apply the knowledge to improve clinical effectiveness and patient safety?" To enhance practicability, the chapters on individual and team factors offer "tips for daily practice" that are meant to provide helpful advice. Every chapter ends with a short "in a nutshell" paragraph summarizing the essential points made in the chapter.

A book like this one requires the combined perspectives of several disciplines. This book grew out of a longstanding cooperation and friendship between a physician with acute medical care background (anesthesia, intensive care, prehospital emergency medicine) providing simulation-based team training at his institution (St.Pierre) and two psychologists who have spent their professional lives doing research in psychology, teamwork, and organizational behavior, and who have taken those findings to develop and provide training to high performance teams in aviation (Simon), crisis management (Hofinger), and healthcare (Hofinger, Simon).

To write this book, each of us shared our expertise with one another so that we could write a cohesive book that is understandable and useful for clinicians seeking to improve their practice and/or provide a useful basic text for those starting in the field. The result we aimed for is a text rooted in the clinical environment of acute clinical care wrapped in a cohesive theoretical framework of cognitive, social, and organizational psychology. The clinical relevance and the practicability of this book have been our major concerns. Since this is our third edition of the book, we are pretty confident that we are doing something that many have deemed valuable.

---

[2]Thanks to Toni Walzer, M.D., from the Center for Medical Simulation and Harvard Medical School in Boston for providing us special expertise and insights for the obstetrics-oriented vignette in Chap. 15.

For us, this book has been a teamwork experience at its best. The process of writing this book has been a challenging yet fruitful time for each of us. All of us contributed to every chapter; we all take the responsibility for the inevitable errors. We have benefitted from feedback on the first and second editions and will continue to be grateful for any remarks concerning the content of this book.

With the advent of the third edition, we continued working to enhance the book with additional information and even added a chapter. As with our endeavors toward the second edition, we found ourselves happily taking the opportunity to collectively revisit, rethink, and rewrite a number of concepts presented in the earlier book. We also continued to improve the writing and sharpen the description of the concepts and examples. While two of us are native German language speakers (St. Pierre and Hofinger), a native English speaker and experienced educational psychologist (Simon) had substantial influence over how the book's content was expressed in terms of the English language and the behavioral science presented in the book. The result, we hope, is an improved and even more worthwhile book that we are anxious to put in the hands of the interested reader.

Erlangen, Germany — Michael St.Pierre
Remseck, Germany — Gesine Hofinger
Boston, MA, USA — Robert Simon

Contents

Part I

Basic Principles: Error, Complexity, and Human Behavior

The first part of this book addresses the relevance of human error as a contributing factor to incidents and accidents in acute medical care. Basic principles of human error, complexity, and human action are outlined.

Chapter 1 focuses on the human factors that provide the potential to trigger critical situations as well as the skills to master them. A review of published data on the incidence of human error and accidents in acute medical care underscores the fact that human behavior dominates the risk to modern socio-technical systems such as healthcare. Nevertheless, we should not view human factors as a weakness in the system; instead, we know that understanding human factors will enhance performance and aid in our ability to control and mitigate errors and mishaps.

Providing healthcare in a high-stakes, time-compressed environment has a number of properties that make it considerably more challenging than decision-making in everyday contexts. Chapter 2 describes the characteristics that have to do with the "complexity of the working environment." The response of healthcare professionals corresponds with the levels of familiarity with a task or an environment and the amount of practice the provider has had with taking care of patients, real or simulated, in that *same stress-filled* physiological state.

Chapter 3 provides workable definitions on error and contrasts two current perspectives (consequential and causal classification) that give rise to two different approaches for dealing with human fallibility, i.e., person-based and system-based approach. Emphasis is placed on the fact that accidents occur as a result of latent conditions that combine with other factors and local triggering events to breach the defensive barriers of the system.

Chapter 4 provides a description of how humans arrive at decisions. The internal logic of one's action is presented and an argument is made on how human behavior does not strictly follow the consistency or objectivity of completely logical thoughts and actions. Instead, behavior is influenced by multiple factors including motivation and emotions. The combination of multiple factors influences decisions and, hence, action.

1 The Human Factors: Errors and Skills

Case Study

During an afternoon shift, two hemodynamically unstable patients are admitted to the cardiac ICU (CCU), one immediately after the other. The resident physician's attempt to stabilize both patients nearly overwhelms him. Because of this, he is unable to give adequate attention to a third patient being anticoagulated with warfarin who had several episodes of coffee-ground emesis during the previous 2 h. After finally stabilizing the two new admissions, the resident prepares for an upper endoscopy, but the third patient suddenly becomes hemodynamically unstable. The patient has a recent hemoglobin value of 6.9 g/dL.

With a working diagnosis of acute upper gastrointestinal (GI) bleeding, the patient receives several peripheral IV lines. Crystalloid infusions are started. Six units of crossmatched packed red blood cells (PRBCs) are ordered from the blood bank. Coincidentally, the blood bank is short of personnel and unusually burdened by multiple orders for blood products. The 6 units of PRBCs are sent together with 2 units of PRBCs for another patient in the CCU. The blood products arrive in the CCU while one of the two recently admitted patients is still being stabilized. After a quick glance at the bag containing the PRBCs, the resident asks the nurse to start the blood transfusion. Within minutes of starting the first infusion of blood, the patient complains of dizziness and shortness of breath and deteriorates rapidly. The resident then focuses his complete attention on the treatment of this patient.

Severe and generalized erythema and edema, together with hemodynamic instability and respiratory distress, indicate a severe anaphylactic reaction. Influenced by a comment from a nurse concerning the transfusion, the physician suspects a transfusion error and stops the infusion immediately. The patient is then anesthetized and intubated. Controlled ventilation is difficult due to severe bronchospasm. Under high-dose continuous infusion of

M. St.Pierre et al., *Crisis Management in Acute Care Settings*,
DOI 10.1007/978-3-319-41427-0_1

catecholamines, aggressive volume resuscitation, and administration of corticosteroids and histamine receptor antagonists, the resident manages to stabilize the patient's hemodynamic situation and to improve the bronchospasm. During the following hours, the patient develops severe disseminated intravascular coagulation (DIC) leading to uncontrollable upper GI bleeding. Despite massive transfusion with coagulation factors and blood products, the patient dies several hours later as a result of his uncontrolled bleeding.

Despite maximum therapeutic efforts by motivated caregivers, an intensive care patient suffered harm from a medical error and died several hours later as a consequence of a transfusion reaction. At first glance, the cardiology resident is most likely to be identified as the responsible agent. After all, he was the person in direct contact with the patient, he gave orders for the transfusion, and he did not adhere to standard treatment protocols, thus displaying negligence in the transfusion process. A closer look, however, reveals additional factors that contributed to the adverse event: a workload that overwhelmed the resident with several patients requiring a rapidly executed high level of care, staff shortage in the blood bank, the simultaneous arrival of packed red blood cells (PRBCs) for two different patients, and the acceptance of final responsibility for the transfusion on behalf of the nurse. None of these factors alone would have been able to compromise patient safety. Taken together, however, the factors combined and managed to breach the defensive barriers within the system. The unlikely temporal combination of several contributing factors on different levels within an organization created a condition where a one single moment of inattention by the resident triggered a deadly outcome. The human error, while quite obvious, was only one link in a longer chain of circumstances.

Faulty individual actions represent only one aspect of human factors in a medical high-stakes environment. It is often overlooked that the remarkable ability to rapidly detect, diagnose, and treat a medical emergency or critically ill patient is rooted in human factors. Healthcare providers can only perform successfully in critical situations because the human factors enable them to do so. Far more often than not, healthcare professionals provide safe and efficient patient care even under unfavorable circumstances.

1.1 Human Factors in Healthcare: The Problem

More than a decade ago, the Quality of Healthcare in America Committee of the Institute of Medicine (IOM) issued a report "To Err Is Human: Building a Safer Healthcare System" (Kohn et al. 1999), which examined the quality of the US healthcare delivery system. The results of the study were alarming and stirred up healthcare systems all around the globe: Year after year, a staggering figure of

44,000 people, and perhaps as many as 98,000 people, died in US hospitals as a result of preventable medical error. Even when using the lower estimate, the number of deaths attributable to preventable medical errors exceeded the mortality rate of severe trauma, breast cancer, and HIV.

The IOM report spurred patient safety initiatives around the globe and triggered an unparalleled endeavor to identify medical errors and design interventions to prevent and mitigate their effect. One of the main conclusions of the report was in diametrical opposition to hitherto existing assumptions within the healthcare community; that is, the majority of medical errors were not a result of individual recklessness or incompetence, but instead were caused by faulty systems, processes, and conditions that predictably led people to make mistakes or failed to help prevent mistakes. The idea of a "systemic approach" to safety was no novelty in a number of other high-stakes industries, but it was a relatively new notion in healthcare. A sizable body of knowledge and successful experiences from other high-risk industries had proven that mistakes can best be prevented by systematically designing safety into processes, moving away from a culture of blaming individuals, and seeking to become open organizations where the best and most reliable solutions to problems were valued regardless of *who* came up with the best ideas.

Five years after the Institute of Medicine's call for a national effort to make healthcare safer, an appraisal of progress warranted cautious optimism as the groundwork for improving safety seemed to have been laid successfully: The tone of conversation in healthcare had changed, attitudes and organizations had been impacted, healthcare leaders had learned a great deal about safety, and competence and knowledge of safety practices had increased. The authors did note, however, that progress was frustratingly slow (Leape and Berwick 2005).

Upon nearing the report's 10-year anniversary, this pioneering spirit has given way to disillusionment; despite a flurry of activity during the first years following the publication, efforts to reduce the harm caused by the medical care system are still too few and fragmented. Little appears to have changed as significant barriers are still encountered when attempting to track progress (Mathews and Pronovost 2008). In most countries, neither a national entity nor a systematic process exists to promote, measure, and track patient safety. Despite a decade of work, there is little reliable evidence that we are any better off today than at the turn of the century when the IOM report was written (Jewell and McGiffert 2009). There is some cause for optimism, however. It is found in the growth of simulation in healthcare, an increased emphasis on teamwork, improved technology such as nearly fail-safe medical administration regimens, improved error reporting systems, and enhanced investigation of errors. One anecdotal finding by the authors is that the phrase *patient safety* has crept into daily use in our healthcare institutions. The technology and culture are changing, but ever so slowly. Challenges remain ahead of us. One of the areas that promises significant results in terms of patient safety and performance improvement is understanding how humans work in stressful environments and then designing our systems and training regimens to accommodate the strengths and weaknesses of the people who function within our healthcare systems.

1.2 What Are the "Human Factors"?

1.2.1 Differing Definitions of "Human Factors"

By the beginning of the twenty-first century, it was common knowledge that human behavior dominates the risk to modern socio-technical systems. We owe this insight to the relentless efforts over four decades of interdisciplinary research groups from the field of cognitive sciences, social psychology, organizational behavior, anthropology, sociology, and reliability engineering. They have been studying aspects of the way humans relate to the world around them with the vision that operational performance and safety in the workplace will be improved through the application of an understanding of human factors in the design of equipment, systems, working methods, and training. The generic term *human factors* has several meanings (Fig. 1.1):

- The *human factors sciences* comprise a variety of scientific traditions mostly rooted in engineering, work science, and psychology. The human factors sciences study anatomical, physiological, psychological, and social aspects of workers in their working environment with the objective of optimizing safety, comfort, and efficiency. It elucidates the interaction of environmental, organizational, and job factors with human and individual characteristics that coincide to influence behavior at work that effect health and safety.
- The application of the theoretical principles, data, and methods to design, development, and deployment of tools, machines, systems, jobs, environments, and services in order to optimize human well-being and overall system performance (for our purposes, system performance includes patient safety) is called *human factors engineering* (HFE) also known as *ergonomics*.
- From a *science of humanities* point of view, human factors are physical, psychological, cognitive, and social properties of an individual that influence interaction with

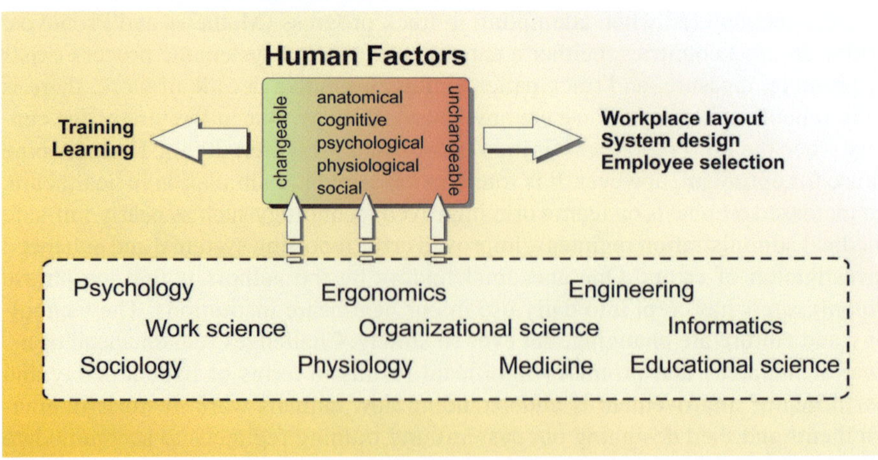

Fig. 1.1 Human factors as scientific discipline and field of application. Some human factors are amenable to training and learning interventions, whereas others can only be addressed by systemic changes

the environment and with social and technological systems. Colloquially, the term *human factors* is often used to differentiate human cognitive or behavioral properties from "technical factors," e.g., design, usability, etc., of systems, machines, and equipment. However, this perspective fails to consider a central issue of human factors because it is not the examination of isolated human properties but rather the *interaction* of humans with their social and technological environment and the way organizational factors influence daily practice and managing critical situations.

- Some aspects of human action regulation (e.g., information processing, decision-making, motivation, emotions, task execution; Chap. 4) and of teamwork can be changed by learning processes and are therefore amenable to training and learning interventions. Other human properties (e.g., basic mechanisms of perception, regulation of attention, fatigue, somatic stress response, personality, etc.), in contrast, cannot be altered by means of learning interventions. Instead, systemic interventions such as workplace layout, system design, and employee selection help to address these shortcomings. Widespread generic terms for the human factors amenable to training interventions are *nontechnical skills* and, less often used, *soft skills* and *para-technical skills*. However, labeling these skills as "nontechnical" seems rather unfortunate, as many communication techniques can and should be learned like any other skills (Chap. 12).

1.2.2 Facts and Fictions: Misconceptions of "Human Factors" in Healthcare

Interest in human factors has increased across healthcare communities worldwide. It is now widely accepted that support of the cognitive and physical work of healthcare professionals and human-centered workplace design help to enhance patient safety. However, there is a growing concern among human factor specialists that there has been an inadequate integration of human factors principles and methods into healthcare, leading to several basic misconceptions (e.g., Carayon et al. 2012; Catchpole 2013; Russ et al. 2013). These misconceptions are not of a mere academic nature but likely hinder healthcare improvement and slow the integration of human factors into healthcare:

- Despite embracing the notion that "safety is a system problem" and the widespread rhetoric of a "systemic approach," the focus within healthcare continues to be on the person and his or her behavior. Superficially, the person-centered approach (e.g., "naming, blaming, shaming") has been abandoned – people are no longer pilloried in public. However, as the response to failure often consists of "re-educating" people, making "human factors training" mandatory, and warning them to be "more diligent," other contributing factors that contributed to an incident are less likely to be fully taken into account and adequately addressed. Ultimately, if the understanding of *human factors* is reduced to *human failure*, the term is only a semantic surrogate for "blaming" (Catchpole 2013).
- A preferred strategy in healthcare is to achieve patient safety by means of right behavior and well-defined processes. This strategy, however, neither identifies

nor removes system hazards, nor does it incorporate human factors engineering design principles to optimize specific work system elements. One of the main reasons for that might be found in the loose relationship between developer, industry, and user. In addition, training is easier to implement and less expensive than changes in the work environment.
- The end user of a system, medical device, or healthcare information technology (IT) – physicians, nurses, paramedics, and patients – is normally not part of the conversation of designers and human factors specialists. This partly explains why established principles of human factors engineering regarding the implementation of medical devices, management, employee working conditions, training, and design are rarely followed (Carayon et al. 2012).

Because this book is mainly directed at healthcare professionals in acute patient care who want to ensure safe patient care even under emergency conditions, the focus of the following chapters will be on psychological and organizational human factors. However, we deem it necessary to emphasize that these human factors have to be addressed in the broader context of how care is delivered within each unit, clinical site, and culture. Only with those considerations in mind will we achieve the desired good results of our collective thoughtfulness.

1.3 Levels of Human Factors

It took the healthcare community a long time to begin to integrate these findings into daily practice. It started to happen after healthcare's close resemblance with other high-risk socio-technical systems had been realized and accepted. In these domains, the analysis of catastrophic breakdowns of high-hazard enterprises (e.g., Three Mile Island, Bhopal, Cernobyl, *Challenger*) revealed a recurrent pattern: 70–80 % of the accidents were not caused by technological failures but instead were the result of inadequacies in problem solving, faulty decision-making, and substandard or nonexistent teamwork.

The remarkably high percentages of human factors-related mishaps are not surprising, considering that people design, build, operate, maintain, organize, and manage these systems. For this reason, human factors sciences address critical issues such as

- *Physical characteristics* (e.g., the negative impact of noise on concentration)
- *Cognitive characteristics* (e.g., perception, attention, information processing)
- *Social/behavioral characteristics* (e.g., in the context of leadership and group process)
- *Engineering and design* (e.g., equipment, physical work environment, task design, work processes, and organizational structures)

The central theme of human factors sciences is that individuals are an integral part of healthcare systems and that their abilities and limitations must be accounted for when optimizing the overall system's performance.

Another central tenet is that human error, in contrast to prevailing assumptions, is not the same as negligence, sloppiness, incompetence, or lack of motivation on the part of the healthcare provider. On the contrary, serious errors are often committed by highly motivated and experienced people (Amalberti and Mosneron-Dupin 1997). Most of the time, human error is the result of normal cognitive processes interacting with systemic factors.

Despite the results from industrial accident investigations, the healthcare community has been slow to participate in discussions of human factors-related errors. Public scrutiny of medical errors was avoided for the sake of reducing exposure to litigation. Only in the past two decades has the medical community begun to find ways to take a broader and more exacting look at medical error. As a result of the increasing openness, the 70–80 % contribution of human error as trigger for incidents and accidents has been confirmed for the medical high-stakes environment (e.g., Cooper et al. 1978; Hollnagel 1993; Reason 1997; Williamson et al. 1993; Wright et al. 1991).

The assessment that the interaction between normal cognitive processes and systemic factors are responsible for critical situations is also true for the dynamics of accident causation in the ICU case study presented earlier in this chapter: A multitude of organizational factors (e.g., human resource allocation, lack of supervision, staff qualification; Chaps. 14 and 15) were hidden as latent failures within the system for a considerable time until they combined with other factors and local triggering events (Chap. 3). The unforeseen combination of factors opened a window of accident opportunity. All those latent factors then needed only a moment of inattention by a healthcare professional to trigger the accident.

In order to fully understand human error and its implications for effectiveness and safety in complex systems, an understanding of the basic principles of human cognition and its effect on individual and team behaviors is indispensable. The same principles apply to management and organizational levels, and on an even larger scale, to the political and legal framework of the healthcare system (Fig. 1.2).

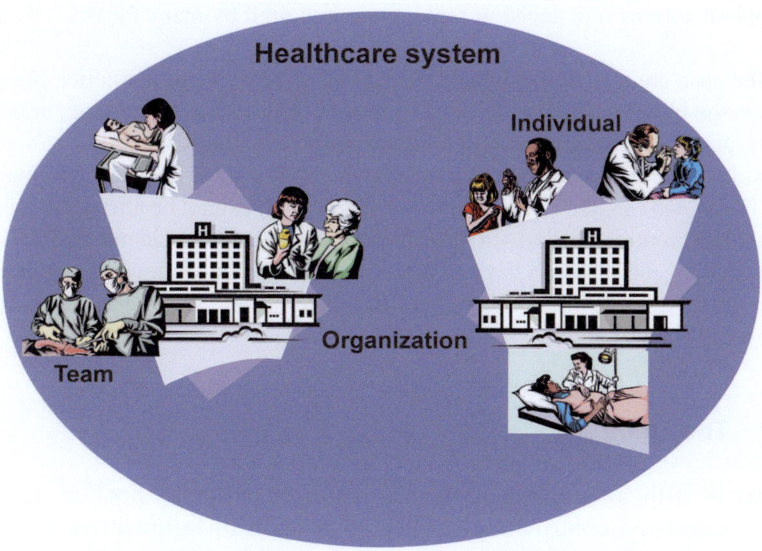

Fig. 1.2 The different levels of patient care that human factors research addresses

1.3.1 The Individual

Although human error can manifest in various ways, there are nevertheless only a few cognitive principles that contribute to these failures. These principles can be identified on the level of perception, information management, and decision-making, but we also must consider emotion and motivation. Some examples that are further explained in Chaps. 4, 5, 6, 7, 8, 9, and 10 are as follows:

- Behavior always follows the "psycho-logic" of action regulation (Chap. 4). There is no such thing as a "purely rational" action.
- Humans do not perceive reality. Instead, humans "construct" their worldview.
- Thinking and reasoning can be related to two distinctively separate cognitive systems developed through evolution ("dual-process account of reasoning"; Chap. 6). One system processes information unconsciously and is associative, effortless, and rapid ("System 1"), whereas the other process is rule based, analytic, controlled, demanding of cognitive capacity, and slow ("System 2").
- Heuristics and cognitive bias lead to a rapid and unconscious termination of the decision-making process. Once the decision is made, the result is not usually cross-checked by conscious thought.
- Humans tend to adjust information to fit their preferred or usual mental model instead of challenging their current point of view. Data is consciously and unconsciously selected and distorted to fit present assumptions.
- Humans try to defend their feeling of competence at nearly any cost. More important than the solution of a problem, as vital as it may be for the patient, may be the necessity of feeling that the situation or a relevant aspect of it is under control.
- Problem solving and decision-making are impaired by many factors.

In the case study, the physician's perceptual error – he did not notice the wrong name on the blood packs – is obvious. Errors in information processing, attentional deficits, and failure in teamwork are not easily observable (Chap. 4).

Besides the aforementioned principles, which are part of the normal human cognitive fabric, we can identify other human factors that cannot be altered by means of learning interventions but which nevertheless contribute to incidents and accidents. These unchangeable factors have to be taken into account, and workplace layout as well as social and technical elements of the system have to be designed to support employees in their daily tasks.

1.3.2 The Team

Compared with an individual, teams represent a larger pool of cognitive resources and can contribute a substantial amount of information, situational models, and proposed courses of action. In addition, all team members can shoulder workload. The physician in the case study lacked this kind of support.

The presence of others, however, can sometimes degrade performance of an individual team member. If basic principles of a successful team process are neglected, or if teams are under stress, internal team dynamics can develop that lead to lower performance (Chaps. 11, 12, and 13). In such a case, the following occurs:

- Team members tend to conform their opinion to the majority in the team.
- Legitimate concerns are not articulated, and criticism is withheld due to perceived hierarchy, obsessive deference to authority, or when a team member is afraid to appear wrong.
- Misunderstanding may result from the use of ambiguous terminology.
- Groups tend to centralize and speed information flow and decision-making when external pressure arises.

In the case study, leadership and communication were flawed. Moreover, the team was not able to share workload well because not enough staff were available. These causation factors show how dependent team performance is on organizational factors.

1.3.3 The Organization

Healthcare delivery is one of the largest and most complex systems in Western culture. The system is composed of subsystems (e.g., prehospital emergency medical service, hospitals, outpatient clinics, manufacturers) with each having a distinct culture and differing financial, technical, and human resources. A common paradox within healthcare organizational goals is to deliver safe patient care and medical excellence versus economy and cost reduction.

In the case study, examples of organizational factors influencing the transfusion error include staffing of the ICU and blood bank as well as the hierarchical culture that prevented the nurse from challenging perceived unsafe decisions.

Organizations can influence the cost and quality of healthcare by influencing the following variables (Chaps. 14 and 15):

- Structure and processes
- Equipment and technologies
- Human resource management
- Teamwork and leadership
- Communication
- Organizational culture

1.3.4 The Healthcare System

Healthcare organizations operate within a political and legal framework that limits the scope for organizing patient care. The influence of these factors is more difficult to trace than individual or organizational factors, but the data presented in the following section shows their large-scale importance. Some of the factors beyond the influence of individual healthcare organizations are:

- The increasing economic pressure on high costs within healthcare
- The funding of healthcare systems (e.g., general taxation, social health insurance, voluntary or private health insurance)
- Work time regulations
- Regulations enacted by governments
- Professional development and the cost associated with training healthcare providers

1.4 Errors in Acute Patient Care

In the mid-1980s, several interdisciplinary research groups started to investigate the issue of human error in medical high-stakes environments. Because of concern about rising costs of litigation and because anesthetists understood that their task characteristics have much in common with those of more widely studied groups in industrial high-risk settings (e.g., pilots, process control), they were the first to initiate collaborations with human factors specialists (e.g., Cooper et al. 1978; Currie 1989).

The past decade has witnessed an increased awareness of the link between normal human decision behavior with suboptimal care and adverse events, which in retrospect are often termed "human error." As clinical decision-making is the most important characteristic of a healthcare provider in an acute care setting and as some kind of decision-making inevitably precedes deliberate action, emergency physicians and anesthesiologists have taken great interest in understanding cognitive and affective dispositions on the quality of decision-making (e.g., Croskerry 2003, 2008; Stiegler and Tung 2013). Contrary to the tacit assumption that the skills associated with decision-making are acquired during postgraduate training and as a natural byproduct of daily clinical work, evidence seems to underscore the fact that the diagnostic process is systematically influenced by heuristics and biases for novices and experienced clinicians alike (Kahneman 2003).

Because the characteristics of the high-stakes medical work environment challenge human problem solving, decision-making, and teamwork considerably (Chap. 2), it is natural to expect the likelihood for diagnostic errors and active failures in acute patient care (e.g., the OR, ICU, and the emergency dept) to be higher than the error rate in routine task environments (e.g., on the ward).

A large body of scientific work is emerging, but a comprehensive overview on errors in acute patient care is not well established. On one hand, too many issues surrounding the identification of errors and adverse events are still unresolved. For example, we do not know the best form of data collection and reporting. To exhaustively track errors, it is not clear what methods are best or are available with our political and legal environment, e.g., retrospective chart reviews, mandatory reportings, solicited voluntary reportings, surveillance systems, or a direct observation approach (Handler et al. 2000)? Thus, the available data comes from a very heterogeneous and idiosyncratic picture. Given the differing methodological approaches to understanding errors, it is impossible to draw completely accurate conclusions about the "real" magnitude of the problem.

It is worth noting that human behavior is often studied using social and behavioral research paradigms. While behavioral research shares a rigorous process and seeks to show causation in its research design, this is often impossible because real-life settings (such as one might need to use to determine types and frequencies of errors) do not allow for enough control to make causation statements. Thus, the social and behavioral scientist depends on an accumulation of evidence shown through a number of studies to be able to identify a phenomenon. In other words, the behavioral scientist often has to rely on a "preponderance of evidence" in order to understand and name a conclusion.

It is with these limitations that we present the following data; neither do they claim completeness nor do they provide an entirely adequate picture of the problem. What we can do is to give the reader an idea of the nature and scale of errors in acute care medicine. What all the publications have in common is that they do not allow for any definitive conclusion as to whether the frequency of errors increases when healthcare providers have to manage critical situations as compared with routine procedures.

1.4.1 Errors in the Prehospital Emergency Medical Service

Prehospital Emergency Medical Service (EMS) is characterized by constantly changing environments, uncertainty, time pressure, and performance in ad hoc teams. Literature on the nature of adverse events in EMS is relatively scant and tends to be focused on the *appropriateness of on-scene performance* and on errors related to skill performance issues. Authors have reported that the majority of events relate predominantly to errors in clinical judgment: the *unreliability of the primary diagnosis* as compared with the discharge diagnosis, as well as the *paramedics' lack of sound ability to determine medical necessity of ambulance transport*.

Skill performance issues included failed out-of-hospital endotracheal intubations (Wang et al. 2009); drug-related errors such as unfamiliarity with drugs due to infrequent use of the medication, dosage calculation errors, or incorrect dosage given; and nonadherence to guidelines or standardized treatment protocols.

Severe diagnostic errors included unrecognized life-threatening conditions, underestimation of the severity of injury, and an on-site diagnosis different from the discharge diagnosis. The majority of data seems to confirm the unreliability of prehospital diagnoses for adult patients and variances from national prehospital medical care strategies (e.g., physician based: Arntz et al. 1996; EMS/paramedic system: Buduhan and McRitchie 2000; Enderson et al. 1990; Esposito et al. 1999; overview in Bigham et al. 2012). For the treatment of the pediatric population, however, some need for further improvement and training of healthcare providers seems to remain (e.g., Esposito et al. 1999; Peery et al. 1999). Current data analyses question the practice of paramedics' determining whether patients require ambulance transport or not (Rittenberger et al. 2005; Brown et al. 2009).

Table 1.1 Incidence of diagnostic and therapeutic errors in prehospital emergency care

Incidence of error	References
22.7 % of out-of-hospital endotracheal intubations fail	Wang et al. (2009)
Incidence of hypoxia (SpO_2<90 %) and hypotension (SBP <90 mmHg) during on-site rapid sequence induction is 18.3 % and 13 % of patients, respectively	Newton et al. (2008)
Self-reported incidence of medication administration errors in 9.1 % of patients	Vilke et al. (2007)
Medical team's scene diagnostic accuracy of spinal injury was 31 %	Flabouris (2001)
8–24 % of all injuries in adult trauma patients are missed	Buduhan and McRitchie (2000), Linn et al. (1997)
Overlooked injuries in the prehospital setting comprised predominantly injuries to the abdomen (17 %), the pelvis (15 %), and the chest (12 %)	Helm et al. (2013)
Pediatric medication dosing errors by emergency medical services (EMS) paramedics occurred in 34.7 % of drug administrations	Hoyle et al. (2012)
9 % of trauma deaths were deemed preventable and 16 % of pediatric trauma patients received inappropriate care	Peery et al. (1999)
Only 36 % of the patients who met criteria for anaphylaxis had epinephrine administered by emergency medical services (EMS)	Tiyyagura et al. (2014)
The incidence of missed injuries in pediatric trauma is 20 %	Esposito et al. (1999)
Severe errors of assessment by the prehospital emergency physician ("Notarzt") occurred in 3 % of cases	Arntz et al. (1996)
EMS on-scene evaluation misdiagnosed 28 % of stroke/TIA patients	Kothari et al. (1995)

Adverse events and near misses appear to be common among EMS providers but, as in other healthcare domains, the culture discourages sharing this information. Confidential interviews revealed that many EMTs felt that substantial departures from existing protocols were common reasons for the occurrence of errors, as well as lack of standardization across EMS units and healthcare facilities. Incompatibilities between equipment were also cited as likely sources of adverse events (Fairbanks et al. 2008).

The question of whether or not emergency medical services care carries an inherently higher risk for committing an error then the provision of patient care in familiar working situations (i.e., in-hospital) has still to be answered. An overview of errors in the EMS is given in Table 1.1.

1.4.2 Errors in the Emergency Department

The emergency department (ED) presents a unique combination of widely divergent patient characteristics, a broad range of illness severity, and variation in practice settings and protocols that distinguish it from "classical" medical disciplines in other acute medical care specialties (Cosby and Croskerry 2009). These characteristics increase the potential for error or patient harm.

First, many *patients* arrive at the ED rather unprepared as they have had an unexpected encounter with trauma or acute illness: ED patients usually do not carry a concise summary of medical problems or a list with current medication with them, nor does the emergency physician necessarily have access to medical records or to referring physicians.

As the illness is seen only through a small window of focus and time, nurses and physicians often rely mainly on communication with the patient and employ quick diagnostic and disposition procedures. Communication itself may be difficult as patients may be fearful, uncooperative, unconscious, or without personal identification. Many patients who seek care in an ED are at increased risk of adverse events because of the serious nature of their illness: In the face of possible acute medical decompensation, there is a lower margin for error and patients who have reached a point of diminished reserves are less likely to tolerate missteps in their management. Despite this need for carefulness, time constraints, emergent problems, and high acuity force clinicians to make decisions with incomplete information and uncertainty, and they must work in a team environment that depends on others to perform as expected.

One of emergency medicine's distinctive features is that there are no limits to the potential number of patients or the types of illness facing the emergency physician at any one time. The large number of possible differential diagnoses contributes to the element of diagnostic uncertainty and may be responsible for the high rate of errors attributed to diagnostic errors (Thomas et al. 2000). In few other workplace settings, and in no other areas of medicine, task complexity, time constraints, and decision density are as high, and the pace of work is as unremitting and uncertain as in an ED. The necessity to handle multiple demands, to constantly reassess allocation of resources, and to prioritize attention to competing demands facilitates errors in care delivery. In addition, constant interruptions (Chisholm et al. 2000), a quick turnaround of patients with insufficient time to be thorough, and inadequate supervision (Hendrie et al. 2007) aggravate the problem.

Because many EDs around the world are not subspecialized, emergency healthcare providers are confronted with nearly any type of injury or disease. This complexity causes the pediatric population to be at higher risk than adults: Staff without specialized pediatric training and with little experience are expected to provide adequate patient care to infants and children, often without the supplies necessary for handling pediatric emergencies (IOM 2006). As EDs in many large cities are overcrowded and operate at or near full capacity, even a multiple-car highway crash can create havoc in an ED. A major disaster with many casualties would be something that many hospitals do not have adequate capacity to handle.

Because of the complex nature of task performance and the complex decision-making that has to be made in a time-compressed environment, teamwork plays an important role in detecting and preventing adverse events. For example, active failures in trauma patient care include problems arising from the interaction of the trauma team with the patient or other team members (Schaefer et al. 1994). Table 1.2 shows some of the typical teamwork-associated problems and errors encountered in the ED.

Table 1.2 Incidence of diagnostic and therapeutic errors in the emergency department (ED)

Incidence of errors	References
The incidence rates of adverse events and near misses are 4.1 % and 5.4 %, respectively. 37 % of the adverse events were judged to be preventable	Camargo et al. 2012
8.6 % of patients experienced a preventable medical error with a twofold higher incidence during higher levels of ED crowding	Epstein et al. (2012)
Literature review shows 1.3–39 % incidence of missed injuries and delayed diagnoses. 15–22.3 % of patients with missed injuries have clinically significant missed injuries	Pfeifer and Pape 2008
3.5 errors per patients with spinal/cerebral injury are committed; errors contribute to neurological disability	McDermott et al. (2004)
2–3 % of patients with acute myocardial infarction or unstable angina are not hospitalized after presenting at the ED	Pope et al. (2000), McCarthy et al. (1993)
3 % of all adverse events occur in the ED; a high rate is associated with negligence in diagnostics	Kohn et al. (1999)
Per adverse event, an average of 8.8 teamwork failures occur	Risser et al. (1999)
27 % of patients with acute myocardial infarction were missed in the ED due to absence of chest pain or lack of ST elevation in the ECG	Chan et al. (1998)
23 % of all airway management cases show performance deficiencies	Mackenzie et al. (1996)
Diagnostic errors occur in 25 % of all admitted patients	O'Connor et al. (1995)
5.9 % of all trauma patient deaths were considered preventable. The most common single error was failure to appropriately evaluate the abdomen	Davis et al. (1992)
In 9 % of patients, injuries are missed during the initial work-up	Enderson et al. (1990)

1.4.3 Errors in the Intensive Care Unit

Critically ill patients require high-intensity care and may be at especially high risk of iatrogenic injury. The underlying comorbidities, acute organ dysfunctions, and the complexity of care processes make this specialty vulnerable and prone to error.

Many reports confirm the notion that adverse events and serious errors involving critically ill patients are common and often life threatening (e.g., Ahmed et al. 2013; Rothschild et al. 2005). Root causes for errors in the ICU are found in the serious nature of the underlying disease as well as in structural, technical, and organizational deficiencies of the unit. Many studies ascribe adverse events to the chaotic arrangement of tubes and lines, limited physical access to the patient, poor lighting, ambient noise, frequent interruptions, insufficiently labeled drugs, medication errors at the administration stage (Valentin et al. 2009), and to problems with medical devices (e.g., Donchin and Seagull 2002; Sanghera et al. 2007). In addition, workload – as measured by the patient to nurse ratio, the occupancy rate, and the ratio of beds per nurse – and poor coordination and communication between physicians and nurses have been shown to be responsible for a multitude of adverse drug events and treatment errors: The case report is one example of the complexity within the intensive care unit. Recently, a review of critical incident studies in the ICU identified a series of contributory factors associated with the lack of specific teamwork skills (Reader et al. 2006). Table 1.3 illustrates the magnitude of the problem of errors in the ICU.

Table 1.3 Incidence of diagnostic and therapeutic errors in the intensive care unit

Incidence of errors	References
In 26.8 % of ICU patients, one or more errors occurred, the most common being insulin administration error. The experience of more than two adverse events was associated with a threefold increase in the risk of ICU death	Garrouste-Orgeas et al. (2010)
1 % of critically ill patients experience permanent harm or die because of medication errors	Valentin et al. (2009)
15 % of ICU patients suffer from adverse drug events (ADE) and medication errors. The most frequent preventable ADE occurred in the prescribing (71.1 %)	Benkirane et al. (2009)
During the first 7 days of hospitalization, 55 % of all high-risk newborn infants have one or more errors. The most frequent error was associated with medication use (84.2 %)	Lerner et al. (2008)
36.1 % of emergency neonatal interhospital transfers had one or more adverse events. 67 % were perceived as being due to avoidable human errors	Lim and Ratnavel (2008)
Adverse drug events occur in 3.6 events per 100 orders; 81 % are considered clinically important	Buckley et al. (2007)
One error for every five doses of medication administered (20 %)	Kopp et al. (2006)
20.2 % of critically ill patients suffer from adverse events	Rothschild et al. (2005)
15 % of patients suffer consequences from an error; 92 % are judged as avoidable	Graf et al. (2005)
13–51 % of all critical incidents pose a major threat for patient safety	Beckmann et al. (2003), Donchin et al. (1995)
One of 10 new patients in ICU is transferred to ICU because of a previous treatment error	Darchy et al. (1999)
The rate of preventable adverse drug events in ICUs is nearly twice the rate of non-ICUs	Buckley et al. (1997), Beckmann et al. (1996), Wright et al. (1991), Giraud et al. (1993)
63–83 % of all critical incidents can be attributed to human error	Cullen et al. (1997)
31 % of all ICU patients suffer iatrogenic complications during their stay in the ICU	Donchin et al. (1995)
For the ICU as a whole, about 1.7 errors per patient per day occur. Twice a day a severe or potentially detrimental error is committed	Donchin et al. (1995)
The majority of adverse events were errors in medication (15–60 %)	Donchin et al. (1995), Giraud et al. (1993)
One of every three errors in ICU is caused by communication problems	Giraud et al. (1993)

1.4.4 Errors in Anesthesia and Postoperative Patient Care

The induction and maintenance of anesthesia, without having any therapeutic benefit in itself, has always been a potentially harmful undertaking. The use of highly potent drugs and the associated loss of consciousness and vital functions bears the risk of harming patients. Beginning in the mid-1950s, anesthetists were the first in healthcare to begin to systematically address the issue of the incidence and nature of perioperative adverse events (Beecher and Todd 1954). The increased insight into the contribution of anesthesia to perioperative morbidity and mortality has led to considerable improvement in the safety and quality of anesthetic patient care. As a consequence of its leading role in the prevention and detection of medical error and in pioneering a patient safety movement, the IOM report referred to anesthesiology as the model for addressing patient safety (Kohn et al. 1999). As a result of major improvements in technology, equipment failure has become a rare event. Nowadays, adverse drug events, circulatory events, problems with airway management, and pulmonary complications are among the most frequent critical situations. Patients in the postanesthesia care unit (PACU) can experience an adverse event from a residual sedative or anesthetic effect, persistent muscle-relaxant effect, inappropriate fluid management, allergic reaction, and upper airway obstruction. Human error plays a significant role in these critical situations and accidents (Table 1.4). Human

Table 1.4 Incidence of diagnostic and therapeutic errors in anesthesia and postoperative patient care

Incidence of errors	References
In a sample of voluntarily reported PACU medication errors, harmful errors were present in 5.8 % of the sample, which included two patient deaths	Hicks et al. (2007)
Retrospective analysis reveals a 0.01 % incidence of medication errors without serious adverse events. In 42 %, syringe swap was the leading cause	Sakaguchi et al. 2008
2.1 % of incidents reported to a National Patient Safety Agency resulted in severe harm or death	Catchpole et al. (2008)
Critical incidents occur in 2.5 % of all pediatric anesthesia cases	Marcus (2006)
The most common presenting problems are related to respiratory/airway issues (43 %), cardiovascular problems (24 %), and drug errors (11 %). Contributing factors included error of judgment (18 %), communication failure (14 %), and inadequate preoperative preparation (7 %)	Kluger and Bullock (2002)
29 % of all critical incidents lead to a major physiological disturbance and require management in intensive care unit	Kluger and Bullock (2002)
A drug administration error occurs at a rate of 1 in 133 anesthetics. Incorrect doses (20 %) and substitutions (20 %) with i.v. boluses of other drugs are the most common errors	Webster et al. (2001)
4 % of all incidents are caused by the patient's unpredictable reactions; 69–82 % of all critical incidents could have been avoided	Arbous et al. (2001)
0.2 % of all patients in the PACU need emergency reintubation; 70 % are directly related to anesthesia management	Mathew et al. (1990)
31–82 % of all incidents are caused by human error, 9–21 % by technical failure	Cooper et al. (1978), Kumar et al. (1988), Currie (1989), Chopra et al. (1992), Webb et al. (1993), Buckley et al. (1997), Arbous et al. (2001), Bracco et al. (2001)

error in anesthesia occurs on the individual level (e.g., judgment) as well as on the interpersonal level (e.g., communication failure) and the organizational level (e.g., standards for preoperative management).

1.5 The Human Factors: Skills for Acute Patient Care

Poor outcomes do occur, but what is perhaps surprising given the complex circumstances of critical situations is that good outcomes happen as often as they do. Human factors are behind faulty systems, processes, and conditions as well as active unintentional failures of healthcare providers. Yet it should not be overlooked that human factors, the way people think and feel and interact with each other and their environment, are an essential resource for safe patient care: Like Janus, the two-faced god of Roman mythology looking in opposite directions, human factors, too, provides both the potential to trigger and the skills to master a critical situation (Fig. 1.3). As a result, human factors should never be equated with "risk factors." Each time mindful healthcare professionals detect, diagnose, and correct a critical situation or an error before it has an opportunity to unfold, it is human factors that prevent patient harm (Fig. 1.4). Correct performance and systemic errors are two sides of the same coin, or, perhaps more aptly, they are two sides of the same cognitive balance sheet (Reason 1990).

There is a growing interest in human factors skills as being crucial for delivering safe and high-quality patient care but which are not directly related to traditional clinical expertise. A growing body of research has shown how critical these skills have become. Safe and successful acute care clinicians must have good *interpersonal skills*, such as communication, teamwork, and leadership, and good *cognitive skills*, such as situation awareness, planning, decision-making, and task management. The

Fig. 1.3 The human factors and the two faces of Janus. Similar to the god of Roman mythology, the human factors have two opposite aspects: They combine to trigger critical situations and at the same time provide the skills to master them

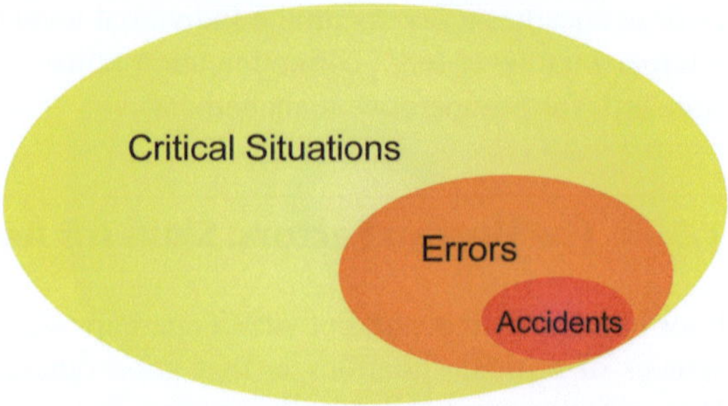

Fig. 1.4 Human factors prevent adverse events. Because healthcare professionals detect critical situations and errors before these can cause accidents, the human factors provide a vital resource for patient safety

aviation industry was among the first to recognize that technical proficiency in pilots was not enough to guarantee safe flight operations and then to identify the most relevant human factors, communication, and teamwork skills (Wiener et al. 1993). Training programs were introduced that taught and reinforced these skills as a set of countermeasures against error. Because the workload profile of anesthetists shows similarities with pilots (i.e., high intensity at task initiation and completion, monitoring for most of the time, and rapid response to critical events), this approach to incorporating human factors, communication, and teamwork skills was adopted for medical care in a high-stakes environment (e.g., Gaba et al. 1994). Because there is increasing evidence that these skills may not extrapolate directly from aviation to the clinical high-stakes environment, several research groups have begun to identify and validate the specific skills important for safety in different high-stakes medical domains (Aggarwal et al. 2004; Flin et al. 2008; Flin and Maran 2004; Fletcher et al. 2003; Reader et al. 2006; Taylor-Adams et al. 2008; Yule et al. 2006).

The resident from the case report, too, experienced both sides of human factors: After having triggered the transfusion reaction, the management of the critical situation was up to him as well. As the critical situation unfolded, he had to manage the emergency by effectively utilizing and coordinating all available resources and team members. In addition to his clinical acumen, he suddenly needed a broad variety of additional skills:

- Rapidly detect and diagnose the nature of the emergency situation.
- Resist the emotional strain caused by the awareness that he himself had triggered the adverse event.
- Call for help.
- Make good decisions under time pressure.
- Know his environment and the resources available.
- Set priorities.
- Lead a team.
- Reassess the situation and dynamically make changes in his plan.

The case study demonstrates another important lesson: Despite maximum effort, the patient suffered irretrievable harm from the adverse event. Even when clinicians have a broad range of human factors and teamwork skills, and although the best technology and medicines are available, even the best emergency care can sometimes still fail to save a patient's life.

One way to understand the relationship between clinical and human factors and teamwork skills is that of a conversation: Clinical skills provide the context-specific vocabulary; human factors and teamwork skills are the grammar that enables a meaningful interaction. The following chapters should be regarded as a kind of "grammar" to help healthcare providers of every profession and specialty engage in a constructive conversation with each other and with the critical situation. The most frequent "grammar errors" will demonstrate possible pitfalls and will hopefully sharpen the providers' focus. The conversation, however, is made difficult by certain characteristics that distinguish emergency situations from any other situation in healthcare. We explore these characteristics in this book.

1.6 "The Human Factors": In a Nutshell

- Human factors are physical, psychological, cognitive, and social properties of an individual that influence interaction with the environment and with social and technological systems.
- Some human factors (e.g., information processing, decision-making, communication, task execution) are amenable to training and learning interventions. Other human properties (e.g., basic mechanisms of perception, regulation of attention, fatigue, somatic stress response, personality, etc.) are unchangeable and have to be addressed by systemic interventions such as workplace layout, system design, standard operating procedures, and employee selection.
- If the understanding of human factors is reduced to human failure, the term is only a semantic surrogate for "blaming."
- The central dogma of human factors sciences is that individuals are an integral part of healthcare systems and that their abilities and limitations must be accounted for when designing and optimizing overall system performance
- Human behavior dominates the risk to modern socio-technical systems: 70–90 % of all errors are due to human factors and teamwork failures.
- The mortality rate of preventable medical error exceeds the number of deaths attributable to severe trauma, breast cancer, and HIV.
- Available data on error in acute care medicine provides a heterogeneous picture. Effective generalizations are limited by limitations on study designs outside of the laboratory and the local and unique structures of healthcare organizations and systems.
- The most frequent human errors in acute healthcare include judgment errors, communication failures, and lack of teamwork.
- Human factors provide the potential to trigger critical situations as well as the skills to master them.
- Human factors skills necessary to manage critical situations include interpersonal skills (e.g., communication, teamwork, leadership) and cognitive skills (e.g., situation awareness, planning, decision-making, task management).

References

Aggarwal R, Undre S, Moorthy K, Vincent C, Darzi A (2004) The simulated operating theatre: comprehensive training for surgical teams. Qual Saf Health Care 13(Suppl 1):i27–i32

Ahmed AH, Giri J, Kashya R, Sing B, Dong Y, Kilickaya O, Erwin PJ, Murad MH, Pickering BW (2013) Outcome of adverse events and medical errors in the intensive care unit: a systematic review and meta-analysis. Am J Med Qual. doi:10.1177/1062860613514770

Amalberti R, Mosneron-Dupin F (1997) Facteurs humains et fiabilité: quelles démarches pratiques? Octares, Touluse

Arbous MS, Grobbee DE, van Kleef JW, de Lange JJ, Spoormans HH, Touw P, Werner FM, Meursing AE (2001) Mortality associated with anaesthesia: a qualitative analysis to identify risk factors. Anaesthesia 56:1141–1153

Arntz HR, Klatt S, Stern R, Willich SN, Bernecker J (1996) Are emergency physicians' diagnoses accurate? Anaesthesist 45:163–170 [German]

Beckmann U, Baldwin I, Hart GK, Runciman WB (1996) The Australian Incident Monitoring Study in Intensive Care: AIMS-ICU. An analysis of the first year of reporting. Anaesth Intensive Care 24:320–329

Beckmann U, Bohringer C, Carless R, Gillies DM, Runciman WB, Wu AW, Pronovost P (2003) Evaluation of two methods for quality improvement in intensive care: facilitated incident monitoring and retrospective medical chart review. Crit Care Med 31:1006–1011

Beecher HK, Todd DP (1954) A study of the deaths associated with anesthesia and surgery. Ann Surg 140:2–34

Benkirane RR, Abouqal R, Haimeur CC, Ech Cherif El Kettani SSS, Azzouzi AA, M'daghri Alaoui AA, Thimou AA, Nejmi MM, Maazouzi WW, Madani NN, R-Edwards I, Soulaymani RR (2009) Incidence of adverse drug events and medication errors in intensive care units: a prospective multicenter study. J Patient Saf 5(1):16–22

Bigham BL, Buick JE, Brooks SC, Morrison M, Shojania KG, Morrison LJ (2012) Patient safety in emergency medical services: a systematic review of the literature. Prehosp Emerg Care 16(1):1–20

Bracco D, Favre JB, Bissonnette B, Wasserfallen JB, Revelly JP, Ravussin P, Chiolero R (2001) Human errors in a multidisciplinary intensive care unit: a 1-year prospective study. Intensive Care Med 27:137–145

Brown LH, Hubble MW, Cone DC, Millin MG, Schwartz B, Patterson PD, Greenberg B, Richards ME (2009) Paramedic determinations of medical necessity: a meta-analysis. Prehosp Emerg Care 13(4):516–527

Buckley TA, Short TG, Rowbottom YM, Oh TE (1997) Critical incident reporting in the intensive care unit. Anaesthesia 52:403–409

Buckley MS, Erstad BL, Kopp BJ, Theodorou AA, Priestley G (2007) Direct observation approach for detecting medication errors and adverse drug events in a pediatric intensive care unit. Pediatr Crit Care Med 8(2):145–152

Buduhan G, McRitchie DI (2000) Missed injuries in patients with multiple trauma. J Trauma 49:600–605

Camargo CA, Tsai CL, Sullivan AF, Cleary PD, Gordon JA, Guadagnoli E, Kaushal R, Magid DJ, Rao SR, Blumental D (2012) Safety climate and medical errors in 62 US emergency departments. Ann Emerg Med 60(5):555–563

Carayon P, Alyousef B, Xie A (2012) Human factors and ergonomics in health care. In: Salvendy G (ed) Handbook of human factors and ergonomics, 4th edn. Wiley, Hoboken

Catchpole K (2013) Spreading human factors expertise in healthcare: Untangling the knots in people and systems. BMJ Qual Saf 22(10):793–797

Catchpole K, Bell MD, Johnson S (2008) Safety in anaesthesia: a study of 12,606 reported incidents from the UK National Reporting and Learning System. Anaesthesia 63(4):340–346

Chan WK, Leung KF, Lee YF, Hung CS, Kung NS, Lau FL (1998) Undiagnosed acute myocardial infarction in the accident and emergency department: reasons and implications. Eur J Emerg Med 5:219–224

Chisholm CD, Collison EK, Nelson DR, Cordell WH (2000) Emergency department workplace interruptions: are emergency physicians "interrupt-driven" and "multitasking"? Acad Emerg Med 7:1239–1243

Chopra V, Bovill JG, Spierdijk J, Koornneef F (1992) Reported significant observations during anaesthesia: a prospective analysis over an 18-month period. Br J Anaesth 68:13–18

Cooper JB, Newbower RS, Long CD, McPeek B (1978) Preventable anesthesia mishaps: a study of human factors. Anesthesiology 49:399–406

Cosby KS, Croskerry P (2009) The nature of emergency medicine. In: Croskerry P, Cosbyy KS, Schenkel SM, Wears LR (eds) Patient safety in emergency medicine. Lippincott & Williams, Philadelphia

Croskerry P (2003) Cognitive forcing strategies in clinical decision making. Ann Emerg Med 41:110–120

Croskerry P (2008) Cognitive and affective dispositions to respond. In: Croskerry P, Cosby KS, Schenkel SM, Wears RL (eds) Patient safety in emergency medicine. Lippincott Williams & Wilkins, Philadelphia, pp 219–227

Cullen DJ, Sweitzer BJ, Bates DW, Burdick E, Edmondson A, Leape LL (1997) Preventable adverse drug events in hospitalised patients. A comparative study of intensive care and general care units. Crit Care Med 25:1289–1297

Currie M (1989) A prospective survey of anaesthetic critical events in a teaching hospital. Anaesth Intensive Care 17:403–411

Darchy B, Le Miere E, Figueredo B (1999) Iatrogenic diseases as a reason for admission to the intensive care unit: incidence, causes and consequences. Arch Intern Med 159:71–78

Davis JW, Hoyt DB, McArdle MS, Mackersie RC, Eastman AB, Virgilio RW, Cooper G, Hammill F, Lynch FP (1992) An analysis of errors causing morbidity and mortality in a trauma system: a guide for quality improvement. J Trauma 32:660–665

Donchin Y, Seagull FJ (2002) The hostile environment of the intensive care unit. Curr Opin Crit Care 8:316–320

Donchin Y, Gopher D, Olin M, Badihi Y, Biesky M, Sprung CL, Pizov R, Cotev S (1995) A look into the nature and causes of human errors in the intensive care unit. Crit Care Med 23:294–300

Enderson BL, Reath DB, Meadors J, Dallas W, DeBoo JM, Maull KI (1990) The tertiary trauma survey: a prospective study of missed injury. J Trauma 30:666–669

Epstein SK, Huckins DS, Liu SW, Pallin DJ, Sullivan AF, Lipton RI, Camargo CA (2012) Emergency department crowding and risk of preventable medical errors. Intern Emerg Med 7(2):173–180

Esposito TJ, Sanddal ND, Dean JM, Hansen JD, Reynolds SA, Battan K (1999) Analysis of preventable pediatric trauma deaths and inappropriate trauma care in Montana. J Trauma 47:243–251

Fairbanks RJ, Crittenden CN, O'Gara KG, Wilson MA, Pennington EC, Chin NP, Shah MN (2008) Emergency medical services provider perceptions of the nature of adverse events and near-misses in out-of-hospital care: an ethnographic view. Acad Emerg Med 15(12):1312–1314

Flabouris A (2001) Clinical features, patterns of referral and out of hospital transport events for patients with suspected isolated spinal injury. Injury 32:569–575

Fletcher G, Flin R, McGeorge P, Glavin R, Maran N, Patey R (2003) Anaesthetists' Non-Technical Skills (ANTS): evaluation of a behavioural marker system. Br J Anaesth 90:580–588

Flin R, Maran N (2004) Identifying and training non-technical skills for teams in acute medicine. Qual Saf Health Care 13(Suppl 1):i80–i84

Flin R, O'Connor P, Crichton M (2008) Safety at the sharp end. A guide to non-technical skills. Ashgate, Farnham

Gaba DM, Fish KJ, Howard SK (1994) Crisis management in anesthesia. Churchill Livingstone, New York

Garrouste-Orgeas M, Timsit JF, Vesin A, Schwebel C, Arnodo P, Lefrant JY, Souweine B, Tabah A, Charpentier J, Gontier O, Fieux F, Mourvillier B, Troché G, Reignier J, Dumay MF, Azoulay E, Reignier B, Carlet J, Soufir L, OUTCOMEREA Study Group (2010) Selected medical errors in the intensive care unit: results of the IATROREF study: parts I and II. Am J Respir Crit Care Med 181(2):134–142

Giraud T, Dhainaut J, Vaxelaire J (1993) Iatrogenic complications in adult intensive care units: a prospective two-center study. Crit Care Med 21:40–51
Graf J, von denDriesch A, Koch KC, Janssens U (2005) Identification and characterization of errors and incidents in a medical intensive care unit. Acta Anaesthesiol Scand 49:930–939
Handler JA, Gillam M, Sanders AB, Klasco R (2000) Defining, identifying, and measuring error in emergency medicine. Acad Emerg Med 7:1183–1188
Helm M, Faul M, Unger T, Lampl L (2013) Reliability of emergency medical field triage: exemplified by traffic accident victims. Anaesthesist 63:973–980
Hendrie J, Sammartino L, Silvapulle M, Braitberg G (2007) Experience in adverse events detection in an emergency department: nature of events. Emerg Med Australas 19:9–15
Hicks RW, Becker SC, Windle PE, Krenzischek DA (2007) Medication errors in the PACU. J Perianesth Nurs 22(6):413–419
Hollnagel E (1993) Reliability of cognition: foundations of human reliability analysis. Academic, London
Hoyle JD, Davis AT, Putman KK, Trytko JA, Fales WD (2012) Medication dosing errors in pediatric patients treated by emergency medical services. Prehosp Emerg Care 16(1):59–66
IOM (2006) Emergency care for children. Growing pains. Committee on the future of Emergency Care in the United States Health System Board on Healthcare Services. Academic, Washington
Jewell K, McGiffert L (2009) To err is human-to delay is deadly. Consumers Health Report Mai 2009. Accessed at http://www.safepatientproject.org/2009/05/to_err_is_humanto_delay_is_dea.html
Kahneman D (2003) A perspective on judgment and choice. Mapping bounded rationality. Am Psychol 58(9):697–720
Kluger MT, Bullock MF (2002) Recovery room incidents: a review of 419 reports from the Anaesthetic Incident Monitoring Study (AIMS). Anaesthesia 57:1060–1066
Kohn L, Corrigan J, Donaldson M (1999) To err is human: building a safer health system. Committee on Quality of Healthcare in America, Institute of Medicine (IOM). National Academy, Washington
Kopp BJ, Erstad BL, Allen ME, Theodorou AA, Priestley G (2006) Medication errors and adverse drug events in an intensive care unit: direct observation approach for detection. Crit Care Med 34:415–425
Kothari R, Barsan W, Brott T, Broderick J, Ashbrock S (1995) Frequency and accuracy of prehospital diagnosis of acute stroke. Stroke 26:937–941
Kumar V, Barcellos WA, Mehta MP, Carter JG (1988) An analysis of critical incidents in a teaching department for quality assurance: a survey of mishaps during anaesthesia. Anaesthesia 43:879–883
Leape L, Berwick DM (2005) Five years after to err is human: what have we learned? JAMA 19(293):2384–2390
Lerner RB, Carvalho M, Vieira AA, Lopes JM, Moreira ME (2008) Medication errors in a neonatal intensive care unit. J Pediatr 84(2):166–170
Lim MT, Ratnavel N (2008) A prospective review of adverse events during interhospital transfers of neonates by a dedicated neonatal transfer service. Pediatr Crit Care Med 9(3):289–293
Linn S, Knoller N, Giligan CG, Dreifus U (1997) The sky is a limit: errors in prehospital diagnosis by flight physicians. Am J Emerg Med 15:316–320
Mackenzie CF, Jefferies NJ, Hunter WA, Bernhard WN, Xiao Y (1996) Comparison of self-reporting of deficiencies in airway management with video analyses of actual performance. LOTAS Group. Level One Trauma Anesthesia Simulation. Hum Factors 38:623–635
Marcus R (2006) Human factors in pediatric anesthesia incidents. Paediatr Anaesth 16:242–250
Mathew JP, Rosenbaum SH, O'Connor T, Barash PG (1990) Emergency tracheal intubation in the postanesthesia care unit: physician error or patient disease? Anesth Analg 71:691–697
Mathews SC, Pronovost PJ (2008) Physician autonomy and informed decision making: finding the balance for patient safety and quality. JAMA 300(24):2913–2915

McCarthy BD, Beshansky JR, D'Agostino RB, Selker HP (1993) Missed diagnoses of myocardial infarction in the emergency department: results from a multicenter study. Ann Emerg Med 22:579–582

McDermott FT, Rosenfeld JV, Laidlaw JD, Cordner SM, Tremayne AB (2004) Evaluation of management of road trauma survivors with brain injury and neurologic disability in Victoria. J Trauma 56:137–149

Newton A, Ratchford A, Khan I (2008) Incidence of adverse events during prehospital rapid sequence intubation: a review of one year on the London Helicopter Emergency Medical Service. J Trauma 64(2):487–492

O'Connor PM, Dowey KE, Bell PM, Irwin ST, Dearden CH (1995) Unnecessary delays in accident and emergency departments: do medical and surgical senior house officers need to vet admissions? J Accid Emerg Med 12:251–254

Peery CL, Chendrasekhar A, Paradise NF, Moorman DW, Timberlake GA (1999) Missed injuries in pediatric trauma. Am Surg 65:1067–1069

Pfeifer R, Pape HC (2008) Missed injuries in trauma patients: a literature review. Patient Saf Surg 2:1–20

Pope JH, Aufderheide TP, Ruthazer R, Woolard RH, Feldman JA, Beshansky JR, Griffith JL, Selker HP (2000) Missed diagnoses of acute cardiac ischemia in the emergency department. N Engl J Med 342:1163–1170

Reader T, Flin R, Lauche K, Cuthbertson B (2006) Non-technical skills in the intensive care unit. Br J Anaesth 96:551–559

Reason J (1990) Human error. Cambridge University, Cambridge

Reason J (1997) Managing the risks of organizational accidents. Ashgate, Aldershot

Risser DT, Rice MM, Salisbury ML, Simon R, Jay GD, Berns SD (1999) The potential for improved teamwork to reduce medical errors in the emergency department. The MedTeams Research Consortium. Ann Emerg Med 34:373–383

Rittenberger JC, Beck PW, Paris PM (2005) Errors of omission in the treatment of prehospital chest pain patients. Prehosp Emerg Care 9:2–7

Rothschild JM, Landrigan CP, Cronin JW, Kaushal R, Lockley SW, Burdick E, Stone PH, Lilly CM, Katz JT, Czeisler CA, Bates DW (2005) The Critical Care Safety Study: the incidence and nature of adverse events and serious medical errors in intensive care. Crit Care Med 33:1694–1700

Russ AL, Fairbanks RJ, Karsh BT, Militello LG, Saleem JJ, Wears RL (2013) The science of human factors: separating facts from fiction. BMJ Qual Saf 22:802–808

Sakaguchi Y, Tokuda K, Yamaguchi K, Irita K (2008) Incidence of anesthesia-related medication errors over a 15-year period in a university hospital. Fukuoka Igaku Zasshi 99(3):58–66

Sanghera IS, Franklin BD, Dhillon S (2007) The attitudes and beliefs of healthcare professionals on the causes and reporting of medication errors in a UK intensive care unit. Anaesthesia 62:53–61

Schaefer HG, Helmreich RL, Scheidegger D (1994) Human factors and safety in emergency medicine. Resuscitation 28:221–225

Stiegler MP, Tung A (2013) Cognitive processes in anesthesiology decision making. Anesthesiology 120(1):204–217

Taylor-Adams S, Brodie A, Vincent C (2008) Safety skills for clinicians: an essential component of patient safety. J Patient Saf 4:141–147

Thomas EJ, Studdert DM, Burstin HR et al (2000) Incidence and types of adverse events and negligent patient care in Utah and Colorado. Med Care 38:261–271

Tiyyagura GK, Arnold L, Cone DC, Langhan M (2014) Pediatric anaphylaxis management in the prehospital setting. Prehosp Emerg Care 18(1):46–51

Valentin A, Capuzzo M, Guidet B, Moreno R, Metnitz B, Bauer P, Metnitz P (2009) Errors in administration of parenteral drugs in intensive care units: multinational prospective study. BMJ 338:b814

Vilke GM, Tornabene SV, Stepanski B, Shipp HE, Ray LU, Metz MA, Vroman D, Anderson M, Murrin PA, Davis DP, Harley J (2007) Paramedic self-reported medication errors. Prehosp Emerg Care 11:80–84

Wang HE, Cook LJ, Yealy DM, Lave JR (2009) Outcomes after out-of-hospital endotracheal intubation errors. Resuscitation 80(1):50–55

Webb RK, Currie M, Morgan CA, Williamson JA, Mackay P, Russell WJ, Runciman WB (1993) The Australian Incident Monitoring Study: an analysis of 2000 incident reports. Anaesth Intensive Care 21:520–528

Webster CS, Merry AF, Larsson L, McGrath KA, Weller J (2001) The frequency and nature of drug administration error during anaesthesia. Anaesth Intensive Care 29:494–500

Wiener E, Kanki B, Helmreich R (1993) Cockpit resource management. Academic, San Diego

Williamson JA, Webb RK, Sellen A, Runciman WB (1993) Human failure: an analysis of 2000 incident reports. Anaesth Intensive Care 21:678–683

Wright D, Mackenzie SJ, Buchan I, Cairns CS, Price LE (1991) Critical incidents in the intensive therapy unit. Lancet 338:676–678

Yule S, Flin R, Paterson-Brown S, Maran N (2006) Non-technical skills for surgeons in the operating room: a review of the literature. Surgery 139:140–149

The Challenge of Acute Healthcare

2

Case Study

At a large inner-city hospital, an anesthesiologist covers the OR as well as the obstetric department. After a busy day, she starts her night shift, during which she is called several times to the delivery ward to insert an epidural in a parturient. At 2:00 a.m., she is called to the emergency department where she is part of a trauma team that takes care of a 32-year-old patient brought to the hospital by EMS following a motor vehicle accident. The victim suffered severe head trauma, maxillofacial injuries, blunt thoracic trauma, an open fracture of the femur, and suspicion of a contained subcapsular hematoma of the spleen.

Following the initial work-up, the patient is transferred to the OR and is simultaneously operated on by trauma surgeons and maxillofacial surgeons. Twenty minutes after the incision, the patient develops increasingly high peak inspiratory pressures, tidal volumes begin to decrease, and saturation drops. The flow-volume curve on the monitor shows an incomplete expiratory phase; however, lung auscultation is normal. Suspecting bronchospasm, the anesthesiologist initiates broncholytic therapy which fails to improve the ventilatory parameters. At the anesthesiologist's request, the surgeons explore the oral cavity and notice that the endotracheal tube is kinked. After unkinking the tube, the peak pressure, tidal volumes, and saturation normalize. Twenty minutes later, the peak pressure increases, tidal volumes decrease, and saturation drops again; however, this time the flow-volume curve does not indicate an obstructive pattern. Instead, lung auscultation reveals diminished right-sided breath sounds. In addition, the invasive arterial line tracing shows a significant decrease in blood pressure. The anesthesiologist attributes these changes to a possible tension pneumothorax which could have occurred at the time of

M. St.Pierre et al., *Crisis Management in Acute Care Settings*,
DOI 10.1007/978-3-319-41427-0_2

insertion of the central line in the right subclavian vein. She communicates her findings to the trauma surgeons, who insert a chest tube. Subsequently, the ventilation, oxygenation, and vital signs return to normal values.

Forty-five minutes later, the patient becomes unstable again. The peak pressure gradually increases, and tidal volumes decrease to 150 ml. The saturation also drops, although at a slower pace than the first two times. The lungs are ventilated with increasing difficulty, and rales are identified on auscultation. Despite increasing the inspiratory pressure, adding PEEP and ventilating with 100 % oxygen, the saturation continues to drop to the 80s. The anesthesiologist contacts the ICU and requests an intensive care ventilator. The new ventilator improves the oxygenation and ventilation, and the patient is rendered stable enough to be transferred to the ICU at 6:00 a.m. The ventilatory parameters are tidal volume of 400 ml, respiratory rate of 14, peak pressure of 32 mbar, PEEP of 15 mbar, and FiO2 of 100 %. Bilateral densities on the chest X-ray confirm early-stage acute respiratory distress syndrome (ARDS).

A multiple-injured trauma patient undergoes an emergency operation in the early morning. After an initial uneventful period, the patient develops a series of ventilatory problems. Each problem leads to a rapid deterioration of the patient's oxygenation status and puts the patient at risk and the anesthetist under time pressure. She has to find the cause of the clinical deterioration and has to rapidly take therapeutic measures before the patient is seriously harmed. The circumstances of this series of ventilation problems, however, are challenging for the anesthetist because the pathophysiological disturbances present with an almost identical set of symptoms and monitor parameters every time, but the underlying cause is always a different one. Furthermore, the physician has difficulty diagnosing the problem because the apparent changes of one organ system are caused by concealed alterations of another system: The significant decrease in the blood pressure is caused by a pulmonary problem (i.e., tension pneumothorax), and a decrease in arterial saturation is due to performance limitations of an anesthesia machine when ventilating a patient with ARDS.

2.1 Medical Emergencies and Critical Situations

Emergencies are among the most challenging situations in medicine. The need for immediate life-saving treatment, the necessity of swift decisions and actions in the absence of complete information, time pressure, the sudden rush of anxiety because of the awareness that a human life is at stake, and the interaction with team members from different specialties all create a potent mix of stressful demands for the healthcare provider. Because emergency situations often appear dramatic and sometimes are characterized by chaos and disorganization, they are clearly not the same as typical situations in daily life. From a cognitive psychologist's perspective, however, an emergency situation represents a specific type of decisional situation within a specific situational context: a situation in which decision-making and task performance have immediate impacts on the current and future state of the situation. Because the future course of events hangs in the balance for good or bad, we call these situations *critical* (Badke-Schaub 2002).

For the healthcare provider, it is basically irrelevant whether the *critical situation* is triggered by an *external* (e.g., trauma, equipment malfunction) or *internal* event (e.g., cardiac dysrhythmia, myocardial infarction, pulmonary embolism, stroke) or by an *error* committed by a healthcare provider (e.g., transfusion error). The requirements and difficulties for successful problem solving and quality patient care are similar. As in the case report, a medical emergency may be composed of multiple critical situations. Each of those critical situations can be analyzed and treated as a separate entity: An unforeseen event interrupts routine patient care and calls forth a decision. Once the critical situation has passed, task performance can return to routine (Badke-Schaub 2002; Fig. 2.1).

Acute critical medical situations are termed "emergencies," or "complications" (Atlee 2007; Gravenstein and Kirby 1995; Taylor and Major 1987), or "crises" (Gaba et al. 1994). The major emphasis of this perspective lies on the clinical picture of an emergency and on the knowledge and skills necessary to manage it. In the discussion exploring patient safety, "adverse event" is another term frequently encountered (e.g., Kohn et al. 1999; Rosenthal and Sutcliffe 2002; Vincent 2002). In this book, we use the term "critical situation," because our focus is on the *cognitive and behavioral aspects* of these situations, and on the factors that influence human decision-making, task performance, and teamwork. "Critical situations" also include minor incidents or minimal events that require rapid decisions to avoid harm to the patient.

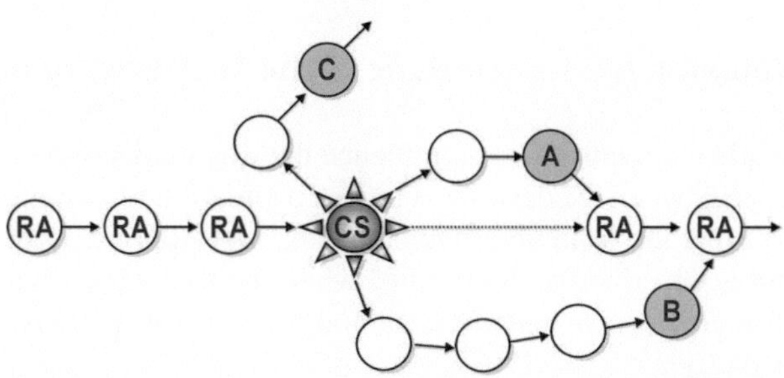

Fig. 2.1 Critical situations. Routine actions (*RA*) are interrupted by a critical situation (*CS*). If this situation is successfully managed, actions will return sooner (*A*) or later (*B*) to routine; however, some decisions result in a deviating treatment pathway for the patient (*C*) (Modified from Badke-Schaub 2002)

2.2 Complexity and Human Behavior

Despite sharing several characteristics with everyday decisional situations, the provision of healthcare in a high-stakes environment has a number of properties that make it significantly different from and considerably more challenging than the provision of patient care in other medical domains. Whereas healthcare providers traditionally have been taught technical proficiency and clinical decision-making, the cognitive process of detecting and correcting critical situations in a high-stakes environment necessitates a broader set of capabilities. The reasons lie in the fact that there are several characteristics that apply uniquely to critical situations in a high-stakes environment.

The case study illustrates several of these characteristics that cognitive psychologists subsume under the term "complexity of a working environment." Complexity has found widespread interest among all fields concerned with human problem solving (e.g., cognitive science, human factors, reliability engineering), because it places many specific demands on decision-makers and affects the kinds and quality of cognitive processes carried out by people. Most of the scientific evidence for decision-making in complex environments comes from outside of healthcare, specifically from industrial or military high-risk environments where human behavior in complex man-made systems has been widely studied. Since the modern healthcare environment has become so complex, the research from these other areas clearly applies to healthcare as well.

Systems theorists and psychologists have advanced several different conceptual frameworks describing the characteristics of complexity. Despite the diversity in definition, there is a general agreement about the basic features of complexity (e.g., Cook and Woods 2001; Dörner 1996; Dörner and Schaub 1994; Frensch and Funke 1995; Perrow 1999; Rasmussen and Lind 1981; Reason 1997; Woods 1988). On the most basic level, complexity has a dual nature, i.e., (a) a characteristic of the task environment and (b) an obstacle for solving problems for the decision-maker.

2.2.1 Complexity: A Characteristic of the Task Environment

There are five salient dimensions that influence the way humans perceive their environment. In general, when we describe a task or a situation as "simple," this usually refers to the fact that the following five characteristics are only weakly expressed. An environment is described as "complex" when the following situational characteristics are strongly represented (Dörner and Schaub 1994; Frensch and Funke 1995; Halpern 2002):

2.2.1.1 Many Variables

Depending on the nature of a critical situation (e.g., multiple trauma, the patient's pathophysiology, previous medical history, invasiveness of procedures), many variables and their interrelation have to be handled. Because conscious reasoning is limited in terms of speed and capacity ("System 2 process"; Chap. 6), people have great difficulty in simultaneously processing multiple critical variables. As a result, when confronted with a large number of variables, it is more likely that decision-makers will overlook important factors and make incorrect assumptions about the state of the system or the patient. Faced with time pressure and information overload people tend to form intuitive judgments and make decisions by using mental shortcuts ("heuristics," "System 1 process," Chap. 6) that focus on one or two salient features of the situation and ignore the rest. In the case study, the anesthetist handled each problem as it happened; but care might well have been compromised had two events happened simultaneously, e.g., kinked endotracheal tube simultaneous to the pneumothorax.

2.2.1.2 Interdependence and Interrelatedness

Because humans can easily get an incorrect or incomplete understanding of the system they operate in, they often overlook the interdependence ("coupling"; Chap. 14) between the variables. Systems such as an operating theater are composed of multiple variables including equipment, medicines, the care team, and the patient. These variables constitute a network of interdependencies, i.e., an action that affects one part of the system will also affect other parts of it. Because of interdependence, action aimed at one variable often affects – sometimes in unknown ways – other variables and aspects of care. For example, the decrease in arterial blood pressure caused by the tension pneumothorax and the desaturation due to performance limits of the anesthesia machine exemplify interdependence. The more links that exist between the variables, the more difficulty decision-makers have in predicting the consequences of their actions. Not regarding or not understanding side effects of actions is a typical error in complex systems. Most importantly, interdependence of variables defines the task environment as *a system*, not as an accumulation of disconnected items. Failure to approach a critical situation from a system's perspective is a major obstacle to successful decision-making under complexity. If a problem solver tries to manipulate variables in isolation, he or she may fail to predict the reaction of the system.

2.2.1.3 Dynamics

Complex situations can unfold over different rates of time. If they are event driven with rapid time constants, such as the above-described critical incident, they are highly dynamic. An emergency situation does not, like in a game of chess, simply wait for a player to make moves. The pace of decision is often determined by events that the decision-maker has no control over. And these events will progress, with or without participation of the actors (Dörner 1996). While the healthcare provider may be busy searching for a solution, the problem changes. This creates the necessity to maintain an up-to-date "mental model" (Chap. 6) of what is often a rapidly changing situation. These unyielding dynamics narrow down the freedom of action: If we wait too long before we act, we will lose opportunities. A therapeutic measure that could help the patient at one point can become obsolete in the near future. Thus, healthcare providers must often implement tentative solutions because time pressure forces them to act before they have gathered complete information or have determined a comprehensive plan. Time pressure, however, is not only forced upon the healthcare provider by external events; it can be an unavoidable consequence of necessary therapeutic actions. For example, once anesthesia has been induced, the patient's ventilation has to be secured, no matter how.

2.2.1.4 Time Delay

Side effects and long-term repercussions are not necessarily obvious right away; instead, they can appear with considerable time delay, thus making it difficult for the healthcare professional to correlate symptoms with the triggering event. For example, the Shaldon catheter was inserted into the right subclavian vein during the initial work-up in the emergency room. Tension pneumothorax, however, did not manifest until several hours later in the operating room. As with interdependence, time delay can obscure the result of therapeutic measures. Whether or not a certain strategy was successful may take quite a while to become apparent and be hidden by the effects of other measures.

2.2.1.5 Irreversibility

Pathophysiological changes in a patient often take a one-way direction. There can be a "too late" for organ systems to recover and a narrow therapeutic window to prevent irretrievable harm. Actions, too, can have irretrievable consequences. When faced with a critical situation, healthcare providers often have one chance only to choose the correct action. Behavior following the principle of trial and error is far too risky and ineffective.

2.2.2 Complexity: An Obstacle for Solving Problems for the Decision-Maker

Complexity is in part defined by the situational characteristics described above. The degree of complexity is defined by the extent of the requirements for successful action. Healthcare providers who have to cope with a complex situation experience characteristics of complexity as obstacles to gathering information, integrating findings, and determining effective actions (e.g., Dörner 1996; Frensch and Funke 1995; Sterman 1994).

2.2.2.1 Uncertainty and Lack of Transparency

Many problems in a medical high-stakes environment are ambiguous and underspecified, e.g., dropping saturation and low arterial blood pressure. What the healthcare provider really wants to know about the patient is often not visible or immediately understandable, and critical information might not be available. Because patients, in contrast to man-made systems, often do not provide detailed information on pathophysiological processes, healthcare professionals are often faced with symptoms that don't point to a specific problem. Problem solvers in acute medical care may not have direct access to information about the situation they must address. They must make decisions affecting a system whose features they can see only partially or unclearly. Monitoring provides access to the patient's underlying condition only via weak external signals and cannot give more than hints as to what the problem exactly might be (Gaba 1992). There is no monitor that can tell the physician, "The sats drop because your patient has started to develop ARDS," or "The peak airway pressure is high because the endotracheal tube is kinked." It is only from understanding ambiguous patterns of different variables that healthcare professionals can draw conclusions concerning the medical problem. Lack of transparency thus injects another element of uncertainty into planning and decision-making. In a medical high-stakes environment, often the main issue in solving a problem is not "What should I do?" Rather, much of the time, the main issue is to lift the veil of uncertainty and lack of transparency and answer the question: "What exactly is the problem" (Klein 1992)?

2.2.2.2 Singularity of the Situation

Once the problem has been defined, for example, by stating a diagnosis, there is another danger waiting for the decision-maker: He or she might miss subtle situational clues that may indicate that a critical situation differs slightly or even dramatically from the mental picture of the provider. Once the provider has developed a mental picture of the condition or event, there is a strong tendency to overlook or reject unobtrusive or contrary evidence. Once a solution has been determined, even when it's incorrect, important details can be missed or not sought – the resulting behavior will take the form "strong-but-wrong" (Reason 1990): When a decision-maker believes the correct diagnosis has been made or the correct actions are underway, established patterns of actions and thought are activated. In these situations, the action will be in keeping with past practice and may not incorporate current situational demands. Rather than choosing an action because it has worked many times before ("*methodism*" Dörner 1996; *"cognitive conservatism"* Reason 1990; Chap. 7), healthcare providers need to seek flexibility and maintain some amount of uncertainty in their approach to decision-making. Thus, *flexibility* is a key characteristic of successful problem solving in critical situations.

2.2.2.3 Information Overload and Lack of Information

In critical situations, much of the information needed at the time of a decision is not yet available. Moreover, multiple sources of concurrent information may overwhelm the healthcare provider. Incoming data has to be assessed for relevance and reliability and integrated into a situational model or discarded. The healthcare provider constantly decides how much information is enough to begin to take action. As the provider begins to take action based on available information, new information becomes available that may confirm or disconfirm a working diagnosis. It is difficult for teams to manage new information that contradicts the current mental picture held by the group, sometimes even when new data points overwhelmingly to a different diagnosis. In order to successfully balance these contradicting requirements, healthcare professionals have to pursue problem-oriented *information management*. The aim of information management is to arrive at a cohesive picture of the situation which is supported by the data available (Chap. 6). The integration of all team members available in this process of generating and evaluating information is a critically important step toward a more consistent and complete mental model of the situation (Salas et al. 1992).

2.2.2.4 Time Pressure

Time pressure limits the possibilities for data collection, problem analysis, goal formulation, and action. For instance, once a patient's oxygen saturation starts to drop, there is a diminishing amount of time left to find out why. During a critical situation, there is no way a healthcare provider can act under time pressure and simultaneously gather complete information. In complex situations, information management will never be complete. Instead, as the need for a rapid decision increases, *transfer of previous knowledge* will replace problem-oriented information management. What will happen is that the provider will rely on mental models from past experience with similar situations to shape current assumptions and guide actions and behavior.

Because reliance on pattern matching from past experience sometimes leads to the wrong action, there is an inherent unreliability to relying exclusively on pattern matching. Moreover, individual emotions are also a part of the healthcare provider's understanding, which may further obfuscate the objective situation and induce a bias on the part of the decision-maker. Relying on pattern matching to guide behavior during a crisis is the hallmark of an experienced and effective provider, but at the same time, it can also induce error in ways that are not well understood by the decision-maker.

2.2.2.5 Risk

Decisions under complexity carry an inherent risk of being incorrect. Even experienced healthcare providers' mental model of reality can be wrong. It can happen that the actions taken will not solve, but rather aggravate, the problem. Therefore, the question for healthcare providers can never be *if* they actually are willing to take risks, but rather under which circumstances they will do so and how much risk are they willing to accept. Unfortunately, judgment of risks can only be based on perceived risk and not on objective facts. Risk assessment during a crisis is therefore a highly subjective undertaking and prone to error. Acute medical care is a high-stakes environment because of the ever-present danger of actually harming the patient with therapeutic measures. The possibility of causing irreversible patient harm by triggering a critical situation and then being unable to manage it suspends like the sword of Damocles over the head of the healthcare provider. On top of the inherent risks associated with taking action (or not taking action) during a critical situation, one moment of inattention can develop into a wrong path. The result of taking an incorrect action during a crisis can result in personal, human, and economic disaster for the healthcare professional and the patient. The awareness of this potential to harm is a major stressor in critical situations (Chap. 9). What healthcare professionals need is the ability to make decisions and take actions in the face of uncertainty.

2.2.2.6 Plurality of Goals

Goals should tell the healthcare professional where to go. They should be "beacons for human action" (Dörner 1996). Goals should help the healthcare provider to regain control over a critical situation and to satisfy as many concurrent needs as possible without creating new problems. The reality of acute medical care, however, is different: Healthcare professionals frequently have to cope with shifting, ill-defined, or competing goals; thus, in a high-stakes medical environment, the formulation of an adequate goal can turn out to be the central cognitive task (Dörner 1996; Chap. 7). Goals can be clear, unclear, explicit, implicit, general, or specific. In addition, sometimes goal criteria are linked inversely: If one goal is satisfied, another goal may fail. For example, to focus on oxygenation by increasing ventilation in the presence of a tension pneumothorax would worsen the hemodynamic situation of a patient. Therefore, complexity makes it necessary that decision-makers pursue multiple goals at the same time. This means that we have to attend to many factors and satisfy several criteria at once. One of the main task requirements when faced with a plurality of goals is the ability to prioritize and integrate.

2.2.2.7 Multiple Players

Teamwork is a characteristic feature of acute medical care. There are barriers to effective teamwork. For example, different healthcare specialties or disciplines may have their own approach to an emergency situation, various standards of performance, and expectations of teammates. Different mental models can result in conflicts if team members fail to communicate appropriately or if team members are overly concerned with "who is right" instead of "what is right." The major prere-quisite for successful teamwork with an interdisciplinary, interprofessional team is the development of a shared mental model among all healthcare professionals involved (Chap. 11). Table 2.1 summarizes the characteristic features of complexity in acute care medicine (Table 2.1).

Table 2.1 Complexity in a medical high-stakes environment

Characteristics of task environment	Characteristics of problem-solving approach
Many variables – People tend to lose track of things	Too much or not enough information – Keep the golden mean
Interdependence and interrelatedness – Conscious reasoning has a rough time	Singularity – Even with decades of experience, expect the unexpected twist
Intransparency – Nobody can know all the details of a situation	Uncertainty – Reckon that it could always be otherwise
Dynamics – The game goes on: with or without you	Time pressure – Time runs on mercilessly
Time delay – Some actions will come back to roost	Risk – You know only in hindsight whether or not you got it right
Irreversibility – Life punishes latecomers	
	Plurality of goals – You can't aim at one thing and one thing only
	Multiple players – Teamwork knows many obstacles

Complexity can be described in terms of characteristics of the task environment and the intrinsic characteristics of the problem-solving approach

2.3 The Challenge of Acute Care Environments

It is early in the morning and the resident had been awake for almost 20 h when she started to take care of the trauma victim. Just when her own biological performance curve had reached its minimum, several vital ventilation problems arose which all fulfilled the criteria of complexity. As a result it wasn't only the critical health condition of the patient and task complexity that posed a threat for patient safety: Characteristic features of the work environment as well as biological limitations reduced the limits of safe performance. As a result, acute patient care is simultaneously jeopardized by several factors. Although certainly many readers will be familiar with working night shifts in a hospital and might have experienced situations comparable to the emergency in the vignette, the fact should not be overlooked that these environmental conditions make acute patient care (in the OR as well as in the ED) different from task execution in other high-reliability organizations (HROs; Chaps. 14 and 16). Such environmental conditions can seriously impact healthcare processes and quality of acute patient care. In critical situations, the error-provoking effects of these conditions may have an even stronger impact and threaten safe patient care. In the following, we will take the "biotope OR" as a distinctive example of such environmental conditions. Some of the factors in the "biotope OR" are changeable, whereas others aren't. All of them, however, have a negative impact on safe patient care.

2.3.1 The Operating Room: An Acute Care "Biotope"

Operating and emergency rooms exhibit all elements of the superordinated hospital system (i.e., entailing interprofessional and interdisciplinary cooperation), but are often confounded by characteristic dynamics and time pressure. Task requirements that promote the development of critical situations or impair the management of manifest crises in the OR are:

- *Economic pressure:* Every OR is under a considerable economic pressure, because the activities that take place in the operating room generate income for the hospital. As a result, there will regularly be a conflict between economic aspects and patient safety concerns. This conflict reduces the margin of safety and promotes the emergence of "routine violations" (Chap. 3).
- *Time pressure:* Every OR is under time pressure, as the scheduled surgical procedures have to be finished within the time frame of daily work. Deviations from this schedule are part of normal daily routine, as emergency operations can interfere with the OR schedule and delay planned procedures. Production pressure increases the risk that anesthesia will be started despite incomplete patient records and hence critical information might be overlooked. In addition, operating times vary considerably as the time necessary for an operation correlates closely with the experience of the surgeon and the complexity of the operative procedure. This makes it difficult to reliably plan the OR schedule, which in turn can further increase time pressure.

- *Using live patients for medical training:* The fact that health professionals are trained during the normal OR activity has a twofold impact on patients' safety and well-being. Firstly, the providers' inexperience increases the variance of anesthesiological and surgical time requirement for the identical procedure and may unnecessarily prolong the time during which a patient is under general anesthesia. Secondly, when patients are used as commodities to facilitate training and when the skills of health professionals are honed by using live patients, the inexperience of the healthcare provider will pose a risk for patient safety: Critical situations may arise more readily if complex and high-risk procedures are performed by novices.
- *Emergencies are an immanent part of the system:* As a result of the patients' underlying disease and of the operative procedure, emergencies arise more frequently in the OR as compared to normal wards and to other high-reliability organizations. Whereas other socio-technical domains try to avoid emergencies at any cost, an OR cannot be closed and emergency procedures can't be postponed to a later date. Consequently, emergency patient care has to be guaranteed even at unsuitable times and under inconvenient circumstances.
- *Transparency of errors committed:* Errors are usually committed in the presence of other healthcare providers and thus are "transparent" in respect to their result (e.g., drug error, surgical bleeding) and their perpetrator. As a result, feelings such as guilt or shame can quickly arise and may increase stress levels and result in a "poor judgment chain" (Chap. 10).
- *Cooperation in a confined space:* Actions are confined to a defined space and the actors are in close contact. In critical situations, a suboptimal interdisciplinary relationship can result in conflict over relational or content components of the situation or a mingling of both. None of the actors can simply leave the room in the midst of an emergency, so professional rivalries, enforcement of personal preferences, power struggle, or plain antipathy can amplify tension in team communication and seriously jeopardize teamwork and patient safety.
- *Differing medical priorities and divergent interests:* Medical priorities differ among different specialties: A problem that may pose a serious challenge for the anesthesiologist may be of only minor interest to the surgeon and vice versa. In addition, the different incentive systems (e.g., in surgery and anesthesiology) perpetuate a diversity of interests and a differing professional culture. Already during routine daily work, the patterns and nature of communications among OR team members who come from surgery, nursing, and anesthesia are characterized by differing dominant themes (e.g., time, safety and sterility, resources, role; Lingard et al. 2002). In the worst of cases, "the other" will not find much appreciation and cooperativeness and an "in-group" and "out-group" thinking may seriously threaten cooperation between the surgical discipline and anesthesiology during an emergency.
- *Traditional self-image:* As a result of the traditional conception of responsibility, the surgeon feels solely responsible for the patient as "his" or "her" patient. Interdisciplinary conflicts about contents may develop into conflicts about "right of ownership." Because of the internalized ideal image of the sovereign special-

ist, a successful operation can be attributed to a good surgeon, whereas a critical situation may amount to the admission of personal failure. Whenever one person's action triggers an uncontrollable situation, it may threaten that person's feeling of competence (cognitive emergency reaction; Chap. 9).

The crucial point about the "biotope OR" is that many of the listed factors lie beyond the influence of any single healthcare provider. Instead, a system-based approach has to be pursued to tackle these issues and blunt the negative impact on patient safety.

2.4 Tackling Complexity: Becoming an Expert

Having listed the key features of complexity, it is important to stress that complexity is not a static or objective characteristic of a task or environment, but instead a subjective one: "Complexity is not a thing per se, complexity is a situation to be investigated" (Rasmussen 1979). Whether or not a situation is perceived as complex and lacks transparency depends on specific individuals and their experiences with the situation. A novice will be overwhelmed by situational and task demands, whereas an expert clinician will display a deep tacit understanding of the situation and will easily move between intuitive and analytical approaches. From this point of view, complexity can be described as a "mental construction" of the clinician. Research on skills acquisition has deepened our understanding of how novices become expert performers in the course of their professional career. One cognitive framework, substantiated by research among pilots, chess players, professional musicians, and automobile drivers, has provided us with a "five-stage model of the acquisition of expertise" (Dreyfus and Dreyfus 1986, 2005). Initially developed to help teachers understand how to assist the learner in advancing to the next level of skills or competencies, the model has practical implications for development and assessment of healthcare providers in routine and complex situations (e.g., Carraccio et al. 2008; Table 2.2). The five stages are:

Stage 1: The novice deconstructs the task environment into its "context-free" features that can be recognized. For some specific circumstances, the novice has learned specific rules and feels responsible to find the correct rule and follow it.

Stage 2: The (advanced) beginner has gained experience coping with real situations. The advanced beginner starts to identify new situational elements and thereby develops an understanding of the relevant context. Decisions and actions are still made by rule application.

Stage 3: The competent has experience but can be overwhelmed by the large number of potentially relevant rules, elements, and procedures they can recognize. The competent starts to learn organizing principles that permit sorting information by relevance. This helps the competent to reduce complexity. Practicing decision-making and taking responsibility helps to move the competent to the next stage.

Table 2.2 Five-stage model of the acquisition of expertise (Dreyfus and Dreyfus 1986, 2005)

	Knowledge	Perception of context	Action	Coping with complexity
Novice	Minimal 'textbook' knowledge without connection to practice	Little situational perception No discretionary judgment	Rigid adherence to taught rules or plans Tends to see actions in isolation	Little or no ability to deal with complexity
Beginner	Working knowledge of key aspects of practice	Situational perception still limited All attributes and aspects are treated separately and given equal importance	Guidelines for action based on limited knowledge of attributes or aspects Sees actions as a series of steps	Appreciates complex situations but only able to achieve partial resolution
Competent	Good working and background knowledge of area of practice	Sees actions partly in terms of longer-term goals	Standard and routine procedures Now sees actions at least partially in terms of longer-term goals	Copes with complex situations through deliberate analysis and planning; little flexibility
Proficient	Depth of understanding of discipline and area of practice	Sees overall "picture" and how individual actions fit within it Perceives and evaluates deviations from normal patterns Sees what is most important in a situation	Decision-making less labored Uses maxims for guidance whose meanings and applications vary according to the situation	Deals with complex situations holistically Decision-making more confident
Expert	Authoritative knowledge of discipline Deep tacit understanding across area of practice	Intuitive grasp of situations Perceives, evaluates, and considers desired actions and alternatives of the overall "picture" Analytic approaches used only in novel situations or when new problems come to light Vision of what may be possible	Uses rules, guidelines, or maxims only as they serve to help solve the perceived problem; they are not given paramount importance	Holistic grasp of complex situations (Sees the "Gestalt") Moves between intuitive and analytical approaches with ease and confidence

Novice to expert: the Dreyfus model of skill acquisition

Stage 4: The proficient will progressively use intuition to realize "what" is happening. By now, this person is able to approach a problem from a perspective arising from multiple real-world experiences. Action becomes easier and less stressful because past experience has taught "what works and what doesn't."

Stage 5: The expert no longer decomposes situations into discrete elements. The expert recognizes situations by reducing a multitude of features into one comprehensive understanding that forms a meaningful whole. In the case report at the beginning of the chapter, the anesthetist's experience provided several meaningful patterns for the specific set of symptoms and monitor parameters; thus, the anesthetist was able to choose from among several possibilities to understand that *Gestalt* (Chap. 6.) It should be noted that the "expert" level does not mean that development stops. Expert practitioners need to evaluate their practice, continue to seek opportunities to maintain their skills, and keep up to date with new evidence.

How then does a novice become an expert? Most people assume that becoming an expert requires extreme or extraordinary ability and that this path can be trodden only by a few. However, current research points in the opposite direction: Experts are always made, not born. It is "nurture" rather than"nature" that is responsible for the level of expertise people will acquire. Research across many fields has shown how expertise can be developed (Ericsson et al. 2007):

- At least for arts and sports performers, a minimum of 10 years (or 10,000 h) of consistent and intense training is required to achieve expertise.
- Experts have to engage in "deliberate practice" – practice that focuses on tasks beyond the current level of competence or comfort – if they want to reach new levels of performance. The development of expertise requires struggle. There are no shortcuts. "To become competent, you must feel bad" (Dreyfus and Dreyfus 1986).
- Having expert coaches makes a difference. If experts coach people, the learning process can be accelerated and higher levels of proficiency can be reached in shorter time. Practice does not make perfect; instead perfect practice makes perfect.
- Real experts very often were motivated students who sought feedback and challenge from their own coaches.

Work on expert systems (computer software designed to provide an answer to a problem, or clarify uncertainties where normally human experts would need to be consulted) typically is grounded on the premise that expertise is based on acquired repertoires of rules and frameworks for decision-making. It was thought that this knowledge could be elicited by "point of care" computers to support clinical judgment and decision-making. Initial enthusiasm, however, has given way to the realization that medical expertise does not work in this fashion. Since intuitive judgment is the hallmark of expertise and expertise is based on the making of immediate and effective situational responses, it cannot be emulated by rule-based software. Therefore, expert systems may improve rule-based performance by supporting human memory (level 3 performance), but they will not lead to better decision-making in the face of complexity (Chap. 10).

2.5 The Skills, Rules, Knowledge (SRK) Framework: Progression Toward Expert Status

The effectiveness of response to a critical situation often is dependent on the degree to which a provider has experienced a similar situation. Familiarity and experience with a situation allows the provider to utilize a conceptual hierarchy of "skills, rules, and knowledge" (Rasmussen 1983, 1987; Fig. 2.2). The skills, rules, knowledge (SRK) taxonomy divides cognitive operations intro three levels of abstraction and defines three ways in which information is processed and actions executed. This distinction has been particularly helpful in characterizing the cognitive mechanisms behind different categories of errors (Chap. 3). When faced with a critical situation, people generally seek to rely on behaviors at the most routine level (i.e., skills). This provides an economical use of the limited resources of attention and conscious thinking (Chap. 6); however, if the routine (skills) level is not effective or relevant, the provider must seek a higher level to find a solution, i.e., rules and knowledge.

When the novice or the experienced clinician is faced with a critical situation, they will differ in the cognitive control mechanisms they need in order to perform

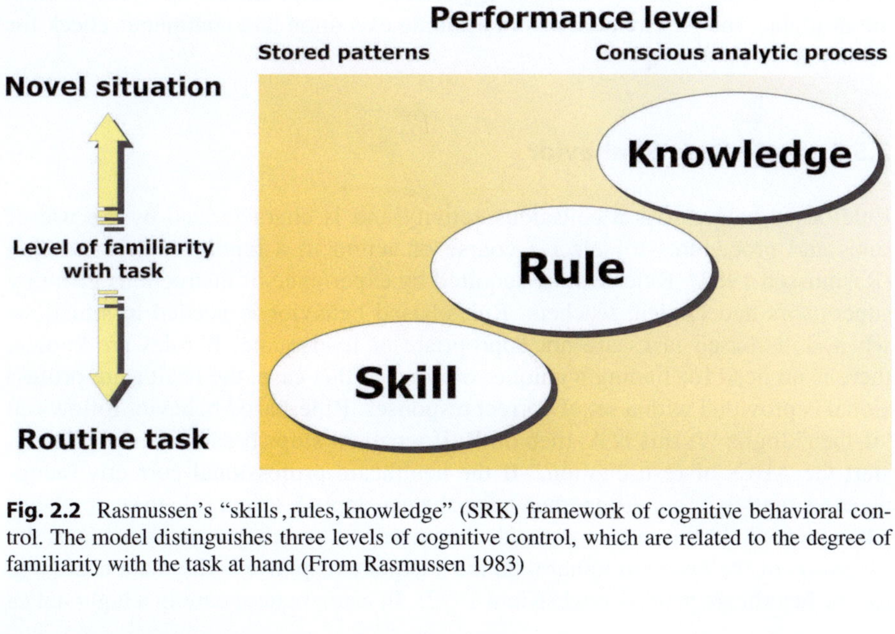

Fig. 2.2 Rasmussen's "skills, rules, knowledge" (SRK) framework of cognitive behavioral control. The model distinguishes three levels of cognitive control, which are related to the degree of familiarity with the task at hand (From Rasmussen 1983)

adequately; thus, novice and experienced providers differ from each other in the following areas:

- Automaticity of response (i.e., highly integrated patterns of behavior)
- Level of abstraction on which problems are represented
- Amount of clinical rules available
- Knowledge available
- Problem-solving strategies

2.5.1 Skill-Based Behavior

A skill-based behavior represents a type of action that requires very little or no conscious control to perform once an intention is formed. This kind of behavior, also known as *sensorimotor behavior*, is smooth and consists of integrated patterns of performance. This type of behavior is characterized by requiring little conscious thought or verbalization, it is "automated." *Automaticity* (i.e., the ability to perform tasks without allocating significant amount of attention) allows humans to free up cognitive resources which can then be used for higher cognitive functions such as problem solving. Because there are a multitude of routine tasks in critical situations that demand skill-based behavior (e.g., routine intubation, placement of peripheral and central IV lines, thoracocentesis, chest compressions), it is predictable when and under which circumstances certain skills are required. Skill-based behavior becomes an issue in critical situations if the healthcare professional does not possess these skills, if they are not available within a team, if he or she applies them wrongly, or if the behavior cannot be applied for whatever reason. However, if skills are available, the requirement lies in accurate execution and continuous check for deviation.

2.5.2 Rule-Based Behavior

Rule-based behavior is a conscious activity and is characterized by the use of rules and procedures to select a course of action in a familiar work situation (Rasmussen 1983). Rules can be acquired by experience or instructions given by supervisors and clinical teachers. Rules-based behavior is needed in situations when skills-based tasks are not appropriate or inadequate. If rules are known, there is no need for finding a unique solution. In this case, the healthcare professional is provided with a set of correct responses. Rule-based behavior follows an "if-then" logic: "If this is A, then do B; if a patient stops breathing immediately, start the ABCs of resuscitation." If the healthcare professional correctly recognizes a situation or condition, then he or she can apply a stored rule to steer toward a known goal. As the case report at the beginning of this chapter demonstrates, the *diagnosis* of the problem rather than the adequate response is the main challenge for the healthcare professional (Klein 1992). In acute patient care in a high-stakes environment, time for thinking is scarce, and wrong actions can cause patients harm; thus, healthcare providers must adhere to as many rules as possible to avoid potential problems.

2.5.3 Knowledge-Based Behavior and Problem Solving

In Rasmussen's rubric, knowledge-based tasks are those that are new, unfamiliar, or unique. Unfamiliarity can have many causes: lack of experience, inadequate clinical training, or simply forgetfulness. Most of the time, however, complexity and coupling create an unexpected and unusual combination of events, thereby giving the healthcare professional an unpleasant surprise. Because they are caused by random and not immediately known factors, critical situations like these cannot be anticipated and learned rules are inadequate. Instead, a more advanced level of reasoning, problem solving, is needed to successfully manage the situation. Healthcare providers need to build a comprehensive model of the situation, form explicit goals based on their current analysis of the situation, make a plan, and execute the plan. The cognitive workload for finding higher-level analogies or analyzing more abstract relations between structure and function is much greater than when using skill- or rule-based behaviors. Successful use of knowledge or problem solving depends heavily upon the performer's fundamental knowledge, diagnosis and analysis skills, and experience with handling critical situations. Because many critical situations unfold without warning, the surprise effect is significant. Errors in managing the critical situation derive from a complex interplay of imperfect rationality, faulty mental models of the situation, a strong emotional component (Tversky and Kahneman 1974; Kahneman et al. 1982), and poor teamwork. Because these critical situations demand a quick response on the one hand, but on the other hand cannot be addressed by precompiled responses, they can rapidly develop into an immediate threat to patient safety and well-being. Fortunately, problem solving under stress can be practiced, for example, by confronting learners and teams with different types of emergencies and allowing them to practice. By regularly training and practicing skill- and rule-based behaviors during critical situations, more cognitive resources can be applied to knowledge-based behavior when faced with an unanticipated event.

2.6 "The Challenge of Acute Medical Care" in a Nutshell

- Healthcare in a high-stakes environment has a number of properties that make it considerably more challenging than decision-making in an everyday context. Cognitive psychologists call these characteristics "complexity of a working environment."
- Complexity has a dual nature: It is a characteristic of the task environment as well as the set of demands imposed on the problem solver.
- The characteristics of a complex task environment are as follows: many features, interdependence, dynamics, time delay, and irreversibility.

- Problem solving in complex environments is rendered difficult by uncertainty, lack of transparency, singularity of the situation, information overload or lack of information, time pressure, risk, plurality of goals, and the presence of many players.
- Operating rooms and emergency rooms exhibit all elements of the superordinated system hospital (e.g., interprofessional and interdisciplinary cooperation) but are often confounded by dynamics and time pressure.
- Complexity is not a static or objective characteristic of a task domain but instead is a subjective one. It is a "mental construction" and depends on the experience of an individual with a type of situation or one with similar task demands.
- The relationship between levels of familiarity and expertise with a task or environment has been conceptualized by Rasmussen's tripartite distinction of "skills, rules, and knowledge."
- Automaticity allows humans to free up valuable cognitive resources, which can then be used for higher cognitive functions such as problem solving.
- Research across domains has shown that large amounts of practicing at the edge of one's expertise will lead one to become an expert. Experts must continually work to eliminate weaknesses.
- Experts are made, not born: The amount and quality of practice are the key factors in the level of expertise people acquired.
- Expertise consists of personal characteristics, skills, and knowledge that distinguish experts from novices. In many domains, there are objective measures of performance capable of distinguishing experts from novices.

References

Atlee JL (2007) Complications in anesthesia. Saunders, Philadelphia

Badke-Schaub P (2002) Kritische Situationen als Analyseeinheit komplexer Handlungen [Critical situations as a unit for analyzing complex actions]. In: Trimpop R, Zimolong B, Kalveram A (eds) Psychologie der Arbeitssicherheit und Gesundheit, Neue Welten – alte Welten [Psychology of work safety and health]. Asanger, Heidelberg, pp 137–142

Carraccio CL, Benson BJ, Nixon LJ, Derstine PL (2008) From the educational vench to the clinical bedside: translating the Dreyfus developmental model to the learning of clinical skills. Acad Med 83:761–767

Cook R, Woods D (2001) Operating at the sharp end: the complexity of human error. In: Salas E, Bowers C, Edens E (eds) Improving teamwork in organizations: applications of resource management training. Erlbaum, Mahwah, pp 255–310

Dörner D (1996) The logic of failure: recognizing and avoiding error in complex situations. Metropolitan Books, New York

Dörner D, Schaub H (1994) Errors in planning and decision-making and the nature of human information processing. Appl Psychol Int Rev 43:433–453

Dreyfus HL, Dreyfus SE (1986) Mind over machine: the power of human intuition and expertise in the age of the computer. Basil Blackwell, Oxford

Dreyfus HL, Dreyfus SE (2005) Expertise in real world context. Organization Studies 26(5):779–792

Ericsson KA, Prietula MJ, Cokely ET (2007) The making of an expert. Harv Bus Rev 85(7):114–121

Frensch A, Funke J (eds) (1995) Complex problem-solving: the European perspective. Erlbaum, Hillsdale

Gaba D (1992) Dynamic decision-making in anesthesiology: cognitive models and training approaches. In: Evans DA, Patel VL (eds) Advanced models of cognition for medical training and practice. Springer, Berlin/Heidelberg/New York, pp 123–148

Gaba DM, Fish KJ, Howard SK (1994) Crisis management in anesthesia. Churchill Livingstone, New York

Gravenstein N, Kirby RR (1995) Complications in anaesthesiology. Lippincott-Raven, Philadelphia

Halpern DF (2002) Thought & knowledge. Lawrence Erlbaum, Hillsdale

Kahneman D, Slovic P, Tversky A (1982) Judgment under uncertainty: heuristics and biases. Cambridge University Press, Cambridge

Klein G (1992) A recognition-primed decision (RPD) model of rapid decision-making. In: Klein G, Orasanu J, Calderwood R, Zsamboka E (eds) Decision-making in action: models and methods. Ablex, Norwood, pp 138–147

Kohn L, Corrigan J, Donaldson M (1999) To err is human: building a safer health system. Committee on Quality of Healthcare in America, Institute of Medicine (IOM). National Academy, Washington

Lingard L, Reznick R, DeVito I, Espin S (2002) Forming professional identities on the health care team: discursive constructions of the 'other'in the operating room. Med Educ 36:728–734

Perrow C (1999) Normal accidents. Living with high-risk technologies. Princeton University Press, Princeton

Rasmussen J (1979) On the structure of knowledge: a morphology of mental models in a man–machine systems context. Technical Report Riso-M-2192. Riso National Laboratory, Roskilde

Rasmussen J (1983) Skills, rules, knowledge: signals, signs and symbols and other distinctions in human performance models. IEEE Trans Systems, Man and. Cybernetics SMC-13(3): 257–267

Rasmussen J (1987) Cognitive control and human error mechanisms. In: Rasmussen J, Duncan K, Leplat J (eds) New technology and human error. Wiley, Chichester, pp 53–61

Rasmussen J, Lind M (1981) Coping with complexity. Technical Report Riso-M-2293. Riso National Laboratory, Roskilde

Reason J (1990) Human error. Cambridge University Press, Cambridge, UK

Reason J (1997) Managing the risks of organizational accidents. Ashgate, Aldershot

Rosenthal MM, Sutcliffe KM (eds) (2002) Medical error. What do we know? What do we do? Jossey-Bass, San Francisco

Salas E, Dickinson TL, Converse SA, Tannenbaum SI (1992) Toward an understanding of team performance and training. In: Swezey RW, Salas E (eds) Teams: their training and performance. Ablex, Norwood, pp 3–30

Sterman JD (1994) Learning in and about complex systems. Syst Dyn Rev 10:291–330

Taylor TH, Major E (1987) Hazards and complications in anaesthesia. Churchill Livingstone, Edinburgh

Tversky A, Kahneman D (1974) Judgment under uncertainty: heuristics and biases. Science 185:1124–1131

Vincent C (ed) (2002) Clinical risk management. BMJ Publishing Group, London

Woods D (1988) Coping with complexity: the psychology of human behaviour in complex systems. In: Goodstein L, Andersen H, Olsen S (eds) Tasks, errors and mental models. Taylor Francis, London, pp 128–147

3 The Nature of Error

Case Study

An anesthesia resident physician in his second year of training anesthetizes a 76-year-old patient scheduled for a laryngectomy and bilateral neck dissection. The medical history reveals coronary artery disease and liver cirrhosis. As a result of the associated coagulopathy, the surgeon has difficulty achieving adequate hemostasis and therefore repeatedly applies epinephrine-soaked swabs to the surgical site. The undiluted epinephrine is rapidly absorbed into circulation and causes sinus tachycardia and polymorphic premature ventricular contractions. Unaware of the surgeon's use of undiluted epinephrine, the resident does not attribute the PVCs to the hemostatic treatment and hence does not urge the surgeon to stop the application. Instead, he decides to treat the arrhythmia with an ampule of lidocaine. Distracted by the ECG, the anesthesiologist does not pay close attention and mistakenly uses an ampule of metoprolol (a β-blocker) instead of the intended dose of lidocaine 2 %. This drug error is facilitated by the fact that both ampules are adjacent to each other in the anesthesia cart and have similar-looking labels. The bolus of the β-blocker leads to cardiac arrest. Immediate CPR is started. After calling the attending anesthesiologist to the operating room, the patient is successfully resuscitated. The patient is discharged from ICU the following day without any neurological deficits.

The analysis of the case report appears to be straightforward: A young resident swaps two cardiovascular drugs and thereby causes a cardiac arrest. One could easily say that he should have been more diligent when he took the drug out of the drawer. To make things worse, the medical indication to give the drug was wrong in the first place. Instead of consulting an experienced colleague, he acted on his own account and jeopardized the patient's life. "Someone who commits such a grave

M. St.Pierre et al., *Crisis Management in Acute Care Settings*,
DOI 10.1007/978-3-319-41427-0_3

mistake," one might suggest, "lacks motivation, competency, and aptitude for an anesthesiologist." But even if this interpretation appears to have strong arguments in its favor, it nevertheless focuses on the person and not on the wrong action and judges a mistake on the basis of its consequences. This approach is unhelpful in generating safety, as we will show in the following chapter. However, we will first look at an everyday example that will help clarify the difference between an erroneous action and a wrong result.

3.1 What Is an Error?

An old lady sits at her window and pursues her favorite pastime: looking down on the street and watching people passing by (Fig. 3.1). For almost a decade, things went uneventfully, but today a mishap occurs: One moment of inattention and her forearm shoves the flowerpot off the window ledge – she commits an error. At best, the consequence of this error is a pile of shards and dirt on the sidewalk. If the worst comes to the worst, she will have to call an emergency medical service because a pedestrian sustained a severe head trauma. Regardless, the severity of the consequence is independent from the underlying cognitive error mechanism (in this case disturbance of attention). External circumstances, related to neither the person nor the error type, determine the outcome of the moment of inattention.

What at first may seem to be commonplace actually turns out to be an example from ordinary life of two distinct perspectives on error. In addition, it perfectly

Fig. 3.1 The difference between error and consequences. One moment of inattention results in a flowerpot being shoved from the window ledge. Although the underlying error mechanism is the same in all three examples, the consequences differ considerably dependent on which floor the old lady lives: basement (*left*) or third floor (*middle*), and even more so if a pedestrian passes below the window exactly in the moment when the pot is shoved from the ledge (Courtesy of Jean Pariés Dédale SAS)

illustrates a fundamental idea of patient safety: One can't understand errors by focusing on the outcome.

One way to look at errors is to classify them by their consequences. *Consequential classifications* emphasize the result of an action. This perspective implies that an action can only be counted as erroneous if it leads to a negative result. If a flowerpot falls out of a second-floor window, it is a much graver mistake than if the same course of events occurs in the basement. Consequential classifications are the most widely used in medicine (e.g., a wrong drug was given to the patient). If people take this viewpoint, their point of interest usually is *what happened* to the patient. Why and under which circumstances the error occurred is of secondary interest to them. In addition, the equivalence between cause and result is assumed: A bad outcome is consistent with a bad process which in turn typically implies insufficient qualification, motivation, or low morale of the person responsible for the incident.

Causal classifications, on the other hand, make assumptions about mechanisms implicated in generating the error. The point of interest in this approach is *why* a planned activity did not result in its intended outcome. In this conceptual framework, the focus is diverted from the outcome of an error and shifted toward possible psychological precursors and systemic interactions that led to the wrong action. People who take this perspective are aware of the fact that factors beyond the reach of the person determine whether an error causes a trivial or grave outcome, e.g., here was no guard railing around the window ledge, house rules did not explicitly prohibit flowerpots on the window ledge, by chance the man has to pass below the window at the exact time the pot reaches the height of his head, etc. If an incident or accident occurs, individual factors of behavior (e.g., perception, information processing, memory, attention), goals and plans, teamwork, and communication are scrutinized for their possible impact. Fig. 3.1 summarizes both perspectives on error.

People do not seem to distinguish between those two perspectives in everyday practice. "A drug error occurred in the OR" seems to be the same as "The resident injected the wrong drug." If only one person seems to be involved in the medication error, a clear cause-and-effect attribution seems justified: His or her wrong actions led to the undesired result. Even in such simple cases, this kind of an assessment is inadequate because most accidents occur in a dynamic setting with multiple healthcare providers involved. In the first perspective, the consequential perspective on error with its focus on what happened, it is relatively easy to find the unwanted result and identify the error. If in looking for causes we try to find *the* wrong action, and *the* (one) person who did it, we speak of the "person-based approach" to errors.

3.1.1 Person-Based Approach

The "person approach" remains the dominant tradition in response to adverse outcomes in healthcare. The long-standing and widespread tradition of the person-based approach focuses on the unsafe acts of people with direct patient contact.

According to the person approach, it is the healthcare provider's fault if something goes wrong. He or she did not have the necessary knowledge, did not pay attention, or was not motivated to do their best. Errors are attributed to missing knowledge or to aberrant mental processes such as forgetfulness, not paying attention, poor motivation, and negligence. As a consequence, assuming that bad things happen because "bad" (i.e., lazy, stupid, or reckless) people committed an error becomes moral issues as well. The result is a culture of "naming, blaming, and shaming."

When viewed from this perspective, solutions to errors lie in improving knowledge (training, education) and in improving motivation by exhortations ("be more careful the next time"), disciplinary measures, or threat of litigation and financial punishment. Personal motivation and becoming a better person and healthcare provider seem to be the keys to error-free performance: "If you concentrate, you will not swap ampules."

From an organizational perspective, this approach is attractive in terms of maintaining the public image of the healthcare institution and because the institution appears relatively blameless. Instead of looking for institutional responsibility with error-prone systems, it is easier and cheaper to target "bad" individuals. The person approach, however, misses the opportunity to enhance patient safety by fixing our systems of care because the approach isolates unsafe acts from their system context. Far from being random, mishaps tend to fall into recurrent patterns. A similar set of circumstances can provoke similar errors, regardless of the healthcare provider involved. This explains why error is not the monopoly of an unfortunate few: Accident analyses from other technological high-stakes environments (e.g., civil aviation, nuclear power, space exploration) demonstrate that it is often "the best people who make the worst mistakes" (Reason 1997). This is sometimes because with growing experience people become complacent, and sometimes it is simply because the most experienced people are given the most difficult jobs. But mostly it is because we tend to put highly trained, competent, and caring people within complex and inherently error-inducing systems. Most of the time, these experts are able to catch an error before it happens or mitigate its effects, but sometimes they cannot. Over and above not being appropriate and helpful, the person approach impedes the pursuit of greater safety by focusing on individuals rather than seeking out and removing the error-provoking properties within our healthcare systems at large.

3.1.2 System-Based Approach

If people advocate a "systemic approach" to the study and prevention of safety-critical errors, the focus shifts from the person at the "sharp end," the one who is directly providing patient care, to include organizational processes and the system as a whole. Instead of looking for the one defining action (and hence the one responsible person) that caused the accident, all levels of the organization are scrutinized for contributing factors. The basic premise in the system approach is that humans are fallible and errors are to be expected, even from the best people in the best organizations. Whenever errors are studied, this should not be done as a separate, pathological category of behavior fragments; the object of study should instead be the cognitive control of behavior in complex environments (Rasmussen 1990). In this conceptual framework, accidents are seen as the result of an unlikely confluence and interaction of several causal streams originating not in the perversity of human nature but rather in an unfortunate interaction with normal cognitive processes and "upstream" systemic factors. Systemic dimensions greatly influence a system's susceptibility to accidents: As soon as socio-technological systems become sufficiently complex, accidents will be inevitable or "normal" (Chap. 14; Perrow 1999). In this view healthcare providers are the inheritors, rather than the instigators, of an accident sequence. The concept of an "organizational accident" replaces the simplistic notion of accepting the explanation for a mishap as "human error" (Reason 1995). Within the systemic framework, countermeasures are based on the assumption that although the human condition cannot be changed, the conditions under which humans work *can* be. The vulnerability of a system can be reduced by strengthening system defenses (resilience; Hollnagel et al. 2006).

Finally, when an adverse event occurs and patients are harmed, the important issue will not be "Who blundered?" but rather "Why and how did the defenses fail? What were the upstream systemic factors contributing to the mishap?" To focus on the system and its weakness will provide valuable information for further improvement. Thus, by changing the focus of accident investigations from finding out "Whose fault is it?," our healthcare system will become more reliable and safer if we ask the following:

- *What* exactly went wrong? What different types of failures occurred? Is a temporal reconstruction of key events possible?
- *Why* did things go wrong? Which psychological mechanisms may have contributed to the development of the accident?
- *In which ways* did the various organizational and human factors *combine* to create the accident?

3.2 How Can Errors Be Classified?

Since Sigmund Freud's *Psychopathology of Everyday Life* (Freud 1901), which searched for the roots of error in the subconscious, the unconscious, and the psychosexual state of the individual, various error taxonomies have been proposed (for an overview: Reason 1990; Senders and Moray 1991; Dekker 2005, 2006; Strauch 2001). There is still no single conceptual framework that appears to give us an agreed-upon and comprehensive picture of human error. There is, however, widespread agreement that speaking of an "error" implies that there was (a) intentional action, (b) aimed at a goal, and (c) at least one alternative existed somewhere in the chain of events that could have been done differently to prevent or mitigate the error. All classifications agree on the distinction between whether something was done wrongly (execution failure) and whether something wrong was done (planning failure).

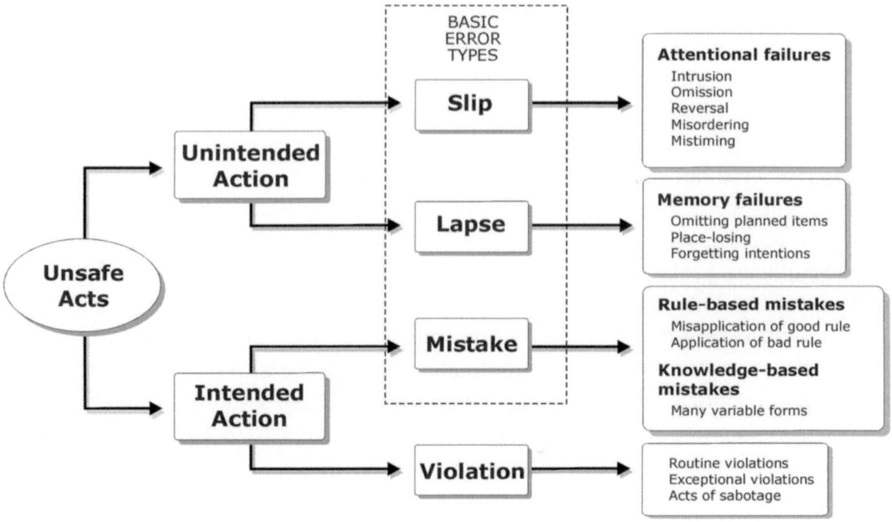

Fig. 3.2 Taxonomy of error according to Reason (Adapted from Reason 1990)

Within the healthcare community, the most influential classification was introduced by the cognitive psychologist James Reason (1990) who proposed three important distinctions (Fig. 3.2):

1. At what level of action control was the error committed? (execution failure vs. planning failure)
2. Was an action executed in the way intended? (Error vs. violation)
3. How long before the accident and at which level of the organization was the error chain started? (active vs. latent error)

In addition, we propose two additional types of error that play an important role in the high-stakes medical environment:

4. Errors in decision-making
5. Errors in teamwork (e.g., faulty communication, insufficient leadership, and inadequate allocation of resources)

3.2.1 Execution Failure Versus Planning Failure

The term *error* applies to intentional actions only: An error is a planned sequence of mental or physical activities that fails to achieve its intended outcome (Reason 1990). The reason for failure can be twofold (Norman 1981):

- *Execution failure*: A planned action fails to achieve the desired outcome because the actions did not go as planned.

- *Planning failure*: A planned action fails to achieve the desired outcome because the plan was inadequate.

3.2.1.1 Execution Failure

In this context the planned course of action is adequate to achieve its objective but the action itself deviates from the intended course. This distinction gives rise to two other working definitions:

Slips result from failure in the execution of an action sequence, often coming from an attentional failure. Slips are potentially observable as externalized "actions not as planned" and occur predominantly with familiar tasks. An example of a slip is setting a defibrillator unintentionally at the wrong energy level.

Lapses are a less obvious form of execution failure and are usually the result of memory failure such as when steps within a sequence of action are omitted because they have been forgotten or overlooked. This happens frequently when there are many steps in a complex process such as placing a central venous catheter.

Because the case study resident's attention was captured for a brief moment by the pathological ECG, he did not pay sufficient attention to the drug he took from the anesthesia cart. A slip was the triggering event of the cardiac arrest in the surgical patient.

3.2.1.2 Planning Failure

Whereas slips and lapses hinder an adequate plan going as intended, the problem of planning failure lies in the inadequacy of the plan itself.

Mistakes are defined as deficiencies or failures in the cognitive processes with which a problem was addressed. Mistakes are independent of whether or not the action was correct or not; mistakes occur when an inadequate plan makes the desired outcome unlikely or impossible.

Mistakes can happen when problem solving is inadequate (knowledge-based mistake) or when the wrong rules are used (rule-based mistake; Rasmussen 1990). In the latter case, mistakes can manifest as:

- The application of a bad rule that remains uncorrected. For example, a provider applies chest compressions during cardiac arrest but at a rate that is incorrect and therefore ineffective.
- The misapplication of a "good" rule, because countersigns (i.e., inputs such as contraindications that indicate that the more general rule is inapplicable) are not taken into account or clinical signs are not detected. The resident's decision to inject lidocaine for the treatment of PVCs is an example of the misapplication of a "good" rule for antiarrhythmic therapy. The resident missed the specifics of the situation: The problematic ECG was not due to the patient's cardiac status, but rather the excessive (but short-lived) plasma level of epinephrine due to the actions of the surgeon. The appropriate rule would have been to simply wait for

the decline of the plasma levels of epinephrine and to request the surgeon to stop administering epinephrine-soaked swabs.

- The non-application of a "good" rule, because the healthcare provider was unfamiliar with the rule or unable to remember it in time. For example, during transport a patient requires intubation. Because the patient recently ate a meal, the paramedic decides to do a rapid-sequence intubation – but fails to provide cricoid pressure during the procedure with the result that the patient regurgitates.

3.2.2 Errors in Problem Solving

Every time a healthcare professional encounters a novel situation that lies outside the range of his or her usual responses, problem solving becomes necessary. Instead of applying familiar rules to a problem, the healthcare provider has to utilize less familiar knowledge to address the situation. Conscious thinking, however, the very "tool" we need for problem solving, is error prone for several reasons:

- Conscious thought works relatively slowly. It has limited capacity ("System 2 processes") and leads us to use our scarce resources as efficiently as possible. We therefore tend to avoid conscious thinking whenever possible and instead take shortcuts or resort to rule-based behavior (Chap. 6).
- In addition to relying on shortcuts (heuristics) and rules, cognitive bias plays an unconscious role in erroneously shortcutting the decision-making process. Far from being pathological, these systematic deviations from rationality are the result of basic principles of action regulation.
- Plans are based on a mental model of the current situation. Unfortunately, mental models are often incomplete or even incorrect. Resulting actions will therefore carry a high risk of being faulty from the start.
- Complexity, uncertainty, and high risk create the uneasy feeling of incompetence. To avoid this feeling, we tend to seek a simple and stable mental model that guards a feeling of competence. Mental models of the world that maintain our feeling of being able to master the situation are selected, and contradictory evidence tends to be discarded (Kahneman et al. 1982; Dörner 1996).

A closer look at the process of problem solving reveals that it can be further subdivided into several steps (Table 3.1; Chap. 10). Errors in problem solving can occur at every step. Research on human problem-solving capabilities has identified several "cardinal errors" (Table 3.2; Dörner 1996).

Errors in problem solving are much more difficult to detect than execution failures, because slips and lapses can become apparent while a person is still acting. Mistakes, however, can pass unnoticed for lengthy periods and become apparent only after planned actions fail to achieve the intended outcome. Even if the issue of faulty planning is raised in an acute care team, the pros and cons of a plan are not known with certainty and can be debated. Chapters 6 and 7 deal with errors on different levels of the outward and visible order of action in more detail.

Table 3.1 Five steps in the organization of complex action

1. Preparedness
2. Analysis of one's own person and the situation
- Monitoring self
- Gathering information
- Building mental models
3. Planning actions
- Formulation of goals
- Risk assessment
- Planning action sequences
- Decision-making
4. Execution of planned action
5. Review effects
- Review actions
- Review and revise strategy
- Self-reflection

Table 3.2 "Cardinal errors" in problem solving

Failure to suspect or anticipate any problems ("planning optimism")
Only information supporting initial assumptions is selected ("confirmation bias")
Skip the process of planning and defining goals and immediately start to act resulting in blind activism
Unawareness of conflicting goals
Not considering side effects, long-term repercussions, and risks
The effects of actions are not reevaluated on a regular basis

3.2.3 Active Errors Versus Latent Conditions

For the understanding of how people contribute to critical situations and accidents, a third distinction is important (Reason 1990, 1997): Errors threatening a patient's safety can be committed by the person treating the patient at the moment or they can be the result of decisions made far away in terms of time or space from the actual patient encounter (e.g., management, equipment manufacturer). These failures lie dormant within the system, and considerable time may elapse before they contribute to an unwanted event. In summary, active errors and latent conditions differ in two points: (a) the place/level in an organization where they occur and (b) the length of time that passes before they reveal an adverse impact on safety.

3.2.3.1 Active Errors

Active errors are committed by people in close proximity to the human-system interface, e.g., when operating medical equipment or at the interface of healthcare provider and patient. These interfaces are the so-called "sharp end" of an organization. Active errors are visible and trigger incidents or accidents directly, thus leading to immediate consequences. Because active errors are easily identified, they are the object of public scrutiny and often lead to sanctions of the "responsible" individual. Swapping similar-looking drug ampules and injecting the wrong drug are examples of active errors by the anesthesiologist.

3.2.3.2 Latent Conditions

Safety-critical decisions can be made by people who are at the "blunt end" of the organization. Blunt-end decisions are made away from the patient and are removed from the patient in terms of time and distance. Blunt-end decisions that have potential to negatively affect patients create "latent errors." These decisions are made at all levels of the organization: Top-level decisions as well as administrative regulations create conditions that facilitate accidents in the workplace. These latent conditions can be hidden in structures (e.g., architecture of acute care facilities, medical equipment, and software), processes (e.g., operational procedures, staff selection and recruitment, qualification, and human resource allocation), and resources (e.g., labeling of ampules) within the organization. In every complex system, at any given moment, an uncertain amount of hidden latent conditions exist. It can take years or even decades for the blunt-end decisions that created them to have consequences for a patient. Until that day, nobody would call them an "error" even though in hindsight, they may have been wrong from the beginning.

A substantial body of scientific evidence has made it apparent that latent conditions pose the greatest threat to the safety of a system as they can interact with active failures to penetrate defensive layers of the system. Healthcare organizations are especially vulnerable because they have to allocate resources to two distinct goals: production and safety. Because financial resources are finite, competing interests between production (i.e., patient care) and safety often are solved in favor of economic goals.

In the case study, the management decision to allocate only one anesthesia provider to every OR without having a spare professional to supervise less experienced staff (the resident physician) is a latent condition for the errors that triggered the critical situation in the case report. Another latent condition for that case – and probably for many others – is the design of the drug ampules that facilitates swapping.

3.2.4 Errors in Teamwork

Teamwork is an essential component of acute patient care. A close relationship exists between good teamwork and successful performance in a high-stakes environment (Schmutz and Manser 2013; Manser 2009; Wheelan et al. 2003). Poor teamwork and communication have emerged as key factors responsible for the occurrence of medical errors (Barrett et al. 2001; Morey et al. 2002). One of the most consistent reasons for poor team organization and poor teamwork is the lack of a shared understanding about the importance of and actions involved in successful teamwork. As a result, conflicts among team members and a breakdown in communication can impair collaboration and result in an under- or misutilization of available resources and the creation of new problems. In addition, team members may not share the same situational assessment and may be reluctant to question actions of teammates even when serious concerns about the adequacy of a diagnosis or treatment exist. The fact that neither the surgeon communicated the application of epinephrine-soaked swabs nor did the anesthesia resident inquire about any unusual procedures by the surgeon is an indicator of poor or nonexistent teamwork in the operating room. Errors in teamwork and their remedial actions are addressed in detail in Chap. 11.

3.3 Proficiency and Probability of Error

At the beginning of their clinical careers, healthcare providers' main concern is to acquire the necessary textbook knowledge and to transfer it to the clinical context. Basic clinical rules are memorized and applied to routine situations. As most beginners are under tutorship or close supervision, they mainly deal with "easy cases," which do not demand too much from them. Thus, the majority of errors will be knowledge based (Fig. 3.3). As the advanced beginner learns to identify new situational elements and starts to apply more and more rules, the probability increases that rule-based errors are committed. When approaching the expert level with its holistic situation assessment and intuitive decision-making, the probability of error due to knowledge deficiency or application of the wrong rule decreases. Instead, absentmindedness increases the likelihood of slips and lapses.

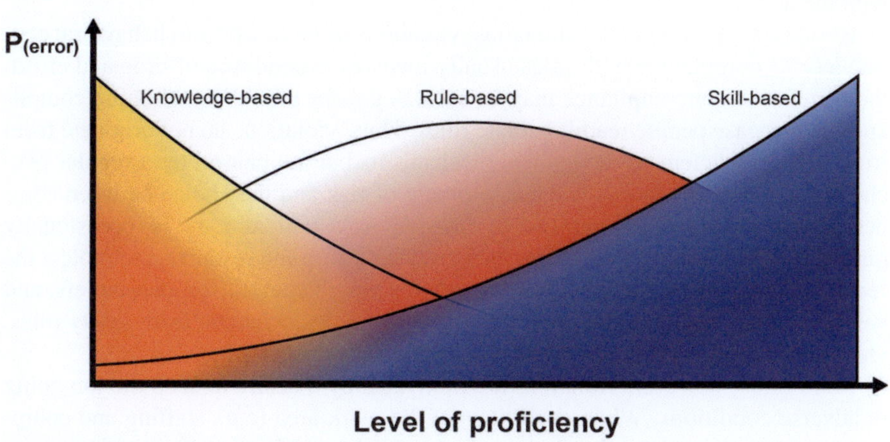

Fig. 3.3 The relationship between probability of error and proficiency depending on the level of expertise. The *y*-axis represents the relative probability of error, whereas the *x*-axis represents the level of provider proficiency. Paradoxically, the more proficient a provider is, the more the error probability increases because skill-based errors are committed due to absentmindedness. Rule-based errors initially increase because beginners tend to be overwhelmed by the excessive number of potentially relevant rules, elements, and procedures (Drawing by J. Reason, reworked with personal permission of the author)

3.4 Violations and Migrations

Up to now unsafe behavior has been addressed from the perspective of individual errors. However, an individual-based analysis of error mechanism fails to capture some of the important human contributions to incidents and system breakdowns. These mechanisms have to be described in terms of the social context and the rules and procedures that regulate behavior: Healthcare providers do not act in isolation but within a regulated social context (e.g., organization, department), which defines a safe working space by providing safe operating procedures, standards, and social norms. Deliberate deviations from written rules and instructions by an individual are called violations.

3.4.1 Violations and Abnormal Routines

Although the term *violation* tends to carry a negative connotation in everyday life, the etiology of violations cannot necessarily be equated with malevolence. *Malevolent acts* (sabotage or vandalism), where harm to the patient, coworker, equipment, or institution is deliberately intended, represent a minority of violations. More often we find actions of individuals that are not intended to do harm but which nevertheless run contrary to existing regulations. *Exceptional violations* are rare and happen only in particular circumstances, usually when unexpected events occur. In the case of unexpected events, an individual attempts to solve a problem in an unfamiliar situation by breaking a rule, but does not fully appreciate the risk associated with the action.

Besides those exceptional situations, violations often result from behavioral economics. As compliance with rules usually involves expenditure of time and effort, the benefits of noncompliance may be seen as greater than those of being compliant – in that case people readily violate rules. Thus, violations do not originate from irrational or deficient psychological mechanisms but are caused by a regular psychological process (Chap. 4): the assessment of risk and the choice between competing intentions. The intention to provide safe patient care is occasionally outweighed by stronger intentions, such as to save time and resources, to protect the feeling of competence, to go to bed as early as possible, etc. Attitudes, beliefs, and values, and not cognitive failures, are responsible for deviations from safety rules. One can err without violating and one can violate without erring.

More often, however, violations are motivated by a desire to keep the job going in adverse conditions. When conditions of the work area (e.g., staffing and equipment) are inadequate but the clinician is expected to perform as if everything were normal, violations are inevitable. These *situational violations* are promoted by the belief that risk associated with forbidden behavior is offset by the clinician's knowledge and skills and that personal knowledge and skills will allow the clinician to maintain adequate control over a difficult situation.

When there are no negative consequences either for the patient or the healthcare worker, the violation is reinforced and learned as a successful behavior. If by that learning process neglecting a safety rule becomes normal, we speak of *routine violations* or *normal violations* (Vaughan 1997).

Routine violations have been studied extensively in recent years (Battman and Klumb 1993; Rasmussen 1997; Lawton 1998; Amalberti 2001; Beatty and Beatty 2004). Violations only occur in systems where constraints and defenses define the lower limit of safe work (Fig. 3.4; boundary between green and yellow). The work space within which clinicians can navigate freely is limited by economic constraints (affordability), by technological constraints (not feasible or not available), and by the individual (physiological and cognitive limits). Within this space there is a point of maximum safety (albeit at the cost of suboptimal performance and fewer degrees of individual freedom; A in Fig. 3.4) and a point of maximum performance (B in Fig. 3.4) at the cost of less safety.

In healthcare there is organizational pressure on individuals to increase performance and enhance patient safety. Thus there is a constant tension in maximizing performance, which moves clinical care to the boundaries of safe operations (C in Fig. 3.4). Violations sometimes actually are expected or tacitly

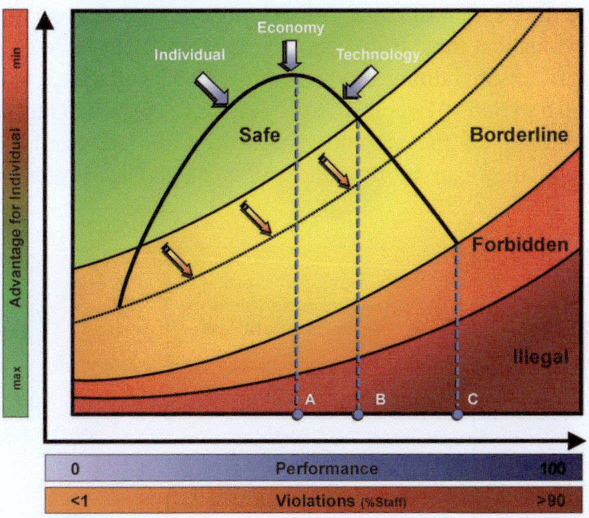

Fig. 3.4 Model of migration of practices based on Rasmussen (1997) and Amalberti et al. (2006). Work space within which human actors provide safe work is limited by safe operating procedures, standards, or social norms on the one hand (*boundary between yellow and green*) and economic, technological, and individual constraints on the other hand (*bell-shaped curve*). Within this space, clinical practice can vary between maximum safety at the cost of suboptimal performance and fewer degrees of individual freedom (*A*) and maximum performance at the cost of less safety (*B*). However, the range of operation in actual practice is wider than the initial space of safe practice. Boundaries of patient safety performance tend to yield to external pressure on production performance and make migration of the system toward less safe areas virtually unavoidable (*dotted line*). Normally, migration is limited to borderline-tolerated conditions of use (BTCUs) in which staff tacitly accepts routine minor violations. Under extreme pressure, violations can cross the line to forbidden space (*C*)

approved by management and the organizational culture. Thus we often hear the phrase in our organizations: "no harm; no foul." If safety regulations are equipped with a lot of "buffer," greater performance is possible without compromising safety too much. But if violations are not sanctioned, clinicians learn during their adaptive search for the best strategy that regulations can be broken without consequences. Secondary advantages for the individual may reinforce such behavior. Thus, initial defenses are likely to degenerate systematically through time. Workers will enlarge the initially safe space of action by migrating toward the "boundary of acceptable performance" (Amalberti et al. 2006). Over time this process of boundary decay leads to a new "unofficial" boundary (Fig. 3.4, dotted line) where deviant behavior becomes routine behavior. As long as no accident occurs, there is no need to recalibrate the system, and the "normalization of deviance" (Vaughan 1997) is maintained by the managements' tolerance and by structural secrecy.

3.4.2 Remedial Strategies for Errors and Violations

From the above description of cognitive and motivational sources of unsafe acts, it has become obvious that there is no single "magic bullet" capable of addressing the entire spectrum of unsafe human action. A different etiology leads to different management (Health and Safety Executive 1995; Fig. 3.5). Slips and lapses can never be completely prevented, but they can be reduced by automation and improved workplace design, and they can be detected and managed by supervision and team

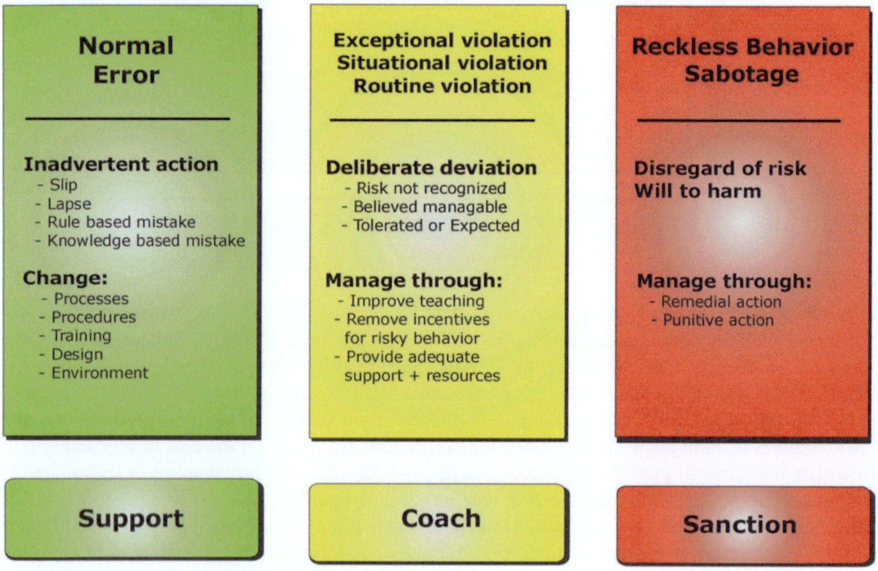

Fig. 3.5 Remedial strategies on error and violations

monitoring. For errors that occur as a result of insufficient knowledge or proficiency, there are several remedial approaches: Teaching can improve knowledge and situation awareness, and skills training can have the potential to reduce errors by improving procedural competence. But both approaches, team monitoring and improved teaching, will have limited effect on the reduction of violations that have an attitudinal basis.

A "natural" tendency within organizations is to respond to incidents with the development of new rules to increase standards. However, creating a body of rules is not sufficient to ensure compliance if the necessary understanding is not communicated – or if the cognitive economy speaks in favor of noncompliance. Thus, violations that are deliberate deviations from the rules require different remediation from those that result from unfamiliarity or inexperience. Because violations naturally reflect the adaptation of professionals in coping with conflicting production and safety demands of their work situations, it is a futile endeavor to completely eliminate them. However, while routine violations cannot be eliminated, they can be *managed* and negative results mitigated. There are certain organizational features that breed a climate of patient safety. These features include encouraging individuals to openly discuss with peers and team members the dangers of reducing an emphasis on patient safety, where clinicians set clear priorities of safety over performance and where organizations have systems that encourage self-checking and team cross-monitoring.

Whereas erring people deserve support and people violating rules are in need of coaching, there should not be indulgence for conscious acts of malevolence. These acts are so contrary to the culture of healthcare and to the value of patient safety that immediate disciplinary or punitive action is management's path of choice.

3.5 The Dynamics of Accident Causation

The adverse consequences of latent error conditions are not revealed until active failures occur. Latent errors remain hidden within the system time until they combine with other factors and local triggering events (e.g., active failures of individuals) to breach the defensive barriers of the system. In order to breach defenses, an unlikely combination of several contributing factors, including the interaction of active and latent failures, on many levels within an organization is required. Unfortunately, the concatenation of these diverse and unusual combinations of events is usually impossible to foresee.

3.5.1 A Window of Opportunity for Errors

The most famous model of accident causation was proposed by James Reason (1990, 1995, 2001), who compared accident causation with a projectile originating in latent decisions made at the higher levels of an organization. In order to cause an accident ("accident opportunity"), the projectile has to penetrate all layers, each of

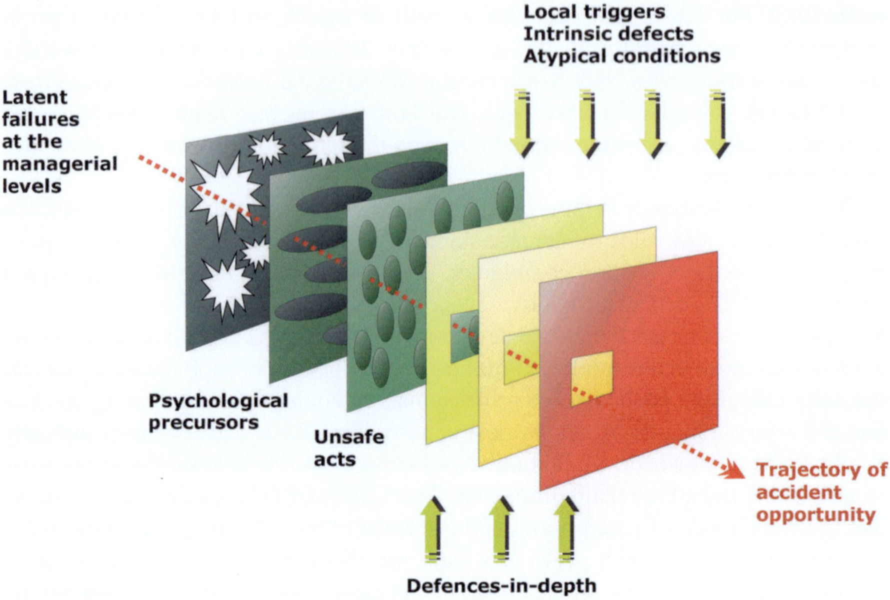

Fig. 3.6 The dynamics of accident causation. A complex interaction between latent failures, active errors, and a variety of local triggering events results in an accident. The trajectory of accident opportunity penetrates several layers in the defensive system. As all the loopholes have to overlay at one time for the accident to happen, the window of accident opportunity is very small (Adapted from Reason 1990)

them representing an organizational, environmental, or personal defense (Fig. 3.6) as follows:

- Latent failures at the organizational level (e.g., faulty management decisions, fallible organizational processes, absence of a safety culture) are transmitted along organizational and departmental pathways to the workplace and create local conditions that promote the occurrence of errors.
- Psychological precursors of unsafe acts are generated by local conditions, personality, and the "psycho-logic" of human action regulation (Chap. 4).
- Unsafe acts can occur due to active failures (e.g., slips, lapses, and mistakes) or violations that combine with the upstream conditions.
- "Defenses in depth" fail (e.g., clinical and behavioral skills, teamwork ability, and technical safety systems), leaving the system vulnerable to the trajectory of accident causation.

If the projectile penetrates several defense layers but is blocked before it can trigger an accident (e.g., a clinician notices an ampule swap before injecting the wrong drug), an *incident* (synonym, critical incident or near miss) has occurred. Thus, incidents are events that reduce the safety margin for a patient. Critical

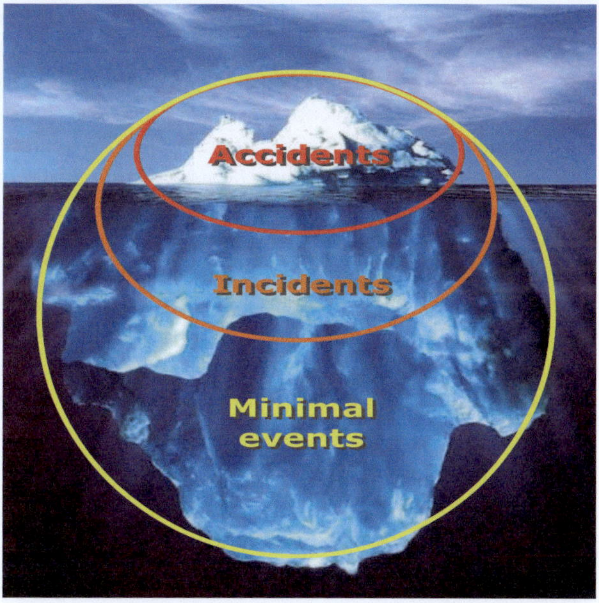

Fig. 3.7 The "incident iceberg"

incidents are like the portions of an iceberg that are hidden below the surface (Fig. 3.7). Accidents, in contrast, represent the tip of the incident iceberg: Much more visible but much smaller in number than incidents. A *sentinel event* is defined by the Joint Commission on Accreditation of Healthcare Organizations (JCAHO) as any unanticipated event in a healthcare setting resulting in death or serious physical or psychological injury to a person or persons, not related to the natural course of the patient's illness.

Fortunately, few unsafe acts result in actual patient injury because system defenses block the trajectory of accident opportunity. If each defense layer is impenetrable, an organization becomes error proof. The reality is different because every layer has loopholes that make the layer vulnerable. In addition, the defenses and loopholes are not static but constantly in motion; for example, the healthcare professional "has a bad day" or a normally reliable piece of equipment fails, etc. Due to this stochastic process, the overlay of loopholes is rendered possible, and a limited window of accident opportunity is opened. All it then needs is an active failure by a healthcare professional and the accident will occur. For instance, for years the pharmaceutical company in our case study produced two highly potent drugs with confusingly similar labels. For years the anesthesia department's policies allowed both drugs to be placed next to each other in the anesthesia cart. There were never any bad consequences to these two practices; it was only when an unsupervised, inattentive, time-pressured, inexperienced resident developed a faulty treatment plan, partly because the surgeon did not convey putting into use a technique that changes vital signs that the "upstream" factors combined with the latent errors produce an accident.

The remedial implication of the model is the notion that the psychological antecedents of unsafe acts (i.e., what goes on in the head of the healthcare professional) are extremely difficult to control. Distraction, inattention, forgetting, and lack of situation awareness are entirely human reactions in a work environment. Active failures are unpredictable in their precise details and therefore hard to manage. And unfortunately automation, while being an important remedy against human error, is often not an option in healthcare. Latent conditions, on the other hand, are by definition present within an organization before the incident or accident occurs. Because nearly all incidents and accidents have organizational and systemic root causes, latent factors are more amenable to diagnosis and remediation than the ephemeral tendencies of those working at the sharp end (Eagle et al. 1992; Gaba et al. 1987). Incidents contain valuable information about latent failures within an organization. One of the major organizational responses in recent years has been to collect and analyze information from incidents and to take adequate measures in response. Incident-reporting systems (IRSs) play a vital part in the quality improvement efforts of healthcare organizations (Chap. 14).

3.5.2 Keeping the Balance: Systemic View and Personal Responsibility

As several seminal publications explicitly pointed to Reason's model of accident causation (e.g., Bogner 1994; Kohn et al. 1999), the so-called Swiss cheese model (SCM) soon gained growing recognition within diverse sectors of healthcare. While this development clearly was a landmark in accident investigation in healthcare, its enthusiastic use sometimes went far beyond what Reason initially had intended; that is, a plethora of accident investigations concluded that nearly every incident or accident necessarily led deep into the roots of the organization. One of the few researchers to question the use of the Swiss cheese model was Reason himself, who warned that the pendulum may have swung too far toward identifying contributions to accidents and incidents that are widely separated in both time and place from the events and clinicians themselves. He posed the question whether the focus on organizational pathology had become too strong and whether consideration should be given to redressing mediation efforts back to the human at the sharp end (Reason 1997; Reason et al. 2006; see also Shorrock et al. 2003). Misapplication of the model can shift the blame backward from a "blame-the-person" culture to a "blame-the-system" culture. In its extremes, actors at the sharp end may be exculpated from responsibility.

Although the healthcare community should still be encouraged to take a holistic view on error and accidents and to analyze human factors throughout the accident sequence, this position should not be used as an excuse for individual negligence or recklessness. "Inadequate defenses," such as an inordinate deference to authority within the team, make the errors more dangerous. However, there will be some errors that overcome even well-planned and maintained defenses. Also, personal issues such as the impact of emotions and motivation on performance (Chap. 4) need to be taken into account: They can be seen as latent factors within the person.

The knowledge of the multiple facets of accident causation is a precondition to designing safer systems: Management factors, personal issues, and workplace design must all be taken into account.

The concept of a "just culture," which has gained widespread acceptance during recent years, tries to readjust the balance between individual and organizational accountability (e.g., Weick and Sutcliffe 2001; Chap. 15).

3.6 Judging Errors: The Benefit of Hindsight

"How come the resident didn't know that high plasma concentrations of epinephrine can trigger ventricular dysrhythmias? For someone anesthetizing patients in the ENT department, this should have been obvious. He immediately should have called for his attending physician for help! It was irresponsible to store the two drugs side by side in the same drawer; everybody knew of the hazardous potential to swap those look-alike ampules!" Hardly any clinician reading the vignette at the beginning of the chapter will be totally immune from this kind of reproachful thinking. Although it is understandable that people have these thoughts, they nevertheless stand in the way of a thorough understanding why a certain situation developed the way it did. Basically, to declare *what should have* been done differently never fully explains *why* something happened. However, it is an everyday experience that incident analyses tend to focus on mismatches between procedure and practice or to propose better alternatives. This tendency to discuss actions that were not taken and alternatives that were not chosen is rooted in the difference of perspective between an actor and a spectator:

- The acting person has an *interior perspective* on the events. How a situation will evolve lies in an unknown future. In the moment, one is confronted with ambiguous problems, uncertain cues, and a general lack of transparency. For the acting person, incoming data is often comprised of unspecified information and unclear meaning of relationships among the data and often does not constitute a clear warning sign of an impending catastrophe. People integrate this information into a mental model of the situation (Chap. 6). Based on this mental model, the decision chosen makes sense at the time.
- The spectator (e.g., employer, reviewer of incident reports, accident investigator) has a twofold advantage. First of all, he or she can take a perspective from the outside on the sequence of events. Secondly, hindsight gives knowledge of the outcome and dangers involved. Hindsight has a way of more easily organizing the evidence pointing to the bad outcome. However, this does not mean that the evidence presented itself that way to people at the time. It actually never does. On the contrary, hindsight turns the opacity, complexity, and dynamics of the real event with its multiple possible pathways into a simple, linear story with an obvious solution, which was not chosen by the people involved (Fig. 3.8). As this simplicity is entirely in the eye of the retrospective beholder, hindsight distorts the judgment of the observer. It confuses our reality with the one that surrounded the people who are under investigation (Dekker 2006). The retrospective observer

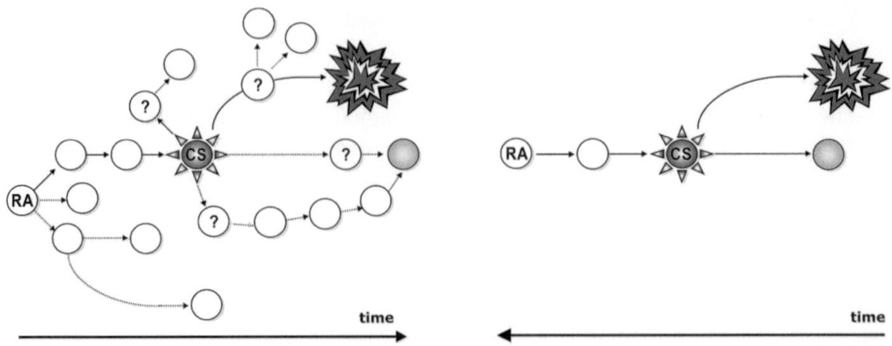

Fig. 3.8 The impact of hindsight bias on the perspective on a sequence of events. A person inside the situation looks ahead (*left figure*; time *arrow* points toward the right). For him or her, a critical situation (*CS*) evolves from routine action (*RA*). Options generated by the decision maker are intended to restore safety (*gray circle*) but are complex, branched, and have an uncertain outcome. The chosen decision leads to the incident (explosion). A retrospective observer who knows about the outcome looks back on the situation (*right figure*; time *arrow* points toward the left). A reconstruction of the sequence of events does not reflect the complexity and opaqueness of the situation and therefore narrows down to the alternative between right and wrong decision (idea adapted from Dekker 2006)

> knows about the outcome of the event and therefore can't understand how people inside the unfolding situation could misread the "obvious" cues presented to them. In addition, once the observer knows that an outcome is bad, he or she can no longer look objectively at the process that led up to it. Knowledge of the severity of outcome further influences a person's judgment of the appropriateness of care. The severity of the outcome affects not only the harshness of implicit judgments but also the willingness to render judgments on people involved (Caplan 1991). Observers often assume that a bad outcome can only be preceded by a bad process ("cause-consequence equivalence"), and so they have great difficulty in believing that actors actually made reasonable decisions when in the end a patient was harmed. In addition, the focus is shifted toward the people at the "sharp end." Latent error-producing conditions are no longer taken into account.

The relevance of the above statement cannot be overemphasized: The retrospective observer looking from the outside knows more than the temporally bound people inside the situation and therefore has a distorted perspective on the event. The underlying psychological mechanisms made by the observer are termed *attribution error* and *hindsight error*.

3.6.1 Attribution Error

When people are confronted with the behavior of other people, they often explain this behavior by a cause-effect pattern: "Because things were such and such, he behaved the way he did."

Attribution to the individual occurs subconsciously and rapidly and is influenced by the amount of available information. Basically, success or failure can be attributed to external factors that are beyond the influence of a person (*external attribution*) or to factors that the actor can control (e.g., effort, skills, *internal attribution*). Evidence suggests that people tend to attribute behavior of other people as internal (e.g., reckless, lazy, incompetent), whereas they believe that their own behavior was primarily influenced by circumstances or characteristics of the situation (Jones and Nisbett 1972). This distortion of the attribution process with its underestimation of situational factors on the performance of other people is called "fundamental attribution error" (Ross 1977). The implication for acute medical care is obvious: As soon as we find ourselves in a critical situation, we will experience our own understanding of the situational demands and the characteristics of the emergency and act accordingly. Oneself does not come into the focus of perception. A spectator, by contrast, for whom the in-the-moment characteristics of the situation are unknown, tends to focus on the person and his or her observable behavior.

3.6.2 Hindsight Bias

Although the analysis of an incident is supposed to explain the past, it is done in the present and thus influenced by the present. Once people know about the outcome of a situation, they are no longer able to assess behavior and underlying intentions the way they would do if they had not learned about the outcome (Fischhoff 1975). Hindsight changes how people look at past decision-making and fundamentally undermines our ability to understand the factors that influenced practitioner behavior. It turns real, convoluted complexity into a simple linear story. Given knowledge of outcome, reviewers will tend to oversimplify the problem-solving situation that was the momentary reality faced by the practitioner. The dilemmas, the uncertainties, the trade-offs, the attentional demands, and the double binds faced by practitioners may be missed or underemphasized when an incident is viewed in hindsight. Outcome knowledge affects an observer's perceptions about motivation and behavior and leads observers to overestimate what others actually did know and which options they actually were able to bring to mind to foresee and prevent unwanted upcoming events (e.g., "He should have paid more attention when drawing the ampules from the cart. He knew that two similar-looking ampules lay side by side"). Because people can imagine that events could have evolved differently, they firmly believe that they should have evolved differently – and thus talk about a reality that did not happen with little relevance to the circumstances of the accident sequence ("counterfactual fallacy"; Miller and Turnbull 1990). Once one knows about the outcome, it is easy to point at "crystal clear" facts that people overlooked but should not have overlooked, what they did not do although they should have done, and what they did not think about but should have. Because hindsight reveals the "true nature" of a situation (e.g., the cause for ventricular fibrillation), the actors' assessment of the situation appears illogical, stupid, premature, etc. Once it is learned that two look-alike drugs routinely lay side by side in the anesthesia cart, it is difficult to understand why the resident did not pay more attention when drawing the ampule.

In hindsight an observer almost always constructs a linear plausible narrative that underestimates the complex reality of the situation confronting the practitioner. Because participants failed to account for information or conditions that "should have been obvious" or behaved in ways that were inconsistent with the (now known to be) significant information, their decisions and actions "inevitably" led to the unwanted outcome. But for the people inside the situation, there was no overarching narrative: Only uncertainty, time pressure, task design, and a dynamic full of elements seemingly coupled with each other (data, perception, problems). A retrospective assessment of the situation is always in danger of creating an unrealistic situation in which the decision maker is solely confronted with the binary decision to err or not to err (Fig. 3.8). If an accident occurs because the people involved did not do "the obvious," the cause is internally attributed.

3.6.3 More Meaningful and Fair: Try to Take the Perspective from Inside the Sequence of Events

A *person-centered approach* makes it impossible for the retrospective observer to understand the reasons why an accident occurred. If you retrospectively judge an event, you don't provide an explanation from the point of view of people within the moment. The reasons for basic questions about why an accident occurred, why the decisions made the best sense at the time to the involved people given their limited information, and how the sequence of events evolved over time do not lie within the observer's reach because one has put oneself out of their range. The way to get at why the actor's decisions and actions made sense can only be obtained by (a) asking questions of what was the actor's mental "reality" at the time and (b) assuming the actor's decisions and actions were being done with good intentions. Instead, the observer tends to create a context that never existed for the people inside the situation.

A person-centered approach can be detected by the language describing human error: Comments usually express indignation, disbelief, and assumptions about a negligent, irresponsible, or thoughtless behavior. They enumerate what the people in question should have seen, should have thought, or should have done in the face of the impending crisis. They implicitly or explicitly impose a "standard of good practice." By referring to this standard, controversial fragments of behavior are matched and found wanting. No attempt is made to understand how the decision could have made sense.

The *system-centered approach*, in contrast, deliberately avoids constructing a referent from outside the accident sequence. Instead it tries to find out what was important to the people inside the situation and why. It tries to reconstruct the world that surrounded the people in question rather than creating an after-the-fact world with little relevance to the circumstances of the accident sequence. Once the decisions and actions that led to an accident are properly located in the context that produced and surrounded the human behavior, the behavior suddenly appears as inherently meaningful and nearly always shows well-intentioned people making decisions that made sense at the time.

As real understanding is only possible when the observer tries to put herself in the shoes of the people in the mishap sequence, the system-centered approach asks:

- How did the world look to the people at the time of the accident?
- How did the situation unfold around them?
- What cues did they get when?
- What goals were they pursuing at that time (not knowing the outcome the observer knows about)?

Answers to these questions help explain why it made sense for these people to do what they did. If it made sense to them, it could make sense to other practitioners as well and could reveal that this type of breakdown may be more common than one would expect. Under similar circumstances, others may make the same decisions and take the same actions. In taking a system-centered approach, people are aware of the fact that "illogical behavior" is only in the eye of the retrospective beholder: The interpretation of incoming data, the mental model, and the actions taken made sense to the actors in question and were aimed at restoring and ensuring the patient's well-being. The meaningful question, both psychologically and in terms of making progress on patient safety, is why were the contradictions and anomalies, plain for all to see in retrospect, but not visible to the team and not interpreted as such at the time.

This system-centered approach does not question the fact that errors were committed and that they jeopardized patient safety or led to patient harm. The perspective of the analysis changes, however: It is now possible to ask how a situation was understood, and why certain actions or the omission of certain actions made sense to the people given the circumstances at the time. Only with answers to these questions can one start to ask how a reoccurrence can be prevented.

3.7 "The Nature of Error": In a Nutshell

- An error is an intended sequence of mental or physical activities that fails to achieve its intended outcome.
- Two distinct perspectives on error exist: consequential classifications ("What is the result?") and causal classifications ("Why did errors occur?"). The two perspectives give rise to two different approaches: the person-based approach and the system-based approach.
- Most cognitive scientists agree on the distinction of execution failure ("something was done wrongly") and planning failure ("something wrong was done").
- Errors are often caused by execution failure *and* planning failure.
- Execution errors are usually skill-based errors. Planning failures can be rule-based errors as well as knowledge-based errors (errors in problem solving).

- Violations are deviations from safe operating procedures, standards, or rules provided by the social and economic context.
- Violations originate from regular psychological process: the choice between competing intentions, e.g., production pressure and patient safety.
- Errors committed actively by a person at the "sharp end" of the system are called "active failures." Errors created as the result of decisions at the "blunt end," far away from the actual patient encounter, are called "latent failures" or "latent conditions."
- Latent conditions remain hidden within the system for unknown lengths of time until they combine with other factors and local triggering events to breach the defensive barriers of the system.
- An incident is an unintended event that reduces the safety margin for a patient.
- The concept of a "just culture" tries to readjust the balance between individual and organizational accountability.
- Errors in teamwork occur as a result of poor leadership, inadequate workload management, and/or inadequate communication.
- Active failures are unpredictable in their precise details and hard to manage; latent failures represent the most suitable cases for adjustment because they are present within the organization before the accident occurs.
- Once a retrospective observer knows about the outcome of an error, he can no longer look objectively at the process that led up to it.
- Given knowledge of outcome, reviewers tend to oversimplify the problem-solving situation that was actually faced by the practitioner.
- Knowledge of the severity of outcome influences a person's judgment of the appropriateness of care. In addition, the severity of outcome affects not only the harshness of implicit judgments but also the willingness to render judgments on people involved.
- A retrospective assessment of the situation is always in danger of creating an unrealistic situation in which the decision maker is solely confronted with the binary decision to err or not to err.
- The system-centered approach tries to reconstruct the world that surrounded the people in question rather than creating an after-the-fact world with little relevance to the exact circumstances of the accident sequence.

References

Amalberti R (2001) The paradoxes of almost totally safe transporting systems. Saf Sci 37:111–136

Amalberti R, Vincent C, Auroy Y, de Saint MG (2006) Violations and migrations in health care: a framework for understanding and management. Qual Saf Health Care 15(Suppl1):i66–i71

Barrett J, Gifford C, Morey J, Risser D, Salisbury M (2001) Enhancing patient safety through teamwork training. J Healthc Risk Manag 21:57–65

Battman W, Klumb P (1993) Behavioural economics and compliance with safety regulations. Saf Sci 16:35–46

Beatty PCW, Beatty SF (2004) Anaesthetists' intentions to violate safety guidelines. Anaesthesia 59:528–540

Bogner MS (1994) Human error in medicine. Lawrence Erlbaum, Hillsdale

Caplan RA (1991) Effect of outcome on physician judgments of appropriateness of care. JAMA 265(15):1957–1960

Dekker S (2005) Ten questions about human error. A new view of human factors and system safety. Erlbaum, London

Dekker S (2006) The field guide to understanding human error. Ashgate Publishing Limited, Farnham

Dörner D (1996) The logic of failure. Recognizing and avoiding error in complex situations. Metropolitan Books, New York

Eagle CJ, Davies JM, Reason J (1992) Accident analysis of large-scale technological disasters applied to an anaesthetic complication. Can J Anaesth 39:118–122

Fischhoff B (1975) Hindsight equals not foresight: the effect of outcome knowledge on judgment under uncertainty. J Exp Psychol 1(3):288–299

Freud S (1901) Psychopatholgie des Alltagslebens. English edition: Brill AA (1914) Psychopathology of everyday life. Unwin, London

Gaba DM, Maxwell M, DeAnda A (1987) Anesthetic mishaps: breaking the chain of accident evolution. Anesthesiology 66:670–676

Health and Safety Executive (1995) Improving compliance with safety procedures. HMSO, London

Hollnagel E, Woods D, Leveson N (eds) (2006) Resilience engineering. Concepts and precepts. Ashgate, Aldershot

Jones EE, Nisbett RE (1972) The actor and the observer: Divergent perceptions of the causes of behavior. In: Jones EE et al (eds) Attribution: Perceiving the causes of behavior. General Learning Press, Morristown

Kahneman D, Slovic P, Tversky A (1982) Judgement under uncertainty: heuristics and biases. Cambridge University Press, Cambridge

Kohn L, Corrigan J, Donaldson M (1999) To err is human: building a safer health system. Committee on Quality of Healthcare in America, Institute of Medicine (IOM). National Academy Press, Washington DC

Lawton R (1998) Not working to rule: understanding procedural violations at work. Saf Sci 28:77–95

Manser T (2009) Teamwork and patient safety in dynamic domains of healthcare: a review of the literature. Acta Anaestesiol Scand 53(2):143–151

Miller DT, Turnbull W (1990) The counterfactual fallacy: confusing what might have been with what ought to have been. Soc Justice Res 4:1

Morey JC, Simon R, Jay GD, Wears RL, Salisbury M, Dukes KA, Berns SD (2002) Error reduction and performance improvement in the emergency department through formal teamwork training: evaluation results of the MedTeams project. Health Serv Res 37:1553–1581

Norman D (1981) Categorization of action slips. Psychol Rev 88:1–15

Perrow C (1999) Normal accidents. Living with high-risk technologies. Princeton University Press, Princeton

Rasmussen J (1990) The role of error in organizing behaviour. Ergonomics 33:1185–1199

Rasmussen J (1997) Risk management in a dynamic society. Saf Sci 27:183–214

Reason J (1990) Human error. Cambridge University Press, Cambridge

Reason J (1995) Safety in the operating theatre, part 2: human error and organisational failure. Curr Anaesth Crit Care 6:121–126

Reason J (1997) Managing the risk of organisational accidents. Ashgate, Aldershot

Reason J (2001) Understanding adverse events: the human factor. In: Vincent C (ed) Clinical risk management. Enhancing patient safety. Br Med J Books, London, pp 9–30

Reason J, Hollnagel E, Paries J (2006) Revisiting the "swiss cheese" model of accidents. EEC-Note 13/06. Eurocontrol, Bruxelles

Ross L (1977) The intuitive psychologist and his shortcomings: Distortions in the attribution process. In: Berkowitz L (ed) Advances in Experimental Social Psychology. Academic, New York, pp 174–220

Schmutz J, Manser T (2013) Do team processes really have an effect on clinical performance? A systematic literature review. Br J Anaesth 110(4):529–544

Senders JW, Moray NP (1991) Human error: cause, prediction, and reduction. Erlbaum, Hillsdale

Shorrock S, Young M, Faulkner J (2003) Who moved my (Swiss) cheese? Aircraft Aerospace 2005:31–33

Strauch B (2001) Investigating human error: incidents, accidents, and complex systems. Ashgate, Aldershot

Vaughan D (1997) The Challenger launch decision: risky technology, culture, and deviance at NASA. University of Chicago Press, Chicago

Weick K, Sutcliffe K (2001) Managing the Unexpected. Jossey Bass, San Francisco

Wheelan SA, Burchill CN, Tilin F (2003) The link between teamwork and patients' outcomes in intensive care units. Am J Crit Care 12:527–534

The Psychology of Human Action

4

Case Study
It is 2:00 a.m. and two police officers are conducting a routine traffic control. Suddenly, the driver of a van starts to shoot at one of the police officers. Being protected by her bulletproof vest, the officer is shot only in her right arm. The second police officer immediately opens fire and shoots the attacker in the chest and abdomen. Two ambulances and an emergency physician in a roving EMS four-wheel-drive vehicle are dispatched and arrive 8 min later at the shooting site. On arrival, the emergency medical service (EMS) finds a 28-year-old alert and oriented female police officer who is bleeding from the brachial artery. She complains of complete loss of sensation and strength in her right arm. No other injuries are found. The paramedics apply a pressure dressing and the bleeding is controlled. The officer's blood pressure is 95/50 mmHg and the heart rate is 90 bpm. Because the physician is busy inserting an intravenous line in the police officer, he asks one of the paramedics to evaluate the injured driver who is lying next to his car. The attacker is tachypneic and obtunded and has weak peripheral pulses. At the physician's orders, an oxygen mask and an intravenous line are placed and volume resuscitation is initiated. Once the police officer is transferred to the ambulance, the physician directs his attention to the attacker who has become unresponsive.

On examination, he finds several bullet entry points in the chest and abdomen. The central pulse is weak and fast. The patient is emergently intubated. No breath sounds are appreciated on auscultation on the side of the bullet holes. Cutaneous emphysema on the same side develops rapidly. The patient is positioned for emergency thoracentesis and a chest tube is placed successfully. An outward rush of air and blood confirms correct chest tube placement. During the emergency transport of the wounded driver, the patient continues to lose blood and has unstable blood pressure. Despite the difficult conditions of a moving ambulance, the physician places additional IV lines and

M. St.Pierre et al., *Crisis Management in Acute Care Settings*,
DOI 10.1007/978-3-319-41427-0_4

repeatedly administers boluses of epinephrine to maintain circulation. It is not until shortly before he arrives at the hospital that the physician becomes aware that he had been so immersed in patient care that he forgot to inform the emergency department about the patient's penetrating chest injuries. As a consequence, the thoracic surgeon arrives with delay in the emergency department to join the resuscitation team. The primary exam confirms the suspected diagnoses of hemopneumothorax and massive intra-abdominal hemorrhage.

Despite surgical intervention, the patient dies in the operating room. The police officer also undergoes surgery during the same night. She recovers but maintains a neurological deficit in her right arm.

An emergency physician is confronted with two patients, one moderately and the other severely injured following a shooting: On the one hand is a hemodynamically stable female police officer with arterial bleeding as a result of a perforating injury of the brachial artery. On the other hand is the male aggressor with shock due to massive intra-abdominal and intrathoracic blood loss. Without having examined both of his patients and then treating them according to medical urgency, he spends almost a quarter of an hour with the less injured police officer, delegating the treatment of the multiple-injured patient to the paramedic. The physician is familiar with the injury pattern and the vital threat to the patient. Nevertheless, he does not address this problem personally until after providing immediate treatment to the police officer. Once he finishes caring for the police officer, he personally begins to spend valuable time with the badly injured patient on site; that is, he decides to "stay and play." This is another error because patients with perforating injuries of the chest are known to benefit from a "scoop-and-run" rapid transport to the closest trauma center with a minimum of treatment done on site.

4.1 The "Psycho-logic" of Cognition, Emotions, and Motivation

The goal of healthcare efforts is effective and safe treatment of patients. Modern medicine aims to provide rational, explainable therapy at any time. That aim implies a model of the "logic of behavior" in which behavior is always determined by logical reasoning (Fig. 4.1a). Problem solving is oriented toward the best possible solution for the problem, nothing more. Apparently, the emergency physician's management in the case report does not follow this model: He first takes care of the comparatively lightly injured person and spends quite a bit of time with her while the more seriously injured patient is treated by a far less capable provider. We can only speculate about the reasons for his behavior. It might be because the patient was the *victim* of a shooting, because she carried a police officer's uniform and was accompanied by a worried colleague, simply because she was young and female, or perhaps because that's

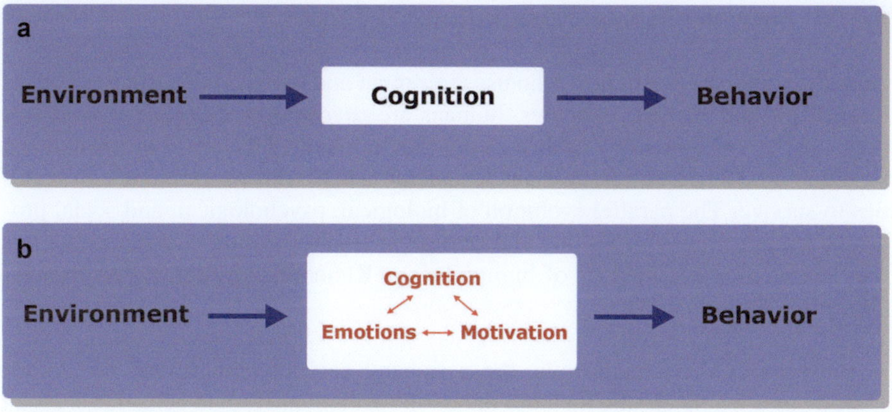

Fig. 4.1 Despite the widespread belief that logical reasoning guides human decision-making in response to environmental stimuli (**a**), evidence favors the notion that an individual's "psycho-logic," which is the idiosyncratic relation between cognition, emotion, and intention, has to be considered to understand decision-making (**b**)

who he approached first. For whatever reason might be the true one, an uninvolved observer might get the impression that a couple of "illogical" factors governed the physician's behavior, and this impression indeed might be true. Human behavior is not exclusively governed by completely rational thinking. Human behavior always results from a complex interplay of cognition, emotions, and motivations mixed with the environment (including available skills). Therefore, it seems appropriate in this context to talk about a "psycho-logic" of our behavior as clinicians (Fig. 4.1b).

The "psycho-logic" of this interaction between reasoning, emotion, and motivation governs all our actions. It is paradoxical because on the one hand, it enables humans to cope with complex and dynamic environments such as anesthesia, intensive care, and emergency medicine. Emotion-based decision-making can be a valuable resource, especially under stress and time pressure (Chap. 9). On the other hand, the "psycho-logic" helps to explain why the emergency physician did not stay "coolheaded" and did not adhere to the advanced trauma life support (ATLS) protocol or other medical guidelines. Unnoticed by himself, his decision-making was likely influenced by his emotions and his personal needs just as much as by rational reasoning. Simply to state that the physician's decisions were "illogical" or "irrational" and that he instead should have been guided by "mere facts" does not address the issue fully.

4.2 Principles of Human Behavior

To better understand the above roughly sketched "psycho-logic" of human emotion and motivation that we will explain in detail later in this chapter, we first need to introduce some basic presumptions about human behavior. These presumptions rely on the work of action psychologists (Dörner 1999; Hacker et al. 1982; Miller et al. 1960).

4.2.1 Biopsychosocial Foundations of Behavior

Humans are *biological beings* who use their mind and body to meet their needs. As a result of their mental capacities, humans are *psychological beings* as well. We perceive our surrounding world in a way that helps us make sense of phenomena surrounding us. In addition, humans are *social beings* who cooperate in communities to survive. The parallel evolution of biological, psychological, and social processes led to a way of reasoning and acting ("action regulation") characteristic for the "biopsychosocial entity" of human being (Kleinhempel et al. 1996; Brenner 2002):

- *Biologically* the human brain, the peripheral nervous system, and the human body as a whole are the medium of action regulation. Human behavior is based on the phylogenetically determined structure of neuronal processes, a fact that becomes quite obvious if, for example, perception (Chap. 5) and the stress reaction (Chap. 9) are considered.
- From a *psychological point of view,* cognition and speech are the main tools for perceiving and regulating human behavior. Speech acts are the result of social relationships and are the most important instrument to regulate these relationships. Furthermore, human cognition is irretrievably connected with emotions and motivations.
- Human beings are essentially bound to living in groups and are biologically oriented to charity and cooperation. Individual psychological development is inseparably connected to *social* development,
- Our social dependence leads us to seek being integrated into a stable social community.

4.2.2 Action

Action is Conditional on External Demands and Internal Psychological Processes The demands of patient care are not entirely rational; our psychological processes, emotions, and motivations also get involved. The range of possible options the emergency physician could have chosen was defined by characteristics of the emergency situation: the site of accident, the kind of injury, the pathophysiological state of the patient, and the available technical and personal resources. They all were fixed determinants at the time the emergency medical team arrived on site.

At the same time, however, his behavior was also determined by the knowledge, thoughts, feelings, and motivations he brought with him or that he developed as a result of his assessment of the situation. Because human action results from reasoning, emotions, and intentions, there is an interaction with any situation. We use the term "psycho-logic" to help understand human action within a context or situation.

Action Is Intentional and Goal Directed Psychology understands action as a sequence of behaviors aimed at achieving a goal. An action in the psychological sense is "the smallest delimitable unit of consciously controlled activity" (Hacker 1986). Actions are influenced by goal-directed mental processes that are fundamentally initiated and sustained by implicit and explicit needs.

Action Can Be Described in Terms of a Control Loop Theoretical models of human behavior assume that mental processes can be described as control loops (Miller et al. 1960). Actions are oriented at an anticipated goal or set point: One tends to keep on doing something until the desired goal is achieved. The goal of the emergency physician developed and became refined when treating the severely injured patient. The main goal was to keep the patient alive. To do this, intermediate goals had to be accomplished, specifically to place IV lines, to intubate, and to insert a chest tube. That way a hierarchical and sequential order of thought is built and sustained until the main goal is accomplished (Hacker 1986).

Action Is a Result of Information Processing The regulation of human action can be understood as a form of information processing (Klix 1971; Dörner 1976). In this view, the concepts of motivation, emotion, and cognition all describe processes of information processing at different levels of the human cognitive system. An important aim of this information processing is to enable people to maintain a relationship with their environment that allows them to fulfill their implicit and explicit needs.

Emotion, Intention, and Reasoning Constitute an Autonomous System Without a total awareness of their existence, the emergency physician's interaction with his environment is influenced by his emotions, intentions, and thought processes. Our conscious self is not always aware of this influence. It even seems not to be necessary for the regulation of action; therefore, we can talk of an autonomous regulation of human action, one that works outside of conscious, in-the-moment awareness.

Human Action Is Embedded in a Social Context It is an essential characteristic of the psychological idea of "action" that individual actions always are "embedded" in a social context. Our individual goals always have a social side. What we think or do serves our individual needs as well as our social relations. Keeping social relations stable and productive is a powerful social need. Maybe one of the reasons for the priority treatment of the police officer was the desire to show respect for a profession that served society.

Action Can Only Be Described on the Level of Visible Behavior The physician's emergency management consists of a multitude of actions that can be observed and described. We can make statements about what he did and when it happened. The external, visible human action is called exactly that action. Actions are observable behaviors.

Of course, we even can form our personal opinion about the appropriateness of some of his actions based on what we see and our judgments, but we cannot know why. The internal powers that drive visible behavior stay hidden. So some of the more puzzling questions will have to remain unresolved: Why did he choose to handle the emergency the way he did? To what extent was he aware of underlying psycho-logic driving his actions? Did he realize he was violating existing treatment protocols? We can apply our theories to reality and try to find answers, but we cannot know for certain all that guided the emergency physician's actions. The theory of human action regulation conceptualizes how cognition, motivation, and emotion are integrated into controlling behavior in complex and dynamic domains of reality.

Action is a result of autonomous, internal information processing following control loops, embedded in social context, driven by the situation and internal needs. To better understand errors in acute care settings, the following premises are helpful:

- *Errors follow the "psycho-logic" of human action regulation.* Every action, even if it is a mistake, is based on an intention and "on purpose." The physician committed an error because he took care of the less injured police officer instead of the multiple-injured patient. This does not imply that the physician explicitly wanted to harm the other patient. It only means that the intentions governing his actions did not properly prioritize the health and safety of the multiple-injured patient. The delayed medical management was caused by other intentions (such as caring for the police officer) being stronger at that moment. When there are competing intentions, the autonomous system is a strong factor in how the physician chooses between them. The main criterion for that choice is not necessarily an external one, that is, the objective reality of the patient's injuries. Fulfilling internal needs, for example, being friendly with a young woman, helping a fellow civil servant, etc., can be as important or more important. Of course, the physician's decision appeared incorrect from a medical point of view, yet his treatment error was caused by a range of normal psychological processes.
- *Errors do not necessarily originate from irrational or deficient psychological mechanisms* but from generally useful psychological process. Errors and mistakes follow, just as correct actions do, the laws of the "psycho-logic" regulation of action.
- *Errors can be avoided.* Despite being rooted in normal psychological processes, errors are not a fate that we must accept. Circumstances that promote and enable error can be analyzed in advance (Reason 1997; Chap. 3). Working conditions and organizational structures can be designed to help avoid and mitigate errors. Moreover, conscious effort and efficient teamwork can often overcome errors resulting from faulty "psycho-logic."

Before we provide more detail regarding the psychological processes that play a role in action regulation, we summarize the characteristics of human action as follows:

- Human action can only be fully understood when considering the "psycho-logic" of human action.

- Human action is the sum total of biological, psychological, and social processes.
- Human action is influenced by the human history of development (phylogenesis), individual development (ontogenesis), and cultural heritage.
- Human action is intentional and goal directed.
- At the visible level, human action can be described in terms of behavior and activities. The underlying processes (emotions, motivations, and cognition) cannot be observed.
- Action can be understood in terms of information processing.
- Erroneous decisions are psychological and rational in the moment and are the result of normal decision-making processes.

4.3 Motivation

4.3.1 From Needs to Intention

4.3.1.1 Requirements, Needs, and Motives

When internal regulation mechanisms are no longer able to regulate the physiological requirements, they are experienced as needs (Fig. 4.2; Bischof 1985). Hunger, for example, is a need based on a requirement for nutrition which cannot be met by the body's own supplies. As soon as a need is perceived (e.g., "I'm hungry"), an action is triggered. During the past decade, several classifications of basic drives have been proposed (e.g., Reiss 2004). Eventually, they can be narrowed down to a few categories of basic needs: existential needs, sexuality needs, social needs (e.g., closeness/affiliation, status, legitimacy), and informational needs (e.g., knowledge, safety, curiosity, and competence; Dörner 1999; Dörner and Güss 2013). The

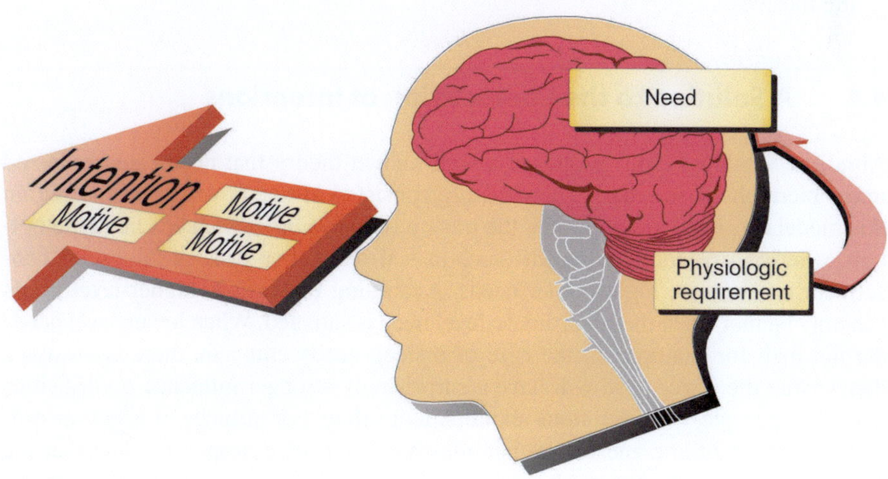

Fig. 4.2 From need to intention

social and informational needs are based on a need for understanding the actual state of the environment. Social needs are driven by the desire for social contact, acceptance by others, and the need to experience a feeling of competence.

A *motive* is a need connected to a goal that seems likely to satisfy a basic need (Bischof 1985). In other words, a motive has a goal connected to satisfying a need. However, for any need there may be several adequate goals or paths to satisfy the need. For instance, one can relieve hunger by choosing to go to the cafeteria or by taking an apple out of one's pocket. People are different – despite having the same basic needs – in how they strive to fulfill needs. Culture, specific previous learning experiences, and the environmental context play crucial roles in the formation of motives.

4.3.1.2 Intentions

Intention is a collective term for all of the various terms used to denote action tendencies, e.g., *wish, aim,* and *intention* (Dörner 1984; Heckhausen and Kuhl 1984). Intentions are a blend of different motives. People tend to meet several needs at the same time, and therefore several motives are active at the same time. For example, if you decide to go to the cafeteria, you could be doing it because you indeed are hungry, but you also might want to go there because you want to meet colleagues, chat, and listen to relevant news. This kind of action goal ("go to the cafeteria") determined by multiple motives is simply called an intention. Thus, an intention is a blend of motives (Fig. 4.2). Intentions are temporal – depending on the actual physiological and psychological state of the organism – and compete with each other (Dörner 1999):

- Humans have physiological and psychological needs.
- Motives arise from a goal that involves satisfying a need.
- Intentions are action-oriented goals that are determined by blending and balancing motives.

4.4 A Solution to the Competition of Intentions

Abraham Maslow (1943) proposed a well-known theory that needs are organized into a hierarchical structure. The structure consisted of five layers of needs. Within this model, depicted as a pyramid, the most basic *physiological* needs lie at the bottom, whereas *psychological* needs (such as self-realization or such things as "concern for others") are higher-order needs. According to Maslow, higher-level needs can only be met when the subordinate-level need is satisfied. When lower-level needs are not met, for example, in the case of a sleep-needy clinician, there is always a danger that the lower need will have a surprisingly stronger influence on decisions than, for example, considerations about patient safety. For instance, it is not uncommon during nighttime anesthesia that anesthesia is started despite the fact that the patient's "NPO time" has not been long enough. The decision "to get on with the operation" is influenced by the anesthesiologist's need to get to bed. Fortunately, this hierarchy of needs is not completely inflexible (e.g., Zimbardo and Gerrig 2012). We all know of situations where we were very hungry or felt an urgent need to go to the restroom but instead kept on going because the patient needed our full attention.

Obviously, needs compete with each other, and the order of execution is not completely defined by their place in Maslow's hierarchy. What happens is that a complex mediating mechanism comes into play. To understand this mechanism, we turn to some other theories (Dörner 1999; Kuhl 1983). The selection of which needs will be met partly depends on the chance of successfully meeting the need in the context of competing needs. Every intention is weighted by an internal mechanism that considers importance, on one side, and a subjective estimate of the manageability of the intention. This weighting process is further mediated by temporal circumstances. If something is unimportant *or* if there is no chance at all of being successful, no action will be initiated.

On the other hand, if something is important or if it is almost certain that one will succeed, action will be initiated. The expectation of manageability is mainly driven by the subjective assessment of competence and control and is highly influenced on the situation as perceived by the individual (Dörner and Güss 2013).

When there are several active intentions, it is always the intention with the highest weighting which will be executed. The result of an internal calculation that determines the strength of a need and the possibility of satisfying that need guides what actions will be manifested. The intention that rises to the top attenuates other intentions. In circumstances where time is limited, the number of intentions also becomes limited. Therefore, less important intentions will not get a chance to manifest into action (Dörner 1999). The fact that relatively less important tasks, such as phone calls, documentation, and other duties, seem to constantly slip the clinician's mind has less to do with forgetting than with the dynamics of intentions. The consequences of competition of intentions in everyday life are usually trivial; for example, you receive a reminder letter to pay a bill. During critical or emergent situations, however, the problem of neglecting an important piece of information or dropping tasks is exacerbated and can become a life-and-death issue. One explanation for this type of error comes from the clinician's strong and unconscious drive to feel competent. Maintaining a sense of competence can interfere with the goal of solving the medical problem. Even though it is difficult to understand or accept because it seems irrational, the drive to maintain a feeling of competence and control is a significant factor in clinical care, especially in acute settings.

4.4.1 "Overall Competence Assessment" and the Need for Control

When an intention is executed, specific motives are acted upon. At the same time, there is another strong and independent need embodied in every intention: the need to experience a feeling of competence. Psychologists sometimes call that the need for control. We have a psychological need to feel able to influence our environment according to the goals we set (e.g., Bandura 1977; Flammer 1990; Dörner 1999).

We want to know with certainty what is happening around us, and we seek clarity of facts and certainty about future developments.

The individual's overall competence assessment tips toward one or another end of a scale: At one end is a feeling of being able to handle the situation, and at the other end is a feeling of helplessness and fear. Another way of stating it is that a difficult situation can be seen as within one's ability to manage (feeling of confidence and competence) or beyond one's ability to manage (feeling of helplessness, frustration, and incompetence). "Helplessness" is the subjectively felt incapability to influence the environment adequately and poses a perceived threat to the human psyche and feeling of well-being (Seligman 1975).

One's current state is routinely perceived as a feeling of competence. For a clinician, once this feeling starts to decrease, for example, when facing a situation wherein one's skills and ability are no longer adequate, the motive of control is activated. Due to its inherent strength, it very often "wins" against other motives. In consequence, behavior is no longer governed by explicit patient-related goals but instead by the subconscious drive for the clinician to regain the feeling of competence.

In summary:

- The concepts of a motive for control and the need for feeling competent describe the need of every human being to achieve clarity about the actual state of the situation, the certainty about future developments, and the capability to influence the environment in accordance with one's own goals.
- The feeling of competence describes the perception of one's own capability to control circumstances.
- The need for competence becomes a driving force in decision-making when the feeling of competence is threatened by circumstances.
- Behavior in complex and dynamic environments is always influenced by reducing uncertainty and gaining control over the situation.
- Emergency situations in high-stakes medical environments are examples of highly dynamic and opaque situations where clinicians may have great difficulties in controlling their environment. As a result, perceived ability to control a situation is reduced and the feeling of competence is at risk. When this is the case, clinicians will attempt to reduce the feeling of inability and try to regain control. These feelings are so strong that the clinician, albeit subconsciously, may have a surprisingly strong intention to regain self-confidence and control. How successful this attempt will be depends on one's ability, the confidence in one's resources, and the quality of the team involved in patient care.

4.4.1.1 Wrong Assessment of Competence

The confidence in our own skills or capability is often misleading. This is especially true in complex situations. For example, if a clinician *overestimates* one's ability to cope with an emergency situation, he or she is more likely to take greater risks because of the (incorrect) feeling of being up to the task. On the other hand, when clinicians *underestimate* their own competence, they have a tendency to act defensively and refrain from taking possibly helpful and necessary steps.

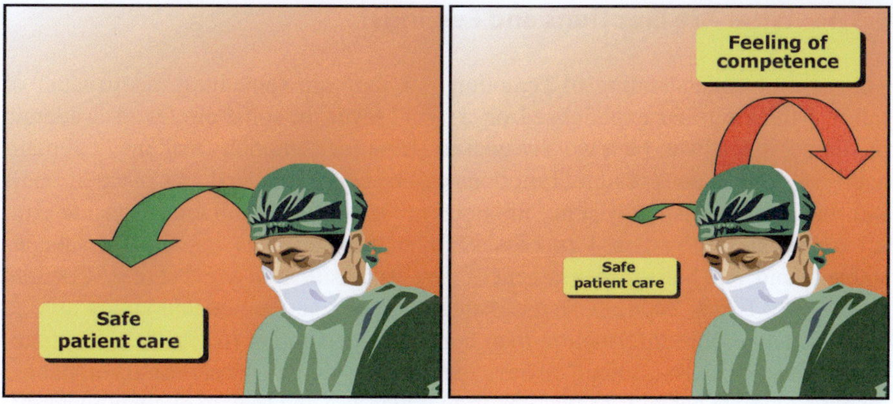

Fig. 4.3 Competence protecting rationality. Normally, safe patient care is the main focus of every healthcare provider (*left*); however, when faced with seemingly unsolvable problems (*right*), healthcare providers will struggle to protect or regain the feeling of competence. As a result, the competence motive, rather than safe patient care, may become the dominant motive

4.4.1.2 "Competence Protecting Rationality"

Complexity in combination with a perceived small prospect of success will diminish the clinician's feeling of competence and activate the need for control. Behavior will be directed at satisfying the competence motive. Normally, the first approach will be to start doing things the clinician knows well or that have proved successful under comparable circumstances. The problem, however, is that the clinician may be subconsciously busier regaining a feeling of competence than actually solving the patient's problem. In such a state, people only want to receive information that does not confuse them or contradict their view of the world and their self-confidence. The unfortunate result may be that only information that confirms the current model of the situation is taken into account and other information is not considered ("confirmation bias"; Chap. 6).

Perceived imminent failure tends to add to uncertainty. The protection of the feeling of competence can then become the dominant motive. Actions are chosen subconsciously not for the patient's sake but for our own defense. The examination of the critical situation on objective grounds becomes secondary. This *competence protecting rationality* (Strohschneider 1999) leads to errors because wrong or less than optimal actions from the patient safety perspective are implemented because of the need to protect a feeling of confidence and control (Fig. 4.3).

4.5 Emotions

In addition to motives, emotions play an important role in regulating human action. While motives determine *what* we do, emotions affect *how* we do it (Dörner and Güss 2013).

4.5.1 What Are Emotions and Feelings?

The general understanding of "emotions" is they are something independent of rational thinking and experienced on a "gut" level. In some circles of academic medicine, it seems to be a worthy goal to strive for "emotion-free" medical management. This is not possible. Emotions can be conceptualized as a piece of one's information-processing system; emotions are a kind of "thinking alongside conscious thinking" (System 1 processes, Chap. 6). Emotions constitute a subconscious, rapid, and holistic assessment of the current situation or event (e.g., Cochran et al. 2006; Evans 2008). This assessment is quick and automated and is able to process much more information than conscious perception (Chap. 5). This "integrated situational assessment" always includes a hedonic component accompanied by physiological activation: We seek to feel pleasure and seek to avoid unpleasantness about a situation (Fig. 4.4; Bach 2009; Scherer and Ekman 1984; Dörner 1999). The situational assessment (with activation and pleasure/displeasure) is experienced as a feeling.

If the emotional and cognitive situation assessments differ from each other, we tend to move toward a sense of confusion, that is, our mind and our gut are telling us different things. But the reason for the confusion is simply that emotions use different and more information than conscious reasoning.

As soon as they are felt, emotions can be further processed just like any other perceived data (Chap. 5). The source of emotions can be analyzed, and their intensity can be changed by means of becoming familiar with their meaning and learning how to incorporate emotional data into guiding action.

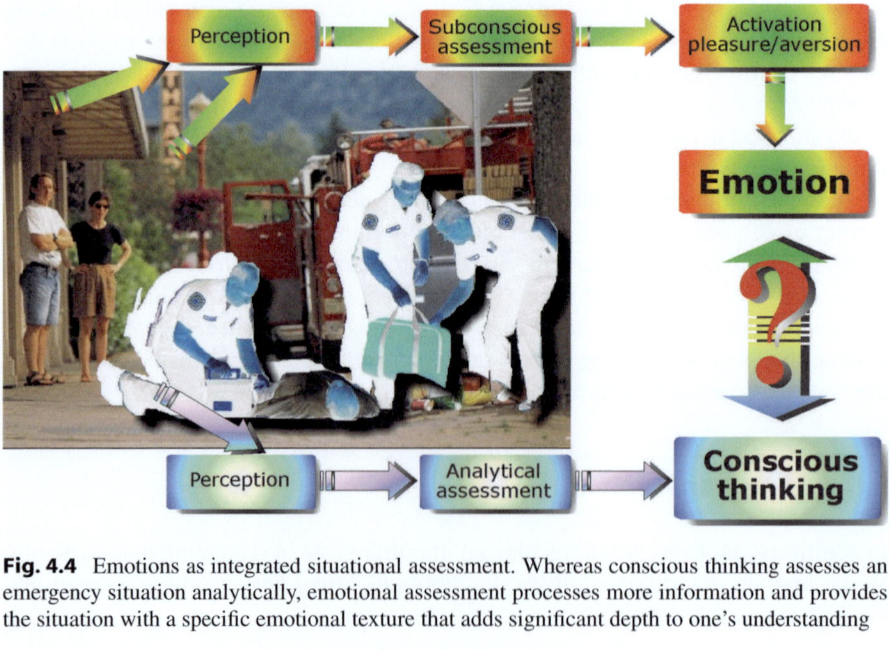

Fig. 4.4 Emotions as integrated situational assessment. Whereas conscious thinking assesses an emergency situation analytically, emotional assessment processes more information and provides the situation with a specific emotional texture that adds significant depth to one's understanding

Feelings accompany behavior and can become a goal of actions. For example, a decision may be delayed because we want to avoid the feeling of failure or an action may be taken because we anticipate the feeling of success.

In situations where cognitive resources are overtaxed or inadequate, humans tend to switch to an emotionally driven style of action (Spering et al. 2005). In this type of situation, emotional assessments are no longer cross-checked with conscious analysis of the situation. On the one hand, swift and risky solutions are taken with no room for reflection. Problems tend to be oversimplified and solutions are considered satisfactory if they "feel right." This can lead to inadequate decisions if the subconscious goal is the maintenance of a feeling of competence or the avoidance of negative emotions. On the other hand, when a highly experienced clinician is following emotionally led actions, it may be the most efficient and correct way of taking action (Zsambok and Klein 1997). The problem, of course, is that the decision-maker/action-taker may "feel right" whether the patient care is simplified and correct or simplified and incorrect.

4.5.2 Emotions and Human Action Regulation

Apart from providing holistic situational assessments, emotions can be further understood as being part of a regulation system that takes two considerations of reality into account: uncertainty because of the *unpredictability* of the environment and the *estimated degree of efficiency* to tackle problems (competence; Belavkin and Ritter 2003). This regulation system modulates parameters that influence the selection of actions (Dörner 1999; Dörner and Güss 2013). Among the parameters influenced by emotions are:

- The general preparedness for action (arousal)
- The thresholds for perceptions and selecting a behavior
- The degree of concurrence between emotional and cognitive processes
- The perceived degree of external factors that release or inhibit correct action

It is an everyday experience that the way a task is performed greatly depends on the emotional state of a person. The execution of a task done angrily can look completely different from the same task done in an even-tempered way. An "angry" mode of action therefore is characterized by an increase in arousal, a decrease in the degree of cognitive checks on action, a little planning, and an incomplete consideration of possible modes of action.

4.5.2.1 Arousal

Certain emotions (e.g., anger, joy, fear) can serve to activate people. This phenomenon, also known as unspecific sympathetic syndrome, increases readiness to explore the environment and to prepare for action. The senses are heightened, muscle tone is increased, and heart rate, blood pressure, and breathing tend to increase

(Chap. 9). Other emotions, such as mourning or hopelessness, reduce arousal. Normally, the chaos of an emergency situation is associated with arousal.

4.5.2.2 Degree of Resolution

In a heightened emotional situation, a cognitive process (e.g., perception, thinking) will run with a different degree of resolution than under normal circumstances and hence with varying accuracy. By "degree of resolution," we mean the level of differentiation and discrimination among dimensions of perception or cognition. "Judging the facts" can happen in a detailed, scrutinizing way or by simply taking in the most salient features of the situation. How well the environmental factors are resolved and considered in making decisions is partly dependent on emotions (via arousal), the importance of the situation, and (subjectively assessed) time pressure. The consequence for the clinician lies in the varying influence our feelings provide. On the extremes, we can develop either a too superficial or a too inclusive, detailed picture of the situation. For example, if one has an aversion for a task, it will reduce the degree of resolution, and the perception of objective reality will be "coarse grained," and the execution tends to be superficial.

4.5.2.3 Selection of Behavior: Concentration

Emotions influence the frequency of changes in intention and the intensity of action. A strong arousal raises the threshold of selecting an alternative motive to replace a leading motive. Thus, the action-guiding motive tends to predominate. If the threshold for selection is high, people will much more likely stick to a task even if the task is not preferred for the patient. If the threshold increases further, it can reach a point where people no longer are able to react to external triggers. Indeed, sometimes neither monitor alarms nor requests from team members can penetrate this "wall of attention." The result, as can be seen in our case report: "The doc goes solo." As long as his concern for the police officer was high, the emergency physician may have considered only the policewoman and "forgot" the second patient for some time. As stated previously, however, it's likely that this was not an issue of a faulty memory but of competing intentions. In contrast, when people feel helpless or have the impression that they are not competent to tackle a problem, the selection threshold for action is decreased. In the hope to bring about positive change, even if it has a small chance of success, they may try whatever comes to mind.

4.5.2.4 Externalization of Behavior

Emotions influence the extent to which attention focuses on external events or on internal cognitive processes (reflection, planning). Thus, emotions have a major impact on the balance between how much a person is driven by perceived events and driven by cognitive processes. For example, angry or scared persons will focus on the stimulus and how to get rid of or control it rather than focus their thinking on the true problem: Shouting at people instead of asking questions may be a result of externalization.

4.6 Knowledge, Memory, and Learning

4.6.1 Knowledge and Schemata

Our knowledge is composed of what we learn and experience. Knowledge is not stored in unrelated bits of information but instead in small meaningful entities, so-called schemata (Selz 1913; Bartlett 1932). Schemata are a cluster of structured data that are stored in the neuronal network of the brain. Schemata contain information that is based on the perceived regularity of the world and one's personal experiences with the environment (Cohen 1989). Schemata underlie every aspect of human knowledge and skills: They give structure to sensory impression (*sensory knowledge*), encode the generic information about our dealings with the environment (know-how; *procedural knowledge*), and represent concepts for the description of objects, facts, and procedures ("know what"; *declarative knowledge*, see Anderson 2005). Schemata are high-order, generic cognitive structures that underlie and organize all aspects of knowledge and skill.

In addition, schemata contain expectations about regularities or changes in the environment: We perceive a situation not only on the basis of momentary stimulus patterns but also based on our expectations about the possible developments of the situation (*horizon of expectations*; Chap. 8). Expectations can be so strong that sometimes we even "see" or "hear" things that we expect but do not happen, such as a confirmation of an order, just because we expect to see or hear it. Because schemata have this interpretative and inferential function, predictable biases in remembering occur. There is a strong tendency to organize our view of the world or a situation in accordance with the general character of previous personal experiences. This characteristic feature of schemata plays a vital role in the way human perception works (Chap. 5).

Procedural knowledge encoded in schemata is the basis for behavior. It consists of "if-then" cycles that are repeatedly compared with expectations about the situation and the outcome of actions (action schemata). The internal logic goes like this: "Given situation A, action B is taken and situation C will be the outcome." When many action schemata are strung together, the result is called a behavioral program or script (Schank and Abelson 1977). People store a range of successful cognitive and behavioral routines as behavioral programs. These are sequences of perception, classification, assessment, decision, and action. The whole chain of a behavioral program can be initiated with relative ease in a familiar and highly practiced situation, or the sequence of steps can be adapted and modified according to situational demands. Among typical behavioral programs common to clinicians, nurses, and paramedics are CPR, the placement of IV lines, and endotracheal intubation.

4.6.2 Memory

With this rough sketch of schemata, we have described a simple model of the human memory (overview in Anderson 2005; Dörner 1984, 1999): Knowledge always consists of schemata stored in neuronal networks. It operates through the interrelation of sensory perception with motor programs and motivation as a behavioral program. The memory items are connected in an associative way that allows for quick and efficient retrieval of relevant information.

As a result of these interrelations, human memory is *active* and adaptive. Memory is not like a computer, where information is stored on a hard disk and retrieved complete and unchanged whenever needed. Instead, concepts stored in memory are constantly rearranged and reorganized depending on the actual needs and the general circumstances; therefore, memories are a reconstruction rather than factual recall. When and in which form information is recollected depends largely on past interactions with the world, emotions, and the current situation. Habits, too, can influence memory. Schemata that are activated more often are more readily available and can be more quickly reactivated.

Human memory is not an entity that can be precisely located in the brain. Most scientists agree that there are different memory functions and they take place in different parts of the brain (see Fig. 5.4; overview in Anderson 2005; Wickens 1992). For example, sensory input (see Chap. 5) is stored for a very short time. However, the contents of this sensory information can be further processed and become meaningful perceptions that can be transferred to immediate working memory and also to long-term memory. Chapter 5 provides a more detailed description of the structure of memory.

Thinking is only possible if people can compare their current experiences with previous ones. We have to be able to access both the long-lasting information in long-term memory and sensory perception that is only momentarily available. The memory items active at a certain moment are the "working memory." The working memory is not a distinct functional entity but instead the description of the momentarily active schemata. There are many complex interactions that occur in the brain on the way from a situational clue (stimulus) to a behavioral response. Chapter 5 provides a more detailed discussion of the interactions between knowledge stored in long-term memory, perception derived from sensory stimuli, and thinking using working memory.

In order to encode experiences into long-term memory, humans are endowed with a "protocol feature" of the events. Protocol memory (Dörner 1999) keeps track of the ongoing mental operations and filters important and relevant details from unimportant and irrelevant "noise." What might be surprising is that among the main criteria for something to be viewed as "important and relevant" are things that lead to success or pleasure. These things tend to find their way into long-term memory. On the other hand, those things assessed as likely to lead to lack of success and to pain tend to be viewed as unimportant or less relevant. Therefore, things viewed as lacking success or painful tend not to be retained in long-term memory. With these main selection criteria, one can see that memory does not function in a machine-logic way but rather "psycho-logically."

4.6.3 Intentions and Memory: Prospective Memory

Totally immersed in the treatment of the traumatized patient, the physician realizes only shortly before arrival at the hospital that he had wanted the team in the ED to call for a thoracic surgeon. He intended to do something, but then forgot his intention. It is only when he imagines his arrival at the emergency room and the people awaiting him that he suddenly realizes that the thoracic surgeon is missing. His *prospective memory* had let him down.

While academic research on different types of memory has a long tradition, research on prospective memory ("intentional memory") is a rather young field of research in the cognitive sciences (Brandimonte et al. 1996). Prospective memory is defined as a psychological process that enables humans to execute previously formed intentions during an appropriate but delayed "window of opportunity" (Harris and Wilkins 1982) or more succinctly "remembering to do things later." In contrast to retrospective remembering, prospective remembering is typically self-initiated and not stimulated by an explicit request to remember. A prospective memory cue is an integral part of ongoing activity and can be missed without the person realizing it (Rothen and Meier 2013). In a strict sense, the term *prospective memory* is misleading, as prospective memory is based on many different cognitive functions and not confined to memory alone. These cognitive functions are:

- Goal formation
- Planning
- Task management
- Attentional control mechanisms

Daily life is filled with prospective memory demands, from remembering where to meet a friend to remembering to take one's medication. As an estimated 50–80 % of all everyday memories are, at least in part, related to prospective memory, it is not surprising that prospective memory failure (colloquially "forgetfulness") makes up more than half of our daily memory problems (Kliegel and Martin 2010): We intend to do something, but then forget to carry out our intentions. Prospective memory failures often give us the vague feeling that we wanted to do something, but have not the faintest clue what that something was. Prospective memory is often initiated during an ongoing activity, and the time between intention and the window of opportunity for implementing what was planned is likely full of unrelated activities. Because prospective memory means self-initiated retrieval of an intention, a person cannot count on help from others but instead must "remember to remember."

Acute patient care is filled with tasks requiring some form of prospective memory: remembering to give antibiotics before operative incision or heparin before transitioning to cardiopulmonary bypass, repeatedly checking serum potassium levels when a syringe pump with potassium is running, or remembering to continue provision of the correct level of anesthesia for a trauma patient when there is an unrelated respirator malfunction immediately after intubation. These memory tasks can be accomplished via monitoring processes, in which people expend attentional resources to either keeping the intention activated while performing ongoing activity or by searching the environment for a prospective memory cue (Harrison et al. 2014). Unfortunately, the ability to remember to execute future tasks can be seriously impaired by many factors inherent to acute patient care: interruptions, distractions, fatigue, cognitive demands of problem solving, multiple task demands, time delays, etc. Intensive care units and emergency departments are busy, interruption-prone clinical environments making them especially susceptible to prospective memory failures. If interrupted, almost 20 % of clinicians may delay or fail to return to a significant portion of interrupted tasks (Westbrook et al. 2010). In addition, task shortening may occur because interrupted tasks are truncated to "catch up" for lost time that may contribute to unsafe acts or errors.

In contrast to civil aviation, where the close connection between accidents and prospective memory failure have been acknowledged (overview in Dismukes (2008)), few researchers have investigated prospective memory and its relevance for patient safety in the acute care setting (e.g., Antoniadis et al. 2014; Dieckman et al. 2009; Glavin 2011; Grundgeiger and Sanderson 2009; Grundgeiger et al. 2013). Of special relevance seem those aspects of work in acute care that have negative effects on prospective memory, e.g., frequent distractions, multiple tasks, delay, fatigue, and interruptions. Frequent interruptions show how the organization of work can influence safety: In one study, repeated interruptions (four during one surgical case or up to ten interruptions per hour) increased the likelihood of prospective memory errors (Antoniadis et al. 2014).

4.6.4 Learning

Learning is inseparable from memory. In everyday experience, learning describes the acquisition of knowledge, skills, and expertise. Different schools within the psychology of learning come from two basic concepts: learning as behavioral change and learning as information processing. The first position looks at learning as a result of personal experience or training (e.g., Zimbardo and Gerrig 2012): *Behavior changes* or *behavioral options* are acquired. The perspective of cognitive psychology understands learning as *information processing that results in a change of thinking and consequently acting*. This change occurs through an increase of our procedural and declarative schemata, in which our behavioral options and our knowledge are organized (e.g., Piaget 1950; Anderson 2005). Learning occurred if information is stored in the memory (deliberately or involuntarily) and can be retrieved. Learning therefore means to expand our repertoire of schemata, i.e., our behavioral options and our knowledge. We constantly learn – every action or every observation that is "relevant" or "pleasant" is stored in our memory and refines the quality and adds to the range of our schemata.

There are many theories on learning (for an overview, see Lefrancois (2005)), but when it comes to learning new behavior, one feature is most prominent and agreed upon by virtually all research groups: *Experience* determines our motivation and behavior. The consequences of actions impact subsequent actions.

When a certain behavior is successful or if it generates pleasant feelings, we will try to repeat it when relevant circumstances appear again. Psychologists refer to this positive feedback as *reinforcement*. In a similar way, actions with an unsuccessful or unpleasant outcome will be avoided. Thus, a close relationship between learning and motivation exists. Other important motivations for learning are the need for a feeling of competence and the need for psychological safety. If actions don't lead to the intended outcome, two possible ways of learning may occur: Either the ineffective behavior is altered or the mental models or goals, which form the basis of the action, are changed. These two processes, which are also called "single-loop learning" and "double-loop learning" (Argyris & Schön 1996), are discussed in more detail in Chap. 16, which focuses on learning within organizations.

Because humans are social beings, we are capable of learning by simply observing other peoples' actions and related consequences. In healthcare, novices learn by observing their more experienced colleagues and by listening to peers and coworkers. In addition to learning medical facts and procedures, novices also become acculturated into the organizational culture. Learning "how things are done around here" means learning how to integrate into that culture (see Chap. 15).

What then do people have to learn to be able to handle critical situations adequately?

Relevant for the acute care setting are:

- *Knowledge*: e.g., pathophysiology, pharmacotherapy, indications, and contraindications of interventions
- *Skills*: e.g., airway management, emergency procedures, communication, teamwork, decision-making, etc.
- *Metacognition*: the ability to analyze and assess one's own thought process and to recognize the impact of "psycho-logic" of human behavior, heuristics, and cognitive distortions
- *Attitudes and values:* e.g., the willingness to ask for help or to learn from mistakes

The above-stated difference between behavioral options and actual behavior has practical implications for the acute care setting. A participant may learn during a team exercise that calling for help early in a critical situation will improve patient safety. "Call for help early!" as a catchy phrase may then be stored as knowledge (extension of schemata), and as a result, the person's attitude toward team support may change. However, whether or not this same person will actually call for help during a critical situation will depend on many factors independent of the learning experience: his or her actual stress level, risk assessment, expected consequences, and the organizational culture (Chap. 15), to name but a few.

Several human factors are not amenable to learning, at least not to learning in the classical sense. These are:

- Functional features of perception (Chap. 5)
- Principles of information processing (Chap. 6)
- Characteristics of human memory
- Characteristics of attention (Chap. 8)
- Basic motives
- Physiological limitations

Nevertheless some of these factors change over the span of life (e.g., deterioration of perceptional threshold and attentional span with increasing age, increased need for sleep in the elderly, etc). Patient safety interventions that take these unchangeable human factors into account will not focus on learning interventions but rather will try to change upstream systemic factors such as changes in workplace setting and routine processes.

Finally, it is important to keep in mind that it is always easier to learn something new from scratch than to unlearn deeply ingrained knowledge and habits and replace those with something new. Habits can become so solidified that people will find great difficulty in changing them or forgetting them altogether (Quinn et al. 2010).

4.6.5 Thinking

"Thinking" encompasses all higher cognitive functions that govern human behavior at the level of planning, expectations, and decision-making. Although very powerful in its operations, thinking is a limited resource because it relies on language processing and thus operates in a sequential mode. People can only think one thought at a time.

Thinking involves interpreting and ordering how information is processed (Selz 1913; Guilford 1967; Klix 1971; Dörner 1976, 1999). Interpreting and prioritizing information is a part of recognition and identification (Chap. 5) including assessment, conceptualization, drawing conclusions, planning, and decision-making. Generally stated, interpreting and prioritizing is problem solving. All these cognitive operations are done with the help of schemata that are constructed, rearranged, amended, and brought to mind in a way that helps us make sense of the world around us.

Thinking without language is possible. It consists of associating schemata according to their emotional match to the situation and to already activated schemata. Analytical thinking, however, is dependent on language. As a consequence, analytical thinking is a relatively slow, sequential working mode as only one thought at a time can be brought to mind (Chap. 6). In addition, attention is required (Chap. 8). Attention, too, is limited. This is certainly clear during a medical emergency; there never seems enough of it to tend to everything! One thing that helps us analyze events quicker is the fact that knowledge is broken down into higher-order and lower-order structures. Organization of knowledge is an essential component of its usefulness (Klix 1971). Associative (emotional-based) and analytical (language-based) thinking works hand in hand to solve complex problems. An idea can emerge from an association and is then analyzed for its meaning.

4.6.6 Metacognition: Thinking About Thinking

Thinking can be applied to itself. We can analyze and assess our own thought process. The concept that individuals are able to see inside their own thought processes, to stand apart, and to "think about their thinking" is called metacognition. The concept was initially developed in the context of educational psychology in the 1970s by John Flavell (1979). It refers to higher-order thinking that involves active control over and regulation of the cognitive processes engaged in learning. As soon as the emergency physician in our case report arrived at the incident site, he likely started reflecting on what he experienced. He started with the situational clues that were readily available and then began searching for additional information. "Do I already know enough about the situation and the patient? Is there anything I still need to know to come to good conclusions?" Metacognition plays a crucial role in the successful generation of situation awareness. If in the aftermath of his mission, our emergency physician asks himself, "How did I reach my decisions? Why did I manage the patient that way? Why didn't I think about a certain issue earlier?" He is engaging in metacognitive activity and has the chance to clarify some of the motives for his actions. This might help him to gain insight into his "psycho-logic" of decision-making and examine the efficacy of his actions. If he reflects on the strategy he applied to the management of the multiple-injured patient, he might be able to identify successful and unwanted behavioral patterns. Metacognition has been described as one of the distinguishing hallmarks of adult human intelligence. It distinguishes adult from child thinking and the thinking of experts from that of novices. Table 4.1 summarizes the components of metacognition that mark an expert.

Table 4.1 Metacognition by experts is characterized by several core features

Metacognition enables people…	
… to have the big picture	Experts excel at forming situation awareness and at detecting when they are starting to lose the big picture. Experts sense decay in situation awareness early and make necessary adaptations. They possess the ability to step back from the immediate problem and reflect on the entire situation with all its ramifications
… to select an adequate strategy	Clinicians are confronted with a wide range of clinical problems and a multitude of possible options to react. Experts can reflect upon their own thinking and select different and novel strategies. These strategies include how decisions are made, where to focus attention, how to improve teamwork, and ways to reduce workload. In addition, experts work to manage their cognitive biases
… to be sensitive to memory limitation	Experts are sensitive to their working and long-term memory limitations and maintain awareness of managing cognitive load. Experts can assess the impact of their level of alertness and their ability to sustain concentration, both of which affect memory. Limitations to memory can be overcome by external cognitive aids that lessen the burden on memory
… to engage in self-critique	Experts know that overconfidence can lead to serious errors. Experts cultivate a capacity for reflection on their decisions and a willingness to reexamine decisions in light of new information or input from team members Expert performance is less variable than that of novices. They can analyze how variations may cause poor performance. In addition, experience allows experts to assess where a plan might have been weak or wrong

Based on Klein (1998)

4.7 Hazardous Attitudes

One of the patterns repeatedly found when accidents are analyzed for root causes is a person's inadequate attitude toward safety and risk. The concurrence of a risky or dangerous situation with an inadequate attitude is often a contributing factor in aviation accidents and healthcare mishaps. These attitudes illustrate the abovementioned "psycho-logic" of human behavior with its interaction of cognition, emotion, and motivation. Attitudes can be seen as a blend of situation assessment (cognition), emotional response (emotion), and an impulse for action (motivation; Hovland and Rosenberg 1960). The cognitions in an attitude have powerful emotional features. Because of the strong emotional component, it is difficult for people to verbalize these cognitions and therefore difficult to bring to one's level of awareness and ability to reflect (metacognition). Furthermore, hazardous attitudes are driven by motives. Attitudes are developed and refined to fit our motives. Five typical hazardous attitudes have been described that account for unsafe response patterns (Jensen 1995). Each of them emphasizes a different motive:

- The *macho attitude*: Courageous actions are supposed to strengthen one's own feeling of competence, especially when team members watch.
- An *antiauthoritarian attitude* is adopted: People want to defy regulations or authority because they cannot stand the feeling of being controlled by other people.
- *Impulsivity* is grounded in the inability to consider options before taking action. To impulsive persons, "just do something, quick" seems superior to leaving any time for reflection.
- *Invulnerability* comes into play when people regard themselves as basically invulnerable. Such people believe mishaps do not happen to themselves; instead mishaps happen to other people who are not as smart or capable. This attitude is especially prevalent in those who have never experienced a major mishap.
- *Resignation* makes people give up quickly when faced with a difficult situation. These persons feel that they have little control to affect an outcome of a difficult situation. Often they take no action whatsoever. Help is expected from others.

These attitudes jeopardize safety in all organizational and industrial sectors. When working with patients, another set of attitudes can impact safety: deprecating and condescending attitudes toward the patient and family. If a nurse says "It's absolutely normal that he's not feeling well after his major GI surgery. Don't worry, I've seen that many times before!" in a belittling reply to a wife's comment about the deteriorating health condition of her husband, it may lead to a delayed detection of an anastomotic leak. Similarly, disrespectful attitudes of senior physicians may impair teamwork with young and unexperienced team members (Chap. 11): "Listen, son, I've been doin' this for over 30 years. I know what I'm doing. Your job is to keep your mouth shut and follow my directions" dismisses the attempt of a medical student who had noticed that the nurse had swabbed a

Table 4.2 The five hazardous attitudes and their antidote

Attitude	Thoughts in emergency situation	"Antidote"
Macho	I can do it, I'll show you!	Showing off is foolish
Antiauthority	Don't tell me what I'm supposed to do	Stick to the rules; they are meant for everybody and the rules can help me
Impulsivity	I have to act now – there's no time	Not so fast – think first. A little thinking before I act will be a worthwhile investment of time
Invulnerability	Nothing will ever happen to me	It can happen to me. Others, just like me, can have a mishap
Resignation	What's the use of even trying?	I can always make a difference; I'm never helpless

From Jensen (1995)

different site from the one written in the OR schedule. Had the senior physician respected the medical student and encouraged airing concerns, wrong-site surgery could have been prevented.

Finally, some physicians tend to over- or underestimate the degree of influence and responsibility they actually have. These attitudes have been termed *responsibility hubris* ("Everything depends on me!") and *responsibility despondence* ("Only others can make a difference!"; Wehner 2014).

Table 4.2 shows the hazardous attitudes and some "antidote thoughts" meant to counteract them by introducing positive mental responses to each situation. Once people discover that they are having hazardous thoughts, they should bring to mind the antidote (Jensen 1995). The main limitation of trying to change hazardous attitudes is that it demands self-reflection ingrained through training or, even more difficult, during action. When hazardous attitudes persist, patient safety can be improved when other team members are in a position that allows for constructive criticism (Chap. 11). A team member's comments may serve as an external trigger for reflection. Because the attitude component of human judgment does respond well to training intervention, training and reflection on action during training should become part of a safety-oriented organizational culture (Chap. 15).

4.8 "Principles of Human Behavior" in a Nutshell

- Human behavior does not strictly follow logical arguments but instead follows an idiosyncratic "psycho-logic."
- "Psycho-logic" implies that a person's interaction with the environment is an interplay of cognition, emotion, and motivation.
- Action regulation is partly autonomous; it's a process without conscious decisions.

- Every action is motivated and is meant to meet one or several needs. Apart from basic needs that secure existence (physiological needs, safety), there are social (proximity, affiliation) and informational (competence, curiosity, aesthetic) motives for action.
- Emotions are an important component of one's integrated situation assessment. Emotions are not language based and are experienced as feelings. Emotions can be described as a modulation of the parameters of action regulation (arousal, selection, resolution level, and degree of externalization).
- Cognition is language based and operates with memory contents organized in schemata.
- Memory is more than passive data storage. Memory is our mental "workbench," the place where our conscious awareness arises. It plays an essential role in our conscious interaction with our environment.
- Prospective memory is a psychological process that enables humans to execute previously formed intentions during an appropriate and later "window of opportunity." Prospective remembering is self-initiated and not stimulated by an explicit request to remember.
- Prospective memory can be impaired by factors present in acute patient care: interruptions, distractions, fatigue, cognitive demands of problem solving, multiple task and patient demands, time delays, etc.
- Learning enlarges our procedural and declarative schemata, that is, our knowledge and behavioral options.
- Among the most salient principles of learning are the following: If the result of an action feels good, we tend to repeat it. If it does not, we will try to avoid it.
- Metacognition describes the concept that individuals are able to examine their own thought processes, to stand apart, and to "think about their thinking."
- Metacognition is a distinguishing hallmark of adult human intelligence and distinguishes adult from child thinking and the thinking of experts from that of novices.
- Safety-relevant attitudes originate from an interaction of cognition, emotion, motivation, and training.

References

Anderson JR (2005) Cognitive psychology and its implications, 6th edn. Worth Publishing, New York

Antoniadis S, Passauer-Baierl S, Baschnegger H, Weigl M (2014) Identification and interference of intraoperative distractions and interruptions in operating rooms. J Surg Res 188:21–29

Argyris C, Schön DA (1996) Organizational learning II: theory, method and practice. Addison-Wesley, Reading

Bach J (2009) Principles of synthetic intelligence PSI: an architecture of motivated cognition. Oxford, New York

Bandura A (1977) Self-efficacy mechanisms in human agency. Am Psychol 37:122–147

Bartlett FC (1932) Remembering. Cambridge University Press, Cambridge

Belavkin RV, Ritter FE (2003) The use of entropy for analysis and control of cognitive models. In: Proceedings of the fifth international conference on analysis and control of cognitive modeling. Universitaets-Verlag, Bamberg, pp 75–80
Bischof N (1985) Das Rätsel Ödipus [The riddle of Oedipus]. Piper, Munich
Brandimonte M, Einstein GO, McDaniel MA (eds) (1996) Prospective memory: theory and applications. Erlbaum, Mahwah
Brenner HP (2002) Marxistische Persönlichkeitstheorie und die 'bio-psychosoziale Einheit Mensch' [Marxist personality theory and the bio-psycho-social entity man]. Pahl-Rugenstein Nachfolger, Cologne
Cochran RE, Lee FJ, Chown E (2006) Modeling emotion: Arousal's impact on memory. In: Proceedings of the 28th Annual Conference of the Cognitive Science Society. Vancouver BC, Canada, pp 1133–1138
Cohen G (1989) Memory in the real world. Erlbaum, London
Dieckman P, Madsen MD, Reddersen S, Rall M, Wehner T (2009) Remembering to do things later and resuming interrupted tasks: prospective memory and patient safety. In: Flin R, Mitchell L (eds) Safer surgery. Analysing behaviour in the operating theatre. Ashgate, Farnham, pp 339–352
Dismukes RK (2008) Prospective memory in aviation and everyday settings. In: Kliegel M, McDaniel MA, Einstein GO (eds) Prospective memory: cognitive, neuroscience, developmental, and applied perspectives. Lawrence Erlbaum, New York, pp 411–431
Dörner D (1976) Problemlösen als Informationsverarbeitung [Problem solving as information processing]. Kohlhammer, Stuttgart
Dörner D (1984) Memory systems and the regulation of behavior. In: Hoffmann J, van der Meer E (eds) Knowledge aided information processing. Elsevier, Amsterdam
Dörner D (1999) Bauplan für eine Seele [Blueprint for a soul]. Rowohlt, Reinbek
Dörner D, Güss D (2013) PSI: A computational architecture of cognition, motivation, and emotion. Rev Gen Psychol 17(3):297–317
Evans JSBT (2008) Dual-processing accounts of reasoning, judgment and social cognition. Annu Rev Psychol 59:255–278
Flammer A (1990) Erfahrung der eigenen Wirksamkeit. Einführung in die Psychologie der Kontrolle [Introduction to the psychology of control]. Huber, Bern
Flavell JH (1979) Metacognition and cognitive monitoring: a new area of cognitive-developmental inquiry. Am Psychol 34:906–911
Glavin RJ (2011) Human performance limitations (communication, stress, prospective memory, fatigue). In: Van Aken (Hrsg): Safety in anaesthesia. Best Pract Res Clin Anaesth 25:2, 193–206
Grundgeiger T, Sanderson PM (2009) Interruptions in healthcare: theoretical views. Int J Med Inform 78:293–307
Grundgeiger T, Sanderson PM, Orihuela CB, Thompson A, MacDougall HG, Nunnink L, Venkatesh B (2013) Prospective memory in the ICU: the effect of visual cues on task execution in a representative simulation. Ergonomics 56(4):579–589
Guilford JP (1967) The nature of human intelligence. McGraw-Hill, New York
Hacker W (1986) Arbeitspsychologie: Psychische Regulation von Arbeitstätigkeiten [Work psychology. Psychological regulation of working activities]. Huber, Bern
Hacker W, Volpert W, von Cranach M (1982) Cognitive and motivational aspects of action. Deutscher Verlag der Wissenschaften, Berlin
Harrison TL, Mullet HG, Whiffen KN, Ousterhout H, Einstein GO (2014) Prospective memory: effects of divided attention on spontaneous retrieval. Mem Cog 42:212–224
Heckhausen H, Kuhl J (1984) From wishes to actions: the dead ends and short cuts on the long way to action. In: Frese M, Sabini J (eds) Goal directed behavior: psychological theory and research on action. Erlbaum, Hillsdale, pp 134–159
Hovland CI, Rosenberg MJ (eds) (1960) Attitude, organization and change: an analysis of consistency among attitude components. Yale University Press, New Haven

Jensen RS (1995) Pilot judgement and crew resource management. Ashgate Publishing, Vermont
Klein G (1998) Sources of power: how people make decisions. The MIT Press, Cambridge
Kleinhempel F, Möbius A, Soschinka HU, Wassermann M (eds) (1996) Die biopsychosoziale Einheit Mensch. Festschrift für Karl-Friedrich Wessel [The bio-psycho-social entity man. Hommage to K.F. Wessel]. Kleine Verlag, Bielefeld
Kliegel M, Martin M (2010) Prospective memory research: why is it relevant? Int J Psychol 38(4):193–194
Klix F (1971) Information und Verhalten Kybernetische Aspekte der organismischen Informationsverarbeitung [Information and behavior. Cybernetic aspects of organismic information processing]. Hans Huber, Bern
Kuhl J (1983) Motivation, Konflikt und Handlungskontrolle [Motivation, conflict, and action control]. Springer, Berlin/Heidelberg/New York
Lefrancois GR (2005) Theories of human learning: what the old woman said. Wadsworth Publishing, New York
Maslow AH (1943) A theory of human motivation. Psychol Rev 50:370–396
Miller GA, Galanter E, Pribram KH (1960) Plans and the structure of behavior. Holt, New York
Piaget J (1950) The psychology of intelligence. Routledge & Kegan Paul, London
Quinn JM, Pascoe AT, Wood W, Neal DT (2010) Can't control yourself? Monitor those bad habits. Pers Soc Psychol Bull 36:499–511
Reason J (1997) Managing the risks of organizational accidents. Ashgate, Aldershot
Reiss S (2004) Multifaceted nature of intrinsic motivation. The theory of 16 basic drives. Rev Gen Psychol 8:179–183
Rothen N, Meier B (2013) Psychophysiology of prospective memory. Memory 22(7):867–880
Schank RC, Abelson R (1977) Scripts, plans, goals, and understanding. Erlbaum, Hillsdale
Scherer K, Ekman P (eds) (1984) Approaches to emotion. Erlbaum, Hillsdale
Seligman ME (1975) Helplessness. On depression, development and death. Freeman, San Francisco
Selz O (1913) Über die Gesetze des geordneten Denkverlaufs [On the laws of the structured thought process]. Spaemann, Stuttgart
Spering M, Wagener D, Funke J (2005) The role of emotions in complex problem solving. Cogn Emotion 19:1252–1261
Strohschneider S (1999) Human behavior and complex systems: some aspects of the regulation of emotions and cognitive information processing related to planning. In: Stuhler EA, de Tombe DJ (eds) Complex problem-solving: cognitive psychological issues and environmental policy applications. Hampp, München, pp 61–73
Wehner T (2014) Qualitat: mit Sicherheit!« - Beides verlangt Verantwortung, beides erzeugt Verantwortungsdiffusion! [Quality and safety: Both ask for responsibility – both create diffusion of responsibility]. Presentation at the Patient Safety Congress, Hamburg 4(4):2014
Westbrook JI, Coera E, Dunsmuir WT, Brown BM, Kelk N, Paoloni R, Tran C (2010) The impact of interruptions on clinical task completion. Qual Saf Health Care 19:284–289
Wickens CD (1992) Engineering psychology and human performance. Harper Collins, New York
Zimbardo G, Gerrig RJ (eds) (2012) Psychology and life. Pearson Education Limited, New York
Zsambok CE, Klein GA (1997) Naturalistic decision making. Lawrence Erlbaum Associates, Mahwah

Part II

Individual Factors of Behavior

Emergent situations demand a different amount and extent of conscious thinking, planning, and decision-making than do routine situations. Whether or not action routines can be applied or new solutions to problems are needed depends mainly on two factors:

- The *complexity* of the emergency situation
- The clinician's *experience* with comparable situations

The less experience a clinician has with a critical situation and the more complex and dynamic the emergency is, the more necessary it becomes to switch from the application of rules to creative problem solving. Conscious problem-solving behavior in anesthesia, intensive care, and emergency medicine can be subdivided into several consecutive steps to organize behavior. Against the background of the "psychologic" of cognition, emotion, and intention, and the awareness of the fact that errors will happen, we look at them in closer detail in Part II. The following chapters focus on factors that influence the individual. The team decision-making process and teamwork are the subject matter of Part III.

The steps involved in the organization of behavior are as follows:

- Information processing and building of mental models (Chap. 6)
- Formation of goals (Chap. 7)
- Planning (Chap. 7)
- Decision-making (Chap. 10)

The chapters corresponding to the steps for organizing behavior are framed by chapters dealing with the unconscious processes governing behavior and thus can enhance or impair it. These processes are:

- Perception (Chap. 5)
- Control of attention (Chap. 8)
- Stress (Chap. 9)

Human Perception: The Way We See Things

5

Case Study

At the end of an uneventful operation maintained by a total intravenous anesthesia (TIVA), a patient starts to buck unconsciously trying to expel the endotracheal tube. Patient movement prompts the anesthesiologist to switch the anesthesia machine from a mandatory to a spontaneous breathing mode. She does this by first selecting the new ventilation mode from the software menu and then pressing a button to activate it. While doing so, the anesthesiologist turns her attention briefly to an unrelated concurrent problem. Shortly after, the anesthesiologist returns her attention to the patient and gets the impression that he is breathing spontaneously: Chest excursions are regular; the capnography curve (expired CO_2) displays a regular pattern; the expiratory minute volume is adequate; and the oxygen-blood saturation remains stable at 100 %. Again, the patient starts to buck and the anesthesiologist decides to extubate the patient. Shortly after extubation, the oxygen-blood saturation begins to drop, and the patient turns cyanotic. It is then that the anesthesiologist realizes that the ventilator is still working in the volume-controlled mode and had not been successfully switched to the spontaneous breathing mode as she intended. She begins to mask ventilate the patient until the patient starts breathing spontaneously a few minutes later.

The anesthesiologist decided to extubate her patient and first needed to test the patient's ability to breathe spontaneously. Because of a handling error, the anesthesia machine was not switched to spontaneous breathing mode and continued to mechanically force ventilate the patient. In the mistaken conviction that the patient was breathing on his own, the anesthesiologist incorrectly interpreted her clinical observation and the information gathered from the monitor as signs of adequate

M. St.Pierre et al., *Crisis Management in Acute Care Settings*,
DOI 10.1007/978-3-319-41427-0_5

spontaneous breathing. She saw regular and deep chest excursions, the flawless pattern of the capnography curve, and an expiratory minute volume close to what she expected. The evidence reinforced her conviction that the patient could be safely extubated. Other minor problems arose that diverted some of her attention for a short while, a period in which she did not realize that her monitor was showing ventilation curves that contradicted her current understanding (e.g., the pressure/time curve and the flow/time curve). Because she accepted her initial perception as being correct and in agreement with her working hypotheses of a spontaneously breathing patient, a critical reexamination of the situation was not initiated until the patient had serious problems.

Human perception has one primary task to fulfill: It has to provide adequate information about that particular part of the external environment on which human survival depends. With this information, we can find navigate territory, avoid danger, and meet our needs. Sensory information enables us to see "where food can be found and where dangers abound." Perception evolved to be "good enough," and does not exactly and flawlessly reproduce an image of the environment. We may think or wish that perception is precise, but it is inexact. We have our limits. The eyes are *not* camcorders or digital cameras that accurately scan all parts of an original image and then store the gathered information in memory to be retrieved when needed. Quite the contrary is true: The original image is not completely scanned, and the resulting information that our sense organs provide is filtered, evaluated, and organized. Although environmental stimuli come to us in many forms (acoustic, visual, olfactory, gustatory, haptic, nociceptive, and vestibulocochlear), only a small set of common principles underlie all sensory processes. Thus, herewith is a discussion of the functional features of perception as exemplified by the visual and acoustic systems. While these two systems are highlighted here, the same mechanisms apply to other sensory processes as well.

The process of visual perception, to start with, can be subdivided into three reasonably distinguishable steps. An example of the pathway of the information content of a capnography curve on the monitor display to the processing in the anesthesiologist's thought: "This patient shows sufficient spontaneous breathing" (Fig. 5.1).

5.1 From Stimulus to Sensation: Sensory Physiology

Environmental stimuli (e.g., sound, light, heat, smells, tastes, tactile stimuli) are "detected" by sensory receptors, specific biological structures that transduce small amounts of environmental energy into generating cellular action potentials. After the reception of the sensory stimulus, the generated sensory signal is encoded and transmitted via neural pathways to specific regions of the spinal cord and the cortex. The interpretation of the sensory input by the central nervous system (CNS) depends on the pathway it takes to the brain, the representation of information in specific areas of the brain, and networking between functional

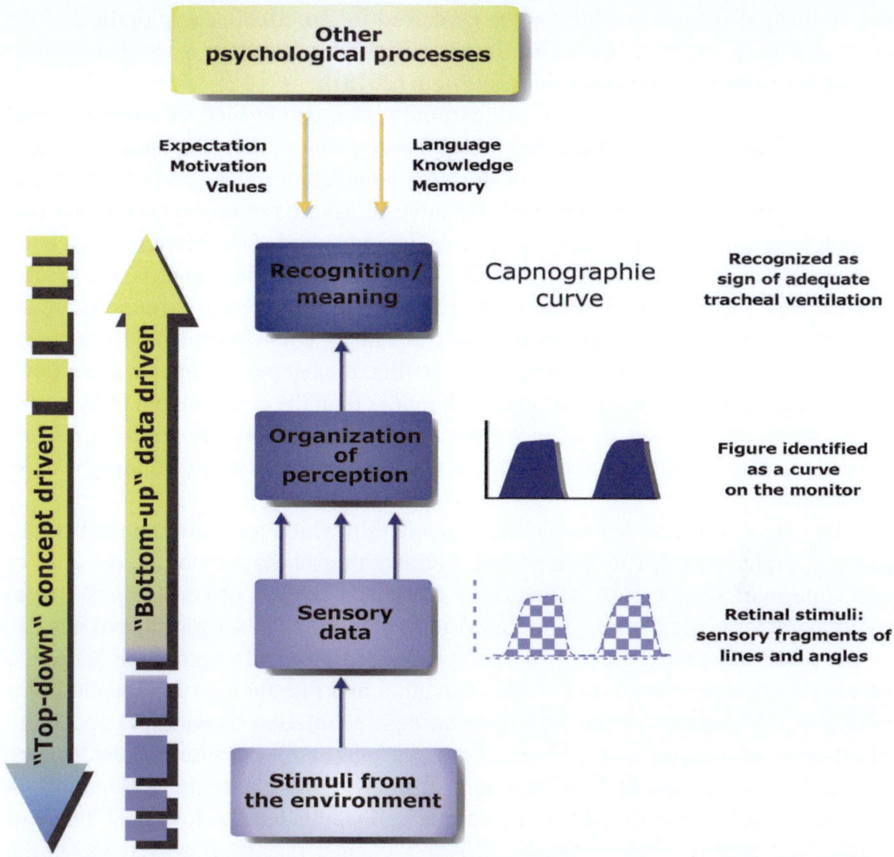

Fig. 5.1 Sensory information reaches us from the outside world as stimuli that are translated into "perception" via a complex multistage process (After Zimbardo and Gerrig 2012). The selection of sensory information is guided by relevant environmental data ("bottom-up") and by expectations and hypotheses formed by past experiences ("top-down"). These processes interrelate in a complex and mostly unexplained way

areas of the CNS. This process describes only the first few steps in the far more complex process of *perception*, in which sensory information is integrated with previously learned information and other sensory inputs. This integration enables us to make judgments about the quality, intensity, and relevance of what is being sensed.

Millennia of human evolution have shaped our sensory organs. Our sensory organs work to reduce the abundance of possible sensory inputs and give us access to a view of reality deemed relevant. This is the main reason why we cannot see ultraviolet light, why we cannot orient ourselves by means of the terrestrial magnetic field, and why we cannot see a mouse from 100 m above the ground as a bird can. Instead, human sensory organs have naturally optimized response to those environmental stimuli that have to be perceived for an effective exploration of the environment (Klix 1971; Ramachandran and Blakeslee 1999; for a detailed description of the sensory physiology, see Goldstein (2013)).

Most sensory organs respond preferentially to a single kind of environmental stimulus. This specificity is due to several features that match a receptor to its preferred stimulus. For the reception of its corresponding stimulus, every receptor has a relative and an absolute threshold. Relative thresholds describe how much two stimuli have to differ from each other to be distinguished. The difference can be in duration, strength, wave length, etc. The stronger the current stimulus, the greater this difference has to be, i.e., the increment threshold to the background is a constant (Weber's law). So when people work in a noisy environment such as a resuscitation room or in a trauma management setting, the beeper volume or a monitor's audio alarm has to be set so that it is much louder than the environment to be heard. If the same alarm is set in a quiet environment such as an OR during a routine operation, it is enough if the alarm is a little louder than the relatively quiet environment.

Absolute thresholds determine the range within which an environmental stimulus (e.g., light, sound) can be detected. Sensory thresholds are not fixed for all of one's lifetime. They can be permanently altered as a result of nerve injury due to trauma or degradation from aging. Short-term alterations in sensory thresholds can be the result of adaptive or motivational processes that regulate attention (Chaps. 4 and 8). We are capable of short-term adaptation and fine-tuning of perception processes to the changes in the environment, e.g., adaptation to darkness and light. Short-term adaptation also prevents "sensory overload" because we are able to ignore or partially ignore less important or unchanging environmental stimuli. A continuous tone tends to fade from hearing, and smells tend to lose their sweet or penetrating quality within minutes. When a change occurs, however, the initial response pattern (e.g., to the alarm or the smell) will reemerge, and the sensory input will become temporarily more noticeable. Inappropriate or badly timed sensory adaptation and fatigue are two highly relevant neurophysiological mechanisms that account for perceptive errors.

5.2 From Sensation to Consciousness: Basic Concepts of Memory

There is a constant stream of environmental and internal data bombarding our sensory system. Our brain cannot process all the data. Data is constantly filtered for relevant information. The cognitive system has to decide which environmental stimuli are relevant and therefore receive closer attention due to their relevance, which stimuli can well be ignored, and when we need to generate a response. Psychologists have conceptualized this kind of information processing into different models that are changing as more is learned about cognition. In this book, we will confine ourselves to components and processes that are commonly agreed upon and that have been substantiated by research (Chap. 4; Fig. 5.2). Overviews about memory

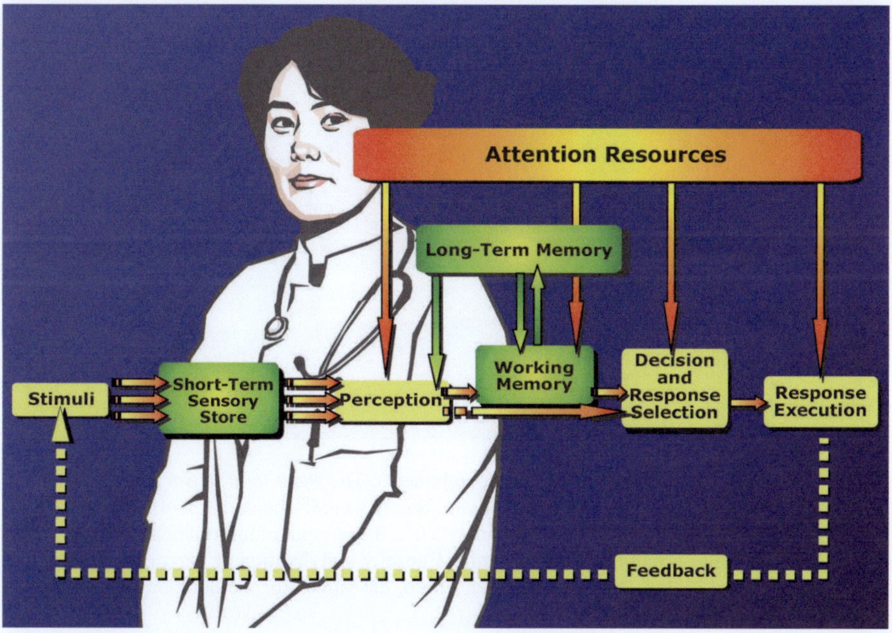

Fig. 5.2 Sensory stimuli enter the short-term sensory store where they are transformed into a form that the perceptual processes within the brain can understand. Processed stimuli are transferred to short-term memory or are acted upon immediately. Short-term memory interacts with long-term memory to develop our perception of the world and to determine our response to these perceptions. Once a response has been executed, a feedback loop provides the sensory system with new stimuli (Adapted from Wickens 1992)

theories can be found in educational books on general psychology (e.g., Anderson 2009; Baddeley et al. 2014).

After an environmental stimulus has been encoded and transmitted to the cortex, it is stored in sensory systems' corresponding *short-term sensory store* (STSS). The STSS has the ability to retain impressions of sensory information after the original stimulus has ceased so that they can be processed further and be "perceived." This sensory storage, also termed sensory memory, has a large capacity for unprocessed information but is only able to hold accurate images of sensory information for a very brief time: The *iconic memory* for vision lasts less than half second, and the *echoic memory* retains an auditory input for about 3–4 s (Fig. 5.3). Given the great number of stimuli impending on our sensory systems at any given moment, we must focus on and attend to specific stimuli that are most relevant to our purpose. The selection is driven partly by data from the environment ("bottom-up") and partly guided from an individual's expectations and concepts formed by past experiences ("top-down") (Fig. 5.1). This selective attention process (Sect. 8.2) forms the basis of situation awareness, an essential component of safe patient care (Sect. 8.4). Selective attention determines which information is consciously processed by our working memory (Chap. 4).

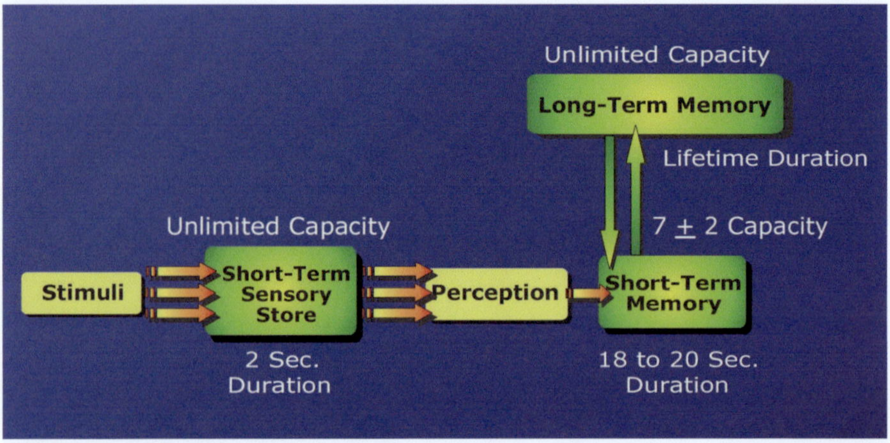

Fig. 5.3 Capacity and duration of memory components. The *short-term sensory store* takes in an unlimited amount of stimuli, but these stimuli are briefly stored. The duration of storage is longer in the *short-term memory*. A good rule of thumb is that the amount of information that can be held is limited to "the magic number" of 7 ± 2 items. Capacity and duration of long-term memory are infinite. Depending on the study and research group, the values for the duration of sensory and short-term memory may vary

5.2.1 Short-Term Memory or Working Memory

The *short-term memory* (STM) receives, holds, and processes information from the STSS before it can be transferred and retained in the long-term memory. The amount of stimuli that can be taken in by our sensory systems is considered to be unlimited. However, the amount that can be taken in is much more than the amount that can be processed. The classic work of Miller (1956) determined the "magical number" of units that can be processed at any one time in the STM as 7 ± 2, but subsequent research has indicated that 5 ± 2 may apply to most of the items we wish to remember, and this number appears to vary among different cultures. Besides having limited storage capacity, the STM also loses information very quickly: Information entering short-term memory "decays" after about 3–30 s unless it is consciously organized and encoded for transfer into long-term memory. STM is also subject to failure induced by distractions and task interruptions that can erase or overwrite information before it can be fully processed. This can lead to failure to complete an interrupted task (*prospective memory failure*; Sect. 4.5). These memory lapses usually create a temporary annoyance in our daily lives, but they can have disastrous consequences in safety critical operations.

Our STM is far more than just passive data storage. The STM plays an essential role in our conscious interaction with our environment. It is, in essence, our mental "workbench," the place where our conscious awareness integrates with the external world. Incoming sensory data is made retrievable and actionable by individual techniques of organization, repetition, and incorporating data from long-term memory (Fig. 5.4):

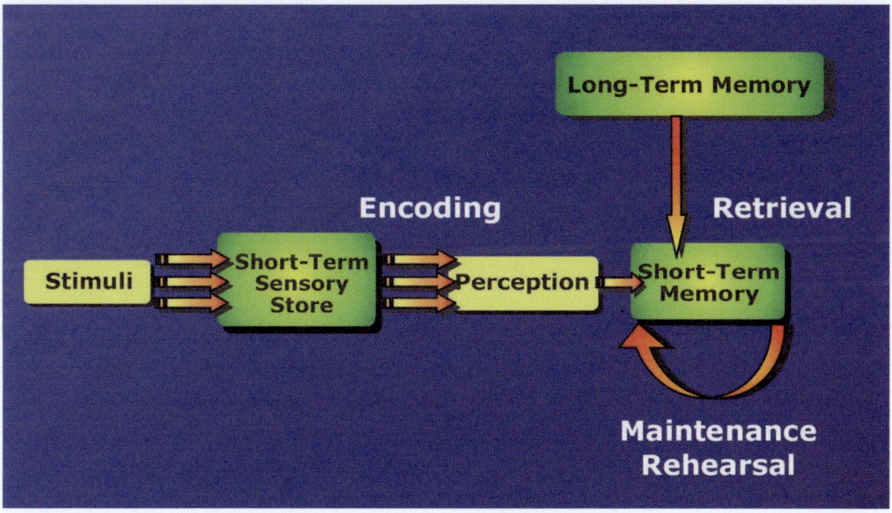

Fig. 5.4 The three basic components of memory and the processes that provide the short-term memory allowing the ability to interact with the environment: *encoding* by restructuring information into usable chunks, *subvocal rehearsal* to retain important information within short-term memory, and *retrieval* of relevant and related information from the long-term memory

- *Encoding*: Sensory stimuli enter short-term sensory store where "attended to" information is organized into a form that can be processed by short-term memory. An effective technique for organizing is to use "chunks," so that the data fits within the confined capacity store of 7 ± 2 "bits." *Chunking* as a memory mechanism can be observed in our day-to-day life: Instead of trying to remember a phone number such as 1-776-240-7911, we might group the numbers as 1776, 2407, and 911. Instead of trying to remember 11 separate digits that go beyond the "magic number," we create a mnemonic with three items that can be memorized easily because each of them carries an additional meaning: the year of America's independence "24-7" and the emergency call 911.
- *Maintenance rehearsal*: As the older name implies, short-term memory has limited storage capacity. Information entering short-term memory "decays" after about 3–30 s unless it is "rehearsed" or otherwise consciously attended to. If the data receives attention, it can be encoded and transferred to be maintained by long-term memory. Rehearsing to transfer information to long-term memory might involve subvocal repetition of the information to be encoded, i.e., we might silently talk to ourselves and repeat the information until we think we have memorized it. However, when such rehearsal is being performed extremely, limited new information can enter consciously. However, no rehearsal is needed for emotionally relevant information, as it can be stored immediately and permanently.
- *Connection to/retrieval of information*: Information can be retrieved from long-term memory to support recall and recognition. Our prior knowledge affects how

we perceive sensory information and our expectations regarding a particular sensory experience guide our interpretation. Thus, well-learned and practiced events can be relatively easily retrieved to support working memory. On the other hand, novel situations present more difficulties for short-term memory because new situations can be connected to incorrect information from long-term memory or simply receive very little support from long-term memory assets.

5.2.2 Long-Term Memory (LTM)

The LTM receives information from STM. For practical purposes, there is no known limit to LTM. The prime advantage of long-term memory is that we do not have to constantly rehearse information to keep it in storage. LTM holds all of the learning and memories of our life experience. It is essentially our life's "database." The knowledge we store in LTM affects our perceptions of the world and strongly influences what information in the environment we attend to: the contents of our memory play an active role in shaping incoming sensory input and creating our response to it. The interaction of the memory or rather knowledge and expectation with different perceptual processes is illustrated in the following.

5.3 "Gestalt" Theory and Meaningful Patterns: The Organization of Visual Perception

Sensory data undergoes an active process of reduction, simplification, addition, combination, and organization. For purposes of this discussion, we will include the organization of visual perception as our example.

Visual data acquisition and processing is not an incoherent data pool but rather a meaningful whole, the so-called Gestalt (Wertheimer 1923, 1925, 1959; Metzger 2006; Eysenck 1942; Koehler 1992; overview in Hartmann and Poffenberger 2006). The German word *Gestalt* has no direct translation in English but refers to "the way a something has been placed or put together" in an "organized structure." Common translations include "form" and "shape," but psychologists have always used the original term. For Gestalt psychologists, *form* is the most basic unit of perception: We do not perceive sensory impressions as fractional particles in disorder, but instead as organized coherent patterns, i.e., as a meaningful "Gestalt." What is "meaningful" or relevant for a person is partially predetermined by evolutionary development and partially the result of one's experience and a lifelong learning process. Thus, when humans perceive something visually, we always pick out form. The whole of this form is more than the sum of its parts; it has meaning. When something is perceived, it is filtered through our experience and our inborn processing patterns. We attribute the meaning of a part within the particular whole in which we think it occurs. This fundamental feature of perception is not restricted to the visual mode.

Gestalt processing can be "transposed" into novel realms and remains identifiable even if crucial parts are altered (Vukovich 2000). For example, from the rhythmical beeps of a patient monitor, we "hear" the heartbeat, or we can "see" a patient breathing in a colored, bell-shaped form on the display of an anesthesia machine. Once we know what to expect, we actually can "see" biological organs rather than a mere array of lines on a paper or a monitor. Forming perceptions into our Gestalt is the way we organize information. This is the only way we can understand something. When something happens that is outside of the possibility of placing it somewhere in our Gestalt, we have great difficulty understanding or retaining it.

Perception neither "reveals" objects and events of the physical world nor is there an objective reality that we can directly access via our sensory systems. Instead, the human brain "constructs" reality by means of a complex interaction of inherited neuronal mechanisms and learned processes of pattern recognition. This reconstruction happens when sensory inputs reach the brain. The result is that an object does not have to be completely scanned before it is perceived as a whole. The reason lies in the characteristics of Gestalt perception. We receive what "makes sense." Two rules describe salient features of Gestalt perception:

- While there are a vast variety of theoretically possible interpretations of sensory impressions, only a few "Gestalten" (the plural of *Gestalt*) are selected during the perceptual process.
- The interpretation of sensory impressions tries to form a Gestalt that is "good," i.e., regular, orderly, simplistic, symmetrical, etc. (*Praegnanz*). If the configuration of perceived stimuli allows for alternative interpretations, our impression will always be the one with a good Gestalt.

Human sensory experience is transformed through this constructive activity into a meaningful whole. A Gestalt will be formed even when the stimuli are incomplete; it will be constructed from whatever information is available. A ticklish example of constructing a whole from incomplete information is the neuropsychological basis for all kinds of optical illusions. From a functional point of view, this constructive activity enables a rapid and sufficient orientation to the external environment. An example is the "subjective Necker cube" (Fig. 5.5) wherein the impression of a three-dimensional cube-like object arises as if it's suspended in space with each "corner" of the cube perceived to be in front of a black disk. The tendency to build a good Gestalt makes us "see" nonexistent white lines on the white background.

Nearly a century ago, Gestalt theory showed the tendency to interpret a visual field or a problem by means of "grouping" similar or proximate objects. The grouping of the stimuli and our natural attempts to view the external world as an "organized whole" follows the laws of organization (Wertheimer 1923; Metzger 2006), with the main factors being the following:

- *Figure and ground*: We tend to organize our perceptions by distinguishing between a figure (important) and a ground (relatively unimportant).
- *Proximity*: Elements tend to be grouped together according to their proximity.

Fig. 5.5 The subjective Necker cube. When carefully observing the figure, the impression of a three-dimensional cube-like object arises that is suspended in space such that each "corner" of the cube is in front of a black "disk." Depending on the observer's interpretation, the cube is either angled to the *right upper corner* or to the *left lower corner* (Adapted from Bradley and Petry 1977)

- *Similarity*: Items similar in some respect tend to be grouped together. The similarity depends on the perceived relationships of shape, color, size, and brightness of the elements.
- *Closure*: Items are grouped together in a way that completes patterns. Missing pieces of the total tend to be added through extrapolation in the generative process of perception.
- *Continuity*: Figures are perceived as combinations of meaningful lines. If there are crossing lines, we perceive them as a pattern of several continuing lines.
- *Simplicity*: Items are organized into simple figures according to symmetry, regularity, and smoothness.

The laws of organization do not operate independently. They influence each other so that the final perception is the result of the Gestalt grouping laws acting in concert. Gestalt theory applies not only to perception and problem solving but also to other aspects of human learning and sense-making.

5.3.1 Hypothesis-Based Perception

There are times when our perceptive power does not recognize an object. When this happens, long-term memory takes the incomplete, unfamiliar, or partially obscured object and unconsciously begins hypothesis testing as to which object this could be. Even the perception of completely presented objects remains incomplete until a hypothesis is satisfied. This process of unconscious hypothesis testing is called hypothesis-based perception (Bruner and Postman 1951). The hypothesis with the highest probability for success is further pursued (Dörner 1999). Through experience and repetition, some hypotheses are readily available and rapidly tested. Things we engage with more often are perceived more quickly and accurately. The most likely hypothesis, given a certain experience and context, is pursued: An expectation is formed about what ought to be seen at a certain point in the visual field, and this expectation is then checked. This cycle (unconscious hypothesis generation compared to perceived object) is repeated until a sufficient number of hits allow for the conclusion that the object has been identified correctly. The process is undertaken rapidly and terminated even when an object might only have been scanned in part. The missing parts are added to the picture – in a way estimated or imagined. Expectations are a powerful drive of human perception and most of the time expectations are fulfilled. We normally see what we subconsciously want to see or are used to seeing, and we hear what we expect to hear. For example, errors frequently occur when a doctor verbally orders a different but similar-sounding drug and the nurse "hears" the expected (but wrong) drug simply because that's what the nurse expected to hear.

Once a hypothesis has been advanced and a perception affirmed, it takes a very deliberate and conscious effort to *re*evaluate the underlying data; strive for a new, more accurate interpretation; then attempt see or hear differently than the first satisfied hypothesis.

5.3.2 Hypotheses Are Knowledge Dependent

The hypotheses that guide the process of perception are based mainly upon knowledge and its components with a strong bias toward previous experience. Common objects are more rapidly identified than unknown ones; a familiar sight is more readily recognized than an unfamiliar one. For example, due to his clinical experience, the anesthetist in this chapter's case study rapidly detected the patient's cyanosis and interpreted it as a clinical sign of insufficient spontaneous breathing. A layperson would have seen nothing but a dark-blue face. In addition to knowledge based on experience, logical reasoning generates hypotheses to guide perception. Sometimes only explicit knowledge about what is to be expected comprises what is actually "seen" (Fig. 5.6).

The mechanism of hypothesis-based perception accepts errors as tradeoff for speed and effortlessness. A multitude of optical illusions readily underscores the fact that our perceptive system can be easily fooled. Nonetheless, the phrase "likely things are likely to happen" is a mostly useful rule for diagnosing common medical problems; it is also the selection rule that our cognitive system naturally applies. From an evolutionary point of view, the ability to rapidly produce workable patterns that serve to understand the environment has advantageous compared to having to scan every aspect of situation, consciously filter important from unimportant information and then test multiple hypotheses for what is perceived. Using patterns as solid evidence and rapidly organizing patters to perceive is far quicker and requires considerably less mental effort. Our

Fig. 5.6 Example for a hypothesis-based perception: Bev Doolittle's painting "The Woods Have Many Faces" (1985). At first, the trees and rock formations are seen as trees and rocks; however, as soon as people are told to look for faces, the individual elements of the picture are reinterpreted differently. A total of 13 faces are "hidden" in the picture

cognitive default mode of an expectation-based perception can only be altered by a comparatively slow and ponderous endeavor at conscious attention control (Chap. 8). It will always take a conscious effort to question present assumptions and to scrutinize what seems obvious. The unexpected cyanosis was an external trigger for the anesthetist to redirect attention to the perceived breathing patient even though there was data that proved a lack of breathing. Errors rooted in expectation-based perception can often be detected by team members because their differing individual experiences predispose them to divergent expectations and perceptions.

The mechanism of hypothesis-based perception also explains why medication errors have a tendency to occur during emergent, critical situations. Time pressure reduces the interval for hypotheses to be accepted. Thus, an insufficient number of hypotheses are considered, or the decision-maker is more likely to estimate or imagine information that is not there. For example, consider a crisis situation where ampules of potent drugs that have a similar appearance have been placed on an anesthesia cart. It is quite plausible for the anesthesiologist to take the drug from its expected place without a second look at the label. Because stress impairs conscious action control (to do things like cross monitoring by a teammate or double checking that the drug is correct), the mistake may go unnoticed with potentially disastrous consequences for the patient. Recently the pharmaceutical industry has come to recognize the importance of packaging medications to help facilitate rapid identification and discrimination between drugs used in operating rooms. For years

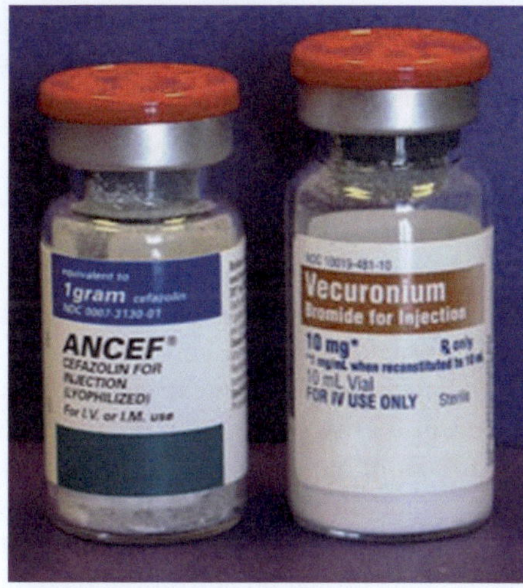

Fig. 5.7 Similarly appearing ampules stored close together in a medication cart combined with faulty drug identity checking can lead to serious medication errors. An example is the swap of vials of cefazolin (an antibiotic) with vecuronium (a long-acting paralytic agent) caused unexplained apnea during general anesthesia (AHRQ 2003)

powerful muscle relaxants such as vecuronium vials were packaged similarly to those of heparin or antibiotics (Fig. 5.7).

The laws of Gestalt, however, are not only useful in explaining action errors. From the knowledge of the laws of Gestalt, human factor considerations can be brought into the design of healthcare environments, e.g., information can be displayed more legibly, vials may be have more distinctive shapes and colors, etc. This approach would be in accordance with basic tenets of human factors engineering.

5.4 Recognition and Creating Meaning

In the third step of the perception process, visual patterns are identified and interpreted, i.e., they are given meaning. Sensory data is selected, processed, and then identified by comparing it with meaningful chunks stored in long-term memory, so-called schemata, and thus classified into recognizable things or sounds. If a person experiences something familiar, the perception is named. At this level, perception receives its meaning and is placed into a broader context. For example, a visual stimulus displayed as a particular capnography curve on a monitor provokes the thought that "this patient is breathing spontaneously" (Fig. 5.1). Only after this last step takes place, after the information has been selected and processed does perception enter consciousness for the first time. Despite the multilevel processing of sensory data at the subconscious level, perception appears to be objective and capturing mere facts. In other words, we believe that what we see, hear, and feel is reality. Because perception feels so completely real, it is counterintuitive for us to question it. This powerful sense of perceiving objective reality makes it difficult for clinicians to apply knowledge about the inherent weakness and fallibility of sensory impressions to care of patients.

5.4.1 That's So Typical! Expectancies

The identification and categorization of perceived data is substantially assisted by mental precepts and expectancies (mind sets). Because some perceptions are more likely to occur within a certain context, they are neuronally preactivated. "More likely" means in this context that in one's personal experience a certain perception has occurred more often in combination with a corresponding sensory impression and therefore has been typical up to now. For instance, a patient's dark-blue face during emergence from anesthesia is more likely to be a sign of inadequate ventilation than the result of either venous congestion or of intravenous methylene blue. Thanks to neuronal preactivation, recognition and identification become faster and show less error. However, unexpected information has to be looked at and considered longer and in greater detail before it can be recognized accurately.

Because preactivation is an experience-dependent phenomenon, experience and knowledge define what is more or less probable in a certain situation. There is danger, however, if past experiences are the main interpretative frame for new sensory information because then we may see what we have always seen. It becomes virtually impossible to "think outside the box" of our initial and ongoing perception. Another way of saying this is that we might only see what we want to see. Because motivational forces (e.g., needs) are a potent trigger for preactivation (Dörner 1999), humans tend to select and interpret sensory information in a way that enables them to have their needs met. If an anesthesiologist wants to extubate a patient as quickly as possible because dinner is waiting at home or because it is 2:00 a.m. and driven to get some bed rest, then interpretation of the capnography curve is more likely to be interpreted as a sign of sufficient spontaneous breathing.

5.5 Perception and Emotion

Perception of events in critical situations is not restricted to cognitive aspects and is always accompanied by emotions (Scherer and Ekman 1984). When people are exposed to environmental changes, a "holistic" emotional assessment of the situation on the basis of previous perceptions will take place – even if the results of this assessment do not surface to conscious processing (Chaps. 4 and 8). Instead, emotions are often quite vague. People usually have difficulty recognizing and articulating them. Because emotions arise in a subconscious perceptive process, they are difficult to analyze on a rational basis. Nonetheless, they are based on perceptions and therefore should be taken seriously. Like the old adage, "Where there's smoke, there's fire," emotions tend to be like "smoke" for a fire that is burning beyond conscious perception. To have an "uneasy" feeling very often means that something is amiss. That is why clinicians are often advised that an uneasy feeling is always worth reflecting upon to better understand why the uneasiness is present. Emotionally driven perceptions are integrated into judgments when making decisions in critical situations, We will get back to this issue in Chaps. 6 and 10.

5.6 Tips for Clinical Practice

The following are tips for clinical practice:

- Perception is always subjective. It's best to rely on four eyes rather than two eyes if the matter is of importance.
- Always be prepared to learn that your perception might actually be deceiving you. Increase the level of resolution in critical situations; it is better to look twice and pay close attention so that you are more likely to discover errors.
- Perception is guided by expectations. Be aware of your expectations and question your decisions. This will enable you to have a less biased approach to a situation.
- Emotionally colored judgments and perceptions play an important role in acute care decision-making. Anticipate their influence!
- Emotions tend to be like "smoke for a fire" that is burning beyond conscious perception. To have an "uneasy" feeling very often means that something is amiss. While experiencing an uneasy feeling, it is always worthwhile to reflect upon why this feeling arose under these particular circumstances.
- Use as many sensory modalities as possible. If you want to get a precise picture of the situation – *hear*, *see*, *smell*, and *feel* how the patient is doing.

5.7 "Perception" in a Nutshell

In summary, the following principles can be derived. Remember, even though much of this chapter used visual or auditory perception as examples, these principles apply to all levels of perception:

- Perception is the process by which sensory information is integrated with previously learned information and other sensory inputs. Integration enables us to make judgments about the quality, intensity, and relevance of what is being sensed.
- Perception enables us to orient and act within our environment. Perception does not result in objective truth, but the perceptive process is oriented to practical results.

- We construct a whole picture from incomplete perceived sensory impressions. This ability is normal and under most circumstances allows us to act effectively.
- Perception happens in three consecutive and interrelated steps:
  1. Processing of sensory stimuli in the sense organs
  2. Organization of perception (Gestalt perception and meaningful patterns)
  3. Recognition and assignment of meaning
- These three processes influence each other and are dependent on our cumulative knowledge and experience.
- Perception is limited by absolute and relative thresholds. Some thresholds are biologically determined; some can be influenced by motivation and conscious control of attention.
- Perception is hypothesis based. Expectancies strongly influence whether a hypothesis is accepted as truth and can foreshorten the process of a complete scan of the environment.
- The underlying hypotheses are based on previous experience and motivation.
- Our cognition does not distinguish between real and constructed data.
- Perception is not precise. Because it is hypothesis based, perception is especially error prone when efficiency and speed are needed.

References

AHRQ (2003) Unexplained apnea during general anaesthesia. http://www.webmm.ahrq.gov/case.aspx?caseID=2#figures. Accessed Aug 2010

Anderson JR (2009) Cognitive psychology and its implications, 7th edn. Worth Publishers, New York

Baddeley A, Eysenck M, Anderson MC (2014) Memory, 2nd edn. Psychology Press, Hove

Bradley DR, Petry HM (1977) Organizational determinants of subjective contour: the subjective Necker cube. Am J Psychol 90(2):253–262

Bruner JS, Postman L (1951) An approach to social perception. In: Dennis W, Lipitt R (eds) Current trends in social psychology. University of Pittsburgh Press, Pittsburg

Dörner D (1999) Bauplan für eine Seele [Blueprint for a soul]. Rowohlt, Reinbek bei Hamburg

Eysenck H (1942) The experimental study of the "good Gestalt": a new approach. Psychol Rev 49:344–364

Goldstein EB (2013) Sensation and perception, 9th edn. Wadsworth Cengage Learning, Belmont

Hartmann GW, Poffenberger AT (eds) (2006) Gestalt psychology: a survey of facts and principles. Kessinger, Whitefish

Klix F (1971) Information und Verhalten. Kybernetische Aspekte der organismischen Informationsverarbeitung [information and behavior. Cyberbetic aspects of organismic information processing]. Huber, Bern

Koehler W (1992) Gestalt psychology: the definitive statement of the Gestalt theory. Liveright Books, New York

Metzger W (2006) Laws of seeing (originally published 1936; translated by Spillmann L, Lehar S, Stromeyer M, Wertheimer M). MIT Press, Cambridge, MA

Miller G (1956) The magical number seven, plus or minus two: some limits on our capacity for processing information. Psychol Rev 63:81–97

Ramachandran V, Blakeslee S (1999) Phantoms in the brain: human nature and the architecture of the mind. Fourth Estate, London

Scherer K, Ekman P (eds) (1984) Approaches to emotion. Erlbaum, Hillsdale

Vukovich A (2000) Christian v. Ehrenfels: "Über 'Gestaltqualitäten'" ["on Gestalt qualities"]. In: Schmale H (ed) Hauptwerke der psychologie. Kröner, Stuttgart

Wertheimer M (1923) Laws of organization in perceptual forms. First published as "Untersuchungen zur Lehre von der Gestalt". Psychol Forsch 4:301–350. Translation published in: Ellis W (1938) A source book of gestalt psychology. Routledge and Kegan Paul, London, pp 71–88

Wertheimer M (1925) Über Gestalttheorie [on Gestalt theory]. Verlag der philosophischen Akademie, Erlangen. Reprint Gestalt Theory 7:99–120

Wertheimer M (1959) Productive thinking (enlarged edition). Harper and Row, New York

Wickens CD (1992) Engineering psychology and human performance. Harper Collins, New York

Zimbardo G, Gerrig RJ (eds) (2012) Psychology and life. Pearson Education Limited, New York

Information Processing and Mental Models: World Views

6

Case Study

At 10:35 in the morning, two ambulances are sent to the site of a rural two-car traffic accident. The first unit that arrives at the scene confirms that two cars are involved and three people have been injured. According to eyewitnesses, the driver of one of the cars lost control of his vehicle, and the two cars had a head-on collision. The two occupants of the second vehicle have only minor injuries, but the driver who caused the accident is comatose. After assessment and triage, the second EMS team focuses on the two mildly injured occupants, one of whom is complaining of paresthesia, likely secondary to a whiplash injury. The unconscious victim is rescued from his vehicle and transferred to the ambulance by the first team. He receives oxygen via face mask and two large-bore intravenous lines are inserted. A normal blood sugar finger stick rules out hypoglycemia as a cause for the unconsciousness. Volume resuscitation is started and the patient is intubated. As the victim shows no external injuries, the working diagnosis at this point includes deceleration injury with severe internal bleeding, injuries to major intra-abdominal organs, and severe head injury. After 2,000 ml of crystalloid solution is infused without any effect on the arterial blood pressure, an epinephrine drip is started. The jugular veins are noted as markedly distended which suggests the possibility of a pneumothorax. However, chest auscultation reveals bilateral breath sounds, and chest palpation shows no rib fractures or subcutaneous emphysema. Thus, the diagnosis of pneumothorax is ruled out. On arrival at the emergency department, the patient continues to be hemodynamically unstable. An ultrasound scan shows no intra-abdominal organ injuries or free intraperitoneal fluid. The chest X-ray reveals adequately ventilated lungs, marked perihilar congestion, normal aortic arch, and significantly enlarged cardiac silhouette.

M. St.Pierre et al., *Crisis Management in Acute Care Settings*,
DOI 10.1007/978-3-319-41427-0_6

Up to this point, 3,500 ml of crystalloid solution has been infused, and the rate of the epinephrine drip has reached 5 mg per hour. A transesophageal echocardiography is performed revealing a dilated left ventricle with severe inferior and apical akinesia. The patient dies shortly after admission to the ICU as a result of severe cardiogenic shock.

A team of paramedics is confronted with a routine call: a motor vehicle accident (MVA) with two lightly injured patients and one severely injured patient. The medical treatment of the patient with clinical signs of volume depletion is routine: oxygen via face mask, the placement of several large-bore IV lines, and volume resuscitation. This emergency situation featured some noteworthy exceptions from "the routine MVA" that were not realized by the EMTs or the physician: neither the unclear circumstances of how the accident happened nor the missing signs of injury nor the sternotomy scar that could indicate previous cardiac surgery received attention. The initial assumption of volume loss as the reason for the arterial hypotension was never questioned. A non-trauma cause, such as an acute myocardial infarction, was not considered. Available information was not searched nor taken into account during the entire operation.

This "blindness to the obvious" is not an unusual phenomenon in clinical medicine. How can it be explained that the physician was unable to see that the external circumstances of the accident could be interpreted quite differently? The answer is that in that moment, her evaluation of the situation and the resulting actions made sense. If it did not make sense, she would have chosen a different strategy. But how did she reach her decision and why did it remain unaffected by conflicting information for such a long time? These questions lead us to the core of human information processing.

Human thinking processes information presented by perception and memory (Chaps. 4 and 5). However, memory items – our knowledge – are not available in the same way as information contained on a computer's hard disk. The selection of relevant memory contents underlies the same principles as perception. Items are classified as "relevant" and thus are more easily and quickly retrieved from memory if:

- They are common.
- They meet expectations and therefore are preactivated.
- They are important.
- They have a strong emotional component.
- They are related in some way to other activated items (associative retrieval).

Thus, selectivity consists primarily in its accessibility, in the ease with which information comes to the mind. Accessibility therefore determines to a high degree what decisions are made: Easily accessible information is considered, whereas information that does not come to mind easily and immediately tends to remain inactive. Unfortunately, the most accessible memory items are not necessarily the most relevant ones for making a good clinical decision (Kahneman 2003).

Conscious thought processes, such as judgment, planning, generation of analogies, or prognostic statements about the anticipated development of events, are based on a multitude of subconscious information processing steps. In this respect, thinking is analogous to perception, in which a multitude of subconscious processes precede conscious perception. Basic cognitive processes that run on the basis of memory architecture are as follows (Lompscher 1972; Selz 1913):

- Identification and classification of objects and events
- Assessment
- Association
- Linking
- Imagination

From the memory retrieval conditions mentioned above and our basic cognitive processes, fundamental principles of information processing can be deduced. These principles explain both the incredible performance of human cognition and some of the roots of our errors in thinking.

6.1 The Organization of Knowledge: Schemata and Mental Models

All human knowledge – sensory, procedural, and conceptual knowledge – can be characterized as a network of sensory and motor schemata and of the concepts of language (Chap. 4). Schemata are chunks of information, "knowledge packages," encoding either generic concepts (e.g., "everything that is needed for starting an IV line") or familiar episodes or scenarios ("how to puncture a peripheral vein"), also known as *scripts* (Schank and Abelson 1977). Schemata exhibit the following fundamental aspects (Bartlett 1932; Anderson 1983):

- They are unconscious mental structures. People are unaware of the fact that both the encoding and storage of information, as well as recall and perception, are guided by meaningful high-level knowledge structures and not by atomistic bits of information.
- High-level knowledge structures are composed of knowledge and past experiences. People try to integrate new material into established knowledge structures; thus, we tend to recognize and classify items similar to what we have already experienced. On the other hand, it is difficult or impossible for us to recognize and classify items that we cannot fit into our knowledge structure.
- Schemata are stored in a hierarchical system with primary rules for solving problems on the top and secondary rules and exceptions to the rules further down in the hierarchy. Whereas novices have only a limited number of schemata, mostly of primary rules, the expert problem solver has stored a multitude of secondary rules and exceptions along with the primary rules.

- Recall of long-term memory actively reconstructs past experiences. Biases in remembering are normal because people tend to interpret presented data in keeping with their own expectations and established habits of thought.
- The recall of schemata follows the principle of economy, which attempts to achieve its goal with the least possible effort.
- This law of economy can actively be overcome by conscious effort and investment of time, both of which are scarce resources in an emergency situation.
- What makes a schema strong is how recently and how frequently it has been used.

The fact that the regularities of the world are organized in our internal representation of the world as schemata explains the inferential and interpretative function of human cognition. It goes beyond the given information. For example, "induction of anesthesia" data can be:

- Identified and assessed ("the patient has lost consciousness and can be ventilated by mask. Everything goes as intended")
- Explained ("unconsciousness is the effect of thiopental")
- Predicted ("once thiopental is injected, the patient will become unconscious")

The entirety of the schemata referring to a certain area of reality is called a mental model (Johnson-Laird 1983). Behind this term stands a picture of the situation based on our experience – a model of a part of the world is represented in our mind. Because mental models organize knowledge in a stable and predictable way, they provide a basis for planned actions. Extensive work in naturalistic decision-making has confirmed that expert individuals rapidly analyze situations by pattern matching against their mental library of prior experience (Klein 1992). A main characteristic of these mental libraries is that information has been contextualized and given meaning. In other words, "knowledge books" in memory are always stored together with the experiential context and with the meaning we gave them. Therefore, knowledge is readily accessed if the current context resembles the original context. A problem arises when people use knowledge stored in memory from a particular context that may be inappropriate for the current situation. This happens especially under the pressures of stress and time, both of which impede reassessment of the situation, as seen in the vignette.

Because mental models contain knowledge derived from past personal interactions with the world, they will always differ between people. In an emergency situation, this requires communication as a means of aligning the mental models of each team member. If this is not accomplished, the odds are high that every team member will think and act in different ways (Chap. 11).

Whenever possible, new information is added to preexisting mental models, i.e., in this way new information is assimilated. Learning in this case means that mental models are enlarged without the need of a structural change. Arterial hypotension in relation to a traffic accident "fits" into the basic model of "volume depletion." Once this model is activated and found acceptable, new information that cannot be integrated into the existing modeling information has a strong likelihood of being not perceived or rejected. Mental models have to be rearranged and have to undergo a structural change to fit the new circumstances (*accommodation*; Piaget et al. 1985). Because humans are creatures of habit and have a strong propensity to maintain existing mental models, rearranging and changing a mental model are unlikely without a strong stimulus to change. And while under stress, we are even more likely to ignore information contrary to our mental model rather than change our image of the world.

6.2 Information Processing: Head or Gut

6.2.1 Dual-Process Theory

The fact that humans are creatures of habit is well illustrated in the way the emergency physician treated the trauma patient. She had experienced situations like this one many times before which made for a confident on-the-spot diagnosis. The physician perceived and developed a mental model that the trauma patient suffered from hemorrhagic shock as a result of internal bleeding and experience had taught this physician that aggressive volume therapy always helped. Her decision was nearly instant and led almost automatically to her therapeutic decision. Because congested jugular veins can be seen in trauma patients under certain circumstances (e.g., when the patient suffers from a tension pneumothorax) and because she could resort to a familiar procedure to fix the cause (the insertion of a chest tube), the physician did not see any reason to question her current mental model and to reevaluate facts and options. It was only in hindsight that she realized that she had committed herself to the incorrect diagnosis and wished she had used a more deliberate and controlled strategy that might have led to different results.

The vignette illustrates alternative modes for solving diagnostic problems. One process is unconscious, rapid, and automatic. It runs efficiently and when used by an experienced clinician is most often correct, or at least nearly correct. The other process is characterized as conscious, slow, and sequential in nature. It permits abstract reasoning and hypothetical thinking. In the mind of a highly experienced clinician, it uses a large library of memories and schemata and is limited mostly by working memory capacity. Although the idea of two distinct kinds of reasoning has been around since psychologists have written about human thought, only in recent years have cognitive scientists proposed two separate cognitive systems, namely, "two minds in one brain" (Evans 2008) with properties of both decision-making coexisting (Table 6.1). According to this view, humans can access both types of reasoning within our cognitive system. The "dual-processing" model of decision-making has gained widespread acceptance in cognitive sciences (for an overview, see Evans (2008), Evans and Stanovich (2013)) and has rendered reasoning independent from working memory capacity.

Research on naturalistic decision-making, such as recognition-primed decision-making (Klein 1998), shows that experts make decisions using both systems. In routine situations and common emergencies, decision-makers size up the situation and quickly recognize which actions make the most sense (System 1). Thus, by

Table 6.1 Distinction between cognitive processes attributed to two differing systems by dual-process theories. The bipartite division of cognitive processes has been corroborated by many research groups

System 1	System 2
Unconscious	Conscious
Intuitive	Analytic
Automatic	Controlled
Implicit, tacit	Explicit
"Gut feeling"	Rational
Rapid	Slow
High capacity	Low capacity
Low effort	High effort
Parallel	Sequential
Holistic	Rule based
Contextualized	Abstract
Domain specific	Domain general
Nonverbal	Linked to language
Independent of working memory	Limited by working memory
Evolutionarily old	Evolutionarily new

relying on their holistic assessment of the situation and the available options, experts actually don't consciously think when they decide – they "just do what is right." Numerous publications found for general audiences often describe this as "gut feelings" or "intuition" (e.g., Klein 2004; Gladwell 2005; Gigerenzer 2008; Kahneman 2012; Chap. 4).

However, when unfamiliar or unusually complex elements arise, System 2 tends to exert oversight on automatic decisions drawn from System 1 and allows abstract reasoning to enter conscious thought. Selection among choices can be considered using mental simulation of the future. Even highly experienced experts cannot rely solely on efficient, unconscious decision-making; on occasion, a situation demands conscious thinking to achieve a "good decision."

Crucial for the understanding of the two process modes seems to be the fact that the intuitive processes ("System 1") consist of numerous neural networks located in the evolutionarily older parts of the brain that support rapid parallel processing of information. Analytical thinking on the other hand is linked to deliberate activation of the cortex and is limited to processing one information strand at a time ("System 2").

System 2 processes take place under conditions where people have greater availability of resources (e.g., time or information). Decisions made under these circumstances tend to be more rational, can be verbalized, and often result in robust decisions. However, System 2 processes do not guarantee right decisions because knowledge may be missing or incomplete and the rules used for reasoning may be wrong. System 2 is the part of our reasoning faculties that becomes increasingly competent as we mature, socialize, and go through formal training. It is refined by training in critical thinking and logical reasoning (Croskerry 2009; Fig. 6.1). System 1 responses occur through prior System 2 learning; repetitive processing of clinical

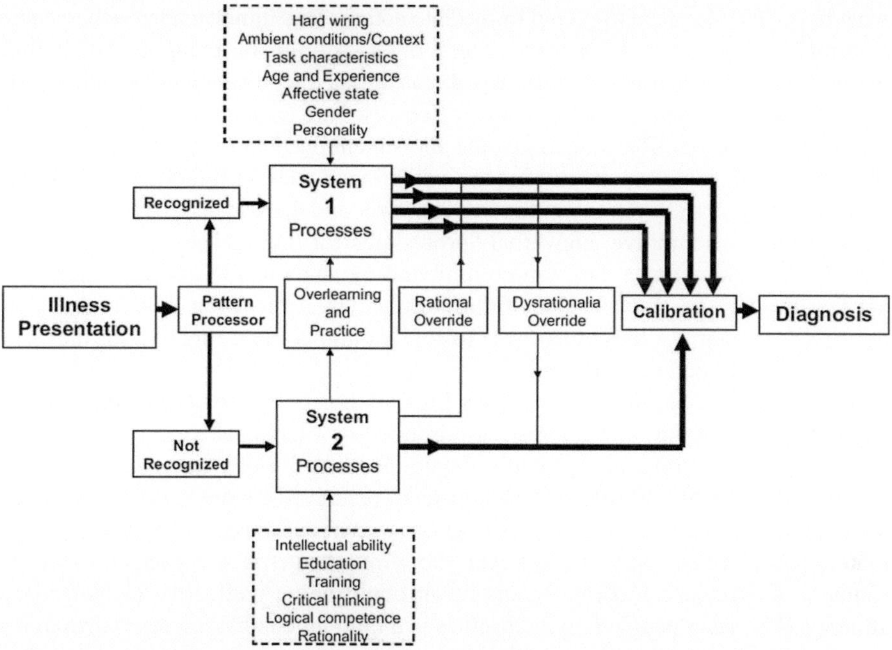

Fig. 6.1 Model for diagnostic reasoning based on pattern-recognition and dual-process theory. The model is linear, running from left to right. The initial presentation of illness is either recognized or not by the observer. If it is recognized, the parallel, fast, automatic processes of System 1 engage; if it is not recognized, the slower, analytical processes of System 2 engage instead. Determinants of System 1 and 2 processes are shown in *dotted-line boxes*. Repetitive processing in System 2 leads to recognition and default to System 1 processing. Either system may override the other. Both system outputs pass into a calibrator in which interaction may or may not occur to produce the final diagnosis (With permission from Croskerry 2009)

presentations and problems by System 2 can eventually lead to a System 1 response. When reasoning falls into System 1, experts find it difficult to verbalize their decision-making; they simply do the right thing.

6.2.2 System 1 Processes and Heuristics

The power of *System 1 processes* lies in the fact that they function autonomously and require almost no precious cognitive resources. Perception is holistic and includes *Gestalt* and emotion (Chap. 5). Actions are triggered associatively. It is a rule of thumb among cognitive psychologists that we spend about 95 % of our time in the intuitive mode of System 1 processes. System 1 is preferred because it saves time and effort. It corresponds to the "principle of economy" (see below). The emergency physician from the vignette illustrates this fact: The trauma patient with his livid skin color in combination with missing visible chest excursions is automatically "seen" as being in a state of respiratory arrest. Bag-mask ventilation is started. Decades of clinical experience have brought her to the point where she no longer needs to think about what to do; the blue face triggered immediate action. This intuitive approach to decision-making is also called a *heuristic*, a term of Greek origin meaning "serving to find out or discover." A heuristic is a strategy that is initiated with partial information with rapid decision-making as one of its goal. Heuristics are an adaptive mechanism that provides significant effort reduction – the abovementioned "principle of economy" – by examining fewer cues, simplifying the weighting of cues, integrating less information, and examining fewer alternatives (Gigerenzer and Gaissmaier 2011).

Heuristics are intuitive, nonverbal "procedures for finding solutions." They are unconscious. Sometimes they can be inhibited by analytical reasoning. Heuristics are not the same as clinical rules of thumb (e.g., "treat first what kills first"; "if in doubt, take it out") – these also help to find solutions more rapidly, but they are explicitly taught and remembered.

Heuristics are ubiquitous in everyday life and mostly lead to satisfactory results. Heuristics that do not serve us well are dropped or altered. The use of a heuristic implies that a person has repeatedly experienced its validity and success of the resulting decisional pattern in a particular set of perceived circumstances. Heuristics are dependent on contextual cues, but the contextual cues need to be only approximately perceived correctly. If, however, the wrong heuristic is chosen or the environment is perceived incorrectly, the result could be an ineffective or dangerous strategy. Whenever people find themselves in a familiar context, perceptual analysis can effortlessly occur without deliberate intention or awareness and lead to judgment and action; decisions and actions are recognition primed (Klein 1992). Heuristics as fast-and-frugal pattern-recognition strategies are inherently neither good nor bad. The price people have to pay for the relatively easy, speedy, and predominantly correct decision-making is our inclination not to verify the data or the decision. Deviations from rationality and the influence of emotions go undetected. This phenomena are called "cognitive bias" wherein we are inclined to make a particular decision and action and tend to accept and defend our current thinking. A bias has a negative connotation; "cognitive disposition to respond" and "affective disposition to respond" have been proposed as alternative terms (Croskerry 2009).

Fortunately, System 2 can verify the content of System 1 decisions by exerting an executive function to override the output of System 1 when necessary. In this way unexamined intuitive judgments can be submitted to verification. This decoupling step serves humans well because taking immediate action on first impressions can sometimes prove catastrophic. The override function of System 2 is a critical feature of cognitive and affective de-biasing (Chap. 10).

6.3 Are We Too Lazy to Think? Economy, Competence, and Safety

Sometimes errors originate from faulty or inadequate knowledge or from an inadequate application of correct knowledge (Chap. 3). Most of the time, however, errors in decision-making appear to originate in the fast, intuitive processes of System 1 which contribute to systematic deviations from rational decisions ("errors of judgment" in popular science; e.g., Dobelli 2013; Croskerry 2008). Underlying the

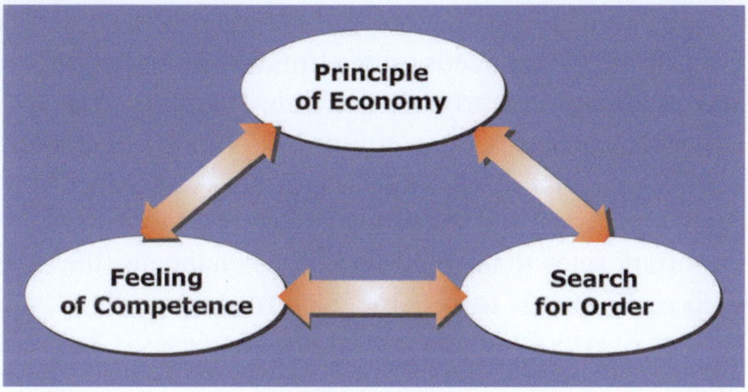

Fig. 6.2 Three basic factors that influence each other in the construction of mental models

descriptive literature are three principles: protecting resources, maintaining a feeling of competency, and searching for order (Fig. 6.2).

6.3.1 Too Lazy to Think: Resource Protection

Conscious thinking (System 2 processes), the tool we need to deal with unknown realities, functions slowly and is limited by working memory. It competes with other stimuli for perceiving, processing, and deciding and uses our limited short-term and working memory resources. Because System 2 requires a great deal of our limited capacity, we tend to avoid conscious thinking and therefore naturally take shortcuts by relying on automated cognition or emotion-based decision-making. Many failings in our thought process are an expression of our tendency to economize. Most of our decisions in everyday life integrate the principle of economy, and the results are satisfactory. Since we are drawn to the principle of economy, we sometimes think we already know something, and we restrict our data gathering and hypothesis generation and testing; it is "business as usual." The same is true for emergency situations: A traffic accident then becomes another one of "these motor vehicle accidents," and arterial hypotension must be caused by volume depletion – as it has been so many times before. What people perceive and think is greatly influenced by what they already know and therefore expect. Using the System 1 approach, only part of the situation is actually scanned and assessed. If it fits or closely fits into an existing mental model, the gaps are efficiently completed by existing knowledge. This principle of completion leads to a highly economical application of thinking, and most of the time, the results are satisfactory. On the other hand, errors can occur when (a) our knowledge is not consistent with reality because it is wrong, or (b) the matching with reality is too superficial, so things are different than they seem to be at first glance.

Another way of protecting cognitive resources is the emotional mode of information processing (*affect heuristic*, Slovic et al. 2002). From an evolutionary perspective, it proved advantageous to use rapid and unconscious judgment to make a decision about whether or not to approach an object by asking a simply, binary question: Does this object give me a good or bad feeling? As a result, reliance on efficient thinking became hardwired. While on many occasions, it saved the life of our ancestors, we also acquired biases toward our first decision and therefore may limit additional information processing, judgment, reasoning, and decision-making.

In everyday life, this mode of behavior is the mostly useful for successful action. It is a strategy that needs only a limited amount of information, leads to good results, and is effective nearly all the time (Hertwig and Todd 2001; Gigerenzer 2000). However, once stress or emotional pressure increases, the principle of economy starts to become even more important (remember, long ago it was often a life or death situation), and we subconsciously allow efficiency and quickness to take more important roles than usual. When this happens, the agreement of the mental model with reality tends to become even more superficial, and the probability for errors, such as overlooking and confusing, increases (Chap. 9).

6.3.2 Beware of Drowning! Guarding the Feeling of Competence

In order to be able to act efficiently, people need a stable mental model to explain the current situation. This is best achieved by constructing and then using an image of reality as long as it seems plausible. While this picture is in place, present assumptions do not have to be questioned, and the course of action can remain unaltered. So, "my mental model is wrong" means "I have to think anew before I can act." However, the notion of "not knowing" also has direct impact on one's feeling of competence. Most human beings prefer not to be confronted with errors or unexpected changes in situation. Instead, we prefer to maintain our mental models as one way to guard our feeling of competence (Dörner 1996).

This strong tendency to guard one's feeling of competence not only explains the stability of mental models but also accounts for the form they tend to take: straightforward and simple models. Strong mental models create a feeling of safety and personal intelligence, whereas complex and differentiated explanations that don't fit our mental model raise doubt and increase insecurity. Therefore, whenever possible, people tend to simplify complex and opaque situations and focus on the predominant problem (Dörner 1996). To a certain extent, this approach to constructing reality makes complete sense because if someone considers himself to be incapable of acting they will hardly act. The motivation to protect one's feeling of competence is an important part of our internal regulation. However, in the attempt to maintain confidence in one's competence in problem solving, people tend to do the following:

- Fail to take notice of data that indicates they are wrong ("fixation error").
- Fail to adequately consider the meaning of developments and long-term consequences of actions during a critical situation. Subjects prefer to attend to a single problem *they have* rather than bother about possible problems they do *not yet have* ("predominance of current problems").
- Fall short of checking the effects of their actions and therefore act "unreasonably" and often end up losing control of the course of events ("ballistic action," Dörner 1996).

In critical situations the urge to guard the feeling of competence can become the dominant motive for action. "Saving face" unconsciously may become more important than saving a patient's life; adequate treatment of the patient's medical problem becomes secondary to the control of one's own feelings. When this happens, we hardly ever notice it. Observers or team members may observe what seems to be irrational or "egotistical" action on the part of the decision-maker, but the decision-maker is typically unaware of the motive to save face. In the mind of the decision-maker, the perception of events and subsequent actions to care for the patient make sense.

Self-reflective examination and critique of one's way of acting are essential means of preventing the need for a feeling of competence to predominate. Unfortunately, self-reflection in these situations is often overlooked.

6.3.3 Certainty and Order: The Avoidance of Ambiguity

Mental models give structure to the world by merging similar experiences and ascribing significance to perceived data. In this way, we create a consistent image of reality. Mental models tend to be cohesive and stable. When a mental model is robust in that it has served us well through a variety of situations, we learn that it enables us to explain the present and to extrapolate into the future. For this reason, people tend to strive for clarity and avoid ambiguity and uncertainty whenever possible (*ambiguity aversion*, Camerer and Weber 1992; Heath and Tversky 1991; Curley et al. 1986).

Structure and order provide a feeling of certainty. It is also important for memory and cognitive processes. Structure is a central feature because structured data can be more readily memorized and retrieved. When we are asked to process a great amount of data, we can only be efficient if these data are somehow structured. Thinking, therefore, can be described as a process whereby we give structure to our environment (Selz 1913). In an acute care setting, this need for a structure in thinking becomes most obvious in the search for an unambiguous diagnosis. In the mind of the physician, eliminating ambiguity and striving for clarity of thinking clear the way for decisive action and the best treatment of the patient.

6.4 Wishful Thinking and Reality: Distortion of Information

In the effort not to question our knowledge, we subconsciously tend to shape information until it fits our mental model of the situation. Shaping the information is subject to confirmation bias and distortion and may truncate data acquisition (Fig. 6.3). All these very human tendencies can lead to an incorrect mental model and the wrong actions for the patient.

6.4.1 Biased Search for Information

We tend to seek pieces of information that reinforce present knowledge or hypotheses (*confirmation bias*, Kahneman et al. 1982). To offset confirmation bias, data that could raise doubts about present assumptions have to be presented with more emphasis than those that reaffirm the prevailing mental model. For instance, if

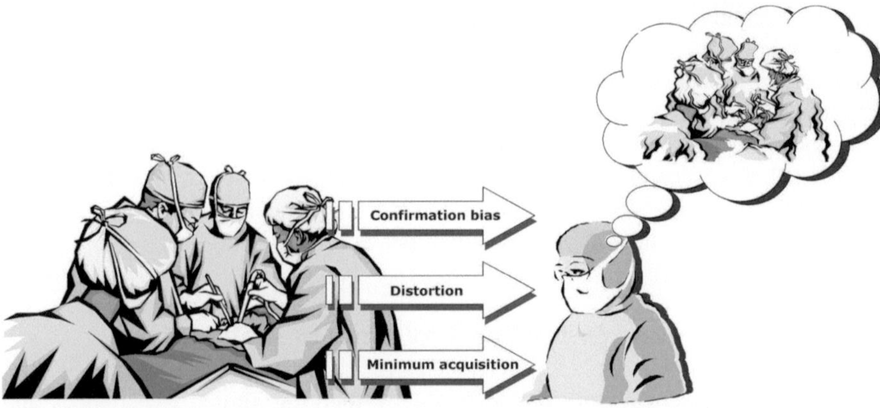

Fig. 6.3 Distortion of information leads to inadequate mental models

someone had mentioned to the EMS team that the patient had complained about retrosternal burning pain prior to the accident, the field diagnosis most probably would have been different. But without early external prompting, it is natural for people not to actively search for information that contradicts the present assumption. The EMS team was no exception to this rule. The only way to avoid this wrong mental model from becoming entrenched is to hold a deep-rooted skepticism about the appropriateness of any initial diagnosis. During a crisis, a good rule to live by is that the odds are high that information has been overlooked; things are not perceived correctly at first; and care is not going as well as it should.

6.4.2 Distortion and Suppression

If critical situations are experienced as a threat to one's feeling of competence, then the need to maintain the current mental model can become practically overwhelming. In this context, ambiguous information is reinterpreted in a way that corroborates present knowledge. This phenomenon can be so intense that people might no longer hear or see new or contradictory information.

6.4.3 Limited Acquisition of Information

The guarding of a feeling of competence is one reason why an inadequate model of reality is held. Another reason for an inadequate mental model is the way information management is handled. The abundance, interrelatedness, ambiguity, and uncertainty of perceptual data (Chap. 2) jointly create a situation of excessive demand for the cognitive system. Once we reach the limits of our cognitive capacity, we will solve the overwhelming problem by reducing information acquisition. Decisions are then based on an insufficient amount of data and therefore result in incorrect diagnosis. When new information is no longer being acquired, it is highly likely that a decision will not be reevaluated until the cognitive load is reduced and new data is considered.

6.5 Filling in the Blanks: Inadequate Mental Models

Resource protection, the guarding of a feeling of competence, and the avoidance of ambiguity are responsible for many mistakes. Other mistakes occur because we often base decisions on handling probabilities and frequencies. This approach, called "frequency gambling," occurs when a decision-maker sees a situation that looks like something they've seen before and acts according to what they've done in the past. Decisions based on probabilities are often correct, but sometimes they are not. A common problem of an inadequate mental model, whether it be from frequency gambling or another factor, is that one's mental model does not correlate with reality. If one is able to collect and process more data, decision-making is likely to improve. Unfortunately, the true data often is not grasped until we look at actions retrospectively when more time is available and more of the existing data can be considered. For example, it was only after the patient transport that the EMS team from our case study realized that they had "bet on the wrong horse" and had not realized the true problem. The amount of literature on faulty decision-making is extensive. In keeping with the theme of this book, we restrict ourselves to a discussion of those forms of error that impact decision-making in the acute care setting.

6.5.1 Fixation Error: Maintaining Mental Models Despite the Evidence

In critical situations, the guarding of competence and excessive cognitive demand can lead to a situation in which the wish for a stable mental model rules behavior. Once a situation assessment has been made, people tend to stay fixed on it even if there is sufficient data pointing in the opposite direction. People develop a cognitive tunnel vision wherein other data, information, or suggestions are not allowed in the tunnel. This error of fixation (DeKeyser and Woods 1990; Gaba 1992) is characterized by a tendency to search for confirming information and to distort perceived data to fit the current mental model (Table 6.2). This becomes most apparent when a certain possibility is rejected at all costs ("everything but this"). Besides the necessity to protect one's mental models, the motive remains the need to control the situation. The motive to remain in control can be characterized as, "If this situation is not what I think it is, then I have to deal with a problem and I might be helpless and fail."

Table 6.2 Fixation errors

Type of fixation error	Meaning
"This and only this"	Persistent failure to revise a diagnosis or plan despite emerging evidence that the diagnosis or plan is incorrect
"Anything but that"	Persistent failure to address a serious problem. Possible explanations for a situation are considered, but the real explanation is rejected before it is taken into account
"Everything's OK"	Persistent belief that there is no danger despite growing evidence to the contrary

Adapted from DeKeyser and Woods (1990)

6.5.2 A Simple Mental Model About Complex Problems

When humans are faced with everyday problems, they seek an appropriate solution by applying simple mental models. In most situations, simple mental models serve us well. Complex problems, however, demand a deep understanding of the situation and the surrounding conditions to find a solution. Because simple models usually work in everyday life, we have a tendency to use them even when we are faced with unusual, hard to understand, complex problems (Dörner et al. 1983; Dörner 1996; Sterman 1994). The potential problems of using simple mental models when the problem is complex are:

- The extent of a problem will be underestimated.
- Overly simple assumptions about the chain of causation will be made.
- Interrelations will be ignored, and single aspects of a problem will be treated as being independent from one another.
- The dynamics of the development will be misjudged. People tend to anticipate the development of variables by means of linear extrapolation. When they suddenly are confronted with a nonlinear development, they will be taken by surprise.

6.5.3 Knowledge Errors

We have knowledge about many things, but sometimes our knowledge is not complete; it may be applied incorrectly or used in the wrong context. For example, a piece of *knowledge* is recalled correctly, but the *application* under the given circumstances is inappropriate. An intensive care physician might diagnose an ECG rhythm correctly but then may err in the selection of the antiarrhythmic drug because the pharmacological profile of this drug is inappropriate to treat this specific dysrhythmia.

More often a person has correct knowledge for a problem that eventually winds up being useless because it does not help to solve the problem at hand. Healthcare providers are prone to fall into this error trap when they act before spending sufficient time creating an adequate mental model of the situation. As in frequency gambling, familiar action schemata are triggered by only a few characteristics of a situation (Chap. 4). Our EMS team pursued an aggressive volume replacement because it is usually indicated in severe hypovolemic shock following a motor vehicle accident. However, the underlying – and unquestioned – assumption was that shock was caused by volume loss and not by a global cardiac failure. Paradoxically, it is experienced clinicians who are especially vulnerable to this kind of misjudgment. Decades of clinical practice have provided them with a wealth of clinical strategies that they apply following a salient cue. Because these behavioral patterns have proven to be successful in past experience, it's unusual to question the initial situational assessment. A behavior that attends to the peculiarity of every single case is replaced by the "methodism" (Dörner 1996; or "cognitive conservatism," Reason 1990) of the "experienced" caregiver. Methodism – seeing new situations in terms of old ones, undertaking established patterns of action that need only be set in motion without much further thought – is far more economical than considering each individual case. Methodism also has the appealing advantage of being reliable and usually effective

The third category of the way knowledge errors occur is when people do not reevaluate a situation in the light of additional information and therefore do not adapt the management accordingly. It can be characterized as, "One's knowledge was correct about some aspects of the situation, but now things have changed." As more information becomes available, it can happen that assumptions about therapeutic options that were initially right become wrong. Because critical situations can change dynamically, the criteria for successful action may change as well. For example, nitroglycerine is the first-line treatment for a patient with stenocardic complaints caused by a myocardial infarction; however, if ischemia increases and contractility is further impaired, nitroglycerin is contraindicated because it causes arterial hypotension. In this case, if the clinician fails to regularly retake the blood pressure, the initial treatment could lead to a potentially fatal treatment error. Situation awareness (Chap. 8; Endsley 1995; Endsley and Garland 2000), the knowledge about where exactly one *is* within a critical situation and about the validity of current assumptions, is a critical ability that can help healthcare providers prevent errors of fixation and correct faulty mental models.

All of these simplified mental models, distortions of the real world, and limited acquisition of information are responses to the psychological impossibility, in terms of both intensity and quality, of perceiving, knowing, understanding, and doing everything ("*bounded rationality*"; Simon 1982). On the contrary, the purpose of mental models is to predict what will happen and what one is going to do and not what is "real."

6.6 Probabilities, Ambiguity, and Risk

Knowing where exactly one *is* within the temporal aspects of a critical situation is prerequisite for successful management: Tasks like being aware of and executing what is most important, putting off some things until later, taking time to plan and adjust the plan, and deciding on and setting up the next stage of care have a time and place. Knowing where *to go* and being able to choose among alternative treatment options are the next logical step in the decision-making process. In order to figure out what to do, it is essential to project an intended course of action into the near future and to estimate probabilities of success or failure.

"Probability" in the psychological sense used here can be defined as subjective conviction that an event will or will not take place or that a statement is true, given the available information (Kahneman et al. 1982). However, subjective conviction may be deceptive because we are imprecise at evaluating risks objectively. Nevertheless, healthcare professionals have to decide how to proceed so the probabilities have to be estimated and weighed as to their desirability. Logically, the relative weight of each option should be a function of the frequency by which an event might occur balanced by the severity of possible consequences. The more often an event occurs and the more severe the impact will be, the more data needs to be taken into account. An illustration of the notion of balancing certainty and risk is presented in Fig. 6.4.

Under optimal circumstances, a reasonable choice can be made from among alternatives as each possible solution results in one and only one certain outcome. Thus, the choice among alternatives is equivalent to a choice among consequences. For example, in the case report, a trauma patient has to be intubated and a hypnotic drug has to be given. Once the drug is injected, the patient will become unconscious. If the anesthetic drug isn't given, no hypnotic effect will occur. The choice to inject the drug leads directly to the consequence "unconsciousness." These kinds of decisions are typically called *decisions under certainty* because we are certain what will happen when the drug is administered (Fig. 6.4).

In other situations, the outcomes of a decision might not be known for sure because one of several outcomes can result from a given action. Sometimes the probabilities of outcomes are roughly known, but very often the probabilities associated are not all known precisely. These kinds of decisions, which comprise the majority of decisions in acute medical care, are typically called *decisions under uncertainty*.

In economic theory there has been a long-standing distinction between "risk" and "uncertainty" (Knight 1921; Ellsberg 1961). *Risk* refers to situations wherein the decision-maker can assign mathematical probabilities to the randomness which with he is faced, e.g., the probability of rolling a six with a die is 1 in 6. *Uncertainty* refers to situations when randomness cannot be expressed in terms of specific mathematical probabilities. Although the "risk versus uncertainty" debate is a long-running and informative debate in economics, we find the distinction between uncertainty and risk clinically helpful when it comes to treating a patient. In the discussion that follows, we use the terms carefully in describing choices in critical situations.

Thus, in contrast to general decision theory, the use of the term *decisions under risk* in healthcare emphasizes the potential harm a patient may suffer. One first tries to minimize harm to the patient while aiming to gain maximum therapeutic effect. The knowledge of potential harm caused by a decision limits decision-making ability. Unfortunately, it is often only in hindsight that the risk of certain actions or

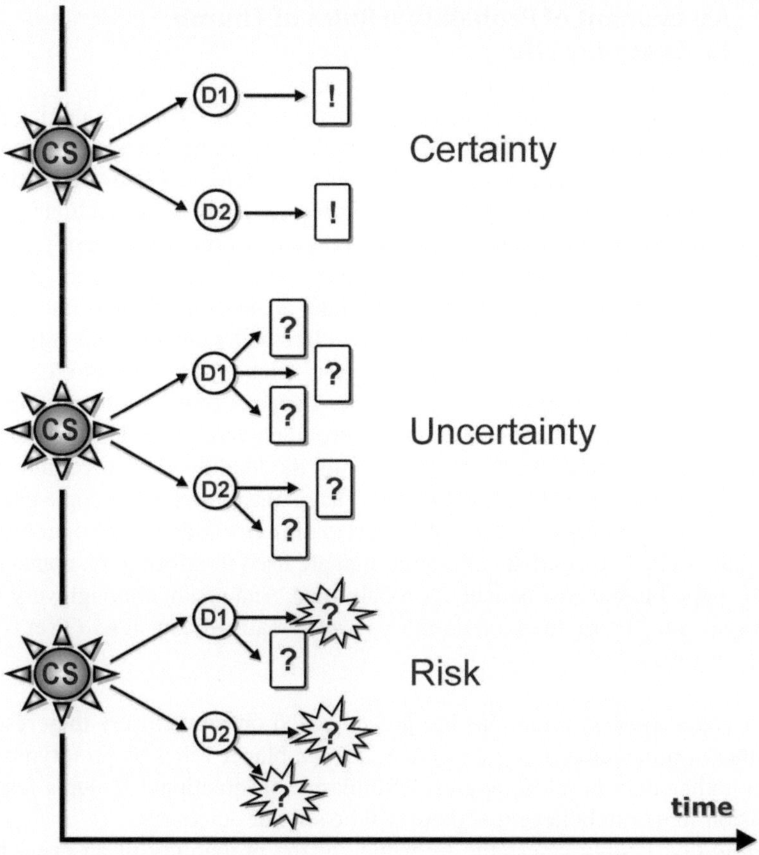

Fig. 6.4 Decisions under certainty, ambiguity, and risk. Triggered by a critical situation (*CS*), decisions (*D*) have to be made. Under conditions of certainty, a choice among alternatives (D1, D2) is equivalent to a choice among consequences ("!," upper trace). Making decisions under ambiguity is characterized by outcome uncertainties ("?," medium trace). Decisions under risk are a subgroup of decisions under ambiguity where the consequence of decisions can harm a patient (*jagged figure*, lower trace)

omissions can be appraised. An example of making a decision under risk can be gleaned from the case report: If the on-scene EMTs decide not to insert large-bore IV lines in the trauma patient, volume resuscitation by smaller lines might suffice to maintain adequate volume status in the case of minor volume loss. The same cautious volume management in a patient with major internal bleeding, however, will most certainly put the victim at considerable risk for intractable traumatic shock. On the other hand, aggressive volume replacement with large-bore IV lines will correctly address the clinical problem of internal bleeding but most certainly will harm a patient when shock is caused by left ventricular failure. Most of the time decisions under uncertainty will entail some degree of risk for the patient.

6.6.1 Assessment of Probability: Rules of Thumb for Everyday Life

People experience difficulties when faced with the task of accurately judging probabilities and predicting values. Most theories of choice assume that accurate decisions can be derived from an assessment of the future outcomes of various options vis-à-vis some type of risk-benefit analyses. However, a detailed and accurate analysis is costly in terms of time and mental effort and in most situations doesn't help very much. Our typical solution is to apply heuristics or our "rules of thumb" to clinical situations. By definition, heuristics doesn't take all the information into account. Moreover, our application of heuristic rules is effected by other considerations such as emotions, fatigue, effectiveness of perception, memory limitations, etc.

This subjective assessment of probabilities happens mostly subconsciously. In routine and in critical situations, healthcare providers tend to base most diagnostic and therapeutic decisions on beliefs concerning the likelihood of uncertain events; numerical probabilities tend not to be used. That is the reason why people generally employ a limited number of rules of thumb to simplify judgmental operations. In general, the same two heuristic principles that are used in information management are also applied to our assessment of probabilities. And again, although very useful in everyday life, these rules of thumb can systematically mislead (Tversky and Kahneman 1992):

- *Representativeness*: Situations are judged based on how closely they resemble another familiar situation. Assessment of resemblance relies on prototypical features rather than on close analysis. Similarity of situational features leads the decision-maker to believe that there will be similar outcomes.
- *Availability*: People assess the frequency or the probability of an event by the ease with which instances or occurrences can be brought to mind. That is, they are easily retrieved from memory, for example, "This happened to me a few days ago and I did … In that situation, everything worked out well." Or, "I just read an article on this condition so I will do … That should work."

6.6.1.1 Representativeness

The assessment that the patient from the case study suffers from a severe volume loss is based on "typical" features of "trauma victim following motor vehicle accident." If a situation contains representative evidence of a certain category, then people may suppose that the situation belongs in this category. The categorization of the emergency situation into the category "motor vehicle accident with multiple casualties" happens on the basis of the similarity with a prototype (*similarity matching*; Reason 1990). Based on this appraisal, the response with the highest probability of success is to start aggressive volume replacement. The reasoning is "It has helped before, why should it fail now?" Applying the heuristic of representativeness has clinically relevant advantages: If the diagnosis "shock resulting from significant blood loss" is derived solely on the basis of weak peripheral pulses in combination with the mechanism of injury without any further detailed examination, then precious time is saved, and volume resuscitation can begin immediately. Unfortunately, the general efficacy of this shortcut can entice people to concentrate on only a few characteristics of the situation and neglect others. The heuristic of representativeness can become even more misleading if it is applied in reverse: "What does not look like a typical myocardial infarction cannot be one." Past experiences taught the medical team that patients with a myocardial infarction "typically" are the result of a call that alerts the EMS team to a cardiac problem. Thus, the EMS team was unprepared to find this medical condition under unusual circumstances. Indeed, a patient with an acute myocardial infarction rarely causes a traffic accident. What is typical for a situation depends on knowledge and experience. The more extensive a mental model of a situation is, the more considerations are likely to be included in the assessment.

6.6.1.2 Availability

The assessed likelihood of an event depends on the ease with which schemata can be retrieved from memory. What people remember most easily influences their belief about probabilities. Lifelong experience has taught us the following:

- Memory items that we have to deal with frequently are recalled better and faster than those we use infrequently.
- Likely occurrences are easier to imagine than unlikely ones.
- Associative connections are strengthened when two events frequently occur together (Tversky and Kahneman 1974).

Because the availability of schemata depends partly on the *frequency* with which they are retrieved, schemata encoding common and frequent situations will be activated more often than schemata of rare events. The frequency heuristic is logically effective most of the time; however, other factors influence the likelihood of memory recall:

- Conspicuity/distinctiveness/salience
- Importance
- Time since last recall

For instance, the fact that many anesthesiologists suspect or at least consider a case of malignant hyperthermia (a very unusual occurrence) as soon as an abnormal increase in end-tidal CO_2 is detected is partly due to the importance of early diagnosis and treatment, and not because of the general incidence of the disease itself.

Novices tend to suspect rare or impressive diseases behind trivial symptoms (so-called fascinomas), as they overestimate the base rate frequency of the disease. To combat this phenomenon, two humorous expressions are often used with novice clinicians "Common things are common," or, "When you hear hoofbeats, think horses, not zebras."

6.6.2 Problems in Dealing with Probabilities

Our inability to deal adequately with probabilities comes not only from a reliance on judgment heuristics, nor is it entirely attributable to motivational effects alone, nor is our lack of ability due to our propensity to lean toward the economy of mental models. Most people simply disregard some basic principles of statistical reasoning that would enable them to estimate probabilities correctly. In the field of healthcare, this is relevant whenever decisions are based on data, such as the choice between different treatments or when taking side effects into account (Gigerenzer 2000 for a collection of examples from healthcare). Even when probabilities are not expressed in numbers, but instead verbally, there are pitfalls that can lead to serious errors:

- "Felt likelihood": The emotional assessment of probabilities ("if I have a good gut feeling the choice cannot be wrong") carries a risk of erroneous decisions.
- "Pseudo-accuracy": If there is a general lack of information, one tends to make assumptions about basic probabilities of risks. Using incomplete information or simply our assumptions about the data, the probability will be wrong. The number only reflects personal assumptions and presumptions. Moreover, if approximations are combined with each other, the errors become larger.
- "Confounding cause and correlation": The joint occurrence of two events does not allow us to know about their causal relationship, e.g., $a \rightarrow b$ or $b \rightarrow a$. It is quite possible that one or both are caused by variable c.
- "Reverse conclusions": If $a \rightarrow b$, this does not automatically imply that if a is not present, then b cannot be present, e.g., "if a myocardial infarction does not happen within a 'typical setting,' then it cannot be a myocardial infarction."
- "Base rate fallacy": One has to know the base rate of the incidence in the population *and* the reliability of a test to determine the probability that a test result is correct. We often neglect the base rate and consider only test reliability.
- "False positives" and "false negatives": Tests that are highly sensitive and include marginal values as possibly positive often lead to false positives (false alarms), i.e., deciding that someone has a fever when they do not. False negatives occur when test results show that there is no out of normal value, when the value is abnormal, e.g., deciding that someone does not have a fever when they do have one. Whether it is worse to wrongly diagnose a disease or overlook a diagnosis is a decision the clinician has to make.

6.6.3 No Risk, No Fun? How to Deal with Risk

Because complexity always includes uncertainty about the result of an intentional action (Chap. 2), risk is an unavoidable component of patient care. Thus, the question for healthcare providers can never be *whether they are willing* to take risks when they treat patients but rather *under what circumstances* they will take risks and for what reasons. As with all decisions under uncertainty, it is important to remember that judgment of risks is based on perceived risk, not on objective facts. Risk assessment is always subjective and prone to error. For actions in an acute care setting, an absolute estimate about risk assessment is not possible, e.g., "Will option X help the patient?" A paradox of in-the-moment risk assessment is that clinicians are generally willing to make decisions regarding relative risk of two actions, e.g., "Is option X more risky than option Y?" Whenever a decision between two actions in a critical situation has to be made, avoiding spontaneity is a good approach. During a crisis situation, the assessment of the risk for a treatment option should involve answers to the following four questions:

- How high is the probability of unwanted events?
- How high is the probability that I will be unable to cope with the situation I am about to create?
- How high is the price to the patient and/or me if I am unable to cope with this situation?
- How high is the price to the patient if I take some time to gather more data?

The safety of the patient depends in large part on the ability of caregivers to make a controlled decision when accepting risk. The degree of risk that a decision presents to the patient will depend on the caregivers' (a) awareness and knowledge about dangers, (b) experience and practice with comparable situations, and (c) actual clinical competence.

Despite the inevitable necessity of engaging in risk-taking actions, the above-stated questions can lead to developing risk-aversive behavior. Risk aversion is the reluctance of a person to engage in actions that have an uncertain payoff. The risk-aversive clinician tends to choose certainty of consequences over uncertainty – even if the uncertain choice has a good probability of benefit to the patient. As should be clear, clinical decisions in crisis situations involve risk taking. This is for certain. We are not advocating that clinicians, especially in crisis situations, avoid or seek risk; we only suggest that decision-makers be as thoughtful as possible about the risks they decide on the patient's behalf.

6.6.3.1 Motivation

It is common that motives other than patient safety enter into medical decision-making. The avoidance of boredom ("no risk, no fun"), the desire to make autonomous decisions irrespective of safety standard ("don't tell me what to do!"), or the desire to become a "hero" by spectacular actions ("now watch me do this!") all lead to an underestimation of risk. The key for successful risk management lies in the realistic assessment of one's own competence and in the control of motivation for risky decision-making. The basic working philosophy should always be to avoid working near one's performance limits because at that point clinical competence is weak and the chances for harming the patient are high. Team members can be a valuable resource addressing the issue of taking unnecessary risks.

6.6.3.2 Heuristics

Identification of an acceptable level of risk constitutes a probabilistic assessment and is done by means of heuristics. The most relevant heuristic for risk assessment is the *rule of availability* (see above). The likelihood of a complication is nearly always inaccurately estimated because the estimation tends to be based on how easily the complication comes to the mind of the clinician. The imaginative drive to envision a complication commonly stems from our own experience, from discussions we have with colleagues, or from a recently read educational article. The probability for a desired or undesired result is *overestimated* if one happened to talk about a similar case just yesterday or if one still has lively memories about an incident that happened not too long ago. On the other hand, risk is generally *underestimated* if one never has experienced a certain complication or if past risky behavior has received positive feedback. In both cases, it is very hard for us to imagine why our patient might be an exception to the rule that comes to mind.

6.7 Tips for Clinical Practice

Both the individual and the team can avoid being trapped by the law of economy and the protection of competence if they intentionally manage the perception and processing of information. The following ideas might seem easy to put into practice, but they require conscious effort and practice to manage our innate thinking habits.

6.7.1 Some Advice About Information Processing and Mental Models

- "Wipe the slate clean." Avoid thinking about legal or social implications; instead direct all attention to the problem. It is of fundamental importance that you start from scratch. Never assume that any single item of your current mental model is fact.
- Critically reevaluate your first hypothesis: The probability that your initial diagnosis has been made by means of heuristics is very high. It is possible that critical aspects of a situation have been neglected; therefore, you should always actively search for information that contradicts and disproves the initial diagnosis. This questioning of an initial diagnosis is all the more important in a critical situation because there may be few possibilities for correction. Because stress further

impairs the ability to search for contradictory data, it should become a habit to ask oneself these questions:
  - Did I overlook facts?
  - Do new data fit my initial assumptions?
  - Have there been any relevant developments recently?
  - Is there any reason why the initial assumption could be wrong?
  - Is there a teammate who might be thinking about this differently?
- The ability to allow for incomplete and incorrect information and conclusions is an important requirement for dealing with complex situations. When newly found evidence might favor an alternative explanation for the clinical problem, then always remember: The ability to admit mistaken assumptions and to revise an initial diagnosis or decision is a sign of wisdom and competence, not of weakness.
- Generate alternatives. You can help avoid fixation errors by making it your habit to explicitly name several possible differential diagnoses or alternative actions every time an idea comes to mind.
- Appreciate that the path to mishaps is paved with false assumptions.
- The ability to admit mistaken assumptions and to revise an initial diagnosis or decision is a confidence and wisdom.

6.7.2 Some Advice on Risk Taking

- Take risks for the right reasons. Risks are best considered when you are calm and thoughtful. Don't take a risk because you are angry, desperate, or frightened. Don't take risks to get revenge or harm someone else.
- Consider the possible loss as well as the gain. That is, assess what the likely consequences of failure will be. Unless you know pretty accurately what both loss and gain will be, you do not understand the risk.
- Be extremely cautious if you have to make a decision about an irretrievable action. For instance, if you want to take the patient's ability to breathe spontaneously by giving a muscle relaxant, then you should always ask yourself: "Do I really want to do that now?"
- Risky decisions should always be made by a person who can cope with the resulting consequences.
- "As an overall philosophy, it is wise to use good judgment to avoid situations in which superior clinical skills must be applied to ensure safety" (Hawkins 1987).
- When possible, take one risk at a time. Divide your actions or goals wherever possible so that you are not combining risks unless absolutely necessary. Simultaneous risky actions increase anxiety, create confusion, and make failure analysis very difficult.
- Always deliberately set a minimum safety level for everything you do and *never* go below it. Remember: If it can't be done safely, it is not worth doing!
- Have a goal. When you take a risk, have a clear purpose in mind so that you will know whether you succeeded or not.

6.8 "Information Processing and Mental Models" in a Nutshell

- Conscious thinking is based upon several basic, subconscious levels of information management processing.
- Knowledge is organized into schemata (e.g., schemata of events, of expectations, of conceptual knowledge) and mental models. They allow for the efficient recognition, interpretation, and extrapolation of events.
- People use two different modes of information processing, which both have strengths and weaknesses: One is a rather analytical, verbally linked process and the other a rather intuitive and holistic one. They complement each other and rely on the same knowledge.
- Many errors originate from basic features of information processing: cognitive economy, protection of the feeling of competence, and the avoidance of ambiguity.
- A heuristic is a strategy that ignores part of the information with the goal of making decisions more quickly, frugally, and/or accurately than more complex methods.
- Heuristics come up against their limits when people come up against their own limits.
- Under stress or high emotional strain, the match between one's mental model and objective reality becomes more and more superficial.
- When stressed, the probability increases for making mistakes like overlooking, mixing up, and mishearing.
- Common problems of information gathering are the selective search for confirming information ("*confirmation bias*"), distortion of information, suppression of unwanted information, and reduced acquisition of information.
- Mental models can be wrong for a given problem. Fixation error, overly simplistic models, knowledge errors, and methodism of the experienced caregiver can affect the problem solving.
- The handling of uncertain information and of probabilities is difficult for most people to do well. People use heuristics, such as *representativeness* and the *rule of availability*, to assess likelihood. Despite their usefulness in everyday life, heuristics can be misleading in critical situations.
- Mental operations with probabilities often lead to erroneous results. True probability calculations often result in counterintuitive solutions.
- Risk taking is unavoidable in acute care settings such as anesthesia, intensive care, and emergency medicine.
- Risks can be over- or underestimated depending on motivation and the heuristics applied.

References

Anderson JR (1983) The architecture of cognition. Harvard University Press, Cambridge, MA
Bartlett FC (1932) Remembering. Cambridge University Press, Cambridge, UK

Camerer C, Weber M (1992) Recent developments in modeling preferences: uncertainty and ambiguity. J Risk Uncertain 5:325–370

Croskerry P (2008) Cognitive and affective dispositions to respond. In: Croskerry P, Cosby KS, Schenkel SM, Wears RL (eds) Patient safety in emergency medicine. Lippincott Williams & Wilkins, Philadelphia, pp 219–227

Croskerry P (2009) A universal model of diagnostic reasoning. Acad Med 84(8):1022–1028

Curley SP, Yates JF, Abrams RA (1986) Psychological sources of ambiguity avoidance. Organ Behav Hum Decis Process 38:230–256

DeKeyser V, Woods DD (1990) Fixation errors: failures to revise situation assessment in dynamic and risky systems. In: Colombo AG, Bustamante AS (eds) Systems reliability assessment. Kluwer, Dordrecht

Dobelli R (2013) The art of thinking clearly. Sceptre Books, London

Dörner D (1996) The logic of failure: recognizing and avoiding error in complex situations. Metropolitan Books, New York

Dörner D, Kreuzig H, Reither F, Stäudel T (1983) Lohhausen. Vom Umgang mit Unbestimmtheit und Komplexität [Lohhausen. Dealing with uncertainty and complexity]. Huber, Bern

Ellsberg D (1961) Risk, ambiguity, and the savage axioms. Q J Econ 75:643–669

Endsley MR (1995) Toward a theory of situation awareness in dynamic systems. Hum Factors 37:32–64

Endsley MR, Garland D (2000) Situation awareness analysis and measurement. Lawrence Erlbaum, Mahwah

Evans JSBT (2008) Dual-processing accounts of reasoning, judgment and social cognition. Annu Rev Psychol 59:255–278

Evans JSBT, Stanovich KE (2013) Dual-process theories of higher cognition: advancing the debate. Perspect Psychol Sci 8(3):223–241

Gaba D (1992) Dynamic decision-making in anesthesiology: cognitive models and training approaches. In: Evans DA, Patel VL (eds) Advanced models of cognition for medical training and practice. Springer, Berlin/Heidelberg/New York, pp 123–148

Gigerenzer G (2000) Adaptive thinking. Rationality in the real world. Oxford University Press, Oxford

Gigerenzer G (2008) Gut feelings: the intelligence of the unconscious. Penguin Random House, London

Gigerenzer G, Gaissmaier W (2011) Heuristic decision making. Annu Rev Psychol 62:451–482

Gladwell M (2005) Blink. The power of thinking without thinking. Back Bay Books/Little Brown, New York

Hawkins FH (1987) Human factors in flight. Ashgate, Aldershot

Heath C, Tversky A (1991) Preference and belief: ambiguity and competence in choice under uncertainty. J Risk Uncertain 4:5–28

Hertwig R, Todd P (2001) More is not always better: the benefits of cognitive limits. In: Hardman D (ed) The psychology of reasoning and decision-making: a handbook. Wiley, Chichester

Johnson-Laird PN (1983) Mental models. Towards a cognitive science of language, interference, and consciousness. Cambridge University Press, Cambridge, UK

Kahneman D (2003) A perspective on judgment and choice. Mapping bounded rationality. Am Psychol 58(9):697–720

Kahneman D (2012) Thinking, fast and slow. Penguin, London

Kahneman D, Slovic P, Tversky A (1982) Judgement under uncertainty: heuristics and biases. Cambridge University Press, Cambridge, UK

Klein G (1992) A recognition-primed decision (RPD) model of rapid decision-making. In: Klein G, Orasanu J, Calderwood R, Zsamboka E (eds) Decision-making in action: models and methods. Ablex, Norwood, pp 138–147

Klein G (1998) Sources of power: how people make decisions. The MIT Press, Cambridge, MA

Klein G (2004) The power of intuition: how to use your gut feelings to make better decisions at work. Crown Publishing Group, New York

Knight FH (1921) Risk, uncertainty, and profit. Houghton Mifflin, New York

Lompscher J (1972) Theoretische und experimentelle Untersuchungen zur Entwicklung geistiger Fähigkeiten [Theoretical and experimental studies on the development of mental abilities]. Volk und Wissen, Berlin

Piaget J, Brown T, Thampy KJ (1985) Equilibration of cognitive structures: the central problem of intellectual development. University of Chicago Press, Chicago

Reason J (1990) Human error. Cambridge University Press, Cambridge, UK

Schank RC, Abelson R (1977) Scripts, plans, goals, and understanding. Erlbaum, Hillsdale

Selz O (1913) Über die Gesetze des geordneten Denkverlaufs [On the laws of structured thought processes]. Spemann, Stuttgart

Simon H (1982) Models of bounded rationality, vol 1. MIT Press, Cambridge, MA

Slovic P, Finucane ML, Peters E, MacGregor DG (2002) The affect heuristic. In: Gilovich T, Griffin D, Kahneman D (eds) Heuristics and biases: the psychology of intuitive judgment. Cambridge University Press, New York, pp 397–420

Sterman JD (1994) Learning in and about complex systems. Syst Dyn Rev 10:291–330

Tversky A, Kahneman D (1974) Judgment under uncertainty: heuristics and biases. Science 185:1124–1130

Tversky A, Kahneman D (1992) Advances in prospect theory: cumulative representation of uncertainty. J Risk Uncertain 5:297–323

Goals and Plans: Turning Points for Success

7

Case Study

After emergency surgery, an obese patient with multiple injuries is transferred from the operating room to the surgical intensive care unit (SICU). The patient's diagnoses include open fractures of the forearm and the femur, blunt chest trauma, a mild head injury, and multiple lacerations. The chest X-ray shows evidence of a lung contusion without any signs of fractured ribs or of a pneumothorax. On admission to the SICU, the patient is adequately ventilated, and his initial hemoglobin concentration is 11.5 g/dL. After 2 h of an uneventful course, the patient suddenly develops increasing peak airway pressure. Despite increasing the inspired oxygen concentration to 70 %, the saturation continues to decrease, and the patient becomes hemodynamically unstable. The resident physician examines the patient, auscultates the lung, and finds decreased chest motion and decreased breath sounds over the right hemithorax. He assumes a diagnosis of pneumothorax without confirming his diagnosis by additional examinations and studies (e.g., chest X-ray). He immediately proceeds to perform a tube thoracostomy through an axillary line incision. Because he has never performed this procedure before and because the anatomy of the patient is less than favorable for an exact identification of anatomical landmarks, he accidentally perforates the liver with the trocar. There is an initial blood return through the chest tube that he interprets as intrapleural bleeding. Despite his intervention, the patient's oxygenation does not improve, and the peak airway pressures do not normalize. Drawing no further conclusions from these observations, no additional interventions are performed at this time by the resident. Over the next 20 min, 1,500 ml of blood drains from the chest tube and the arterial blood pressure continues to drop. The resident inserts two large-bore intravenous lines and rapidly infuses crystalloid and colloid solutions. At the same time, he asks the nurse to prepare an infusion pump with epinephrine, to check the arterial blood gas, and

M. St.Pierre et al., *Crisis Management in Acute Care Settings*,
DOI 10.1007/978-3-319-41427-0_7

to request packed red blood cells (PRBCs) and fresh frozen plasma (FFP) from the blood bank. The resident finally calls for his attending physician, but before he arrives in the SICU, the patient goes into cardiac arrest. Cardiopulmonary resuscitation (CPR) is immediately started, and spontaneous circulation returns. From the location of the thoracostomy site and from the clinical course, the attending physician diagnoses intra-abdominal bleeding from a perforated liver and immediately organizes an emergency exploratory laparotomy. Following massive volume resuscitation of blood products and crystalloid, the patient is stabilized and transported to the operating room. Laparotomy confirms the diagnosis of a massive hemorrhage from a laceration to the liver. The surgeons succeed in controlling the bleeding and the blood pressure improves. As a result of the massive transfusion of blood products, the patient develops transfusion-related lung injury (TRALI) and requires mechanical ventilation for several weeks. An intraoperative bronchoscopy reveals a large blood clot, which almost completely obstructs the right mainstem bronchus as the cause for the initial problem. After removing the clot, the saturation and airway pressures normalize rapidly.

A physician-in-training was confronted with a ventilatory problem in an intensive care patient. He interpreted the presenting constellation of symptoms (increased airway pressure, absent breath sounds over the right lung, and slowly decreasing saturation) as signs of a tension pneumothorax. Although there were several more differential diagnoses for this symptom constellation and although the patient was in no immediate danger, the resident started to act on his first diagnosis. He neither searched for alternative causes for the clinical problem nor did he request a second opinion. He performed a thoracostomy without supervision by an experienced colleague and did not adequately consider the possibility of a complication. When the complication occurred, he did not recognize it for what it was: a punctured liver. The clinical course led to the patient's cardiac arrest that required immediate cardiopulmonary resuscitation. Because of a massive volume replacement and red blood cells, CPR was successful. As a result of this massive transfusion, however, the pulmonary situation of the patient deteriorated and he developed full-blown acute respiratory distress syndrome. The real trigger for the situation, a blood clot in the right main bronchus, could have been removed bronchoscopically with very little risk to the patient. Because the resident prematurely formulated the goal "insert a chest tube" and because he subsequently planned and executed the insertion poorly, he put the patient's life at risk. Setting goals and planning actions did not adequately take place.

Goals and plans are thoughts about the future – anticipated events, developments, and actions. As such, *goals* are states that satisfy needs or, more precisely, mental representations of such states. *Plans* in turn are the avenues to reach those states. Because humans are able to imagine needs that lie in the future, plans and their corresponding goal-oriented actions are not always linked to current needs, e.g., one can sit down and start learning for an exam scheduled to take place in a couple of months.

In acute medical care, pursued goals primarily serve the patient's well-being, for example, adequate oxygenation in the clinical vignette. As a result, actions taken are not intended to satisfy clinicians' existential needs (e.g., hunger, sleep), but rather serve imagined needs of another person. However, non-physiological needs such as informational or social needs do have an effect on action (Chap. 4). In other words: A current motive may have less to do with the patient's actual pathophysiological state and more to do with unconscious needs of the healthcare provider. Although these motives are always operant, healthcare providers are not necessarily aware of their existence and hence impact – in contrast to medical goals, which can be well defined. It should be noted that the stronger a goal touches a person's self-concept (e.g., regaining a feeling of situational control), the more resolutely he or she will pursue its fulfillment. The ability to detect and reflect upon the influence of non-patient-centered goals on one's own thinking (*metacognition*; Chap. 10) is a skill that will improve the quality of decision-making.

Goals are an essential part of the planning process, and the elaboration of goals poses cognitive demands that are different from those of planning. Also, different types of mistakes occur during the formulation of goals than during the process of planning. Thus, goals and plans are treated separately here.

7.1 Setting and Elaboration of Goals

Thinking about goals might seem superfluous for any person involved in acute and emergency healthcare. After all, why should one bother formulating goals if the necessity to maintain and regain vital functions is more than obvious? Goals that point in a certain basic direction, such as "to normalize ventilation" in the adipose multiple-injured patient, are called general goals. There is seldom doubt or conflict about this kind of goal. However, because a patient's condition can change quickly and dangerously, good quality goals must have a temporal and fluid nature. General goals have to be translated into specific goals and then manifest into plans of action. This is where, in our case study, the intensive care resident physician got in trouble.

The patient had a medical problem that could lead to different treatment goals. On the one hand, the symptoms could be caused by a tension pneumothorax. This is a life-threatening condition that's best treated by a rapid decompression of the intrapleural air. A specific goal would then be the immediate decompression of the tension pneumothorax. There are, however, several other less rapidly progressing causes that could be responsible for the symptoms. Thus, a specific goal here could be "analyze causes before treating." This goal was not considered. In order to identify and reflect upon possible differential diagnoses, the physician would have had to spend time that he might not have believed available if the clinical condition were indeed deteriorating rapidly. If his goal was to act immediately and therefore to insert a chest tube by himself, then this goal was in retrospect quite a poor one because the procedure can be tricky and can cause complications, especially when performed by an inexperienced person. It appears that the goal of acting immediately must have seemed reasonable to the resident. Another goal that arguably could have competed for his attention might have been "maximum patient safety." If this goal was preeminent, the resident might have called an experienced colleague for help. Lastly, in our example, the resident may have had an educational goal of "gaining experience with invasive emergency procedures." As can be imagined, the intensivist-in-training is likely balancing all these diverse goals as well as others we might not be able to imagine.

The need to pursue multiple goals (Chap. 2) is one of the main problems in an acute care setting. Having many goals means that people have to attend to many factors and satisfy several criteria when they act. In addition, it is quite possible that goals can be negatively linked: Satisfying one criterion may preclude satisfying another. The dilemma of having many, and perhaps competing, goals is intensified because there is nearly always a lack of a complete understanding of the situation; reality is not obvious. Increased airway pressure, irregular breath sounds, and a slowly declining saturation signal are changes that can have several different causes. Our case study is one of countless examples that demonstrate how the data clinicians use to formulate goals are incomplete and opaque. When people do not know what exactly the problem is, they have difficulty in defining the right goal. The vague and inaccurate setting of goals is not the only source of error in this case study.

The intensivist, like all clinicians and physicians, formulated explicit goals like the well-being of the patient. At the same time he was pursuing implicit goals intended to meet very personal needs (Chap. 4). To feel competent, to try something new (e.g., the insertion of a chest tube), to protect self-esteem, to be successful – all these motives subconsciously influence the formation of goals and hence the intensivist's decision for or against a certain procedure. The fact that personal motives influence decisions is unavoidable and not necessarily bad. It only leads to problems if, as in the case study, non-issue-related motives start to uncontrollably govern behavior. Non-issue-related goals become especially apparent when actions lead to medical problems or other errors.

7.1.1 What Is a Good Goal?

To reach a goal means to accomplish some desirable result of our activity and to have certain needs met. Goals tell us which way to go; they serve as "beacons for our actions" (Fig. 7.1; Dörner 1996). Because people learn which goals to pursue under certain circumstances, changes in environmental conditions as well as changes in the underlying knowledge can alter current goals (Sun 2009; Chap. 4). Good goals are those goals that help to satisfy as many concurrent needs as possible without creating new problems. The goals of the intensive care physician did not meet these criteria. Whenever one is confronted with a complex problem (see

Fig. 7.1 Goals as beacons for action

Frensch and Funke (1995) on complex problem solving), the difficulty of formulating an adequate goal should not be underestimated. Sometimes goal setting turns out to be the central cognitive task because it will so greatly impact further planning and decision-making (Dörner 1996). Good goals, while they may be hard to determine, can successfully direct action.

Good goals have the following attributes (von der Weth 1990):

- *Positive*: Goals should be formulated positively whenever possible. Simply to avoid something or to make a situation "different" lacks specificity and would be inadequate as a guidepost for planning and action. With a positive goal, however, we want to achieve some definite condition.
- *Specific*: A clearly specified goal has well-defined criteria and can be described very precisely. The criteria can be exact numerical values ("given a FiO_2 of 0.7, the saturation shall rise above 95 %") or qualitative statements ("the airway pressures shall lie within the range of normal").
- *Structured*: General goals consist of multiple specific goals. For example, to achieve normal airway pressures (general goal), certain changes have to be envisaged (change in lung physiology, respirator settings). Moreover, goals can be further subdivided into partial goals that become increasingly specific until they can give rise to action.
- *Prioritized*: Goals need to be prioritized according to importance and time. Are there goals that we want to achieve under all circumstances? On the other hand, what should be avoided at all costs (normocapnia vs. peak airway pressure)? What are we willing to sacrifice?
- *Realistic time frame*: The formulation of a good goal has to consider the time available to execute the tasks associated with it. Setting unrealistic schedules will make it impossible to obtain a goal and serves to demotivate people from the start.

- *Checked for conflicts and contradictions*: Which goals are mutually exclusive? This attribute is especially important if undesirable side effects are possible. For example, experimenting with a new or unfamiliar invasive procedure and ensuring patient safety links goals that are mutually exclusive. One should not realize only in hindsight that reaching one goal has made it difficult or impossible to satisfy the other.
- *Allow for flexibility*: Situations often develop in unpredictable ways. Not defining rigid goals too early in the course of action allows for a flexibility that seizes opportunities as they emerge.

Characteristics of good goals are as follows:

- They are positive.
- They are specific.
- They are structured.
- They are prioritized.
- They set a realistic time frame.
- They are checked for conflicts and contradictions.
- They allow for flexibility.

7.1.2 Problems with Setting Goals

The conscious formulation of goals is rarely exercised in everyday practice. But in critical situations maintaining this bad habit can have unpleasant consequences because a faulty formulation of goals may result in ineffective action. Experiments to elucidate the problems of goal setting have identified several critical issues (e.g., Dörner and Pfeifer 1993; Dörner 1996; Dörner and Schaub 1994; Schaub 1997), as described below.

7.1.2.1 No Formulation of Goals: Action Counts

The formulation of goals serves to gain or regain control over a critical situation. However, if the level of stress experienced by an individual or team exceeds their coping capacity, often goal formulation is abandoned, and actions are taken without appropriate consideration for their effects ("*actionism*"). Without having set a goal, spontaneous ideas become the basis for short-term plans and immediate actions: To be able to do something gives a good feeling in a difficult situation. The process of planning is then not guided by goals to be achieved but by the awareness of the immediate effects of one's actions. People tend to demonstrate their competence by taking powerful actions even if they are ill-considered. Good teamwork suffers in the context of taking action without goals. With no goals in mind or announced, actions become uncoordinated and evaluation of actions is inadequate. When goals are not formulated and announced, hindsight analysis usually shows that team members all have different ideas of what needed to be done and how they should have assessed the efficacy of their actions.

7.1.2.2 No Priorities Set

Complex and time-critical situations will always create more than one goal to be addressed. These goals can conflict with one another because the variables may be negatively linked such that achieving one goal may make it impossible to succeed with another; because a given time frame may allow for only one goal to be pursued; or because available resources (e.g., personnel, material) are inadequate to meet all demands of a situation. Therefore, when it is impossible to solve all the problems at once, a way has to be found to organize the list of problems according to their importance and urgency. Prioritization has to take place and verbalized to the team before actions are planned, delegated, and executed. If, as often happens, the team leader eases the task of dealing with multiple problems by delegating responsibility, it will be helpful to be aware and communicative about whether he or she is "delegating problems" for people to solve or "dumping responsibility" because the leader cannot figure out what to do. It is common for a physician who is unclear about the priorities of his or her tasks to thrust a multitude of orders on the crisis team. It is then up to each team member to decide which of these many orders to tackle first. Their priorities, however, are governed by different motives. For instance, they may decide to solve the problems on the basis of competence or personal preference; or they might do what was said last or what brings them out of this particular situation as quickly as possible. These selection criteria may not be the correct criteria to solve the most important or urgent problem.

Inadequate analysis of problems and inefficient setting of priorities will sometimes lead to "repair-service behavior" (Dörner 1996). Like a plumber who runs from one leaking pipe to the next, we address problems according to urgency and immediate awareness. The main consequence of repair-service behavior is that the wrong or minor problems might be solved: Criteria such as obviousness or personal competence determine the selection of a problem and action. Repair-service behavior is a reactive behavior and means that the clinicians will always stay behind the game. If problems are not addressed adequately, in the proper order and according to agreed-upon goals, improper actions may go unnoticed and add to the crisis in unpredictable ways. Unless we anticipate such problems and plan to address them, they will take us by surprise. As repair-service behavior does not take the future development of a situation into account, it is unsuitable to deal with the dynamics of complex systems.

7.1.2.3 Unawareness of Conflicting Goals

As complex situations are characterized by the interrelatedness of many system variables (on-scene situation, pathophysiology of the patient, motives of the different providers and professional groups involved), there will be some goals that are in themselves justified but which are mutually exclusive – be it the parallel technical and medical rescue operation on site or the diagnosis and therapy during resuscitation of a trauma patient in the emergency room. There is always the possibility of conflicting goals, which can only be resolved by purposefully collaborating and agreeing on priorities. If those conflicting issues are not addressed appropriately, the solution to a problem will be left to chance, to hierarchy, or to time pressure.

7.1.2.4 Lack of Clarity

The most frequent problem that occurs in setting goals is that they are often incomplete and therefore lacking in clarity. When goals are unclear, they provide inadequate guideposts for planning and action. Furthermore, unclear goals lack a criterion by which a team can decide with certainty whether progress is being made or whether the goal has been achieved. Unfortunately, goals that are incomplete or not well articulated can leave providers with a false sense of control and good progress. Lack of goal specificity creates an atmosphere of teamwork where it remains unclear what should be done by whom. Teams may willingly accept unclear goals as they hardly ever create conflict; or they may accept unclear goals because no team member really knows what to do; or they may accept unclear goals because no one wants to question the leader. Setting goals in such a manner is more a strategy for conflict avoidance than an adequate preparation for providing patient care.

7.1.2.5 Missing Awareness About "Psycho-logic" Goals

Explicitly formulated and communicated clinical goals are the manifestation of our drive to do something to help our patients. It should be noted, however, that goal setting is subject to the same "psycho-logic" as other action decisions. There will always be motives and implicit goals such as protection of competence, control, personal status, fear of failure, competition, or simple convenience. It lies in the "psycho-logic" of human behavior that there are no "mere factual" decisions. Self-regulation (how to take care of oneself), social regulation (how to connect and communicate with other people), and the principle of economy (how to use the resource "thinking" as economically as possible) play a vital role in everything we do. Clinicians who are aware of their "nonfactual" goals are better able to understand how they might affect goal setting and take better control that way. Too often our implicit goals remain hidden from ourselves and are only detected in hindsight or by team members who feel empowered to speak up.

7.1.2.6 Early Adoption of Final Goals

Once a final goal is set, it tends to persist, even if new information contradicts the worthiness of the goal. In our case example, the obvious facts that neither peak airway pressure nor oxygenation improved when the chest tube was inserted did not make the resident doubt the adequacy of his goal. There may be multiple reasons for maintaining that goal. One reason may be the belief that to change an opinion might generate an appearance of lacking competence. A lack of competence is something most people do not easily admit. When doubts are not allowed to arise, behavior can become rigid and no longer open to the situation's real developments.

7.1.2.7 Fixation on Negative Goals

By setting negative goals (what should be avoided) instead of positive goals (what should be achieved), people often try to defuse a critical situation with an unworthy or incorrect goal. For example, a clinician may decide that "the oxygenation should not deteriorate further". However, it could be found later that the problem was an increasingly severe myocardial infarction. Thus, there are a number of other necessary positive clinical options that should be undertaken. Unfortunately, when negative goals are formulated and executed, what needs to be achieved can remain unrealized. Even worse is that intense mental occupation with a negative goal may aggravate or precipitate an unwanted event. Frequent mistakes in setting goals are:

- No clear formulation of goals
- No priorities set
- Unawareness of conflicting goals
- Lack of clarity
- Missing awareness about "nonfactual" goals
- Early adoption of final goals
- Fixation upon negative goals

7.2 Planning

Planning is a mental activity. It is "probationary action" (Freud 1911); one might also describe it as an imagined approach to a desired goal (Funke and Fritz 1995). Defining an appropriate goal is part of the planning process. Planning becomes necessary every time behavior other than sensorimotor or rule-based behavior is required (Chap. 2).

Planning means (Hacker 1986; Strohschneider 1999):

- To identify available options
- To assess the options (risks and benefits, possibility of execution)
- To string individual actions together and schedule each step (who, when, what, where)

In planning, we consider what we might do. We may think through the consequences of certain actions and mentally check whether those actions will bring us closer to our desired goal. Once a goal has been selected, we ideally take action, and depending on the action's results, refine our approach. When setting goals and constructing a plan of action, we consider the circumstances, possible consequences of an action, whether there might be a better alternative, and the risks of actions. That way planning can lead to a priori learning – people can adapt to a situation that has not yet occurred (Dörner and Güss 2013). Planning has a big advantage: It is absolutely safe because it is not real. It is like sending up a mental "trial balloon": Even if it pops, nobody will be hurt. However, it's not being real is also a disadvantage of planning. Planning also takes time, which might be in short supply. And we only know afterward whether or not a plan worked out!

A plan can refer to an isolated action or to a sequence of actions. In any case the planning sequence comprises the three elements "condition for task X – action X – result of action X." For example, "If it is possible to insert another IV line in this adipose patient, he can immediately receive 250 cc of a crystaloid solution and then his blood pressure will increase." If a certain action may lead to several possible

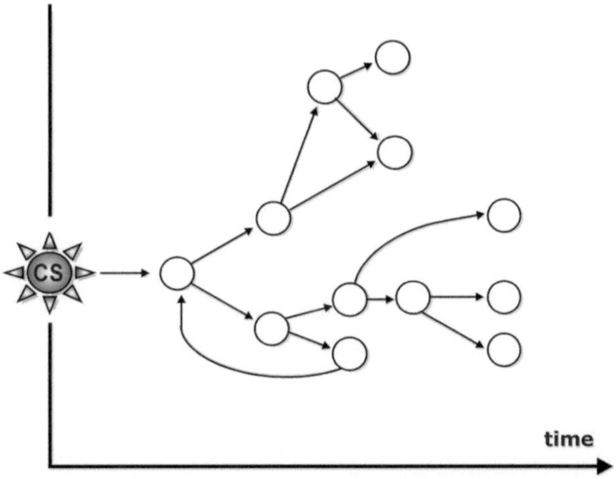

Fig. 7.2 Branching structure of a planning process (After Dörner 1999). The starting point where the plan originates is a critical situation (*CS*). *Arrows* represent actions. *Circles* indicate the goals that subjects hope to achieve with those actions

results, a plan will branch out in different directions. For example, "If it is possible to insert another IV line in this adipose patient, then we can start volume therapy. If we do not succeed, then we will try the other arm or proceed with a central venous approach." A plan can follow different paths depending on circumstances (Fig. 7.2). Because the precise sequence of actions usually cannot be determined in advance in an acute care setting, consistent planning of all possible branching would soon result in an unmanageable tree. Therefore, it is wise not to predefine too many steps in advance, but instead plan ahead to an important goal or partial goal and then adjust based on how things actually develop ("muddling through" Lindblom 1959).

The process of planning can be viewed in two ways: forward planning and "reverse" planning (Dörner 1996).

In forward planning, we begin at the beginning and think from the momentary situation. We consider the current state of the patient and decide how to proceed. This is a very "natural" form of planning. In its best form, we plan, then act, and then adjust.

To plan in "reverse" means to plan with the goal as starting point. Reverse planning requires that we have a clear goal in mind and then develop adequate intermediate goals. If the ultimate goal is unclear or unobtainable, we will not have a solid structure for taking action. Since the ultimate goal is usually not known during a crisis, it might be the main reason why people show little spontaneous enthusiasm for this kind of planning. Many clinical problems require both kinds of planning, shifting back and forth between the forward and the reverse mode.

An additional complexity in the planning process emerges from the fact that the medical treatment of critically ill patients is given in an interprofessional setting. It is common for different disciplines and specialties to have different views on the correct treatment plan. Truly effective treatment plans will include consideration and possible incorporation of a variety of expertise. The implications with regard to conflict in a team environment are discussed in detail in Chap. 11.

7.2.1 Appropriate Planning in Complex Situations

Complex emerging situations in acute care medicine are characterized by ambiguity and high internal dynamics (Chap. 2): Just like the resident in the case study, we often do not know enough about the patient to be able to plan adequately. Compounding the difficulty with constructing an adequate plan, the situation develops independently while we might be busy reflecting upon the problem. Finally, because the situation is ambiguous and dynamic, the consequences of our actions are not so easily identified, e.g., for quite a long time the resident was convinced that he had successfully placed a chest tube. All these characteristics lead to the fact that it is practically impossible to develop a comprehensive plan that includes all the eventualities that can occur. Planning in a crisis does not equal predefining the entire path from the current situation to the final goal in all its details. It will always be necessary to adjust plans according to the patient's condition or the development of the situation. While flexibility is one of the central requirements for planning in complex situations, it is possible to formulate some basic rules for good planning. Despite the complexities, good planning in the context of acute care medicine is absolutely necessary.

7.2.1.1 Includes Checks and Branches

Developing and executing one single path that works from the starting point to the final goal are unrealistic. A good plan will include branching points. One good way to know whether an alternative approach (a branching point) is needed is to include a check or test to see if an action worked. If the action worked or did not work, the plan proceeds or is adjusted accordingly. If these checks are made mindfully and carried out diligently, branching points are obvious and helpful. When intermediate goals have been formulated, they can serve as branching points. If a particular intermediate goal has not and cannot be reached, the plan should be reformulated. In our case study an intermediate goal could have been the normalization of ventilation parameters following chest drainage. The fact that they remained unchanged could have made the resident physician think again.

7.2.1.2 Considers Side Effects and Long-Range Consequences

Good plans do not end when a goal has been reached or even when the patient appears stable. Every treatment contains the risk of unwanted side effects and long-range consequences. One main requirement for successful planning is not only to envisage the treatment path but also to reflect on the unwanted consequences of our actions that may only arise with great delay. Quite obviously, in the case study the side effects and long-range consequences of actions were not considered when planning for a thoracostomy.

7.2.1.3 Includes Sufficient Resources in Reserve

Because critical situations are dynamic, it is necessary to plan for resources to address contingencies. An obvious example is to call a rapid response team when a patient's respiration rate drops. It is quite probable that situations will develop differently than planned. Resources in reserve in the acute care setting are manpower and material resources. In a time of scarce resources in our health systems, our buffer against an unforeseen turn in the patient's condition may be harder to obtain, at least in a timely fashion. Planning without buffer increases the risk to our patients. A good plan will include obtaining the resources needed immediately and will include timely requests to obtain reserve resources in case something unforeseen occurs.

The characteristics of good planning are that it:

- Includes checks and branches
- Considers side effects and long-range consequences
- Includes sufficient resources in reserve

7.2.2 Mistakes and Problems with Planning

Complexity and dynamics make planning difficult and imprecise. Even with its inherent limitations, it is still worthwhile. Herewith is a discussion regarding some common planning mistakes (Dörner 1996; Dörner and Schaub 1994; Schaub 1997; Strohschneider 1999; Strohschneider and von der Weth 2001).

7.2.2.1 Missing Planning: Methodism

If a clinical rule has been employed successfully in the past, there is a strong tendency for healthcare providers to apply it again and again. Thus, past experiences can lead to rigidity and an overreliance on rule-based problem solving, an approach referred to as "methodism" (Dörner 1996; Reason 1990 uses the term "cognitive conservatism"). Clinicians who take this approach are thinking along these lines: "I know this kind of situation; I have experienced it before and I know exactly what to do!" By acting on the basis of what has proved successful in the past, the planning process is skipped, and established patterns of actions are activated. What can happen is that such rules, though perfectly adequate in certain circumstances, may be misapplied if the situation differs slightly in important ways from previous situations. Because the differences may be subtle and unobtrusive, important details may be missed or not considered. The resulting behavior will take the form of "strong but wrong" (Reason 1990).

7.2.2.2 Planning with Only One Emphasis and Without Alternatives

The decision-maker only considers one single action without taking branching or alternatives into account. Sometimes this has to be done because of great time pressure. However, in the case study, one could reasonably argue that there was enough time to do some planning. The resident assumed that there was a successful puncture of a pneumothorax and apparently had no alternative or backup plan. In this case, the resident had to completely restart the planning process once an idea proved unsuccessful.

7.2.2.3 Planning Without Considering Side Effects or Long-Term Consequences

It is important to understand the links among goal criteria. "You cannot do only one thing" may sound like a truism but contains a deep truth for the management of complex situations. Every action has immediate and long-term effects that should be taken into account before acting. Because the patient's immediate and future well-being is at stake during a crisis, good planning involves taking into account the tradeoff between short-term clinical gains and long-term "cost." The treatment cost (in terms of the patient's well-being) should not be higher than that of the disease. This maxim is frequently disregarded because it leads to doubts about the appropriateness and consequences of one's treatment and will cost time and mental effort. But if we act without this kind of planning and unwanted side effects occur, we will have failed to plan correctly.

7.2.2.4 Not Enough Planning

To subdivide a general plan into many partial goals requires a lot of mental capacity. Because mental capacity is a precious resource in complex situations, we may be inclined to formulate vague plans with no branching, not enough thought to what resources are needed, etc. Within certain limits, this is a sound approach. For example, if a patient stops breathing after complaining of chest pain, chest compressions should begin immediately without formulating a plan. However, "underplanning" typically leads to poor team formation, lack of role clarity, and oftentimes fixation because no progress checks and branching have been considered.

7.2.2.5 Overconfidence in Planning

When wishful thinking starts to prevail and considerations for what to do in case of failure are no longer thought of, excessive optimism governs our behavior, e.g., "insertion of the chest tube will go well because it has to go well." The perception of feedback from the system (e.g., bleeding, unchanged ventilation status) was not explored nor well understood by the resident because he was confident that his plan was successful. We tend to choose to perceive what we expect to see because we presume that the plan will be successful. The most serious variant of unjustified confidence in planning is the complete disregard for thinking about complications (e.g., the perforation of the liver) or that other critical situations could actually arise. In case of a complication, we are then totally and unpleasantly surprised and have to do two complex things: build new plans under time pressure and cope with our feelings of failure.

Common mistakes in planning are:

- Missing planning and automatically relying on past practice: Methodism
- Planning without alternatives
- Planning without considering side effects or long-term consequences
- Not enough planning
- Overconfidence in planning

7.3 Tips for Clinical Practice

7.3.1 Goals

- Set realistic goals. Decisions are good only insofar as they are good ideas and there is enough time to put them into practice.
- Focus on clarifying your goals and be explicit about the criteria by which you can decide whether the goal has been achieved.
- Prioritize your goals and enlist assistance accordingly.
- Be self-critical about nonmedical motives and goals that might govern actions.
- Whenever possible, state goals in a positive sense. Be explicit about the state you want to achieve; it is more important and more informative to team members than the state you want to avoid.
- Always remember that you can never do just one thing and never focus on just one isolated goal. Always expect and plan to manage multiple and sometimes conflicting goals.
- Use communication about the treatment goals as a chance to improve teamwork. Verbalizing goals and providing feedback is the only way to ensure coordinated action.

7.3.2 Planning

- Hope for the best but prepare for the worst! If you consider a "worst-case" scenario in your planning process, it is far less likely that unexpected developments will catch you off guard.
- Build in checks to see whether something is working or not. Consider next steps for success and branches for failures.
- Always remember: It can happen to you, too! Even the most experienced healthcare worker often will suffer from inadequate planning. What appears to be a lack of planning in retrospect is much more likely to be due to the natural difficulty of planning in complex situations than with personal incompetence.
- Always plan with alternatives and sufficient buffer (time, resources, staff).
- Take unwanted side effects and long-term side effects into account. Ask yourself: If I choose this action, what negative outcomes could possibly happen down the road?
- Never forget that planning is a mental activity. It requires strength and can become tiresome. Sufficient rest and energy are vital to good planning, especially in critical situations. Wherever possible, the most experienced person should delegate all manual activities to team members to have his or her mind devoted to spend all available mental energy for planning and managing.

7.4 "Plans and Goals" in a Nutshell

- Goals are states that satisfy needs or, more precisely, mental representation of such states. Plans in turn are the avenues to those states.
- To have a goal means to know how certain needs can be met. Good goals are those that can satisfy many needs at the same time without creating new problems.
- The more deeply a goal touches a person's self-concept, the more resolutely he or she will pursue its fulfillment.
- Goals tell us which way to go; they serve as "beacons for actions."
- Good goals are set as general, intermediate, and partial goals, and they are prioritized and checked for conflicts.
- Goals should be stated as a positive goal; clarified as necessary and acknowledged by the team and have criteria by which a decision can be made about whether or not a goal has been achieved.
- Goals take into account the need for flexibility in dynamic situations.
- Common problems in setting goals are "actionism" (acting too quickly), lack of prioritizing, lack of clarity about conflicting goals, missing specificity and structure, overly rigid definitions of final goals, and fixation upon negative goals.
- Personal, nonmedical goals may have great but subtle influence on our actions. Most notably, protection of one's feeling of competence can govern behavior in critical situations.
- Planning is necessary for every clinical action. Clinicians should have a plan even for rule-based actions.
- Planning is a form of mental rehearsal for approaching a goal. To plan means to search for and assess options for action and then outline concrete steps.
- Because of the complexity in acute and emergent care, comprehensive and long-term planning is inaccurate. Good planning under emergent circumstances is moderately branched, includes sufficient buffer, and is checked for possible side effects and long-term consequences.
- Common problems in planning are methodism, planning without alternatives, planning without considering side effects or long-term consequences, underplanning, and overconfidence in planning.

References

Dörner D (1996) The logic of failure. Recognizing and avoiding error in complex situations. Metropolitan Books, New York

Dörner D (1999) Bauplan für eine Seele [Blueprint for a soul]. Rowohlt, Reinbek bei Hamburg

Dörner D, Güss D (2013) PSI: a computational architecture of cognition, motivation, and emotion. Rev Gen Psychol 17(3):297–317

Dörner D, Pfeifer E (1993) Strategic thinking and stress. Ergonomics 36:1345–1360

Dörner D, Schaub H (1994) Errors in planning and decision-making and the nature of human information processing. Appl Psychol Int Rev 43:433–453

Frensch PA, Funke J (eds) (1995) Complex problem-solving: the European perspective. Erlbaum, Hillsdale

Freud S (1911/1961) Formulierungen über die zwei Prinzipien des psychischen Geschehens [Two principles of psychological regulation]. Gesammelte Werke, Band VIII. Fischer, Frankfurt am Main

Funke J, Fritz A (1995) Über Planen, Problemlösen und Handeln [On planning, problem-solving, and action]. In: Funke J, Fritz A (eds) Neue Konzepte und Instrumente zur Planungsdiagnostik. Deutscher Psychologen Verlag, Bonn, pp 1–45

Hacker W (1986) Arbeitspsychologie [Work psychology]. Deutscher Verlag der Wissenschaften, Berlin

Lindblom CE (1959) The science of muddling through. Public Adm Rev 19:79–88

Reason J (1990) Human error. Cambridge University Press, Cambridge

Schaub H (1997) Decision-making in complex situations: cognitive and motivational limitations. In: Flin R, Salas E, Strub ME, Martin L (eds) Decision-making under stress: emerging themes and applications. Ashgate, Aldershot, pp 291–300

Strohschneider S (1999) Human behavior and complex systems: some aspects of the regulation of emotions and cognitive information processing related to planning. In: Stuhler EA, de Tombe DJ (eds) Complex problem-solving: cognitive psychological issues and environment policy applications. Hampp, Munich, pp 61–73

Strohschneider S, von der Weth R (eds) (2001) Ja, mach nur einen Plan: Pannen und Fehlschläge – Ursachen, Beispiele, Lösungen [Problems in planning – examples, causes, solutions]. Huber, Bern

Sun R (2009) Motivational representations within a computational cognitive architecture. Cogn Comput 1:91–103

von der Weth R (1990) Zielbildung bei der Organisation des Handelns [Elaboration of goals in action regulation]. Peter Lang, Frankfurt am Main

Attention: The Focus of Consciousness

8

Case Study

A resident physician finishes his last night shift at the end of a week of night calls. It is 5:00 a.m. and the last few hours have been particularly straining because of several unstable patients. The resident is very tired but conscientiously decides to do rounds on his patients one more time before getting some rest. While evaluating a patient whose hemodynamic status has recently worsened, he is emergently called to another patient who has been inadvertently extubated during positioning. When the resident arrives at the bedside, the patient is being mask ventilated by a nurse, and the oxygen saturation is 85 %. The physician takes over the ventilation and asks the nurse to prepare for reintubation. Because the patient is agitated and resists mask ventilation, the resident decides to give him a bolus of fentanyl and midazolam from the infusion pump. Immediately after the injection, the patient becomes severely tachycardic and hypertensive. The heart rate is 180 bpm and the blood pressure is 260/150 mmHg. A quick glance at the infusion pump labels makes the resident realize that he has mistakenly delivered a bolus of epinephrine instead of fentanyl. Upon recognition of the error, the patient's hemodynamic response is rapidly brought under control with boluses of nitroglycerin. His vital functions return to normal soon after. The patient is then uneventfully intubated.

After 1 week of night shift in an ICU, a fatigued physician was faced with an emergency. The call for help reached him in a moment when his attention was focused on another problem. Tired and still immersed in thought, he had to switch tasks and manage an emergency situation where he had to concentrate on mask ventilation and simultaneously deal with an agitated patient and prepare for reintubation. In this context, he wanted to give a bolus of an analgosedative drug to the patient manually and unintentionally manipulated the wrong infusion pump and applied a high dose of a catecholamine. Due to an immediate intervention with a vasodilating drug, further patient harm due to an excessive increase in heart rate and arterial blood pressure was prevented.

M. St.Pierre et al., *Crisis Management in Acute Care Settings*,
DOI 10.1007/978-3-319-41427-0_8

8.1 The Control of Action: Attention, Vigilance, and Concentration

Human thinking, perception, and action can be consciously controlled and influenced. Conscious control is vital for problem solving and for actions that require precision and that potentially impact the patient's short- and long-term well-being. The relevant central resource, the process by which we focus our awareness, is called *attention*. It enables us to be completely present in a certain task. Attention, however, is also a vulnerable and limited resource. If it decreases or, as in the case study, is substandard due to fatigue, then people often suffer a loss of control over their behavior. Mistakes are more readily committed. Furthermore, attention is a precious commodity because there are limitations on how much attentional capacity we have.

Human factors research has proposed (a) phasic and tonic activation, permanent attention, and vigilance as *characteristics of attention* and (b) tiredness, fatigue, and monotony as *disturbance of attention*.

8.1.1 Attention

Due to a moment of inattention, an intensive care physician injected a bolus of a wrong drug. He did not notice the mistake until the monitor alarm made him aware of a dangerously high blood pressure and heart rate. Although he was focusing his attention on the emergency situation, one part of his actions escaped his attention, namely, the injection of the drug. How then should we conceptualize "attention?" "Everyone knows what attention is," psychologist William James stated as early as 1890. "It is the taking possession by the mind, in clear and vivid form, of one out of what seem several simultaneously possible objects or trains of thought. Focalization, concentration of consciousness are of its essence. It implies withdrawal from some things in order to deal effectively with other" (James 1890). Despite this early and understandable explanation, there is no clear agreement on definition to the present day (e.g., Eysenck and Keane 2000; Styles 2006). Instead, several metaphors are used to describe certain aspects of attention (Zimbardo and Gerrig 2007). The three most distinct metaphors are those of a spotlight, a filter, and a bottleneck.

8.1.1.1 Metaphors of Attention

The *spotlight* metaphor conceptualizes: *Not everything that is present in the situation is consciously perceived by humans*. We can only look at, listen to, and reflect upon that which is within the focus of attention. The "spotlight attention" is intimately connected with consciousness; however, information that is not within the focus of attention is not lost; it still can enter perception, be processed, and then become apparent as emotions. This happens in a cryptic form because emotions are flash-like, holistic summaries of situational assessments and do not explain themselves (Chap. 4).

The metaphor of a *filter* emphasizes the fact that *not everything that humans perceive enters consciousness* (Chap. 5). The most popular conceptualization of this theory is Broadbent's metaphor of a bottleneck (Broadbent 1958): Because

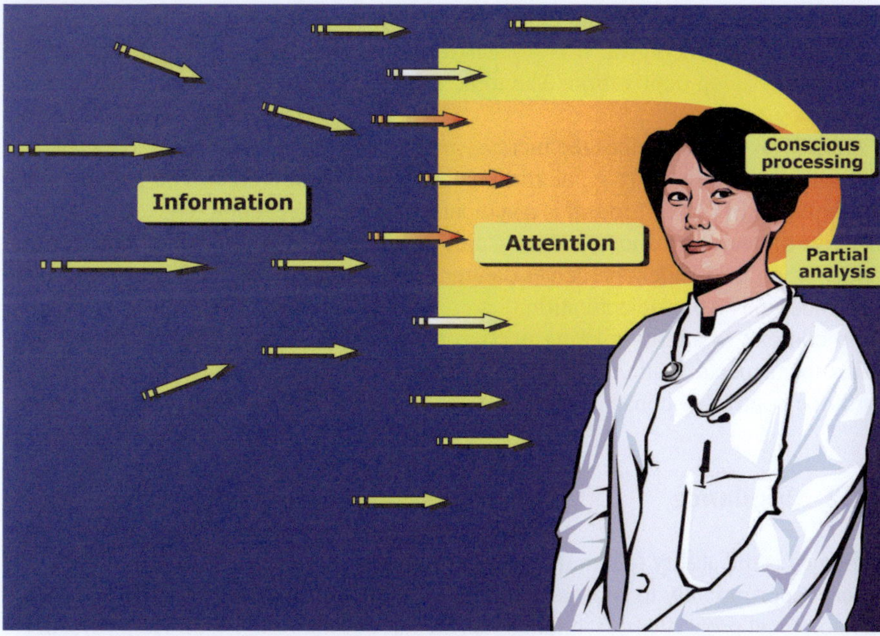

Fig. 8.1 Modified bottleneck metaphor of attention: As attention is a limited resource ("the bottleneck"), every piece of information has to be processed on a conscious level or it will be lost; however, some information, although not perceived consciously, will be partially analyzed

attention is a limited resource, every piece of information that is not consecutively processed on a conscious level, and hence passes through the *bottleneck*, is lost. A modified version of the bottleneck theory is empirically supported by neurophysiological findings: Although the conscious processing of information depends on attention, other sensory inputs, even if they are not consciously perceived, will be partially analyzed (Fig. 8.1). Partial analysis is accomplished through neuronal networks other than the cortex. A neuronal network connection can perceive unconsciously received data with respect to relevance and fit them into existing schemata (Ramachandran and Blakeslee 1999). If a perception is judged to be "relevant," an involuntary orientation toward the source of the sensory stimulus occurs (*orientation response*; Sokolov 1963). The monitor alarm caused by a violation of the blood pressure limit is such a source of a sensory stimulus that caused a reorientation of the resident's attention. For him, the sound of the alarm was a relevant perception that fit into an existing schema and directed him to turn his attention to data outside the focus of his immediate attention.

8.1.1.2 Physiology of Attention

The physiological correlate for attention is the activation of the central nervous system. According to the quality of activation, two basic forms of attention can be discerned: a *tonic* and a *phasic* arousal.

Tonic arousal describes the wakefulness of a person. This arousal is not accessible by conscious control. It is regulated by the circadian sleep-wake rhythm and impaired by sleep deprivation. The tonic arousal of the resident was low when the emergency occurred.

Phasic arousal describes the increase in central nervous system (CNS) activation that follows a stimulus (e.g., alarm) signaling imminent danger. The physiological consequence of phasic arousal is a sympathoadrenergic reaction with a concomitant increase in heart rate and blood pressure, dilated pupils, and increase in skin resistance. When the resident perceives danger for his patient via the BP alarm, his attention undergoes a phasic activation.

In contrast to attention being unconsciously focused by central nervous activation, other aspects of attention, namely, vigilance, selection, and sharing, can at least partly be controlled consciously.

8.1.2 Vigilance

Vigilance is the ability to remain alert and watchful for extended periods of time and to react appropriately to occasional stimuli. The first to conduct research into neurophysiological properties of vigilance was the famous neurologist, Sir Henry Head. He proposed at the beginning of the last century that vigilance is "the extent to which the activities of a particular portion of the central nervous system exhibit at any moment signs of integrative and purposive adaptation" (Head 1923). During World War II, the Royal Air Force recruited psychologist Norman Mackworth to study the efficiency of radar operators. Triggered by the field-generated experience that airborne radar and sonar operators on antisubmarine patrol missed weak signals on their displays particularly toward the end of a watch, Mackworth sought to determine by systematic study why and when this phenomenon occurred. He found that the accuracy of signal detections declined by about 15 % after only 30 min and then showed a more gradual decline over the remainder of the watch period. This quintessential finding of detection performance, described as vigilance decline over time, is also known as the *vigilance decrement* (Mackworth 1948; Mackworth 1970). His explanation, which was followed by most cognitive psychologists, was that vigilance decrement was caused by the mentally undemanding and understimulating nature of the tasks operators had to perform. From this traditional point of view, vigilance tasks were benign assignments that did not require much from the observer. However, more recent research has proven conventional wisdom to be wrong. Modern studies provide powerful converging evidence showing that vigilance assignments impose substantial demands on the information-processing resources of observers and are therefore associated with a considerable level of subjective workload and stress (Warm et al. 2008). The findings of high information-processing demand during vigilance tasks support the view that attention is the limiting resource and that the workload imposed by vigilance tasks drains our information-processing resources. Thus, instead of "being a bore," extended vigilance tasks actually impose a high cognitive demand.

Interest in vigilance has increased in high-risk enterprises because of the prevalence of automation. Technological advancements have shifted the roles of workers from active controllers to that of system supervisors who serve in a fail-safe capacity in which they need only react when problems arise. In some respect the task description of a "system supervisor" is true for many domains in acute medical care. Whereas the beginning of anesthesiology, to name one example, was characterized by a strong clinical interaction between patient and physician or nurse, this has changed during recent decades. Observation of monitors and vital sign displays has replaced the "hand on the pulse," and the number of displays, alarms, and waveforms on high-end monitors has risen from approximately four in 1970 to as many as 23 in 2000 (Beatty 2000).

Because many pathophysiological changes often develop over an extended period of time, patients tend to decompensate gradually. Thus, an early awareness of impending changes is of paramount importance. The vigilant observation of patient status and monitors is an important task for healthcare providers in acute and emergency healthcare settings. In light of this fact, and with an eye toward a little sense of humor, several anesthesia societies from around the world have accommodated by integrating *vigilance* into their society's maxim ("vigila et ventila"; stay vigilant and ventilate).

Performance decrements during lengthy vigilance tasks manifest as decreases in reaction time and a drop in visual or auditory alarm detection probability (Krueger 1994). During lengthy surgeries, vigilance decrements can become a problem for surgical residents who may have to perform monotonous tasks or for anesthesia providers who must continuously monitor patient vital signs, assess the possible impact of a variety of parameters and physical changes, and administer drugs. Vigilance is one of the key characteristics in the successful prevention of critical situations (Howard and Gaba 1997). Performance shaping factors that increase (e.g., stress) or reduce (e.g., fatigue) the level of activation will impair vigilance.

8.1.3 Concentration

Concentration is the long-term focus of attention on a specific, consciously selected segment of reality (Zimbardo and Gerrig 2007). Concentration depends on the ability to pay *selective attention* by which disturbing stimuli are blocked out and a conscious selection of relevant stimuli is made. To fully concentrate on one aspect of reality, the actual motive to concentrate and focus attention over long period has to be guarded from concurrent motives that strive for activation (Chap. 4). In addition, concentration demands that we increase the threshold for perceiving irrelevant stimuli that could distract us. Concentration requires both the inhibition of irrelevant stimuli *and* unwanted motives to continue maintaining a chosen focus.

8.1.4 Divided Attention

The term "divided attention" is used if someone has to accomplish two or more tasks at the same time (Eysenck and Keane 2000). Most people are unable to consciously process data in a parallel manner. They can only execute several tasks if only one of them demands conscious thinking and all the others can be processed automatically

(Schneider and Shiffrin 1977). The intensive care physician from the case study is no exception to this rule. His attention is focused on successful mask ventilation and the preparation for reintubating the patient. The bolus application of the assumed analgosedative drug, however, is done automatically without looking closely at the infusion pump. If a task such as the bolus application is executed automatically, then attention will only turn toward the automatism at certain "control points" to check the correct execution. For the remaining time, the physician's attention is focused on mask ventilation and the planned intubation. These tasks demand conscious thinking. However, because the intensive care physician is tired, these tasks demand more of his attention than usual. As a consequence, he misses "control points" of the drug administration and depends on the automatism of manipulating the pump to be executed without a sufficient amount of conscious control.

Dealing with several tasks simultaneously without a loss in efficiency is more likely possible if different sensory modalities are involved. The physician can more easily give orders and at the same time listen to the signal of the pulse oximeter. Analytic thinking, in contrast, requires his full concentration and therefore shielding of his attention from all other tasks.

The necessity to divide attention between multiple concurrent tasks is not only an inherent characteristic for certain medical emergencies but is also characteristic of the task environment of acute medical care provision as a whole. The skill of trying to divide attention is made even more difficult because healthcare professionals are often "interrupt driven" (Antoniadis et al. 2014) in their task performance and have to manage many "break-in tasks" (Chisholm et al. 2000). Attentional control mechanisms and divided attention are also relevant if previously formed intentions are executed during an appropriate but delayed "window of opportunity" (*prospective memory*; Harrison et al. 2014; West et al. 2011; Smith 2003 Chapter 4). Prospective memory cues are detected via monitoring processes, in which people expend attentional resources either by keeping the intention activated while performing ongoing activity or by searching the environment for the prospective memory cue. Such cues can be:

- *Time based* (e.g., "at 1:00 p.m. I have a meeting with the executive director")
- *Event based* (e.g., "the next time I meet my colleague, I will ask him whether he got the broken stretcher repaired")
- *Action based* (e.g., "as soon as I'm finished dictating the medical report, I will have another look at the newly admitted patient in room 014")

A transformation of time-based cues into event-based cues (e.g., by setting an alarm on one's mobile phone) helps to make the prospective memory more independent of limited attentional capacity.

8.1.5 Attentional Capacity: A "Bucket Theory"

The necessity of dividing attention between different tasks is always there in healthcare. So, could we do some training to enlarge our attentional capacity? Research done with pilots (Wickens 1984) in order to design effective aircraft cockpits shows that we are dealing with a certain amount of attention that a human has and can share between different tasks. This view of attentional capacity propounds a "bucket theory of attention" because every person has a certain amount of attentional capacity. It cannot be enlarged at will, but it can be managed differently.

There are different theoretical approaches to attentional capacity in psychology. Most authors think of attention as a central bank of resources that is available for all tasks requiring mental effort. A competing model is that of multiple specialized resources, specific to a modality (e.g., seeing, hearing). Both models, however, agree that the overall capacity of attention is limited.

This view has a lot to do with performance in teams and explains why it is important for a person managing a medical incident (e.g., code leader) to keep her hands off the patient, to not "do" anything but just "think." That way the precious resource of "attentional capacity" is being used for an important role. Clinicians often have been so overtrained to perform certain tasks; they often think these tasks do not require much of their attention. But this is incorrect. For example, we might find an anesthesiologist squeezing a bag valve mask while trying to run a code. Even though the anesthesiologist may not be aware that squeezing the bag is taking away from his attention, some amount of attentional capacity is being used. The better alternative would be to step back, think, and spend 100 % of the attentional capacity on running the event.

8.2 Open for News: Background Control and the Horizon of Expectations

An essential precondition for many tasks in acute and emergency healthcare is the ability to completely focus on the actual intention. Because certain tasks require great precision and skill, the current activity may require most of our attention. However, concentration on one task should never become absolute; otherwise, it could become impossible to detect opportunities for other good intentions or imminent complications and dangers. Background control is the mechanism by which our cognitive system tries to avoid this pitfall (Dörner 1999). The term, *background control*, describes the phenomenon wherein people tend to scan their environment on a regular basis for relevant and new clues. This is done by allowing attention to take a broad view of the situation and then having it return to its primary task.

Background control happens without conscious planning. If a task is very important or when the stress level rises, background control is reduced or completely abolished. Background control is also influenced by the feeling of competence. If someone feels incompetent, they may either start to control their environment less to prevent threatening events from being discovered (called "encapsulating"), or they may start to scan quite frequently, which appears to be volatile, inconsistent, and unfocused behavior.

The extent to which people attend to background control depends on the safety of the environment, the difficulty of the current task, and one's expectations about the progress of events ("horizon of expectations"; Fig. 8.2). The horizon of expectations is a prognosis about the expected; it extrapolates present circumstances to predict the future. In the case study, the physician's horizon of expectations

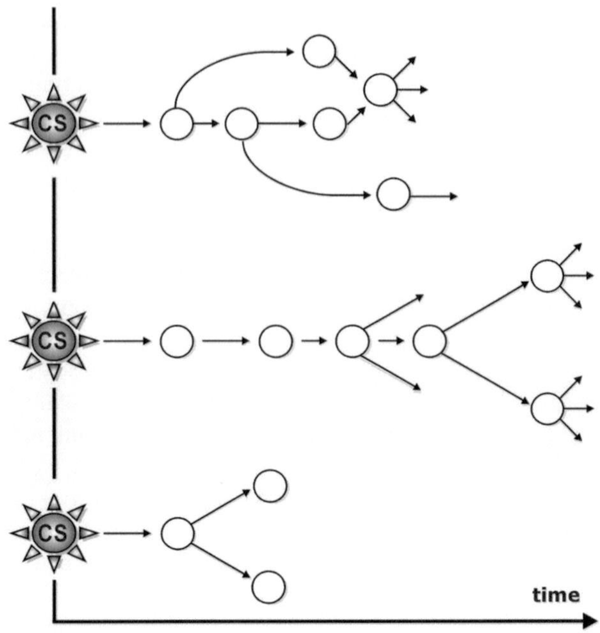

Fig. 8.2 Horizon of expectations (After Dörner 1999). Every critical situation (*CS*) is extrapolated into the future. *Circles* represent events and the arrows alternative actions or developments. The further away from the present an event is, the more options are thinkable and expectations become increasingly imprecise

consisted of continuing the unproblematic preparation for reintubation. The moment the horizon of expectations broke (because of the increase in the patient's heart rate and arterial blood pressure alarm), he was surprised and possibly even frightened. Attention was immediately focused toward the infusion pumps (orientation response), and then he reflected on the situation: What happened? Why are things not going as expected?

The horizon of expectations is a necessary component for the regulation of attention. Expected events take less of our attentional capacity. Occasional attention controls are enough to refresh and verify the situational picture. Events, however, that cannot be predicted with certainty have to be tracked more closely. The greater the uncertainty about expectations concerning the future (uncertain horizon of expectations), the more often people have to control and attend to the background.

8.3 Situation Awareness

Human factors research has shown the importance of situation awareness (SA) as a central factor for error reduction within complex technical systems. Situation awareness is usually defined as "the perception of the elements in the environment within a volume of time and space, the comprehension of their meaning and a projection of their status in the near future" (Endsley 1995; Fig. 8.3). "Knowing what is going on so you can figure out what to do" is a catchy summary for situation awareness (Adam 1993). Situation awareness is especially important in work domains where a

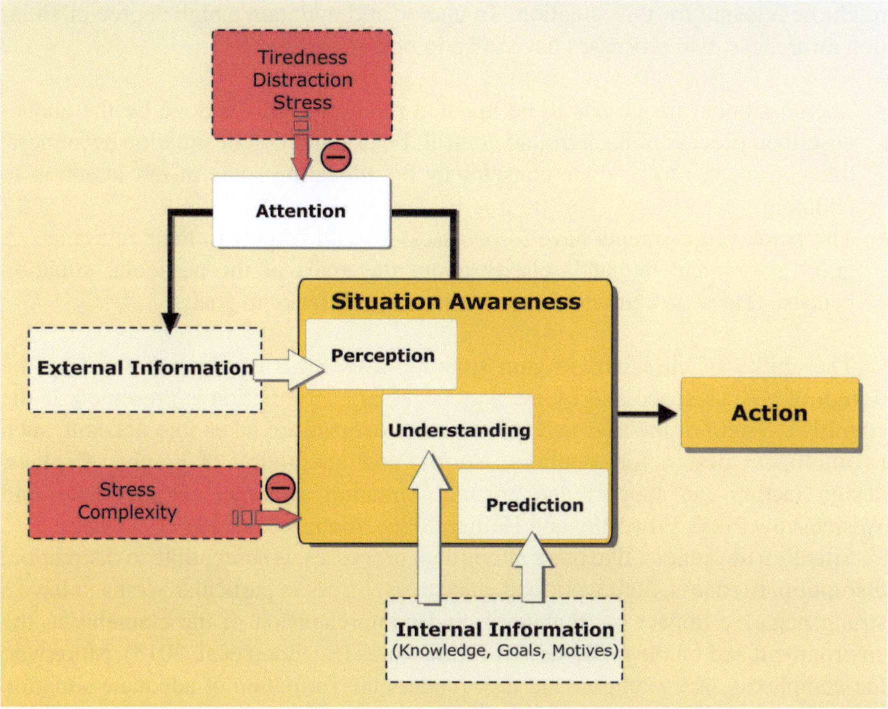

Fig. 8.3 Situation awareness involves being aware of what is happening in the vicinity, comprehending the relevance of aspects within the current situation, and predicting the future status of the situation. Tiredness, distraction, stress, and complexity of the situation impair the formation of adequate situation awareness

highly dynamic environment generates high information flow and poor decisions can lead to serious consequences.

One result of research into situation awareness is that people have to be oriented to the entirety of their environment to be able to control it (Endsley 1995, 2000, 2004; Carskadon-Banbury and Tremblay 2004; Stanton 2010). A crucial prerequisite for good situation awareness is metacognition, the concept that individuals are able to reflect on their own thought processes, to stand apart, and to "think about their thinking." Metacognition builds situation awareness by allowing the healthcare provider to ask the following questions (e.g., Endsley 1995):

- What is the big picture? What is happening and which items determine the present situation?
- What do the current actual events signify?
- In which directions could the situation evolve?

To develop and maintain situation awareness, people first have to construct an image of the current situation by detecting objects, parameters, and events that might be relevant for this situation. To update and maintain a high degree of situation awareness, two processes have to be in operation:

- The situational image has to be updated regularly. This is done by the above-described process of background control. For the buildup of situation awareness, this control has to be done consciously by allocating some of our attention to updating.
- The perceived elements have to be assessed with respect to their relevance. A good assessment demands clarity about the goals of the particular situation because relevance can only be determined in reference to goals.

The ability of clinicians to gain situation awareness can be enhanced by the design of a work space and by the way necessary information is presented. If the cognitive system of the user and behavioral processes are taken into account, such as intelligent design for monitors, alarms, and integration of graphic displays, design factors can support and enhance situation awareness (e.g., Drews and Westenskow 2006; Edworthy and Hellier 2006; Michels et al. 1997).

Situation awareness, like other attentional processes, is susceptible to distraction, disruption, tiredness, high workload, and stress. Stress in particular seems to have a strong negative impact on perception and comprehension of the elements in the environment and on the prediction of future status (Sneddon et al. 2013). Moreover, the complexity of a situation and task renders the formation of adequate situation awareness difficult.

Just as individuals have situation awareness, members of a team will possess situation awareness required for their respective responsibilities as well as information requirements relevant to all team members. Research refers to situation awareness in team operations as "shared situation awareness" or "team situation awareness." One of the main tasks in team formation and function is the creation of such shared situational awareness, of a shared mental model of the situation. Developing shared mental models for a problem creates a context for making decisions that uses the cognitive resources of the entire team (Stout et al. 1997; Vidal and Roberts 2014). Such shared knowledge enables each person to carry out his or her role in a timely and coordinated fashion, helping the team to function as a single unit with little negotiation of what to do and when to do it (Sorensen and Stanton 2013; Chap. 11). On the other hand, a lack of shared knowledge correlates with team errors (overview in Schmutz and Manser 2013).

8.4 Disturbances of Attention

Conscious control of actions can be impaired by many factors. Some disorders, somatic as well as psychiatric (e.g., depression, schizophrenia), change the regulation of attention. Furthermore, some people habitually show an insufficient regulation of attention (*cognitive failure;* Broadbent et al. 1982). These disturbances appear to be relatively stable personality traits and are not covered in this chapter. In the context of this chapter acute alterations in attention due to tiredness, fatigue, monotony, and "encapsulation" are examined. These impairments are common problems in caring for patients in the acute care environment, decrease general performance, and may cause mistakes.

8.4.1 Can I Stay in the Game?: Fatigue

The term *fatigue* describes the diminished ability to perform both cognitive and physical tasks that require mental or muscular work. Fatigue is a protective physiological function signaling that the margin of effective performance has been reached. Fatigue appears as a reversible reduction in the physical and mental performance and is accompanied by feelings of physical exhaustion (muscular fatigue) and by the subjective feeling of tiredness (mental fatigue). In contrast to monotony, the effects of fatigue can only be compensated for by rest, not by a change in activity. Fatigue has various effects on physiological outcomes and on mental and behavioral performance (Zimbardo and Gerrig 2007; Dinges 1995; Rosekind 1995), among others:

- Alertness, attention, and vigilance are reduced. People are able to sustain concentration on a task for a shorter than usual period of time.
- Reduced motor performance (fine motor skills and eye-hand coordination) and a decreased effectiveness of motor tasks (speed and accuracy are reduced).
- Slowed reaction time and decision-making. In order to reduce effort, rule-based decisions are preferred over knowledge-based decision-making (principle of economy; Chap. 6).
- Impaired memory function manifested as a reduced ability to learn and to recall items.
- Motivational alteration of the thinking process: People become careless in the formation of opinion, increasingly tolerant of their own mistakes, and prone to hasty decisions.
- Change in social behavior with disrupted communications, uncontrolled affects, and a reduced inclination to share information with team members.
- Alterations in visual perception ranging from changes in the sensitivity threshold to perceptual anomalies (e.g., illusions, hallucinations) in the case of prolonged severe sleep deprivation. In addition, the degree of resolution of perception can decrease, which may lead to important details being missed.
- Somatic symptoms emerge and appear as an increase in heart rate, shallow breathing, a reduction in muscle tone, and an increase in oxygen consumption. These symptoms emerge even if the level of physical work remains stable.

Fatigue and its recovery follow exponential curves, albeit reciprocally: The decrement in psychomotor performance begins slowly and becomes more manifest the longer a mental or physical strain is sustained. In contrast, the recreational effect of a break is strongest in the first minutes of the break. Then the rate of recovery decreases. Therefore, many short breaks are more effective than a single long one.

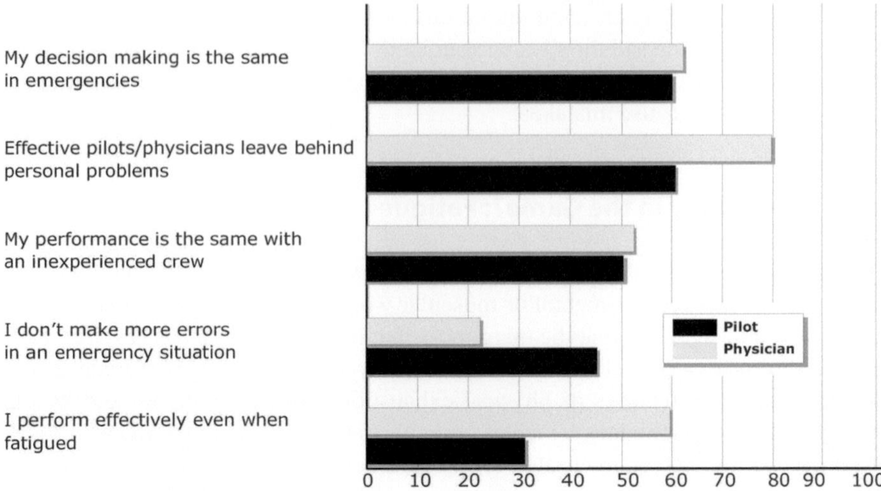

Fig. 8.4 Percentage of physicians and pilots who had an unrealistic attitude toward their performance limits. Two of three physicians denied any detrimental effect of fatigue on their performance (From Helmreich and Merritt 1998)

There is a significant discrepancy between subjective reports of fatigue and alertness and objective measures of physiological status (Howard et al. 2002). The feeling of tiredness is perceived much later than the actual decline in the physical performance or mental capability. Physicians seem to be especially prone to this kind of misjudgment. In contrast to other professional groups (e.g., pilots, nurses), physicians often believe that they can perform flawlessly even when fatigued (Fig. 8.4; Flin et al. 2003; Helmreich and Merritt 1998).

Because the feeling of tiredness is an unreliable indicator of actual fatigue, people often react to this feeling only when their performance has already decreased. This is one of the reasons why breaks are often taken too late. Recovery then takes more time than when breaks are taken early and regularly. With respect to patient safety, it is important to obtain ample and timely breaks.

8.4.2 I'd Rather Be in Bed: Sleepiness and Sleep

Fatigue demands rest. It is caused by physical and cognitive work or by prolonged stressful situations. Sleepiness is caused by the need to sleep and prompts people to go to bed and thus to recover. In sleep medicine, however, the terms *fatigue* and *sleepiness* are often used interchangeably. More precisely, fatigue is referred to as "on-the-job sleepiness" or "daytime sleepiness" (Caldwell et al. 2008; Monk 1991). Sleepiness, in the strict sense, is part of the natural sleep-wake cycle that is synchronized to a circadian rhythm of approximately 24 h. This circadian rhythm's timekeeper is located in the suprachiasmatic nucleus

(SCN) of the human brain. The rhythm is biphasic with a state of increased sleep tendency at night and during early afternoon (circadian lulls) and periods of maximal wakefulness during late morning and late evening. Light is the major factor that ties this rhythm to activity during the day and sleep at night. Additionally, various physiologic variables and hormones either rise or fall at various times throughout the 24-h period.

Sleep deprivation occurs when an individual does not obtain the quantity of sleep needed to restore their central nervous system to a fully rested state. Sleep deprivation can occur on a long- or short-term basis. Chronically reduced sleep (e.g., restricted to less than 5 h per day) creates a cumulative "sleep debt" that will impair physiological and cognitive performance within a week (Dinges et al. 1997). The concept of sleep debt has been crucial for countering the notion that healthcare professionals can accommodate to less sleep through constant sleep deprivation in conjunction with adequate motivation and professionalism (e.g., by expecting novices to work 36 h every other day with only one night in between; Caldwell et al. 2008). Tiredness is nature's toll, unswayable by pride or professionalism. With increasing age, the need for sleep does not decrease; on the contrary, the amount of slow-wave sleep phases decreases, the probability for nocturnal awakening rises, and sleep becomes less restorative.

Impact of Sleep Debt

Sleep debt manifests well before a week of disrupted sleep. One single night of sleep deprivation is sufficient to impair performance comparable to the effect of ethanol ingestion. One night's loss of sleep can cause performance-impairing and memory decrement effects that are equally potent to alcohol and significantly more potent in its sedative effect. Two hours of sleep loss has an equivalent sedative effect to the ingestion of three 12-oz (360 ml) servings of beer. A sleep loss of 8 h corresponds to the effect of consuming ten 12-oz beers (Roehrs et al. 2003). In a study, following 17 h of wakefulness, the performance on psychomotor tests was comparable to the effect of a blood alcohol concentration of 0.5‰. After 24 h of sustained wakefulness, psychomotor ability further decreases to performance comparable to that of a person with a blood alcohol concentration of 1.0‰ (Dawson and Reid 1997; see also Arnedt et al. 2005; Ware et al. 2006; Van Dongen et al. 2003). Moreover, sleep-deprived house staff has a higher risk of sleep-related driving accidents when driving home after a night shift. This finding led to the recommendation that management should provide "post-call" sleeping facilities for all personal working night shifts (AAGBI 2013).

Despite the general effect of sleep deprivation on performance, some individuals are more fatigue resistant than others. There seems to be a relationship with their chronotype (or "circadian type," "diurnal preference"). People who prefer to be active early in the day ("morningness") are often more affected by sleep deprivation than people who are most alert in the late evening hours ("eveningness"). Thus, personal characteristics of being "larks" or "owls" seem to affect psychomotor performance in the work environment (Caldwell et al. 2008).

Night Shift

On-the-job sleepiness is a constant threat to safe performance in healthcare because many healthcare professionals work nonstandard schedules and consistently fail to obtain sufficient sleep. Recently, 70 % of residents working in the ICU demonstrated a severe degree of sleepiness despite reductions in work hours (Reddy et al. 2009). Individuals are at increased risk for on-the-job sleepiness if they:

- Have to work long hours in a given shift
- Have to work long shifts for several consecutive days
- Have unpredictable or irregular shift schedules
- Did not obtain sufficient sleep immediately prior to the work shift
- Suffer from cumulative sleep debt

Several studies have shown that working the night shift increases the likelihood of accidents with every consecutive night (Knauth 1995; Spencer et al. 2006). Night services and on-call duties make clinicians susceptible to error (Landrigan et al. 2004; see Howard et al. 2002; Samkoff and Jacques 1991 for overview). Research on the performance of surgeons (Taffinder et al. 1998; Grantcharov et al. 2001), anesthesiologists (Howard et al. 2002), and residents (Barger et al. 2006) following sleep deprivation corroborated the notion that the incidence of errors increases as a function of sleepiness. Although there is no clear correlation between sleepiness and direct harm to patients, surveys support this notion. For instance, in an interview study with anesthesiologists, more than half of the group was able to remember one or more clinical errors they had committed as a direct result of extreme sleepiness (Gaba et al. 1994; Gravenstein et al. 1990). Similar results have been reported from other clinical areas (Baldwin and Daugherty 2004).

In recent years, attempts have been made to mitigate the adverse effects of shift work on the circadian rhythm by designing ergonomic shift systems (overview in: Flin et al. 2008; Nelson 2007). Elements of such worker-friendly shifts are:

- Forward shift rotation: Scheduling shifts on consecutive days so that they advance forward through a 24-h day is preferable (e.g., first shift in the morning, second in the afternoon, third as night shift).
- Shift changeover: Providing 24 h of coverage using shifts of 10-, 8-, and 6-h duration is more sleep-friendly than scheduling three 8-h work periods.
- Scheduling on-call duties no more frequently than one in every five nights.
- Napping for short periods: Naps during nighttime hours can minimize changes in circadian rhythms (Smith-Coggins et al. 2006). Given the difficulty of introducing naps in most clinicians' night shifts (e.g., emergency department), it would mandate at least double clinician coverage to increase napping opportunities.

One problem with sleep deprivation seems to be that subjects can be physiologically sleepy, even near pathological levels, without being aware of their progressively impaired alertness and increasing cognitive deficits. In an experimental setup, every second subject believed that they had stayed awake during the entire study period while EEG/EOG measurements showed they had fallen asleep (Howard et al. 1995). Besides having a major impact on the ability to perform adequately, sleepiness also interferes with personal lives during training programs (e.g., residency programs), leaving many personal and social activities and meaningful personal pleasures deferred (Papp et al. 2004).

Another source of errors during nighttime is *sleep inertia*. Sleep inertia describes the fact that an abrupt awakening from deep sleep (e.g., when a pager beeps) is characterized by a decline in motor performance and a subjective feeling of grogginess. Reaction time performance is directly related to sleep stage at awakening, e.g., persons awakened during the deepest sleep have the slowest reaction times. Furthermore sleep inertia has a strong motivational impact as it urges people to return to sleeping. Although the effects of endogenous epinephrine in an emergency can partially counter sleep inertia, recovery to full orientation can take up to 20 precious minutes. Until then healthcare providers give less than optimal care during crisis management. Sleep inertia studies show there is no easy solution to the problem of waking up "impaired." Both working through the night and sleeping when being on call can lead to errors.

Disruptive circadian rhythm is the cost individuals have to pay for shift work and on-call duty. For this reason, many healthcare professionals try to treat their lack of synchronization by using alertness-enhancing or sleep-promoting substances. Caffeine is the most common alertness-enhancing drug. Caffeine increases vigilance and improves performance in sleep-deprived individuals, especially if they normally do not consume high doses of caffeine. It has no serious side effects but can interfere with daytime recovery sleep if it is taken toward the end of the night shift. Modafinil has been shown to significantly attenuate fatigue-related performance decrements throughout 40 h of continuous wakefulness. It has low abuse potential but its long duration makes it difficult to synchronize its effect with the 24-h circadian rhythm. Amphetamines (e.g., dextroamphetamine) have the greatest potential for abuse and should therefore not be used by healthcare providers to treat fatigue resulting from sleep deprivation. In a recent nationwide survey, 6 % of anesthesia residents admitted to taking "something other than caffeine" to stay awake while on call (Hanlon et al. 2009).

One might expect that the lack of rest incurred by working night shifts would facilitate daytime sleep. But because the circadian rhythm is disrupted, many people have trouble sleeping when their natural circadian rhythm tells them it is time to be awake. Thus, clinicians often use substances to assist obtaining much needed sleep. Among the most commonly used substances promoting sleep are melatonin, an endogenous hormone that varies in a 24-h cycle and signals "biological night," and zolpidem, a nonbenzodiazepine hypnotic. Older sleep medications (e.g., benzodiazepines) should be avoided because they carry a high potential for abuse. The use of pharmacological sleep aids by clinicians is widespread. For example, 20–30 % of emergency physicians reported regular use of sleep-facilitating substances (e.g., alcohol, antihistamines, sleep adjuncts, and benzodiazepines) to help them sleep around a night shift (Bailey and Alexandrov 2005; Handel et al. 2006).

To solve these problems associated with sleep deprivation and performance decrements, it is likely that healthcare professionals, especially the ones who must make high-stakes decisions under time-limited conditions, will need to assert their right to lead healthy lives themselves. The long-term cumulative effects of sleep deprivation hastens the onset of professional burnout and limits the number of years that highly trained individuals can practice their craft (Nelson 2007).

8.4.3 Much Ado About Nothing: "Alarm Fatigue"

Acute patient care is unthinkable without patient monitoring systems used to continuously monitor vital signs and to quickly detect critical and life-threatening conditions. Although modern alarm systems fulfill this requirement, problems in their real-world clinical application diminish their usability: Artifacts of moving patients (e.g., ambulance vehicle, intensive care) and surgical manipulation (e.g., electrocautery) as well as too narrowly set alarm thresholds create a high percentage of clinically irrelevant alarms. Studies have indicated that the presence of false-positive alarms ranges from 80 to 99 % (overview in Borowski et al. 2011). The high number of false-positive device alarms leads to a desensitization of caregivers, which results in inadequate or even complete lack of responses to alarms. The problem of excessive alarms resulting in alarm fatigue is sometimes called "cry wolf effect" (Bretznitz 1984; Schmid et al. 2011). The dimension of the problem may be illustrated by the fact that within a 4-year period the US Food and Drug Administration (FDA) Manufacturer and User Facility Device Experience database (MAUDE) received 566 reports of patient deaths that were related to disabled, silenced, or ignored device alarms (FDA 2011). Strictly speaking, alarm fatigue is not caused by disturbance of attention but results from motivational protection of attention. Whenever something repeatedly demands attention and proves to be false, it will lose its importance. Once audible alarm sounds lose their relevance, the horizon of expectations changes: An orientation reaction toward the alarm source does not take place, and caregivers continue to pursue their current task. Ergonomics and human factors engineering has identified several ways of improving currently used alarm systems (Borowski et al. 2011):

- "Softer" alarm melodies instead of single piercing alarms
- Vibrotactile alarms allowing silent notification of a responsible provider
- Networking of alarm devices
- Algorithms that reduce the number of false alarms (e.g., alarm delays, online signal extraction, etc.)
- Intelligent alarm systems (e.g., context-aware alarms, alarms based on root cause analysis, diagnostic alarms)
- Improvement in the knowledge of healthcare providers regarding the function of the alarm system (e.g., user-friendly manuals, self-explanatory systems, and adequate training)

8.4.4 Nothing to Do: Monotony

Monotony is a state of reduced mental and physical activity (Ulich 2001). This condition arises when people are in an environment with few relevant stimuli and have to frequently repeat uniform tasks that demand their attention. These tasks cannot be automated, but they do not demand hard thinking either. In contrast to fatigue (which demands recovery), monotony disappears as soon as the task is altered: "seconds of terror" dispel "hours of boredom." Monotony is best addressed by a change in tasks. Listening to music or undertaking physical exercise can mitigate monotony. Monotony is not usually a big problem in the context of acute and emergency healthcare. Tasks such as monitoring and surveillance may be boring, but they do not create monotony; instead, they demand vigilance.

8.4.5 Tightly Focused: Too Much Concentration and Missing Background Control

Up to now we have described how too little arousal impairs attention. But the contrary can be true as well: Excessive concentration on a task can interfere with an appropriate distribution of attention. If people are too preoccupied with a task, then the occasional scanning of the environment for relevant information (background control) will be significantly reduced. We then are no longer open for other relevant clues and are less likely to notice when another problem emerges that may become important. This is like wearing blinders (Chap. 9 on the influence of stress).

8.5 Tips for Clinical Practice

- Take the effects of fatigue seriously. The feeling of wakefulness can be deceptive. Do not wait until you feel tired before getting some rest. Take scheduled breaks.
- If you are unable to work safely, you should take measures to rest or go home.
- If you work in a team, you can avoid fatigue by relieving each other from time to time.
- Before you appoint a task to someone, make sure that the person is paying attention.
- Ensure that important actions can be performed without interruption.

8.6 "Attention" in a Nutshell

- Attention is the conscious focus of perception and thinking on an object.
- When attention is being focused, information can enter consciousness via a second, indirect way: the preconscious processing and test for relevance that is experienced as emotion.
- Relevant stimuli lead to an automatic orientation of attention.

- Vigilance is the ability to maintain attention for extended periods of time and to react to rare and accidentally occurring stimuli.
- Concentration is the extended focus of attention on a specific, consciously selected segment of reality. Concentration includes selective attention, guarding from concurrent motives, and an increase in the perception threshold.
- The "horizon of expectations" is a (subconscious) forecast about the expected; it is an extrapolation of the present into the future.
- Situation awareness is the ability to perceive and assess a situation and anticipate its future development: "Knowing what is going on so you can figure out what to do and what will likely happen when you do it."
- Situation awareness, like other attentional processes, is susceptible to distraction, disruption, tiredness, high workload, and stress.
- Fatigue is a reversible reduction in performance. Its effect can only be remedied by rest, not by a change in activity.
- Fatigue is a protective physiological response that cannot be overcome by motivation, training, or willpower.
- Tiredness is caused by the need to sleep and is a natural function of our circadian rhythm.
- Tiredness is a physiological process. It is nature's toll, unswayable by pride or professionalism.
- Feeling fatigued does not exactly correlate with the actual physiological impairment of fatigue, i.e., people often subjectively experience fatigue after fatigue has already set in and performance has already decreased.
- People cannot reliably self-judge their level of fatigue-related impairment.
- Sleep deprivation occurs when an individual does not obtain the quantity of sleep needed to restore their central nervous system activity to a fully rested state.
- After 24 h of continuous wakefulness, the psychomotor ability of a subject decreases to a performance comparable to that of a person with a blood alcohol concentration of 1 ‰.
- Physicians are prone to misjudgment about their achievement potential. They often believe themselves to be unimpaired even when fatigued.
- Monotony is a state of reduced mental and physical activity.
- There are wide individual differences in fatigue susceptibility.
- There is no one-size-fits-all "magic bullet" (other than adequate sleep) that can counter the effects of inadequate sleep for every person in every situation.
- There are valid counter-fatigue and sleep strategies that will enhance safety and productivity when correctly applied.

References

AAGBI Association of Anaesthetists of Great Britain & Ireland (2013) Fatigue and anaesthetists 2013. London. Zugriff unter. http://www.aagbi.org/sites/default/files/webversionfatigue04.pdf. Apr 2014

Adam EC (1993) Fighter cockpits of the future. Proceedings of 12th IEEE/AIAA Digital Avionics Systems Conference (DASC). pp 318–323

Antoniadis S, Passauer-Baierl S, Baschnegger H, Weigl M (2014) Identification and interference of intraoperative distractions and interruptions in operating rooms. J Surg Res 188:21–29
Arnedt TJ, Owens J, Crouch M, Stahl J (2005) Neurobehavioral performance of residents after heavy night call vs after alcohol ingestion. J Am Med Assoc 294:1025–1033
Bailey B, Alexandrov L (2005) A survey to describe sleep-facilitating substances used by Canadian emergency physicians. CJEM 7(2):93–102
Baldwin DC, Daugherty SR (2004) Sleep deprivation and fatigue in residency training: results of a national survey of first- and second-year residents. Sleep 27:217–223
Barger LK, Ayas NT, Cade BE, Cronin JW, Rosner B, Speizer FE, Czeisler CA (2006) Impact of extended-duration shifts on medical errors, adverse events, and attentional failures. PLoS Med 3:e487
Beatty P (2000) Advances in patient monitoring. In: Weissberg P (ed) Horizons in medicine 12. Royal College of Physicians of London, London, pp 395–407
Borowski M, Görges M, Fried R, Such O, Wrede C, Imhoff M (2011) Medical device alarms. Biomed Tech 56:73–83
Bretznitz S (1984) Cry wolf: the psychology of false alarms. Lawrence Erlbaum, Hillsdale
Broadbent DE (1958) Perception and communication. Pergamon, London
Broadbent DE, Cooper PF, Fitzgerald P, Parkes KR (1982) The Cognitive Failures Questionnaire (CFQ) and its correlates. Br J Clin Psychol 21:1–16
Caldwell JA, Caldwell JL, Schmidt RM (2008) Alertness management strategies for operational context. Sleep Med Rev 12:257–273
Carskadon-Banbury S, Tremblay S (2004) A cognitive approach to situation awareness: theory and application. Ashgate, Aldershot
Chisholm CD, Collison EK, Nelson DR, Cordell WH (2000) Emergency department workplace interruptions: are emergency physicians "interrupt-driven" and "multitasking"? Acad Emerg Med 7:1239–1243
Dawson D, Reid K (1997) Fatigue, alcohol and performance impairment. Nature 388:235
Dinges DF (1995) The performance effects of fatigue. In: Fatigue symposium proceedings. National Transportation Safety Board/NASA Ames Research Center, Washington, DC, pp 1–2
Dinges DF, Pack F, Williams K, Gillen KA, Powell JW, Ott GE, Aptowitcz C, Al P (1997) Cumulative sleepiness, mood disturbance, and psychomotor vigilance performance decrements during a week of sleep restricted to 4–5 hours per night. Sleep 20(4):267–277
Dörner D (1999) Bauplan für eine Seele [Blueprint for a soul]. Rowohlt, Reinbek
Drews FA, Westenskow DR (2006) The right picture is worth a thousand numbers: data displays in anesthesia. Hum Factors 48:59–71
Edworthy J, Hellier E (2006) Alarms and human behaviour: implications for medical alarms. Br J Anaesth 97:12–17
Endsley MR (1995) Toward a theory of situation awareness in dynamic systems. Hum Factors 37:32–64
Endsley MR (2000) Situation awareness and measurement. Erlbaum, Mahwah
Endsley MR (2004) Situation awareness: progress and directions. In: Banbury S, Tremblay S (eds) A cognitive approach to situation awareness: theory and application. Ashgate, Aldershot, pp 317–341
Eysenck MW, Keane MT (2000) Cognitive psychology, 4th edn. Psychology Press, Hove
FDA Patient safety news (2011) Alarming monitor problems: preventing medical errors. Excess via. http://www.fda.gov/MedicalDevices/Safety/AlertsandNotices/TipsandArticlesonDeviceSafety/ucm222022.htm. Am 15 Apr 2014
Flin R, Fletcher G, McGeorge P, Sutherland A, Patey R (2003) Anaesthetists' attitudes to teamwork and safety. Anaesthesia 58:233–242
Flin R, O'Connor P, Crichton M (2008) Safety at the sharp end. Asgate, Burlington
Gaba DM, Howard SK, Jump B (1994) Production pressure in the work environment: California anesthesiologists' attitudes and experiences. Anesthesiology 81:488
Grantcharov TP, Bardram L, Funch-Jensen P, Rosenberg J (2001) Laparoscopic performance after one night call in a surgical department: prospective study. Br Med J 323:1222–1223

Gravenstein JS, Cooper JB, Orkin FK (1990) Work and rest cycles in anesthesia practice. Anesthesiology 72:737
Handel DA, Raja A, Lindsell CJ (2006) The use of sleep aids among emergency medicine residents: a web based survey. BMC Health Serv Res 19:136
Hanlon JG, Hayter MA, Bould MD, Joo HS, Naik VN (2009) Perceived sleepiness in Canadian anesthesia residents: a national survey. Can J Anaesth 56(1):27–34
Harrison TL, Mullet HG, Whiffen KN, Ousterhout H, Einstein GO (2014) Prospective memory: effects of divided attention on spontaneous retrieval. Mem Cog 42:212–224
Head H (1923) The conception of nervous and mental energy. II. Vigilance: a psychological state of the nervous system. Br J Psychol 14:126–147
Helmreich RL, Merritt AC (1998) Culture at work in aviation and medicine. National, organizational and professional influences. Ashgate, Aldershot
Howard SK, Gaba DM (1997) Human performance and patient safety. In: Morell R, Eichhorn J (eds) Patient safety in anesthetic practice. Churchill Livingstone, London, pp 431–466
Howard SK, Gaba DM, Rosekind MR (1995) Evaluation of daytime sleepiness in resident anesthesiologists. Anesthesiology 83:A1007
Howard SK, Rosekind MR, Katz JD, Berry AJ (2002) Fatigue in anesthesia: implications and strategies for patient and provider safety. Anesthesiology 97:1281–1294
James W (1890) The principles of psychology. Henry Holt, New York
Knauth P (1995) Speed and direction of shift rotation. J Sleep Res 4:41–46
Krueger GP (1994) Fatigue, performance and medical error. In: Bogner M (ed) Human error in medicine. Erlbaum, Hillsdale, pp 311–326
Landrigan CP, Rothschild JM, Cronin JW, Kaushal R, Burdick E, Katz JT, Lilly CM, Stone PH, Lockley SW, Bates DW, Czeisler CA (2004) Effect of reducing interns' work hours on serious medical errors in intensive care units. N Engl J Med 351(18):1838–1848
Mackworth NH (1948) The breakdown of vigilance during prolonged visual search. Q J Exp Psychol 1:6–21
Mackworth JF (1970) Vigilance and attention. Penguin, Harmondsworth
Michels P, Gravenstein D, Westenskow DR (1997) An integrated graphic data display improves detection and identification of critical events during anesthesia. J Clin Monit 13:249–259
Monk TH (1991) Sleep, sleepiness and performance. Wiley, Chichester
Nelson D (2007) Prevention and treatment of sleep deprivation among emergency physicians. Pediatr Emerg Care 23(7):498–503
Papp KK, Stoler EP, Sage P, Aikens JE, Owens J, Avidan A, Phillips B, Rosen R, Strohl KP (2004) The effects of sleep loss and fatigue on resident-physicians: a multi-institutional, mixed-method study. Acad Med 79:394–406
Ramachandran V, Blakeslee S (1999) Phantoms in the brain: human nature and the architecture of the mind. Fourth Estate, London
Reddy R, Guntupalli K, Alapat P, Surani S, Casturi L, Subramanian S (2009) Sleepiness in medical ICU residents. Chest 135(1):81–85
Roehrs T, Burduvali E, Bonahoom A, Drake C, Roth T (2003) Ethanol and sleep loss: a "dose" comparison of impairing effects. Sleep 26(8):981–985
Rosekind MR (1995) Physiological considerations of fatigue. In: Fatigue symposium proceedings. National Transportation Safety board/NASA Ames Research Center, Washington, DC, pp 1–2
Samkoff JS, Jacques CH (1991) A review of studies concerning effects of sleep deprivation and fatigue on residents' performance. Acad Med 66:687–693
Schmid F, Goepfert MS, Kuhnt D, Eichhorn V, Diedrichs S, Reichenspurner H, Goetz AE, Reuter D (2011) The wolf is crying in the operating room: patient monitor and anesthesia workstation alarming patterns during cardiac surgery. Anesth Analg 112:78–83
Schmutz J, Manser T (2013) Do team processes really have an effect on clinical performance? A systematic literature review. Br J Anaesth 110(4):529–544
Schneider W, Shiffrin RM (1977) Controlled and automatic human information processing: I. Detection, search, and attention. Psychol Rev 84:1–66

Smith RE (2003) The cost of remembering to remember in event-based prospective memory: investigating the capacity demands of delayed intention performance. J Exp Psychol Learn Mem Cogn 29:347–361

Smith-Coggins R, Howard SK, Mac DT, Wang C, Kwan S, Rosekind MR, Sowb Y, Balise R, Levis J, Gaba DM (2006) Improving alertness and performance in emergency department physicians and nurses: the use of planned naps. Ann Emerg Med 48(5):596–604

Sneddon A, Mearns K, Flin R (2013) Stress, fatigue, situation awareness and safety in offshore drilling crews. Safety Sci 56:80–88

Sokolov E (1963) Perception and conditioned reflex. Pergamon, Oxford

Sorensen LJ, Stanton NA (2013) Y is best: how distributed situational awareness is mediated by organisational structure and correlated with task success. Safety Sci 56:72–79

Spencer MB, Robertson KA, Folkard S (2006) The development of a fatigue/risk index for shift workers. HSE Books, London

Stanton NA (2010) Situation awareness: where have we been, where are we now and where are we going? Theor Issues Ergon Sci 11(1):1–6

Stout RJ, Salas E, Fowlkes JE (1997) Enhancing teamwork in complex environments through team training. Group Dyn 1:169–182

Styles E (2006) The psychology of attention. Psychology Press, Hove

Taffinder NJ, McManus IC, Gul Y, Russell RC, Darzi A (1998) Effect of sleep deprivation on surgeons' dexterity on laparoscopy simulator. Lancet 352:1191

Ulich E (2001) Arbeitspsychologie [Work psychology], 5. Vdf. Schäffer-Pöschel, Zürich/Stuttgart

Van Dongen HP, Maislin G, Mullington JM, Dinges DF (2003) The cumulative cost of additional wakefulness: dose–response effects on neurobehavioral functions and sleep physiology from chronic sleep restriction and total sleep deprivation. Sleep 26(2):117–126

Vidal R, Roberts K (2014) Observing elite firefighting teams: the triad effect. J Contingencies Crisis Manag 22(1):18–28

Ware JC, Risser MR, Manser T, Karlson KH (2006) Medical resident driving simulator performance following a night on call. Behav Sleep Med 4:1–12

Warm JS, Parasuraman R, Matthews G (2008) Vigilance requires hard mental work and is stressful. Hum Factors 50(3):433–441

West R, Scolaro AJ, Bailey K (2011) When goals collide: the interaction between prospective memory and task switching. Can J Exp Psychol 65:38–47

Wickens CD (1984) Processing resources in attention. In: Parasuraman R, Davies DR (eds) Varieties of attention. Academic, New York, pp 63–102

Zimbardo P, Gerrig R (2007) Psychology and life, 18th edn. Allyn and Bacon, Boston

Stress

9

Case Study

An emergency dispatch center notifies a local emergency department about a child who has fallen from a third-story window. About 15 min later, the ambulance team arrives in the resuscitation bay with a 15-month-old male. Complete spine immobilization is in place and the patient is receiving oxygen via a non-rebreathing mask. A trauma team composed of an emergency medicine (EM) resident, a surgical resident, a neurosurgical resident, an X-ray technician, and two nurses assumes care of the child. Due to an emergent situation on the ward, the anesthesiologist is unavailable to join the team. As per hospital policy for trauma codes, the EM resident assumes the role of trauma team leader. Unfortunately, both surgery and EM residents have had limited experience with pediatric trauma patients. The primary survey reveals an unresponsive patient with severe head and facial injuries. The patient is tachypneic and has weak central pulses and sluggishly reactive pupils. The paramedic reports that the child was briefly unsupervised and had fallen from a third floor window. While the surgery resident performs bag-mask ventilation, one of the nurses attempts to place a peripheral IV line, but her efforts are unsuccessful. During this period, the ECG shows two episodes of bradycardia. It is not until the second nurse suggests an intraosseous needle that the EM resident considers changing his plan.

Although he has had no previous experience with a drill-inserted device, he succeeds in establishing an intraosseous access on the first try. General anesthesia is induced with atropine, midazolam, and ketamine in order to maintain spontaneous ventilation. The intubation is more difficult than expected due to blood and secretions in the oropharynx. After multiple attempts, the child is intubated. However, the saturation immediately begins dropping. A markedly distended abdomen suggests an esophageal intubation and the endotracheal tube is withdrawn. The oxygen saturation improves

M. St.Pierre et al., *Crisis Management in Acute Care Settings*,
DOI 10.1007/978-3-319-41427-0_9

again with bag-mask ventilation, and successful reintubation is confirmed with capnometry. Auscultation reveals bilateral breath sounds and discrete rales, most likely due to aspiration of blood and mucus. With bagging, peak airway pressures are high and the oxygen saturation remains at 89 %. Following the insertion of an orogastric tube and suctioning, the abdomen deflates, peak airway pressures normalize, and the oxygen saturation rises to 100 %. Forty minutes after presenting to the emergency department and the initial resuscitation, the patient is transported to the CT scanner for further diagnostic evaluation.

A small trauma team provides care to a seriously injured infant. The team leader is an emergency medicine resident who has little experience with pediatric trauma management. This emergency situation is a significant challenge for him, i.e., first experience with an intraosseous drill, correct calculation of dosage, and nasotracheal intubation, and the patient's young age adds even more emotional strain. Combined, these factors put the physician under enormous stress. The stress is further increased due to his difficulty in performing time-critical procedures such as obtaining IV access and intubation. Due to the prolonged period to gain initial stabilization, it takes nearly one hour before the patient is sufficiently stable to be transported to CT.

9.1 What Is Stress?

For an inexperienced resident physician, caring for a seriously injured child is stressful. The resident in the vignette is confronted with a situation that brings him to the edge of his expertise and clinical competence as well as his emotional resilience. In this case, the cause of the acute stress is obvious. It is the clear awareness about the gap between his own capabilities and the available resources and the demands for pediatric trauma management. In addition, other contributing factors include the sight of a severely injured child, the consecutive experience of failure, time pressure, and responsibility for life and death. Several other unknown factors may also further decrease his ability to manage the situation adequately (e.g., trouble at home, recent illness, long working hours, night shifts, insufficient sleep, a never-ending flood of paperwork, keen competition among colleagues, insufficient support from his supervisors). All of these permanent strains accumulate to chronic stress which impairs human performance in the long term.

Generally, stress is a state of physical and psychological activation in reaction to external demands. These demands require a person to change or adapt behavior immediately. The resulting state of activation prepares the clinician for goal-directed action. The term *stress* was not originally restricted to a negative connotation (Selye 1936; Semmer et al. 2005); it simply describes the body's activation and mental arousal. For the young physician, however, the stressful situation is accompanied by strong, unpleasant emotions. He experiences the demand for change in behavior as a threat, because he feels that there is an imbalance between the demands of the emergency situation and the available resources.

9.1.1 When Does Stress Start? It's a Matter of Appraisal!

9.1.1.1 Appraisal of Situational Demands

A central feature of emergency and critical care is that healthcare providers can find themselves in a novel situation from one moment to the next. For the physician in this case, treating a pediatric trauma patient in this context is a situation he has not yet experienced. Every time people are suddenly in a novel situation, they appraise it in a rapid, subconscious, and holistic way. Cognitive appraisal theory (Lazarus and Folkman 1984) postulates that situations are evaluated in terms of their significance for personal well-being. Two basic appraisal issues can be regularly identified when faced with a new situation. The primary appraisal is: "How much is at stake in the encounter? Does this situation threaten my goals; is it neutral or even favorable for me?" The secondary appraisal is: "Do I view the situation as within my abilities and available resources?"

Whether or not a person appraises a situation as "threatening" depends a great deal on skills, knowledge, and available resources; on ethical values and world views; and on the person's physical and emotional state. Because the physician has little experience with pediatric emergencies, he feels threatened. What the case study didn't reveal is that it wasn't only the actual encounter with the patient that triggered his anxiety. As soon as he learned about the patient, he previewed the upcoming events in the trauma bay in the light of his inadequate clinical experience. Thus, *anticipation* of excessive situational demands suffices to create stress (Ulich 2001; Semmer 1997). An experienced emergency physician, on the contrary, who has broad clinical experience with infants and toddlers, may feel calm and confident that he will have the situation under control. In that case, his anticipation of the incoming trauma patient might actually increase motivation and performance. Critical for the understanding of the psychobiological genesis of acute stress is the realization that stress is generated by *subjective perception* of a particular event. "If a person appraises his or her relationship to the environment in a particular way, then a specific emotion, which is tied to the appraisal pattern, always follows" (Lazarus 1991).

Once an encounter is assessed as personally relevant, a secondary appraisal follows that is an equally holistic and subconscious assessment of adaptational demands raised by the situation. It includes an assessment of coping resources and what can be done to mitigate harm: "What can I do about it? Will I be able to handle this emergency, or does it exceed my resources?" Depending on this appraisal, different strategies will be applied to deal with the stressful situation (Fig. 9.1). Stress in personally relevant encounters develops to the extent that situational demands exceed perceived coping resources.

The physician can only manage this situation if his own resources (e.g., experience, skills, equipment, team members) meet or exceed the demands of the clinical

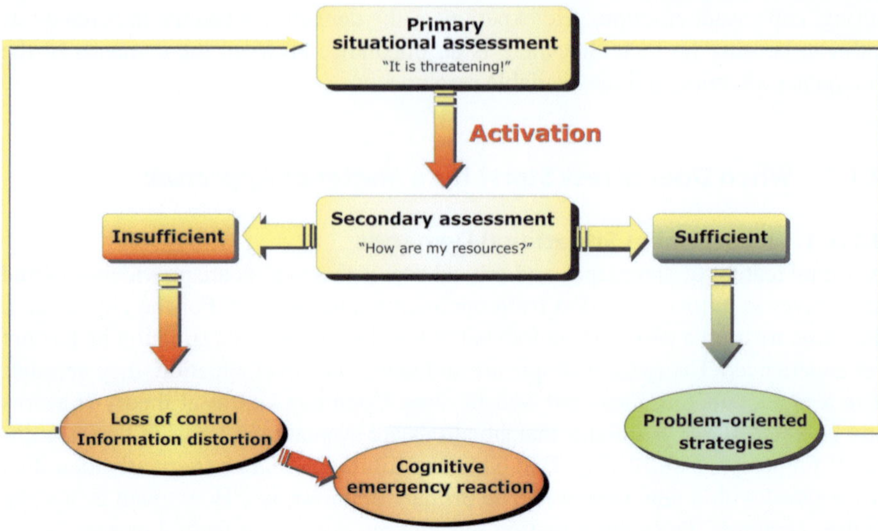

Fig. 9.1 Primary and secondary assessment of a situation (After the model of Lazarus 1991)

event. Another subjective factor in a crisis that determines whether or not available resources suffice depends highly on the current management goal (Chap. 7). If the emergency physician's primary goal was to transfer the multiply injured child out of the ER expeditiously, he might be more confident than if his goal is to adhere flawlessly to Pediatric Advanced Trauma Life Support guidelines.

In the case example, making goals explicit and breaking them down into intermediate goals would likely have increased the possibility that one or several of these goals will not have been met. If the physician had planned to obtain IV access within 2 min, to intubate the child on the first attempt, and arrive in the CT scanner within 10 min, he certainly would have failed on every single goal. Unfortunately, stress increases when goals are threatened. Goals in question can range from goals concerning *identity* ("I want to be an excellent physician in every possible situation") over *global* goals ("I want this child to survive") to *explicit* goals ("I want to intubate this child"). If stakes are high, as in the case of life-threatening injury, goals are especially important to the caregiver, and it causes a great deal of stress if they are threatened.

9.1.1.2 Stressors

Whether or not a factor actually causes stress is first and foremost a question of appraisal. Beyond that, several other factors can equally increase the likelihood of a practitioner becoming stressed, independent of personal characteristics (Semmer 1997). Such sources of workplace stress are called *stressors*. Generally, stressors are environmental conditions, events, or external stimuli that most people experience as a threat to important goals or to physical, emotional, social, or ethical integrity. Stressors appear to be situation dependent. Acute stressors arise only in critical

Table 9.1 Example acute and chronic stressors in the acute care setting

Acute stressors	Chronic stressors
A plethora of acoustic alarms The high rate of dropping saturation signal	Excessive working hours
Time pressure, production pressure ("surgery has to start right now")	Chronic sleep deprivation
Complexity of the work environment (Chap. 2)	Constant economic production pressure (e.g., fast changing of patients in the OR)
High-stakes environment; responsibility for a patient's life	Bureaucracy
Insufficient knowledge or experience Uncomfortable ethical dilemma	Lack of support by supervisors
Committed errors (Chap. 3)	Dependence on goodwill of supervisors Required number of procedures for specialty training
Fatigue (Chap. 8)	Competition among colleagues
Constant interruptions of routine procedures (Chap. 6)	Professional identity: inadequate error culture and unrealistic dogmas ("no patient shall ever die on the table")
Working in a bad team climate (Chap. 11) Unclear distribution of competence Fear of medical-legal consequences	Constant confrontation with death and suffering

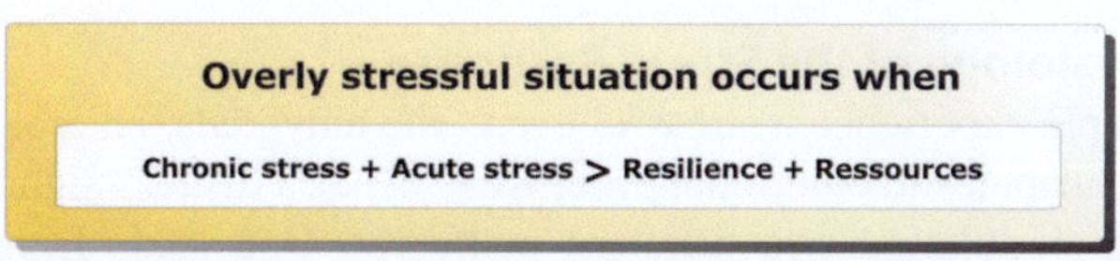

Fig. 9.2 Factors that may cause excessive stress in an emergency situation. If and to what extent a person is overstrained by a situation depends on the interplay of all four factors

situations, whereas chronic stressors are characteristics of the work environment (Table 9.1).

Literature distinguishes between physical, environmental, social, emotional, ethical, and cognitive stressors – among others. Physical stressors, for example, include thirst, hunger, pain, sleep debt, and lack of oxygen; environmental stressors within the workplace include heat, cold, strong odors, and noise – conditions that are not that uncommon in urgent and emergent care environments.

Acute and chronic stressors have an additive effect (Fig. 9.2). An immediate consequence is that healthcare workers who are constantly exposed to chronic stressors are less able to tolerate periods of high workload, emergencies, or other unusual problems than people who infrequently experience chronic stressors (Jackson 1999). Thus, one way of helping people to cope better with acute stress is to reduce or eliminate as many chronic stressors as possible.

9.1.2 The Stress Response: Fight or Flight

The stress response (Cannon 1928; Selye 1936) is a stereotypical physiological response of the human organism to different external challenges or threats. The purpose is physical integrity and survival. When the external balance is challenged, the organism changes its internal balance accordingly. Whenever an organism is confronted with a threat, the high physiological arousal that is part of the stress response rapidly mobilizes resources to deal with the threat by either fighting it (if the danger is perceived as weaker than one's own strength), by running away (if an attack comes from a stronger foe), or by simply doing nothing when a choice between the two options is impossible (*fight, flight, or freeze response*). This threat does not necessarily have to be another living being; any sensory stimulus perceived as dangerous for the physical integrity or for personal goals can trigger the stress response.

In the setting of acute and emergency medical care, however, this "fight, flight, or freeze" response no longer serves its purpose: When confronted with a severely injured child, physically "fighting" with an adversary makes no sense. Moreover, since healthcare providers are obligated to care for their patients under all circumstances, flight or freeze is not a viable option either. Critical situations in healthcare do not require the resources that the stress response naturally mobilizes. On the contrary, the response mode may create more problems than it solves.

In addition to fight, flight, or freeze response, humans demonstrate social responses to stress (e.g., *tend-and-befriend*, Taylor et al. 2000). If social contacts are supportive and comforting, stress responses decline.

9.1.2.1 Physiology of the Stress Response

Whenever people experience a stressful event, the amygdala, an area of the limbic system that contributes to emotional processing, sends a distress signal to the hypothalamus thus stimulating two different pathways. One leads from the anterior hypothalamus that generates an arousal of the sympathetic branch of the autonomic nervous system (ANS) and to a release of epinephrine from the inner part of the adrenal gland and then from the adrenal medulla into the bloodstream. As a result, oxygen delivery to the brain, skeletal muscles, and the heart increases. As the initial surge of epinephrine subsides, the hypothalamus activates the pituitary and the adrenal gland. This second component of the stress response system is known as the HPA axis. The HPA axis leads to the release of adrenocorticotrophic hormone (ACTH) into the blood. ACTH activates the outer part of the adrenal gland, the adrenal cortex. Consequently, cortisol and aldosterone levels rise, which in turn induce gluconeogenesis and inhibit regenerational processes. The stress response originates from the evolutionary priority to supply the organism with as much energy as possible so that it could deal effectively with threats (Semmer 1997). Cannon (1928) accordingly referred to the stress reaction as "physiological emergency reaction." It manifests many unpleasant physiological symptoms which nevertheless are vital for survival ("somatic" in Table 9.2).

Once the danger is over, the physical indicators subside within the next 15 min; however, while the stress response optimizes gross motor skills, fine motor skills are

Table 9.2 Behavioral, emotional, somatic, and cognitive indicators of acute stress

Indicators of acute stress		
*B*ehavioral	*Fight or flight*	*Freeze*
	Externalization of behavior	Apathy
	Aggressiveness	
*E*motional	Anxiety	Fear of loss of control/failure
	Irritability	Panic
	Emotional outbursts	
*S*omatic	*Stress response* (Cannon 1928)	
	Increase in heart rate	Tremor
	Increase in blood pressure	Increased tonus of skeletal muscles
	Increased breathing frequency	Urge to urinate and empty bowels
	Increased perspiration, cold skin Dry mouth	Gastrointestinal sensations ("butterflies in stomach")
*T*hinking	Impairment of memory	Information overload
	Impairment of judgment	Loss of situation awareness
	Impairment of decision-making	Withdrawal to automatism and rules
	Cognitive tunnel vision	"Blank mind"
	Reduction of complexity	

Based on Flin et al. (2008)

impaired by tremor. This tremor can further increase problems in stressful situations, particularly when fine motor skills are necessary (e.g., insertion of an IV line, emergency surgical procedure).

9.1.2.2 Alteration in Thinking, Emotion, and Behavior

If physical changes, such as tremor, dry mouth, and increased heart rate, were the only noticeable effects of the stress response, people might still be able to manage every emergency successfully. Improved concentration on the task would help compensate for the physiological drawbacks. However, the stress response also induces characteristic changes in the way people think, feel, and behave. It is possible to classify the indicators of acute stress effects during the stress response into four categories, which can be readily remembered by the acronym "BEST": behavioral, emotional, somatic, and thinking (Table 9.2; based on Flin et al. 2008).

Basically, "fight or flight" also modifies cognitive processes and impairs our ability to recall data from memory, to analyze and reason, and to judge and make decisions. Fight and flight require first and foremost: (a) focused attention and (b) decreased resolution and limited processing of information.

If our attention is focused on a single task, then we concentrate primarily on essential aspects required to bring the task to completion. The threshold to select another task increases, which basically limits distraction and helps us stay on task (Chap. 4; Dörner 1999). This cognitive change, however, has several drawbacks. If attention is so focused that other potentially relevant information is screened out, it becomes increasingly difficult to maintain situational awareness (Hancock and

Szalma 2008). Effective situational awareness depends on a situational image that is updated regularly. In other words, focusing competes with background control (Chap. 8); we do not see or hear normally easy to detect information that might be important to us. In hindsight, people sometimes describe this experience as having had a "perceptual tunneling."

In addition to a narrowed perception, focusing also implies a *narrowing of the process of thinking*. Because only the problem at hand matters, short-term goals guide behavior. Future complications, potential problems, and unexpected developments may not be considered when planning the next steps (Schaub 1997; Semmer 1997; Dörner and Schaub 1994; Dörner and Pfeiffer 1993). Stress makes it increasingly difficult for people to choose between alternative courses of action. As information processing becomes coarse and superficial under stress, we prefer simple explanations for problems as well as quick and easy solutions. To make matters even worse, our resulting behaviors will not only be shortsighted but also strongly guided by emotions. We dispense with a deeper reflection on and analysis of a situation and make decisions without fully considering options and consequences. When stressed, we plan less and revert to automatisms and rules. As a result, only preexisting, well-practiced behavioral programs are activated because they provide for fast action with limited cognitive load. This is true even in novel situations which actually demand more than usual processing. Under stress, people tend to do what they *know* best and have practiced the most rather than what might *be* best.

Stress-related alterations in thinking and emotions increase the likelihood for errors in many ways. Indeed, once an error has occurred, stress levels may increase further and promote more errors. A chain of poor judgments may be triggered (Chap. 10).

9.1.2.3 Transfer of Stress into Other Situations

Once a person realizes that the threat has passed, the parasympathetic nervous system helps restore equilibrium. This physiological return to normal usually takes only several minutes and has little residual effect. The elimination of stress hormones, however, takes longer than the actual situation, leading to a hangover of activation. Often, the mental preoccupation with an emergency outlasts the actual critical situation and consequently leads to a prolonged elevated stress level. Stress can thus be carried from one situation to the next and also from the workplace into private life and vice versa. In this way, stress can accumulate (Semmer 1997).

9.1.3 Chronic Stress

If the stimulus for a stress response remains active, the acute stress reaction ("alarm reaction") will gradually turn into a general adaptation syndrome (Selye 1956). This "resistive reaction" enables the organism to adapt to prolonged stressful conditions. A state of apparent resistance against the stressors is achieved by increasing cortisol levels, which can result in essential hypertension, an elevated heart rate, high blood sugar levels, and a weakened immune system. Regenerative processes are inhibited.

If this arousal remains for weeks or months, resistance is no longer possible, exhaustion follows, and physical and mental health are in danger.

9.1.3.1 Results of Long-Term Stress

The manifestations of chronic stress, too, can be categorized by the acronym "BEST" (Table 9.3). It is important to realize that humans can manifest a wide range of symptoms with a multitude of combinations. Thus, there is no such thing as *the* classical stress disease; in fact, every organism yields at its most vulnerable point. In addition to direct effects, stress also tempts people into unhealthy behavior such as smoking, alcohol, or drug abuse and an unbalanced diet.

The effects of chronic stress add to acute stress and thus can have a negative impact on patient safety (Fig. 9.2). Although all healthcare providers should be familiar with the effects of stress on their personal performance, an attitude of personal invulnerability seems to be a valued professional attribute, especially among physicians. When compared with other professional groups, a higher percentage of physicians held unrealistic attitudes about their performance capabilities when faced with various kinds of stressors. Half of doctors endorsed the unrealistic attitude that his or her decision-making was the same in routine situations as well as in emergencies (Fig. 8.4) (Sexton et al. 2000; Flin et al. 2003).

9.1.3.2 From Long-Term Stress to Burnout

When chronic work stress in a healthcare setting is maintained for a long period of time (e.g., long working hours, many on-call duties, insufficient sleep, bureaucracy, unsympathetic superiors), maladaptive response patterns can develop. This response has a far-reaching impact on a healthcare provider's emotional health and attitude

Table 9.3 Behavioral, emotional, somatic, and cognitive indicators of chronic stress

Indicators of chronic stress		
*B*ehavioral	Absenteeism	Distraction
	Apathy	Hostile behavior
	Carelessness	Nervous tics, grinding teeth, chewing fingernails
	Addictive behavior (e.g., alcohol and smoking)	
*E*motional	Anxiety	Depression
	Worry	Confusion
	Cynicism	Emotional instability
	Bad temper	Crankiness
*S*omatic	Chronic fatigue	Neglect of physical appearance
	Health complaints (e.g., chronic infections)	
*T*hinking	Lack of concentration	Forgetfulness
	Poor attention	Poor time management

Based on Flin et al. (2008)

toward life: the burnout syndrome. New York psychologist Herbert J. Freudenberger coined the term "burnout" to explain the process of physical and mental deterioration in professionals working in areas such as healthcare, social work, or emergency legal services (Freudenberger 1974). Subsequently, burnout syndrome was defined as a sustained response to chronic work stress comprising three dimensions (Maslach 2003):

- *Emotional exhaustion*: An intense feeling of emotional exhaustion. As emotional resources are depleted, workers feel they are no longer able to provide care for others. Emotional exhaustion is the hallmark of burnout.
- *Depersonalization*: Negative feelings and cynical attitudes toward the recipients of care. A callous or even dehumanizing perception of others can lead healthcare providers to believe that their patients somehow deserve their condition.
- *Lack of personal accomplishment*: Tendency to evaluate oneself negatively, particularly with regard to one's work with patients. The prevailing feelings are those of low accomplishment and professional failure.

In addition to the dimensions, Maslach proposed a classical sequence for the development of burnout syndrome as a response to occupational stress. The stages are (Maslach 1982):

- *Overcommitment*: There is no healthy distance to work; people tend to "give everything."
- *Beginning exhaustion*: The onset is slow. Early symptoms include a feeling of emotional and physical exhaustion. A sense of alienation, cynicism, impatience, negativism, and feelings of detachment develop to the point that the person begins to resent the work he or she is involved in as well as the people who are a part of that work. There is a constant feeling of tension, and errors are committed with higher frequency.
- *Increased exhaustion*: Healthcare providers start to develop hostile feelings and a negative attitude toward both their own profession and their patients. The personal engagement at work is reduced, "burnout-related absenteeism" increases, and emotional reactions such as feelings of guilt, self-pity, and helplessness emerge.
- *Feeling burned out:* If the stress level remains high, a feeling of depleted energy and an inner distance from work will emerge. The ruling feelings are shutdown, numbness, mood swings, helplessness, and desperation. Individuals who once cared deeply about fellow human beings will insulate themselves to the point that they no longer care at all. Psychosomatic disorders increase in frequency and can lead, as a worst-case scenario, to a nervous breakdown and to reactive depression.

From early on, researchers observed that burnout mainly occurred in professionals working in areas such as social work, education, and healthcare, all of which share the commonalities of a high emotional strain and little chance to significantly influence working conditions (Elfering et al. 2005). According to a popular model (*effort-reward imbalance*, Siegrist et al. 2004; Siegrist 2012), burnout can especially develop if people experience a strong mismatch between the "effort/costs" of their work (e.g., time pressure, responsibility, workload, etc.) and the resulting "reward" (e.g., appraisal, status, salary, etc.).

Healthcare professionals generally have psychological morbidity rates higher than the general population (Tennant 2001). From among the different medical specialties, however, intensivists seem to be especially vulnerable to burnout as they often take care of patients for long periods of time as compared to paramedics or emergency medicine technicians who hand over their patients to the next provider. Approximately one of every two intensivists is in danger of high-level burnout (Embriaco et al. 2007). In the same study, organizational factors such as workload (the number of night shifts per month, a long period of time between nonworking weeks, night shift the day before the survey) and impaired relationships (such as conflict with a physician or nurse colleague) were associated with a higher incidence of burnout. However, factors related to the severity of illness of patients were not associated with psychological morbidity.

9.1.4 Moderate Stress Can Boost Performance

Stress does not only have negative aspects. On the contrary, in order to be able to perform at all, people need a certain level of stress. The cortico-cerebral activation that is part of the stress response sets us in motion and enables us to focus. Moderate stress results in improved performance provided the person has ample resources to manage the situation or task. If the level of stress exceeds available resources, performance declines.

An underchallenge – a complete lack of stress – leads to poor performance. Additionally, underchallenge and boredom can be stressors themselves. We feel tense and even angry, which can also lead to errors.

Precisely how much stress people need for ideal performance depends highly on the individual and the task involved. Every task has an optimal level of arousal; too-high and too-low levels of stress will result in suboptimal performance (Fig. 9.3).

Improved performance is one positive aspect of stress. A second important function of stress is the promotion of learning. Every stressful situation carries an implicit message for the individual: You will either have to change the situation (e.g., by finding a solution) or modify your thinking and behavior. It is this kind of pressure that leads to learning. Without the necessity for change, people hardly ever reconsider their cognitive models. We naturally prefer to revert to the known and familiar rather than scrutinizing the obvious and finding new solutions.

9.2 Stress Outside the Normal Range

In the previous passages, we provided a brief overview of the physiological and mental effects of everyday stressors, both acute and chronic. In acute and emergency care settings, however, the level of stress can strain healthcare providers beyond their limits, which results in a characteristic narrowing of thinking and

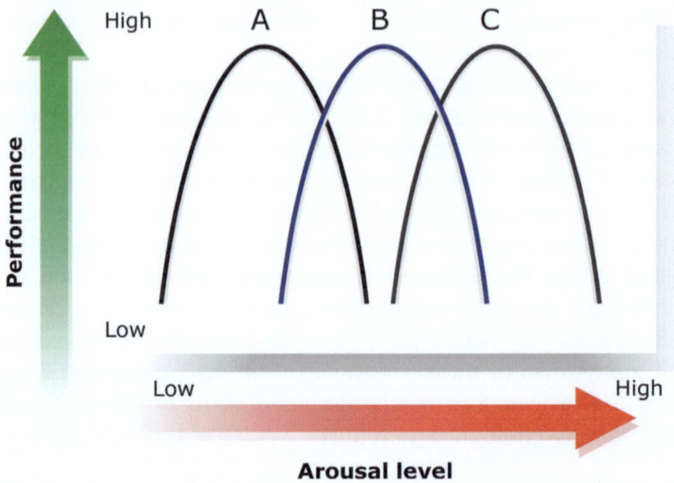

Fig. 9.3 Relationship between activation and performance. An optimal performance in any given task depends on the degree of activation and the nature of the task. *A*, *B*, and *C* represent tasks or individuals in relation to a task with increasing difficulty (After Yerkes and Dodson 1908)

behavior. The term *cognitive emergency reaction* refers to the psychological alterations that result from the physiological reactions in stressful situations (Dörner 1996; "*intellectual emergency reaction*" in Reason 1990).

9.2.1 Overwhelmed: The Cognitive Emergency Reaction

Whenever things go very wrong and problems become uncontrollable and impossible to solve, people's feeling of competence (Chap. 4) is seriously threatened. Because humans need a minimum feeling of competence in order to maintain their ability to act, they defend it at any cost. For this purpose, the cognitive system is "shut off." Maintaining the feeling that the situation is under control – or at least some relevant aspect of it – becomes even more important than the solution, as vital as it may be. As a result, people try to avoid any additional strain on their feeling of competence (e.g., doubts about the mental model or the adequacy of a plan). They end up seeing only what they want to see (distortion of information; Sect. 6.3) and use the resource of "conscious thinking" (e.g., reflection, planning) as economically as possible (principle of economy; Chap. 6). The cognitive emergency reaction shows the symptoms outlined below.

9.2.1.1 Externalization of Behavior

- People focus less on internal cognitive processes (e.g., thinking, planning) than on overt behavior (Chap. 4).
- The greater the reduction in thinking and planning processes, the more behavior will be guided by external triggers and less by goals. This results in erratic actions.

9.2.1.2 Quick Fixes

- People regress to familiar schemata of thinking and acting (methodism).
- Quick and simple solutions are preferred.

9.2.1.3 Inappropriate Reduction of Complexity

- Simple and reductionist mental models are formed.
- One's own (reductionist) situational model is defended against any other point of view. This results in dogmatism, bossiness, rejection of criticism or doubt, and the avoidance of the word *but*…
- New information will no longer be taken into account and analyzed; contradicting information will be viewed selectively. In the end, we may even defend our mental model against reality.
- Ignorance or the bad motives of other people are made responsible for problems rather than the complexity of the situation or environment (personalization).

9.2.1.4 Abandoning Self-Reflection

- Self-reflection is markedly reduced. Subjects no longer pause to evaluate the progress of previous actions. Instead, task performance is reduced to a series of disconnected actions.

Healthcare professionals are generally unaware of the way their decision-making and emergency management are affected by the cognitive emergency reaction.

9.2.2 Devastated: Post-traumatic Stress Disorder (PTSD)

Due to his lack of experience with pediatric emergencies, the emergency medicine resident's pediatric encounter was overshadowed by fear of failure. Patient management became protracted. The intraosseous approach should have been considered and executed earlier. Had that been done, successful intubation might have been executed before the airway became more complicated due to accumulating blood and fluids. After significant delay, the patient is transported to the CT scanner for further diagnostic evaluation. By and large not the most proficient emergency management, but at least the resident was able to keep the child alive. But what if an esophageal intubation had gone unrecognized and led to cardiac arrest? Then feelings of helplessness, shame, and the awareness that he was responsible for a dead toddler likely would have increased stress to an almost unbearable level.

Severe trauma – including death – in the pediatric age group is among the most stressful and upsetting events healthcare professionals can experience. Research indicates that work with seriously ill or injured children breaks down natural defenses and emotional distancing and regularly leads to strong identification with the victims (Alexander and Klein 2001; Clohessy and Ehlers 1999; Dyregov and Mitchell 1992; Laposa and Alden 2003; Mahony 2001; Sterud et al. 2008).

Witnessing or being actively involved in an event that produces intense feelings of fear, helplessness, shame, and horror can traumatize individuals and can lead to post-traumatic stress disorder (PTSD). PTSD is an anxiety disorder that can develop after exposure to a terrifying event or situation outside the normal range of human experience (APA: American Psychiatric Association 1994). In acute care medicine, experiences such as major disasters, severe polytrauma with dismemberment, suicide bombing, severely burned patients, death after prolonged resuscitation, and providing care to a patient who is a relative or close friend who is dying are likely PTSD trigger events (Gallagher and McGilloway 2007; Laposa and Alden 2003; McCammon et al. 1988; Van der Ploeg and Kleber 2003). Around 25–30 % of people experiencing a traumatic event may go on to develop PTSD. In recent years, research on the development of PTSD has been extended from individuals who were victims of traumatic events (e.g., survivor of terrible accident, rape victims) to individuals who routinely deal with horrifying events as part of their jobs. These include disaster workers, paramedics, and emergency room personnel. Although disaster workers seem especially prone to develop PTSD due to the magnitude of the traumatizing scenarios they experience, research indicates that frequently occurring "minor" critical accidents can accumulate to trigger PTSD. Whereas the estimated prevalence of PTSD among the general adult population in Western countries lies around 3–4%, 20–30 % of adult critical care nurses (Mealer et al. 2009) and of pediatric acute care nurses (Czaja et al. 2012) fulfill criteria of PTSD as defined by the American Psychiatric Association (APA). For emergency medical personnel, the incidence of workers with symptoms that fulfill the criteria for PTSD has been reported as high as 10–22 % across a variety of countries and healthcare systems (Anderson et al. 1991; Clohessy and Ehlers 1999; Grevin 1996; overview in Donelly and Siebert 2009). Twelve percent of emergency room professionals exhibit symptoms consistent with a diagnosis of PTSD, suggesting that they, too, are at increased risk for developing PTSD (Laposa and Alden 2003).

The most characteristic symptoms of PTSD defined by the Diagnostic and Statistical Manual of Mental Disorders version 4 (DSM-IV) of the American Psychiatric Association (APA 1994) are of an intrusive nature. A person re-experiences the traumatic event, showing symptoms that include:

- *Dissociative reactions* (e.g., flashbacks) in which the person acts or feels as if the event were recurring
- *Intrusive memories* that bring up questions and wishful thinking on which people tend to dwell (rumination) but which do not help them come to terms with the event (e.g., Why did this happen to me? What could I have done differently? I wish things could be undone!)
- *Frightening thoughts* that similar events could happen to oneself or one's family
- *Nightmares* in which the content and affect of the dream are related to the event
- *Marked physiological reactions* to reminders of the traumatic event (e.g., increased heart rate, sweating, tremor)
- Persistent *avoidance of reminders* of the trauma is another core symptom of PTSD. This includes *suppressing thoughts*, feelings, or physical sensations that

arouse recollections of the traumatic event and *avoiding* activities, events, objects, or places resembling or associated with the event.

PTSD is characterized by negative alterations in cognitions and mood as well as symptoms of hyperarousal. This makes PTSD also relevant for patient safety. If healthcare professionals feel detached from their job, patients, and colleagues, this most certainly affects patient care and teamwork.

Assessment of PTSD presents significant challenges in many domains of healthcare. Many healthcare professionals avoid talking about their problems even when associated complaints exist. Time pressures and a job culture that emphasizes distancing oneself from emotional reactions make it unlikely that they will find adequate support at work if difficulties arise. Whether or not a person actually gets PTSD depends on a number of personal, social, support, and environmental factors.

In light of the fact that traumatic events and terminal illness are part of the fabric of acute healthcare, it is no surprise that 10–20 % of providers respond with maladaptive strategies that eventually lead to PTSD. Several practical steps have been advocated to identify and support healthcare professionals at increased risk for PTSD (Mitchell 1983; NICE 2005), including distancing, confronting, and talking about the event following the emergency.

9.3 Teams Under Pressure

Teams basically respond to stress much like an individual. They guard their (collective) feeling of competence and avoid being overwhelmed by destructive emotions. In addition to the abovementioned reactions, team members show behavioral patterns that can further compromise patient safety (Sect. 11.2) as follows (Badke-Schaub 2000):

- Early abandonment of data collection
- No reflection on the problem
- No discussion about goals
- No search for alternative strategies
- Group pressure to suppress disagreement
- Risk shift
- Diffusion of responsibility
- Lack of team member coordination
- Call for a strong leader

When team leaders are stressed, team dynamics and team effectiveness are impaired in two broad ways. Firstly, leaders will feel compelled "to do something" in order to maintain a sense of control and a feeling of competence. As a result, they delegate less and perform many tasks by themselves. Secondly, their thinking and behavior focuses on their own personal actions instead of the team as a whole. There is less communication about goals and plans; the "leader goes solo" (Chap. 13).

9.4 Coping Mechanisms

The idea of "coping mechanisms" was first conceptualized by Lazarus and Folkman (1984; Lazarus 1991), who defined coping as "those changing cognitive and behavioral efforts developed for managing the specific external and/or internal demands judged as exceeding or surpassing the individual's own resources." Coping strategies have customarily been classified according to the specific method by which a problem is addressed (active/assertive vs. passive/avoiding), reflecting the "fight-or-flight response" on a cognitive level.

- *Active cognitive*: The assessment and reevaluation of one's understanding of a stressful situation. Potentially stressful events as well as painful emotions can be reinterpreted and thereby lose their destructive impact.
- *Active behavioral*: Observable behaviors, which are aimed at controlling and managing a stressful situation.
- *Avoiding*: The refusal to face a problematic or stressful situation.

Other classifications emphasize the distinction between problem-focused coping and emotion-focused coping (Lazarus and Folkman 1984; Edwards 1988). Problem-focused coping is directed at defining the problem, generating solutions, choosing among them, and acting; emotion-focused coping moderates the emotional response to stressful events.

Various studies have related coping strategies with burnout and other consequences of occupational stress in healthcare settings. As a general rule, active and problem-oriented strategies are healthier for the individual in the long run and provide greater capacity for coping with difficult situations. Coping strategies focused on avoidance have been shown to be linked to all three components of burnout. Which strategy people choose in the end depends highly on the situation itself and on the preferred coping mechanism, which is largely determined by a person's personality and his or her previous learning experiences (Weber 2004). Further, the coping strategy can also reflect the self-conception of a person's cultural surrounding. For example, the overt expression of strong emotions (e.g., joy, anger, and infuriation) is natural in southern European countries. In such cultural settings, strong emotions are self-evident parts of interpersonal communication and do not indicate exceptional personal involvement of the person speaking. In most parts of Asia, however, an untamed expression of feelings would create quite a different response. In this cultural context, an expression of strong emotions outside the family might be considered inappropriate and impolite.

9.4.1 Emotion-Focused Coping Mechanism: Yelling at People?

Acute stress is a trigger for strong emotions. In order to reduce the impact of these strong emotions on decision-making and action, it can become necessary to deal with one's own emotions first (e.g., by consciously calming down and reflecting) before addressing the actual problem. The unreflective approach to letting off steam by yelling at team members may provide short-term relief from emotional pressure but will be counterproductive for any further effective teamwork. If emotions are not dealt with appropriately, their unfiltered expression can damage acceptance by others and destroy functional social relationships (Billings and Moos 1984). People do not willingly support and cooperate with a person who publicly devalues them.

An emotionally charged situation can be perpetuated by the opposite approach as well: An active cognitive coping strategy that pays too close attention to the present emotional state may actually amplify negative emotions. A person who intensely experiences their own activation (e.g., "I'm really mad at this person") will certainly integrate this perception into future situational assessments (Baumeister et al. 1994). Situational assessment, emotion, and arousal, followed by additional situational assessment, can lead to a vicious circle. An appropriate way of dealing with any strong feeling would be to "filter" these emotions in advance and then to bring them into the situation in a cooperative and nondestructive way (e.g., by telling team members that you are angry and why, but without attacking them personally). This approach might be characterized as "having your emotions instead of your emotions having you." However, there is a major requirement for this kind of processing of emotions: It only works if people have a minimum of self-control and if this self-control is not impaired by too much stress. This, unfortunately, will bring us right back to some points made earlier.

9.4.2 Cognitive Coping Mechanism: Try to See Things Differently!

If task demands exceed available resources and stress levels rise, it seems logical to consider the possibility of reducing the difficulty of a task. A situation may be made more manageable for the healthcare provider by reinterpreting the facts. Then he or she might have a realistic chance of success since the available resources might just be enough to manage the crisis. Many healthcare professionals in acute medical care apply these cognitive strategies unconsciously (Larsson and Sanner 2010). While rethinking the problem at hand in a different way may work well, there are some characteristics of acute medical care that place limits to this approach: If a goal is utterly unrealistic in the first place, it might be more than appropriate to strive for increased realism. This approach has particular applicability when dealing with chronic stressors and certain personality traits (e.g., perfectionism). For healthcare providers who are faced with a critical situation, however, this strategy is of limited value. If a patient could reasonably be expected to survive a medical emergency, then certain goals cannot be abandoned lightly. Despite being tempted by a strong "flight response," it was no option for the emergency resident in the vignette to stop in the middle of the trauma resuscitation and to say to himself: "Well, I always knew this case was too much for me; I'd better stop treating the infant now."

In an effort to reinterpret a situation, the cognitive coping strategy can actually do more harm than good since people start losing confidence in their capabilities and in any realistic chances for success. As a result, pessimism takes over and people no longer expect improvement. Instead of trying to control a situation, they resign themselves to failure and withdraw from constructive action. If healthcare professionals repeatedly experience such situations, they may start to develop the hazardous attitude of resignation (Chap. 4).

Coping strategies have not only short-term advantages or disadvantages; there is a price that likely has to be paid in the long run depending on the coping mechanism. This is especially true for inappropriate strategies that temporarily ameliorate the stress response. Some examples of costly coping mechanisms:

- Yelling at coworkers reduces emotional pressure but is devastating to functional and healthy relationships.
- Becoming less ambitious and reducing personal goals to a minimum greatly relieves a person of chronic stress but may actually hinder his or her medical training and subsequent professional development.
- Trying harder under unsatisfying work conditions can lead to burnout.
- Smoking may help people to calm down but will eventually lead to serious health problems (Semmer 2003).

9.4.3 Resilience: A Fourfold Strategy

The fact that some individuals can quite obviously tolerate more stress than others can be explained by resilience. Resilience in cognitive psychology (as opposed to the concept in high-reliability theory; see Chap. 14) refers to the positive capacity and the dynamic process of people to cope with significant stressors without developing manifest psychological dysfunction, such as mental illness or persistent negative mood. In addition, the term can be used to indicate that people have an adaptive system that uses an experience with stress to develop resistance to future negative events. Relevant psychological literature on resilience is not consistent in its use of the term *resilience* or *psychological resilience*. Synonyms or closely related terms are *hardiness, resourcefulness, adaptive coping, thriving, sense of coherence,* and *mental toughness*.

Several features characterize resilient people:

- Cope well with high levels of ongoing disruptive change.
- Are highly committed to their goals and fully engaged in their activities as they see the situation as meaningful rather than random or pointless.
- See problems as opportunities and as a positive challenge.
- Believe that they can influence the situation (internal locus of control) and that success is not dictated by external factors (external locus of control).
- Have the capacity for seeing small windows of opportunity and making the most of them.
- Have a "where there's a will, there's a way" attitude.
- Are able to "hang tough" when things are difficult.

- Are able to "bounce back" easily from setbacks and "recover from almost anything."
- Accept failure and errors as a normal part of life and do not see them as a confirmation of their own inability.
- Are flexible enough to adapt to a new way of working when an old way is no longer possible or effective.
- Generally express a positive attitude toward life without being naïve.
- Have a healthy social support network.

The core features of resilience are also known as the "3 Cs of resilience": control, challenge, and commitment.

Less resilient individuals find themselves worn down and negatively impacted by life stressors and often envy people who seem to have much more inner strength to cope with adversity. However, resilience is not a fluke; it generally emerges in people who have developed the abovementioned attitudes and cognitive and emotional skills over time. Strategies to enhance resilience in at-risk populations such as healthcare professionals can be seen as positive, proactive, preventative, and potentially cost-saving approaches to minimize psychological dysfunction (e.g., PTSD). Basically, all coping strategies can be grouped into three broad categories (Kaluza 2004, 2012):

- *Problem oriented* (e.g., problem-solving strategies, resource allocation)
- *Cognitive* (e.g., change in attitude, "inner alertness," self-instruction)
- *Regenerative* (e.g., relaxation, sports, and other physical activities)

Research literature suggests that no single method of coping guarantees success. Rather, individuals are best served by using a flexible repertoire of methods. Starting points to enhance resilience can be derived from the four factors in Fig. 9.4.

9.4.3.1 Reduction of Chronic Stress

Stress management in acute healthcare is easier if chronic stress is managed. Helpful strategies include:

- Developing a relaxed and easygoing attitude toward life, thus minimizing stress outside of work.

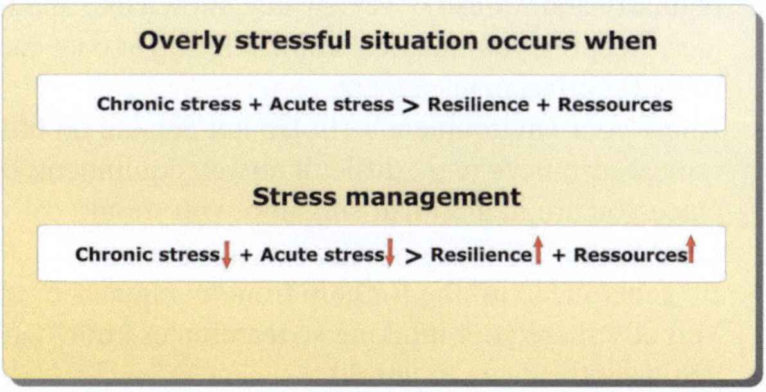

Fig. 9.4 Factors that lead to excessive stress in a critical situation and practical aspects of how the resistance to stress might be increased

- Identifying those factors that are personal stressors. Become familiar with the way you react to these stressors.
- Achieving work-life balance: Alternate times of stress with times of recreation.
- Living healthy: Good food, enough sleep, and moderate sport help to build resources needed in stressful times.
- Seeking help: Coaching, counseling, or therapy might be useful to reduce chronic stress.

9.4.3.2 Reduction of Acute Stress

Some helpful tips may help you to reduce stress in an acute emergency:

- Make it a habit to plan with foresight. Always try to stay ahead of the game. Use periods of low workload to prepare for potential upcoming events or procedures (e.g., by preparing for possible intubation, etc.).
- Try to stay in active control of your behavior. As soon as stress increases, this will be one of the first things you will abandon.
- Try to apply good strategies of action (Chap. 10) whenever possible.
- Try to minimize the narrowing impact of the stress reaction on your thinking: Step back and take a different perspective; scan your environment and ask yourself, "What else could be important?"
- Make sure that you pursue realistic goals. A realistic goal is one that you and your team can achieve given the specific context of a critical situation.
- Try not to be emotionally overwhelmed by a problem. Of course, it is easier said than done: "Don't panic!"
- If you have committed an active failure, try to see it as an isolated event and not as a confirmation that you are incompetent or lack the necessary capabilities.
- Sometimes, it is helpful to apply a body-oriented strategy: Step back, pay attention that you feel "firmly grounded" at the place you stand, and start to breathe consciously and in a controlled way.

9.4.3.3 Increase Your Resources

- You can best practice the management of critical situations and team behavior in a realistic yet safe environment. Simulation-based training programs are available for a variety of acute medical care specialties (Chap. 15).
- Knowledge and skills help to reduce stress. You should practice critical skills regularly and refresh or review key knowledge and train problem-solving strategies. Keeping your medical knowledge up to date can further improve your capability for crisis management.
- Know your environment well. Do not depend on others to tell you where to find critical resources (e.g., difficult airway equipment, defibrillator).
- Once you are in a critical situation, you should call for help early and get sufficient resources.
- Be generous in asking for help from teammates or other experts.
- Verbally share your thinking so teammates know what you are thinking and how you want the event to unfold.

9.4.4 Leading Teams Out of Stress

Your team is the most important resource in a critical situation. Whether it is the acquisition of knowledge, the development of situational models, the formation of goals, and the execution of tasks, team members can support each other to complete key tasks. Good communication is a necessary prerequisite and promotes a good team climate. Effective leaders distribute the resource "team" adequately among the different tasks and maintain an overview of the situation. Furthermore, leaders help their team arrive at a shared mental model by naming the problem and by sharing the course of action. Team members under stress need clear orders as well as respectful communication (Chaps. 12 and 13).

9.5 The Role of Organizations in Reducing Stress

From a work psychology perspective, the role of an organization in the development and management of stress is just as important as the behavior of individuals and their coping strategies. Modification of stressful working conditions can have a long-term impact on employees and is much more effective than trying to change individual behavior. In the acute and emergency healthcare setting, many acute stressors are part of the job and cannot be changed: the sight of critically ill or injured patients, the experience of suffering and death, personal tragedies, and an occasional feeling of helplessness. Some chronic stressors, such as night shifts and on-call duties will remain an inevitable part of any healthcare system. Other stressors, however, can and should be changed. Organizations can reduce job stress and foster effective stress management by implementing the following (Sauter et al. 1990):

- Adapt workload and workplace to the capabilities and resources of the workforce.
- Align work schedules and outside-the-job demands (e.g., flexible working hours, job-sharing).
- Create a climate of support: All areas of a healthcare organization should provide the emotional support and assistance that personnel require in order to accomplish assigned tasks. People should be able to voice concerns and call for help at any time without any fear of negative reactions from others; better is to encourage speaking up and asking for help.
- Clear mechanisms should be in place to find needed help.
- Promote the recovery of employees by providing regular breaks and access to food and beverages, maintaining work schedules, and providing appropriate on-call rooms or staff rooms. Following periods of high workload, allowances should be made for recovery.
- Provide a constructive atmosphere for dealing with critical situations, such as debriefings.
- Foster learning through continuous healthcare professional education, regular seminars, and supportive morbidity and mortality conferences.

9.6 "Stress" in a Nutshell

- Stress causes a deep-seated response in the human organism intended to secure physical integrity and survival. It prepares the organism for a rapid and goal-directed action.
- Stress is not an external event that befalls people out of nowhere. Instead, the stress response results from a person's active perception of a situation and the ensuing subconscious and holistic assessment.
- Whether or not a situation will trigger the stress response depends largely upon the (subconscious) situational appraisal ("Does this situation threaten my goals?" "Is it neutral or favorable?") and upon appraisal of available resources ("Will I be able to manage this critical situation?").
- The stress response prepares people physically and mentally to either fight a threat by means of a quick and goal-directed action (if the danger is perceived as weaker than one's one strength) or to escape from the danger (if an attack from a stronger force seems inevitable). If a choice between the two options seems impossible, people might "freeze" by simply doing nothing ("fight, flight, or freeze response"). This is true even in acute and emergency healthcare settings, where neither fight nor flight is a viable option.
- The indicators of the stress response can be grouped into four categories, which can be readily remembered by the acronym "BEST": behavioral, emotional, somatic, and thinking.
- Stress not only alters an individual's physiological parameters but also psychological response patterns (e.g., thinking and feeling). Thus, it is one of the most important factors influencing human cognitive functions and analysis-driven decision-making.
- When stressed, attention is focused on the actual problem ("cognitive tunnel vision"), and information processing becomes less robust.
- Stress hampers the perception of sound choices from among alternatives and leads to simple explanations and quick solutions to complex problems.
- The physical reactions of stress (e.g., tremor) can contribute additional stress to a critical situation by impairing fine motor skills.
- A moderate level of stress results in an improved performance; too much stress has the opposite effect.
- Chronic work stress in a healthcare setting may ultimately lead to a maladaptive response pattern with a strong impact on a person's emotional health and attitude toward life, known as the "burnout syndrome."
- The three dimensions of burnout are emotional exhaustion, depersonalization, and a feeling of professional failure.
- If healthcare providers are overwhelmed by a critical situation, a characteristic narrowing of thinking and behavior follows. This cognitive change is called the "cognitive emergency reaction."
- Post-traumatic stress syndrome (PTSD) is an anxiety disorder that can develop after exposure to a terrifying event or situation outside the normal range of human experience.

- Research indicates that 10–20 % of paramedics and emergency room personnel respond to traumatic experiences with maladaptive strategies that eventually lead to PTSD.
- The "3 Cs" of resilience are control, challenge, and commitment. People with a "hardy" personality view critical situations as being under their control and as a challenge rather than as a threat. They are committed to finding a solution because they see the situation as meaningful rather than random or pointless.
- Maintaining a feeling of competence may override the real objectives of patient management.
- Teams respond to stress much like an individual and expend effort in maintaining a feeling of competence. In addition, team members display other behavioral patterns, which can further compromise patient safety.
- The role of organizations in the development and prevention of stress is just as important as individual behavior and related coping strategies.

References

Alexander DA, Klein S (2001) Ambulance personnel and critical incidents: impact of accident and emergency work on mental health and emotional well-being. Br J Psychiatry 178(1):76–81

Anderson HS, Christensen AK, Petersen GO (1991) Post-traumatic stress reactions amongst rescue workers after a major rail accident. Anxiety Res 4:245–251

APA: American Psychiatric Association (1994) Diagnostic and statistical manual of mental disorders (DSM-IV), 4th edn. American Psychiatric Association, Washington, DC

Badke-Schaub P (2000) Wenn der Gruppe Flügel fehlen: Ungeeignete Informations- und Entscheidungsprozesse in Gruppen. [Dysfunctional processes of information management and decision-making in groups]. In: Mey H, Lehmann H, Pollheimer D (eds) Absturz im freien Fall oder Anlauf zu neuen Höhenflügen. vdf. Zürich, pp 113–130

Baumeister RF, Heatherton TF, Tice DM (1994) Losing control: how and why people fail at self-regulation. Academic, San Diego

Billings AG, Moos RH (1984) Coping, stress, and social resources among adults with unipolar depression. J Pers Soc Psychol 46:877–891

Cannon WB (1928) Bodily changes in pain, hunger, fear, and rage. Appleton – Century – Crofts, New York

Clohessy S, Ehlers A (1999) PTSD symptoms, response to intrusive memories and coping in ambulance service workers. Br J Clin Psychol 38(3):251–265

Czaja AS, Moss M, Mealer M (2012) Symptoms of posttraumatic stress disorder among pediatric acute care nurses. J Pediatr Nurs 27(4):357–365

Donelly E, Siebert D (2009) Occupational risk factors in the emergency medical services. Prehosp Disaster Med 24(5):422–429

Dörner D (1996) The logic of failure. Recognizing and avoiding error in complex situations. Metropolitan Books, New York

Dörner D (1999) Bauplan für eine Seele [Blueprint for a soul]. Rowohlt, Reinbek

Dörner D, Pfeiffer E (1993) Strategic thinking and stress. Ergonomics 36:1345–1360

Dörner D, Schaub H (1994) Errors in planning and decision-making and the nature of human information processing. Appl Psychol Int Rev 43:433–453

Dyregov A, Mitchell JT (1992) Work with traumatized children – psychological effects and coping strategies. J Trauma Stress 5:5–17

Edwards JR (1988) The determinants and consequences of coping with stress. In: Cooper CL, Payne R (eds) Causes, coping, and consequences of stress at work. Wiley, New York, pp 22–48

Elfering A, Grebner S, Semmer NK, Kaiser-Freiburghaus D, Lauper-Del Ponte S, Witsch I (2005) Chronic job stressors and job control: effects on event-related coping success and well-being. J Occ Organ Psychol 78(2):237–252

Embriaco NE, Azoulay E, Barrau K, Kentish N, Pochard F, Loundou A, Papazian L (2007) High level of burnout in intensivists: prevalence and associated factors. Am J Respir Crit Care Med 175(7):686–692

Flin R, Fletcher G, McGeorge P, Sutherland A, Patey R (2003) Anaesthetists' attitudes to teamwork and safety. Anaesthesia 58:233–243

Flin RH, O'Connor P, Crichton M (2008) Safety at the sharp end. A guide to non-technical skills. Ashgate Publishing, Burlington

Freudenberger HJ (1974) Staff burnout. J Soc Iss 30:159–165

Gallagher S, McGilloway S (2007) Living in critical times: the impact of critical incidents on frontline ambulance personnel-a qualitative perspective. Int J Emerg Ment Health 9(3):215–223

Grevin F (1996) Posttraumatic stress disorder, ego defense mechanism and empathy among urban paramedics. Psychol Rep 79:483–495

Hancock P, Szalma JL (eds) (2008) Performance under stress. Ashgate, Aldershot

Jackson SH (1999) The role of stress in anaesthetists' health and well-being. Acta Anaesthesiol Scand 43:583–602

Kaluza G (2004) Stressbewältigung. Trainings manual zur psychologischen Gesundheitsförderung. Springer, Berlin/Heidelberg

Kaluza G (2012) Gelassen und sicher im stress, 4th edn. Springer, Berlin/Heidelberg

Laposa JM, Alden LE (2003) Posttraumatic stress disorder in the emergency room: exploration of a cognitive model. Behav Res Ther 41(1):49–65

Larsson J, Sanner M (2010) Doing a good job and getting something good out of it: on stress and well-being in anaesthesia. Br J Anaesth 105(1):34–37

Lazarus RS (1991) Emotion and adaption. Oxford University, Oxford

Lazarus RS, Folkman S (1984) Stress, appraisal, and coping. Springer, Berlin/New York

Mahony KL (2001) Management and the creation of occupational stressors in an Australian and a UK ambulance service. Aust Health Rev 24:135–145

Maslach C (1982) Burnout. The cost of caring. Prentice-Hall, Englewood Cliffs

Maslach C (2003) Burnout. The cost of caring. Malor, Cambridge, MA

McCammon S, Durham TW, Allison EJ Jr, Williamson JE (1988) Emergency workers' cognitive appraisal and coping with traumatic events. J Trauma Stress 1:353–372

Mealer M, Burnham EL, Goode CJ, Rothbaum B, Moss M (2009) The prevalence and impact of post traumatic stress disorder and burnout syndrome in nurses. Depress Anxiety 26(12):1118–1126

Mitchell JT (1983) When disaster strikes…the critical incident stress debriefing process. J Emerg Med Serv 8:36–39

NICE: National Institute of Clinical Excellence (2005) Post-traumatic stress disorder (PTSD): the management of PTSD in adults and children in primary and secondary care. Clinical Guideline 26. Accessed at http://www.nccmh.org.uk/guidelines_ptsd.html

Reason J (1990) Human error. Cambridge University, Cambridge

Sauter SL, Murphy LR, Hurrell JJ (1990) Prevention of work-related psychological disorders. Am Psychol 45:1146–1158

Schaub H (1997) Decision-making in complex situations: cognitive and motivational limitations. In: Flin R, Salas E, Strub ME, Martin L (eds) Decision-making under stress. Emerging themes and applications. Ashgate, Aldershot, pp 291–300

Selye H (1936) A syndrome produced by diverse nocuous agents. Nature 138:32

Selye H (1956) The stress of life. McGraw-Hill, New York

Semmer N (1997) Stress. In: Luczak H, Volper W (eds) Handbuch Arbeitswissenschaft [Handbook work science]. Schäffer-Pöschel, Stuttgart, pp 332–340

Semmer N (2003) Individual differences, stress, and health. In: Schabracq MJ, Winnubst JA, Cooper CL (eds) Handbook of work and health psychology, 2nd edn. Wiley, Chichester, pp 83–120

Semmer NK, McGrath JE, Beehr TA (2005) Conceptual issues in research on stress and health. In: Cooper CL (ed) Stress medicine and health. CRC, Boca Raton, pp 1–44

Sexton JB, Thomas EJ, Helmreich RL (2000) Error, stress, and teamwork in medicine and aviation: cross sectional surveys. Br Med J 320:745–749

Siegrist J (2012) Effort-reward imbalance at work – theory, measurement and evidence. Universität Düsseldorf: Eigendruck. Verfügbar unter. http://www.uniklinik-duesseldorf.de/fileadmin/Datenpool/einrichtungen/institut_fuer_medizinische_soziologie_id54/ERI/ERI-Website.pdf. Accessed 16 Jan 2016

Siegrist J, Starke D, Chandola T, Godin I, Marmot M, Niedhammer I et al (2004) The measurement of effort-reward imbalance at work: European comparisons. Soc Sci Med 58(8):1483–1499

Sterud T, Hem E, Ekeberg O, Lau B (2008) Occupational stressors and its organizational and individual correlates: a nationwide study of Norwegian ambulance personnel. BMC Emerg Med 8(16):1–11

Taylor SE, Klein LC, Lewis BP, Gruenewald TL, Gurung RA, Updegraff JA (2000) Biobehavioral responses to stress in females: tend-and-befriend, not fight-or-flight. Psychol Rev 107(3):411–429

Tennant C (2001) Work-related stress and depressive disorders. J Psychosom Res 51(5):697–704

Ulich E (2001) Arbeitspsychologie [psychology of work], 5th edn. Vdf/Schäffer-Pöschel, Stuttgart/Zürich

Van der Ploeg E, Kleber RJ (2003) Acute and chronic job stressors among ambulance personnel: predictors of health symptoms. Occup Environ Med 60:i40–i46

Weber H (2004) Explorations in the social construction of anger. Motiv Emotion 28:197–219

Yerkes RM, Dodson JD (1908) The relation of strength of stimulus to rapidity of habit-formation. J Compar Neurol Psychol 18:459–482

Strategies for Action: Ways to Achieve Good Decisions

10

Case Study

On the pediatric cardiology ward, the on-call pediatric resident is called to evaluate a 6-year-old patient complaining of nausea and dizziness. The child is 5 days status post cardiac surgery. His symptoms had started about 2 h earlier and worsened gradually. By the time the resident arrives at the bedside, the patient's clinical condition has deteriorated further, and he has signs of impaired consciousness. The pediatrician obtains vital signs and applies monitors. The blood pressure is 60/40 mmHg and the ECG shows sinus tachycardia with a heart rate of 130 bpm. The saturation fluctuates between 88 and 92 %. Knowing that the chest drain had been removed the day before, the physician next listens to the lungs, which reveals diminished breath sounds over the left lung and distant heart sounds. In addition, she notes marked distension of the child's neck veins. At this point, she considers the most likely diagnoses to be either tension pneumothorax status post removal of the chest drain or pericardial tamponade. Supplemental oxygen via facial mask and a fluid bolus of 250-ml crystalloid solution are administered, but the child remains unstable. The resident considers intubation, but is concerned about the detrimental effects of positive pressure ventilation on hemodynamic parameters. She decides to optimize the patient's status first. An epinephrine infusion is started and the blood pressure improves. The patient is now stable enough for transfer to the pediatric intensive care unit. There, transthoracic echocardiography shows a large circumferential pericardial fluid collection and right ventricular diastolic collapse. With the diagnosis of pericardial tamponade, the patient is immediately taken to the operating room for an exploratory thoracotomy.

M. St.Pierre et al., *Crisis Management in Acute Care Settings*,
DOI 10.1007/978-3-319-41427-0_10

A pediatrician is confronted with an emergency in which the leading symptoms can be due to variety of causes. From clinical examination alone, she gets no further clues about the etiology of the clinical deterioration. What makes this situation particularly challenging is the fact that some therapeutic actions (e.g., intubation, insertion of a chest tube) might actually worsen the patient's condition. If her initial diagnosis proves wrong, the wrong intervention may do considerable harm to the young patient. Although her first impulse is to intubate the child immediately, she does not give in to her gut reaction but reconsiders the intuitive decision. She concludes that neither vital signs nor the dynamics of the situation demand immediate action and thus postpones the intubation. Instead, she manages to stabilize the patient, which in turn buys her time to perform the necessary diagnostic procedures. As soon as the cause for the clinical deterioration becomes evident, therapy can be tailored to the specific pathophysiology of acute cardiac tamponade.

Given the urgency and ambiguity of the situation, the resident showed remarkable foresight and thus prevented further harm to her patient. Her behavior illustrates the fact that human factors should never be equated with "risk factor" as they provide both the potential to trigger critical situations and the skills (e.g., situation awareness, problem solving, planning, decision-making, task management) to master them.

10.1 Five Steps of a Good Strategy

For the pediatrician, a decompensating post-op cardiac patient represents a novel situation to which she simply cannot apply familiar rules. She is faced with several puzzling questions: "What actually *is* the problem?" and "What am I *supposed* to do about it?" Instead of simply activating behavioral programs, she deliberately applies problem-solving strategies. However, conscious thought – the very "tool" humans need to deal with unknown realities – has a limited capacity and is quite slow due to inherent sequential information processing. In time-critical situations, ad hoc decision-making becomes tempting in order to alleviate the burden of thinking too hard.

Novices may prematurely apply rules that seem to fit for a given situation. Experts may do the same. But for experts, holistic situation assessment and potential courses of action come to mind more easily based on previous successful encounters under similar circumstances. However, as experts may not examine these circumstances critically, they may overlook crucial situational clues that suggest important deviations from the expected pattern. If this is the case, experts will succumb to "methodism of the experienced." Because both groups need to make sound decisions, novices as well as experts can benefit from a clear understanding of how decision-making works.

Deconstructing this decision process into systematic steps can help novices and experts improve their actions in complex and dynamic contexts. The literature offers several decision-making aids for critical situations (e.g., Runciman 1988; Gaba

1992; Risser et al. 1999; Small et al. 1999; Murray and Foster 2000). All of them contain, in one way or another, the following five steps of a good strategy:

1. Preparedness
2. Self- and situation assessment
   - Self-monitoring
   - Defining the problem
   - Gathering information
   - Building mental models
3. Planning actions
   - Formulating goals
   - Assessing risk
   - Planning
   - Making decisions
4. Executing action according to the plan
5. Review of effects
   - Reviewing actions
   - Revising strategy
   - Self-reflection

10.2 "Head" or "Gut": Which Shall We Follow?

Given the acute clinical deterioration and ambiguity of the vital signs in the vignette above, it would have been entirely possible that the resident would follow her first impulse. Instead, she showed foresight and prevented further harm to the child. Under different circumstances, her decision-making could have led to different outcomes. Possible scenarios include:

- *Spontaneous, "gut-feel" decision combined with clinical inexperience:* The little experience the pediatrician gained with airway management in respiratory compromised children may have led to the formation of a behavioral rule: "If the saturation drops and does not improve when applying a face mask with oxygen (e.g., S_pO_2 levels stay below 90 %) and if the patient continues to be in a state of reduced alertness, I have to intubate my patient immediately!" Because she did not have previous opportunities to form clinical exceptions to this rule (e.g., in the context of acute cardiac tamponade), the child's reduced alertness in combination with the low sats could have been a clear indication for an endotracheal intubation. The combination of a perceived plausibility for intubation with stress and time pressure most certainly could favor the execution of her "gut-feel" reaction with the likely consequence of ongoing clinical deterioration (a "strong but wrong" decision).
- *Spontaneous, "gut-feel" decision due to clinical experience*: A global assessment of the situation as being cardiac tamponade would have led her to avoid invasive ventilation as long as possible. By doing so the experienced pediatrician would likely prevent further exacerbation of the clinical situation.

Thus, contrary to popular belief, "spontaneous" or "intuitive" decision-making is not universally "bad" or "misleading." In both instances, the novice and experienced physicians follow their intuition. The difference lies in the spontaneous initial assessment, the accuracy of which is usually based on experience (Dreyfus and Dreyfus 2000). For experienced clinicians dealing with familiar situations, "spontaneous decisions" often provide satisfactory, workable options.

- *Inexperience and analytic decisions:* At the other end of the spectrum, the pediatrician may be a beginner and thus lack any knowledge or experience to interpret the situational clues. Being aware of her deficits, she may avoid any spontaneous reaction. Instead, her decision-making would involve many conscious steps of analytical problem solving (System 2 process). She would initially analyze the situation and try to find and apply rules. Given the unclear situation, the physician may become overly cautious and reluctant to act. If she acts, that action will likely be anchored on only a few salient clues (e.g., drop in saturation). In the extreme, the combination of inexperience and thorough analysis could result in "paralysis by analysis" and impede any decision-making.
- *Combined strategy of pattern recognition plus deliberate consideration:* Somewhere along the spectrum between gut-feel decisions and painstaking analysis lies an approach that combines the strength of both processes. The pediatrician could use heuristics to generate options, and then, before acting upon her first impulse, use analytic cognition to exert an executive function and submit her hitherto unexamined intuitive judgments to verification. This "override function" of conscious deliberation, which can prevent humans from taking immediate action on first impressions, appears to be a critical feature in good decision-making.

10.3 Heuristics and Cognitive Bias: Beware of What Guides You

But how do you arrive at applying such strategy? Can conscious deliberation be trained and learned? The need appears to be obvious: Although diagnostic reasoning and clinical decision-making are essential aspects of clinical performance, these skills are seldom part of professional education or postgraduate training. As a consequence, nurses, ambulance staff, and clinicians have to make decisions with far-reaching consequences on a daily basis without being aware of how their reasoning can be made vulnerable by systematic deviations from rational decisions and by the influence of emotions ("cognitive bias"). *Systematic* in this context implies that "bias," like the aforementioned heuristics, results from basic principles of human behavioral regulation and thus comprises mental phenomena that shape and characterize everyday thinking. For example, people tend to over- rather than underestimate their actual knowledge of a situation, take credit for success but blame failure on external circumstances, judge attractive people more competent than the average person, and are motivated more by the danger of losing something rather than by the prospect of gain (Dobelli 2013). To obviate the notion that "bias" refers to pathological entities, the terms *cognitive disposition to respond* (CDR) and *affective dispositions to respond* (ADR) have been proposed (Croskerry et al. 2013).

Systematic deviations from rational decisions obey the principle of economy, which allows the decision-maker to swiftly arrive at "good enough" solutions. Table 10.1 gives an overview of the most frequent heuristics and cognitive biases and relates them to basic cognitive principles as presented in this book (Table 10.1).

10.4 Improving the Decision-Making Process

10.4.1 Self-Monitoring

The cognitive intervention of self-monitoring is a strategy that helps improve clinical reasoning and decision-making by allowing the decision-maker to analyze his or her decision-making process. Self-monitoring of the decision-making process can help the decision-maker to identify cognitive and affective dispositions to respond and to manage their impact through deliberate reflection (Graber et al. 2012; Trowbridge 2003). In order to do so one must:

- Have *knowledge* about the major classes of heuristics and cognitive biases used in decision-making.
- Be able to reflect upon the way in which heuristics, affective biases, and cognitive biases might exert an influence on his or her *thought processes and behavior* (metacognition).
- Have set *triggers* that signal one to stop pursuing a pattern-recognition path and instead deliberately analyze the problem at hand.
- *Approach the decision-making in a systematic way* and use decisional aids where appropriate.

This deliberate, conscious consideration of alternatives requires time and cognitive resources. Even if the "perceived urgency of the situation" suggests otherwise, the time to stop and think is almost always available:

- Initial treatment focuses on vital symptoms and not on clinical diagnoses. Following algorithms helps to stabilize the patient.
- When faced with diagnostic uncertainty, the primary goal is to strive for a clinical condition that offers many different possibilities for actions that have a high probability of success ("maximum efficiency and divergence," see below). Corollary: the time for deliberate problem solving is well invested considering how quickly premature commitment to a single treatment path may destroy future options.
- Establishing forced consideration of alternatives does not necessarily take long – one critical question like "Could this be anything else?" may suffice.

Table 10.1 Overview of the most frequent heuristics and cognitive biases and their underlying cognitive principles

Heuristics and cognitive biases	Relevance	Cognitive principle
Availability	People estimate the frequency or probability of an event on the basis of the ease with which it comes to mind (e.g., how easily it can be remembered)	Principle of economy
Representativeness	People estimate the frequency or probability of an event on the basis of prototypical characteristics of the situation	Principle of economy
Anchoring	People perceptually lock on a salient feature of the initial presentation and then fail to adjust their initial prognosis in the light of later and contradicting information	Search for order
Confirmation bias	People tend to see (and seek) pieces of information that reinforce present knowledge or hypotheses rather than refuting them	Search for order Avoidance of ambiguity Distortion of information
Fundamental attribution error (correspondence bias)	Dispositional factors (internal attribution) rather than situational factors (external attribution) are held responsible for behavior of others or illness of patients	Locus of control, internal vs. external
Framing effect	The way a problem is framed (e.g., as gain or loss for the patient) has a strong influence on decision-making and risk assessment	Risk aversion
Affect heuristic (visceral bias)	People make decisions based on an intuitive emotional ("affect") assessment. If they have pleasant feelings about something (e.g., a patient, a decision), they see the benefits as high and the risks as low and approve. If a decision "feels wrong," they disapprove	Aversion to unpleasant feelings
Sunk-cost fallacy	The more effort and commitment people have already invested in a particular matter (e.g., in a treatment path), the harder it becomes to revise or abandon that plan, even if there is ample evidence that they are wrong. It becomes almost impossible to admit: "I was mistaken!" or "This therapy is not helping the patient!"	Feeling of competence
Premature closure/ search satisficing	People tend to close their decision-making process as soon as the first plausible explanation for a problem has been found. This bias is reflected in the maxim: "The most commonly missed fracture in the ED is the second one!"	Principle of economy
Overconfidence bias	People overestimate systematically their knowledge and prognostic abilities. Too much confidence is placed in opinion instead of gathered evidence. As a result, people act on incomplete information and intuition	Feeling of competence

Table 10.1 (continued)

Heuristics and cognitive biases	Relevance	Cognitive principle
Hindsight bias	If people know the outcome of an event, their perception is profoundly influenced, and a realistic appraisal of what exactly happened is no longer possible. This is true for the appraisal of one's own behavior as well as the behavior of others	Expectation-based perception Basic properties of human memory
Halo effect	Positive feelings in one area cause ambiguous or neutral traits to be viewed positively: If people like one aspect of another person (e.g., attractiveness, social status), they will have a positive disposition toward unknown characteristics of that person, such as intelligence or competence	Expectation-based perception Search for order Avoidance of ambiguity
Commission bias	Under stress and time pressure people tend toward action rather than inaction. More important than the solution of a problem is the upkeep of a feeling of control over a situation. This is true even if actions are not indicated or are an act of desperation	Feeling of competence

In addition, situational analysis should always go hand in hand with self-monitoring. Decision-makers should be aware of their tendency to allow feelings about a patient or an interaction with colleagues to affect care decisions. To detect circumstances that might bias one's thinking, one could ask questions such as, "How does this patient make me feel? Is this a patient I like or don't like for any reason? Does this situation make me angry? Do I feel tempted to prove that I can do something?"

10.4.2 Strategies to Improve Decision-Making

A systematic way to introduce specific debiasing techniques into the decision-making process is the application of cognitive self-monitoring strategies. These strategies attempt to minimize influences of nonrational decision preferences by creating rules to induce self-monitoring of decision-making processes, thereby "forcing" the clinician to consider alternatives (hence *cognitive forcing strategies*). Such strategies require a *trigger* that signals clinicians to toggle from an intuitive thinking disposition to an analytic strategy as well as appropriate knowledge of solutions and strategic rules as part of the *reasoning process* (Croskerry et al. 2013; Stiegler and Tung 2014).

In the context of healthcare, several cognitive forcing strategies have been proposed (Croskerry 2002; Graber et al. 2012; Stiegler and Tung 2014; Stiegler and Ruskin 2012):

- *Systemic deconstruction:* Radiologists use systemic deconstruction as a strategy to combat confirmation bias when they interpret every X-ray in the exact same systematic way. Thus, they force themselves to focus their attention on all structures and possible findings and not only on the clinical question asked. A similar approach in emergency medicine is the primary assessment of trauma patients with the "ABCDE" algorithm taught in Prehospital Trauma Life Support and Advanced Trauma Life Support courses.
- The "*3D Rule*" for diagnoses and therapeutic interventions ("Rule of Three," Stiegler and Ruskin 2012): Whenever a clinical change occurs, clinicians base their initial treatment on representativeness and availability heuristics. However, if this treatment is repeated without effect, a differential of at least three other diagnostic possibilities must be entertained before a third attempt at the same intervention (e.g., a third dose of a drug) is undertaken. Three diagnoses before a *3rd* dose can be memorized as "3D." Even if the probability of other causes is not that high, a forced consideration of alternative explanations for a given problem can help to prevent, among other things, fixation errors, premature closure, and confirmation bias.
- *Rule out worst-case scenarios:* Whenever a clinician is confronted with a vital problem (e.g., patient with shortness of breath), he intuitively will consider the most common causes for this presentation first. The "rule out the worst-case scenario" approach, however, will redirect the clinician's attention to diagnoses with significant consequences, even if they are statistically rare.
- *Make use of the "universal antidote":* Another helpful strategy for minimizing the influence of intuitive decision preferences is to develop the habit of asking the simple question, "Could it be anything else?" every single time one arrives at a preliminary assessment. By forcing the decision-maker to explicitly search for arguments that could falsify her current working diagnosis, this strategy constitutes a powerful antidote to combat the principle of economy with its tendency for confirmation bias and fixation errors.
- *Reevaluate during patient handover:* A patient handover is a specific clinical situation that might increase vulnerability to specific biases. Healthcare providers who get a patient handed over by another team or person are in danger of accepting an unchecked diagnosis together with the patient (diagnosis momentum). Clinicians will be even more likely to succumb to biased reasoning and stereotyping if the patient appears repulsive (e.g., signs of self-neglect, acute alcohol intoxication, massive obesity, psychiatric disorder). In situations with a higher risk for biased reasoning, it can be helpful to support decision-making by a set of probing questions:
  - Am I working on a pathophysiologic state (e.g., shortness of breath) or did I already commit myself to a diagnosis (e.g., asthma attack)?

  - If I have committed myself to a diagnosis, was the diagnosis suggested to me by another person (e.g., the patient, a paramedic, a nurse, a physician) and did I just accept it, or did I match it with the patient's clinical presentation?
  - Is this a patient I don't like or like too much, for some reason? Am I in danger of stereotyping and therefore unwilling to take further diagnostic or therapeutic steps?
  - Did I consider other organ systems besides the obvious ones?
  - What could be the most serious diagnosis and the worst-case scenario I certainly should not miss?
- *Use cognitive aids* whenever possible. Checklists and guidelines designed for medical emergencies can compensate for shortcomings in human memory (e.g., retrieval of inert knowledge, working memory for calculations, and prospective memory for future tasks) and thus may help to improve patient outcome (Goldhaber-Fiebert and Howard 2013).

10.5 Maximum "Efficiency and Divergence"

The moment our pediatric resident makes first contact with her patient, she can only assess the patient's current clinical status. Foreseeing dynamic developments or the influence of therapeutic actions is not possible. Although the patient's condition is serious, it does not warrant immediate invasive procedures (e.g., intubation, chest tube). Instead of performing potentially harmful interventions, the physician supports the patient's hemodynamic state, thus keeping several options open as long as possible. She decides against intubation given the possible detrimental effect of positive pressure ventilation on cardiac preload in patients with impaired ventricular filling. Instead, she starts a continuous infusion of catecholamines to increase blood pressure. Blood pressure and oxygen saturation stabilize, which buys time to determine the pathophysiological cause for the critical situation. Once the reason for the clinical deterioration becomes evident, the resident can take specific therapeutic steps. An integral part of patient care in a high-stakes environment should be avoiding premature commitment to a single treatment path – especially when it is potentially harmful or irreversible. Healthcare providers should nevertheless deliberately strive for clinical conditions of "maximum efficiency and divergence" (Fig. 10.1; Oesterreich 1981). A situation characterized by high efficiency and divergence offers many different possibilities (hence, "divergence") for actions that have a high probability of success ("efficiency"); thus, intermediate goals set according to this criterion target clinical conditions with many degrees of freedom. In these situations, clinicians can move efficiently in many different directions

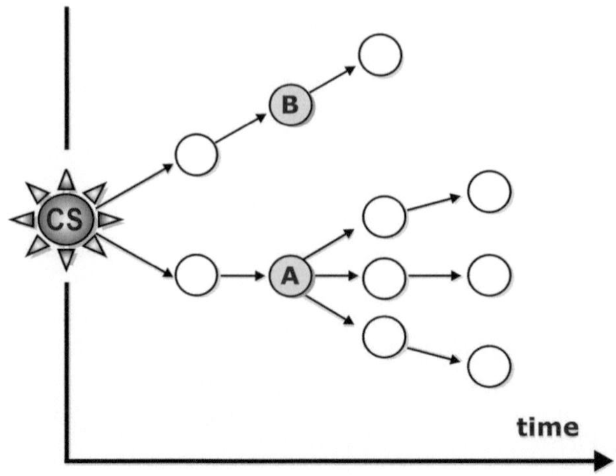

Fig. 10.1 "Maximum efficiency and divergence" as a strategy for good action (Oesterreich 1981). Patient treatment is thought of as the sequence of different clinical situations (*circle*). In critical situations (*CS*), there are usually several options for action from which to choose. Some goals (*B*), however, have only 1° of freedom, and therefore the development will go in one direction only. If a condition of maximum efficiency divergence is targeted (*A*), many different possibilities for actions are kept open

10.6 "Good Decisions" in the High-Stakes Environment of Acute Medical Care

The pediatric resident in our case wants to make "good decisions" about the decompensating cardiac surgery patient. However, she faces the challenge of making "good decisions" in a context where complexity, ambiguity, and dynamic changes make sound decision-making more difficult. Given these limitations, what characterizes "good decisions" in a high-stakes environment?

A "good decision" in an emergency situation achieves is characterized by the following:

- Promotes safe, efficient, and effective task management.
- Considers the current situation with all relevant contextual features, including time limitations and availability of finite resources.
- Respects human factors, such as limited information-processing capacity and the influence of motivation and emotion on behavior, and doesn't overstrain a person, recognizing the limits to mental and physical workload and variable resistance to stress.
- Leads to a timely and feasible course of action.
- Anticipates complications of treatment or diagnostic interventions.
- Integrates both "gut feeling" and analytical approaches. Evidence suggests that novices, too, should heed a "bad feeling" about a decision or management strategy.

It is important, however, to note that good decisions are not equivalent to the following:

- *Good results:* Decision-making is concerned primarily with how people arrive at certain conclusions. "Shortcuts" and guideline violations may result in good outcomes and thereby reinforce the same hazardous attitudes that lead to the decision in the first place. On the other hand, an element of risk for patient safety and potentially poor outcomes always remains despite good decisions. For example, when debriefing an unsuccessful cardiopulmonary resuscitation, team members may nonetheless conclude that all decisions and actions were correct. Finally, after a critical event, clinicians may say in hindsight: "It was pure luck that things turned out all right!"
- *Good intentions:* Good intentions do not guarantee good outcomes. Inherent risks and the probability of success should be assessed for all planned actions. An emergent intubation of the post-op cardiac patient would have been performed with the best intentions, but might have caused more harm than good. Additionally, intentions should match reality. If we consider a specific course of action, it is only worth considering it if we have the necessary skills and resources to make it happen.
- *Best possible decisions:* Once the stress of a critical situation wears off and team members share their thoughts on critical issues, some previously unconsidered options may arise. Unfortunately, in time-critical situations, these key pieces of information, ideas, and opinions were not available at the time, and therefore "the best possible decision" was not possible at all. Bearing in mind this critical restriction and the power of the hindsight bias may help prevent nagging thoughts of "I could have/should have/would have done otherwise or better."

Situational demands may exceed assets in critical situations. Specific skills may be required, correct rules may have to be applied appropriately, or a completely new solution has to be found (Chap. 2). Whether or not a decision in the high-stakes environment of acute medical care is "good" depends on whether or not it meets the requirements of the emergency situation.

10.7 Decisional Aids

Experience from other complex work environments demonstrates that decisional aids can actually help people structure and organize their decision-making and thereby reduce the tendency for hasty decisions (Benner 1975; Orasanu and Connolly 1992; Jensen 1995). Structured decision-making processes have been shown to improve safety in high-risk environments. Decisional aids are mnemonics often formulated as acronyms (i.e., pronounceable words formed from the initial letter of each of the constituent words) to facilitate learning and recall. When uncertain or ambiguous circumstances require judgments or decisions, decisional aids help organize one's thoughts and prevent impulsive actions, use of shortcuts, and neglect of important facts. Before acting, a brief deliberate pause is recommended to reconcile the final decision with the implicit knowledge from prior experience: Does the plan feel right as well?

Table 10.2 Decisional model "DECIDE"

	Question/statement	Meaning
Detect	"Something has changed!"	The decision-maker detects that a change has occurred that requires attention
Estimate	"Does this change have any significance for me?"	The perceived change is assessed for its significance for the patient and for the future course of events
Choose	"I will choose a safe action!"	The decision-maker explicitly decides to choose the safest possible option
Identify	"Which reasonable treatment options do I have?"	The option with the fewest risks and the highest probability for success is chosen
		In addition, a "plan B" is mapped out in case the first choice should fail
Do	"I will act on the best options!" "What effect did the action have?"	The action is planned and executed
Evaluate		The effect of the action is evaluated
		The intended and actual course of action is compared
		Ask yourself: Has the situation changed? Is this plan still appropriate?
		If necessary, return to "Detect" or "Identify"

After Benner (1975)

10.7.1 Decisional Aids for Time-Critical Problems

Two six-element decision-making models from high-risk nonmedical industries have been adapted to acute medical care and shown to be helpful:

- DECIDE from the domain of firefighting (Table 10.2; Benner 1975) safety in a critical situation is the focus of this model.
- FOR-DEC from the domain of civil aviation (Table 10.3; Hoermann 1995) emphasizes risk-balanced decision-making while avoiding ad hoc decisions.

Both decisional aids describe a "closed-loop" process: As soon as an action has been executed, thinking goes back to the beginning and the situation is reviewed. In both cases, if the situation has changed and if an action did not bring the intended result, decision-makers start again. Because these acronyms describe decisional aids, they presume clear goals, which is why neither model includes *goal setting*. In medical emergencies, priorities and short-term goals such as securing the airway or providing CPR are clearly important. In other situations, however, attention may have to focus on other goals and priorities. By implementing the question, "What are our goals and priorities?" into the "Facts" part of FOR-DEC, this critical aspect of decision-making receives appropriate attention. Importantly, these decisional aids empower all team members to share the same approach to decision-making and action. Once the decision-making process of FOR-DEC or DECIDE becomes the implicit structure of problem solving of all team members, collecting data,

Table 10.3 Decisional model "FOR-DEC"

	Question/statement	Meaning
Facts	"What is the problem?!" "What are our goals and priorities?"	The need for a decision is detected
		The situation is analyzed and facts are collected
		The urgency is assessed: How much time do we have until a decision must be made? From among many possible goals and priorities, a limited set is chosen
Options	"What different options do we have?"	All team members contribute their point of view on available options
Risks/benefits	"What are the pros and cons for every option?"	The benefits and the probability for success as well as the risk of each option mentioned are evaluated
		The degree of uncertainty is estimated
– **D**ash	Phase transition	The dash has two functions: "Mental pause" – when pros and cons have been weighed: Does the decision process feel right? Transition from the team phase to the team leaders' decision
Decision	"This is what we will do!"	A decision is made by choosing the best option. The best option has the fewest risks and the highest probability of success
		At the same time, a "plan B" is formulated in case the first plan fails
		Before the plan is executed, the situation is rechecked: Is the initial analysis still appropriate?
Execution	"Who will do what and when?"	The decision is executed
Check	"Is the decision still correct?"	The action is checked. A critical comparison of the factual and intended effect is made
		If necessary, the decisional process returns to "facts"

After Hoermann (1995)

generating management options, and assessing risk will be tasks that lie with the team as a whole rather than with solitary individuals. This is teamwork at its best.

10.7.2 Decisional Aids for Complex Problems with Moderate Time Pressure

Healthcare providers are at times confronted with only moderate time pressure to solve highly complex problems. Intensive care patients whose clinical condition deteriorates over several hours may fall into this category. In such cases, formulating clear goals is of great importance. The model shown in Fig. 10.2 has been successfully implemented into the organizational behavior within other high-risk domains (Dörner 1996; Dörner and Schaub 1994). The arrows indicate that the steps do not have to be

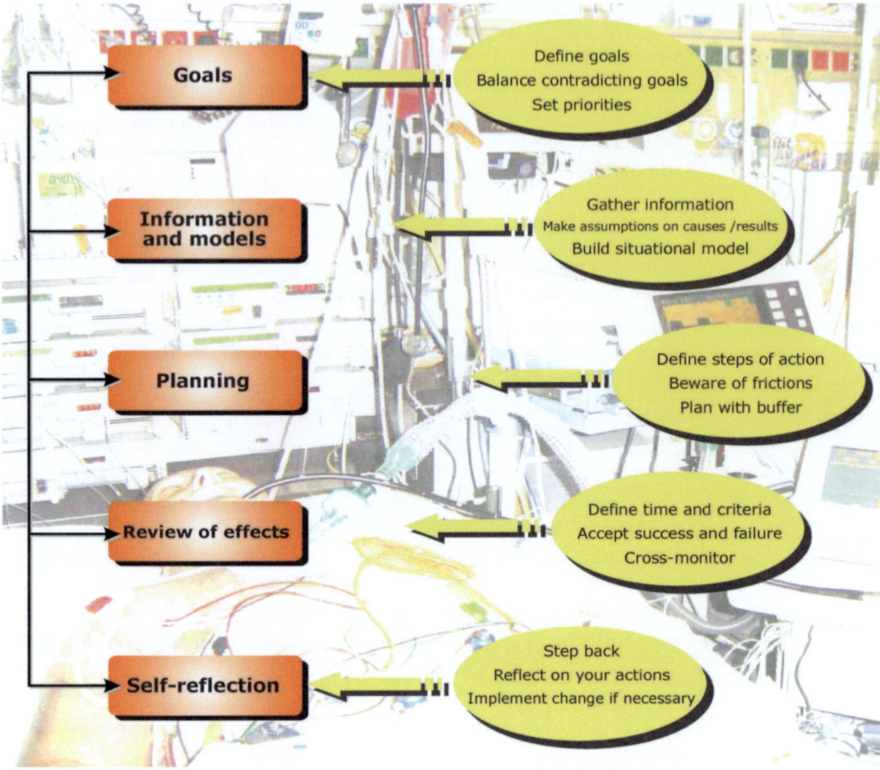

Fig. 10.2 Action organization: a decisional model for situations with moderate time pressure and high complexity (Modified after Dörner 1996)

processed in sequential order. Depending on the problem, it may be necessary to spend considerable effort gathering information before intermediate goals can be defined; or it might become necessary to revise goals during planning due to changing conditions. The model of action organization works more like a checklist and reminds people to spend an adequate amount of time organizing complex actions.

Goals, *plans*, *models*, and the handling of information are the topics of Chaps. 6 and 7.

Review of effects is assessing the results of action, a central feature of any decisional aid. Several factors impede effective review of effects. Time delay and the concurrent effects of many actions can make it difficult to attribute clinical effects to the result of single actions. Also, the review of effects is a form of information management, and therefore restrictions to information management described in Chap. 6 apply. Finally, performing only a superficial review of effects or avoiding it all together may stem from a motive to protect the feeling of competence, especially if failure is likely.

Self-reflection describes the conscious analysis of one's own behavior (alone or as part of a team) that elicits reasons for success or failure and identifies modifications for future actions. However, self-reflection is uncomfortable, and finding an appropriate time for it during an emergent crisis may be problematic. After a critical situation, other issues may arise, and often people only reluctantly return to analyze past events. Nevertheless, self-reflection is essential for those working in complex domains because it enables us to learn consciously and to change our behavior.

10.8 Strategies for Coping with Error

10.8.1 Detect Errors Early

Errors and mistakes do not arise from faulty cognitive mechanisms but instead from useful psychological processes and limited cognitive capacity. This explains why it is normal for humans to make mistakes; however, mitigating the effects of inevitable mistakes that affect our patients requires early detection and correction. These are difficult tasks for the person who committed the error. We tend to overlook the elements that lead to the error, and, if we do reflect on our actions, we often come up with the same answer. We have a hard time looking at things differently. We readily accept our way of thinking even if the available data only loosely matches our mental model. This tendency to see things with this bias leads us to easily overlook our own errors. Fortunately, specific strategies applied to critical situations improve error detection rates.

The following suggestions are for individuals; organizational error management will be a topic of Chap. 14.

10.8.1.1 Anticipate Error: "It Can Happen to Me!"

Because we are prone to commit errors of one sort or another, it is necessary to anticipate them in our own behavior. A self-critical attitude and an awareness of the ever-present possibility of errors can help us suspect error as the cause for any discrepancy between actual and intended courses of action.

10.8.1.2 Improve Your Perception: Look for Contradictions in Your Model

Any action that provides immediate physical feedback can help identify an error (e.g., accidental puncture of the carotid artery when trying to insert a central IV line). Much more difficult, however, is error detection in situations in which feedback about success or failure is lacking. It reduces insecurity and, despite evidence to the contrary, encourages the feeling that the critical situation is under control. Decision-makers should actively search for information that could refute the current situational model or that could indicate plans are not going as intended. In order to question one's assumptions in an emergent situation (in which clear knowledge about what to do is comforting), it should become routine in less critical situations to search for pieces of information that contradict or even disprove current assumptions about the situation.

10.8.1.3 Be Aware of the "Sunk Cost Fallacy"

Decisions in acute medical care are often made under time pressure and high uncertainty. However, as the situation evolves, clinical signs can indicate that the initial decision was wrong or less than optimal and the resulting therapy therefore inadequate. Unfortunately, the more people have already invested in a matter (e.g., by searching for confirmative evidence for the diagnosis or having initiated an unusual or an expensive therapy), the more clinicians are inclined to stick to a chosen strategy – even if there is ample evidence against it. As a result we have a tendency to intensify efforts to make the chosen strategy successful because stopping seems unreasonable after all we have already invested. Under these circumstances, it is nearly impossible to admit "I was off track!" or to conclude "Our current strategy is not helping the patient!" The reason for this lies in the need for control and our motive to protect a feeling of competence (Chap. 4): the psychological need to feel able to influence our environment according to own goals, to know with certainty what is happening around us, and to have clarity of facts and certainty about future developments. Even when we have the feeling that the current clinical state strongly suggests that our efforts are based on faulty assumptions and wrong, the motive of control can become active and outplay rational arguments. Therefore, whenever one realizes that one has an uneasy feeling or come to a dead end with a therapy but still feels the urge to continue, one should ask the simple question: "Do I want to continue because I have the facts on my side or am I continuing because I have a hard time admitting that I was mistaken?"

10.8.1.4 Ask Team Members for Feedback

Other team members are the most valuable resource for detecting inadequate plans or erroneous actions. In fact, such cross-monitoring and speaking up are among the most powerful and effective means to enhance patient safety (Risser et al. 1999). However, healthcare providers seem reluctant to accept the fact that two pairs of eyes see more than one and that the responsibility for making diagnoses and plans lies with one individual. The interplay between complexity, cognitive economy, and ambiguity aversion makes it so hard for clinicians to detect and assess changes in their environment. Fig. 10.3 depicts this fact: As soon as routine action (RA) is interrupted by a critical situation (CS), people start to ask themselves "What exactly is the problem?" and to search for information. In addition, they assess the urgency of the situation: "Is there still time left for data collection, or do I have to act now?" Once a person has made a diagnosis and begins to act (A), the mental model will be based on the current data available. Cognitive economy impedes any effort to change this model. A team member entering the situation later in the course of events (B) is far less likely to be bound by preconceived ideas or assumptions. B's unbiased assessment may promote a fresh understanding of the situation. *Those who enter the situation afresh at some later point are not so theory bound, at least initially. The nakedness of the emperor is readily seen by those who have not come to believe him clothed* (Reason 1990).

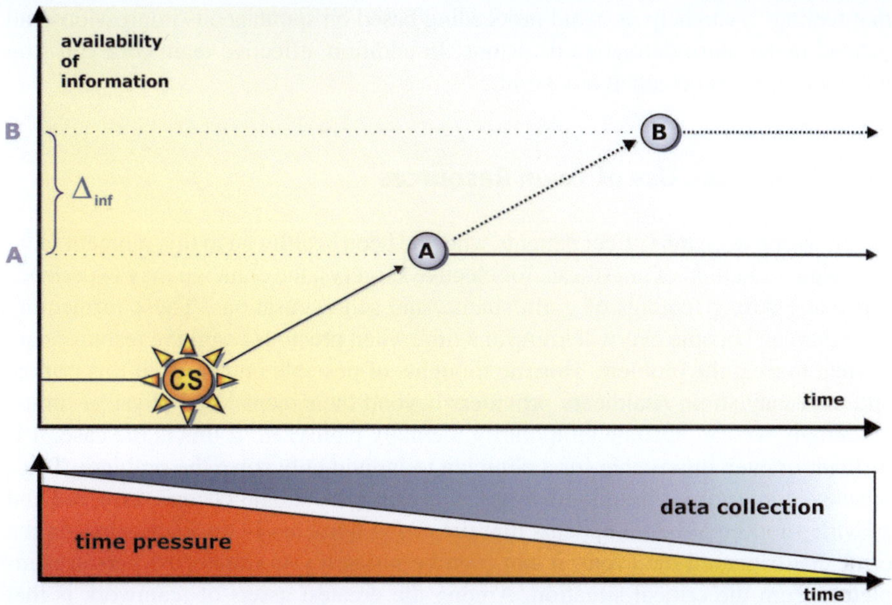

Fig. 10.3 Time pressure, data collection, and the advantage of having a second person entering a critical situation. The resulting mental model will likely comprise more of the situation and may result in a different diagnosis and plan. Time pressure (*red wedge*) and data collection (*blue wedge*) are inversely correlated. Corollary: There is no such thing as complete data collection under time pressure

10.8.2 Mitigate the Effects of Errors

10.8.2.1 Break the "Poor Judgment Chain"

One single error does not usually result in a fatal outcome in a critical situation. It is only the sequence of poor decisions and the inability to recognize and correct them early that leads to accidents and patient harm.

Poor decisions can (a) reduce the safety margin for effective management, (b) undermine personal feelings of competence, and (c) create feelings of shame and guilt, and thereby increase stress levels.

For these reasons, a single error increases the probability for additional errors, thereby resulting in a poor judgment chain (Jensen 1995). Once errors add up and the situation threatens to become unmanageable, people start acting "mindlessly." But we are not helpless victims to this mechanism; we can learn to assess critically the impact that errors have on our judgment and decisional processes. If we are aware of our own behavior and of how we make decisions, we may face critical situations with less fear of becoming helpless in the face of committed errors. Adopting an ongoing critical self-perception (e.g., "I am aware of a feeling of frustration because of the error I committed and I feel an urge to just do something to get rid of that feeling!") can help us avoid proceeding based on spontaneous impressions and instead make more deliberate decisions. In addition, effective teamwork can stop the poor judgment chain at any point.

10.8.3 Making Use of Team Resources

When wrong decisions affect patients who had been healthy up to this moment (e.g., following induction of anesthesia for elective surgery), the clinician may experience especially strong feelings of guilt, shame, and self-accusations. These tormenting thoughts can become overwhelming at a time when precious cognitive resources are needed to treat the problem. Horrific thoughts of possible outcomes of this critical situation may strain healthcare providers beyond their mental and physical limits; essentially we can become temporarily mentally paralyzed. If this is the case, it is difficult or even impossible for a clinician to individually solve the problem. Thus, whenever an error is committed, other team members should become involved and provide support. When it appears that the erring clinician is stuck focusing on the error that triggered the event, it can even be necessary to excuse the person completely from the critical situation. Among the greatest assets of teamwork is that team members who enter a critical situation later are not as emotionally involved and have a better chance of recovering from an error by reconsidering the diagnosis, plan, and execution.

10.8.4 Coping with Errors

In summary, to detect errors early, it is important to do the following:

- Anticipate error: "It can happen to me!"
- Improve perception and awareness – be doubtful, look for contradictions, and be aware of a feeling that "this might not be working."
- Ask team members for feedback.

To mitigate the effects of errors, the two points are especially relevant:

- Be aware of the dangers of the "poor judgment chain."
- Use the team as a resource.

10.9 Tips for Clinical Practice

- Apply decisional aids (e.g., DECIDE, FOR-DEC) when working in a team environment.
- Be aware of your gut feeling in critical situations; a "bad" feeling should never go unheeded.

- Practice using decisional aids in advance if you want to be able to apply them in critical situations; under stress we resort to familiar patterns of thinking and behavior so things that aren't practiced will not be available during a crisis.
- "Doing nothing" is a decision; giving more time, even a small amount extra, to think and decide is sometimes the best thing you can do.
- Correct mistakes immediately – rectification outranks justification!
- Call for help early. Ask available colleagues to join you in the critical situation; the welfare of our patients is preeminent.
- Create open channels of communication! Solicit input from colleagues irrespective of rank or title. Make it your habit to thank team members for *any* feedback about your performance or suspected errors. Thank them for their contribution. The long-term benefit will be that others will view you as a trustworthy professional and someone to whom they can offer unsolicited ideas and support. Their comments will become extremely helpful in detecting, avoiding, and recovering from errors and mistakes.
- As a team member, an effective technique is to share an observation and pair it with their point of view about it without judging the person to whom you are giving feedback.

10.10 "Strategies for Action" in a Nutshell

- A good decision in high-stakes acute care settings meets the needs of the emergency situation.
- Heuristics are neither inherently good or bad nor are they necessarily rational or irrational. Whether or not they are helpful depends on the context of the application and the structure of the environment.
- Deviations from rational decisions and the influence of emotions ("cognitive bias") simplify clinical decision-making. Both come from basic human behavior and are comprised of mental phenomena that shape and characterize our everyday thinking.
- The cognitive intervention of self-monitoring is a strategy that helps to improve clinical reasoning and decision-making by allowing the decision-maker to analyze one's decision-making process.
- Part of a good strategy is to avoid committing to a single treatment path too early. Instead, strive for clinical conditions with as many degrees of freedom as possible. From there, it is possible to move efficiently in different directions.
- A condition that offers several possibilities each with a high probability of success is called "maximum efficiency and divergence."
- A good strategy has five steps: preparedness, analysis of the situation, goal setting and planning of actions, execution of action, and review of effects.
- The systematic application of decisional aids (e.g., DECIDE, FOR-DEC) can help decision-makers organize their thoughts and prevent impulsive actions.
- Experience-based knowledge reaches consciousness as a feeling or intuition. It should be taken into account as well as analytical approaches.

- Decisional aids enable all team members to share the same approach to decision-making and action. Applying an agreed-upon approach to decision-making or using cognitive aids in a critical situation is a team responsibility that does not lie with a single individual.
- It is impossible for healthcare providers to be error-free in caring for patients; however, once an error occurs, it is important to avoid a "poor judgment chain."

References

Benner L (1975) D.E.C.I.D.E. in hazardous materials emergencies. Fire J 69:13–18

Croskerry P (2002) Achieving quality in clinical decision making: cognitive strategies and detection of bias. Acad Emerg Med 9:1184–1204

Croskerry P, Singhal G, Mamede S (2013) Cognitive debiasing 1:origins of bias and theory of debiasing. BMJ Qual Saf 22:ii58–ii64

Dobelli R (2013) The art of thinking clearly. Sceptre Books, London

Dörner D (1996) The logic of failure. Recognizing and avoiding error in complex situations. Metropolitan Books, New York

Dörner D, Schaub H (1994) Errors in planning and decision-making and the nature of human information processing. Appl Psychol Int Rev 43:433–453

Dreyfus HL, Dreyfus SE (2000) Mind over machine: the power of human intuition and expertise in the era of the computer, 5th edn. Blackwell, Oxford

Gaba D (1992) Dynamic decision-making in anesthesiology: cognitive models and training approaches. In: Evans DA, Patel VL (eds) Advanced models of cognition for medical training and practice. Springer, Berlin/Heidelberg/New York, pp 123–148

Goldhaber-Fiebert S, Howard SK (2013) Implementing emergency manuals: can cognitive aids help translate best practices for patient care during acute events? Anesth Analg 117(5):1149–1161

Graber ML, Kissam S, Payne VL, Meyer AND, Sorensen A, Lenfestey N, Tant E, Henriksen K, LaBresh K, Sing H (2012) Cognitive Interventions to reduce diagnostic error: a narrative review. BMJ Qual Saf 21:535–557

Hoermann HJ (1995) FOR-DEC. A prescriptive model for aeronautical decision-making. In: Fuller R, Johnston N, McDonald N (eds) Human factors in aviation operations. Proceedings of the 21st conference of the European Association for Aviation psychology (EAAP), vol 3. Avebury Aviation, Aldershot. pp 17–23

Jensen RS (1995) Pilot judgement and crew resource management. Ashgate Publishing, Burlington

Murray WB, Foster PA (2000) Crisis resource management among strangers: principles of organizing a multidisciplinary group for crisis resource management. J Clin Anesth 12:633–638

Oesterreich R (1981) Handlungsregulation und Kontrolle [Action regulation and control]. Urban and Schwarzenberg, Munich

Orasanu J, Connolly T (1992) The reinvention of decision-making. In: Klein G, Orasanu J, Calderwood R, Zsamboka E (eds) Decision-making in action: models and methods. Ablex, Norwood, pp 3–20

Reason J (1990) Human error. Cambridge University Press, Cambridge

Risser DT, Rice MM, Salisbury ML, Simon R, Jay GD, Berns SD (1999) The potential for improved teamwork to reduce medical errors in the emergency department. The MedTeams Research Consortium. Ann Emerg Med 34:373–383

Runciman WB (1988) Crisis management. Anaesth Intensive Care 16:86–88

Small SD, Wuerz RC, Simon R, Shapiro N, Conn A, Setnik G (1999) Demonstration of high-fidelity simulation team training for emergency medicine. Acad Emerg Med 6:312–323

Stiegler MP, Tung A (2014) Cognitive processes in anesthesiology decision making. Anesthesiology 120:204–217

Stiegler MP, Ruskin KJ (2012) Decision-making and safety in anesthesiology. Curr Opin Anaesthesiol 25(6):724–729

Trowbridge RL (2003) Twelve tips for teaching avoidance of diagnostic errors. Med Teach 30:496–500

Part III

The Team

Part II dealt with the "psycho-logic" of cognition, emotion, and intention and the different factors that influence a healthcare provider's behavior in a critical situation. Patient care, however, is seldom an individual's enterprise: There are always people from different professional groups and specialties involved. Teams are more than just the sum of individuals. Teams have their own strengths and weaknesses and can develop a specific dynamic. Part III deals with teamwork in a high-stakes environment from a human factors point of view.

The main questions are:

- What requirements do teams in an acute care setting have to meet?
- What are the typical team-related errors?
- What are the characteristics of good communication in critical situations? What are typical communication problems?
- What role does leadership play in the successful management of emergency situations? What characterizes a good leader and what problems may arise with leadership?

Teamwork does not only depend on the people involved in direct patient care but also on the organization in which the team works. The organization sets the organizational frame for teamwork and allocates resources to care. Organizations that encourage good teamwork vis-à-vis the culture and organization, such as enabling regular team meetings and providing team training and practice using simulation, are likely to see safer and more effective patient care. The implementation of teams into the greater concept of "an organization" is the subject matter of Part IV.

The Key to Success: Teamwork

11

Case Study

A worker in a printshop attempts to remove a foreign object from moving print cylinders. During a brief moment of inattention, the cylinders catch the sleeves of his shirt and both of his arms are drawn into the machine. Despite a nearly instantaneous shut down of the equipment by one of his colleagues, both arms are trapped up to the elbows. Because of the unusual circumstance, EMS dispatch decides to send a physician to the scene along with the ambulance. When the emergency physician, a senior resident in emergency medicine, arrives at the scene with two paramedics, he finds a patient with a reduced level of consciousness standing in front of the print cylinders. The worker's colleagues are supporting him in a standing position. With the help of the paramedics, the physician places a large-bore peripheral IV line in a vein of the dorsal foot and starts volume resuscitation. With repetitive small boluses of ketamine and midazolam, the patient receives adequate analgesia and sedation, while the two paramedics with help from two workers construct a small temporary platform adjacent to the print cylinders. Assessment of the situation by the machine technician reveals a difficult and protracted disassembly. Since the printshop is not far from the local hospital, the emergency physician contacts the operating room and requests a surgeon and anesthesiologist to come to the scene. Because the patient is young and an amputation would impose severe risks, the emergency physician and surgeon decide not to amputate the patient's extremities. Meanwhile, the fire department arrives and, after the anesthetist has deepened the analgesia and sedation, help the machine technician with the difficult task of disassembling the press. Two hours later, both arms are freed from the printing machine. Sudden pulsating bleeding is stopped by the inflation of upper extremity tourniquets that the paramedics had placed on both arms before they were released from the machine. The patient is intubated on site and transferred to the operating room. Due to the rapid and coordinated rescue and surgical intervention, both extremities are saved with a good degree of functionality.

M. St.Pierre et al., *Crisis Management in Acute Care Settings*,
DOI 10.1007/978-3-319-41427-0_11

Both the trauma mechanism as well as the pattern of injury of this occupational accident pose complex demands on the medical treatment of the entrapped patient. The temporary team of physicians from different specialties, paramedics, fire rescue workers, and employees of the printing plant successfully coped with the challenge because all the necessary tasks were managed by sharing and contributing the skills and experience of all team members. Together, they achieved teamwork at its finest.

11.1 The Team

11.1.1 Why Teamwork Has Come into Focus Only Lately

Teamwork is the cooperative effort by members of a group or team to achieve a common goal. Wherever ill or injured people are cared for, healthcare providers will take care of their patients in groups of two or more people. Therefore, teamwork is an inherent feature of healthcare; there is virtually no modern healthcare without teamwork. Despite this fundamental feature, the medical community traditionally neglected this issue until a few years ago. The reasons for that are manifold.

First, the widespread tendency of the healthcare community not to think in team concepts may reflect a *deep-seated cultural issue*: Many team members in Western societies are children of a culture that has come to cherish the individual human being in an unprecedented way. The pursuit of individual happiness and the fulfillment of personal agendas are unchallenged goals of our culture and have strongly affected the way we perceive human relationships.

Secondly, compared to other high-risk industries such as nuclear power and aviation, healthcare has been slow to regulate itself. The traditional culture, now slowly changing, has been that physicians are largely independent practitioners who make decisions with little oversight or accountability.

In addition, the foundations for a preference of individual proficiencies over social competence are laid early on. From birth through college, we nurture and praise the individual accomplishments of our children, as well as admire their cognitive faculties and the new skills they acquire. Collectively, we communicate the message that the most important is what an individual can successfully accomplish single-handedly. The basic presumption that individual technical expertise will guarantee a desirable outcome has further found expression in the medical and nursing educational cultures. Healthcare providers have been taught isolated technical tasks or clinical algorithms but have not been taught to perform in a team environment nor familiarized with basic concepts of communication and team performance (Leonard et al. 2004). In short, contemporary Western culture has produced a medical community wherein medical quality and safety have historically been viewed as dependent on the performance of expert individual practitioners.

While there has been extensive scientific work on requirements for successful teamwork within other industries and professions, the medical community has only recently started to address and implement relevant teamwork concepts.

Perhaps one of the reasons for this translational gap is that healthcare providers traditionally favor "hard facts" over any kind of "soft science" originating from human factors research or from psychology and organizational studies (Rice 2009). Thus, it has been silently assumed that effective communication and teamwork are adequate for daily clinical practice. Simply put, teamwork has not been a valued skill in the medical community. It is only in the last decade or so that parts of the healthcare community have come to accept the fact that healthcare provides no exception to the rule that a team of experts does not make an expert team. The necessary teamwork skills, like any other skills, have to be learned and practiced (Chap. 16).

Another important reason has been identified as a contributor to insufficient team performance and miscommunication: the *power relationships* that exist in healthcare. In nearly all healthcare organizations, there exist different groups or workers and clinicians with traditionally different statuses. Healthcare organizations tend to be dominated by a strongly hierarchical structure with a concept of leadership that resembles more of an authoritarian, military-like model rather than the mature interaction of adult healthcare providers (Firth-Cozens 2004). Ideally, critical information should flow freely among all team members, with all – regardless of professional status – empowered to ask questions and to voice concerns if they believe that a planned action may result in less than optimal care or harm the patient. However, unbalanced power relationships result in a steep "authority gradient" (Chap. 12). Open dialogue within the team is impaired or even rendered impossible. The authority gradient creates a team climate that globally discourages employees to come forward with questions and concerns and often denies them the ability to fully exercise their skills in service to the patient.

Considering the prevalence of this mindset, it is not surprising that for decades the concept of teamwork has largely been reduced to a gathering of people who give and take orders. But even when a teamwork concept is embraced, physicians and nurses nevertheless have different attitudes about the teamwork they experience with each other, including issues such as suboptimal skills with regard to conflict resolution and interpersonal communication (Makary et al. 2006; Thomas et al. 2003; Undre et al. 2006). Furthermore, there seems to be a difference between novice and senior physicians of the same discipline (Flin et al. 2006) and between physicians of different disciplines (Ummenhofer et al. 2001).

Teamwork failures have increasingly been noted as causes of mishaps in healthcare. This is partly due to the fact that there is more awareness of human factors these days than before. The other reason for increased attention to teamwork is that medical mishaps and error analyses have shown that as much as 50–70 % of medical errors are due to failures in communication and teamwork. When looking at healthcare mishaps, it's clear that clinical skills, drug administration, and device-related errors are less and less of a factor; and human factors and communication are increasingly found to be a primary or contributing factor. This phenomenon is exactly what happened in aviation: as the field experienced significant technical advances, the proportion of mishaps owing to teamwork and communication failures grew to as much as 70–80 %.

11.1.2 Why Teamwork Is Necessary

Fortunately, the past decade has witnessed an increasing concern among specialties involved in acute medical care about the fundamentals of successful teamwork. Stimulated by a large body of evidence from other high-stakes environments (e.g., civil and military aviation, military command operations, nuclear power plants, offshore oil platforms), healthcare providers started to analyze the antiquated approach to teamwork within their own fields of expertise and have tried to adopt and integrate team training measures.

From a task perspective, this approach to teamwork is long overdue. Many tasks impose mental and physical demands that are too strenuous even for the most experienced individual to perform in isolation. Furthermore, the required tasks in highly technical and specialized environments demand that different groups of professionals cooperate if a problem is to be dealt with successfully. The case study at the beginning of this chapter represents such an interprofessional team approach.

The strongest support, however, for a cultural change and for a focus on teamwork in healthcare comes from the extensive body of research that has been directed at identifying the factors that contribute to an undesired patient care event. Working groups from different healthcare environments have identified unequivocally a close relationship between teamwork and performance in a high-stakes environment (e.g., Weaver et al. 2014; Reader et al. 2006; Jain et al. 2006; Risser et al. 1999, 2000; Wheelan et al. 2003). Poor teamwork and weak communication between members of healthcare teams have emerged as key factors in poor care and medical errors (Barrett et al. 2001; Morey et al. 2002). An observational study in the OR showed that 30 % of communication incidents were faulty and led to consequences for the patient (Lingard et al. 2004). Another survey carried out in hospital emergency showed that insufficient teamwork was responsible for 43 % of all medical errors (whereby 8.8 errors were made in average per patient). In addition, team members often failed to question actions of teammates, even when serious concerns about the adequacy of a diagnosis or a treatment existed (Fig. 11.1; Risser et al. 2000).

One of the consistently found reasons for poor team formation and teamwork is the lack of a shared understanding about the necessity and function of teamwork. As a result, emerging conflicts among team members and a breakdown in communication impair collaboration and result in an underutilization or misallocation of available resources.

Despite the delayed introduction of teamwork concepts in healthcare, there is a growing awareness of the significance of communication and team coordination for efficient task management in critical situations and the need to strive for the cultural change that is needed to support a new approach to providing care in a teamwork environment. Interviews with all specialties of acute medical care have yielded comparable results: Healthcare providers in the operating room (e.g., Flin et al. 2003a; Helmreich and Schaefer 1994; Schaefer et al. 1995; Sexton et al. 2006), emergency departments (e.g., Barrett et al. 2001; Cole and Crichton 2006; Morey et al. 2002; Risser et al. 1999), adult intensive care units (e.g., Brown et al. 2003; Kaissi et al. 2003; Ohlinger et al. 2003; Reader et al. 2006; Sherwood et al. 2002;

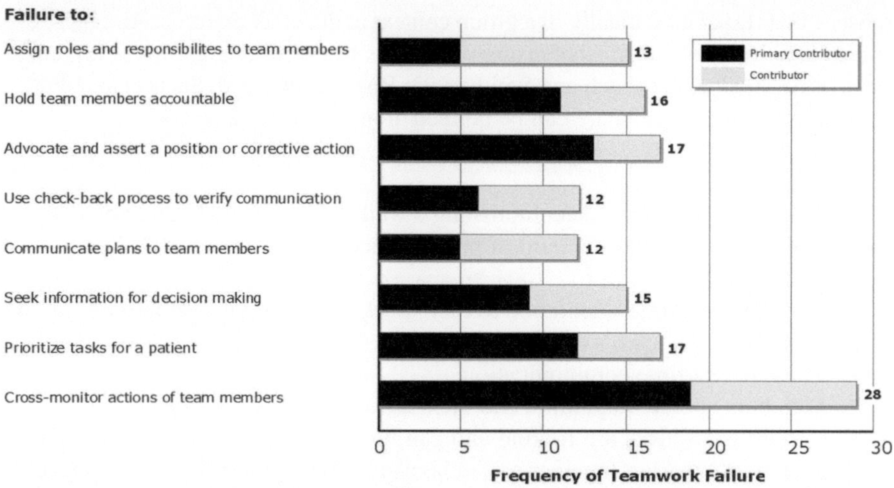

Fig. 11.1 The most frequent teamwork errors. Depicted is the data of 54 cases from 11 cooperating hospitals of retrospective emergency department closed-claims review where poor teamwork was judged to have contributed to clinical error (From Risser et al. 2000)

Thomas et al. 2004), pediatric intensive care units (Brown et al. 2003), labor and delivery units (Guise and Segel 2008), and preclinical emergency medicine (Matera 2003) acknowledge the importance of human factors issues and conclude that training measures are necessary to improve their teamwork skills and enhance patient safety.

The fact that the incidence of unwanted events correlates with the quality of the teamwork can also be proved reversely: In several studies, quality of acute medical care was improved, and error and incident rates were reduced through effective communication and good teamwork. Therefore, it has become clear that there is a correlation between the quality of team processes on the one side and treatment processes and patient outcomes on the other (overviews in Weaver et al. 2014; Schmutz u. Manser 2013; Salas et al. 2008). For this reason, the promotion of team skills and widespread systematic team training is fundamental for patient safety within acute medical care.

11.1.3 What Is a Team?

Although the term *team* has been used repeatedly in the preceding text, it is worthwhile to clearly define the type of team found in acute care. The definition of the term *team* has been the subject of lengthy and controversial discussions within the scientific community. Research in team psychology has provided differing conceptual frameworks and theories concerning the nature of teams and team performance. Types of teams can be conceived to fall on a continuum, with highly structured, interdependent teams at one extreme and teams whose members interact minimally and perform most of their tasks individually in a group context at the other extreme. And there are shared definitions of "team" that distinguish teams from working groups or organizations (Kriz 2000; Katzenbach and Smith 1993; Risser et al. 2000; Salas et al. 1998).

A team in acute healthcare can be defined along three dimensions:

1. Mission and Goals
   - Teams are oriented to accomplishing a well-defined, time-bound objective.
   - There is a definable standard of performance.
2. Performance
   - Teams have a time orientation to their work. There is an identifiable start and stop time for a team's tasks and mission.
   - There is real-time communication.
   - Members operate in parallel and their actions must be coordinated.
   - Certain team tasks are routine and can be choreographed or scripted. Other aspects of working together are ad hoc and can be guided by teamwork rules and principles.
   - Decision-making takes place (planned or on the fly) that affects the team's actions and performance.
   - Teams manage their resources through awareness of team members' workloads.
   - It is possible to plan and critique performance.
   - A team can improve its performance through practice.
3. Membership
   - Individuals can identify themselves as a member of the team.
   - Team membership is structured. Team members understand the roles of leader and follower. There are opportunities for emergent leadership and followership roles depending on the demands of the situation and team member skills.
   - Team membership is initially defined by the skills of each member. There is partial overlap of skills among at least some of the team members so that workload can be distributed.
   - Based on structure and skill criteria for team membership, it is possible to partition responsibilities.
   - During the temporal life of the team, the team's mission is superordinate to the goals of the individual.

11.1.4 The Strength of Teamwork

Whenever people work together as a team in complex situations and under time pressure, it is expected that team performance will exceed the sum of individual actions. Several reasons account for the strength of teamwork:

- Different talents and abilities can be used strategically as strengths and not as a factor of competition.
- Larger amounts of cognitive and attentional capacity are available because of the many eyes, ears, and minds involved. More information can be gathered and

processed. With this, more substantiated decisions are possible when communication works well.

- More views and alternatives can be brought to light. It is possible that a more comprehensive picture of the current situation will emerge. This in turn helps the team leader plan and make decisions.
- Mutual monitoring can help notice individual and team errors.
- Shared workload can help prevent work overload of an individual and make sure that all planned and required tasks can be executed in a timely manner.
- Mutual support can encourage and enable team members to master even the most difficult situations.

11.2 Team Performance: Input Factors

Team performance research has been able to define major factors that affect the way a team will cope with a given task. Integrating these data into a conceptual framework, several theoretical models have been proposed (for an overview, see Salas et al. (1998)). Despite the diversity of the models, they share an understanding that defines team performance as the result of how (process, throughput) a team utilizes its human and technical resources given a specific situational and task context (input factors). Results of team performance (output) in healthcare are first of all safe patient care, but also error incidence, working climate, and team member satisfaction (Salas et al. 1998; Mickan and Rodger 2000; Paris et al. 2000). Knowledge of these factors is necessary for the advancement of teamwork training programs in healthcare. Additionally teamwork knowledge can help sensitize healthcare professionals and healthcare educators to team processes that can serve as guidelines for strategies in team training (Chap. 16). It is recognized that teamwork skills and knowledge are not a substitute for clinical skills, rules, and knowledge; they are the tool with which clinical skills are used. Fig. 11.2 is a conceptual depiction of an integrated model of team performance in a healthcare high-stakes environment.

The input factors for team performance can be subdivided into:

- Individual characteristics
- Team characteristics
- Characteristics of the task (“emergency”)
- Characteristics of the performance environment

11.2.1 Individual Characteristics

Every team member brings a set of individual characteristics (attitudes, motivation, personality) and individual skills (experience and skills in clinical care, communication, and human factors) to the team. In addition to individual skills, team members need team skills. Team skills are a set of skills that individuals must develop to

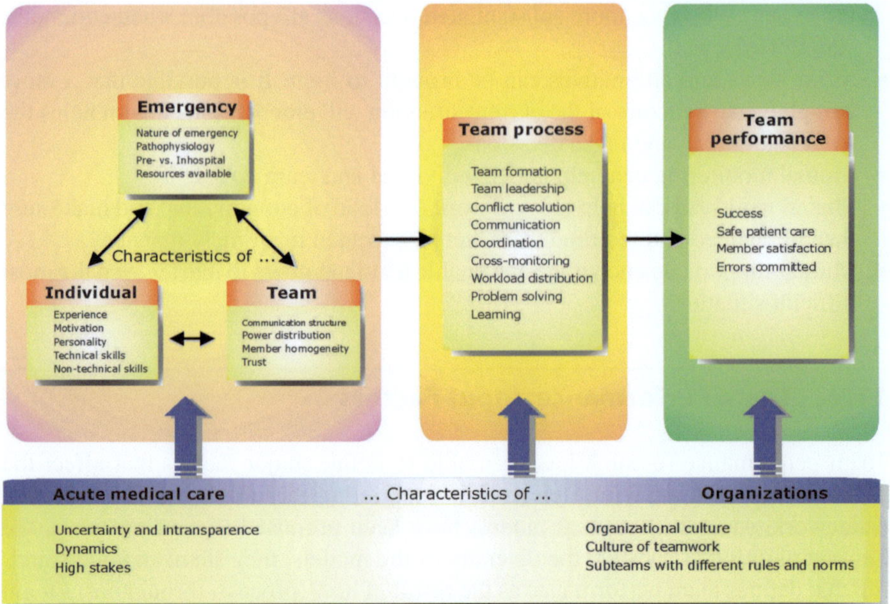

Fig. 11.2 Integrated model of team performance in a medical high-stakes environment. Successful teamwork is the result of an interaction of work and task characteristics, team characteristics (individual, team), and the team process over time. The organizational and situational characteristics influence input and process. The model is based on the theoretical framework of Salas et al. (1998)

function effectively in a team: effective communication, adaptation to varying situational demands, compensatory behavior, mutual performance monitoring, and giving and receiving feedback (Burke et al. 2004). These team skills ensure that team members' abilities will be complementary and combined to manage resources and to form professional relationships that enhance team performance. Thus, sometime soon (and in acute healthcare settings, this should be very soon), clinicians will experience a merging of clinical skills with teamwork skills to perform successfully.

In actuality, the individual's personal performance on the team can be understood as the product of three factors: individual characteristics, individual skills, and teamwork skills.

Another way to define this is: Personal performance on the team = individual characteristics × individual skills × teamwork skills. Describing team performance as a product shows that each factor is necessary. Personality conflicts and varying levels of individual proficiencies can degrade team performance.

Certain skills have been identified that characterize a successful team player. A successful team player can:

- Listen and participate actively
- Ask the right questions

- Hold an opinion and then change points of view
- Assess and value the qualities of other team members
- Assess what he or she can do best and appreciate where others have more experience and skills
- Keep to an agreement and identify with a task
- Be self-critical
- Solve conflicts in a constructive way

Teams whose members perform in a team-oriented and cooperative way are demonstrably more successful than teams with team members who equate success with competition (Driskell u. Salas 1992).

11.2.2 Team Characteristics

General team characteristics define the team as an entity: team size, group cohesiveness, intra- and inter-team cooperation, power distribution within the team, communication patterns among team members, and the homogeneity and heterogeneity of the team members. For these factors, desirable attributes have been described for teams in a high-stakes environment such as industrial or military teamwork. The research is based mainly on established teams that have a life span of weeks or months in the formation of an identity.

Acute healthcare specialists, however, are more like teams in aviation because healthcare teams usually work with "temporary" teams that are gathered in a random fashion ("*ad hoc teams*"). For instance, the odds are low that the same group of emergency medical technicians, physicians, and firefighters will ever again be dispatched for another medical emergency.

As a result, successful teams in high-stakes healthcare environments show, in addition to the general characteristics of teams, a range of additional features and problems:

- *Teams in an acute medical care setting often have to organize themselves "on the fly:"* The acute healthcare setting requires the organization of caregivers – who may be strangers from diverse disciplines who do not know one another's roles or special skills and may even be uncertain about one another's goals – into "ad hoc" teams (Murray and Foster 2000). Task demands ("treating the patient") and social demands ("getting acquainted with each other") have to be implemented in parallel and without any delay. In the example case, the team met for the first time in the printshop while the severely injured patient needed immediate attention.
- *The team is defined functionally:* The task distribution during the parallel medical treatment and technical rescue operation is specified by profession and status and does not have to be negotiated. Nevertheless, some changes in function can be made during the treatment. For instance, the emergency physician assigned the induction and maintenance of anesthesia to the anesthesiologist and left the

treatment of the extremity to the surgeon. The fact that role expectancies do not have to be negotiated anew in every single case is important for the strength of ad hoc teams (*action teams*; Manser 2009), in which team members have little or no experience working together, e.g., operating room, intensive care unit, EMS, and emergency departments.

- *Teams in an acute healthcare setting are hierarchical*: Hierarchy is necessary because in most emergent or acute emergencies there has to be one responsible decision-maker. Hierarchy supports the management of critical situations by clear paths of information flow and decision-making. Hierarchy can hinder problem solving, on the other hand. For instance, instead of actively participating in the acquisition of data and contributing to finding the best treatment options, team members might be inclined to leave everything to the team leader.
- *The team often consists of various specialties or disciplines with specific rules and different ways to handle a situation:* Multidisciplinary teamwork is a characteristic feature of acute healthcare. The major prerequisite for successful teamwork with an interdisciplinary or interprofessional team is communication to develop a shared understanding of the situation and what must be done.
- *External circumstances can render teamwork difficult:* Teamwork in acute healthcare has to function under emotional strain, often coordinating with strangers and in less than ideal physical circumstances. EMS, firefighter/rescue personnel, and various clinical specialists in this chapter's scenario could not provide acute medical care in the tidy and ordered interior of an ambulance or hospital but were literally bound to a small temporary platform adjacent to the print cylinders.
- *Decision-making is embedded in performance:* Team tasks differ in the centrality of decision-making in their activities (Orasanu and Salas 1993). While decision-making can be the central task for some teams (e.g., tactical command and control), teams in an acute healthcare setting have to decide and take action at the same time. If attention focuses strongly on a physical task, this will impair the decision-making process and increase the chances for ineffective or error-prone care. Thus, it is best to explicitly allocate decision-making and task performance among the team.

11.2.3 Task Characteristics

Tasks arise due to an outside set of stimuli to which a team must respond in a coordinated and timely fashion. The team's response depends highly on the characteristics of the task assigned: Tasks differ in their complexity (Xiao et al. 1996), in task organization (i.e., the degree of interdependencies that exist between various subtasks), and in task structure (i.e., the manner in which subtasks are assigned to and shared by various team members and different professional groups). These task characteristics have a strong impact on the communication structure of a team. If few interdependencies exist among subtasks (i.e., low demand for task organization), team members will focus almost exclusively on performance of their assigned subtask. An example would be a domestic fire with the firefighters making their way through smoke-filled passages to rescue people who are trapped in the burning structure while the Emergency Medical Team is treating patients with smoke inhalation in the safety of the ambulance. However, if subtasks of teams are highly interrelated (as in the case of the printshop injury), the communication structure has to be elaborate and comprehensive to synchronize the different subteams. In the case of the printshop mishap, team members must communicate frequently and clearly to coordinate the flow of individual work.

Another aspect of the task is what resources are at hand. External and internal resources can limit or expand the possibilities for successful team performance. Equipment, staffing, and availability of special treatment options have an impact on whether or not a decision can be executed.

11.2.4 Characteristics of the Performance Environment

Task characteristics become especially important in the environment of high-stakes healthcare. The foregoing case study calls attention to several characteristics of the environment healthcare providers find themselves in:

- The task environment is characterized by dynamic complexity, uncertainty, and tight coupling, i.e., wherein decisions carry substantial risk in a time compressed environment. There are several unique features that characterize decision-making and action in a healthcare high-stakes environment. They are explained in detail in Chap. 2.
- External circumstances affect teamwork. Time and space matter in healthcare. Decisions have to be made under time pressure – the patient trapped in the press has little time to wait for the team to organize. "Space" in acute healthcare incidents often means "little or no space" – the treatment of the patient on site or in an ambulance demands the ability to work in close physical proximity to teammates and to coordinate actions with precision. In preclinical trauma patient care, prehospital providers may have difficulty accessing the victim. In the present case study, the treatment of the patient cannot be performed in the familiarity of an ambulance. Instead the victim's entrapped arms demand care that has to be provided in an unusual and unfamiliar setting. The problem of inaccessibility also applies in a moderate way to patients on ICUs whose access may be impeded behind respirators, monitoring lines, and instruments, and a multitude of tubes and IV lines.
- The task type can vary considerably. Thus, acute care teams must have or be able to access a broad spectrum of clinical skills, rules, and knowledge. In every healthcare specialty, providers can be confronted with a great variety of medical or trauma emergencies. In addition, several specialties (e.g., anesthesia, emergency medicine) have to deal with a broad spectrum of patient characteristics (e.g., from neonatal to geriatric multimorbid patients) demanding very different sets of clinical abilities.

11.3 Team Process

Team processes are intertwined with the way team members communicate and coordinate their activities. Team processes have been an important focus for team research because they determine whether teams will be effective or ineffective. The individual characteristics that make a team member a good team player have already been listed. However, a successful outcome of teamwork requires adequate interaction of all team members involved. Several models (Fleishmann and Zaccaro 1992) have identified team process factors that enable, support, and enhance team performance (Table 11.1). Team processes are a management tool to expedite high-quality care to patients. They give caregivers increased control over a constantly changing environment and form a safety net that helps protect patients and healthcare providers from the consequences of inevitably occurring errors (Sexton 2004). Teamwork will only function in critical situations if team processes are exercised and perfected

Table 11.1 Characteristics of a good team process in a medical high-stakes environment

Team process factor	Action
Team formation and positive team climate	Develop a "we" feeling
	Demonstrate mutual respect in all communications
Establish team leadership	Encourage leadership behavior in non-routine situations
	Establish a team leader
	Assign roles and responsibilities
Solve conflicts constructively	Try to see the positive aspects of a conflict
	Avoid struggle for power with team members
	Focus on "what is right" not "who is right"
Apply problem-solving strategies	Whenever appropriate, use problem-solving strategies (e.g., FOR-DEC, DECIDE)
Communicate and share mental models	Create a "psychologically safe" environment for team members to speak up
	Offer and request information
	Develop and verbally maintain a shared mental model
Coordinate task execution	Profit from implicit coordination and strive for explicit coordination
	Coordinate planned actions
Cross-monitor teammates	Monitor teammates' performance
	Address critical issues
	Anticipate possible results
Share workload and be true to your performance limits	Monitor the workload of team members
	Offer backup behavior
	Communicate clearly, when you have reached your performance limit
Improve team skills	Engage in informal and formal team training measures (personal feedback, team debriefing, simulation)

After the MedTeams Project; Risser et al. (2000)

through frequent practice – that is, we have to practice teamwork so that in an emergency we can rely on it.

11.3.1 Team Formation and Positive Working Climate

Good teamwork provides the foundation to accomplish daily operational task objectives, but it does not simply "happen." Rather, it must be taught, consciously implemented, reinforced, and maintained. Teamwork grows in a trustful, cooperative climate that has to be nurtured, for example, by respectful communication. Only within a psychologically safe work environment will employees mention seemingly "unimportant" information or concerns about the safety of planned actions. Team formation is a leadership task *and* the task of every single member. The cohesion within the team and respectful interpersonal relationships play a vital role in the successful management of a critical situation.

11.3.2 Establish Team Leadership

The clinical leadership role in an in-hospital emergency is usually assigned to a physician, whereas in the case of on-scene management, the leadership role can vary between different people (e.g., emergency physician, EMS team leader, chief firefighter), depending on which task is being executed at the moment (e.g., medical treatment, technical rescue). In some emergencies (i.e., cardiac arrest in the general ward), the performance environment may be noisy and chaotic, with many people involved. When emergent events occur in unusual places or under unusual circumstances, it is common to have confusion about who is the clinical leader. In this case, the person best capable of managing the crisis should actively take the role of clinical team leader. This is especially important for situations with an unrehearsed group that is called together in an emergency from different disciplines and professional groups (Murray and Foster 2000). This kind of emergent leadership behavior should be encouraged in unstructured situations. But in routine tasks where roles and functions are clear, it should be crystal clear if who is the clinical leader.

Many hospitals are adopting an organizational approach to high-stakes situations and have two leaders with different functions. One is the clinical leader, usually a physician, who leads the multidisciplinary team in the clinical care of the patient. The other is an event manager, often a nurse, who takes charge of resourcing the event, e.g., calling for pharmacy and respiratory therapy, allowing people into the room and asking others to leave, calling for equipment, etc.

Good leaders change their focus frequently between ensuring that clinical tasks are executed and that team coordination is maintained. A good clinical leader seeks to prevent overload of individual team members by distributing responsibility and workload in a well-balanced way and insists on good two-way communication. A good event manager ensures that the right people, equipment, and medications are available.

11.3.3 Solve Conflicts in a Constructive Way

Conflicts are an inherent part of team performance. Whenever different people assess a situation, different points of view will emerge because everybody has unique motivations, knowledge, and information about the situation. In this respect, conflicts are necessary, helpful, and constructive. The contribution of diverse opinions can support a team to get a more comprehensive picture of a situation. However, if conflicts turn into power struggles, they become destructive: "Who's right" instead of "what's right" is the kind of conflict that will invariably and severely impair team performance. As a general rule, *relational conflicts* should not be addressed in an emergency situation but rather in a follow-up discussion, when stress has eased and emotions have calmed down. In contrast, *task-related conflicts* (e.g., the choice of the right treatment) should always be resolved even if it seems cumbersome. In addition, each team member should feel empowered to speak up and voice concerns so that all arguments and all information flow into decision-making. While the contribution of the team members is crucial for decision-making, professional conflicts are not solved democratically. The leader makes the decisions and is responsible for them.

11.3.4 Apply Problem-Solving Strategies

The medical care of the patient with two entrapped arms is not an everyday problem. As a result, the practical approach to this problem cannot be deduced from a rule but instead needs team-based problem solving. Critical situations with moderate time pressure are best solved when a problem-solving strategy is applied. One way to strengthen this process is to apply problem-solving strategies that contain all essential steps. Two example strategies, DECIDE and FOR-DEC, were discussed in Chap. 10.

11.3.5 Communicate and Share Mental Models

Only the information that team members verbally communicate to their teammates will contribute to the overall situation awareness and to decision-making (Leonard et al. 2004). Only when team members feel psychologically safe within the team environment will they speak up when they have information or concerns. By psychologically safe, we mean that individuals feel safe to state their observations and concerns without fear of being ridiculed or embarrassed and that they will be respected and valued team members. Good communication in critical situations is aimed at creating a shared mental model of patient-related and operational issues, thereby "getting everyone on the same page."

The term "shared mental model" (Chap. 10) refers to the team members' knowledge and beliefs concerning the task, the relevant environment, the role and functions of each team member, and the available resources (Cannon-Bowers et al.

1993). When team members reach a shared understanding of these factors, they can coordinate their actions and, through ongoing communication and updates, adapt to the demands of the task and the team.

Developing shared mental models for a problem creates a context within which decisions can be made and the cognitive resources of the entire team can be exploited (Stout et al. 1999). Such shared knowledge enables each person to carry out his or her role in a timely and coordinated fashion, helping the team to function as a single unit with minimal negotiation of what to do and when to do it. The greater the degree of accuracy and overlap among team member mental models, the greater the likelihood that the team members will predict, adapt, and coordinate with one another successfully, even under stressful or novel conditions. Essential for the accuracy and commonality of the situational picture are regular updates of the members' mental models.

If teams want to achieve a shared mental model, they need time to communicate verbally, ideally before the start of the common task, e.g., during a team time-out before a surgical operation. Questions that help to build shared mental models:

- What is the patient's problem? What exactly are we going to do to help the patient?
- Who is on the team, what are our names, and what are our roles?
- What are the expectations for sender and receiver when speaking up and sharing information?
- What resources do we have? What resources might we need and how will we get them if needed?
- What problems might we expect during the procedure and, if they happen, what is the plan for managing and ameliorating them?
- Who in our team is responsible for which subtasks?

To maintain a common understanding, team situation awareness (Chap. 8) is needed. Team members should regularly scan the environment for relevant cues and patterns and then communicate information to the team. It is incumbent on all team members to help each other integrate new information into the team's existing knowledge structures and plans. A noteworthy axiom is that there is no chance that team members will see things similarly unless things are verbalized. Put another way, "Assumptions are the bedrock of mishaps in high-performance, high-stakes teams."

11.3.6 Coordinate Task Execution

Coordination of actions is necessary because of time pressure, differing technical knowledge and roles, and the need for parallel operations by team members. Shared mental models allow teams to anticipate, without too much talking, each other's resource needs and actions (implicit coordination), especially when workload becomes high and the amount of communication naturally decreases.

However, if teams rely too heavily on implicit coordination, they are prone to suddenly find themselves overwhelmed by a problem exactly because an individual's or the team's unspoken expectancies are not met. A good team process will be characterized by team members defining the problem much more explicitly, volunteering relevant information, articulating plans and strategies, discussing contingencies, explaining the rationale for a decision to all teammates, and by allocating and coordinating responsibilities within the team (explicit coordination).

11.3.7 Cross-Monitor Teammates

Complexity, coupling, and opacity increase the likelihood of errors. In order to mitigate the effects of inevitably occurring patient safety errors, healthcare providers should be encouraged to monitor their team members. They should ask critical questions and voice concerns if one believes that an action may harm the patient ("four-eyes principle," cross-monitoring) or if a plan or task may be less than optimal. If the clinical work environment actively embraces the idea of mutual monitoring for errors regardless of rank, discipline, or specialty, cross-monitoring will reduce clinical errors considerably. One caregiver's error can often be prevented or corrected by another caregiver. Cross-monitoring and speaking up implies a working climate of open communication and a willingness to accept help from others, irrespective of their professional status, i.e., a climate of "what's right" needs to predominate instead of "who's right." In an environment where this is not the case, slips, lapses, poorly executed actions, and faulty plans will go unnoticed or remain unchallenged. In a high-stakes performance environment where human fallibility is known and accepted to be always present, cross-monitoring has the power to provide a safety net that can protect both the patient and the caregiver.

11.3.8 Share Workload and Be Mindful of Performance Limits

Mutual monitoring is not confined to the detection of errors but also includes the workload status and the performance limits of each team member. High workload has been widely shown to degrade performance in individuals and to have a negative effect on team performance. In addition, high workload conditions increase the need for explicit coordination among team members (Urban et al. 1995). Critical situations can bring healthcare providers to a point where they may be overwhelmed by the task load and personal stress. Therefore, team members should make it a habit to monitor the workload of other members and to offer help early and readily. On the other hand, when team members feel that their personal limit is reached, they should communicate this to the team, e.g., "Things are going too fast for me, please slow down" or "I'm not ready yet, please do not continue. I'll tell you when"). Do not hesitate to ask for help!

11.3.9 Improve Teamwork Skills

Teamwork is not an automatic consequence of placing healthcare professionals together in the same shift or room. Teamwork depends highly on the set of social and interpersonal skills discussed in this book that should be taught in training programs in a systematic and efficient way. In order to achieve this objective, any training effort should be underpinned by a properly developed skills framework. Ideally, this skills framework should

- Have empirical data to substantiate learning activities and objectives
- Developed into structured skill and team taxonomies to facilitate instruction and
- Include feedback to the team vis-à-vis post-case debriefings that explores and rectifies gaps in team performance

Based on the framework of the European aviation marker system NOTECHS (NOn-TECHnical Skills; Flin et al. 2003b), several very similar sets of behavioral markers have been developed for healthcare. These adaptations of NOTECHS include ANTS for anesthetists (Fletcher et al. 2003), NOTSS for surgeons (Yule et al. 2006), OTAS for surgical teams (Healey et al. 2004), and UTNR for neonatal resuscitation teams (Thomas et al. 2004). Other frameworks include TeamSTEPPS (AHRQ 2008), MedTeams (Morey et al. 2002), and others.

Numerous healthcare team training programs have been developed and implemented in response to the patient safety crisis. Some of these programs are specialty-specific (e.g., anesthesia, obstetrics, pediatrics, emergency medicine), whereas others are multidisciplinary. Two complementary categories of team training have become widely used: programs that rely heavily on state-of-the-art simulators and others that primarily use didactic classroom team training (Overview in: Hunt et al. 2007; Sundar et al. 2007). With the recent advent of virtual worlds, a third team training opportunity is emerging that enables participants to engage in a multiplayer mode with standard in-hospital scenarios (Youngblood et al. 2008; Theodoropoulos et al. 2007) as well as with trauma and mass casualty scenarios in city buildings and on streets (Dev et al. 2007).

Whereas most of the simulation-based team trainings have adapted courses from Crew Resource Management (CRM) conducted in commercial and military aviation (e.g.; ACRM; Howard et al. 1992), classroom-based programs offer interactive training that incorporates facilitated discussion, role playing, case studies, behavior modeling, and knowledge testing. Many of the principles that are advocated and behaviors that are taught are similar across programs. The strongest team training programs will offer a combination of classroom and simulator training.

Although research unequivocally supports the notion that teamwork skills can be learned and systems can be designed to enhance team performance (e.g., Morey et al. 2002), the acquisition and maintenance of team behaviors requires a supportive organizational culture, sufficient time, and regular refresher and reinforcement training opportunities. Unfortunately, culture trumps training. A number of central aspects of team training (e.g., open communication, cross-monitoring, and speaking up across the authority gradient when necessary) run counter to the prevailing professional culture in most institutions. Thus, a critically important challenge facing the success of team training efforts will be to have leadership that clearly values clinical teamwork and to provide sustained on-the-job support and reinforcement.

11.4 Why Teamwork Can Go Wrong

Given that teams represent increased cognitive resources compared with individuals, we might take it for granted that teams perform better than individuals: After all, they represent multiple ears, eyes, and brains that can contribute a substantial amount of information, situational awareness, and proposed courses of action. In addition, workload can be shouldered by all team members. Yet the presence of others can actually degrade the performance of an individual team member. If basic principles of a successful team process are neglected or if teams operate under stress without support from other team members, internal team dynamics will develop that lead to lower performance of the whole team than what might have been expected from the sum of its parts (Badke-Schaub 2000; Schulz and Frey 1998; Orasanu and Salas 1993). What do we know about the underlying mechanisms?

11.4.1 Deficits of the Individual

Some teams fail to perform well because individual team members lack clinical or team skills. When individual skills are deficient, other team members must compensate accordingly. There are two problems that arise in this type of situation. First, team members must become aware that there is a skill deficiency. This is not always easy to know because clinically weak members often do not think of themselves as weak or may be unwilling or too uncomfortable to state their deficiency or lack of confidence. The second problem is that other team members, once they become aware of the deficiency, must spend some of their valuable attentional, cognitive, and physical resources to fill in where the team is weak.

While having sufficient clinical skills is one important aspect of having a strong team, there are other factors to consider as well. First, a team needs to be adequately structured for an individual to know what he or she is supposed to do, i.e., there must be role clarity. Second, team members must be willing to try to be good team players. There are people who simply don't want to or can't perform well in a team environment for reasons such as:

- Individual characteristics such as personality or behavioral characteristics (e.g., self-centeredness, excessive perfectionism)
- Absence of skills that support the team process (e.g., communication skills, physical limitations such myopia or late-onset hearing impairment). For exam-

ple, if a team leader lacks the necessary communication and leadership skills and ability, teamwork will become virtually impossible.

Besides being unable to be a good team player, there is also the possibility that a team member is unwilling to work with other members of a team. This may be the case if team members:

- Are forced to work as part of a team, although they actually prefer to work alone
- Have to cooperate with people they dislike
- Try to solve an interpersonal conflict with other team members (often from other specialties of professional groups) by means of a patient case
- Seek to use a team for their own interests
- Use their role within a team to resolve power issues
- Do not work with full motivation but let others do the work and benefit from teammates' efforts ("social loafing")

11.4.2 Deficits of the Team

11.4.2.1 Communication Deficit

Dynamic exchange of information and resources and coordination of actions are vital if a critical situation is to be managed successfully. Without communication, it is impossible to develop a shared understanding of the situation and to act in concert. If critical information is not shared, decisions will be made on the basis of less complete data. Misunderstandings can arise when mental models are not shared. Lack of communication leads to a failure to announce intended tasks and to a reluctance to challenge assumptions about the appropriateness of actions taken by other team members (Stout et al. 1999). Due to the vital importance of communication regarding team activity, Chap. 12 deals with the subject extensively.

11.4.2.2 Unclear Specification of Responsibility

If leadership is not clearly established in an unstructured situation, and if teams fail to agree on responsibilities in critical situations, we will see a diffusion of responsibility (Darley and Latane 1968): Some tasks (e.g., the easiest or least risky) tend to be addressed by several team members, although one person might have been enough and other tasks may remain undone because everybody expects somebody else to take care of it. When roles are not clear, time limits for critical tasks may pass without action because team members are unaware of their responsibilities nor the need for timely execution of assigned tasks. If several healthcare providers are in charge of an emergency without having agreed on a team leader, then the tendency for risky decisions may increase because nobody will have to fully account for the clinical care (*risk shift*; Kogan and Wallach 1969).

11.4.2.3 Shared Misconceptions

Teams and team members may develop different and unspoken conceptions of how the team should function. Some examples include:

- Teams can develop a tendency to follow a "majority rules" approach in their decision-making instead of rational arguments.
- Our psychological cognitive and affective dispositions to respond (Chaps. 6 and 10) can affect the entire team.
- Team members may assume that other members of the team know what to do without verbally coordinating decisions and actions.
- Individuals naturally tend to perceive that others on the team see things exactly the same way even though this is practically never correct.
- Successful teams, ones who've worked together before, may succumb to an *illusion of unanimity* and invulnerability. The internal reasoning goes along this line: "If every single team member agrees with a solution, it cannot be wrong." The pitfall is that because all team members are in agreement, they see no further need to discuss other possible options. Thus, the search for solutions is abandoned too early. Expert opinion from outside the team is not requested and the team unknowingly suspends its rational judgment.

11.4.2.4 Development of Peer Pressure

If group cohesion is highly valued by the team, dissent and discussions are easily seen as a threat. Proposals from a leader unite the team in a course of action so they are not challenged. Once the majority of the team members have formed an opinion, they will stick to it even when faced with contradicting information that proves an opinion wrong and unrealistic. Criticism by dissenting members is suppressed; disagreement is seen as disruption. Team members are ignored or bullied instead of rationally convinced. The danger of peer pressure lies in the failure to rationally explore potential decisions and actions because only those pieces of information that confirm a decision or course of action are used in the decision-making process. In the context of peer pressure, the problem is that once a treatment path has been chosen, the team can become surprisingly inflexible to change because nobody expresses doubt or asks critical questions.

11.4.2.5 "In-Group" and "Out-Group"

The feeling of togetherness and mutual support can stimulate teams into exceptional and outstanding performance; however, if this feeling of togetherness becomes excessive, teams tend to set boundaries between themselves and other teams. This can also happen between subteams: "We" are right, "they" are wrong; "we" know best, "they" do not. Teamwork under these circumstances no longer encompasses all parties involved – group interests may unconsciously outweigh the interest for the patient's health.

11.4.2.6 Groupthink

Groupthink is a term applied to situations wherein a highly cohesive group subjected to considerable pressure tries to minimize conflict and reach consensus

Table 11.2 Eight symptoms indicative of groupthink

Illusion of invulnerability	Creates excessive optimism and encourages extreme risk taking
Illusion of unanimity	Resulting from self-censorship of deviations, and augmented by the false assumption that silence means consent, team members believe that all team members hold a common view
Collective rationalization	Discounts warnings, which might lead to reconsidering assumptions before recommitting to past decisions
Unquestioned morality	Inclines members to ignore the ethical or moral consequences of decisions because of unquestioned belief in the group's inherent morality
Stereotyped view	Characterizes the opposition as too evil for genuine negotiation or too weak and stupid to effectively oppose the group's purposes
Direct pressure	Discourages dissent by any member who expresses strong arguments against any of the group's stereotypes, illusions, or commitments
Self-censorship	Reduces deviations from the apparent group consensus, reflecting each member's inclination to minimize to himself the importance of his doubts and counter arguments
Self-appointed mindguards	Attempt to protect the team from adverse information that might shatter their shared complacency about the effectiveness and morality of their decisions

Adapted from Janis (1972)

without critically testing, analyzing, and evaluating all options (Janis 1972; Table 11.2). Although group cohesion has been shown to be the most important antecedent to groupthink, it will lead to groupthink only if one of the following two antecedent conditions is present:

- Structural faults in the organization: insulation of the group, lack of tradition of impartial leadership, lack of standard operating procedures, homogeneity of members' social background and ideology
- Provocative situational context: high stress from an emergency situation, recent failures, excessive difficulties with the decision-making, ethical dilemmas

In the context of acute medical care, provocative situational factors can prevail. The effect of acute stress and the feeling of incompetence can severely degrade a person's individual and teamwork abilities and propagate groupthink. Chapter 9 addresses the pathology of teamwork in emotionally strained situations.

11.4.2.7 The Organizational Context

The organizational context or environment surrounding a team plays an important role in groupthink. For example, although the emergency physician, the emergency medical technicians, and the firefighters were dispatched from different sites and from different organizational cultures, they are nevertheless embedded in larger organizations (e.g., hospital, EMS organization, fire department). An organization can impact teams working in their sphere of influence via:

- Structure of leadership
- Working climate, corporate identity
- “Us vs. Them” thinking, sometimes called “tribalism” in healthcare
- Safety culture
- Resource allocation

If the institutional culture tolerates disrespectful interactions among the different disciplines and specialties, this will negatively affect cooperation. Healthcare providers may not support one another more than absolutely necessary and a real team spirit will not develop. On the other hand, if senior healthcare providers (e.g., physicians, nurses) ask their coworkers to monitor their decisions and actions and give feedback on any concerns, then a top-down model encouraging safe behavior will develop.

Organizational deficiencies do not always lead immediately to bad teamwork. Highly motivated teams can compensate for these problems for a long time. For instance, during unusual, temporally bound situations like a staff shortage for a shift in an intensive care unit, personal commitment to patient care can increase. In the long run, however, this strategy will prove to be weak. Healthcare workers will become overstrained, motivation will diminish, and job satisfaction will decrease. And staff burnout will likely increase (Chap. 9).

On the other hand, the organizational context can support and reinforce competent teamwork by creating a supportive safety culture and by providing sufficient resources in terms of training, staff, equipment, and working conditions. This will positively affect the stress level of team members and the quality of team performance. A comprehensive information system, a functional educational system, and a reward system for safety-conscious performance can further propagate effective teamwork in a high-stakes environment. Chapter 15 covers this topic in greater detail.

11.5 Tips for Daily Practice

- If you want to benefit from a good team process in a critical situation, you need to rehearse team skills on a frequent basis. In an emergency situation, only well-developed habits and skills will be available (i.e., behavior that has been practiced time and again).
- Make respectful interactions a routine practice.
- When differences of opinion arise, focus on “what’s right” not “who’s right.”
- Clarify roles and functions in an emergency. You cannot manage without role clarity.
- People cannot read your mind. State your perceptions and opinions clearly!
- You will not succeed if you do not talk! Talking is the way team members develop and maintain a shared mental model.

- Employ a simple concept to effectively manage workload: Watch out whether your teammates need help or information and ask for help or information for yourself.
- Teamwork and leadership are tightly connected. Many team problems are really problems of insufficient leadership.
- Everybody who is involved in the immediate care of the patient belongs to the team.

11.6 "Teamwork" in a Nutshell

- Teamwork is the cooperative effort by members of a team to achieve a common goal.
- Teamwork is an inherent feature of healthcare.
- High-quality, safe patient care depends on outstanding teamwork.
- Poor teamwork and communication breakdowns between members of healthcare teams are involved in most of the mishaps in healthcare.
- Research conducted in a wide variety of work environments, such as aviation, special forces, athletic teams, etc., have identified a close relationship between teamwork and performance in a high-stakes environment.
- Member interdependency and the need for coordination are key characteristics of a team.
- Superb individual clinical skills do not guarantee effective team performance. Corollary: a team of experts does not make an expert team.
- Communication is at the core of team performance. With it, teams will form readily and perform well; without it, they may not function as a team at all.
- Team performance (output) is the result of how a team utilizes (process) its available human and material resources given a specific situational context (input factors). The results of good team performance are safe patient care, low error incidence, good working climate, and team member satisfaction.
- There are identifiable team process factors that enable, support, and enhance team performance. These processes can be identified, taught, and mastered.
- If people manage to work together as a good team, then the team's performance in complex situations and under time pressure is much more effective than the actions of an individual.
- Teams in acute medical care have their own characteristic features and specific problems; in other words, learning about teamwork in other industries such as nuclear power, commercial aviation, etc., will not solve a problem of weak teams in healthcare.
- Teamwork can fail because team members lack clinical skills.
- Individual clinical skills and knowledge are not sufficient for successful team performance; the collective resources of the team must be appropriately organized and utilized through interaction processes.
- Communication is used to build shared situational mental models that are especially important when conditions demand nonhabitual responses. Once shared

models have been created, they provide a context for interpreting information, making decisions, taking actions, and adjusting a plan.
- A high level of situation awareness also provides a basis for predicting the needs of other team members.
- The old adage, "There is no I in TEAMWORK," it turns out, is well supported by research.
- The presence of others who are perceived by teammates as a threat or as being rude and disrespectful can degrade the performance of an individual team member. Dysfunctional personal relationships will negatively impact team performance.
- Teamwork behaviors and skills are teachable.
- Expert teams have been trained in both task work and teamwork skills.
- Organizations can reinforce good teamwork by creating a culture of mutual respect among caregivers, valuing patient safety, and by providing sufficient resources in terms of staff, training, and equipment.

References

AHRQ (2008) TeamSTEPPS. Strategies and tools to enhance performance and patient safety. AHRQ Pub. No 06-0020-2

Badke-Schaub P (2000) Wenn der Gruppe Flügel fehlen: Ungeeignete Informations- und Entscheidungsprozesse in Gruppen [Inadequate decision-making and information processing in groups]. In: Mey H, Lehmann Pollheimer D (eds) Absturz im freien Fall oder Anlauf zu neuen Höhenflügen. Vdf, Zürich, pp S 113–S 130

Barrett J, Gifford C, Morey J, Risser D, Salisbury M (2001) Enhancing patient safety through teamwork training. J Healthc Risk Manag 21:57–65

Brown MS, Ohlinger J, Rusk C, Delmore P, Ittmann P (2003) Implementing potentially better practices for multidisciplinary team building: creating a neonatal intensive care unit culture of collaboration. Pediatrics 111:482–488

Burke CS, Salas E, Wilson-Donnelly K, Priest H (2004) How to turn a team of experts into an expert medical team: guidance from the aviation and military communities. Qual Saf Health Care 13(Suppl 1):i96–i194

Cannon-Bowers JA, Salas E, Coverse S (1993) Team mental models in expert team decision making. In: Castellan N (ed) Individual and group decision making. Lawrence Erlbaum, Hillsdale, pp 221–246

Cole E, Crichton N (2006) The culture of a trauma team in relation to human factors. J Clin Nurs 15:1257–1266

Darley JM, Latane B (1968) Bystander intervention in emergencies: diffusion of responsibility. J Pers Soc Psychol 8:377–383

Dev P, Youngblood P, Heinrichs WL, Kusumoto L (2007) Virtual worlds and team training. Anesthesiol Clin 25(2):321–336

Driskell JE, Salas E (1992) Collective behavior and team performance. Hum Fact 34:227–288

Firth-Cozens J (2004) Why communication fails in the operating room. Qual Saf Health Care 13:327

Fleishmann E, Zaccaro S (1992) Toward a taxonomy of team performance functions. In: Swezey R, Salas E (eds) Teams: their training and performance. Ablex, Norwood, pp 31–56

Fletcher G, Flin R, McGeorge P, Glavin R, Maran N, Patey R (2003) Anaesthetists' Non-Technical Skills (ANTS): evaluation of a behavioural marker system. Br J Anaesth 90(5):580–588

Flin R, Fletcher G, McGeorge P, Sutherland A, Patey R (2003a) Anaesthetists' attitudes to teamwork and safety. Anaesthesia 58:233–242

Flin R, Lynne M, Goeters KM, Hörmann J, Amalberti R, Valot C, Nijhuis H (2003b) Development of the NOTECHS (non -technical skills) system for assessing pilots' CRM skills. Hum Fact Aeros Safet 3(2):95–117

Flin R, Yule S, McKenzie L, Paterson-Brown S, Maran N (2006) Attitudes to teamwork and safety in the operating theatre. Surgeon 4:145–151

Guise JM, Segel S (2008) Teamwork in obstetric critical care. Best Pract Res Clin Obstet Gynaecol 22(5):937–951

Healey AN, Undre S, Vincent CA (2004) Developing observational measures of performance in surgical teams. Qual Saf Health Care 13(Suppl 1):i33–i40

Helmreich R, Schaefer H (1994) Team performance in the operating room. In: Bogner M (ed) Human error in medicine. Erlbaum, Hillsdale, pp 225–253

Howard SK, Gaba DM, Fish KJ, Yang G, Sarnquist FH (1992) Anesthesia crisis resource management training: teaching anesthesiologists to handle critical incidents. Aviat Space Environ Med 63(9):763–770

Hunt EA, Shilkofski NA, Stavroudis TA, Nelson KL (2007) Simulation: translation to improved team performance. Anesthesiol Clin 25(2):301–319

Jain M, Miller L, Belt D, King D, Berwick DM (2006) Decline in ICU adverse events, nosocomial infections and cost through a quality improvement initiative focusing on teamwork and culture change. Qual Saf Health Care 15:235–239

Janis I (1972) Groupthink. Psychological studies of policy decisions and fiascos. Houghton – Mifflin, Boston

Kaissi A, Johnson T, Kirschbaum MS (2003) Measuring teamwork and patient safety attitudes of high-risk areas. Nurs Econ 21:211–218

Katzenbach JR, Smith DK (1993) Teams. Der Schlüssel zu Hochleistungsorganisationen [Teams. The key to high-performance organizations]. Redline Wirtschaft, Vienna

Kogan N, Wallach MA (1969) Risk taking. Holt, New York

Kriz WC (2000) Teamkompetenz. Konzepte, Trainingsmethoden, Praxis [Team competence. Concepts, training methods, practice]. Vandenhoeck and Ruprecht, Göttingen

Leonard M, Graham S, Bonacum D (2004) The human factor: the critical importance of effective teamwork and communication in providing safe care. Qual Saf Health Care 13(Suppl 1):i85–i90

Lingard L, Espin S, Whyte S, Regehr G, Baker GR, Reznick R, Bohnen J, Orser B, Doran D, Grober E (2004) Communication failures in the operating room: an observational classification of recurrent types and effects. Qual Saf Health Care 13:330–334

Makary MA, Sexton JB, Freischlag JA, Holzmueller CG, Millmann EA, Roven L, Provenost PJ (2006) Operating room teamwork among physicians and nurses: teamwork in the eye of the beholder. J Am Coll Surg 202:746–752

Manser T (2009) Teamwork and patient safety in dynamic domains of healthcare: a review of the literature. Acta Anaesthesiol Scand 53:143–151

Matera P (2003) The power of teamwork. J Emerg Med Serv 28:26

Mickan S, Rodger S (2000) Characteristics of effective teams: a literature review. Aust Health Rev 23:201–208

Morey JC, Simon R, Jay GD, Wears RL, Salisbury M, Dukes KA, Berns SD (2002) Error reduction and performance improvement in the emergency department through formal teamwork training: evaluation results of the MedTeams project. Health Serv Res 37:1553–1581

Murray WB, Foster PA (2000) Crisis resource management among strangers: principles of organizing a multidisciplinary group for crisis resource management. J Clin Anesth 12:633–638

Ohlinger J, Brown MS, Laudert S, Swanson S, Fofah O (2003) Development of potentially better practices for the neonatal intensive care unit as a culture of collaboration: communication, accountability, respect, and empowerment. Pediatrics 111:471–481

Orasanu J, Salas E (1993) Team decision-making in complex environments. In: Klein G, Orasanu J (eds) Decision-making in action: models and methods. Ashgate, New York, pp 327–345

Paris CR, Salas E, Cannon-Bowers JA (2000) Teamwork in multi-person systems: a review and analysis. Ergonomics 43:1052–1075

Reader T, Flin R, Lauche K, Cuthbertson BH (2006) Non-technical skills in the intensive care unit. Br J Anaesth 96:551–559

Rice MM (2009) Teams and teamwork in emergency medicine. In: Croskerry P, Cosby KS, Schenkel SM, Wears RL (eds) Patient safety in emergency medicine. Lippincott Williams & Wilkins, Philadelphia, pp 177–180

Risser DT, Rice MM, Salisbury ML, Simon R, Jay GD, Berns SD (1999) The potential for improved teamwork to reduce medical errors in the emergency department. The MedTeams Research Consortium. Ann Emerg Med 34:373–383

Risser DT, Simon R, Rice MM, Salisbury ML (2000) A structured teamwork system to reduce clinical errors. In: Spath PL (ed) Error reduction in health care. A system approach to improving patient safety. AHA, Chicago, pp 235–278

Salas E, Dickinson TL, Converse SA, Tannenbaum SI (1998) Toward an understanding of team performance and training. In: Swezey RW, Salas E (eds) Teams: their training and performance. Ablex, Norwood, pp 3–30

Salas E, DiazGranados D, Klein C (2008) Does team training improve team performance? A meta-analysis. Hum Factors 50:903–933

Schaefer HG, Helmreich RL, Scheidegger D (1995) Safety in the operating theatre, part 1: interpersonal relationships and team performance. Curr Anaesth Crit Care 6:48–53

Schmutz J, Manser T (2013) Do team processes really have an effect on clinical performance? A systematic literature review. Br J Anaesth 110:529–544

Schulz S, Frey D (1998) Wie der Hals in die Schlinge kommt: Fehlentscheidungen in Gruppen [Erroneous decision-making in groups]. In: Ardelt-Gattinger E, Lechner H, Schlögl W (eds) Gruppendynamik. Anspruch und Wirklichkeit der Arbeit in Gruppen [group dynamics – ideal and reality of work in groups]. Verlag für Angewandte Psychologie, Göttingen, pp S 139–S 158

Sexton JB (2004) The better the team, the safer the world: golden rules of group interaction in high risk environments: evidence based suggestions for improving performance. Swiss Re Centre for Global Dialogue Rüschlikon/Gottlieb Daimler Karl Benz Foundation, Switzerland/Ladenburg

Sexton JB, Makary MA, Tersigni AR, Pryor D, Hendrich A, Thomas EJ, Holzmueller CG, Knight AP, Wu Y, Pronovost PJ (2006) Teamwork in the operating room: frontline perspectives among hospitals and operating room personnel. Anesthesiology 105:877–884

Sherwood G, Thomas E, Bennett DS, Lewis P (2002) A teamwork model to promote patient safety in critical care. Crit Care Nurs Clin North Am 14:333–340

Stout RJ, Cannon-Bowers JA, Salas E, Milanovich DM (1999) Planning, shared mental models, and coordinated performance: an empirical link is established. Hum Factors 41:61–71

Sundar E, Sundar S, Pawlowski J, Blum R, Feinstein D, Pratt S (2007) Crew resource management and team training. Anesthesiol Clin 25(2):283–300

Theodoropoulos A, Kneebone R, Dornan B, Leonard R, Bello F (2007) Development and evaluation of a virtual intensive therapy unit – VITU. Stud Health Technol Inform 125:467–469

Thomas EJ, Sexton JB, Helmreich RL (2003) Discrepant attitudes about teamwork among critical care nurses and physicians. Crit Care Med 31:956–959

Thomas EJ, Sherwood GD, Mulhollem JL, Sexton JB, Helmreich RL (2004) Working together in the neonatal intensive care unit: provider perspectives. J Perinatol 24:552–559

Ummenhofer W, Amsler F, Sutter PM, Martina B, Martin J, Scheidegger D (2001) Team performance in the emergency room: assessment of inter-disciplinary attitudes. Resuscitation 49:39–46

Undre SN, Sevdalis AN, Healey S, Darzi A, Vincent CA (2006) Teamwork in the operating theatre: cohesion or confusion? J Eval Clin Pract 12:182–189

Urban J, Bowers C, Monday S, Morgan B (1995) Workload, team structure and communication in team performance. Mil Psychol 7:123–139

Weaver SJ, Dy SM, Rosen MA (2014) Team-training in healthcare: a narrative synthesis of the literature. BMJ Qual Saf 23(5):359–372

Wheelan SA, Burchill CN, Tilin F (2003) The link between teamwork and patients' outcomes in intensive care units. Am J Crit Care 12:527–534

Xiao Y, Hunter WA, Mackenzie CF, Jefferies NJ, Horst R (1996) Task complexity in emergency medical care and its implications for team coordination. Hum Factors 38:636–645

Youngblood P, Harter PM, Srivastava S, Moffett S, Heinrichs WL, Dev P (2008) Design, development, and evaluation of an online virtual emergency department for training trauma teams. Simul Healthc J Soc Simul Healthc 3(3):146–153

Yule S, Flin R, Paterson-Brown S, Maran N, Rowley D (2006) Development of a rating system for surgeons' non-technical skills. Med Educ 40(11):1098–1104

Speech Is Golden: Communication

12

Case Study
Late one afternoon, a hospital's code team responds to a "code blue" on a general surgical ward. Upon their arrival, the patient is unconscious; two nurses are performing cardiopulmonary resuscitation (CPR), while several bystanders observe the events in disbelief. The responding ICU physician has the impression that the resuscitation is chaotic and uncoordinated. He announces in a loud voice that he will be running the code and ensures that the nurses are performing effective, well-coordinated CPR. He then delegates specific tasks to other team members. Several minutes later, a surgeon arrives and the intensivist gives her a brief update on the situation. The two physicians initially entertain the diagnosis of massive pulmonary embolism as the cause for the pulseless electrical activity, but soon learn that the patient had just had an uneventful splenectomy. Suspecting hemorrhagic shock, the intensivist orders aggressive fluid resuscitation. During active CPR, a large-bore central venous access is established and after 2000 ml of crystalloid fluids and repeated epinephrine doses, there is return of spontaneous circulation with an adequate blood pressure. The surgeon calls the operating room (OR) to schedule an emergent exploratory laparotomy, requests the emergency release of blood products from the blood bank, and ensures that a cell saver is prepared for the OR. The patient stabilizes and is transported to the OR, where the intensive care physician gives a concise report to the receiving team and answers their questions. The hemoglobin concentration upon arrival is 3.8 g/dl. During the operation, the surgical team identifies a disengaged splenic ligature and controls the bleeding. Intraoperatively, the patient receives 9 units of packed red blood cells, 12 units of fresh frozen plasma, and 2 units of platelets. The postoperative course is complicated by acute renal failure that resolves over several weeks. The patient recovers completely and goes home without any neurological deficits.

M. St.Pierre et al., *Crisis Management in Acute Care Settings*,
DOI 10.1007/978-3-319-41427-0_12

A code team responds to a cardiac arrest, and a group of variably experienced physicians, nurses, and staff from the general ward manages the medical emergency. In his role as team leader, the critical care physician must cope with several parallel tasks: He assigns tasks to the team members, coordinates the resuscitation efforts, gathers all available information to determine the cause of the cardiac arrest, and assesses responses to his interventions. In addition, he initiates preparations for an emergency operation while, at the same time, supervising the resuscitation efforts. He hands over the patient to the OR team and shares all relevant information. The fact that the patient survives the cardiac arrest without any neurological impairment can largely be ascribed to the successful teamwork and the good communication during the emergency situation.

12.1 Organizing the Chaos: Functions of Communication

The most fundamental function of communication is to deliver a message from one individual to another. The case study, however, highlights a key feature of good communication in critical situations. Much more than just talking, communication has to fulfill several important functions during a crisis. The communication patterns necessary in this context differ from those used in everyday conversations. Communication in a high-stakes medical environment fulfills several essential functions that we discuss in this chapter.

12.1.1 Building and Maintaining Team Structure

In the case study, the intensivist structures the team, a role authorized a priori by virtue of his profession. He assigns functions and roles to team members and delegates more complex tasks such as CPR and easier tasks such as running an errand. As our case shows, every healthcare team needs structure to manage complex medical tasks successfully. Lifesaving critical care is usually performed by multiple caregivers from divergent professions and specialties ("*ad hoc teams*"; Chap. 11). The team members may not know each other, their roles, and special skills nor understand each individual's goals, task demands ("performing ACLS"), and social demands ("getting acquainted with each other"), which must all run in parallel (Murray and Foster 2000). As a process, team formation clarifies who takes on which role and who follows whose instructions. The team structure is determined partly by professional roles and partly by explicit verbal allocation and coordination of responsibilities within the team. The explicit nature of this communication is important especially if "equal-rank" team members are present (e.g., experienced nurses and physicians). A successful team explicitly negotiates the leadership role and allocates responsibility without making assumptions about lead and follower roles. If a core team has already formed (as in the case of a code team joining staff on ward), communication helps outside staff members find their role while promoting and maintaining the team structure.

12.1.2 Coordinating Team Process and Task Execution

From an operational perspective, communication enables achievement of task objectives and coordination of team efforts. The team leader in the case study coordinates work flow by assigning tasks in accordance with the team members' abilities. By concentrating all available resources on crisis management and avoiding unessential actions, the team leader builds a sense of confidence in his team. This confidence is particularly important for inexperienced teams as they execute their critical task. A leader unfamiliar with an emergency situation and with the current team needs to invest some time and thought to ensure coordination among team activities. However, coordination is not confined to a top-down process; coordination also implies that each team member is aware of other teammates' actions and task completion. Moreover, team members can self-identify their roles with permission of the team leader.

12.1.3 Enabling Information Exchange

Information exchange is the third function of communication that contributes to successful team performance during high-stakes events. Effective information exchange is a critical element for adequate situational assessment and development of good action strategies.

12.1.4 Facilitating Relationships

A general characteristic of human communication is that it takes place in a social context. Communication, therefore, fulfills a fourth, ever-present function during the entire event because it facilitates and creates relationships among the team members.

Three main factors influence how these relationships are formed:

- The professional roles and necessary qualifications the participants embody
- Which behaviors they display
- Their expectations of each other and of their communication

The first three functions of communication (team structuring, coordination, information exchange) are unthinkable without this "being in a relationship." It is impossible to exchange information with a mere matter-of-fact attitude without simultaneously establishing a relationship between team members in this information exchange. This aspect has direct consequences for safe delivery of patient care: If a leader confidently and expertly steps into the leader role and displays a calm and decisive attitude in an emergency, he or she creates a team climate characterized by confidence, reliability, trust, and a willingness to take responsibility. By always behaving this way, the leader cultivates a reputation of a safe and competent clinician with whom other people enjoy to work. Team members develop positive expectations of their leader, which, in turn, characterize (and indeed facilitate) subsequent interactions. On the other hand, if a leader is viewed as being arrogant and bossy, team members expect this attitude in the future. If such an "arrogant" leader gives brusque commands and treats others rudely and with disrespect during a critical situation, team members will see their expectations confirmed – a vicious circle of expectations, perception, interpretation, and reaction arises. If the "competent, confident, calm and decisive" leader displays the same brusque behavior, the team likely will interpret this differently. Since they appreciate this leader's normally affirmative personality, they simply excuse curt utterances as unintended. Thus, issues of relationship and communication are inextricably bound together.

Basic functions of communication in an acute medical care setting are:

- Building and maintaining team structure
- Coordinating team process and executing tasks
- Exchanging information
- Facilitating relationships

12.2 Understanding Communication

A number of disciplines have studied communication resulting in various theories and myriad findings. All theories share the notion that communication deals with information and interaction. In the following section, we outline some basic psychological concepts that are relevant to communication and then explain two of the field's useful theories.

12.2.1 Basic Assumptions About Communication

There are many theoretical frameworks about and definitions of what actually constitutes communication (Griffin 1999; Miller 2005) and even more practical tips and suggestions on how to communicate well in everyday life (Knapp and Daly 2002; Hargie 2006). Throughout this book, the following assumptions form the basis of our understanding of the term *communication*:

- Communication is mostly *intentional*. A person deliberately interacts with another person. This interaction can occur verbally or nonverbally (e.g., head nods, smiling, frowns).

- Communication involves *at least two people* and implies that one person's thinking and behavior is brought into the relationship with the other person.
- Communication as a central form of human behavior *depends on the situational context*. Each time a person talks and behaves, this behavior is perceived and interpreted by another person. In addition to perceiving, the observer can relate this behavior to him or herself irrespectively of the sender's intention. For example, some of the nurses in our case study who stand by awaiting instructions but whom the critical care physician does not explicitly address could interpret his behavior as an indication that "the physician is ignoring us." This example illustrates one of the basic assumptions underlying communication theory, namely, that communication has to be seen in a much broader context than mere verbal exchange: "We cannot not communicate" (Watzlawick et al. 1996).
- As we have no direct access to the mind of others, communication can *never be a mere transfer of information* from one person to another (Maturana and Varela 1992). Although the sender has many options to state his or her intention in a given situation as clearly as possible, he or she cannot know for certain how others understand or will respond to it. During the resuscitation in the case study, the critical care physician asks one of the student nurses from general ward to fetch a central line from the crash cart. Because the nurse does not know what he means, his request – "Could you please go and get me a central line from the crash cart?" – has insufficient informational value for the student nurse to direct her behavior in accordance with the physician's intention. Thus, the physician cannot achieve his goal with the student nurse because his statement did not contain the necessary information.
- We cannot determine how our counterparts will interpret words and behavior since *"meaning" is not an agreed-upon variable* that is transmitted along with the words spoken. Because every message is subject to personal interpretation of the receiver, the result of this process may differ considerably from the sender's initial intention.
- Cooperation within a team very often produces stable and relatively reproducible *patterns of team communication* (Watzlawick et al. 1996). Communication patterns can be more or less appropriate for the demands of the actual situation. But if a team is accustomed to discussing all pros and cons before implementing a therapeutic intervention, this helps provide optimal care for a critically ill patient.
- A *dysfunctional communication pattern* is one in which people have good intentions, but the interaction creates an unproductive and destructive system. A common example is the widespread tendency to blame other people for communication problems while refusing to share part of the responsibility. In this way, the behavioral patterns of both communication senders and receivers form results in poor understandings and conflict within the team. If two people cooperate (and communicate) ineffectively, the reason lies not in problematic personalities (e.g., choleric surgeon, hysterical nurse) but in communication patterns that likely can be improved.

12.2.2 Sources and Squares: Theories of Communication

Several theoretical models conceptualize communication as the transmittal of signs and contents. In the context of team performance in a high-stakes environment, two models are especially suited to explain both regular and problematic aspects of human communication.

12.2.2.1 The Shannon-Weaver Transmission Model of Communication

In 1949, Claude Shannon and Warren Weaver, two engineers – not psychologists – working for Bell Telephone Labs in the United States, formulated a technical model of communication to help develop a mathematical theory of communication. They proposed that all communication must include five components if a message is to be transmitted successfully (Fig. 12.1):

- Information source: It produces a message.
- Transmitter: It encodes the message into signals.
- Channel: Signals are adapted for transmission via a channel.
- Receiver: It "decodes" (reconstructs) the message from the signal.
- Destination: Where the message arrives.

The model is relatively straightforward and easily understood. It is useful to use the Shannon model to juxtapose it to the complexity of human communication in high-stakes, high-stress situations. A crucial prerequisite in this model is that both transmitter and receiver share a common set of rules, symbols, and sounds about how to encode and decode the message. The quality of reception is affected by the kind of channel (which does not have to be speech), by the channel capacity, and by perturbations (e.g., noise). Apart from its obvious technological bias, this model nevertheless emphasizes certain interpersonal communication problems arising from channel interference due to factors such as noise. Interference with the message traveling along the channel may lead to a change in the signal during transmission; at times the signal may not even be received at all. For example, if an emergency setting is loud and chaotic, a leader's instructions or a team member's feedback can easily be misunderstood or missed altogether. A second interference factor is channel overload. Channel overload is not due to noise but instead when signal exceeds channel capacity. In the context of high-stakes medical care, this can happen easily

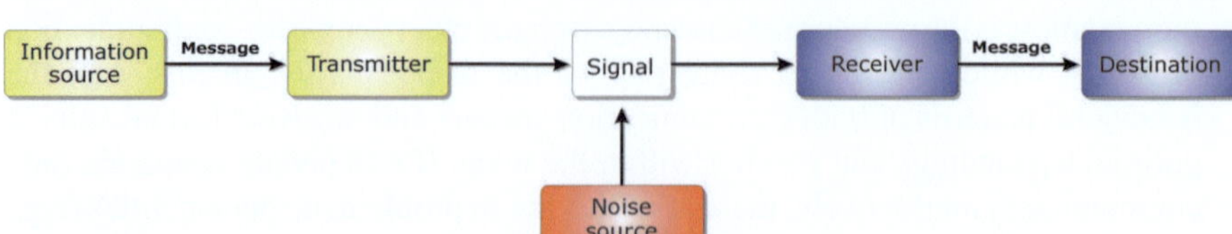

Fig. 12.1 Sender – channel – receiver. The Shannon-Weaver transmission model of communication (From Shannon and Weaver 1949)

if all team members talk at the same time. Messages (and not noise) overload the "verbal communication" input channel, and the receiving person must filter "relevant information" from the incoming data (Chap. 8). In the process, crucial information can be misunderstood or lost. Another important aspect pertains to the message itself. Shannon's original paper was about information theory and discussed the transmission of information. However, human communication is much more than merely transferring information: Human beings do not process information but instead process *meanings*; thus, if the model is applied to human communication, problems arise with the assumption that meanings of a message can be encoded, transferred, and decoded. In addition, Shannon's model suffers from its obvious linearity: It views communication as a unidirectional process, although human communication relates to the combination of verbal and nonverbal interaction between at least two subjects.

One last distinction, the physical context, is helpful when juxtaposing this model to the high-stakes medical environment (Kanki and Smith 1999). While the location of a communication event may not affect the information content of the message, it often affects the quality of transmission, impact, efficiency, and nature of the communication process. If sender and receiver are together in the same room, face-to-face communication can take advantage of the shared experience and nonverbal cues like facial expression and gestures. In the absence of shared visual information, as on a phone call, supplementary sources of information are eliminated. Remote communication can only utilize verbal and paraverbal (e.g., intonation, phrasing) cues. If communicators are remotely located and speak via intercom, as can happen with physicians from different departments, or via radio when EMTs contact the dispatch center or medical control, closing the communication gap (readback/hearback) is absolutely essential to ensure information transmission.

12.2.2.2 The Four Aspects of a Message

In contrast to technical models, psychological models of communication describe the interactions between subjects who communicate with each other. Psychological models include and distinguish between:

- The content of a message (content component)
- The relationship subjects have with each other (relational component)
- The way a message can be interpreted (interpretational component)

Communication is not merely a matter of sending and receiving but also of what is said, how it is said, and how the actors understand what has been said (Bühler 1934; Searle 1969). Psychological models emphasize that we do not communicate merely on the grounds of factual information; instead, "communication = content + relationship" (Griffin 1999). Moreover, apart from expressing the relationship between sender and receiver, every message also contains a (hidden) statement about the sender ("self-revelation"; Watzlawick et al. 1996).

The "square model" of communication based on work by Schulz von Thun (1981, 2000; English in Campbell and Bagshaw 2002) can help to explain misunderstandings and perhaps give us some insight into common difficulties. In this model, every message has four aspects, such as the four sides of a square: content, self-revelation, the relationship between the actors, and appeal (Fig. 12.2; Table 12.1).

These four aspects of a message are equally relevant for the person talking and the person listening. One could say that we talk with four mouths and listen with four ears, and we open them more or less widely, depending on our – not always conscious – intentions (Fig. 12.3). Which aspect of the four the sender emphasizes

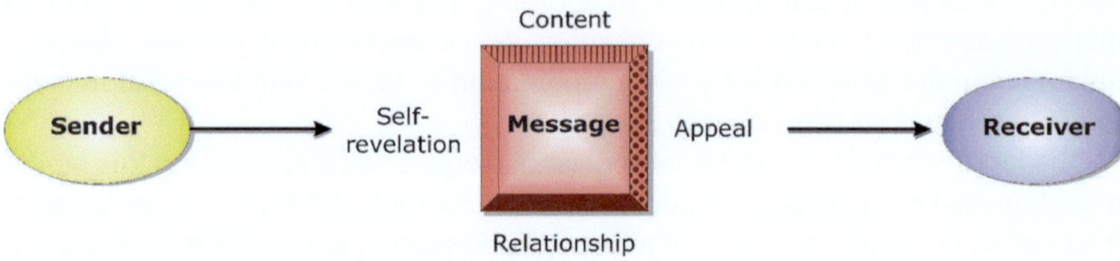

Fig. 12.2 The four aspects of a message. Schulz von Thun's psychological "square model" of interpersonal communication (From Schulz von Thun 1981)

Table 12.1 The four aspects of a message: The "square model" of communication (From Schulz von Thun 1981)

Content	Information about facts, objects, and events
Self-revelation	Information about the sender as person: This can either take the form of a voluntary self-presentation or an involuntary self-revelation
Relationship	Information about the relationship between sender and receiver: The sender reveals how he or she sees the receiver and their relationship by the words chosen, intonation, and nonverbal signals
Appeal	Information about an appeal to act: Every message tells the receiver what he or she is supposed to do or not do

From Schulz von Thun (1981)

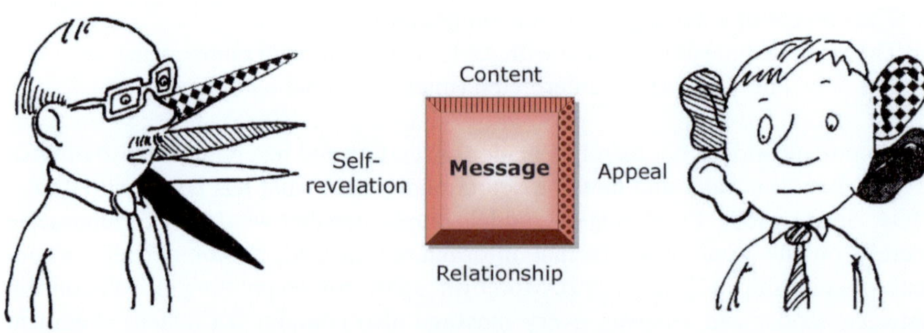

Fig. 12.3 The "four beaks" and "four ears" model (From Schulz von Thun et al. 2000). Both sender and receiver of a message can emphasize one of the four aspects of a message. The sender has no dependable means to predict the receiver's understanding of the message

(i.e., which mouth speaks the loudest) depends on his or her thoughts, intentions, and communication abilities. The receiver in turn reacts to each aspect of the message. Which of these aspects the receiver emphasizes (which ear listens more or less intently) will be rooted in his or her present mental state of mind, expectations, anxieties, and previous interactions with the sender. The sender, however, has little influence on the listener's mind and therefore has difficulty in predicting the receiver's response to the message.

A clinical example might help to clarify this matter (Fig. 12.4). After a patient has been weaned from cardiopulmonary bypass at the end of a coronary artery bypass operation, the cardiac surgeon turns to the anesthesiologist and says: "The blood pressure is dropping! How high is your epinephrine running?" From the surgeon's point of view (sender of the message), the message content refers to an observable change in hemodynamics and the resulting question about an appropriate catecholamine therapy. At the same time, his question also includes an appeal to the anesthesiologist. His request might or might not be the same if he said, "Have a look at your infusion pump and tell me the infusion rate." His question reflects his momentary mental state (self-revelation). One possibility could be that the question expresses his concern about the patient's current pathophysiological state and possible consequences if the hemodynamic situation does not improve quickly; however, on the relational side, the surgeon may want to clarify the responsibility for all tasks. He could reveal to the anesthesiologist by the choice of his wording, intonation, and nonverbal cues what he thinks about his anesthesiologist counterpart: "This is my patient, and as the responsible person, I have no confidence in your ability to manage this situation. I have to be the one to tell you to increase the infusion rate; I think this case is too difficult for you."

The anesthesiologist (receiver of the message), however, will listen with his "four ears" to the different aspects of the message and open some ears more widely than others. If the content aspect is perceived as the most important one to him, he

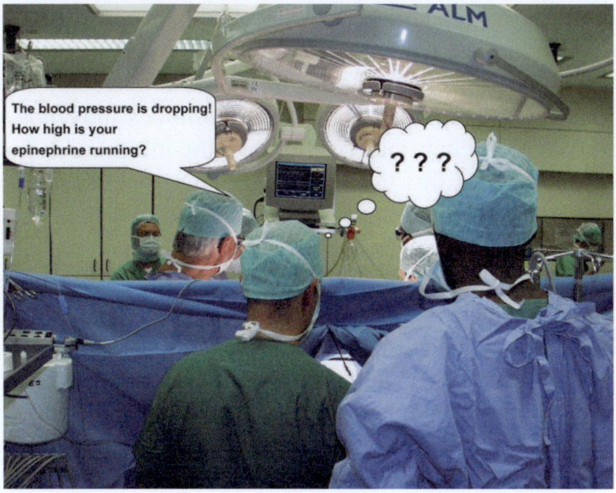

Fig. 12.4 Interpersonal communication during a critical situation while weaning from cardiopulmonary bypass. The anesthesiologist's reply to the cardiac surgeon's question will depend on the four aspects of the message (content, self-revelation, relationship, appeal) and how the anesthesiologist emphasizes the aspects in the moment

will respond to the question by stating the facts and telling the surgeon the infusion rate; however, if in the question the receiver hears the self-revelation of concern about the patient's well-being, then he might answer the question by mitigating the surgeon's concerns: "I'm taking care of the problem and have just increased the infusion rate of epinephrine. I'm confident that the blood pressure will normalize so you can actually continue to operate." Maybe the anesthesiologist has a very sensitive ear for the relational aspect of the message. In this case, he will consider the question as meddling with his area of responsibility and will hear disrespect for his capabilities. The answer then might be: "Mind your own business."

The reader might try to read aloud the sentences in the example. Observe the tone of your voice and the emotions that go with it depending on your intentions, and imagine the reaction of a counterpart.

12.2.3 It's Not Only What You Say, It's the Way You Say It: Verbal, Paraverbal, and Nonverbal Communication

Human communication uses different channels in parallel to transfer information. Besides the words we choose (verbal communication), we also transmit a message through the tone, pitch, and pacing of our voices (paraverbal communication) and communicate through gesture, posture, facial expression, and eye contact (nonverbal communication). Communication can use many behavioral patterns; even silence can be "telling." People on the receiving end of a message will infer from all three channels the information they believe is relevant in the current situation. Information conveyed via nonverbal channels can "speak" to people much more directly than words and thus have the greatest impact. Nonverbal and paraverbal information can help the receiver understand the meaning of a message in its larger situational context. Nonverbal information is like a commentary or an instruction manual for the spoken sentences. The surgeon's question, "How high is your epinephrine running?" together with a frown on his face could be interpreted by the anesthesiologist as an expression of doubts about his competence. The same words spoken in a calm and friendly manner would signal "I'm confident, you'll manage it!" This interpretation takes place subconsciously; the nonverbal and paraverbal channels are much more colored by attitudes and emotions and are mostly below the threshold of conscious control than the information processing of the verbal channel. If we feel that the verbal and nonverbal channels are at odds with each other because the words convey one meaning and the nonverbal information indicates another meaning (*incongruence*), we tend to subconsciously place greater importance on the nonverbal and paraverbal cues. When in doubt, we lean toward believing the tone, facial expression, gestures, and body language rather than the spoken word.

Another type of incongruence is that messages can often be subject to several ways of interpreting a message. In that case, we usually choose the one we expected or the one most probable in that situation. Incongruence, in short, leaves space for the receiver's interpretation. The result reflects the receiver's self-perception, anxieties, and expectations and not necessarily the sender's original intent. Thus, it is important to remember that spoken messages align with the paraverbal and nonverbal channels to maximize the chances for congruence by the receiver.

12.3 General Disturbance of Communication

The clinical vignette from the top of the chapter describes an acute medical emergency during which communication structures, guides, and coordinates the team activities. The outcome of this team process is rewarding; the patient survives his cardiac arrest and can be discharged from the ICU without any neurological deficits. It is not uncommon, however, that communication fails and then compromises effective and safe patient care. The disturbances can be rooted in any of the following:

- The characteristics of the message
- The process of receiving and interpreting the information
- The relationship of dialogue partners

12.3.1 Misunderstanding

In the acute care setting, people communicate to call attention to their observations, thinking, intentions, and goals of action. If the sender transmits information or instructions and a team member reacts in a way that is different from what the sender intended, a misunderstanding occurs. Under familiar and routine conditions, misunderstandings are less frequent because both sender and receiver have similar mental models about what behavior would be best under the circumstances. Even if the message is transmitted incompletely (e.g., because of a noisy environment) and the receiver catches only half of the words, the situational context and expectations enable the receiver to fill in the missing words to guess the sender's meaning correctly. However, it is different in novel and ambiguous situations because neither sender nor receiver can rely on familiar mental models. The situation has to be identified, assessed, and explained, and future development has to be predicted (Chap. 6). Because this process depends highly on emotions, motives, available knowledge, and experience, the sender's and receiver's result may overlap to varying and unreliable degrees. The gap in a shared mental model increases the likelihood for misunderstanding.

In casual conversation, small misinterpretations are tolerated – sometimes even taking on the form of intentional ones (e.g., jokes, ironic remarks). In a high-stakes environment, however, where complex tasks, ambiguity, and time pressure necessitate effective teamwork, small misunderstandings and communication inefficiencies may have unwanted consequences.

12.3.1.1 Linguistic Ambiguity

Verbal messages can be misunderstood because phonation, grammar, dialect, and unaccustomed accents add ambiguity to sentences. The intended meaning must be derived from the situational context. If interference like noise, time pressure, and distraction complicates the process of understanding, then the interpretation of ambiguous sentences is prone to error.

12.3.1.2 No "Square Clearness"

Successful communication is a "four-dimensional" affair, as every message contains four different aspects for both the sender and the receiver. Humans verbalize with "four mouths" and listen with "four ears" and thus will unconsciously select one of the four aspects (Fig. 12.3). Misunderstandings arise if the listener emphasizes a different aspect of the message than the one intended by the sender. This subconscious selection takes place even if the message was transmitted completely and without channel interference. If we want to avoid these kinds of misunderstandings, we have to communicate in a congruent way. If, for example, somebody is overly busy and is asked if help is needed, a mixed message is conveyed by saying, "I'm fine," but with a desperate tone indicating being overwhelmed. In this example, the needed help may or may not be forthcoming.

12.3.1.3 Different Mental Models

Misunderstanding on a more complex level occurs if a team member's mental model and related plans for action differ from those of his or her teammates. This can easily happen if there is no explicit sharing of mental models. As a result, the team will be governed by the faulty assumption that all members are on the same page. They will think they are taking care of the same patient, but may be treating "a different problem." When mental models have limited overlap, the likelihood that team members predict, adapt, and coordinate with one another successfully is greatly reduced. If observations, assessments, and expectations concerning future developments are not shared, then team members will have no certainty about the team's situational picture nor teammate's expectations. Moreover, when the sender and receiver have different situation awareness and mental models, inappropriate actions may be the response to a sender's information, and treatment plans can develop in different directions.

12.3.2 Relational Problems

Most behavior in communication is strongly dependent on social and individual relationship patterns. We speak of symmetric relationships if the persons involved are equal in position, and communication is based on "equal power." The hallmark of complementary relationships is that one person is higher in the hierarchy and one is lower. Communication is affected because of "differences in power" (Griffin 1999). Relationships in the healthcare setting will have both types of power (Watzlawick et al. 1974).

Because communication is the way of relating to other human beings, a person's lifelong interpersonal interactions lead to personal assumptions and differentiated categories of how he or she thinks people behave and which personality traits they carry. Hence, when two people meet for the first time, they subconsciously compare the perceived behavior of their counterpart with predetermined categories. If this process happens too quickly or rigidly, people end up being pigeonholed after only a few moments of interaction. The next time these two people meet, they will have certain expectations about the behavior of their counterpart – expectations that are only reluctantly challenged. This is the reason why the "first impression" (be it negative or positive) can have such a great impact on successful communication. A person's assumptions about his or her counterpart create a strong bias for subsequent encounters. If a positive first impression is mutual, it will help to foster a positive and constructive team climate. If the first impression is negative, a series of misunderstandings can arise from differing perceptions, assessments, categorizations, and expectations. Expectations rule perception which in turn determines receiver reaction. Unfortunately, we are seldom aware of our bias toward other people and typically do not question the appropriateness of our expectations. Instead, we tend to ascribe the difficulties we have with certain people to their faulty characteristics. We do not believe that it is the problematic interaction (of which we are one part) but instead we ascribe problems to the personality of the other person. Based on an expectation-driven interaction, it becomes clear why we find so many flawed communication patterns in the workplace. The most frequently encountered dysfunctional interactions are:

- Symmetric escalation
- Complementary communication
- Reactance

12.3.2.1 "Tit for Tat": Symmetrical Escalation

Symmetric communication describes a normal pattern of interaction based on the equivalence of both partners. Two people communicate symmetrically if the behavior of one person is mirrored by the behavior of the other; both partners strive for a reduction of differences (Griffin 1999). However, if the relationship between communication partners is tense or if one has a competitive personality, the relational pattern will become prone to misunderstandings. In this context, individuals compete for control. The result is symmetric escalation with the motto, "What you can do I can do as well!" A cardiac surgeon who had started training in anesthesia before changing specialties may try to compete with his anesthesia counterpart in a symmetrical communication pattern. His statement, "When I started my training we constantly had our finger on the pulse and could detect a low blood pressure without all these technical gadgets," could be answered by "It's exactly the technology that I now employ that makes it possible for you to perform operations on increasingly sicker patients." If both people continue this symmetrical pattern, they may place a priority on the ongoing tit-for-tat argument instead of maintaining awareness of the patient's hemodynamic problems.

12.3.2.2 "What Goes Around Comes Around": Complementary Communication

Power differences of the communication partners may complement each other. One person's actions create the condition for the other person's actions, e.g., "order – execute," "ask – answer." Beyond hierarchical structures or power gradients, the perception of an individual's behavior can provoke a corresponding behavior in the other person. A dependent nurse may "force" her team leader to supervise her task execution closely and encourage the physician to give very detailed instructions even if the senior nurse actually dislikes this kind of what she perceives as controlling behavior. The more controlling the leader behaves, the more dependently the nurse confines herself to task execution without engaging critical thinking. Thus, the unconscious subordination of one person leads to the dominance of the other. This dysfunctional communication pattern can become habitual within the complementary relationship. Once the pattern is established, expectations become stronger and more ingrained and therefore increasingly more difficult to change. Quite possibly, both partners actually are unhappy with this forced behavior; it may contradict their personal values, preferences, and the ideals of their professional roles. Other complementary interactions in healthcare include the physician-patient relationship and the teacher-student relationship. To be sure, these relationships and communication patterns can be complementary in a satisfactory way, but power differences may become problematic.

12.3.2.3 "Don't You Tell Me What I'm Supposed to Do!": Reactance

Humans show great variability in their acceptance of rules or regulations. We also have an attachment to our individual practice patterns. If we view those practice patterns as being threatened or eliminated, we tend to react poorly. Whether the relationship is complementary or symmetrical, it is possible that the receiver may feel pressured (complementary) or manipulated (symmetrical).

As a general rule, people will do what they view to be in in accordance with their values and self-interests. In a complementary relationship, subordinates will have an unpredictable level of tolerance, but tend to be mindful of the power of superiors. In a symmetrical relationship, peers feel more empowered to obey rules and make decisions independent of peers. Good leaders and peers will try to avoid crossing the boundary of tolerance in subordinates and peers. Examples of techniques of crossing the boundary in a complementary relationship might occur when a person is heavily pressured to accept a certain view or attitude or in a symmetrical relationship when the sender does not intend to manipulate but the receiver has a keen sense of the empty appeal of a message. In both cases, people will likely demonstrate behavior in contradiction to a demand, rule, or regulation, which intends to communicate, "Don't you tell me what I'm supposed to do!" In more general terms, a negative reaction is a learned protective function. It results in mental and physical activation aimed at resisting other people's manipulative efforts and reconstituting a person's perceived behavioral freedom and freedom of choice (Brehm and Brehm 1981). Behavioral reactions that are negative include:

- Defiance
- Refusal

- Intentional failure
- Aggression
- Passive-aggressive
- Arrogance

Communication patterns governed by negative reactions can play a major role when a healthcare provider receives instructions from a teammate of another professional group (e.g., nurses from physicians) or when questions or instructions come from colleagues of other specialties. For example, a cardiac surgeon's asking an anesthesiologist "How high is your epinephrine running?" might trigger a negative reaction in someone who hears, "I'll tell you how to do it." In this example, the anesthesiologist may have an emotional response to the perceived manipulative and insulting question and reply "I know how to treat my patient!"

12.4 Poor Communication in Critical Situations

Many problems in team performance can be traced to the abovementioned interpersonal communication difficulties that are found in both routine and critical situations. As critical situations in high-stakes medical contexts pose specific demands, they also present specific opportunities for failure. Several communication patterns have been identified that can contribute to faulty team performance in critical situations (Cushing 1994; Ungerer 2004).

12.4.1 Unspecified Receiver

In critical situations, every message should be directed to a specific person. If questions or instructions are put forward to no one in particular, then there's a good chance that no one will feel concerned or responsible. The necessary process of ensuring that messages are correctly received and understood by the right person is often neglected, especially when task load is high. Most team members actively avoid additional responsibility for more tasks as they reach or exceed their personal limit. If none of the team members actively receive an instruction, then diffusion of responsibility occurs (Chap. 11). Poor communication with an unspecified receiver can be recognized in phrases such as "could somebody…," "does anybody…," and "We should do…."

12.4.2 Problems with Speech: Articulation and Terms

Ineffective communication results from poor articulation or mispronunciation. Talking in a low voice, speaking very quickly, mumbling, and talking in unfinished sentences, with a strong accent, or with faulty grammar, contribute to misunderstanding.

Replacing medical terms by colloquial terms and unofficial jargon creates an "insider language" which may not be a problem among team members who know each other. However, when unfamiliar healthcare workers or those from other disciplines or specialties become involved, using colloquial language and nontechnical terminology can lead to misunderstanding. To avoid misunderstanding, the healthcare provider needs to use standard terminology as much as possible or, at the least, clarify the meaning of idiosyncratic terms and expressions.

12.4.3 Information Overload

A constant danger in critical situations is overloading a message with information. If this happens, the receiver has to decide which part of the message is important. The criteria for this decision are guided by the receiver's personal experience and expectations. It often does not reflect the sender's intentions, again resulting in misunderstanding. The following signs may indicate an information overload (Ungerer 2004):

- Rapid sequence of instructions for unrelated actions
- Minimal pause between sentences (<2 s)
- More than one verb and object per sentence
- Long lists with numbers or dosage instructions
- Aggressive and pressured speech
- Long and detailed instructions
- Several questions embedded in one question

12.4.4 Becoming Tight-Lipped

In critical situations, precise and unambiguous language is essential. However, if team members barely communicate, this threatens team processes and may even result in a complete communication breakdown. Worse still, if team leaders become tight-lipped, the entire team risks losing its shared mental model ("doc goes solo"). Typical indicators of an overly muted critical event include:

- Abandonment of explanations
- No response to team member's questions
- No active communication about background information
- Closed questions
- Monosyllabic answers
- Long periods of silence

12.4.5 "Resolving" Conflicts by Passivity or Aggressiveness

Team member communication styles aimed at resolving conflict and solving group questions can be placed along a continuum according to the degree to which they reflect a concern for one's own well-being at the possible expense of others, or vice versa (Jentsch and Smith-Jentsch 2001). The following behaviors on both ends of the continuum result:

- *Passive*: Worded in the form of questions, passive verbalizations often convey a watered-down expression of the sender's true intentions. Critiques are "sugar-coated," and statements are indirect, i.e., "beating around the bush" instead of addressing the critical issue directly. As a result, valid and critical points are not understood, do not carry the weight they should, and do not catch the attention of team members and the leader.
- *Aggressive*: Aggressive statements are direct and unambiguous and therefore leave no doubt about the sender's intentions. Unfortunately, they generally take the form of accusatory, disrespectful, or even rude remarks. They are perceived as a form of hostility and defensiveness. In this context, team members find it difficult to consider or accept input or critique in this form, even if it is true. The result of the perceived aggressive behavior is that team members often do not reveal information deemed potentially useful for fear of unleashing additional aggressive behavior from the teammate.
- *Assertive*: The divine "middle of the road" between these extremes of conflict resolution is discussed in greater detail below.

12.4.6 Poor Listening

Communication is not a one-way street. Careful active listening, inquiring through questions to gain clarity, and responding appropriately are skills just as important for effective communication as those needed to transmit information and instructions. Effective listening can be jeopardized in many ways. Indicators of poor listening are listed in the following summary (Jensen 1995; Transport Canada 1997):

- *Interrupting*: People who constantly interrupt a conversation are probably paying more attention to their own opinion and intentions than to what the other person is saying. They have preplanned their response and use short pauses to advance their own point of view.
- *Diverting*: People change the direction of the conversation by picking up irrelevant issues. Because they have not perceived the core problem, they pay undue attention to surface details rather than focusing on the substance of what is being said. Any key word may suffice to trigger the detour to other areas of interest.
- *Debating*: There is a fine line between challenging what someone says in order to obtain clarification, insight, or more information and arguing for the sake of arguing. People tend to debate if they are more interested in winning an argument than in hearing the other person's position. In addition, some people want to play devil's advocate and take the other side no matter what team members say.

- *Quarreling*: If a conflict moves from the content level to the relational level, then personal differences manifest in verbal fighting with the other person. A conversation can rapidly turn into a dispute, and both partners may be more interested in battling with each other than in solving the problem.
- *Becoming defensive*: In order to defend one's feeling of behavioral freedom, an opinion is dismissed. Moreover, because people often feel pressured to accept another's view, they reject both the person and the corresponding opinion.
- *Tuning out*: When people think that their communication partner is not worth listening to and that they already know their counterpart's opinion, or when they are preoccupied with their own position, they will tune other people out instead of listening.

12.4.7 Mingling Relational and Content Components

Team members often allow relational and content components of a message to mingle. This happens when relational messages are consciously or unconsciously hidden in a harmless phrase yet carry emotional content as perceived by the receiver, or if someone refuses a proposal simply because it comes from a person he or she does not like or respect. This mingling of messages results in a breakdown in communication because receivers are likely to attend to the relational message and react primarily to the emotional content. Reasons for this mingling include:

- Antipathy among team members
- A working climate of disrespect
- Compelling others to adhere to personal preferences and habits
- Intolerance for human error
- Power struggle for social status

Although a discourse may apparently be concerned with facts and goals, subtle relationship messages can emerge like "pinpricks from below" (Fig. 12.5). Any team member can deliver messages in the form of "pinpricks," even those who allegedly have a lower social status.

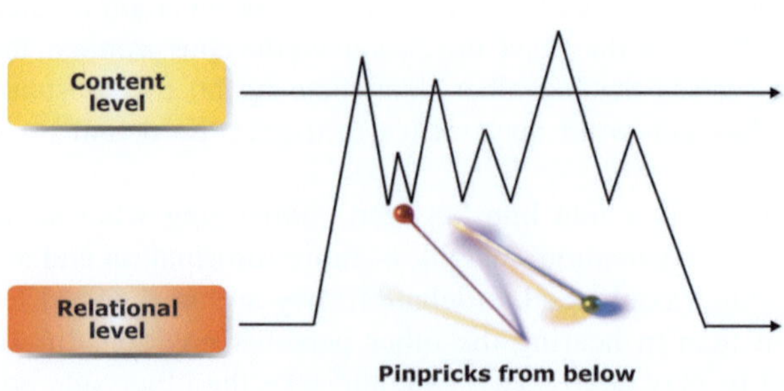

Fig. 12.5 A discussion about facts can be disturbed by subtle devaluing messages on the relationship level ("pinpricks from below") (From Schulz von Thun 1981)

Typical examples of how the relational and the content component can be interwoven in a critical situation are:

- *Making decisions alone:* If someone acts without consulting team members in the decision-making process, the message sent might be construed as "I don't value your contribution. I can decide without you!"
- *Enforcing decisions through loudness:* If leaders have the attitude that "the loudest argument wins," they could be transmitting the message, "I disrespect you; the only thing that counts is me and my opinion."
- Request something innocent and reasonable with a *subtle disparaging remark mixed in:* Antipathy can take the form of subtle relational messages, such as "John, could you please do something useful and go get the bronchoscope?"
- *Open insult:* If stress and the experience of failure lead to a loss of self-control, rude or even hostile remarks can follow. Remarks of this kind indicate a lack of respect and esteem for others. The cost to repair a relationship shattered in this way is hard to estimate but can be immense.

12.4.8 Clarifying Relationships at the Wrong Time

Negative relationship messages have no place in critical situations; however, when they do occur, the relationship component should be settled after the critical situation. This approach is not defensive or conflict avoiding; instead, concern for patient care during a critical situation predominates the clarification of relationship issues. Even if communication style in a critical situation becomes unpleasant from time to time (e.g., loud and harsh commands) and team relations become strained, the following rule applies: first cope with the emergency situation and then discuss personal and relational issues so that communication can be more effective next time.

12.5 Safe Communication in Critical Situations

12.5.1 Give Luck a Bit of a Boost

Considering the multiple possible pitfalls in human communication and the fact that we all talk with "four mouths" and hear with "four ears" (Fig. 12.3), it might seem difficult to believe that we are ever successful delivering a message from one person to another. Constructive communication might seem to be a fortunate exception rather than the rule. However, there are some basic techniques that improve personal communication skills and communication in critical situations.

12.5.2 Communicate Congruently

Verbal, paraverbal, and nonverbal messages should all correspond with each other. If a disconnect exists between those messages, the receiver of a message can no longer be sure which message he or she should trust. All speakers can consciously try to provide a congruent message by matching body language, nonverbal signals, and the words spoken.

12.5.3 Select the Same Aspects of a Message

Communication partners can try to select the same aspect of a message and make that their shared objective. If the content component is in the foreground, then both partners should use their "content mouth" and "content ears." If the self-revelation is especially important, then it helps if both partners meet on a basis of personal "I-statements" by saying things that reveal their state of mind, e.g., "I think," "I plan," "I see," "I hear," "I will do chest compressions," etc.

12.5.4 Listen Actively

The general understanding of "listening" is that it is a passive undertaking. An effective countermeasure is active and purposeful listening. Active listening is hard work and is more than just incessant attention. Active listening means that every team member takes responsibility for working to understand the point of view of his or her teammates. This is the case when, for instance, a team member uses the word "concern" in a remark. Recognizing the verbal triggers, the receiver can positively respond by asking: "Why exactly are you concerned? What makes you feel uncomfortable? Why might you be thinking this is a safety issue?" By listening actively, team members do not make assumptions about a teammate's intention or expect others to be good at conveying what they really mean; instead, they are proactive and take up the point until unclear issues are resolved. Our personal filters, assumptions, judgments, and beliefs distort what we hear. Our understanding of a team member's message can differ dramatically from what he or she intended to say; therefore, as an active listener, we can use feedback as a means to ensure mutual understanding by restating what we think we heard and by asking "Did I understand you correctly?" Active listening is a communication skill that requires acceptance and active attention for the person speaking too. Only if these prerequisites are met can people more accurately follow another's speech, enquire with greater focus, and influence the conversation by nonverbal signals. Active listening facilitates the exchange of information and increases the likelihood that the listener will understand what the other person means. The following habits and behaviors indicate an active listener (Transport Canada 1997):

- *Be patient*: Wait with your response until the other person has finished speaking. Do not interrupt. While the other person is talking, try to hear what his or her position is.

- *Ask questions*: Once the other person has finished speaking, ask for clarifications, details, and explanations.
- *Observe and hold eye contact*: Observe body language and listen closely to nonverbal and paraverbal signals. In this way, we can learn a lot about what the other person is really trying to communicate.
- *Paraphrase and mirror*: Repeat important details (doses, names, and times) verbatim; otherwise, repeat in your own words what you understood. This can help to clarify your own thoughts as well as let the sender know how well he or she has been understood. One useful rule is to verbally repeat all medical orders, e.g., "Yes, I will get the chest tube," and verbally acknowledge all operational orders, e.g., when asked to get a blanket, "I'll get it."
- *Be supportive*: Encourage, show respect, and say "thank you" when information or assistance is provided. This will help to create a supportive team climate.

12.5.5 Raise the Issue of Communication Failure

Raising the issue of communication failures is often uncomfortable for team members, but addressing our failures is the best way to avoid them in the future. One of the most common ways that team members avoid the very real emotional and relational components of communication is to discuss only the facts and goals of verbalizations and fool ourselves that the relationship is only about the clinical content.

If after the critical event, communication partners discuss the way they interact and how they interpret each other's words, they can best avoid precarious situations and promote productive cooperation and mutual respect. Talking about the situation in which communication occurs is called *meta-communication*.

Besides the importance of teams productively reviewing their communication and including emotional and relational aspects, there are some rules for good communication style in critical situations:

- Communicate congruently.
- Select the same aspects of a message.
- Address communication issues at an appropriate time.
- Speak unambiguously.
- Close the loop when receiving a communication.
- If ordering or asking and the communication loop is not closed, ask the person to acknowledge.
- Brief team members.
- Search actively for information.
- Share information.
- Advocate for the best patient care.
- Voice concerns respectfully and honestly.
- Listening actively.
- Debrief after an event and include the topics of teamwork and communication.

12.5.6 Speak a Clear Language

12.5.6.1 Speak Unambiguously, Avoid Ambiguity

Language is never completely devoid of ambiguity. For this reason, clarity at the content level is a sign of good communication; a shared phraseology is helpful. Each speaker should explicitly identify the intended receiver of information by making eye contact and addressing the person by name. Information should be provided concisely and using simple sentences with few items. Complex sentences with several verbs and objects can be confusing, especially during a critical event. All difficulties, negative trends in vital signs, and unexpected problems should be stated clearly, e.g., "I cannot find a vein for an IV."

12.5.6.2 Close the Communication Loop

Communication can fail for various reasons: What the listener hears can be different from what the speaker said, and the listener's understanding can differ from the speaker's intention. A good way to avoid misunderstanding and to achieve verified mutual understanding is for the receiver to cross-check his understanding with the senders' intention by closing the communication loop. Fig. 12.6 illustrates how to close the communication loop: During induction of anesthesia, the physician orders a nurse, "Please give 0.2 mg Fentanyl IV." The nurse then repeats what he has heard ("readback"): "0.2 mg of Fentanyl IV."

Thus, the physician knows that his instructions were correctly understood. To acknowledge the correctness of the nurse's understanding, the physician confirms ("hearback"): "Yes, 0.2 mg Fentanyl IV." Now the nurse, too, knows that he understood the instruction correctly and only then should inject the drug. Readback/hearback, or "closing the loop," is an efficient way of helping teams achieve a verified mutual understanding of the situation and of helping healthcare providers avoid errors arising from informational gaps and misunderstandings. This is all the more important in a high-stakes environment where complexity, uncertainty, and time pressure increase the likelihood of errors occurring. It is better to identify misunderstandings by closing the loop than by detecting them during or after task execution. Although the process may seem awkward and cumbersome at first, it can become a fluid part of messaging and decision-making in critical situations if it is an accepted and valued by the team and has been practiced repeatedly. As stated many times before, only when procedures have become habit through practice and daily interactions will team members be able to apply them in the heat of an emergency situation.

12.5.7 Brief Team Members

Briefings, although a standard practice in many high-stakes environments (e.g., civil aviation, military command), are uncommon in clinical medicine. Spending a few minutes on briefing and planning at the beginning of a shift can get everyone on the same page, help to avoid surprises, and positively affect how the team works together (Leonard et al. 2004). Shared mental models are the basis for joint action (Chap. 11). For this reason, briefing the team in advance along general lines on the planned

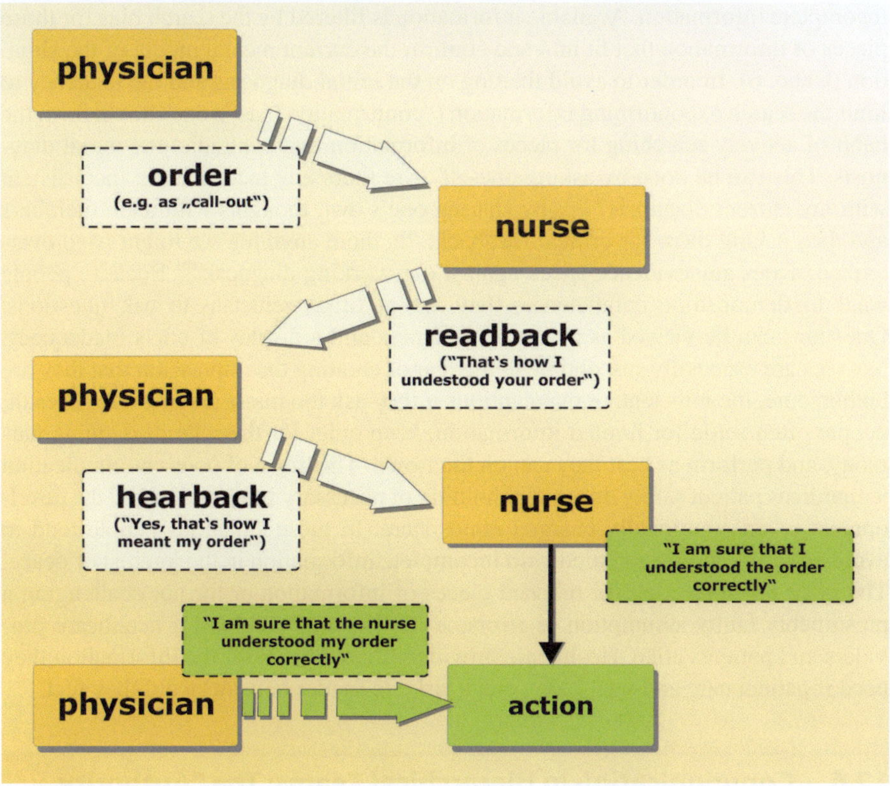

Fig. 12.6 Closing the communication loop consists of the elements "order," "readback," and "hearback." Both communication partners can be certain that their mutual understanding of the situation is verified by the communication partner and is not based on assumptions or expectations

course of action is highly recommended. Briefing is especially useful for critical actions that may have several alternate pathways (e.g., difficult airway management, exchanging endotracheal tubes, coordination of medical management). The shared mental model achieved via a team briefing allows every team member to assess the effectiveness of planned actions, think ahead, initiate planned actions and assess results. If a critical situation has a low-workload phase, performing a situational update and forecasting the possible developments of the situation are an excellent use of time. Briefing proactively focuses individual plans and intentions, helps to align mental models, and creates opportunities for inquiry, concerns, and suggestions.

12.5.8 Search Actively for Information

Good information forms the basis for good decisions, so seeking and gathering information are vital activities for safe patient care. At the outset of critical situations, healthcare providers must often base their initial diagnosis or decisions on incomplete information. Available information is filtered by the search bias for those pieces of information that fit into and confirm the current mental model of the situation (Chap. 6). In order to avoid fixating on the initial diagnosis and the tendency to limit the search to confirming information ("confirmation bias"), one should form the habit of actively searching for pieces of information that contradict the initial diagnosis. This can be done by asking oneself "Are there any facts that are inconsistent with my current diagnosis?" or by sharing one's own thoughts with team members and then asking them for critical feedback: "Is there anything we might have overlooked? Does any evidence speak against our working diagnosis?" Because people want to demonstrate competence, they are at times reluctant to ask questions. Questions can be viewed as a sign of weakness and a display of one's inadequacy. Novices are especially susceptible to the fear of creating the impression that they are bothersome, incompetent, or overcautious if they ask too many inquiries. As a result, people often settle for limited information, keep quiet for the sake of ongoing harmony, and perform as best they can on their own. This form of poor communication jeopardizes patient safety due to withholding of necessary information and the development of an emotionally charged atmosphere. In these situations people tend to avoid conflicts and are satisfied with incomplete information in the interest of peace. The price for not asking for relevant pieces of information or for not challenging a presumably faulty assumption or erroneous action may be high for healthcare providers and patients alike. Healthcare providers should press for the information they need if patient care and well-being are at risk, no matter how awkward they feel.

12.6 Communication in Hierarchical Teams: The "Authority Gradient" and the Need to Speak Up

12.6.1 The Authority Gradient

Efficient teamwork is essential for the delivery of high-quality, safe patient care not least because it is the main safety net for the early detection and mitigation of errors committed by individual team members. These team members can be nurses, students, technicians, and residents, as well as attending physicians. If safety-relevant errors are to be detected and mitigated in a timely fashion, then critical information must be allowed to flow freely among all team members. Irrespective of their professional status, team members must feel empowered and encouraged to cross-monitor, to ask questions, and to voice concerns if they believe that a decision or a planned action is not clear or suboptimal or may harm the patient. However, it is exactly the difference in professional status and the associated authority gradient that can have a major negative impact on optimal information exchange and team coordination (Belyansky et al. 2011; Cosby 2010). The term *authority gradient* was coined by Hawkins (1987) (as *Trans-Cockpit Authority Gradient*) in the context of aviation crew resource management (CRM) training, and the Institute of Medicine report "To Err Is Human" introduced the concept to medicine. Authority gradients are most likely to influence decisions and actions in systems that are hierarchical. Healthcare has been characterized for most of its history by a strongly hierarchical structure. As a consequence, teamwork in healthcare had more in common with an authoritarian, military-like concept of leadership than with the mature interaction of adult healthcare providers. For decades the concept of teamwork had largely been reduced to a gathering of people who give and take orders and basically split the team into those who did the brainwork and those who simply did as they were told. There are some who call this concept of unequal power, and its negative impact on safe patient care the "Berlin Wall" of patient safety (Walton 2006). Despite recent progress, medical hierarchies in most of today's healthcare institutions are still best characterized as the dual combination of a power gradient between a superior and a subordinate and a knowledge gradient between teacher and learner.

However, although the term *authority gradient* usually conveys a negative influence from authoritative figures, it seems inappropriate to equate authority with communication barrier per se. It should rather be kept in mind that team members experience a "relational hierarchy" along with the "professional hierarchy." Thus, it is usual that attending physicians can be perceived as competent, approachable, and even loved within their institution rather than autocratic, inaccessible, and despotic. Authority and "authority gradient" do not inevitably lead to a breakdown in communication but rather represent a potent risk factor. It may be expected that autocratic and feared attending physicians receive minimal support from their teams.

Blind trust can hinder residents and nurses from challenging superiors just as much as blind obedience can (St.Pierre et al. 2012). In a concrete situation, a team member's decision to voice patient-related concerns rather than to remain silent most probably will depend on his or her perception of the superior and on associated fears about the leader's reaction (Table 12.2).

Leaders in turn may discourage subordinates from providing information and assisting with tasks and avoid speaking up for fear of being criticized and of being considered incompetent. This fear should be baseless, because

Table 12.2 An example list of possible reasons why team members fear to speak up when concern arises about patient care. And an example list of why leaders have difficulty being questioned by subordinates

Team members possibly fear that…	Leaders possibly fear that…
…their questions will be interpreted as incompetence, as the answer is "obvious" …they will experience negative social consequences due to their questions …they exceed their scope of practice and competence …they will appear to be a know-it-all and egotistical …they may not know how to find the right words to express a respectful way of questioning and challenging their superior	…their authority is being undermined and incompetence is implied …challenge will encourage subordinates to continuously meddle in their decision-making …in an emergency there will be too much debating and not enough action …hierarchies will be loosened when they are needed most

patient-relevant concerns of team members generally do not relate to competence or expertise but more likely address the influence of human factors (e.g., misunderstanding, inattention, distraction, fixation, information deficit, fatigue) on decision-making.

12.6.2 Advocacy, Assertiveness, and Inquiry

Several studies were able to demonstrate a correlation between insufficient communication and poor patient outcome (e.g., Taylor-Adams and Vincent 2000; Wilson et al. 1995). As a result, healthcare drew on positive experience from other high-risk industries and developed training concepts that sensitize employees to their responsibility for assuring patient safety and in voicing concerns and doubts when necessary (e.g., AHRQ 2007; Barrett et al. 2001; Risser et al. 1999). Despite conceptual differences, most programs share basic assumptions regarding the individuals' responsibility for patient safety.

- *Advocacy*: Independent of his or her position within the hierarchy, every healthcare professional is responsible for the patient's care and well-being and cannot dispense with this responsibility. In this perspective the employee is the patient's advocate and speaks up when he or she has concerns.
- *Assertiveness*: For effective teamwork, it is crucial that ambiguity can be addressed, and intentions and actions of each team member can be questioned at any time. This requirement explicitly includes senior staff members (Chap. 13). Team members have to voice their concerns actively and assertively until they can be sure that their content was heard, understood, and adequately considered by the leader (Lorr and More 1980; Jentsch and Smith-Jentsch 2001). The objective is that all patient care and safety-relevant facts can contribute to the leader's opinion formation before a decision is made. Because team members will have to carry out a decision, they want to be convinced by facts and not forced by authority. Assertiveness is not the same as aggressiveness, however. Assertiveness means to clearly communicate feelings, ideas, requests, and concerns without humiliating or hurting the communication partner (Table 12.3). Honesty and fairness are crucial parts of assertiveness.

- *Inquiry*: Team members must never rely on assumptions regarding the mental model of the other, e.g., "I guess the attending knows what she is doing," and instead should cross-check one's personal assumptions with other's perspective. This is true for team members who want to know the reason for a potentially wrong or dangerous action. And it applies to the leader who wants to address verbal prompts or concerns voiced by team members.

Therefore advocacy, assertiveness, and inquiry do not imply that a team member seizes leadership and makes decisions in a leader's stead. Rather, it means that patient care and safety-relevant information and concerns can be clearly voiced at

Table 12.3 Differences between assertive and aggressive behavior

Assertive behavior	Aggressive behavior
Focused on problem solving	Focused on confrontation
Interested in other's opinion	Ignores other's opinion
Self- and team enhancing	Self-enhancing at other's expense
Expresses feelings about self	Expresses depreciation of others
Influences others	Chooses for others
Tries to hurt no one (including self)	Wants to hurt others
May achieve desired goal; if not, will negotiate	Achieves desired goal at any expense
Uses a conversational tone	Speaks loudly
Makes good eye contact	Stares and glares at others or ignores input altogether
Adopts an open posture and expression	Stands rigidly, crosses arms, invades others' personal space
Tries to participate in groups	Tries to control groups

any time and regardless of hierarchical structures. Team members do not question authority per se; instead the concern is voiced about the decision or planned action.

12.6.3 Overcome Speechlessness

Teams need a common language to address conflicts and communicate their degree of concern. With a shared formal method to settle disputes, residents and nurses may be more likely to speak up when they believe patient care may be compromised, and superiors may more readily recognize verbal prompts from team members that alert them to suboptimal or contraindicated care. Ideally, a conversational technique of stating clearly what one heard or saw and their concern (e.g., advocacy) in combination with genuine interest in the superior's point of view (e.g., inquiry) should be used to overcome communication barriers between peers, specialities, disciplines, and the hierarchy.

Even without time pressure, many subordinates find it difficult to question senior decisions (McCue and Beach 1994; Sutcliffe et al. 2004) or to resolve a conflict raised during a surgery (Coats and Burd 2002; Belyansky et al. 2011). This problem is aggravated in the case of immediately impending and irreversible actions or during dynamically evolving critical situations. In these situations team members have limited time to address the decision-maker with their patient concerns and to prevent potential patient harm. Conflicts with acute, time-bound relevance to safety are one of the most challenging situations in patient care.

Several strategies and tools to enhance performance and patient safety in conflict situations have been proposed. One example is TeamSTEPPS developed by the Agency of Healthcare Research and Quality (AHRQ 2007). A constructive approach for addressing and resolving conflict includes assertive statements using "CUS words" (i.e., "concerned, uncomfortable, safety issue"). Actually, CUS implies an escalation of statements starting with a vague "gut feeling" (uncomfortable: "something feels wrong but I don't know exactly what it is"), followed by a reasonable concern (concerned: "because of XYZ I don't think that this action is right!"), and ramps up to verbal intervention (safety issue: "Stop! If you continue we may harm or kill the patient"). CRM training (Chap. 16) sensitizes team members (including leaders) to actively listen and to take up the point every time they hear one of the CUS key words.

The essence of appropriate assertiveness is being able to state your case without making the other person defensive. The following communication strategy has been proposed and widely used (Jensen 1995; Transport Canada 1997; AHRQ 2007):

- *Make an opening*: Use the other person's name.
- *State the problem* (*real or perceived*): Define the problem.
- *State your concern*: Make the issue yours, and describe it with an "I" statement. "The way I see it…" is more productive than "Sir, you are wrong!" Be as clear and concise as possible. Do not assume that your communication partner has the same perceptions and associations you have. Make clear that *you* consider the issue at hand to be patient care and well-being. Your counterpart should realize that you perceive *something* is wrong and not that *he* or *she* is wrong.
- *Offer a solution*: If possible, suggest at least one solution to the problem. State what you would do rather than what your communication partner should or shouldn't do. If you don't have any good ideas of what's best, ask for a short "time out" to think and figure out what to do next. Do not assume that your communication partner has considered the aspects that you find obvious.
- *Reach agreement on next steps*: After you have simply put forward your point of view, ask for feedback: "What do you think?" It is important your communication partner acknowledges that he or she heard and understood your concern.
- *Reach an agreement* through collaboration if possible.

First attempts to implement these communication strategies into training concepts for perioperative medicine show promising results (e.g., Hunziker et al. 2011; McLaughlin et al. 2006).

12.6.4 "Two-Challenge Rule" in Healthcare?

To assist subordinate crew members in resolving the basic question of whether or not to voice concern or to intervene, the "PACE" operational methodology has been proposed in aviation (Besco 1999). PACE skills enable subordinate flight crew members to use proven, operationally based procedures to effectively intervene when a captain is not performing up to reasonable professional standards.

The acronym stands for:

- *Probing* for a better understanding
- *Alerting* captain of the anomalies
- *Challenging* suitability of the present strategy
- *Emergency* warning of critical and immediate dangers

The first two steps represent the first challenge. The last two steps represent the second challenge of the "two-challenge rule." The two-challenge rule allows one crew member to automatically assume the duties of another crew member who fails to respond to two consecutive challenges, i.e., does not respond or does not respond with an answer that makes sense. This right is derived from the assumption that a pilot who does not respond appropriately after two callouts jeopardizes flight safety and that the responsibility for the safety and effectiveness of a flight is in the hands of the whole crew, not only the pilot.

In face of its effectiveness in aviation, there has been some debate in healthcare over whether it is appropriate or acceptable for a trainee or nurse to assume control from a supervising attending. The main difference between both domains lies in the fact that in aviation, the two-challenge rule regulates the interaction between two similarly qualified people (e.g., pilot flying and pilot not flying). For obvious reasons this rule cannot be applied in exactly the same way in healthcare. However, a translation of the two-challenge rule from aviation to healthcare can empower team members to "stop the line" if they sense or discover a possible safety breach. When an initial assertive statement is ignored, team members should feel the responsibility to voice concerns once more to ensure that they have been heard. The team member being challenged must acknowledge that the concern has been heard. If the safety issue still hasn't been addressed, a stronger course of action has to be taken. If taking over control is not an option, then calling for a second opinion of another senior physician or senior nurse or utilizing the institutional chain of command has been recommended as equivalent in healthcare (e.g., AHRQ 2007; Cosby and Croskerry 2004).

Because the two-challenge rule can be problematic in certain aspects and carries the potential to disrupt clinical routine, it is advisable to clarify framing conditions before introducing such a procedure. Otherwise team processes and patient safety are jeopardized (Prineas 2011):

- *Seek support by faculty and senior leadership*: Inform faculty and leadership that trainees are being taught this concept as well as this type of language. Leaders have to be informed that this language is not meant to undermine their authority but rather is used as a patient care and safety strategy independent of the person addressed.
- *Propagate and use standardized language*. By doing so faculty can more readily recognize and respond to words and assertive statements in real clinical settings.
- All employees must *use* the language exclusively *in the interest of the patient*. Each person involved has to be aware of this preeminent responsibility and should not pursue a personal agenda.
- Implement the two-challenge rule *as part of a broader patient safety approach*. Ideally, communication training (e.g., as part of clinical simulation) precedes the introduction into clinical practice.

The notion that the two-challenge rule could and should be implemented in healthcare was supported by the Institute of Medicine's report, "To Err Is Human"

(Kohn et al. 1999). Since the report, there have been several successful initiatives to implement a two-challenge approach by twice pairing an advocacy-inquiry and then taking some action (e.g., Morey et al. 2002; Pian-Smith et al. 2009).

12.7 Communication After Critical Incidents

12.7.1 Don't Forget to Debrief and to Give Feedback

Critical, time-pressured situations demand rapid decision-making. Under these circumstances, it is common that time to address a conflict is hard to find. To prevent a breakdown in relationships, unresolved conflicts should be addressed systematically in a debriefing. Because giving feedback requires a calm atmosphere and sufficient time, it should be given after a critical situation in an environment that focuses on what's right and not who's right.

Feedback on statements and behavior of the team and its leader are appropriate. Feedback is an ideal tool for clarifying a misunderstanding and offers boundless learning opportunities. To make feedback an essential part of team communication, team members need to feel safe and be sure that feedback is valued and will be used constructively. Communication among equal (symmetrical) healthcare providers and the resulting feedback is generally rich in positive and negative aspects. Feedback from subordinates to people higher up in the hierarchy tends to focus on appreciation and positive behavior but mostly avoids addressing problems. To avoid this pitfall, it is a good strategy for a leader to ask explicitly for feedback concerning his or her behavior and for constructive advice, e.g., "What did I not do well and any advice about how I could improve for next time?" The following guidelines may be helpful for constructive feedback:

- Show a respectful attitude – everybody can learn from feedback.
- Choose an appropriate time and place.
- Give feedback when the receiver is ready for it.
- Give both positive and negative feedback. They are both valuable.
- Never embarrass anybody.
- Keep in mind that everyone is trying their best.
- Choose the environment; some things should be private; other things should be for the group; debrief away from patient care areas; try to find a less noisy/busy area.
- Make your feedback precise and objective, and give the other person time to reply and explain their thinking, i.e., don't "hit and run."
- Address observable behavior – not characteristics or unobservable motivations of a person.
- Use "I" statements whenever you communicate observations, e.g., I saw, I heard, and I think.
- If possible, suggest an alternative behavior and see what the receiver thinks.
- Set a good example: Take feedback willingly and show gratitude for it.

12.7.2 Address Conflict in a Constructive Way

Conflicts arise in different ways. First, people experience the same situation differently and have divergent mental models, opinions, plans, and intentions. Secondly are personal issues such as a prior negative experience, feeling less than competent, personal difficulties with another member of the team, etc. Conflicts become even more complex when it is a blend of both.

If a conflict is related to medical issues, it generally can be resolved by reviewing and discussing data, opinions, or evidence. In this context, the best point of view can be identified and pursued, or, perhaps, conflicting intentions can be prioritized, and both can be addressed. It is also quite possible that both points of view are dismissed in favor of a third superior possibility. When a conflict is resolved in a constructive way, a more comprehensive picture of reality and better solutions nearly always emerge.

12.7.3 Address Relational Conflicts

If personal conflicts surface during critical situations, motives such as protecting the feeling of competence can quickly govern behavior. Who is right will become more important than what is right. Emergency situations often contain disagreements because to some lesser or greater degree, everyone perceives things in their own way. Failing to see a teammate's point of view as reasonable or as worthy as our point of view, we might stubbornly take an immovable position – and so might our teammate! Team members and leaders should try to work at the relationship level once the critical situation has passed. There are no easy rules of thumb about how to resolve differences, but the knowledge of some basic guidelines may improve the ability to resolve conflict.

The following attitudes and behaviors are characteristic of constructive conflict resolution:

- *Listen well*: Try to see a conflict as an unsolicited opportunity to hear and learn additional points of view.
- "*The problem is the problem*!" Instead of attacking your counterpart, you should tackle the problem.
- *The patient should be the winner* and not one of the healthcare providers involved in the conflict. Conflicts should not be a struggle with an adversary; instead it should be an opportunity to find the best solution. It can be a win-win situation and a learning opportunity for all persons involved.
- *Bring out the differences*: It is helpful to clarify the areas of both agreement and disagreement. Often, there will be less disagreement than initially expected, and discussions will usually include the fact that everyone was trying their best to take care of the patient.

- *Acknowledge feelings*: People often take strong positions because of feelings rather than logic. When feelings are brought up, consider them to be worth examination and as discussion.
- *Respect every team member*: Leaders should always express respect and appreciation for their team members raising issues or concerns.
- *Seriously consider suggestions and options*: If the leader disagrees with other team members and decides on a different course of action, the leader should ensure that others know that opinions and suggestions have been considered.

12.8 Tips for Daily Practice

- Practice good communication and good listening; let it become a habit in your daily life. You will profit from this habit in critical situations.
- Be aware of your appearance and bearing. The first impression you make on other people (be it negative or positive) has an impact on successful communication.
- You cannot expect people to read your mind, so state what you are thinking, share your opinions clearly, and voice your concerns.
- Remember: Nothing is so simple that it cannot be misunderstood.
- Things said are often not things heard and things heard often are not things understood.
- Whenever you feel uncomfortable or concerned that patient safety is at stake, state your concern, and challenge authority in a respectful, nonthreatening, and supportive way. Make sure that critical information is addressed.
- If you are in doubt: Ask!
- Good decisions are based on good information. You have to actively seek, organize, and share information if you want to ensure safe patient care.
- Use advocacy, assertiveness, and inquiry when confronted with safety-relevant issues. Avoid questioning the authority of the decision-maker; instead focus on the rationale underlying his or her current decision.
- In an emergency, active listening is a critical skill.
- In critical situations, the odds are high that the initial mental model is incomplete or faulty. It's a good practice to search actively for information that contradicts your current assumptions.

12.9 "Communication" in a Nutshell

- In the context of a high-stakes medical environment, communication has a fourfold function: It enables and maintains team structure; it coordinates the team process and task execution; it enables information exchange; and it facilitates relationships.
- Human communication takes place in a social context. For this reason, it is impossible to exchange information in a mere matter-of-fact manner without

simultaneously establishing a relationship between the persons participating in the information exchange.

- "Communication = content + relationship + perceptual filters."
- Communication is not simply about transmitting but also receiving, including ensuring that the transmission was understood as intended.
- Communication is much more than mere verbal exchange. Every action can be interpreted by others and thus can transport a message intentionally or unintentionally: "One cannot not communicate."
- Human communication uses different channels in a parallel way, including verbal, paraverbal, and nonverbal cues.
- If the verbal and nonverbal channels are incongruent because words convey one meaning and the nonverbal or paraverbal information indicates something different, the receiver will place greater importance on the nonverbal cues.
- Good communication uses verbal and nonverbal cues congruently. Every speaker can provide a congruent communication by matching body language, nonverbal signals, and the words spoken.
- The meaning of a message cannot be transmitted; instead, it is "reconstructed" by the receiver. If a message is transmitted incompletely, then listeners will try to "complete" the message by making their own interpretation of the unclear aspects.
- Symmetrical relationships are those in which the persons involved are equal in position. Complementary relationships are based on differences in power, with one person being higher in hierarchy than the other.
- General disturbances of communication can be rooted in the *characteristics* of the message, the *process* of sending, receiving, and interpreting, and in the *relationship* of the dialogue partners.
- Communication becomes dysfunctional when the people involved have good intentions but the interaction creates an unproductive and destructive system.
- The most common dysfunctional communication patterns are symmetrical escalation, complementary communication, and defensive behavior.
- A misunderstanding occurs if the receiver of a message reacts differently to information or instructions than the sender intended.
- Effective listening is a key communication skill and can be jeopardized in manifold ways.
- Active listening means taking responsibility for understanding the point of view of another person.
- A safety process that ensures messages are clearly received and understood requires "readback" (i.e., the receiver says what she or he has heard) and "hearback" (i.e., the sender acknowledges whether or not the readback was correct).
- Assertiveness means advocating your position emphatically until concerns about the adequacy of decisions or actions of other team members can be addressed. The goal of assertiveness is to prompt other team members to diligently reconsider before a decision is made or an action taken.
- Only if a communication pattern has been practiced repeatedly in everyday and stressful (e.g., simulation) situations can it become a fluid part of the fabric of messaging and decision-making in critical situations.

References

AHRQ (2007) TeamSTEPPS. Strategies and tools to enhance performance and patient safety. Curriculum Kit disc wallet AHRQ Pub. No. 06-0020-3. Accessed at www.ahrq.gov

Barrett J, Gifford C, Morey J, Risser D, Salisbury M (2001) Enhancing patient safety through teamwork training. J Healthc Risk Manag 21:57–65

Belyansky I, Martin TR, Prabhu AS et al (2011) Poor resident-attending intraoperative communication may compromise patient safety. J Surg Res 171:386–394

Besco RO (1999) PACE: Probe, Alert, Challenge, and Emergency action. Bus Commer Aviat 84(6):72–74

Brehm S, Brehm JW (1981) Psychological reactance – a theory of freedom and control. Academic, New York

Bühler K (1934) Sprachtheorie: Die Darstellungsform der Sprache [Speech theory]. Fischer, Jena

Campbell RD, Bagshaw M (2002) Human performance and limitations in aviation. Blackwell Science Ltd, Oxford, UK

Coats RD, Burd RS (2002) Intraoperative communication of residents with faculty: perception versus reality. J Surg Res 104:40–45

Cosby KS (2010) Authority gradients and communication. In: Croskerry P, Cosby KS, Schenkel S, Wears R (eds) Patient safety in emergency medicine. Walters Kluwer Lippincott, Philadelphia, pp 195–204

Cosby KS, Croskerry P (2004) Profiles in patient safety: authority gradients in medical error. Acad Emerg Med 11:1341–1345

Cushing S (1994) Fatal words. Communication clashes and aircraft crashes. University of Chicago Press, Chicago

Griffin E (1999) A first look at communication theory, 4th edn. McGraw-Hill, Boston

Hargie O (2006) Handbook of communication skills. Routledge, London

Hawkins F (1987) Human factors in flight. Ashgate Publishing Company, London

Hunziker S, Johansson AC, Tschan F et al (2011) Teamwork and leadership in cardiopulmonary resuscitation. J Am Coll Cardiol 57:2381–2388

Jensen RS (1995) Pilot judgement and crew resource management. Ashgate, Aldershot

Jentsch F, Smith-Jentsch KA (2001) Assertiveness and team performance: more than "just say no". In: Salas E, Bowers CA, Edens E (eds) Improving teamwork in organisations. Applications of resource management training. Erlbaum, Mahwah, pp 73–94

Kanki B, Smith G (1999) Training aviation communication skills. In: Salas E, Bowers CA (eds) Improving teamwork in organisations. Erlbaum, Mahwah, pp 95–127

Knapp ML, Daly JA (2002) Handbook of interpersonal communication (abridged). Sage, London

Kohn L, Corrigan J, Donaldson M (1999) To err is human: building a safer health system. Committee on Quality of Healthcare in America, Institute of Medicine (IOM). National Academy Press, Washington, DC

Leonard M, Graham S, Bonacum D (2004) The human factor: the critical importance of effective teamwork and communication in providing safe care. Qual Saf Health Care 13(Suppl 1): i85–i90

Lorr M, More W (1980) Four dimensions of assertiveness. Multivar Behav Res 14:127–138

Maturana HR, Varela F (1992) Tree of knowledge. The biological roots of human understanding. Shambala, Boston

McCue JD, Beach KJ (1994) Communication barriers between attending physicians and residents. J Gen Intern Med 9:158–161

McLaughlin SA, Bond W, Promes S et al (2006) The status of human simulation training in emergency medicine residency programs. Simul Healthc 1:18–21

Miller K (2005) Communication theories: perspectives, processes, and contexts, 2nd edn. McGraw Hill, New York

Morey JC, Simon R, Jay GD, Wears RL, Salisbury M, Dukes KA, Berns SD (2002) Error reduction and performance improvement in the emergency department through formal teamwork training: evaluation results of the MedTeams project. Health Serv Res 37:1553–1581

Murray WB, Foster PA (2000) Crisis resource management among strangers: principles of organizing a multidisciplinary group for crisis resource management. J Clin Anesth 12:633–638

Pian-Smith MCM, Simon R, Truong RD, Baboolal H, Raemer DB (2009) Teaching residents the two-challenge rule: a simulation-based approach to improve education and patient safety. Simul Healthc 4(2):84–91

Prineas S (2011) Safety critical communication. In: Cyna AM, Andrew MI, Tan SGM, Smith AF (eds) Handbook of communication in anaesthesia and critical care. A practical guide to exploring the art. Oxford University Press, Oxford, UK

Risser DT, Rice MM, Salisbury ML, Simon R, Jay GD, Berns SD (1999) The potential for improved teamwork to reduce medical errors in the emergency department. The Med-Teams Research Consortium. Ann Emerg Med 34:373–383

Schulz von Thun F (1981) Miteinander reden [Talk with each other]. Bd 1. Rowohlt, Reinbek bei Hamburg

Schulz von Thun F, Ruppel J, Stratmann R (2000) Miteinander reden. Psychologie für Führungskräfte [Talk with each other: psychology for leaders]. Rowohlt, Reinbek bei Hamburg

Searle JR (1969) Speech acts. An essay in the philosophy of language. Cambridge University Press, Cambridge

Shannon CE, Weaver W (1949) The mathematical theory of communication. University of Illinois Press, Urbana

St.Pierre M, Scholler A, Strembski D, Breuer G (2012) Do residents and nurses communicate safety relevant concerns? Simulation study on the influence of the authority gradient. Anäesthesist 61:857–866

Sutcliffe KM, Lewton E, Rosenthal MM (2004) Communication failures: an insidious contributor to medical mishaps. Acad Med 79:186–194

Taylor-Adams S, Vincent CA (2000) Clinical accident analysis: understanding the interactions between the task, individual, team and organisation. In: Vincent CA, deMol B (eds) Safety in medicine. Pergamon Press, Amsterdam, pp 101–116

Transport Canada (1997) Human factors for aviation: advanced handbook. Transport Canada Civil Aviation Resources, Ottawa

Ungerer D (2004) Simple speech: improving communication in disaster relief operations. In: Dietrichs R, Jochum K (eds) Teaming up: components of safety under high risk. Ashgate, Aldershot, pp 81–92

Walton MM (2006) Hierarchies: the Berlin Wall of patient safety. Qual Saf Health Care 15:229–230

Watzlawick P, Weakland JH, Fisch R (1974) Changing a system. Norton, New York

Watzlawick P, Beavin J, Jackson D (1996) Pragmatics of human communication: study of interactional patterns, pathologies and paradoxes. Norton, New York

Wilson RM, Runciman WB, Gibberd RW, Harrison BT, newby L, Hamilton JD (1995) The quality in Australian health care study. Med J Aust 163(9):458–471

Leadership 13

Case Study

A 12-year-old boy sustains a bicycle accident resulting in an open fracture of the mandible. Because the patient has a full stomach and mouth opening is reduced due to pain, the anesthesia resident decides to perform a rapid-sequence induction with thiopental and succinylcholine. The intubation is successful and uneventful, and anesthesia is maintained as a total intravenous anesthesia (TIVA) with propofol and remifentanil.

After 30 min of uneventful anesthesia, the saturation begins to drop slowly and sinus tachycardia develops. Under the assumption of insufficient anesthetic depth, the resident increases the concentration of propofol and remifentanil. The intervention, however, does not affect the tachycardia. The anesthesia resident checks the IV line to rule out soft tissue infiltration and auscultates both lungs. Breath sounds are equal bilaterally. Meanwhile the patient requires 70 % oxygen to maintain saturations above 95 %. Because the resident is unable to find any apparent cause for the clinical deterioration and because of the danger of the situation, he calls for help from his attending physician.

When the attending physician enters the operating room a few minutes later, the patient is receiving a minute volume of 9.5 l/min to maintain the end-expiratory CO_2 at 45 mmHg. Infrequent monomorphic premature ventricular contractions are noted on the ECG. The attending tells the resident to insert an arterial pressure line into the radial artery and to obtain an arterial blood gas. The lab results show a combined respiratory and metabolic acidosis with a mild alveolo-arterial difference in the partial pressure of oxygen and a potassium concentration of 5.6 mmol/l. Based on the induction of anesthesia with succinylcholine in conjunction with the current clinical picture and the lab findings, the attending physician decides to interpret the clinical deterioration as symptoms of malignant hyperthermia and to treat it accordingly.

M. St.Pierre et al., *Crisis Management in Acute Care Settings*,
DOI 10.1007/978-3-319-41427-0_13

The patient's body temperature is 37.2 °C (99 °F). He informs the maxillofacial surgeons about the seriousness of the condition and asks them to interrupt the operation. Dantrolene is dissolved in solution and administered to the patient. The arterial blood gas is monitored closely, and the appropriate treatments for pH abnormalities and hyperkalemia and renal protection are initiated. Cardiovascular stability is maintained by catecholamine support. Due to an increase in the patient's temperature to 39.7 °C (103.4 °F) over 20 min, the attending anesthesiologist initiates external cooling procedures which are accomplished by the surgeons and OR technicians.

Twenty minutes after the administration of dantrolene, the heart rate begins to drop slowly, and the acid-base status begins to improve. Minute ventilation and FiO_2 are gradually reduced. Once the treatment begins to indicate a reassuring response by the patient, the attending physician contacts the pediatric intensive care unit (PICU) and requests a bed for the patient. He informs the pediatric intensivist about the clinical course, the measures taken, and the current clinical status. An hour later, the patient is further stabilized and is transferred to the PICU. Over the course of the next day, the patient develops a compartment syndrome of the left lower leg requiring reoperation. The anesthetic is trigger-free for malignant hyperthermia and proceeds uneventfully. The patient is extubated postoperatively and is transferred from the PICU to the general ward on the following day. He is discharged from the hospital without any residual symptoms. The patient and his family are tested for their susceptibility to malignant hyperthermia, and both the patient and his younger brother have positive results.

13.1 The Case for Leadership

Successful team performance in healthcare and good leadership are two sides of the same coin. Teamwork in teams that are organized hierarchically cannot function properly without a sound concept of leadership, and vice versa.

When talking about leadership in a high-stakes healthcare environment, the status of a critical situation needs to be differentiated from that of everyday life. Nevertheless, both leadership approaches cannot be considered completely independent from each other. It is likely that many of the same senior healthcare providers will be responsible as leaders for their staff members in routine situations as well as in emergency situations. Whether or not leadership in a medical emergency succeeds will depend to a great extent on the daily interactions of the leader with the team. What then are the core functional competencies of a leader and which behaviors are required to lead successfully? Which personal characteristics and abilities are required to bring out the best in teams? How can leaders attain above-average results while maintaining an environment of trust, motivation, and high job satisfaction? Of the extensive body of research on this topic (overview, e.g., Bass and Stogdill 2007; Manser 2008), the results most important for acute healthcare are summarized in what follows.

13.1.1 Leadership in Everyday Life

Leadership in everyday life has a threefold purpose. First, leadership is directed at the *activities* of staff members. This is done by:

- Assigning tasks
- Defining goals
- Helping to provide the necessary resources
- Monitoring the execution and the results
- Resolving team conflicts

Second, leadership in healthcare has a lot to do with a leader's ability to *assess* clinical skills and the training status of staff members. Leadership comprises creating learning opportunities for each staff member and supporting their career. Therefore, leaders in healthcare should always be concerned about human resource development efforts. By assuming a leadership position, healthcare providers volunteer to motivate staff members, to value their individual personality, and to empower teammates to increasingly take responsibility for their working environment. Leaders inspire staff members by who they *are*, what they *know*, and what they *do*.

A third aspect to leadership, specific for high-stakes environments, has been proposed by the Institute of Medicine report (Kohn et al. 1999) and many other publications: Leaders in healthcare should also be *role models* for a patient safety-oriented approach to patient care. In order to mitigate the effect of inevitably occurring errors in patient safety, leaders should create a working environment where healthcare providers feel encouraged to be alert to threats to patient safety, to voice concerns if they believe that an action may harm the patient ("advocacy and assertiveness," Chap. 12), and to monitor task performance and workload of their team members (cross-monitoring, Chap. 11).

Hierarchy of authority frequently inhibits people from expressing themselves. Effective leaders flatten the hierarchy, create familiarity, and manage to create an environment that feels "safe" for team members to speak up when they have information or safety concerns. By inviting team members to contribute their thoughts and ideas, a leader can facilitate a shared mental model of patient-related and operational issues (Chap. 11). This is done by communicating (verbally and nonverbally) a message of support and empowerment, and conveying an understanding of the paradox of errors is normal in the medical high-stakes environment (Table 13.1), while we do whatever we can to mitigate or eliminate those errors.

Some of the basic principles of leadership in everyday life are:

- *Set an example:* Be a good role model for your staff, set a high standard for personal conduct, and adhere to this standard in all situations. Sincerity, integrity, and ethical demeanor are trust-inspiring characteristics, and communicate to the team that you are a safe person with whom to work. Team members not only want to hear what they are expected to be or to do; they also want to see it lived out in *your* life as well.

Table 13.1 The most important words a leader can speak (author unknown)

The six most important words: "I admit I made a mistake"
The five most important words: "You did a good job"
The four most important words: "What is your opinion?"
The three most important words: "If you please"
The two most important words: "Thank you"
The one most important word: "We"
The least important word: "I"

- *Promote speaking up* with observations, concerns, and questions. Actively encourage proactive coordination behaviors in your team members (Edmondson 2003). What you sow in "times of peace," you will reap "when the heat is on."
- *Be technically proficient:* As a leader, you must know your job and have a solid familiarity with all task demands.
- *Know your staff members by name* and look out for their well-being.
- *Be supportive, advocating, and empowering:* Believe in people and communicate that belief.
- *Think and behave in team concepts:* Communicate to your staff that it is *we*, not *me*, who do the job.
- *Keep your staff informed:* Practice good communication skills (Chap. 12).
- *Foster a sense of responsibility* within your staff.
- *Help resolve conflicts within a team:* Recognize areas of tension between individuals, and help them apply conflict resolution techniques (Chap. 12).

13.1.2 Leadership in a Critical Situation

The case study of a malignant hyperthermia (MH) is an example of a time-critical medical emergency that necessitated leadership in an emergent situation for successful management. In contrast to leading people in everyday life, effective leadership behavior in a critical situation is more centralized. The requirements for leadership in an emergency situation are described in greater detail below.

13.2 Leadership Theories

13.2.1 Approaches to Leadership

There are diverse definitions of leadership that focus either on the position of the leader (singular or collective) or the purpose, process, and hallmarks of leadership. Most definitions come from an industrial or management setting and cannot readily be applied to healthcare. Leadership in the context of acute medical care can be defined as the process where a person assumes responsibility to influence and direct the performance of other team members by utilization of all available resources toward the achievement of a defined goal. A leader in a critical situation can be identified and defined as a team member whose influence, at least temporarily, on group attitudes, performance, and decision-making exceeds that of other members of the group. Research on the nature of leadership has proposed several theories, which all emphasize certain aspects of leadership. The earliest theories emerged during the first part of the twentieth century and focused on the qualities that distinguished leaders from followers. Subsequent theories looked at other variables such as situational factors and skill level. For the context of healthcare in a high-stakes medical environment, the following theories are relevant ones (e.g., Bass and Stogdill 2007).

13.2.2 "Great Man" Theories

This theoretical approach may still be rarely encountered among senior physicians as the deluded self-perception of a person with respect to his leadership abilities. This theory originally assumed that the capacity for leadership is inherent and that great leaders are born, not made. The historical roots to this theory are based on the results of early research on leadership where the leaders studied often came from the aristocracy, which contributed to the notion that leadership had something to do with "breeding" and the right genes. The leadership style of people who have this "great man" self-assessment adheres to the idea of this notion of personal distinctiveness. While the weak reasoning that postulates this idea of leadership might seem nearly ludicrous, there are a surprising number of situations where it seems to be the primary rule used to select who will be responsible for leading a critical event. As a result, teamwork with such a leader often proves to be far less than optimal.

13.2.3 Trait Theories

If we had to choose in an emergency whom we would like to follow as a leader, it's quite likely that certain individuals come easier to mind than others. Personal experience has taught us that these people, besides having a firm clinical foundation, seem to be made of "the right stuff" even under the most adverse circumstances. Under the guiding assumption that the "right stuff" must be identifiable in terms of certain qualities and traits, research focused in the 1940s and 1950s on the discovery of these alleged inherent characteristics (Stogdill 1948). However, the results were inconsistent and only showed that different leadership traits predominated in different situations. Because trait theory was unable to identify future leaders and only confirmed those persons who already were recognized by their peers as being leaders, researchers lost interest. Since the 1980s the trait theory of leadership regained some popularity by introducing concepts of charisma and charismatic leadership. Among the major problems with trait theories is the fact that traits useful for leadership usually have a downside (such as suppressing others, overconfidence), and no theory has yet stated "how much" of these traits really makes a good leader. Furthermore, trait theories promote the idea that adults are as they are, which makes educational efforts, such as developing leadership skills, seem worthless from the start. Also, the focus on traits implies that all persons need to lead in the same way regardless of the tasks or the environment in which they perform.

13.2.4 Behavioral Theories

In contrast to the static character of the trait perspective that conceptualizes leadership as a set of properties possessed by certain individuals and residing *in* them, behavioral theories take a process stance, claiming that leadership is a phenomenon that *resides in the interactions* between leaders and followers and makes leadership available to everyone (Northouse 2012). As a process, leadership can be observed in leader behaviors and can be learned. According to behavioral theories, among the skills a leader must have are interpersonal skills, conceptual skills, and technical skills. This approach opens broad possibilities for leadership development, assessment measures, and training interventions because, as the theories go, good leaders will develop through a never-ending process of self-study, education, training, and experience. In addition, poor leadership behaviors can be identified that contribute to teamwork failure, thus adding a second layer of understanding. This approach seems to confirm personal experience; most healthcare professionals can compare their present performance to the time when they first started the job and will find that their leadership ability indeed has improved. But behavioral theories tend to completely ignore the possibility that trait theories and the influence of personality add something to our understanding of leadership. After all, not every person will be able to learn and demonstrate appropriate leadership behavior.

13.2.5 Styles of Leadership

Leadership style is the manner and approach of providing direction, implementing plans, and motivating people. As seen by the employees, it includes the total pattern of explicit and implicit actions performed by their leader (Newstrom and Davis 1993). The first major study of leadership styles was performed by a research group led by Kurt Lewin, who was able to establish three different styles of leadership (Lewin et al. 1939). These styles differ in the degree of employee orientation (relationship and person orientation) and task orientation (performance orientation) (Blanchard et al. 1985).

The *laissez-faire style* (from the French: "just let things happen") is characterized by a low task focus and a low person focus. The *laissez-faire* leader steps back from the leadership role. The leader's involvement in decision-making is minimized, thus allowing people to make their own decisions and to do as they think best. This leadership style is sometimes called a "delegation" or "free rein" style, although the "delegation" comes more often from the leaders' unwillingness to lead than a deliberate act of delegating responsibilities to staff members.

If a leader has a *democratic (participative) leadership style*, then his or her primary focus is the well-being and the needs of the team members. The execution of task requirements is subordinate to the preeminent goal of team harmony and coherence. The democratic style is characterized by discussions in which the tasks are democratically discussed and divided. The leader tries to listen to as many voices as possible and to compromise when necessary so that everyone feels okay about decisions and plans. Team members may be involved in the decision-making even in situations where quick and unambiguous commands of the leader are necessary.

In clear contrast to the democratic approach is the *autocratic leadership style*, which is defined by unilateral control with a strong focus on the execution of the leader's view of task demands and efficacy, but with little concern for people. In the autocratic style, the leader may use pressure, threats, and any method that seems to work to achieve conformance. Leaders are viewed as having the solutions to problems; decisions are made without consultation; tasks are distributed with a detailed description of the procedure; and task execution is monitored closely. Communication is almost entirely top-down with a clear and hierarchical decision structure. The authoritarian leadership style is often perceived by team members as being arbitrary and paternalistic. An autocratic style can work in a performance environment where there is no need for input on the decision, where the decision would not change as a result of additional input, and where the motivation of people to carry out subsequent actions would not be affected whether they were or were not involved in the decision-making. This is clearly not the case in acute medical care. A modified autocratic style with its clear command structure can be effectively applied during cardiopulmonary resuscitation or during the management of natural or human-made disasters such as mass casualties (e.g., Koenig and Schultz 2016). The modification allows for feedback and the volunteering of information. In the context of high-stakes, time-critical healthcare, however, the autocratic leadership style causes the highest level of discontent among team members and generates an information-poor environment instead of the needed information-rich environment.

An *integrative leadership style* combines a high focus on task execution with an equally high attention to the relations with and among team members. The concern of the leader is directed at the execution of tasks *and* the integration of team members. Leaders engage in discussing, convincing, and explaining to achieve a high degree of mutual agreement and shared mental models (Chap. 11). Depending on the dynamics of a situation, the integrative style in a high-stakes medical environment can either be directive (authoritative) or cooperative (Fig. 13.1).

A final task-vs.-person orientation is of practical importance: the difference between a transactional and a transformational leadership style. In brief, transactional leadership is based to a varying extent on the underlying assumption that people are motivated – and made compliant – by reward and punishment. As a result, employees receive a salary and other benefits, and the employer in turn gets authority over the subordinate.

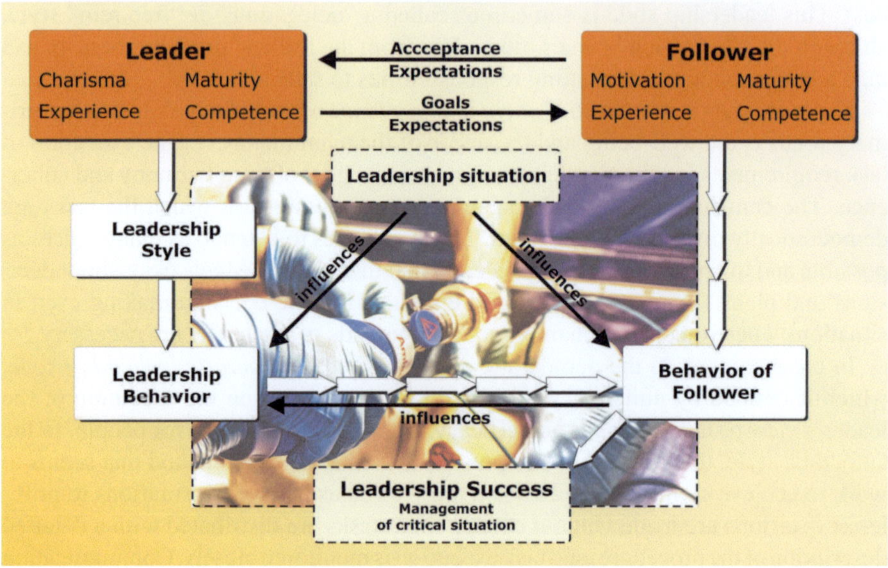

Fig. 13.1 Model of integrative leadership in a high-stakes medical environment. A leaders' personality, leadership style and behavior, the interaction with followers, and characteristics of the leadership situation have a major influence on leadership success

13.2.6 Transformational Leadership

While transactional leadership has more of a "telling style," transformational leadership pursues a "selling style." Leadership expert James MacGregor Burns introduced the concept of transformational leadership as a process where "leaders and their followers raise one another to higher levels of morality and motivation" (Burns 1978). Unlike in the transactional approach, this process is not based on a "give-and-take" relationship, but on the leader's personality and on his or her articulation of an energizing vision and challenging goal. Bernard M. Bass later further developed the concept of transformational leadership (Bass 1985): Evaluating managers tagged as high performers by their superiors as well as by their followers, they were able to define essential characteristics of successful transformational leadership. According to this research, a leader …:

- … *has charisma*: Influence is a result of integrity and fairness, provides a vision and a sense of mission, sets clear goals, instills pride, and gains respect and trust by "walking the talk."
- … *inspires*: Communicates high expectations and inspires people to reach for the improbable, uses symbols to focus efforts, expresses important purposes in simple ways, encourages others, stirs the emotions of people, and gets people to look beyond selfish interests.
- … *stimulates intellectually*: Promotes intelligence, rationality, and careful problem solving.

- … *gives individual consideration*: Gives personal attention, treats each employee individually, coaches, and advises.

As a result, transformational leadership occurs every time leaders broaden and elevate the interests of their employees, generate awareness and acceptance of the purpose and mission of the team, and stir their employees to look beyond their own self-interest for the good of the group. Studies were able to show an association between transformational leadership styles and positive outcomes in comparison to other leadership styles. Transformational leadership is positively associated with employee outcomes including commitment, role clarity, and well-being (e.g., Judge and Piccolo 2004; Michaelis 2009).

Many authors argue that by defining transformational behavior and by implementing it into leadership training, leaders-to-be can learn the techniques and obtain the qualities they need to become transformational leaders (Avolio and Bass 2004). But although transformational leadership has been in focus for some years (e.g., Gardner et al. 2010), it is still unclear under which conditions this leadership style works best.

13.2.7 Shared Leadership Theory

All of the above theories share one general assumption: Leadership must be exercised by one individual in order to be effective. However, a growing body comprised of positive research evidence from manufacturing firms, management, school administration, and more recently in aviation and the military has challenged this conventional assumption. Models have successfully been implemented where the leadership task is distributed among team members rather than focused on a single designated leader. This shared leadership, defined as "a dynamic, interactive influence process among individuals in groups for which the objective is to lead one another to the achievement of group or organizational goals"(Pearce and Conger 2003), has been advocated as an alternative way of reducing task overload and improving team performance of complex tasks. Although not a novel invention (Gibb 1954), the theory of shared responsibility has only recently been applied in the context of acute healthcare (Flin et al. 2003; Klein et al. 2006; Künzle et al. 2010; Tschan et al. 2006; Xiao et al. 2004). The results have been promising: In certain cases, shared leadership appears to facilitate performance in complex tasks given that no individual team member possesses all the resources necessary to address all task demands. Thus, shared leadership is likely to be an effective strategy to overcome the one-and-only-one leader approach – especially if task complexity is high. The distribution of leadership in situations with high task load induced by nonroutine events according to the skill sets rather than formal leadership ranking is very similar to the concept of "deference to expertise" from high-reliability theory (14.2.3), where decision-making is allocated to the person with the most expertise and is separated from formal hierarchy. Although the importance of sharing leadership behavior among team members in low workload situations is corroborated by research evidence, its role in high-stress situations remains unclear. Shared leadership runs contrary to a widespread and established notion that explicit leadership by the most experienced clinician is paramount to deal with severely injured patients. Further research is warranted to help clarify the role of shared responsibility in acute care medicine.

13.2.8 Followership: No Leadership Without Exemplary Followers

For decades, followership has been an understudied topic in organizational science. Whereas organizational literature is full of studies on leadership styles and characteristics, the preoccupation with leadership seems to have kept researchers from considering the nature and the importance of the follower in successful organizations. The underlying assumption was that good or bad leadership almost exclusively accounts for organizational outcomes. One important reason why "followership" hasn't been researched could be the negative connotation people give to the term *follower*. Whereas *followership* may be defined as the ability to effectively follow the directives and support the efforts of a leader to maximize a structured organization, the term is often stigmatized as denoting passive, weak, and conforming behavior (Alcorn 1992). While followership has taken a backseat to leadership for a long time, the last decades have witnessed a growing interest in followership (e.g., Kelley 1988). Research groups have started proposing concepts that do not reduce followers to passive people carrying out commands. In contrast, recent leadership theories emphasize the agreed-upon cooperation of leaders and followers in achieving common organizational goals (e.g., Yukl 2010). These goals can only be achieved if there is buy-in on the part of the follower. In a sense it is at the discretion of the follower to decide whether or not he or she will accept a certain person as leader. If he or she does not accept the leader, then followership be less than optimally executed and may fail altogether – not much gets done and what does get done may not be what the leader wants. Thus, the "only-leadership-count" stance within the tradition of literature on organizations ignores the fact that effectiveness of a leader is largely dependent on the willingness and consent of the followers to accomplish their leader's goals. Without followers, there can be no leaders.

Besides enabling an organization to meet its objectives, followership is important for patient safety efforts in that "being led" is not a passive process and following does not imply dispensing with independent, critical thinking. On the contrary, "exemplary followers" are neither passive nor conformist team members but provide a level of independent thinking that can prevent groupthink (Chap. 12) or spontaneous group decisions. In addition, courageous and honest exemplary followers will voice concerns and doubts and respectfully challenge their leaders, if they believe that patient safety is jeopardized. Without this safety net of competent and thoughtful followership, no healthcare organization can fulfill its commitment to safe patient care processes.

Finally, following and leading are not mutually exclusive characteristics. In some aspects, every leader is still a follower within his or her organization and vice versa:

Registered nurses train student nurses and are accountable to their head nurse; residents teach medical students and have attendings as their leaders. Attendings lead a team of nurses and residents in an emergency, but in turn are accountable for their actions to the head of the department.

13.2.9 Situational Leadership

In the last four decades, situational and contingency theories of leadership have been developed. Based on the work of Fiedler (Fiedler 1967), these models look at the impact of various factors to determine how leaders optimally function in different situations. The underlying assumption is that there is no one best way to influence people and that different types of situations call for different leadership behaviors. No single optimal psychological profile of a leader can be validated. Good leadership is adaptive with respect to a multitude of external conditions. The effectiveness of a given pattern of leadership behavior is contingent upon the demands imposed by the situation and by the followers' overall maturity. Depending upon how a leader assesses a follower's task maturity (i.e., the *ability* to perform a task) and his or her psychological maturity (i.e., the *willingness* to perform a task), differing levels of *directive* and *supportive* behavior can be effectively applied (Fig. 13.2). The extent to which leaders direct and support followers lends itself to categorizing four different leadership behaviors (Hersey and Blanchard 1977):

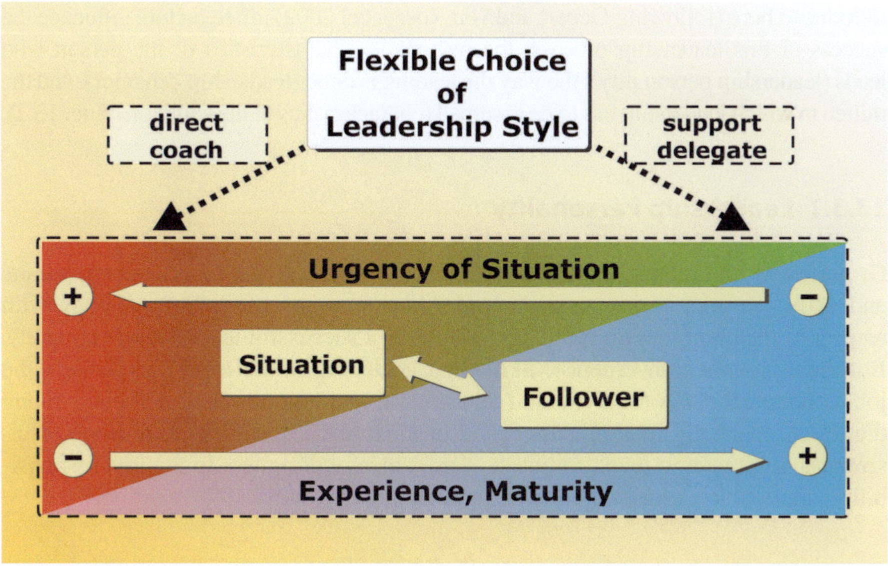

Fig. 13.2 Situational leadership in acute medical care. Leaders choose their style contingent upon the demands imposed by the urgency of the situation and by the follower's experience, maturity, and willingness

1. *Telling* is where the leader demonstrates high directive behavior and low supportive behavior.
2. *Selling* is where the leader demonstrates high directive behavior and high supportive behavior.
3. *Participating* is where the leader demonstrates low directive behavior and high supportive behavior.
4. *Delegating* is where the leader demonstrates low directive behavior and low supportive behavior.

As a result, leadership in everyday life differs from leadership in a critical situation. For example, having experienced ICU nurses as team members will evoke a different leadership behavior as compared to managing a crisis with an inexperienced trainee. The challenge for a leader, however, is to know when to apply which behavior and, conversely, to abandon a certain style when it is no longer warranted. Special caution is warranted when a highly directive "telling" style is used with experienced team members or for trivial tasks because it influences safety-relevant behavior (Zohar 2002). A follower may feel patronized and show recalcitrant behavior (Chap. 12) or may withdraw mentally from a situation. Versatility and adaptability are primary requirements needed for successful situational leadership. Fortunately, they can be trained and learned.

13.3 A Conceptual Framework for Leadership

Most likely, successful leadership in a high-stakes medical environment depends on a synthesis of these theories (e.g., the situational leadership model). In the frame model introduced here (following Gebert and von Rosenstiel 2002), three factors influence the success of this leadership process: the personality characteristics of the person who leads (leadership personality), the way the leading is done (leadership behavior), and the milieu in which leadership has to be assumed (characteristics of the situation) (Fig. 13.2).

13.3.1 Leadership Personality

Grounded in trait theory, there have been many different studies of leadership traits and skills. Results of research on leadership have not yielded consistency with respect to the combination of characteristics of a successful leadership personality. But there is some convergence. Skills that leaders need are technical skills in the job, conceptual skills (analytic and decisional), and human relation skills. Among the traits repeatedly identified as found in most leaders are self-confidence, decisiveness, high energy level, initiative, dominance, willingness to assume responsibility, intelligence, creativity, and being organized (Stogdill 1974).

13.3.2 Leadership Behavior

One factor has consistently been identified as an ingredient of successful leadership behavior: communication. To lead, one must communicate – with team members and external resources (e.g., laboratory services, intensive care units from other departments, blood bank). Communication, however, is not an end in itself. Its purpose is to build a team out of individuals and to enable successful task performance. Current theories describing successful leadership behavior have been presented in the preceding paragraphs.

13.3.3 Leadership Situation

Healthcare providers in an acute medical care setting find themselves in a variety of situations that require an adaptive and flexible leadership repertoire. For instance, a surgeon may teach a young resident during an operation in the morning, be part of a trauma team at noon, and lead a quality improvement meeting in the late afternoon. Among the most profound difference in situations is between leadership in everyday life and leadership in an emergency. Because leadership situations differ from each other, different styles of leadership need to be applied. Healthcare providers should be aware of the diversity of styles, learn and practice in various situations, and become experts at adapting their leadership behavior according to the demands of the event (McCormick and Wardrobe 2003).

13.3.4 The Followers

For a leader and the team to effectively accomplish goals, followers must have the ability and willingness to fully participate in the team and to engage with the leader. Followers who provide a level of independent thinking and who know about their responsibility to speak up when they believe that patient care is compromised or jeopardized are an indispensable asset for achieving optimal patient care. Because followers are often learners as well, good leaders are aware of how to dynamically transfer leadership responsibility. The transfer may take place because the leader needs to attend to a task or to give an inexperienced colleague some supervised practice or because another clinician is equally or more qualified to lead in a particular situation. Two important aspects of leadership change are necessary: Be explicit about the change so the whole team is aware, and ensure that the team's situational awareness remains high. Observations of teamwork behaviors have shown one other important aspect in a team success: Leaders and followers have a "contract" of sorts that is an explicit and agreed-upon understanding of their roles. Followers then enable, support, and enhance team performance (e.g., Klein et al 2006).

13.3.5 Leadership Success

Leadership behavior has consequences. Whether or not leadership in an emergency is successful has traditionally been viewed as mostly dependent on the clinical course of events; that is, leadership was assessed primarily in terms of survival and recovery of the patient. The teamwork was viewed as far less important. By which route the goal of survival and recovery was reached was irrelevant. However, the past decade has witnessed an increasing interest in the *process* of leadership. Successful leadership is no longer only a question of patient outcome, but also that of a leader's interaction with the team members. Current research and thinking is that effective leadership promotes better patient outcomes. Furthermore, effective leadership promotes a working and cultural environment that treats healthcare providers with respect and as mature, competent, and caring adults. When treated in this way, teams perform better.

13.4 Leadership Problems in Critical Situations

Leadership problems in acute and emergent healthcare can most often be traced to one or both of these core problems: (1) A leader does not explicitly assume responsibility for the leadership position, does not attain the team's explicit agreement, and/or (2) does not act according to sound leadership principles. The failure to take and agree on responsibility and to lead can lead to suboptimal or unsafe results as described below.

13.4.1 Without a Leader: When Nobody Shows the Way

If the leader does not fulfill the formal leadership function with the corresponding leadership behaviors, patient treatment in an emergency is jeopardized. Because decision-making in the high-stakes medical environment is based on an instructive leadership style, an indecisive leader will cause loss of coordination, failure to execute necessary tasks, and time delay. Recent research demonstrated that despite having sufficient knowledge and training, teams managing a cardiac arrest were unable to follow guidelines successfully with the major obstacles being those of poor leadership and a lack of explicit task distribution (Marsch et al. 2004). This lack of leadership can partially be compensated for if team members are familiar with the tasks at hand and with each other because they have been working together for a while. In this case shared mental models, although not as good as they could be, allow each team member to anticipate each other's resource needs and actions (*implicit coordination*, Chap. 11).

13.4.2 Misled into Action

The main tasks of leadership in an emergency situation are to generate a shared comprehensive mental model of the situation, to define priorities and partial goals, and to coordinate the actions of all team members. This means that leaders have to refrain from operative actions. Unfortunately, leaders are not immune from a stress-related urge to act ("do something now"). Once leaders have been drawn into executing tasks (e.g., inserting a central IV line, giving drugs, adjusting the ventilator settings), the leader's attention has been drawn away from the demands of effective leadership, and therefore it is most likely that the leader will lose sight of "the big picture." Studies exploring the relationship between team leadership skills and quality of cardiopulmonary resuscitation in an adult cardiac arrest simulation were able to demonstrate a positive association between team leadership skills and quality indicators of effective CPR (e.g., better technical performance, shorter pre-shock pause, and lower total hands-off ratio; Yeung et al. 2012). If it should become necessary for the leader to perform a task (e.g., inserting the central IV line because the resident failed), this should only be a short temporal exception, and the leader should explicitly have someone else take over leadership while distracted with a task. When the task is finished, the leader can explicitly resume leadership responsibilities.

13.4.3 Tasks Executed? Failure to Monitor

The leadership process is a goal-oriented, recurrent, closed-loop cycle of thinking, deciding, and acting. Due to this iterative structure, preceding actions influence ongoing leadership decisions and team actions. A crucial part of the process of leading lies in monitoring whether an instruction has been understood and executed and, if so, what the results are. If leaders fail to maintain and close the loop, subsequent decisions will be based on assumptions and expectations, but not on real data.

13.4.4 Strain: Leadership and Emotional Pressure

The anesthesiologist in the case study is confronted with a series of parallel task demands. He has to grapple with the unclear diagnosis of the medical problem, has to gain knowledge of the available resources, must satisfy the team's need for adequate communication, and has to be aware of and regulate his own emotional reactions. Although the demands present an enormous challenge, trained and experienced leaders can cope with them. If a leader is unable to cope with the demands, the trap of the "cognitive emergency reaction" (Chap. 9) becomes a potential problem. Cognition and behavior will then no longer be directed at leading the team but instead at regaining the feeling of competence. Another frequently observed and unwanted behavior is that the "leader goes solo." Under stress, decision-makers tend to focus on their own thinking and acting. In this condition, team members are excluded from participating in the leader's mental model of the situation; thus, they have no idea what the leader thinks, plans, or expects for support (Driskell and Salas 1991).

13.4.5 Change in Leadership: Change in Function

Healthcare providers in an acute medical care setting are sometimes forced to switch functions. For example, in the case study, the resident assumed the role of leader in the case of malignant hyperthermia until the attending physician arrived, a "code blue" might be led by the physician on the ward until the resuscitation team can take over the case, etc. In both cases team members have to conform to the altered conditions and have to adapt their behavior. The key to successfully changing leaders or roles during an event is to be verbally explicit about the change. To adjust to changing conditions, the team must be aware of leader and role changes. Explicitly announcing and verifying roles as they change is just as important as being explicit and verifying situation updates, decisions, and task execution.

13.4.6 "I'm in the Driver's Seat!": Leadership and Power

Teams in an acute medical care setting tend to view themselves as hierarchical. A hierarchical team implies a power gradient. Teams that attempt to reduce the authority gradient and view the leader as having one job among a number of other important jobs tend to share information better. Problems often arise if a leader assumes a strong autocratic leadership style. If a leader wields power insistently and consistently, team members get the impression that the leader understands all there is to know about the situation and knows exactly what decisions and actions need to take place. If the function of a team member is continuously relegated to receiving orders, this can lead to hidden resistance, passivity, and suboptimal teamwork. Team members might refuse to "be led" or to fully cooperate with the leader. Lack of information sharing and trust can lead to a breakdown of teamwork with attendant costs in the patient's safety and well-being. On the positive side of the coin is that a power gradient, if wielded judiciously and respectfully, can be in the interest of the team because during a critical situation where team members may be confused about the big picture, leadership can be very effective. However, no matter what style of leadership is used, active participation and volunteering of information should be encouraged by the leader.

13.4.7 "There Is Only Room for One of Us!": Conflict for Leadership

When several leaders with a comparable position in hierarchy meet in an emergency (e.g., resuscitation on general ward, acute bleeding in the OR, trauma in the emergency department), the leadership position can become ambiguous. If there is no standing rule about the allocation of responsibility, it is helpful when the respective leaders agree explicitly on the most appropriate leader. It is less important what decision rule is used for deciding who is the leader, whether it be the most experienced person or the trainee needing to practice; what is important is that the leadership role and allocation of responsibilities be explicitly negotiated and agreed.

13.4.8 Handing Over Responsibility: The "Revolving Door" Effect

During the management of the malignant hyperthermia in the case study, the resident handed over leadership the responsibility to the attending physician. This handing over of responsibility generally corresponds with the necessary knowledge, expertise, and clinical skills of the leader and is done by turning over all relevant information. On the other hand, sometimes leaders take over responsibility too abruptly or implicitly. The resident could be sent away, ignored, or verbally "pushed away." Because in this way the information the resident could share is lost, negative consequences for patient care are likely. Relevant information about the clinical developments, important clues, procedures performed, and laboratory data requested will not be available for future treatment. When a new leader is designated, team members must convey crucial information instead of leaving without providing information (*revolving door effect*). Having a new team leader has advantages because the new leader might have a fresh and less biased perspective. On the other hand, the advantage of having a new leader can be undone if team members stop participating in problem solving and information sharing.

13.4.9 Invulnerable: Immunization Against Criticism

Leaders can make incorrect diagnoses, order questionable procedures, make mistakes, etc. Because a leader's decisions in everyday life often go unchallenged, an immunization against criticism of team members can take place. Consequently, decisions a leader makes in critical situations might also be immune to criticism. Ideally, the interaction of team members with their leader should be characterized by a sound balance of respect and assertive behavior. The price for not understanding or not challenging a leaders' faulty decision can be high. Leaders can and should actively encourage team members to share their thoughts and to voice concerns. Leaders need to actively solicit feedback and concerns from team members. A powerful leadership technique is for the leader to announce that speaking up when an action or decision is wrong or doesn't make sense is an expectation of all team members. For this technique to work, the leader has to follow up with demonstrable appreciation when team members speak up, whether they be right or wrong in their concern.

Leadership Problems

- Leadership role is not assumed.
- Relying on assumptions about who is in charge or that people know what needs to be done.
- Losing sight of the big picture.
- Failure to monitor.
- Overstrained with a situation (cognitive emergency reaction).
- Getting involved in clinical tasks while holding a leadership role.

- Exerting power with an autocratic style.
- Failing to resolve conflicts with peers.
- Assuming responsibility abruptly and thereby displacing team members who have valuable situational knowledge ("revolving door" effect).
- Immunity from criticism.

13.5 Leadership Tasks in a Critical Situation

The life-threatening situation from the case study forced the attending physician to provide leadership in a critical situation. His leadership behavior exemplified the relevant tasks of a leader in a critical situation. Seven interrelated tasks seem especially vital for success in such a setting:

- *Organize the team;* encourage, promote, and facilitate good teamwork .
- *Apply problem-solving strategies,* verbally.
- *Articulate clear goals.*
- *Make decisions* using input from team members.
- *Delegate and coordinate* task execution.
- *Monitor workload balance* within and across the team.
- *Reevaluate* the situation regularly and verbally.

The items overlap to some degree with the characteristics of a good team process that we encountered earlier (Chap. 11.3). In this respect, it is noteworthy that successful teamwork is the responsibility of *every* single team member.

13.5.1 Organize the Team, Encourage, Promote, and Facilitate Good Teamwork

Good teamwork does not happen simply by assigning healthcare professionals together in the same shift. Similarly, formal positions with inherent authority do not necessarily result in effective leadership. Instead, good teamwork and leadership depend on a set of social and interpersonal skills of both leader and followers (Chap. 11) and flourish only in a trustful, cooperative climate. In contrast to leadership of single-discipline teams engaged in routine production tasks, leadership in interdisciplinary action teams is characterized by a set of distinctive features:

- Leadership in emergent acute care settings differs from leadership in other professional areas because often there is little time for members to get accustomed to each other. Instead of being able to brief the entire team prior to the mission, it is common for leaders to organize their team "on the fly."
- Leaders face the challenge of having strangers from a variety of professional groups, and clinical disciplines cooperate in ad hoc teams. Thus, leaders are

faced with task demands ("patient treatment") as well as social demands (familiarization, developing some form of team etiquette, establishing and reinforcing communication patterns, etc.).

- Whenever possible, leaders should not participate "hands on" in patient treatment but rather make it their top priority to build a structured team and free their resources for thinking, decision-making, and situational reassessment. While it is often senior team members who are assigned the task of leadership, their capabilities might be needed in certain situations (e.g., difficult airway, central IV line, venous access in neonates and infants). As soon as possible, leaders should try to regain their "hands-off" position.
- Effective leaders in most situations help provide the needed resources for team members. In the case of emergent acute care settings, responsibility for resource management in terms of equipment, personnel, and communication with outside functions such as lab, radiology, etc., needs to be assumed by another team member. This person is often called the event manager.
- Effective teamwork with its central behavior components of workload distribution, mutual performance monitoring, feedback, closed-loop communication, and backup behavior is the mainstay of efficient patient care. Effective leaders cultivate desired team behaviors and skills when they openly share information and explicitly empower members to speak up, give constructive and timely feedback, and challenge the leader's thoughts and actions when appropriate.
- What team members expect from their leader is leadership behavior, not formal authority. Ideally, leaders renounced their individuality in the service of a reliable standard of excellent care, thereby embodying the transition from the mindset of craftsman to that of an equivalent actor (Amalberti et al. 2005).
- Leaders set the tone for their team, for better or worse. Integrity, friendliness, fairness, adherence to moral standards, and interpersonal skills may not directly impact task execution in every single case, but they certainly play a crucial role in generating team cohesion.

13.5.2 Apply Problem-Solving Strategies Verbally

The purpose of leadership is to influence and direct the performance of team members toward the achievement of a defined goal (Murray and Foster 2000). However, before a leader can formulate a goal, the immediate and underlying problems have to be understood. In acute healthcare settings, problem solving can be impaired by the complexity of the situation and by stress. Therefore it is highly recommended that leaders have a structured and well-practiced approach to problem solving (e.g., the five steps of a good strategy, Chap. 10) rather than solving the problem on the basis of minimal informational input and by relying on heuristics. In addition, provocative situational factors (e.g., acute stress, feeling of incompetence) can severely degrade a leader's judgment and create a vulnerability to peer pressure.

13.5.3 Articulate Clear Goals

Leaders carry the main responsibility for ensuring that their team achieves its clinical goals. These goals serve as "beacons for our actions" that should satisfy as many concurrent needs as possible without creating new problems. When team members know what the leader wants them to accomplish, they can go about seeing a bigger picture of what they are supposed to do and can take more responsibility for obtaining the teams goals. Clear goals lead to clear priorities. When goals and priorities are in place, material and personnel resources can be timed and allocated efficiently and effectively by competent team members. On the other hand, when goals and priorities are not articulated clearly, critical situations can run out of control because multiple individuals, concentrating on only their part of the situation, will likely execute uncoordinated, unplanned, and often contradictory tasks.

13.5.4 Make Decisions with Input of Team Members

Teams in acute care medicine must respond to unexpected events in a coordinated way. A shared mental model is the single most important prerequisite for successful coordination of team efforts (Stout et al. 1999). Having a shared mental model of a situation means that team members have a common understanding about the task or problem at hand, the resources, the team members' abilities and skills, and the situational context (Chap. 11). Shared knowledge enables each team member to carry out his or her role in a timely and coordinated fashion, helping the team to function as a single unit with little negotiation of what to do and when to do it. The greater the degree of accuracy and overlap among team member mental models, the greater the likelihood that they will coordinate with one another successfully, even under stressful or novel conditions. Leaders are responsible for generating and sharing mental models. In routine situations team members should be encouraged to share their thoughts and impressions with the leader. In time-critical situations with no room for prior discussions, input should be collected on the fly: Leaders should verbally state their current mental model to the group (e.g., "I think our problem is… the main risks are… the strategy is…") and at the same time encourage team members to challenge these assumptions if they don't make sense or if they seem incorrect (e.g., "Does anyone see it differently … am I missing anything … ?").

13.5.5 Delegate and Coordinate Task Execution

To be an effective leader, it is imperative that responsibilities or assignments be delegated to members of the team. The process includes four steps:

- Decide what to delegate.
- Decide to whom to delegate.

- Communicate clear expectations.
- Request feedback, and close the loop.

The attending physician bore responsibility to ensure that all team members direct their efforts toward effective treatment of the malignant hyperthermia. For this purpose the leader provided partial goals deduced from medical knowledge and set priorities according to the situational demands (Chap. 7). The leader communicated the plans to the team in an appropriate way and distributed individual responsibilities to team members according to their skills and knowledge (to the extent that the leader knows them). Using specific rather than general delegation, the leader avoided the trap of requesting "someone" to do "something." Besides being specific, delegation of responsibility should be descriptive rather than prescriptive: Recognizing that there is often more than one way of executing a task, leaders should have tolerance for team members in their individual method of fulfilling their area of responsibility provided that the method is compatible with the desired outcome (Iserson 1986). To establish a closed feedback loop, leaders should request feedback on task execution, explicitly encouraging members to state problems or negative outcomes (e.g., "I'm having difficulties with the central IV line. I accidentally punctured the carotid artery already twice"). Ideally, team members provide this feedback without being asked.

13.5.6 Monitor Workload Balance Within and Across Teams

Team members differ with respect to their capabilities and experience. Therefore the identical task may be conceived and executed differently by different team members. Leaders should be aware of the performance limitations of each member and carefully monitor workload balance. Emotions, too, can create a sudden disequilibrium calling for a redistribution of workload. For example, during the management of the malignant hyperthermia in the example case at the beginning of this chapter, the resident was overwhelmed with the situation because he blamed himself for choosing succinylcholine as a muscle relaxant for the induction of anesthesia. Because of his emotional turmoil, he repeatedly failed at inserting a central IV line into the jugular vein. To break this poor judgment chain, the attending physician assigned the resident to a different task and had him supported by an emotionally stable team member. Managing workload is part of a leader's comprehensive task of team management. By drawing upon and allocating people, knowledge, information, materials, and time, a leader can prevent work overload situations that compromise situation awareness and increase the risk of errors.

13.5.7 Reevaluate the Situation Regularly and Verbally

The last step in the process of leading a team during critical situations is regular reassessment of the situation. Reevaluation comprises the team process as well as external circumstances: Reevaluating the team implies mutual cross-monitoring whether information has been understood and tasks have been executed. Teams can support their leaders by providing ongoing voluntary feedback. It is critical for the leader and team members to keep in mind that we cannot ensure a shared mental model unless it is verbalized. Only through verbal updates and review will the team remain coordinated. Ideally reevaluation is not a one-way street with the leader constantly demanding updates from followers, but rather a mutual interaction between both parties. Because complex situations can unfold over different rates of time and in different directions, a healthcare provider may be busy searching for a solution to one thing when another problem emerges. Thus, faced with event-driven dynamics with rapid time constants, team leaders will have to keep track of developments within the patient and within the team. Both team monitoring and reevaluation of external circumstances are prerequisite to maintaining an up-to-date "mental model" and to anticipating future developments.

13.6 Tips for Daily Practice

- If you want to lead, you must respect people and show appreciation. Leadership only works if leaders have a genuine interest in fellow human beings and if they show their appreciation. Make sure everybody counts and everybody knows they count. Without this core value of "liking people," nobody should strive for a leadership position.
- Leadership starts in everyday life. When confronted with a critical situation, leaders can only rely on well-established behaviors and a team climate that has been established in the normal course of life.
- Leadership does not flow automatically from a hierarchical position. True leadership is manifested only if a person is qualified in terms of leadership behavior.
- Good leadership is adaptive with respect to environmental conditions. The effectiveness of a given pattern of leadership behavior is contingent upon the demands imposed by the situation and by the followers' overall capabilities.
- Always remember: In critical situations, leadership is paramount. If there is more than one leader, there is no leader.
- Delegation has to be specific. Statements like "Could someone get a chest tube" risk that no one will get a chest tube.
- The leader sets the tone for the entire team. Loudness and yelled orders are the hallmark of disorientation and disorganization and may be perceived by team members as a sign of disrespect.
- The patient is the one with the emergency, not you and your team. Even with limited time, restricted resources, and high stress, leaders should convey the feeling that the patient's welfare is of prime importance. Put another way: The decisions and actions the team takes are not about "who" is right, but "what" is right.
- Instead of succumbing to groupthink, the leader should make each individual in the group think.

13.7 "Leadership" in a Nutshell

- Leadership in the context of acute events in healthcare can be defined as the process whereby a person influences and directs the performance of other team members by utilization of all available resources toward the achievement of a defined goal.
- A leader can be defined as a team member whose influence on group attitudes, performance, and decision-making exceeds that of the other members of the group.
- Leaders are taught and practice to lead, not born to lead.
- In the context of healthcare in a high-stakes environment, four leadership theories are relevant: the "great man" theory, trait theories, behavioral theories, and situational and contingency theories.
- The success of the leadership process is determined by the person who leads (leadership personality), the way this leading is done (leadership behavior), the attitudes and abilities of the followers, and the situation in which the leadership role is enacted.
- Leadership behavior can be described as existing on a grid with relationship orientation and task orientation as the two dimensions.
- Four leadership styles can be developed within this grid: the "laissez-faire" style, the democratic style, the authoritative style, and the integrative style.
- Leadership tasks in critical situations comprise coordination, delegating responsibilities, formalizing information flow, determining the structure of the team, stabilizing emotions, and representing the team to others.
- Leaders involved in an intense healthcare situation will need an "event manager" to help ensure that resources are available and to coordinate with others within the organization.
- Successful leadership depends on the skills of the leader *and* the teamwork skills of each team member.
- A leader must have conceptual skills, technical skills, and interpersonal skills.
- Effective leaders delegate so that they can regulate. During high workload periods, the team leader should manage clinical progress, and team members should manage the technical tasks.
- No single leadership style is best for all situations. Different styles of leadership are more appropriate for certain types of decision-making.
- Situational leadership is a holistic leadership concept that perceives, respects, informs, coaches, and motivates staff members as unique human beings.

References

Alcorn DS (1992) Dynamic followership: empowerment at work. Manag Q 33:9–13

Amalberti R, Auroy Y, Berwick D, Barach P (2005) Five system barriers to achieving ultrasafe health care. Ann Intern Med 142:756–764

Avolio BJ, Bass BM (2004) Multifactor leadership questionnaire, manual, 3rd edn. Buros Institute of Mental Measurements, Lincoln

Bass BM (1985) Leadership and performance beyond expectations. Free Press, New York

Bass BM, Stogdill RM (2007) Bass and Stogdill's handbook of leadership: theory, research, and managerial applications, 3rd edn. Free Press, New York/London

Blanchard KH, Zigami P, Zigami D (1985) Leadership and the one minute manager: increasing effectiveness through situational leadership. William Morrow, New York

Burns JMG (1978) Leadership. Harper & Row, New York

Driskell JE, Salas E (1991) Group decision-making under stress. J Appl Psychol 76:473–478

Edmondson AC (2003) Speaking up in the operating room: how team leaders promote learning in interdisciplinary action teams. J Manag Stud 40(6):1419–1452

Fiedler F (1967) A theory of leadership effectiveness. Harper & Row Publishers, McGraw-Hill, New York

Flin R, Fletcher G, McGeorge P, Sutherland A, Patey R (2003) Anaesthetists' attitudes toward teamwork and safety. Anaesthesia 58:233–242

Gardner WL, Lowe KB, Moss TW, Mahoney KT, Cogliser CC (2010) Scholarly leadership of the study of leadership: a review of the leadership Quarterly's second decade, 2000–2009. Leadersh Q 21(6):922–958

Gebert D, von Rosenstiel L (2002) Organisationspsychologie [Organizational psychology]. Kohlhammer, Stuttgart

Gibb CA (1954) Leadership. In: Lindzey G (ed) Handbook of social psychology, vol 2. Addison-Wesley, Reading, pp 877–917

Hersey P, Blanchard KH (1977) Management of organizational behaviour: utilizing human resources. Prentice-Hall, Englewood Cliffs

Iserson KV (1986) Critical leadership. J Emerg Med 4:335–340

Judge TA, Piccolo RF (2004) Transformational and transactional leadership: a meta-analytic test of their relative validity. J Appl Psychol 89(5):755–768

Kelley RE (1988) In praise of followers. Harv Bus Rev 66(6):142–148

Klein KJ, Ziegler JC, Knight AP, Xiao Y (2006) Dynamic delegating: shared, hierarchical, and deindividualized leadership in extreme action teams. Adm Sci Q 51:590–621

Koenig KL, Schultz CH (2016) Disaster medicine. Comprehensive principles and practices, 2nd edn. Cambridge University Press, New York

Kohn L, Corrigan J, Donaldson M (1999) To err is human: building a safer health system. Committee on Quality of Health Care in America, Institute of Medicine (IOM). National Academy Press, Washington, DC

Künzle B, Kolbe M, Grote G (2010) Ensuring patient safety through effective leadership behaviour: a literature review. Saf Sci 48:1–17

Lewin K, Lippitt R, White RK (1939) Patterns of aggressive behaviour in experimentally created "social climates". J Soc Psychol 10:271–299

Manser T (2008) Teamwork and patient safety in dynamic domains of healthcare: a review of the literature. Acta Anaesthesiol Scand 53:143–151

Marsch SCU, Müller C, Marquardt K, Conrad G, Tschan F, Hunziker P (2004) Human factors affect the quality of cardiopulmonary resuscitation in simulated cardiac arrests. Resuscitation 60:51–56

McCormick S, Wardrobe J (2003) Major incidents, leadership, and series summary and review. Emerg Med J 20:70–74

Michaelis B (2009) Transformational and charismatic leadership effect on performance outcomes. An analysis of linking mechanisms and boundary conditions. Dissertation. Available under http://archiv.ub.uni-heidelberg.de/volltextserver/volltexte/2009/9886/pdf/Dissertation_Michaelis_UB_041009.pdf

Murray WB, Foster PA (2000) Crisis resource management among strangers: principles of organizing a multidisciplinary group for crisis resource management. J Clin Anesth 12:633–638

Newstrom JW, Davis K (1993) Organizational behavior: human behavior at work. McGraw-Hill, New York

Northouse PG (2012) Leadership: theory and practice, 6th edn. Sage, Thousand Oaks

Pearce CL, Conger JA (2003) All those years ago. In: Pearce CL, Conger JA (eds) Shared leadership: reframing the How's and Why's of leadership. Sage, Thousand Oaks

Stogdill RM (1948) Personal factors associated with leadership: a survey of the literature. J Appl Physiol 25:35–71

Stogdill RM (1974) Handbook of leadership: a survey of the literature. Free Press, New York

Stout RJ, Cannon-Bowers JA, Salas E, Milanovich DM (1999) Planning, shared mental models, and coordinated performance: an empirical link is established. Hum Factors 41:61–71

Tschan F, Semmer NK, Gautschi D (2006) Leading to recovery: group performance and coordinative activities in medical emergency driven groups. Hum Perform 19:277–304

Xiao Y, Seagull FJ, Mackenzie CF, Klein KJ (2004) Adaptive leadership in trauma resuscitations teams: a grounded theory approach to video analysis. Cogn Tech Work 6:158–164

Yeung JH, Ong GJ, Davies RP, Gao F, Perkins GD (2012) Factors affecting team-leadership skills and their relationship with quality of cardiopulmonary resuscitation. Crit Care Med 40(9):2617–2621

Yukl GA (2010) Leadership in organizations, 7th edn. Prentice Hall, Upper Saddle River

Zohar D (2002) The effects of leadership dimensions, safety climate, and assigned priorities on minor injuries in work groups. J Organ Behav 23:75–92

Part IV

Error and Safety in Organizations

The fourth part of this book focuses on the influence of organizations on the performance of healthcare professionals in a high-stakes medical environment. At first sight many of these factors are beyond the responsibility of healthcare providers: The organizational culture, basic concepts of patient safety, or principles of staff development seem to be set variables that the individual must accept as they are; however, knowledge about the many ways an organization can impact patient safety can assist healthcare professionals in understanding basic mechanisms of accident evolution and may help to sharpen the focus for latent conditions in one's own work environment.

When there are medical errors, usually one or more care providers are associated with the event. The overall conditions for "patient safety" often depend on the last line of defense, i.e., hospital or rescue staff. Therefore, it is helpful to understand the connections between the organization and the individual, such as the causation factors and mechanisms of a mishap and the relevance of latent factors.

Chapter 14 outlines a systemic view of organizations and discusses several influential organizational theories on error: safety culture as the "DNA of safety"; the human factors approach, which emphasizes the inevitability of errors in organizations; the theory of "normal" accidents that are caused by the design of systems; and high-reliability theory, from which healthcare can benefit. In addition, relevance and limitations of learning from aviation are discussed. As examples of factors that influence the actions of the doctors and nurses "at the sharp end" of the system, we present concepts of workflow management, medical device technology, and personnel management.

Chapter 15 deals with the reduction and management of complexity. Standardization as a tool for error prevention and checklists as a formalization of standards are discussed with regard to their benefits and limitations. Human factors-oriented system designs and knowledge management are examples for general strategies to push organizations toward patient safety.

Chapter 16 deals with learning in and of organizations. Concepts from other high-risk domains such as the "reliable organization" and the "learning organization" may be beneficial for the medical sector as well, because they hold the possibility of changing the mindset of employees for their daily work. However, complex organizations such as hospitals cannot be changed with simple “recipes for success” or isolated measures. Instruments such as incident reporting systems and case studies and training in high-stress environments that replicate real-world conditions such as can be done in simulation are important ingredients; and regular team training with debriefings should be an integral part of organizational development. Given the current economic situation, it is even more important that the issues of patient safety, error prevention, and reliable behavior are on the personal agenda of every healthcare provider.

Organization, Errors, and Safety

14

Case Study
In the early afternoon a 32-year-old worker falls from the top of a 4-m scaffold and impacts the ground with the right side of his body. Emergency medical services (EMS) evaluate the patient, who is found to be alert and hemodynamically stable. He is transported to the emergency department of a nearby hospital for further evaluation. There, overseeing six emergent cases, the emergency physician is extremely busy, while additional patients are waiting. On arrival, the patient's blood pressure and heart rate are within normal limits, and the lungs are clear to auscultation. The patient's chief complaint is localized pain on the right side of his chest worsening with deep breathing and movement. The patient undergoes a chest X-ray (CXR) in the radiology department. The radiology technician who is in the habit of identifying patients based chiefly on their last name erroneously distributes the wrong films. The patient's CXR, because they are from a different patient, shows a set of normal findings. The patient returns to the emergency department accompanied by a student nurse who has been asked to monitor the patient, while the rest of the staff helps with other cases. In the course of the following half hour, the patient becomes increasingly short of breath and anxious. The emergency physician is called by the student nurse to assess the patient. He reviews the CXR films and, after ruling out any chest and lung pathology, prescribes boluses of morphine as required for pain control. Shortly after morphine is administered, the patient becomes obtunded. The pulse oximeter, brought into the room by the nurse shortly before, shows an oxygen saturation of 79%. Bag-mask ventilation is immediately initiated. After an uneventful intubation, the emergency physician notices decreased breath sounds on the right side of the chest and subcutaneous emphysema. While preparing for chest tube insertion, the patient's oxygen saturation abruptly drops to the 40s. The ECG monitor displays ventricular fibrillation. A defibrillator is immediately obtained; however, the shock is

M. St.Pierre et al., *Crisis Management in Acute Care Settings*,
DOI 10.1007/978-3-319-41427-0_14

delayed due to the unfamiliarity of the operators with the new version of the device. Eventually resuscitation efforts prove successful and the patient regains spontaneous circulation. The CXR is examined again and the swap discovered. The correct films are reviewed, and multiple rib fractures and a right-sided pneumothorax identified.

A construction worker fell from the top of a scaffold and was transported by EMS to an emergency department. At the time of admission, the emergency department was understaffed and overcrowded. Due to the hectic workflow, the one available physician performed a very quick, basic clinical check before heading for the next patient. Because the initial clinical findings suggested serial rib fractures, the physician ordered a CXR. At the radiology department, the CXRs were swapped, and the patient returned to the emergency department with the wrong images. Because the patient carried the CXRs and because the family name on the film is identical to the patient's name, no suspicion arose that the films could be wrong. Neither first name nor date of birth was verified. Thus, the actual severity of his injuries was overlooked. Moreover, an inexperienced student nurse was assigned to the patient, and pulse oximeter monitoring was not initiated. When the patient's clinical status deteriorated, the resident physician was unable to correlate the symptoms with the normal radiological findings. Because the CXRs showed no pathology, the resident neither crosschecked the radiological findings by repeating the clinical examination (e.g., by chest auscultation) nor did he closely reexamine the CXR (e.g., by verifying the patient's name); instead, he ordered pain therapy with morphine, which worsened the clinical situation. It is only after a successful intubation that new clues emerged (e.g., decreased breath sounds, subcutaneous emphysema) which pointed to a pneumothorax. The situation was complicated by the fact that controlled ventilation precipitates a tension pneumothorax which rapidly develops into cardiac arrest. Moreover, the defibrillator in the emergency department has been on the floor for only 2 weeks, and everyone had not yet been trained in its use.

Although at first sight the circumstances of this event indicate a series of unfortunate events, their occurrence is not accidental: The organizational structure of this hospital allowed the successive occurrence of seemingly isolated factors to come together for this specific case. What at first glance may appear to be the result of the faulty behavior of a few healthcare providers (e.g., radiology technician, student nurse, resident emergency physician), on closer inspection the picture that emerges is the contribution of flawed processes and structures within this hospital. Also contributing to the substandard care were other organizational factors – such as time budgeted for each patient or training provided on medical equipment.

To illustrate this statement, we explain what an organization is and how it can be described in a point of view that includes human factors and patient safety considerations.

14.1 Organizations as Systems: Different Perspectives

Of all organizations in Western culture, healthcare delivery has certainly become one of the largest, most complex, and costliest of all. Although healthcare delivery is usually not thought of as a system, being *a socio-technical system* is one of its most distinctive characteristics. A socio-technical system is defined as the way human behavior, an organization's complex infrastructures, and technology interact. The socio-technical system "healthcare" has many component subsystems: prehospital emergency medical services; hospitals (with their further subdivision into departments, wards, divisions, teams, programs); outpatient clinics; pharmacies; laboratories; manufacturers; government agencies; and patient organizations. Each of these represents a distinct culture with its own goals, values, beliefs, and norms of behavior on one hand and financial, technical, and unique human resources on the other. Most of the problems within healthcare organizations do not exist in isolation; they interrelate with each other. In order to solve any specific problem within a subsystem, it is necessary to take a broader perspective, where local issues are seen as part of a coherent whole. *Systems thinking*, the "discipline for seeing wholes, recognizing patterns and interrelationships, and learning how to structure those interrelationships in more effective, efficient ways" (Senge 1990), has been applied to industrial and management issues for a long time. However, systems thinking as applied to healthcare has only recently been applied to addressing our unique organizational issues.

"Thinking in system" implies analyzing the totality of the system instead of the individual system elements within the organization, so that the interaction of relations and structures comes into focus.

What then, exactly, is an organization? Within social sciences, many theoretical frameworks have been proposed for defining organizations: what organizations *are*, how they should *function*, and what actions can be taken if they do not function well. Several major schools of thought have evolved, each with its own perspective about characteristics of organizations, as described below:

- Organizations are systems that are distinguishable from their environment. They are linked in a variety of relationships with their environment, and they form internal structures in which people and technology interact as socio-technical systems. The technical and social systems of an organization have their own history, are subject to change, and follow their own laws.
- From a *structural perspective*, organizations are created and exist primarily to accomplish specific goals. The organizational structure as well as processes and rules are determined mainly by the organization's goals, technology, and environment. Behavior in organizations is intentionally rational and governed by "norms of rationality;" hence organizations are "rational systems" (Gouldner 1959). System theorists would say that "a hospital 'has' an organization." If the management of an organization adopts a structural perspective, it will emphasize that goals, tasks, technologies, and structures are the primary determinants of organizational behavior; the needs, capacities, and self-interests of individuals or

groups are less significant. The ongoing optimization and improvement of individual expertise and performance, and of cooperative processes, is best accomplished through the exercise of authority and rules, not by fostering individual creativity or participation. Organizational problems usually reflect inappropriate structure and can be resolved through redesign and reorganization.

- While the structural perspective places rationality as its central motive, the *human resource approach* focuses on the relationship between organizations and people (e.g., Argyris 1957; Argyris and Schön 1996). In this framework, people are the most critical resource; organizations exist to serve human needs instead of humans existing to serve organizational needs. Topics central to self-concept of an organization include motivation, attitudes, participation, and teamwork. As a result, an organization is a permanent arrangement of social elements with a formal structure. The organizational members not only pursue factual goals but also personal interests (e.g., career, power, individual development, and education). If we say "the hospital 'is' an organization," we emphasize the fact that people in organizations try to satisfy different needs and motives and are ready to align their behavior to shared values and norms. Such a hospital would place great value on the compliance with social rules. Organizational problems result from poor synchronization of human and organizational needs: Organizations become ineffective when people feel exploited, or both. When organizations become dysfunctional, effective remedial efforts strive for a state where organizations can achieve their goals effectively, while humans derive rewards and meaning from their work.
- The *functional perspective* on organizations centers on the process of organizing as the main leadership task. This framework tries to identify and strengthen all processes wherein useful organizational structures, rules, and processes are created. If an organization takes this perspective, the core belief will be that an organization will never have reached its final structure; instead, constant reevaluation, reorganization, continuous improvement, and rationalization remain central tasks. One pitfall of this approach of constant reevaluation and improvement is that organizational problems and therefore their solutions may be rooted in an incomplete understanding of the way the organization functions under a variety of circumstances.

Each perspective points to important phenomena in organizations and provides a useful analytic framework of how structures, processes, people, and tasks interact. The outlined perspectives should be taken as complementary rather than independently exclusive: Every organizational event can be interpreted in a number of ways, because organizations are "multiple realities" (Bolman and Deal 1984). Despite obvious differences, social scientists nevertheless agree that organizations generally develop as instruments for attaining specific goals. Organizations emerge out of situations in which people recognize a common or complementary advantage that can best be achieved through collective action; thus, by their very nature, organizations imply the integration and structuring of activities directed toward goal accomplishment. Organizations are consciously coordinated and deliberately structured social entities – a group of people intentionally organized to construct or compile a common tangible or intangible product or service (Alvesson 2002; Bedeian 1984; Black 2003; Bolman and Deal 1984). The goals an organization tries to achieve can either be deliberate and recognized (explicit, as in a mission statement) or may operate unrecognized "behind the scenes" (implicit). Explicit goals of healthcare organizations can be safe patient care, medical excellence, or cost reduction, whereas implicit goals may comprise personal agendas of management, directors, or professional groups within the organization.

In order to balance contradicting goals and to accomplish specific goals, organizations have to coordinate recurrent tasks by setting up task plans. These task plans can be more or less complex and comprise a multitude of separate decisions that make the punctual allocation of people, material, and other resources at the correct destination possible. At the early stages of organizational development, most of these task plans tend to emerge spontaneously, reflecting a balance between effort and result. An evident vitality and spontaneity distinguishes these task plans, similar to blood flowing through vessels, providing an organism with nutrients; however, when organizations exist for some time, experience with solutions to recurring problems will be reflected in formalized structures, hierarchies, functions, and task descriptions. The constant blood flow of spontaneous and fresh ideas will gradually turn into a "thrombus of clotted decisions."

Finally, as human organizations are social systems with an essential social character, they show identifiable boundaries between members and nonmembers. By defining who belongs to the organization and who does not, organizations create an "inside" where people cooperate, share common rules, and agree upon the way power and responsibility are distributed, and an "outside" to which it can respond as a collective body.

14.2 Safety Culture: The DNA for Safety

14.2.1 Organizational Culture and Safety Culture

Throughout human history, whenever groups of people gathered together, they had to face two basic challenges: Individuals had to be integrated into an effective whole, and the group had to adapt effectively to the external environment in order to survive. As groups found solutions to these problems over time, they engaged in a kind of collective learning that created a set of shared assumptions and beliefs we call "culture." The same process of collective learning takes place when people work together on a day-to-day basis. In the case of an organization, this culture is referred to as "organizational culture." It combines all features that make an organization or a company distinctive as a stable social system: deeply embedded values, norms, and expectations that accrued over time and which are now shared by the members of a particular organization. In addition, the values of the founders and the variations of values that managers and clinical directors also add shape the staff's beliefs and attitudes.

Organizational culture is:

- *Implicit:* The basic beliefs are generally reflected by the members and are accepted as given.
- *Collective:* These shared beliefs lead to consistent behavior.
- *Conceptual:* The underlying values and beliefs provide the members of the organization with an orientation in the world.
- *Interactive:* “How we do things around here” is sometimes implicitly, sometimes explicitly communicated to all new employees.
- *Emotional:* If the members are part of a culture, they will be influenced holistically.
- *Historically grown:* The current culture developed through learning over time.

We can summarize organizational culture as “the way we do what we do, how we think about it and how we feel about it.”

14.2.2 The Three Levels of Culture by Edgar Schein

The organizational psychologist Edgar Schein developed the most famous approach to organizational culture (including safety culture) in the late 1980s (Schein 2004). In his model, organizational culture consists of three different levels. Not all of them are easily accessible to an observer who wants to get to know this organization (or wants to learn something about its safety culture) (See Table 14.1.).

Basic underlying assumptions are the driving force behind every action and are usually not questioned or discussed. They become relevant for safety if an organization wants to change. Due to the emotional value of the basic assumptions, people will resist any kind of change.

Based on the underlying assumptions are *espoused values* – the organization’s stated values and rules of behavior. These are expressed, for example, in mission statements. The common assumptions are not necessarily identical with every publicly propagated value. It is possible that the two levels do not match, because values are propagated that do not fit with the resulting behavior. Although the hospital in the case study publicly advertised, “Our focus is on you, the patient,” the crowded waiting room of the emergency department and the scarce staffing speak in a way that shows disdain for the patients’ needs and an indifference with regard to the patients’ safety. The last level consists of the *observable* behavior, structures and processes that are visible also to an outsider (“artifacts”).

So, if we look at basic assumptions regarding safety in an organization, at the values and opinions employees have regarding safety, and also how safety for both staff members and patients is taken into account in structures and procedures, then we are dealing with “safety culture.”

This concept of a specific aspect of organizational culture was first used in the report of the International Atomic Energy Agency (IAEA) on the Chernobyl disaster in 1986 (INSAG-1 1986). The IAEA defines safety culture as “that assembly of

Table 14.1 Different levels of organizational culture and their relevance for patient safety

Levels	Meaning in general	Example for safety culture	Suitable measuring instruments for patient safety
Visible characteristics ("artifacts")	Observable behavior and appearance of the organization and its building The interpretation is difficult because there is no clear interpretation rule	Technical status of medical devices Hand disinfection Standard operating procedures (SOPs) Safety checklists The presence of incident reporting system The presence of morbidity and mortality conference Number of near misses	On-site inspections Safety audits Document analysis Observations
Publicly propagated values and opinions ("espoused values")	Form the justification for action Can be and generally are communicated to employees	Official mission statement Propagated goals and strategies Attitude and behavior of the senior management with regard to safety Safety precautions Existing risks and risk behavior Workload Communication strategies during safety incidents	Questionnaires on safety climate (e.g., SAQ, HSC) Self-assessment (e.g., MaPSaF) Interviews
Basic underlying assumptions	Form the core of the culture Basic assumptions about human activity and relationships Value of human life in terms of resource utilization and investments	Ideas about human nature (e.g., religious or humanistic) Work ethic Attitude toward change and learning Profit orientation	Not immediately apparent, must be derived from the expressed values and artifacts Partial approximation is possible though interviews

Following Schein (2004)

characteristics and attitudes in organizations and individuals which establishes that, as an overriding priority, nuclear plant safety issues receive the attention warranted by their significance" (INSAG-4 1991). Safety culture can be also defined as "the product of individual and group values, attitude, competencies, and patterns of behavior that determine the commitment to and the style and proficiency of an organization's safety… programs" (HSC 1993). In summary, it can be stated that safety culture has the following characteristics (after Guldenmund 2000):

- It is relatively stable, multidimensional, and holistic in construct.
- It is based on shared cultural norms in the work environment.
- It affects the perceptions and behavior of the employees and constitutes practices.
- Thus, it influences the safety in organizations.

To express that safety (and not the avoidance of errors) is the goal, it is better to use the term *safety culture* than *error culture* in the context of healthcare delivery. Safety culture implies that structures and procedures of the organization, workplaces and equipment, qualifications of employees, and communication and decision-making are designed in service to allow *safe behavior at all workplaces at all times*.

Thus it is evident that patient safety cannot be delegated to individual officials such as safety managers or quality managers. Safety can only be achieved if all employees are aware of safety issues. Safety then becomes a "dynamic non-event" (Weick 1991). *Non-event* as it refers to the continuous absence of an accident and *dynamic* in so far as safety is not a permanent condition and is achieved over and over again. In this struggle, employees should be aware of their high responsibility for the patients and "don't forget to be afraid" (Fig. 14.1; Reason 1997).

14.2.3 Safety Culture and Safety Climate

Safety culture or lack thereof tends to have lasting features that aren't easily changed. However, a direct measurement of safety culture is hardly possible. It requires an in-depth analysis of the organization. This analysis can be structured by the three levels of culture in Schein's model (Guldenmund 2000). However, the

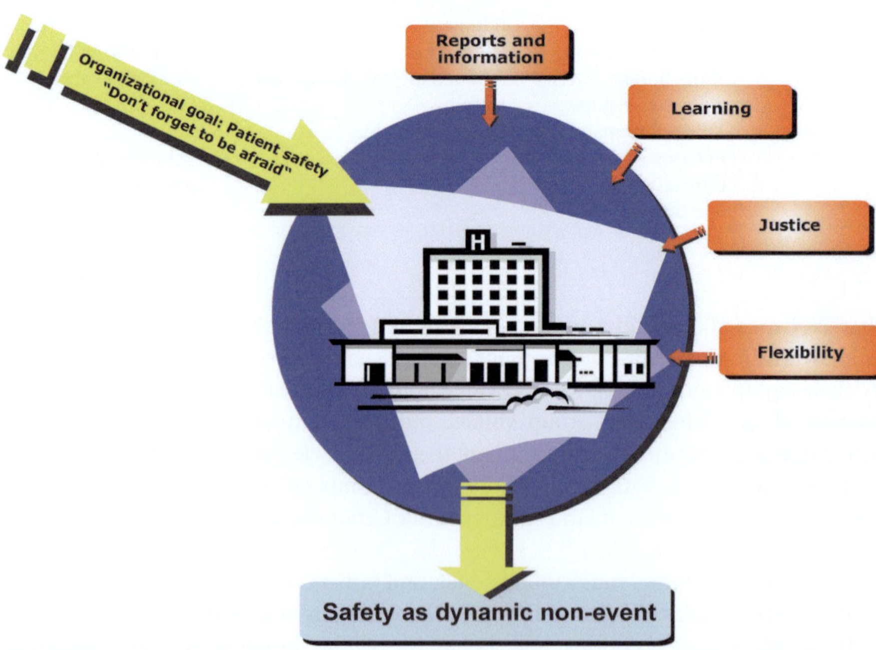

Fig. 14.1 Elements of a safety culture. Safety is not a static feature of a system but rather the dynamic absence of critical events for which a person or team has to continuously strive

different levels vary regarding their accessibility for observers, and therefore different measurements are needed (Table 14.1). When trying to access the unobservable characteristics of a safety culture (basic assumptions) by questionnaires, the result will be insight into the "safety climate."

The concept of "safety climate" is often linked with the concept of "safety culture," but has a different meaning (Denison 1996; Mearns and Flin 1999). The term safety climate best describes a snapshot of the current employees' perceptions, attitudes, and beliefs about risk and safety, typically measured by questionnaire surveys. As it refers to a situation and its link to thoughts, feelings, and behaviors of organizational members, it is temporal, subjective, and often subject to direct manipulation by people with power and influence.

The most common and validated instruments in medicine are the Hospital Survey on Patient Safety Culture (HSPSC), the Manchester Patient Safety Assessment Framework (MaPSaF), and the Safety Attitudes Questionnaire (SAQ). However, the interpretation of these data regarding safety culture is difficult because organizations can form subcultures that depend on the specific context of different groups.

14.3 The Development of Safety Culture

Based on mounting evidence that better safety culture is related to lower incidence of adverse events (Hofmann and Mark 2006; Naveh et al. 2005; Neal and Griffin 2006; Singer et al. 2009; Vogus and Sutcliffe 2007) and higher reporting rates of incidents (Cohen et al. 2004; Gandhi et al. 2005), the moderation and development of safety culture in healthcare has attracted a great deal of research attention from a range of academic disciplines. As a defining feature of a culture is its relative stability over time, an effective safety culture cannot be developed overnight. Rather, organizations adapt gradually to changes in environments and develop their (safety) culture in response to successes, failures, or regulatory requirements. The necessary paradigm shift toward valuing safety and integrating it into the culture often encounters considerable resistance within an organization. Since cultural change is driven by leadership, the safety-related attitudes of leaders play a crucial role in this cultural change and development. Leaders can trigger cultural change, but it takes the entire organization to make the change.

A marker for organizational culture and thus a predictor for an organization's maturity with respect to safety is information flow and, in particular, an organization's general way of coping with information that suggests an anomaly or contradicts prevailing assumptions. In some organizations, information flows well, and elicits prompt and appropriate responses. In others, it is hoarded for political reasons, not subjected to organizational scrutiny and understanding, or it languishes due to bureaucratic barriers. By examining key aspects of dealing with safety-related information, development phases can be described within an organization (Fig. 14.2; Parker et al. 2006). The model reflects the dynamic and multidimensional nature of safety culture and how it develops (Table 14.2). Some aspects of the model, such as incident reports or workplace safety, are discussed in Chaps. 15 and 16.

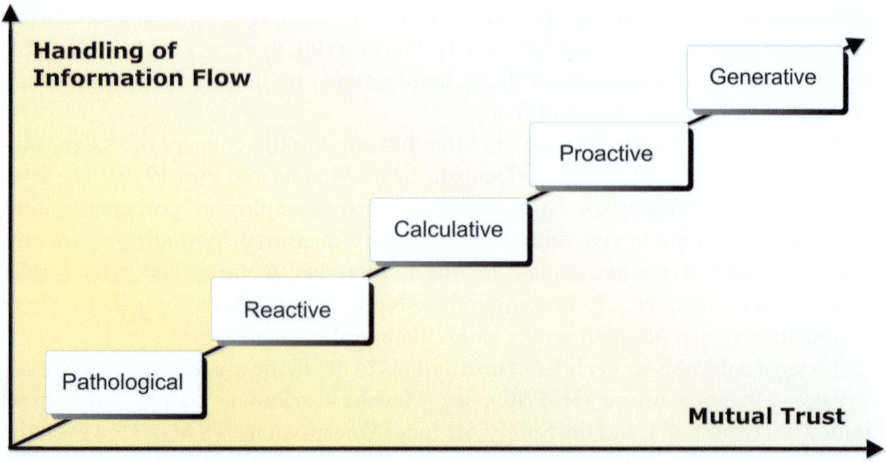

Fig. 14.2 Framework for developmental aspects of safety culture (following Parker et al. 2006)

It should be noted that the safety culture of an organization is not developed homogeneously – there are always more and less “mature” parts of an organization: “Safety culture is local” (Singer et al. 2009). In addition, the connection between organizational culture and behavior isn’t deterministic: Even in organizations with a pathological safety culture, there are individuals for whom safety is a top priority and who swim against the stream.

14.4 Safety Culture Is an Informed Culture

Because medical work involves teams, shared information will provide the glue that keeps the team focused and coordinated to pursue patient safety. Thus, “safety culture” is an “informed culture” (Reason 1997). Those who manage and operate the system have current knowledge about the human, technical, organizational, and environmental factors that determine the safety of the system. Values and beliefs, relationships, learning, and other aspects of organizational safety culture are all about sharing and processing information.

The main elements of an informed culture are (Reason 1998; Parker et al. 2006; Weick and Sutcliffe 2015):

- *The existence of a safety information system* (e.g., incident reporting system): An informed culture collects, analyzes, and disseminates information from incidents and near misses as well as from regular proactive checks on latent conditions of the system.
- *The existence of a reporting culture*: Informed cultures want to get the most out of the “free lessons” that incidents provide. An informed culture is free of blame and open for communication, promoting willingness to report on errors and

Table 14.2 Different stages of organizational development and corresponding key aspects of safety culture

	Stages of safety culture, low to high				
	Pathologic	Reactive	Calculative	Proactive	Generative
Commitment to safety	"Who cares, as long as we don't get caught?"	"Look out for yourself" is the rule	People know how to pay lip service to safety, but practical factors prevent complete follow through	Commitment to safety is developing, but attitude is not universal	Levels of commitment and care are high. Standards are defined by workforce
What causes accidents?	Individuals are blamed, and it is believed that accidents are part of the job	There are attempts to remove "accident prone" individuals. Systemic causes are considered but have no consequences	Management has a "them" rather than "us" mentality. An individual perspective is preferred over a systemic perspective	Management looks at the whole system, including processes and procedures	Blame is not an issue. People take a broad view looking at the interaction of systems and individuals
Hazard and unsafe act reporting	There are no reports	Reports are simple and focus on who or what caused the situation	Reports follow a fixed format. The number of reports is what counts	Reporting looks for "why" rather than just "what" and "when." Quick submission is appreciated	All levels actively access and use the information generated by reports in their daily work
How are incidents reported, investigated, and analyzed?	Investigations only take place after a serious accident	Investigation is aimed only at immediate causes. Focus is on finding guilty parties	Search for causes is usually restricted to the local workforce	Information and lessons learned are shared within the organization. There is little creativity in imagining how the real underlying issues could affect the business	Investigation and analysis are driven by a desire to obtain a deep understanding of how accidents happen

(continued)

Table 14.2 (continued)

	Stages of safety culture, low to high				
	Pathologic	Reactive	Calculative	Proactive	Generative
What happens after an accident?	The priority is to limit damage and get back to production	Management is annoyed every time an accident occurs. Reports are not passed up the line if it can be avoided	Workers report their own accidents. Management is worried about the impact on business statistics	Investigation focuses on underlying causes, and the results are fed back to supervisory level	Management shows personal interest in individuals and the investigation process
Work-site job safety techniques	There are no techniques. "Look out for yourself!"	After accidents, a standard hazard management technique is brought in to fix the problem. After introduction, there is limited systematic use	Commercially available techniques are introduced without being initiated by previous accidents, but lead to little action	Job safety analysis is accepted by workers as being in their own interest	Job safety analysis is revised regularly using a defined process. People are not afraid to tell each other about hazards
Competency training	Training is seen as a necessary evil, and people attend when it is compulsory	Training is aimed at the person: "If we can change their attitude, everything will be all right"	Lots of standard training courses are given. There is some on-the-job transfer of training	Leadership fully acknowledges the importance of tested skills on the job	Issues like attitudes become as important as knowledge and skills. Needs are identified and methods of acquiring skills are proposed by workers
Rewards for good safety performance	None is given or expected – staying alive is reward enough. There are only punishments for failure	There are only disincentives for poor safety performance. The understanding that positive behavior can be rewarded has not yet arrived	Some lip service is paid to good safety performance	There are some rewards for good performance. Evaluation is process-based rather than on outcomes	Recognition itself is seen as high value. Good safety performance is intrinsically motivating

Following Parker et al. (2006)

violations. Leadership and management decide upon the reporting method (e.g., written or verbal information, information upon request or spontaneously delivered, anonymous, etc.).

- *A present culture of trust*: Providing safety-related information is rewarded.
- *The willingness and competence to learn from what has happened*: Learning includes drawing the right conclusions from the safety system and implementing reform when it is required.
- *Prevailing justice*: In the aftermath of every single incident or accident, the focus is not on individual blame; instead, great care is taken to analyze the event for latent errors. Nevertheless, a clear line is drawn between acceptable and unacceptable behavior. There is no general amnesty for errors. Every member within an organization is aware of the fact that disrespect for standard operating procedures, violations of safety rules, and substance abuse during work will not be tolerated. A culture in which all acts are immune from punishment would lack credibility in the eyes of the workforce. Defining which actions will be rewarded and which will be punished communicates what is of central importance to the organization.
- *Flexibility*: During emergency situations, decisions will be made by frontline experts at the "sharp end." The advantage of this procedure is that decisions can be made without having to wait for confirmation from higher levels of authority. Every member is aware of which decision-making competence is expected and he or she will act accordingly. Leaders within the organization encourage other members to display flexibility during their decision-making in critical situations.

14.5 Organizations, Human Error, Reliability, and Ultra-safety

Organizations try to achieve specific goals that can be achieved through collective action. Often, processes that lead to unsafe behavior, near-incidents, and accidents disturb the achievement of these objectives. This fact has led organizational psychologists to address some basic questions: Why do errors occur in organizations? Why are socio-technical systems safe or unsafe? Are there abilities or competencies that enable people to work consistently in a reliable and safe manner? How do organizational frameworks and human behavior interact in the pathogenesis of incidents? As a result of this discussion, a number of models were developed that deal with error and error mitigation in organizations. The most relevant for acute medicine include:

- The human factors engineering approach
- The theory of "normal" accidents
- The theory of high-reliability organizations
- The theory of ultra-safe systems

14.5.1 The Human Factors Engineering Approach

Before scientists started to systematically deal with the emergence of incidents and the contributing role of human error, the normal way of handling an incident was to identify the person whose improper action had led to the undesirable result and to exclusively hold this individual liable (*person approach*, Chap. 3).

Human factors research has relentlessly pointed to the fact that active failures (Chap. 3) rarely arise solely from negligence but are more likely the consequence of error-provoking circumstances (e.g., equipment design, software development, architecture of workplace Norman 1988; Vicente 2004). Errors are seen as "the downside of having a brain" (Chap. 4; Helmreich 1998) rather than pathological cognitive processes that could be overcome by improved effort or diligence.

From a human factors-oriented perspective (*systemic perspective*), one wrong action rarely leads to an adverse event. Instead, preconditions and actions at all levels of an organization make a system "vulnerable" so that one wrong or unsafe action can trigger an incident. In a vulnerable system, similar circumstances will lead to similar errors, regardless of the person involved in the action. This vulnerability lies primarily in error-producing work conditions (e.g., the design of the workplace, architecture, device, and software design; Norman 1988; Vicente 2004). "Human error" therefore depends not on characteristics of individuals but on the socio-technical systems in which humans work (Chap. 1).

The contribution of the human factors approach to safe patient care and error reduction in a high-stakes medical environment can be seen in three key areas (Moray 1994; Vicente 2004):

- Design of safe systems
- Ergonomics
- Importance of teamwork

Formal structures, hierarchies, functions, and task descriptions within an organization can be seen as an "accumulation of clotted decisions." From this perspective, latent conditions for errors (Reason 1990a, b, 1997) are the "accumulation of clotted *unsafe* decisions," often the decisions of those with no direct patient contact, such as systems engineers, managers, and others at the "blunt end" of an organization, who do not set safety as the top priority or who, despite setting safety as the top priority, involuntarily create conditions that weaken a system's protective barriers. Their decisions are embedded in organizations and can have considerable short- and long-range effects on patient safety. "Organizational accidents" result from the interaction of a chain of latent failures, breaches in the defenses, and often involve momentary errors by the healthcare professional. Because almost all organizational accidents result from faulty systems that set people up to fail (Kohn et al. 1999), one of the main research areas of human factors engineers has been the analysis of *system design*.

The second main field of work within human factors research has been the application of scientific information concerning human limitations to the design of objects, systems, and environments for human use: the field of *ergonomics* (Carayon 2006). The design of medical equipment and the architectural layout of rooms influence the likelihood of mistakes. Due to inappropriate design of equipment and software, healthcare professionals are "forced" to commit errors, or they are hindered from working safely and efficiently by such things as cable clutter, wires, hoses, and lines running across the floor.

The information-processing capacity and decision-making capability of individual healthcare professionals have severe limitations within a high-stakes medical environment and are exacerbated under time pressure. In addition, poor *teamwork* and breakdowns in communication between members of healthcare teams can be key factors in poor care and medical errors. As a result, human factors theory has emphasized the importance of group-level interactions and the use of multidisciplinary teams to detect, prevent, and manage error-associated incidents (e.g., Entin and Serfaty 1999).

Human factors engineering tries to optimize the relationship between humans and systems by designing systems and human-machine interfaces that are robust enough to reduce error rates and mitigate the effects of errors within the system.

14.5.2 Normal Accident Theory

In the aftermath of the accident at the Three Mile Island nuclear power plant in 1979, Yale University sociologist Charles Perrow introduced the idea that as soon as technological systems become sufficiently complex, accidents will be inevitable or "normal." This conceptual framework has come to be known as Normal Accident Theory (NAT; Perrow 1984, 1994, 1999). Perrow explained his theory by introducing two related dimensions – interactive complexity and loose/tight coupling – which he claimed together determine a system's susceptibility to accidents.

Interactive complexity and coupling. The system dimension of interactive complexity is characterized by a multitude of positive and negative feedbacks between its components, most of these not visible or not immediately comprehensible. Unfamiliar or unexpected sequences of events may evolve in manners unpredictable to the designers or the users of the system. As a result, apparently trivial events may accumulate consecutively, with potentially severe consequences: The "harmless" habit of a radiology technician to refer to patients using only their family name can then contribute to the events leading to a cardiac arrest in a young trauma patient.

The concept of coupling describes the proximity of connections or transitions between system components. Coupling can be either tight or loose. If a system is tightly coupled, high interdependency exists: Each part of the system is tightly linked to other parts, and subcomponents of a tightly coupled system have prompt and major impacts on each other. In the absence of buffers, a change in one part of the system can rapidly affect the status of other parts. As a result, the quick response of system components to disturbances in another system may have disastrous consequences. The impairment of venous return by an increase in intrathoracic pressure, as in the case of a tension pneumothorax, would be a pathophysiological example of tight coupling. In addition, tight coupling and interactive complexity raise the odds that a healthcare provider's intervention will worsen a critical situation. For example, the extent of the lung damage became evident only after the physician had intubated the patient, thereby precipitating the tension pneumothorax.

In contrast, if loose coupling exists, the system components either work relatively independently of each other or the system itself possesses sufficient buffers to absorb the effect of failures or unplanned behavior without causing destabilization. According to NAT, systems with interactive complexity and tight coupling will experience unforeseen and unpreventable accidents.

As Charles Perrow formulated his theory as an explanation for disasters due to system accidents in socio-technical systems, he came to the conclusion that safety could be ensured only by renouncing risky technologies (e.g., nuclear energy).

14.5.3 High-Reliability Theory

The pessimistic view of NAT is that accidents are inevitable and normal. In contrast, representatives of the theory of high-reliability organizations (HROs) show in their analysis of several case studies that even complex organizations with tight couplings can work reliably and safely without accidents by following certain organizational and communication rules. These case studies include large organizations in industries with complexity levels that are similar to hospitals such as aircraft carriers and nuclear power plants (LaPorte and Consolini 1991; Roberts 1990; Weick and Sutcliffe 2015).

These high-reliability organizations achieve their high safety standards through mindful attention to ongoing operations. HROs resemble other organizations in their input processes, but differ through their adoption of a widespread precautionary attitude toward usual and unusual operations. HROs are committed to *mindfulness* as a means to manage challenges. High-reliability theory offers an optimistic approach and emphasizes that organizations can contribute significantly to the prevention of accidents through good organizational design and management. The high-reliability theory identifies the important role played by the cultural features in an organization that places high value on "error-free performance." The processes by which HROs mindfully pursue their goal are characterized by an "informed safety culture" (Reason 1997) and several other characteristics (Roberts 1990; Weick and Sutcliffe 2015). Naturally, there are exceptions; however, research on HROs shows that it is possible for an organization to work safely even under adverse conditions if the following ideas guide action.

14.5.3.1 Features of Reliable Organizations

- High-reliability organizations are marked by *anticipation*: They respond early to weak signals with high attention.
- *Preoccupation with failure*: HRO employees are preoccupied with minor incidents and rare events rather than with accidents or complete failures. Because even the slightest incident indicates possible weakness in the system, every

opportunity to learn is made real. This is evident in frequent incident reviews, the reporting of errors no matter how inconsequential they are, and employees' obsession with the liability of success. Employees in HROs are skeptical, wary, and suspicious of long and quiet periods of success, always anticipating the danger of complacency and inattention. Sensitive to the fact that any decision or action may be subject to faulty assumptions, they are "chronically worried about the unexpected." They hope for the best but anticipate the worst.

- *Reluctance to simplify interpretations*: HROs are just as preoccupied with complicating their simplifications as they are with probing their failures. The relentless attack on simplifications can be seen by the preference for discovering and describing complex models about internal and external events. It is assumed that simple mental models and expectations produce simple sensing and rash decisions. Instead, HROs employ varied and complex sensors to register and control complexities, i.e., "It takes variety to control variety."
- *Sensitivity to operations*: Normal work routines are constantly scrutinized for potential weaknesses of the system. The necessary sensitivity required here is accomplished by building "a dense web of communication." Every staff member is provided with detailed real-time information on what is happening and what ongoing operations require for error-free performance. Sensitivity to operations permits early identification of problems so that action can be taken before problems become too substantial.

Despite all efforts to anticipate and take preventive measures, critical events will occur. The mindset necessary to cope with these critical situations differs from the one needed to anticipate their occurrence. Once they are faced with critical situations, HROs will apply at least two processes that enable them to contain and recover from problems. These processes include:

- *Deference to expertise*: In a typical hierarchical structure, important decisions are made by high-ranking decision makers. Although hierarchical patterns of authority exist, authority within HROs always shifts toward the area of required expertise, not toward seniority or rank. The designation of who is "important" in a certain critical situation changes according to the decision maker's specialization and "migrates" to the person or team with expertise relevant to the problem at hand.
- *Commitment to resilience*: To be resilient is to be mindful of errors as they occur and correct them before they worsen and cause more serious harm. Organizations that are committed to resilience always expect the unexpected. To reduce the likelihood of such an occurrence, focus is laid on developing general resources to cope and respond swiftly. A resilient mindset seeks cure rather than prevention; mitigation rather than anticipation. Attention is concentrated on knowledge and resources that relieve, lighten, moderate, reduce, and decrease surprises. While *anticipation* encourages people to think and then act, *resilience* encourages people to act while thinking to implement lessons learned from error (Hollnagel et al. 2006). Resilience in the context of HROs denotes a different meaning than resilience in the context of response to stressful events (Chap. 9).

Reliability-enhancing organizations encourage people to discuss the current state of the system, deviations, personal intentions, minimal events, and the occurrence of error. A climate of openness and trustful relationships between employees and leadership are prerequisites. The constant reflection upon decision-making, past and present, can prevent an effect of normalization when dealing with deviance. "Normalization of deviance" (Vaughan 1997) conceptualizes the gradual shift in what is regarded as normal after repeated exposures to "deviant behavior," i.e., behavior straying from correct and safe operating procedures. Corners get cut, safety checks bypassed, and alarms ignored or turned off, and these behaviors become not just common but stripped of their significance as warnings of impending danger. Normalization of deviance is likely to occur within an organization if deviating events, deviating behavior, or violations of rules do not receive immediate negative feedback. In the absence of a controlled punitive system, safety hazards will slowly turn into an acceptable risk.

In summary, the theories all address the issue of patient safety and human fallibility from a systemic perspective. All three theories provide helpful insight into the dynamics of error occurrence in a high-stakes medical environment and focus on a different set of organizational dynamics (Table 14.3).

Table 14.3 Three theories addressing error and safety in terms of "system" issues

Theory	Key ideas around issue of errors	Key organizational factors implied by the theory to reduce error	References
Human factors theory	"Latent" conditions and active errors combine in a system to cause accidents	Decreased complexity; feedback loops; system redundancies; team cooperation; rapid response capability; operator communication; information systems; decentralized decision-making	Reason (1990a, b) Rasmussen (1982) Gaba (1989) Helmreich et al. (1999)
Normal accident theory	Errors in complex systems are unavoidable; no design is foolproof; risk is determined by the level of coupling between tasks and complexity of interactions	Control over personnel; close proximity of elites to operating systems; no centralization; use of buffers between steps in process; information and feedback around critical phases and errors	Perrow (1984, 1994, 1999)
High-reliability theory	Complex organizational processes can be designed and operated for reliable performance	A "culture" of reliability and safety; system redundancies; training and education; decentralized decision-making; clear goals; measurement and feedback; the use of routines	LaPorte (1982) Roberts (1990) Schulman (1993) Rochlin (1993) Weick and Sutcliffe (2015)

From Hoff et al. (2004)

14.5.4 Ultra-safe Systems

The likelihood of dying or being injured while working varies between different socio-technical systems. Systems that almost never produce accidents (such as the nuclear industry or civil aviation) can therefore be considered as "ultra-safe" (Amalberti et al. 2005). It should be possible to identify the strategies and tools responsible for this success and apply them to healthcare so that healthcare organizations can be as safe as aerospace and other ultra-safe domains. However, the main difference between healthcare and these other domains lies not in the availability of tools, but rather in the willingness of the high-risk sectors to say goodbye to deep-rooted assumptions and beliefs regarding individual action and autonomy. Ultra-safe systems to a high degree owe their safety to standardization of processes and the acceptance of necessary changes in attitudes and traditions. Comparing healthcare with ultra-safe systems, there are five barriers that must be eliminated to reach maximum safety in healthcare (Amalberti et al. 2005):

- *Acceptance of limitations on maximum performance*. When the prevailing attitude is "attain a specific high level of production, no matter what it takes," the system in question is very unsafe. Healthcare has a strong emphasis on productivity to keep costs low. Low safety levels do not necessarily arise from incompetent actors; more often they are incurred by experts who challenge the boundaries of their own maximum performance.
- *Abandonment of professional autonomy*. The psycho-logic of human action demonstrates that it is natural for an individual to pursue personal goals. Competing personal interests in patient care arise when the autonomy of two individuals collide. Strict regulations and a growing movement toward educating healthcare professionals in teamwork have reduced the autonomy of healthcare professionals and thereby improved safety in healthcare, but there is still much to be done in this area.
- *Transition from the mindset of craftsman attitude to that of an equivalent actor*. A ubiquitous phenomenon in healthcare is the fact that patients choose their physician (e.g., surgeon, pulmonologist, cardiologist) in the belief that the result of a planned procedure will vary according to their choice. This view is typical of a craftsman market. Healthcare professionals must face the difficult transition of abandoning their status and self-image as craftspeople and instead adopt a position that values equivalence and standardization. Individuality in processes has to be renounced in the service of a reliable standard of excellent care. Anesthesiology seems to come close to this characteristic: No patient chooses a hospital or outpatient clinic just because he wants to have anesthesia delivered by a specific anesthesiologist. However, standardization and the equivalent actor principle require stable conditions for activity, which are less common in intensive care units and emergency departments with the variation in patient acuity and staffing.
- *Need for system-level arbitration to optimize safety strategies*. Increased pressure from medical malpractice liability and media scrutiny has created a need for

system-level arbitration. There is a clear tendency of professionals and their unions to overprotect themselves in the face of legal pressures and threats of litigation. Healthcare professionals are no different – they fear for their own position and act accordingly in pursuit of maximum (personal) safety. The perverse effect of this is that litigation-avoidance decisions primarily absolve them from responsibility but may not be in the best clinical or economic interests of the patient. To change this, the acceptance of residual risk has to be endorsed.
- *Need to simplify professional rules and regulations.* With increasing safety, the visibility of risk is increasingly hidden within system complexity. The potential of any new technique or regulation to strengthen safety diminishes. Thus, the probability is high that these decisions and regulations are made without clear proof of their benefits, and may even introduce frictions and contradictions among existing regulations and policies.

Unfortunately, none of the theories provide the needed solution for healthcare's pressing safety problems. The challenge for healthcare will be to find ways of adapting these theories to the structure, needs, and constraints of patient care. Simply copying safety "models of success" from other high-stakes environments will not work (Thomas and Helmreich 2002).

14.6 Aviation as a Model? Parallels and Limits

A highly reliable, ultra-safe socio-technical system that is used again and again as a reference for patient safety is civil aviation. While in the 1970s flying was still a risky business, the number of air traffic accidents in 2013 was, despite the continuously increased number of flights, at a historic low: Were a passenger to fly every day, they would have to spend about 6,500 years in the air before being involved in a fatal accident. This impressive development despite growing air traffic is the result of a cultural and technical transformation of the system.

14.6.1 Parallels to Healthcare

Although the consistent implementation of concepts for risk management in many other socio-technical systems has also led to a dramatic decline in the accident rate (e.g., nuclear power, petrochemical industry) and these could also offer many points of comparison, physicians seem to be drawn to almost exclusively search for viable concepts in aviation: "Pilots show doctors how errors can be avoided" or "Doctors learn from pilots" are stereotypical newspaper headlines expressing the opinion that doctors (especially anesthesiologists and emergency room personnel) have a lot in common with pilots. For years pilots have been welcome speakers at medical conferences, and if a doctor shows detailed knowledge of instruments and procedures in the cockpit during a talk on patient safety he or she harvests admiration. The reasons for this continuing appeal of civil aviation to healthcare are manifold:

- *Role model for improving safety*: Healthcare can only dream of the level of safety of civil aviation. In 2010–2014, the 5-year average of fatalities due to safety problems in commercial aviation jet planes was 353 persons/year, compared to 517 fatalities/year in 2009–2013 (IATA 2015, 2016). In 2015, the number of fatal accidents was 0 (IATA 2016), although there were two total hull losses due to terrorism and crime. Other statistics show slightly different rates, depending on the types of planes, regions, and incidents included. All show a superb level of safety (e.g., Boeing 2015). In contrast, 2–3 % of patients undergoing surgery died (Pearse et al. 2012).
- *Comparable socio-technical environment:* In both domains, teams of highly specialized experts interact with advanced technology in high-risk situations. Errors may have a significant impact on the safety of the persons entrusted to them and have financial, legal, and political consequences (Kao and Thomas 2008).
- *Comparable cognitive and social requirements*: Those healthcare domains dealing with patients with rapidly deteriorating health conditions that must be diagnosed with the use of technology and be treated in a team require decisions under uncertainty and complexity. Since pilots face similar challenges in emergency situations and dealing with it has been part of their training for decades (crew resource management (CRM) training), adaptations for acute medicine have been successfully implemented from early on (first in anesthesia, but now becoming more widespread in emergency care, critical care, operating room teams, obstetrics, and others).

In the interests of patient safety, a number of aviation concepts have been transferred to the healthcare domain (Helmreich 2000; Toff 2010; Levy et al. 2014; Lewis et al. 2011; Kao and Thomas 2008; Ornato and Peberdy 2014). These include:

- Addressing human factors (Chap. 1)
- Simulator training and adapting crew resource management principles (Chap. 16)
- Development of behavioral markers for assessing behavioral and teamwork skills (Chap. 2) for different acute medical disciplines
- Standardization of processes: implementation of checklists (e.g., World Health Organization's "Safe Surgery Saves Lives" initiative) and establishment of standard operating procedures (Chap. 15)
- Joint briefings (Chap. 11)
- Establishment of incident reporting systems (Chap. 15)
- Reduction of work hours to reduce the influence of fatigue (Chap. 8)

14.6.2 A Bumpy Comparison: Doctors and Nurses Face More Challenges than Pilots

In the initial euphoria, several medical publications presented healthcare and civil aviation as two socio-technical systems with many similarities. In the last few years, however, the focus has moved to the considerable differences between the two

(Rampersad and Rampersad 2007; Ricci et al. 2012; Rogers 2011; Shaw and Calder 2008; Webster 2002). Although healthcare should still learn from aviation and hasn't finished testing and adapting its safety concepts (Gaba 2011), regulatory or organizational frameworks should be considered, and differences need to be clearly named to avoid unrealistic expectations and to integrate procedures into healthcare in a useful way. That such a critical, meaningful connection between aviation and healthcare remains fascinating and exciting is proven by the book *Why Hospitals Should Fly* (Nance 2008), which led the US bestseller lists for many weeks.

One oversight may be that the cognitive demands required for effective acute care medicine likely are more similar to those of military pilots. For reasons unknown, this fact is not reflected in patient safety literature.

Since the comparison of acute healthcare and aviation is often limited to specific aspects, the main differences between civil and military aviation and acute medicine will be compared more fully below (Table 14.4). This makes it possible for readers to see where their own organization might learn from aviation and which know-how may be useful and transferable.

In our opinion, task requirements are similar in many ways. The workplace and the environment of the system, however, are not. Work in acute healthcare and in aviation is vulnerable to deficits in skills such as situation awareness, decision-making, communication, leadership, and teamwork. Decision-making under uncertainty is especially highly demanding.

In addition to the admiration of the ethical dimension of demonstrating consistently high standards of safety, it is a sobering thought that airlines invest in the safety of their passengers and crew members primarily due to economic reasons and regulatory aspects. These factors do not predominate in the healthcare domain.

14.7 Organizational Sources of Error

14.7.1 Key Systems Issues for Addressing Error and Safety in Acute Medical Care

Published more than a decade ago, the Institute of Medicine's (IOM) report "To Err Is Human: Building a Safer Healthcare System" (Kohn et al. 1999) has triggered an unprecedented effort within the healthcare community to identify interventions that might decrease medical errors and enhance patient safety. A system-based approach to reducing error and the need for a strong patient-safety environment have begun to replace the focus on alleged incompetent or misguided individuals. Consequently, the medical community has directed empirical research to the linkages between organizational dynamics, medical error, and patient safety. A review of the clinical and health service literature was able to identify the most discussed or analyzed organizational variables (Hoff et al. 2004). At present, however, there seems to be little scientific evidence for asserting the importance of one single individual, group, or structural variable in error prevention. From among the analyzed variables, the following seem especially relevant for initiating latent errors in a medical

Table 14.4 Comparison between the "workplace cockpit" in civil and military aviation and acute healthcare

	Workplace acute healthcare mostly in hospital	Workplace cockpit in civil aviation	Workplace cockpit in military aviation
Characteristics and job	Risks are an integral part of care and are taken based on the potential benefit and ideally after the patient's informed consent. Accordingly, various outcomes are anticipated and acceptable	There will not be any risks. A safe flight is the only acceptable outcome	A distinction is made between peace operations and mission operations. In peace operations only limited risks are taken (*train as you fight*). During mission operations, risks to pilots and aircraft are taken into account
	The team is usually responsible for one patient at a time. An error concerning the patient has no physical consequences for the team	The crew is responsible for many passengers They may die themselves as a result of an error	The crew is (depending on the type of aircraft) responsible for crew members, and mission success Crews can die as a result of errors or enemy actions. Armed combat aircraft potentially kill innocent people (collateral damage)
	Patient care is performed by various team members in different locations with partially overlapping actions. Knowledge about diagnosis and treatment must be passed on at the interfaces	A flight has a defined start and a defined end and is performed by a crew From this flight nothing will be taken to the next shift For long-haul flights, a replacement crew is on board. Handover then takes place in-flight	Short missions with a known target are performed by a team (which may also include formations of several planes). On missions with an unknown destination, extensive handovers at the target area with target instructions are necessary. Missions can overlap, so that handovers from aircraft to aircraft can be necessary
	Emergency procedures must be performed immediately; patient condition can't be optimized first and treatment can't be postponed	If the weather conditions are not safe or any function of the plane is out of order the flight is canceled	In peace operations, same as civil aviation During combat, flight takes place in unfavorable circumstances based on risk assessment

(continued)

Table 14.4 (continued)

	Workplace acute healthcare mostly in hospital	Workplace cockpit in civil aviation	Workplace cockpit in military aviation
Regulatory structures and training	Nearly all regulatory authority comes from a number of nongovernment, volunteer organizations	Main regulatory body (e.g., Federal Aviation Agency) is responsible for manufacturers, airlines, and flight personnel	In the United States, each branch of the military has a central authority for training, licensing, and aircraft certification and publishes operations manuals for pilots and maintenance
	Since the late 1990s, sporadic attempts have been made to enhance human factors and organizational design and to utilize behavioral and teamwork training to enhance individual and team performance	Since the late 1970s, a structured and systematic approach has been made to enhance human factors and organizational design and to utilize behavioral and teamwork training to enhance individual and crew performance	Since the late 1980s, a structured and systematic approach has been made to enhance human factors and organizational design and to utilize behavioral and teamwork training to enhance individual and crew performance
	No psychometric testing of candidates. Selection largely based on previous academic performance	Rigorous selection with psychometric testing of candidates	Rigorous selection with psychometric testing of candidates
	Simulator training is optional Not all hospitals have simulators or access to such	Simulator training is the main pillar of education in modern education programs All airlines have access to simulators	Simulator training is an integral part of the training The percentage of real flight hours during training is significantly higher than in civil aviation
	Available simulators (patient, virtual reality task trainer) have limited validity. The complexity of widely variable biological systems is large. Current simulator technology provides very poor fidelity	Available simulators have excellent validity, since the behavior of technical systems can be reproduced predictably	Available simulators have limited wartime validity, since the complexity of the mission and centrifugal forces are difficult to simulate

Table 14.4 (continued)

	Workplace acute healthcare mostly in hospital	Workplace cockpit in civil aviation	Workplace cockpit in military aviation
	Learning on live patients; learning curve of the learner is associated with risk for the patient	Learning in the flight simulator; learning curve of the pilot for obtaining the "type rating" without danger to passengers Operation with passengers, "line training," is performed after qualifying in a simulator	Learning is approximately 15 % in a flight simulator; 85 % in a real aircraft Risk to man and machine exist during the training
	Patient care is often done without adequate supervision and even scheduled supervision is not available because of other responsibilities	Constant supervision by experienced pilots Semiannual and annual check flights and medical exams and standardized assessment of pilots' mental fitness to fly	Constant supervision during training After taking the exam supervision is only indirectly ensured Annual check flights and medical assessment for pilots
	Simulator training is voluntary and accomplished in irregular intervals	Semiannual/annual mandatory simulator training	Semiannual and annual mandatory simulator training
	Defined behavioral markers for some disciplines No pass/fail standards	Defined behavioral markers Required by the government and defined by the airline company. Relevant for pilots' permission to fly	Defined behavioral markers, each branch of the military sets its own regulations for pilot assessment
Team	Teams in acute healthcare are usually large (e.g., emergency room surgery) and relatively heterogeneous (many specializations) Often changing daily, with personally unknown team members	The cockpit team usually consists of only two persons Together with cabin crew relatively homogeneous team (2 professional groups) Often changing daily, with personally unknown team members	Combat aircraft cockpit team consists of two pilots or a single pilot; however, increasing number during formation flying (maximum 4 aircrafts per formation) Fixed or formed team policy determined by military branches

(continued)

Table 14.4 (continued)

	Workplace acute healthcare mostly in hospital	Workplace cockpit in civil aviation	Workplace cockpit in military aviation
	Competencies of the team members are not identical and depend on training and experience Procedures are often only known by single team members; little redundancy Knowledge base is mostly complementary and not substitutive	Skills of the pilots are largely identical, but depend on experience Procedures can be carried out both by the captain and first officer redundantly Knowledge base within the cockpit is identical	*Combat aircraft:* the competence of a two-man crew is up to 80 % different; only singular in single-seat jets, redundancy in the formation Some procedures can be carried out by either the front-seat pilot or the rear-seat weapons system officer. The degree of redundancy varies by type of aircraft and mission Knowledge base is complementary and only partly substitutive *Transport aircraft:* Like civil aviation
	No regular mandatory team or communication training for medical teams	Crews receive regular mandatory team and communication training (CRM)	Crews receive regular mandatory team and communication training (CRM)
	No or little standardized communication	Standardized communication in the cockpit and with air traffic control (ATC)	Standardized communication in the cockpit and with air traffic control (ATC)
	In an emergency there is often unclear leadership because of heterogeneous formation of teams	Clear hierarchy and leadership during an emergency	Clear hierarchy and leadership during an emergency
	Little language standards, no defined working language Frequently multicultural teams; problems in cooperation because of different languages and culture	Worldwide language standards and common working language (English) Frequently multicultural teams, also dealing with language problems	Worldwide language standards and common working language (English) Rarely multicultural teams in the cockpit. Formations might be multicultural, especially during allied operations

Table 14.4 (continued)

	Workplace acute healthcare mostly in hospital	Workplace cockpit in civil aviation	Workplace cockpit in military aviation
Aircraft and human	People are not constructed. Their current pathophysiology must be concluded from ambiguous signals	Aircraft are constructed; their current system state can be optimally represented for the operator	Aircraft are constructed; their current system state can be optimally represented for the operator
	The human body is not produced in series. People differ in their demographic conditions, comorbidities, and course of disease	Aircraft of one series is nearly identical and interchangeable in their flight behavior	Aircraft of one series is nearly identical and interchangeable in their flight behavior
Control of the processes and work environment	Heterogeneity of patient care. Guidelines are often only reluctantly and with great latency introduced in everyday life. There are no government guidelines except for payment regulations. Guidelines promulgated by volunteer professional organizations. Availability of "standard operating procedures" for incidents not standardized or required	High degree of regulation by airline company and government approved "standard operating procedures" for all routine situations and expectable incidents. Compliance is required. Procedures are executed as a checklist	High degree of regulation by "standard operating procedures" for all routine situations and expected incidents. Compliance is required. Procedures are executed as a checklist
	Process variability is often necessary; idiosyncrasies due to caregiver differences, patient condition, team, and clinical environment	Process variability is undesirable and not part of the professional self-image of pilots	Process variability in routine flight operations is undesirable. Processes at the tactical units require great flexibility to survive during operations. Strategic and tactical advantage through flexibility is part of the professional self-image of fighter pilots

(continued)

Table 14.4 (continued)

	Workplace acute healthcare mostly in hospital	Workplace cockpit in civil aviation	Workplace cockpit in military aviation
	Doctors and nurses in acute healthcare must often overcome emergencies and develop expertise Checklists/algorithms for some emergencies in some institutions available	Pilots regularly train for emergencies that they may never experience Emergencies are processed using checklists	Pilots regularly train for emergencies that they may never experience. Probability of occurrence of emergencies is higher than in the civil aviation sector as the aircraft are operated closer to their limits Emergencies are processed using checklists
	The negative impact of fatigue on performance is systematically underestimated So far, there is insufficient change in working conditions due to knowledge about fatigue effects	The negative impact of fatigue on performance is part of the training and regulatory requirements The economic pressure to perform while fatigued is secondary to regulations	The negative impact of fatigue on performance is part of the training and regulatory improvements. Implementation of measures to take account of fatigue is still lacking during combat operations
	Work environment is usually known	Problems may occur in unfamiliar territory/environment; in this case, few resources and support options	Problems may occur in unfamiliar territory/environment; in this case, few resources and support options
Learning from mistakes	Incident reporting systems of varying quality are currently in place or being established almost everywhere Still, only a small number of incidents are reported, and thus learning opportunities are missed	Incident reporting systems are in place (e.g., Aviation Safety Reporting System from NASA) and are used as an information base for improvement of aviation safety	Incident reporting systems are in place for all branches of the military and are used as an information base for improvement of aviation safety

Although all three domains share similarities, the differences are significant and should be considered when attempting to transfer practices in aviation to acute healthcare. As can be seen, many of the differences are fundamental

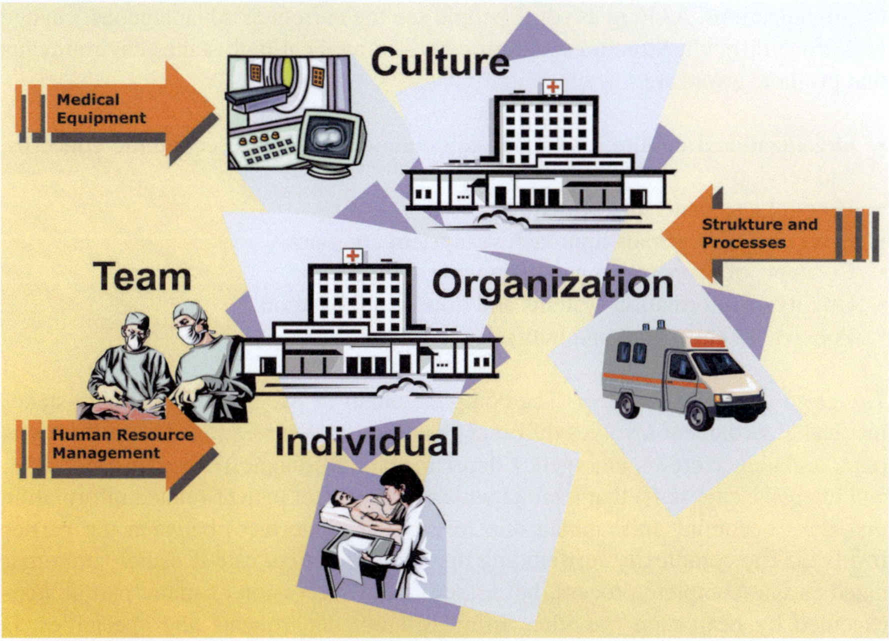

Fig. 14.3 Organizational sources of latent errors in a medical high-stakes environment

high-stakes environment (Fig. 14.3; Cooper et al. 1978; Flin and Maran 2004; Morell and Eichhorn 1997; O'Connor et al. 2002):

- Structure and processes
- Equipment-related incidents
- Human resource management
- Teamwork and leadership
- Communication
- Organizational culture

Here, we describe structures and processes, equipment problems, and human resource management. Teamwork, communication, and leadership are topics discussed in Chaps. 11–13. The significance of organizational culture is pursued in Chap. 15, in addition to formal teamwork training interventions and simulation-based team training.

14.7.2 Structures and Processes

Medical and legal requirements are changing constantly. Consequently, organizations must adapt their structures and processes continuously. Historically grown structures underlie a certain inertia that causes a typical resistance to change within the organizations. As long as some people see the current as advantageous, change will prove difficult. Structures and processes in medical high-stakes environments that promote errors are:

- Organizational culture: particular combinations of safety, economic concerns, and service
- Hierarchies, leadership principles
- Error concepts: person approach vs. system approach
- Concepts of cooperation and teamwork
- Quality of information systems and flow of information
- Policies for shift work and hours of work

The Organizational Problem The complete chain of patient care in a high-stakes medical environment involves different groups of staff across several organizations (e.g., ambulance crews, emergency department staff, diagnostic departments, labs, and intensive care staff) that interact and create relevant patient-related information that risks becoming mishandled due to the many interfaces between the parties involved. The complexity surrounding the fact that patient care is usually not organized as one complete process, but rather as the succession of many partial steps executed by healthcare providers from different departments and specialties, is summarized as an *organizational problem*: The shared goal of safe patient care can only be reached if specialists are willing to work together and if coordinated actions are aided by the organizational structure and resources. A lack of organizational coordination is a normal feature of every organization.

The circumstances which lead to harm in the young trauma patient have their roots in such organizational problems. An organizational problem is best addressed by creating structures and implementing strategies that improve the interaction and collaboration among healthcare professionals and the services in which they work (Fig. 14.4). In order to achieve this goal, an organization needs concepts for:

- Reliable communication at the numerous interfaces
- Interdisciplinary teamwork
- Leadership performance
- Efficient knowledge management

Because optimizing knowledge transfer and cooperation of specialists are required, the organizational problem is a problem of standardization, coordination, and motivation. Thus, organizations must continue to address standardization, motivation, and cooperation at the interfaces between different disciplines and services. Just like in the example of the emergency department, other subsystems of acute care (OR, emergency room, recovery room, intensive care, preclinical patient care) obviously have to deal with the same problems, i.e., various professions and services are responsible for their share in the overall tasks of patient care. A significant part of the work is therefore information exchange and coordination, e.g., patient handoffs, visitations, shift changes, briefing, case conferences.

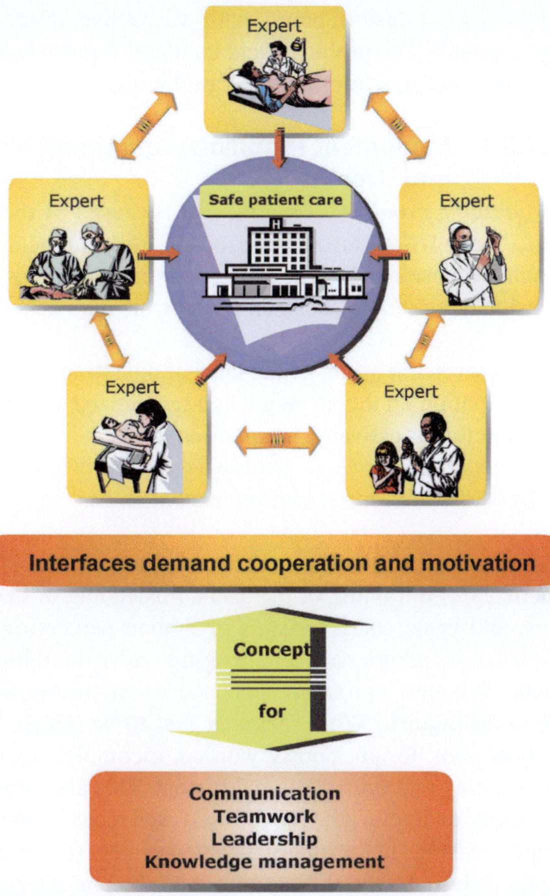

Fig. 14.4 The organizational problem. Every expert has his or her own knowledge, experience, and motives, which are needed for constructive cooperation with experts from other specialties. The interfaces between professional groups demand cooperation and motivation as well as an institutional concept for communication, teamwork, leadership, and knowledge management

In addition to this inherent organizational problem, there may be conflicting goals. Despite the explicit goal of safe patient care, each department and specialty may pursue goals unique to the discipline or service that may not well-serve overall patient well-being. Goal conflicts are exacerbated especially when resources are restricted. The understaffing of the emergency department in the case study may have been due to a conflict between best medical and economic considerations, which was resolved in favor of short-term economic savings.

14.7.3 Medical Equipment-Related Incidents

Equipment-related incidents represent only a minority of incidents in a high-stakes medical environment (9–20 % of all incidents; for anesthesia: Chopra et al. 1992; Cooper et al. 1978, 1984; Currie 1989; Webb et al. 1993; for intensive care: Valentin et al. 2006). Nevertheless, they can have serious consequences if the equipment is highly invasive or life supporting, and if tight coupling exists between patient and device (e.g., infusion pump with vasoactive drug, ventilator, cardiopulmonary bypass pump). The problems and incidents reported can be divided into two groups: equipment malfunctions and user problems.

14.7.3.1 Equipment Problems: Equipment Malfunction and User Error

An *operating problem* is an error that is caused by the design features of the device itself, like software errors or errors in the documentation (e.g., incomprehensible manual because of machine-made translation). A *user error* is due to the action (or omission of action) of the user. User errors may occur when:

- The user is not aware of the current operating mode of the device.
- Information on the display is not recognized or is misinterpreted.
- A function is activated unintentionally.
- Expected actions (e.g., acknowledgement of a setting change to allow it to take effect) are not (or not in time) executed.

User errors are therefore errors in operating the system. Causes lie in a lack of experience and training of the users, misleading or inadequate design of user interfaces, and basic characteristics of human perception and information processing which can be additionally challenging under the influence of stress, distraction, or fatigue. Whether a problem is caused by the user or by the equipment can be difficult to distinguish: What seems at first to be human error may turn out to be the result of poor design, poorly worded, incomplete or misleading user guidance, or poor training and organizational factors. This also applies to the delayed defibrillation in our example: The model used was recently purchased and installed without training sessions in the emergency department (organizational factor). It had a completely different way of operating than the previous models and was unfamiliar to everyone in the team. Instead of the operation of a panel, labeled with "1, 2, 3," they had to use a flip-out monitor and search for the correct functions (poor design and user guidance).

14.7.3.2 Development Problems: Learning to Understand the User

The safety of medical devices has steadily improved in the recent decades because of the advent of standards, accident prevention regulations, and improved technology. Due to the application of safety standards, technical defects of medical devices have become rare. The increasing quality of medical devices, however, often comes together with more functions which usually leads to more complex requirements for operating and maintaining the device. This increased complexity is on the one hand due to competition, as manufacturers implement (sometimes unnecessary) special features to secure a market advantage. On the other hand, decision makers in hospitals or rescue organizations are often inclined to favor devices with more features to get more features for the same money. Users are thus confronted with new devices in which one key may have different functions depending on what state the machine is in. This requires additional knowledge and awareness to know the correct branch point within the state of the internal software hierarchy that is in effect at the time. Therefore, many users dislike and reject devices that host special functions since special functions can often prevent basic and everyday tasks from being performed intuitively. A consequence of this increasing complexity is that undesirable events due to technical defects in the equipment become less important, while user errors become a significant risk.

Since safety features of the devices cannot protect from all risks of user error, usability becomes more important as a safety feature. Usability refers to the extent to which a product can be used by specified users in a specified context to achieve specified goals with effectiveness, efficiency, and satisfaction. Often manufacturers assume that the user will learn to understand the internal logic of the device, rather than developing the device according to ergonomic principles so that the device can support a more natural logic held by the user. To assess whether a medical device has a reasonable performance, the following factors must be considered:

- Intuitive and understandable operation.
- Low learning and training costs.
- Clear dialogue between human and machine.
- Understandable user manual.
- Clear information and assistance with dysfunctions and alarms.
- The application context of the unit is adequately considered.

The last point especially has become the focus of medical device manufacturers in recent years. Most human errors in the operation of medical devices can be attributed to the failure of the developer to consider early in the development process the users' expectations and needs and the requirements that the device will be exposed to in everyday life. In particular, it is often overlooked that users of a new device will:

- Apply it in *unusual* and *unexpected ways*. Manufacturers need to know the user to make sure that the product behaves appropriately even when used in unanticipated ways.
- Experience the control keys, labeling, and operating modes as *confusing or too complex*. Manufacturers should not rely on user training or manuals to make the complexity understandable, even if these are statutory: The best devices are those that do not demand extensive training and user memory to be used safely.
- *Deprive* them of their *safety functions* by muting the alarms or permanently disabling them. Often the reason alarms are disabled is that they have no therapeutic effect or no meaning beyond an initial warning or alarm when there is no impending danger, and the frequency of alarms (false and/or real) is experienced as a nuisance by nurses and physicians alike (Chap. 8).

Apart from medical consequences of application errors, poor usability also leads to:

- Increased process times and errors
- Poor utilization of functionality
- Frustration and dissatisfaction of users
- Need for repeated training and dependence on manuals for safe operation
- Follow-up costs (treatment and compensation) for incidents involving patients or users

14.7.4 Human Resource Management

Accessible healthcare requires well-trained and motivated healthcare team members comprised of the right skill mix and of an adequate size to be able to deliver safe, high-quality care. Over the past decades, however, healthcare services have been losing their competitiveness as employers. Moderate revenues concurrent with increasing workload and unsatisfactory career perspectives have contributed to an increasing reluctance to enter healthcare and lower morale among the workforce. As a result, healthcare organizations have increased their efforts to develop human resource concepts contingent on organizational needs as well as economic and political circumstances. The theoretical underpinnings as well as practical techniques of managing a workforce are provided by (mostly non-clinician) human resource management (HRM) specialists. In today's healthcare systems, HRM tries to cover the gap between the economic demands of today's healthcare and the individual employee's needs and objectives. HRM takes a positive view of healthcare professionals, assuming that virtually all concerned wish to contribute to safe patient care. Given the importance of skilled and motivated healthcare professionals for an efficient and safe delivery of patient care, and for the avoidance of errors, HRM has to serve six key functions:

- *Determination of staff requirement*: Long-term organizational goals determine the quantity of trained healthcare professionals needed; however, whether or not the planning can be put into practice is highly dependent on the way the organization solves the short-term conflict of available financial resources and staff requirements. A suboptimal solution of the competing priorities leads to staff shortage, long working hours, and a decline in morale or a financially ineffective organization.
- *Staff recruitment and selection*: A thorough job analysis is required to determine the level of technical skills, competencies, and necessary flexibility of a potential employee. Despite the availability of adequate diagnostic tools for staff selection, current practice still seems to be that employees are hired according to personal diagnostic standards of clinical leaders and other responsible persons. As a result, certain personality traits may accumulate systematically and predominate within an organization. For example, if the head of a department has a conflict-avoiding personality, he or she will prefer to hire conflict-avoiding staff

members. This tendency in turn may create a certain team climate where members are reluctant to advocate their position or voice concerns even when the interests of a patient are at stake.

- *Clinical job assignment:* Staffing assignments are often responsible for misallocation of human resources. For example, problematic aspects in staff assignment are constant changing schedules for operations with surgeons operating or anesthesiologists anesthetizing patients whose medical history they are unaware of. Even worse, healthcare providers are assigned tasks that exceed their knowledge and experience, such as emergency physicians with limited experience with pediatric patients being responsible for any patient delivered to the emergency department.
- *Evaluation of clinical performance*: HRM strategies include the design of compliant, consistent, and effective competency-assessment programs. Healthcare professionals typically are not held accountable for providing evidence-based, best practice care.
- *Promotions and remuneration*: In the face of a tightening market for qualified healthcare professionals, healthcare employers often find themselves in a seller's market wherein they have to compete for employees by offering attractive financial rewards, extensive individual choices about care and fulfilling job opportunities.
- *Human resource development*: Producing better-trained healthcare professionals with relevant qualifications and higher clinical proficiency is best done by applying principles of knowledge management (Chap. 15) and by integrating formal teamwork training interventions (Chap. 16) into quality improvement efforts. So far, few employers in the healthcare sector have implemented a systematic human resource development strategy, and even fewer have stuck with modern strategies once started. An active strategy can help to build the long-term attachment and morale of employees.

Human resource management affects patient safety directly, despite the fact that decision-makers typically have no direct patient contact. This is quite obvious in the case study: The concatenation of unfortunate circumstances might not have occurred if the emergency department had been adequately staffed with physicians and qualified nurses; however, the strategic decision to provide a unit with enough qualified staff will only be made if patient safety is an organization's top priority.

In addition to the human resource issues, this century has seen another vital challenge emerge for the provision of acute medical care: On a national scale, issues such as hospital emergency planning and disaster preparedness have come into focus. The constant threat of mass casualties caused by natural disasters, large technology failures (such as the Fukushima Nuclear Plant), terrorist bombings, and bioterrorism pose a completely new challenge for the provision of emergency medical care.

From what we said about the organizational topics "structures and processes," "medical devices," and "human resource management," it is clear that organizations influence the actions of individuals and teams in many ways. Latent conditions on the organizational level in tightly coupled acute healthcare become evident when local conditions coincide with unsafe acts. This can lead to a failure of the safety barriers and result in a mishap.

14.8 Organization, Errors, and Safety in a Nutshell

- Although healthcare delivery is usually not thought of as a system, its most distinctive characteristic is its uniqueness as a socio-technical system, defined as the way human behavior and an organization's complex infrastructures interact.
- Organizational theory has different perspectives on organizations: the structural perspective, the human resource approach, and the functional perspective.
- Organizations develop as instruments for attaining specific goals: They emerge in situations where people recognize a common or complementary advantage that can best be served through collective action.
- Culture describes how groups think and act. Organizational culture is made of basic assumptions, espoused values, and expectations and is observable in behavior and artifacts.
- Safety culture is a part of organizational culture. A mature safety culture implies that all structures and procedures of an organization, the workplaces and the equipment, qualification and training, and communication and interaction are designed in a way that allows working safely at all times.
- Safety and reliability in an organization need responsible persons (like safety managers), and for all staff members to consider themselves as being responsible.
- Patient safety is based on an "informed culture." Information about errors is reported; there is a clear distinction between errors and violations of rules; errors are used for learning; safe patient care requires that management has knowledge about human factors and safety principles.
- The human factors approach studies human abilities and characteristics as they affect the design and operation of equipment, systems, and jobs. From a human factors perspective, "human error" is not mainly a property of humans – it is a property of systems that includes and interacts with humans.
- The Normal Accident Theory states the idea that when technological systems become highly complex, accidents become inevitable and therefore "normal."
- High-reliability theory emphasizes that organizations can contribute significantly to the prevention of accidents through good organizational design, effective management, and ongoing mindful attention to ongoing operations.
- Ultra-safe organizations accept limits to human and organizational performance and avoid overregulation; the individual feels as part of a team instead of being an independent agent.
- Key system issues for addressing error and safety in acute medical care include structure and processes, equipment-related incidents, HRM, teamwork, leadership, communication, and organizational culture.

References

Amalberti R, Auroy Y, Berwick D, Barach P (2005) Five system barriers to achieving ultrasafe health care. Ann Intern Med 142(9):756–764

Alvesson M (2002) Understanding organizational culture. Sage Publications, London

Argyris C (1957) Personality and organization. Harper & Row, New York

Argyris C, Schön DA (1996) Organizational learning II: theory, method and practice. Addison-Wesley, Reading

Bedeian AG (1984) Organizations. Theories and analysis. Saunders College Publishing, New York

Black RJ (2003) Organisational culture: creating the influence needed for strategic success. Dissertation.com, London

Boeing (2015) Statistical summary of commercial jet airplane accidents. Worldwide Operations, 1959–2014. Online available: www.boeing.com/news/techissues/pdf/statsum.pdf. Accessed 29 Apr 2016

Bolman LG, Deal TE (1984) Modern approaches to understanding and managing organizations. Jossey-Bass, San Francisco. Burke CS, Salas E, Wilson-Donnelly K, Priest H (2004) How to turn a team of experts into an expert medical team: guidance from the aviation and military communities. Qual Saf Health Care 13 (Suppl 1):i96–i194

Carayon P (Hrsg) (2006) Handbook of human factors and ergonomics in health care and patient safety (human factors and ergonomics series). Erlbaum, Mahwah

Chopra V, Bovill JG, Spierdijk J, Koornneef F (1992) Reported significant observations during anaesthesia: a prospective analysis over an 18-month period. Br J Anaesth 68:13–18

Cohen M, Kimmel N, Benage M, Hoang C, Burroughs T, Roth C (2004) Implementing a hospital-wide patient safety program for cultural change. Jt Comm J Qual Saf 30(8):424–431

Cooper JB, Newbower RS, Long CD, McPeek B (1978) Preventable anesthesia mishaps: a study of human factors. Anesthesiology 49:399–406

Cooper JB, Newbower RS, Kitz RJ (1984) An analysis of major errors and equipment failures in anesthesia management: considerations for prevention and detection. Anesthesiology 60:34–42

Currie M (1989) A prospective survey of anaesthetic critical events in a teaching hospital. Anaesth Intensive Care 17:403–411

Denison D (1996) What is the difference between organisational culture and organisational climate? A native's point of view on a decade of paradigm wars. Acad Manage Rev 21(3):619–654

Entin EE, Serfaty D (1999) Adaptive team coordination. Hum Factors 41:312–325

Flin R, Maran N (2004) Identifying and training non-technical skills for teams in acute medicine. Qual Saf Health Care 13(Suppl):i80–i84

Gaba DM (1989) Human error in anesthetic mishaps. Int Anesth Clin 27:137–147

Gaba DM (2011) Have we gone too far in translating ideas from aviation to patient safety? –No-. BMJ 342:198–199

Gandhi TK, Graydon-Baker E, Huber C, Whittemore A, Gustafson M (2005) Closing the loop: follow-up and feedback in a patient safety program. Jt Comm J Qual Patient Saf 31(11):614–621

Gouldner AW (1959) Organizational analysis. In: Merton RK, Broom L, Cottrell LS (eds) Sociology today. Basic Books, New York

Guldenmund FW (2000) The nature of safety culture: a review of theory and research. Safety Science 34:215–257

Helmreich RL (1998) The downside of having a brain: reflections on human error and CRM. University of Texas Aerospace Crew Research Project Technical Report 98–04

Helmreich RL, Merritt AC, Wilhelm JA (1999) The evolution of crew resource management in commercial aviation. Int J Aviat Psychol 9:19–32

Helmreich RL (2000) On error management: lessons from aviation. BMJ 320:781–785

Hoff T, Jameson L, Hannan E, Flink E (2004) A review of the literature examining linkages between organizational factors, medical errors, and patient safety. Med Care Res Rev 6:3–37

Hofmann DA, Mark B (2006) An investigation of the relationship between safety climate and medication errors as well as other nurse and patient outcomes. Personnel Psychology 59(4):847–869

Hollnagel E, Woods DD, Leveson N (eds) (2006) Resilience engineering. Concepts and precepts. Ashgate, Aldershot

HSC (Health and Safety Commission) (1993) Third report: organizing for safety. ACSNI Study Group on Human Factors. HMSO, London

IATA (2016) Safety report 2015. IATA, Montreal

IATA (2015) Safety report 2014. IATA, Montreal

NSAG-1 (International Nuclear Safety Advisory Group) (1986) Summary report on the post-accident review meeting on the chernobyl accident. International Atomic Energy Agency, Vienna

INSAG-4 (International Nuclear Safety Advisory Group) (1991) Safety culture. International Atomic Energy Agency, Vienna

Kao LS, Thomas EJ (2008) Navigating towards improved surgical safety using aviation-based strategies. J Surg Res 145:327–335

Kohn L, Corrigan J, Donaldson M (1999) To err is human: building a safer health system. Committee on Quality of Health Care in America, Institute of Medicine (IOM). National Academy Press, Washington, DC

LaPorte TR (1982) On the design and management of nearly error-free organizational control systems. In: Sills DL, Wolf CP, Shelanski VB (eds) Accident at Three-Mile Island: the human dimensions. Westview, Boulder/Colorado, pp 185–200

LaPorte TR, Consolini PM (1991) Working in practice but not in theory: theoretical challenges of high reliability organizations. J Publ Admin Res Theory 1:19–47

Levy PD, Dancy JN, Stowell SA, Hoekstra JW, Arthur CL, Wilson CH, Bednar JM, Dorman T, Hiestand B (2014) Lessons in flying: crew resource management as a quality improvement method for acute coronary syndromes care. Crit Pathw Cardiol J Evid Based Med 13(1):36–42

Lewis GH, Vaithianathan R, Hockey PM, Hirst G, Bagian JP (2011) Counterheroism, common knowledge, and ergonomics: concepts from aviation that could improve patient safety. Milbank Quart 89(1):4–38

Mearns KJ, Flin R (1999) Assessing the state of organizational safety – culture or climate? Cur Psychol 18(1):5–17

Moray N (1994) Error reduction as a systems problem. In: Bogner MS (ed) Human error in medicine. Erlbaum, Hillsdale, pp 67–91

Morell RC, Eichhorn JH (eds) (1997) Patient safety in anesthetic practice. Churchill Livingstone, New York

Nance JJ (2008) Why hospitals should fly: the ultimate flight plan to patient safety and quality care. Healthcare Press, Bozeman

Naveh ET, Katz-Navon N, Stem Z (2005) Treatment errors in healthcare: a safety climate approach. Manage Sci 51(6):948–960

Neal A, Griffin M (2006) A study of the lagged relationships among safety climate, safety motivation, safety behavior, and accidents at the individual and group levels. J Appl Psychol 91(4):946–953

Norman DA (1988) The psychology of everyday things. Basic Books, New York

O'Connor RE, Slovis CM, Hunt RC, Pirrallo RG, Sayre MR (2002) Eliminating errors in emergency medical services: realities and recommendations. Prehosp Emerg Care 6:107–113

Ornato JP, Peberdy MA (2014) Applying lessons from commercial aviation safety and operations to resuscitation. Resuscitation 85(2):173–176

Parker D, Lawrie M, Hudson P (2006) A framework for understanding the development of organizational safety culture. Saf Sci 44:551–562

Pearse RM, Moreno RP, Bauer P, Pelosi P, Metnitz P, Spies C, Vallet B, Vincent JL, Hoeft A, Rhodes A (2012) Mortality after surgery in Europe: a 7 day cohort study. Lancet 380:1059–1065

Perrow C (1984) Normal accidents: living with high-risk technologies. Basic Books, New York

Perrow C (1994) Accidents in high-risk systems. Technol Stud 1:1–38

Perrow C (1999) Normal accidents. Living with high-risk technologies. Princeton University Press, Princeton

Rampersad C, Rampersad SE (2007) Can medicine really learn anything from aviation? Or are patients and their disease process too complex? Sem Anesth 26:158–166

Rasmussen J (1982) Human errors: a taxonomy for describing human malfunction in industrial installations. J Occup Accid 4:311–335

Reason J (1990a) Human error. Cambridge University Press, Cambridge

Reason J (1990b) The contribution of latent human failures to the breakdown of complex systems. Phil Trans R Soc Lond 327:475–484

Reason J (1997) Managing the risks of organizational accident. Ashgate, Aldershot

Reason J (1998) Achieving a safe culture: theory and practice. Work & Stress 12(3):239–306

Ricci M, Panos AL, Lincoln J, Salerno TA, Warshauer L (2012) Is aviation a good model to study human errors in health care? Am J Surg 203:798–801

Roberts KH (1990) Managing high reliability organizations. Calif Manage Rev 32:101–113

Rochlin GI (1993) Defining "high reliability" organizations in practice: a taxonomic prologue. In: Roberts KH (ed) New challenges to understanding organizations. Macmillan, New York, pp 11–32

Rogers J (2011) Have we gone too far in translating ideas from aviation to patient safety? Yes. BMJ 342:198–199

Shaw J, Calder K (2008) Aviation is not the only industry: healthcare could look wider for lessons on patient safety. Qual Saf Health Care 17:314

Schein E (2004) Organizational culture and leadership, 3rd edn. Jossey-Bass, San Francisco

Schulman PR (1993) The analysis of high reliability organizations: a comparative framework. In: Roberts KH (ed) New challenges to understanding organizations. Macmillan, New York, pp 33–54

Senge P (1990) The fifth discipline: the art and practice of the learning organization. Doubleday, New York

Singer S, Gaba D, Falwell A, Lin S, Hayes J, Baker L (2009) Patient safety climate in 92 US Hospitals: differences by work area and discipline. Med Care 47(1):23–31

Thomas EJ, Helmreich RL (2002) Will airline safety models work in medicine? In: Rosenthal MM, Sutcliffe KM (eds) Medical error: what do we know? What do we do? Jossey-Bass, San Francisco, pp 217–234

Toff NJ (2010) Human factors in anaesthesia: lessons from aviation. BJA 105(1):21–25

Valentin A, Capuzzo M, Guidet B, Moreno RP, Dolanski L, Bauer P, Metnitz PG (2006) Patient safety in intensive care: results from the multinational Sentinel Events Evaluation (SEE) study. Intensive Care Med 32:1591–1598

Vaughan D (1997) The challenger launch decision: risky technology, culture, and deviance at NASA. University of Chicago Press, Chicago

Vicente KJ (2004) The human factor. Revolutionizing the way people live with technology. Routledge, New York

Vogus TJ, Sutcliffe KM (2007) The Safety Organizing Scale: development and validation of a behavioral measure of safety culture in hospital nursing units. Med Care 45(1):46–54

Webb RK, Russell WJ, Klepper I, Runciman WB (1993) The Australian Incident Monitoring Study. Equipment failure: an analysis of 2000 incident reports. Anaesth Intensive Care 21:673–677

Webster CS (2002) Why anaesthetising a patient is more prone to failure than flying a plane. Anaesthesia 57(8):819–820

Weick KE (1991) Organizational culture as a source of high reliability. Calif Manage Rev 29:112–127

Weick K, Sutcliffe R (2015) Managing the unexpected. Sustained performance in a complex world. Wiley, New York

Strategies for Patient Safety

15

Case Study

The labor and delivery unit was unusually busy, and the resident was especially concerned about two of the patients he was watching closely. Patient A with a vertex/vertex twin pregnancy at 37 weeks of gestation had been in labor for 26 h. Patient B was full term with a Category 2 fetal heart tracing and intermittent decelerations. The resident consulted his attending physician about Patient B's fetal heart tracing, and it was decided that Patient B could be allowed to continue to labor with very close surveillance.

It was clear to the resident and attending physician that both of these patients might require a cesarean section (C-section). The decision was made to transfer Patient B to a specific labor room that can be quickly transformed into a second operating room for the unit. This transfer was standard procedure in the unit and in accordance with hospital policies. In addition, it is required that the anesthesia care team be informed that the patient may require an emergency C-section so they can set up their anesthesia equipment in that room in advance. The anesthesia care team would then remain in standby. For unknown reasons, this call was never made.

In the meantime, the resident and attending physician reevaluate Patient A with the twin gestation. Despite regular adequate uterine contractions and the patient's pushing efforts, the presenting twin has not descended further into the birth canal. The patient now has a prolonged second stage of labor. Although the fetal heart tracing remains a reassuring Category 2 with average variability and no decelerations, given the patient's state of exhaustion they agree that she cannot push effectively any longer. The station of the presenting twin is too high for a safe operative vaginal delivery. The patient is relieved and gives her informed consent for the C-section. The resident informs the anesthesia care team and the scrub nurses and asks them to come to the operating room for an "urgent" but not "emergent" C-section on Patient A.

M. St.Pierre et al., *Crisis Management in Acute Care Settings*,
DOI 10.1007/978-3-319-41427-0_15

Preparations for Patient A's twin delivery by C-section are suddenly interrupted by the charge nurse informing the obstetricians that Patient B's fetal heart tracing is showing a severe bradycardia at 80 bpm. The midwives are not able to resolve the fetal bradycardia despite oxygen administered to the patient, fluid bolus, and changes of position. The attending physician calls for an emergency C-section for Patient B in her convertible labor room. Preparations for Patient A's C-section are put on hold and she is informed of this by the resident.

Chaos can be heard in the labor room as the midwives and other staff try to help set up Patient B's labor room for the C-section. Instrument kits are being opened and set up. The fetal heart rate is still in the 80s. In an effort to improve the fetal bradycardia by decreasing the frequent uterine contractions, one of the midwives starts a subcutaneous infusion of a tocolytic β2-agonist. The patient is being positioned in her bed as a midwife preps the abdomen and inserts a Foley catheter. The resident orders the charge nurse to inform the anesthesiologist about the change in plans and that urgency has increased to "emergency C-section" as he begins to scrub. When the anesthesia and surgical team finally do arrive, it becomes obvious that they had not been notified about the change of rooms and instead had been waiting in the regular operating room for the patient to arrive.

The resident feels badly that he was not clear about Patient B possibly needing a C-section to be done in this room in the first place and can't think how that important piece of information was missed. The anesthesia care team had no opportunity to set up their equipment, and they are working at maximum speed to get everything done safely under significant time pressure. The attending obstetrician is very concerned about the fetal bradycardia and is calling loudly for staff from the neonatal intensive care unit to be paged stat. The resident is thinking that he should have suggested bringing Patient B into the operating room once he found out that nothing was set up in this room, but he's afraid to speak up with everyone so upset and now the patient is already prepped and draped.

After completion of all preparations, anesthesia induction and intubation are done without difficulty. A few minutes after incision, a term male infant is delivered and handed over to the neonatology team. Everyone is relieved when after less than a minute of positive pressure ventilation, the infant begins to cry.

During the course of surgery, uterine atony is noted by the obstetrical team and requires significant uterotonics: oxytocin infusion and uterine massage, followed by methergine and then prostaglandin F2α. The patient has more bleeding than usual and the anesthesiologist decides to start a second i.v. line. It is only then that he notices the infusion pump with the tocolytic β2-agonist was never turned off. After disconnecting the tocolytic, uterine tone recovers and bleeding is minimal. The remainder of the surgery is uneventful.

Following the emergency C-section in the labor room, both teams proceed directly to the operating room to perform the C-section on Patient A under spinal anesthesia. Delivery of vigorous twin girls takes place without complications.

In a debriefing conducted shortly after the event, there is emphasis on the positive outcome. It turns out that neither the obstetric physicians nor the midwives had been aware of the existence of an interdisciplinary agreement, which regulates the commissioning of anesthetic equipment in the case of a possible cesarean section. Ignorance of existing standards, inadequate surgical preparation of the patient without the anesthesia team having time to set up their equipment and go through their checklist, and the lack of situational awareness due to the need to focus on tasks, stress, communication, and teamwork errors, including failure to speak up and failure to inform the anesthesia team of all medications administered, were discussed. The good outcome was not confused with good team performance. Transparent discussion of the teamwork and communication failures helps the team realize that it was the clinical experience of all involved in the case and perhaps a bit of luck that may have saved Patient B from a more serious adverse event.

15.1 The Organization's Mission: Patient Safety

For organizations, the temptation may be great to assess the safety of their patient care only by the outcome: As long as patients aren't harmed, there is no cause for concern. It is easily overlooked that in the unfolding of an incident such as the described emergency C-section, individual factors can add up in unpredictable ways (e.g., oblivion, stress, lack of communication), especially at the interfaces of professions and disciplines. Acute care medical organizations cannot rely on circumstances leading to a beneficial patient outcome. For safe patient treatment, hospitals need a functioning safety culture. However, this does not evolve by itself: Safety must be an ongoing and cross-functional management and leadership task for hospitals. Facing this task under the current conditions is a major challenge for hospitals. If a hospital is capable at any time of supporting patient-safe work conditions at any workplace, then we can call the hospital a reliable organization.

15.1.1 Working Safely: Reduce, Cope with, or Manage Complexity?

In order to increase patient safety, healthcare organizations are basically faced with two possibilities: For one, they can try to minimize the variability of processes and thus the complexity of tasks (Fig. 15.1.). That would mean reducing or avoiding uncertainty that leads to errors. Reduction of complexity can be achieved when dealing with routine processes, where activities will take place in a stable environment (Grote 2015). This applies, for example, to many aspects of patient care in

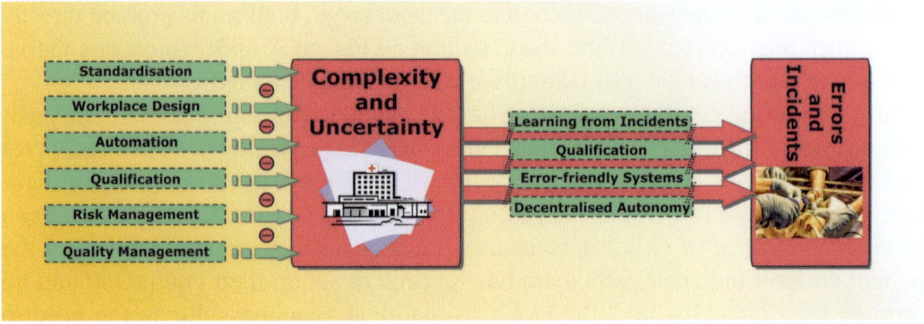

Fig. 15.1 Strategies for safety: reduction of complexity as well as the ability to cope with complexity and uncertainty are part of making an organization resilient and enhancing patient safety

general wards where elements of care, long-term medication, ordering and evaluation of diagnostic tests, and perioperative treatment pathways for elective patients can be designed as routine processes. Ways to achieve this mainly are:

- Standardization
- Workplace design and automation
- Staffing patterns and distribution of expertise
- Qualification of employees
- Quality management and risk management

In many areas of acute care, however, stable and routine conditions are not necessarily present. Lack of transparency, uncertainty, complexity, and dynamic change limit the possibility of planning and standardization. In these areas, an organization can enhance safety only by strengthening the ability to deal with complexity and uncertainty. This is the second path to patient safety: The focus changes from "preventing and managing errors" to "preventing and managing complexity."

In recent years, more and more healthcare organizations have developed into high-reliability organizations (AHRQ 2008; Bagnara et al. 2010; Resar 2006). Reliable organizations of course try to avoid errors as much as possible. Because they are aware of the inevitability of human errors, they do not expect flawlessness. Instead, they try to make the system more robust ("resilient") against the effects of errors: Mistakes shouldn't lead to patient harm.

This is done by:

- Employees' qualification
- Learning from incidents and errors
- Error-resistant system design
- Decentralized autonomy, as in high-reliability organizations (HROs)
- Mindfulness of processes among all workers

In theories of high reliability, accepting the fact that complexity will always be a central characteristic of the work environment is part of the strategy used to reduce complexity (Grote 2015). The idea of a central control of systems is abandoned and replaced by local control at the sharp end. By giving operational control to the employees, the entire system should become safer. Since these ideas are still fairly new to healthcare, it remains to be seen just how well the concept of local control will work in the actual implementation.

This chapter deals first with risk management and quality management. Then we will discuss standardization as a means to reduce complexity and avoid errors. Contrasting this approach, organizational development, knowledge management, and human factors-oriented system designs are discussed as approaches that accept complexity. Learning in organizations is discussed in Chap. 16, with a focus on education and training as well as learning from mistakes, incidents, and accidents.

15.1.2 Clinical Risk Management and Quality Management

In recent decades, efforts to improve processes in healthcare have led to quality management systems. Since the turn of the millennium, clinical risk management increasingly supplements this. It can be debated whether quality or safety is the higher-level concept and to which one "patient safety" belongs. The answer probably depends on one's professional background and current concerns. In the context of patient safety in acute medicine, it is important to know that all these efforts share the common goal of working as safely and effectively as possible. Whether "safe" is a part of "good" or "good" a part of "safe" will therefore not be discussed here.

15.1.2.1 Clinical Risk Management

Until recently, risk management in healthcare was only known as an economic function. Only in recent years has the concept of "clinical risk management" emerged. The economic point of view has the following definition: Clinical risk management is a prevention system that will reduce the risks of patient care and pursues the goal of continuous improvement of the quality of care and patient safety and serves as the defense against unjustified patient claims against the hospital. This practice follows the same cycle as business risk management: identify risks – evaluate risks – control/manage risks – monitor risks (e.g., Vincent 1996; ASHRM and Carroll 2010).

Clinical risk management seeks to identify hazards for patients before they happen. Risks are analyzed and evaluated: Which risks can be avoided? Which risks are unavoidable in medicine? Which risks can be tolerated? Many surgical procedures, drug therapies, and diagnostic procedures carry an inherent risk and thus patients are always at some degree of risk. So, it seems intolerable to increase their risk by unsafe working systems and faulty processes. The reality of healthcare, however, looks at the problem differently: Money and human resources are limited, and the allocation of scarce resources is all about priorities and therefore the distribution of risks. Therefore, clinical risk management techniques accept some risk within its approach.

Risk management asks, "What is the worst-case scenario in our patient care?" A powerful tool to anticipate incidents and avoid errors is readily available: The imaginative creation of "worst-case scenarios" in which healthcare professionals, their team, or the entire organization rehearses their readiness to cope with a situation. This approach, also known as the "scenario-based risk identification" principle from risk management, is especially helpful with unusual problems and events. Similar to planning (Chap. 7), the scenario analysis of a hypothetical situation can help people think through the implications and consequences of their potential actions. Real events often serve as a basis for such scenario planning. For example, the communication failure described in the case study can be analyzed for specific risks that might arise in the context of interdisciplinary emergency care of cesarean section patients. Since the exact same case won't occur in the same constellation again, it is important to apply imagination and ask: How could a similar trajectory of the event (Reason 1990; Chap. 3) pass through all safety barriers? What else could have happened? How can the occurrence of similar constellation and series of events be prevented? These questions can be asked independently of formalized risk management, so every person's imagination is an important safety resource.

It is also part of clinical risk management to implement preventive measures and raise employee awareness for the risks to encourage learning from mistakes (Chap. 16). Risk-minimizing measures may then manifest vis-a-vis the creation of standards, education and training, the design of workplaces and equipment, or personnel management. In this way, risk management seamlessly merges with overall safety management.

15.1.2.2 Quality Management

"Quality management" means to design all processes in an organization in such a way that the results or products are all of good quality. In acute care, quality means first and foremost the quality of the treatment, but also the safety of the treatment. Quality also includes well-being, sustainable use of resources, cost-effectiveness, compliance with laws and standards, etc. To manage quality implies knowing how the processes should be, which in turn means that there are criteria for good quality within the organization.

The term *quality management*, like the term *risk management*, was initially introduced by business and industry. Quality management is defined as concerted activities to direct and control an organization aimed at improving the quality of products produced or services offered. The four main components include quality planning, quality assurance, quality control, and quality improvement. Quality management is focused not only on product and service quality but also on the means to achieve it.

In the medical context, the "product" and "service quality" are the patient's health and the quality of medical care. It should be noted that this is not about the optimum, i.e., best possible quality, but a predefined level of quality. Effort and results have to be balanced, just as in risk management. Therefore, quality in the medical field is also defined as "sufficient and appropriate medical care," which means it meets demands, is oriented to the quality of life, professionally qualified, but also is economic, with the aim to raise the likelihood of desired health outcomes in individuals and in the population.

The focus of quality assurance is on the structure (e.g., resources, personnel, facilities, equipment) and the processes involved (e.g., the actual activities of patient care, information management, teamwork, and leadership) as well as on the resulting outcome (e.g., wellness, length of stay, morbidity, mortality; see Eichhorn 1995).

Continuous quality improvement (CQI), a related but somewhat different term, activities aim at delivery of the highest-quality care. By focusing on latent errors and poor system design, CQI tries to eliminate preventable morbidity and mortality as far as possible. The main instruments for CQI are regular clinical audits and the establishment of quality circles.

15.1.2.3 Methods for Risk and Quality Management

Clinical quality management (QM) and risk management (RM) make use of many different methods. We introduce two methods that can be implemented in everyday care in hospitals beyond the formal QM and RM audits and quality circles.

A clinical audit is a systematic and objective evaluation of an organization (e.g., department, hospital, relief organization) that aims to improve patient care. Aspects of patient care – including structure, processes, and outcomes – are selected and evaluated against explicit criteria and, where necessary, changes are implemented at an individual, team, or service level. Audit procedures include collecting, analyzing, interpreting, and documenting information. Auditors are either external auditors (independent staff assigned by an auditing firm) or internal auditors (healthcare providers from within the organization hired to assess and evaluate its system). Clinical audits are initiated and supported by the Board of Directors or top management.

Clinical audits in a medical high-stakes environment should focus on the structures and processes that are most likely influenced by latent errors: medical equipment (including maintenance), the preparation of planned procedures, patient positioning, drug administration, and the application of protocols and standard operating procedures (SOPs; Eichhorn 1995; O'Connor et al. 2002).

A *quality circle* (QC) is a small volunteer group of healthcare professionals who meet at regular intervals to identify, analyze, and resolve workplace and patient care-related issues (e.g., Robson 1989). QCs are usually led by a supervisor or a senior healthcare professional who acts as a moderator. The QCs neither decide on changes nor put improvements into practice, but they present ideas and suggestions to the management on how to improve the quality of healthcare processes and patient safety. QCs are driven by two principles: that employees can often make better suggestions for improving work processes than management and that employees are motivated by their participation to make improvements. Employee acceptance of the QC process is highly dependent on the extent to which management acts favorably on suggestions from the QC.

15.2 Complexity Reduction, Error Avoidance: Standardization

A view still widespread in the healthcare system is that safe patient care is the responsibility of the individual. However, this view ignores the fact that healthcare takes place in a particular organizational context with specific processes that need to be taken into account. An important approach to reduce the variety of possible system configurations and treatment alternatives is standardization. Standardization in medicine encompasses medical devices and IT systems as well as diagnostic and therapeutic processes and communication. On the other hand, outcome standardization – a common thing in industry – is not always possible when dealing with the anatomy and physiology of humans.

Medical devices and *IT systems* are standardized by legal and professional frameworks and manufacturer initiatives. The aims are:

- To increase user and patient safety
- To increase the simplicity and compatibility of system components
- To achieve technical and organizational interoperability of medical devices and IT systems through data and transmission standards

The standardization of *processes* can take place within an organization (e.g., nursing and therapy standards in intensive care units, clinical treatment paths within a hospital) or outside the organization by national societies (e.g., in the form of guidelines) or by international initiatives (e.g., WHO "High 5 s Project"; Leotsakos et al. 2014). Standardization of processes aims at:

- The reduction of process variability, so that the quality of care, safety, and resource consumption are independent of healthcare personnel, time, and place
- Ensuring that treatment follows the best method known at the time and minimizes care that is idiosyncratic to the practitioner (*equivalent actor* vs. *craftsman attitude*; Amalberti et al. 2005; Chap. 14)
- Supporting the training of new employees, who all get acquainted with the same procedures from the beginning
- Strengthening teamwork through shared mental models for processes

15.2.1 Standard Operating Procedures

A standard operating procedure, commonly abbreviated as SOP, is a detailed, written instruction aimed at achieving uniformity of the performance of a specific function. Standard operating procedures exist for routine operations as well as for emergency situations. The SOPs for emergency situations should enable a structured approach to a critical situation and be flexible enough to meet situational demands. They emphasize the medical and technical steps and are complemented by general steps of organized action (Cooper et al. 1993). The advantage is that SOPs describe successful guidelines for coping with an emergency situation. As a result, the individual has less to figure out, which puts less stress on memory and, when designed well, provides especially welcome guidance in time-critical situations. Standardization is not only for specific medical management of certain diagnoses but should also be for daily procedures and information transmission (e.g., patient hand-off between the OR and recovery area, shift change in the ICU) and at the interface of interdisciplinary work. In the domain of intensive care medicine, evidence is mounting that standardization has an enormous potential to improve patient care and outcome and to reduce ICU and hospital length of stay as well as healthcare expenditures (Hasibeder 2010).

A lasting effect may be more likely if standardization is part of a larger scheme of efforts aimed at improving the safety culture of an organization (see below).

15.2.2 Standardization of Communication

Experience from other high-stakes environments (foremost civil and military aviation) has provided ample evidence that a standardization of communication techniques can help to reduce misunderstandings in noisy and stressful situations (Conell 1996). Standard terminology (comparable to that of civil aviation) and the resulting avoidance of misunderstanding can help to reduce errors. Standards for communication processes ensure that messages are clearly "received" and understood. These standards are termed *callouts*, *readbacks*, and *hearbacks*. A callout is a concise statement in a defined terminology. Readback and hearback are a redundant procedure aimed at verifying that both sender and receiver understand what the communication partner has said (Chap. 12).

Standard phraseology is not yet widespread in medicine. Announcements such as "Please step back, I will defibrillate!" most closely match a callout, but the phraseology doesn't have any cross-organizational reliability. The wording used in the case study, *urgent cesarean section*, is another example: Everyone in the participating teams may know that a cesarean section must be performed within 30 min. Communication conventions have emerged organically and locally in medical organizations but not necessarily consistent. Moreover, there is no industry-wide "seal of approval" as in aviation. Healthcare professionals, generally unfamiliar with the technique used in civil aviation, tend to dismiss communication standards as unnecessary. Nevertheless, if healthcare professionals in a high-stakes medical environment want to reduce misunderstanding, the establishment of communication standards would be a promising way to go. These standards would have to become a habit in daily practice; only then would healthcare professionals be able to use them effectively in critical situations.

15.2.3 Standardization of Patient Handover

The handover that includes relevant information and transfer of responsibility of a patient from one unit to another or from one caregiver to another in the same unit is a significant and error-prone process. Patient handovers take place between emergency services and emergency department, between emergency room and normal wards, between ICU and operating room, but also at every change of shift of nursing staff and physicians. Despite the importance of this process, there are few studies that examined inhibiting and promoting factors for the process of patient handover. Recent studies suggest that a structured handover (e.g., checklists, iSBAR) can help to reduce information loss (Dawson et al. 2013; Segall et al. 2012; Riesenberg et al. 2009). Checklists give handover of patients a structure, but they typically do not convey all important aspects of patient care. Therefore, they shouldn't be the sole basis for the communication of information. Limitations of checklists will be discussed below.

15.3 Tool with Untapped Potential: Checklists

Until recently, healthcare has relied heavily on clinicians' ability to recall critical information during a medical emergency. During stressful situations, however, levels of cognitive function are compromised, resulting in a variety of planning and execution failures (Sect. 3.2), decreased compliance with standard operating procedures, and decreased proficiency.

Many inherently risky industries, such as aviation, aeronautics, and nuclear power have tried to overcome this limitation by mandating the use of and adherence to cognitive aids such as checklists and protocols. Typically, a checklist is a list of action items or criteria arranged in a systematic manner, allowing the user to record the presence/absence of the individual items listed to ensure that all are considered or completed (Hales and Pronovost 2006). Main objectives of a checklist are memory recall, standardization and regulation of processes, and its use as a diagnostic tool. Well-designed checklists standardize what, how, and by whom interventions are done. Under circumstances where the use of checklists is highly regulated and considered mandatory for practice, a checklist becomes a protocol and its completion from memory considered a violation (e.g., in civil aviation; Helmreich 2000).

15.3.1 Functions and Forms of Checklists

Checklists can support individuals and teams during:

- Preparation and execution of routine tasks
- Structuring of teamwork
- Problem solving

Working with checklists requires at least a partial standardization of processes. The great advantages of appropriately used checklists are that they give certainty of action, direct the attention to the task at hand, and help the team to build shared mental models and support each other (Fig. 15.2).

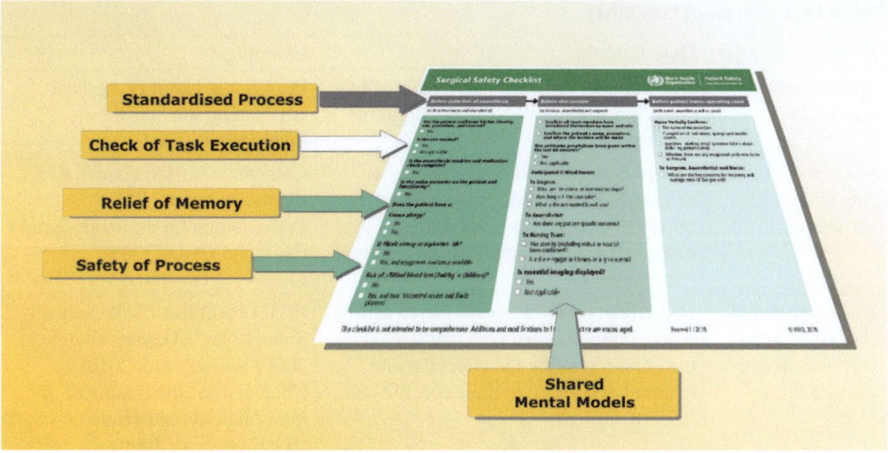

Fig. 15.2 Functions of a checklist that support the individual and the team

Checklists for *routine tasks* in complex systems contribute to a correct and complete execution of safety-relevant tasks. All steps involved are explicitly listed and have to be checked off in given order. Typical routine tasks that can be supported by checklists are machine checks and job preparation tasks. The obstetric department of the case study has a checklist for changing a labor room into an operating room. Also the WHO "Surgical Safety Checklist" (Haynes et al. 2009) is a routine tool. Evidence from many studies suggests that the implementation of that checklist in a locally adapted form improves the perceived quality of teamwork and helps reduce errors in teams (Lyons and Popejov 2014). But there have been other studies that do not find a reduction in morbidity or mortality after introducing the checklist (Urbach et al. 2014). It is likely that using the checklist establishes an opportunity for communication within the team where relevant information is transferred. In addition, safety awareness and safety culture can be improved. But when checklists are used incorrectly or when the team rejects them, the positive impact is lost and there can even be negative effects on teamwork (Russ et al. 2013).

Checklists for unexpected problems can support a structured approach to diagnose a problem or find the cause of an event.

Different from routine tasks or simple problems, in emergencies, a checklist cannot guide every step of action. For that reason, the term cognitive aid may be preferred. One aim of an emergency cognitive aid is to make sure that relevant information is available independently from memory (e.g., dosage, rarely used drugs, telephone numbers) and that critical steps in treatment are guided by best practices (Goldhaber-Fiebert and Howard 2013). Another function is to direct the problem solver's attention to those phases of problem solving that could get lost in action (e.g., setting priorities, risk identification, or control of action). And finally, cognitive aids help formation and functioning of teams in medical emergencies (Marshall 2015).

Table 15.1 Forms of checklists

Form of checklist	How it works	Example
Static parallel checklists	One person completes the checklist by checking a series of read and do items	Pre-use checkout of medical equipment, the anesthesia machine checklist
Static sequential checklists with verification	One person (or a computer) reads a series of items ("challenge"), and the other person verifies completion of the task or that items are within parameters ("response")	Catheter insertion checklist (Pronovost et al. 2006) Preparations for cesarean section (Hart and Owen 2005)
Static sequential checklists with verification and confirmation	Used most often in a team-based setting where team members are challenged by the person reading the checklist and respond according to their specific task	WHO checklist "Safer Surgery Safes Lives" (Haynes et al. 2009; Weiser et al. 2010) Checklist for the treatment of malignant hyperthermia (Harrison et al. 2006)
Dynamic checklists	Guide complex decision-making in emergencies using the format of a flowchart, and act as verification after execution of a task without necessarily leading users to a specific conclusion	Algorithms for BLS and ACLS Algorithms for the management of crisis under anesthesia (Runciman and Merry 2005) Algorithms for the management of the difficult airway

There are several forms of checklists. Some forms require a strict sequence of action; others just remind the user of relevant items. Some are made for individual physicians or nurses; others require teamwork. In some checklists, the control of every step is required. Table 15.1 shows the most common forms of checklists (Table 15.1, following Winters et al. 2009).

15.3.2 Barriers Against Checklists or Cognitive Aids

Whereas healthcare organizations have begun to follow aviation by promoting teamwork and implementing theories of crew resource management into the fabric of healthcare, they have been slow in adopting the policies of employing cognitive aids and checklists in both routine and emergency circumstances (Hayashi et al. 2007; Klopfenstein et al. 1998; Laboutique and Benhamou 1997; Langford et al. 2007; March and Crowley 1991). Thus, the reinforced standardization of processes by introducing mandatory checklist completion seems to be a more difficult task in medicine than in aviation. This is despite growing evidence from medicine that using checklists appropriately improves patient safety. Operational difficulties as well as cultural barriers may contribute to this difficulty. Below are some examples of thinking that are barriers to the use of checklists:

- *Humans can't be standardized by checklists*: Human physiology is far more varied and underspecified than structures and processes in the industrial setting. The resulting variations in the patient population make standardization of processes, which constitutes the basis in designing and implementing a standardized checklist, difficult.

- *Emergencies can't be standardized by checklists*: Medical emergencies often follow an unpredictable and disorganized pattern, which makes it difficult for a checklist to cover all directions/ramifications in which a critical situation may evolve. For this reason, it is more appropriate to speak of cognitive aids.
- *Only what you know by heart is yours*: For many healthcare professionals, reliance on cognitive aids is considered second best choice as compared to reliance on one's own memory. Worse, some physicians feel that checklists insult their intelligence and consider the use of checklists an admission of weakness and convey a lack of skill and knowledge.
- *Checklists limit decision-making*: Healthcare professionals place high value on their professional autonomy. Attempts to standardize routine and emergency tasks are often viewed as limiting professional judgment and as threat to autonomous decision-making.
- *Once I realize I need a checklist, it's too late*: Sometimes it is difficult to know when to start using a checklist in the course of action. Also, in a team, the responsibility for starting or reading the checklist may not be clear.
- *Checklists are unwieldy*: Often, hospitals or departments lack effective technical strategies to make checklists readily available to everyone. Alternatives to unhandy paper-based checklists or handbooks could be software-based tools for cell phones and devices as well as electronic checklist systems implemented into the electronic monitoring or documentation system (Sawa and Ohno–Machado 2001).

15.3.3 Limitations of Checklists

15.3.3.1 Example: Patient Handover

Checklists can give structure to patient handover; however, as the sole basis for the communication of information, they entail the risk that important aspects of the complexity and mystery of patient care may not be communicated (Cohen et al. 2012). This is because people describe the situation depending on the circumstances, either on the basis of universal, context-independent principles ("paradigmatic") or through a story in which something special is expressed ("narrative"). Checklists as a paradigmatic representation are therefore suitable for simple or very complicated processes, but not for the description of complex facts that need to be told as a story (Hilligoss and Moffatt-Bruce 2014): *Simple* procedures (such as cooking a meal or starting a patient monitor) require little expertise and can be standardized and formulaic. *Complicated* processes (such as the preparation and implementation of an organ transplant or the entire treatment path of a patient from his hospital admission to discharge (DeVries et al. 2010)) consist of many individual sequences, but all can be structured by using checklists. *Complex* processes (such as the treatment of a hemodynamically unstable child with a congenital heart defect) are characterized by the interaction of many system components. Only a holistic perception, as given in a narrative account, enables an adequate description of the situation.

15.3.3.2 Example: Safety Initiatives and Culture

Based on the stunning decline of catheter-related infections after the introduction of a checklist in 103 intensive care units (Michigan Keystone ICU Project, Pronovost et al. 2006) and the dramatic reduction of perioperative morbidity and mortality that could be observed after the introduction of the "Surgical Safety Checklist" in participating hospitals (Haynes et al. 2009), the press and parts of the healthcare sector were excited about the "small and simple checklists" that appeared to be the long-sought solution for the problem of patient safety risk. However, those who were responsible for this achievement contradicted this point of view (e.g.Bosk et al. 2009). Checklists were only one component of a broader program with the goal to change the culture of an intensive care unit, emergency room, or operating room. A much greater challenge than the definition of the necessary content of the checklist was to understand the social, political, organizational, psychological, and emotional barriers that needed to be overcome before scientific evidence could be applied in the form of a checklist. The real challenge for the introduction of a checklist is not simply in its creation but to overcome all the barriers to employing the checklist. The fallacy behind the concept of a "simple, small checklist" thus lies in the assumption that a *technical tool* (checklist) can solve a *sociocultural problem*.

15.3.4 Developing and Implementing Checklists

One of the great dangers of checklists is that they can easily be compiled and readily be applied to virtually every aspect of patient care. Under the well-intentioned assumption that checklists can prevent errors, mitigate harm, and reduce the costs associated with errors, an excessive mandated use might make the system overly complex and burdensome and impede the quality and speed of care delivery. In addition, it may generate an insidious clinical condition in the user: "checklist-fatigue syndrome."

Other risks seem to be associated with the introduction of checklists as well: Every time a system is changed to improve safety, we may defend against some known risks but unwittingly introduce new ones. An additional problem with checklists is that it may not be evident which checklist is the appropriate one to use. For instance, when an airplane's landing gear won't deploy, pilots know to go to that checklist in the manual. In clinical care, when a patient's blood pressure drops and the heart rate increases, it is not entirely clear which checklist should be employed. If checklists are not revised and updated on a regular basis, new scientific evidence will not be incorporated, hindering patients from getting state-of-the-art care. If clinicians adhere too strictly to checklists and become dependent upon these tools for their judgment, they may apply them even to clinical situations with incomplete evidence where the exercise of critical thinking would be more appropriate.

Because little is known about which specific checklists are truly linked to safety levels, how many checklists are too many, and when we have overburdened the checklist users, a systematic approach seems warranted before introducing a new checklist. The recommended steps to develop checklists include the following (Winters et al. 2009; Marshall 2013):

- Review existing literature.
- Understand the needs and workplace of the user.
- Include a multidisciplinary group in the design.
- Perform pilot testing in a simulated environment before full-scale implementation.
- Use an iterative approach for rigorous validation of the impact on service delivery: Benefits should be demonstrated rather than assumed.
- Reevaluate and update checklists periodically based on new scientific data and on feedback from caregivers.

In addition to following the recommended steps, it is sensible to apply principles from human factors engineering (Degani and Wiener 1993).

- List the most critical items at the beginning of the checklist whenever possible.
- Avoid long checklists when possible. Subdivide long checklists into small meaningful sections.
- Pay close attention to usability, including the time it takes to complete the checklist, and potentially negative effects of changes in practice.

15.4 Management of Complexity: Acute Medical Care of the Future

15.4.1 Promote Change

If acute medical organizations want to make patient safety an integral part of their corporate culture, they need to promote change in their processes, their self-concept, and the interactions of their members. Change always happens, and organizations continuously adapt to new circumstances. But if change is to be deliberate and systematic, it needs a framework and a roadmap. Such a framework is offered by concepts of *organizational development* that have been tried and tested in other industries (Senge 1990; Argyris and Schön 1995; Nonaka and Takeuchi 1995). Organizational development means to strategically plan and systematically change an organization with the goal of increasing effectiveness in problem solving. Organizational development must be planned long term and involve the employees. Starting points for programs of organizational development are new demands of the organization. Since organizations are not developed from the outside, but move toward their own targets, change can only come from inside. Core issues of the development of organizations are knowledge, learning, quality, leadership, and flexibility. For acute medical care, important goals are patient safety and patient satisfaction, a transparent treatment chain, employee participation, and dedication to quality. Organizational change aims at those processes by which the "core service," patient care, is provided. The most important resources in successful development processes are always the employees, specifically their knowledge, skill, and motivation (see Chap. 16).

15.4.2 Knowledge Management

In the process of changing into a "learning organization," healthcare organizations will have to face the challenge of facilitating knowledge sharing and learning among the organization's members. Industry has addressed these issues by drawing heavily on theories of process and knowledge management. There is no generally agreed-upon definition of *knowledge management* (KM). Most often, the term refers to a range of systematic practices that support and achieve "the creation, sharing, retention, refinement, and use of knowledge; generally in an organizational context" (Edwards et al. 2005). One of the unifying elements across most KM theories is a shared understanding of knowledge as *the* intellectual capital and as a central factor in achieving improved performance and competitive advantage (Bali and Dwivedi 2006). Knowledge in this context includes both the experience and understanding of the people within the organization and its information artifacts, such as documents, guidelines, protocols, and reports, available within the organization (Stefanelli 2004).

Modern information technologies (IT) have provided organizations with the necessary tools to create and distribute knowledge within their sphere of influence, thus promoting the learning process of their members. These IT solutions include expert systems, e-learning, knowledge bases, corporate intranets and extranets, and other health IT infrastructures (e.g., computerized physician order entry, decision support systems; Handler et al. 2004); however, it is not enough to simply collect data. Only after information has been selected and processed to meet defined criteria is it usable knowledge in terms of KM. From this perspective, KM can be regarded as the art and science of transforming data into useful knowledge.

In view of this, which knowledge exactly is of interest for KM systems? Despite the diversity of their theoretical frameworks, most KM practitioners share the distinction between tacit and explicit knowledge (Nonaka and Takeuchi 1995):

- *Tacit knowledge* is subconscious and internalized knowledge and involves physical as well as perceptual skills (e.g., complex surgical interventions, situation assessment, diagnosing an X-ray). It is "know-how" knowledge held only in minds of organizational members. When tacit knowledge is employed, individuals are unaware of what they know and how they obtain particular results.
- *Explicit knowledge*, in contrast, is conscious and can be codified: A person is fully aware of what he or she knows and is able to communicate this information to others (e.g., calculating the IV dose of a drug, generating differential diagnoses). An example of external explicit knowledge is best practice recommendations.

The task of KM is, on the one hand, to convert internalized tacit knowledge into explicit codified knowledge in order to share it with other members of an organization. In a second step, the knowledge offered by a KM system has to be retrieved, understood, and internalized by individuals. This way, explicit knowledge is absorbed and results in new personal tacit knowledge. On the other hand, KM theories try to solve the problem of how an organization needs to be designed to facilitate knowledge processes. In other words, how the "right" information can be brought to the "right" people at the "right" time to enable the "right" actions.

In this context, acute medical organizations have to ask themselves:

- What cultural and structural barriers stand in the way of systematic knowledge management?
- How can knowledge be generated from the vast amount of medical information (e.g., publications)?
- How can knowledge be distributed and shared? Which method is best suited for which kind of knowledge?
- How can information technology be profitably and effectively used in this process?

An essential feature of acute medicine is that people from different departments or specialty units within the larger organization interact (e.g., emergency services and emergency room up to the intensive care unit) and continuously generate new information. As important pieces of information may be lost at the various interfaces, structured knowledge management can help to improve the interaction and cooperation. A systemic approach in which acute care medicine is thought of as a process with many participating organizations will help clinicians to incorporate the knowledge and to correctly channel the information required by the treatment chain (Edwards et al. 2005).

Safety-oriented knowledge management thus contributes to an informed and reliable corporate and healthcare culture. This brings us full circle to the topics discussed in Chap. 14.

15.4.3 System Design: Human Factors and Patient Safety

If future organizations of acute medicine want to treat patients safely, they have to keep in mind the principles of human factors in the design of processes and technological systems. This abstract-sounding statement means that the work system and all its components must be designed in a way to make safe work possible at *any workplace* at *any time*. In addition to safety, it is necessary for the health and well-being of employees to be taken into account.

Human factors-oriented system design includes considering human qualities and abilities as it organizes their interactions with technology, materials, jobs, and facilities. The following propositions are intended to illustrate what it would mean to translate these guiding principles for hospitals and healthcare facilities.

15.4.3.1 Management for Safety: Human Factors Knowledge and the Integration of Expertise

Decisions regarding the working conditions under which patients are treated are taken at the management level. Thus, patient safety is also a key responsibility of leaders. To set a framework that is safe for both patients and staff, management needs medical-technical knowledge and an understanding of human factors. Currently, it is rare to see new hospital or healthcare equipment or technologies being systematically chosen with human factors as an essential consideration. To do so will require an integration of management, employee participation, learning, and training (Carayon et al. 2012).

Knowledge of human factors is now mainly used to explain accidents and incidents (Chap. 16). For improving patient safety, it should come into play much earlier: Significant and expensive decisions can hardly be reversed if one learns *after* an accident that they weren't adapted to human characteristics and abilities. Structural parameters (e.g., location and arrangement of the trauma room) or large equipment purchases are examples for this. If human factors knowledge in hospitals is to be truly useful, human factors expertise must be involved from an early stage in the acquisition process as well as continuously in the processes of planning, design, training, and clinical use.

15.4.3.2 Human Factors for Patient Safety in Purchasing

The relevance of the design of medical devices for patient safety has been shown in many studies, especially concerning infusion pumps (reviewed in Vincent et al. 2014). For user-centered design of equipment, there is ample knowledge from decades of ergonomic research. The design of devices and operating concepts is, of course, beyond the direct reach of hospitals. But through purchasing policy and by contact with equipment manufacturers, some influence can be exercised. The uniformity of operating concepts in a hospital can be controlled within the organization (probably with short-term financial disadvantages) so that confusion by the variability of devices can be eliminated. But for that, buyers need to know about the potential sources of error and the role of system design for patient safety.

15.4.3.3 Human Factors Aspects of Workplace Design

It's not only about medical devices! The whole working environment should be designed in a way that is useful for workflows that allow for safe working conditions. A relevant example for workplace design in hospitals from a human factors point of view is the placement of hand sanitizer dispensers. Birnbach et al. (2010) pointed out that the compliance of physicians significantly increased when the dispensers were placed in their sight field. Such human factors interventions are powerful because they are effective, independent of individuals, their motivation, or their knowledge (of course, factors such leaders as role models continue to be important). Workplace design is also often less expensive than training to change behaviors. It needs to be implemented once, while behavioral changes must be practiced again and again due to staff turnover and to reinforce best practice.

15.4.3.4 Human Factors Aspects of Hospital Work Processes

Equipment and workplaces are the "hardware" of work. In the case study, the syringe pump is mounted below eye level – an arrangement that invites it to be overlooked under stress. However, on the "software" side, human factors interventions are also necessary and useful for patients and staff. This means designing work processes so that they correspond to human capabilities. An example of this is the avoidance of interruptions. To be interrupted while working on a task by another task can cause a person to forget operations or objectives of the first (interrupted) task (prospective memory failure Sect. 4.5). Human factors considerations can form work processes in a way to make interruptions rare. The reorganization of such processes requires knowledge of attention and memory processes. Even if interruptions are not completely preventable, it is still possible to lessen their effects. One method is to pause a few seconds before continuing the interrupted task because it helps to fully refocus on it (Brumby et al. 2013).

Obviously not all processes can be optimized in a human factors way in a hospital, especially in acute medicine. In the case study, a cesarean section had to be performed in a labor room without the resources of a real OR. Even in optimally designed hospitals, surgeries will have to be performed at night, although the error rate is known to increase significantly at night, especially from 2 to 5 o'clock. Such situations should be limited to emergencies. The current tendency to shift elective surgery to the late night hours may be economically feasible, but for patient safety and the health of employees, it is not. Whenever work must take place under unfavorable conditions, special attention should be paid to strengthen as many barrier layers as possible (Chap. 3). For example, good teamwork and good workplace design can help so that the increased probability of error does not lead to accidents.

15.4.3.5 Whole System Standards

Designing processes implies standardization. As shown in the example of introducing checklists, new processes cannot simply be thrown into a system. To make them work, the entire system must be considered. In the case of the checklist, that concerns issues such as communication, handovers, the effects of status and hierarchy, workload and disruptions, costs, problems in media changes from paper to computer, and others. To think through all of these aspects takes time and resources – but without that, standards will not be effectively and usefully implemented.

Standard processes need to be practiced which means that training is a critical component of systems change and improvement (Russ et al. 2013). Of special importance are processes that were altered or that must be mentally available in case of an emergency (handovers, resuscitation). These processes have to be learned, simulated, and practiced in everyday life. And yet, training and human factors aspects are a rather weak intervention (see Chap. 16 for more details) compared to truly ergonomic work conditions and processes.

15.4.4 Resilience in Acute Medicine

Since the beginning of the millennium, the concept of *resilience*, often in connection with the ideal of a high-reliability organization, has been much discussed in safety research (e.g., Hollnagel et al. 2006). The term, which means elasticity, adaptability, or flexibility, has its roots both in materials science and in engineering as well as in psychology. Originally, it described the ability of a material to be deformed and afterward to bend back to the original shape. In psychology, resilience is understood as the qualities or skills that enable a person to adapt to adverse conditions and to recover from trauma or bad events (e.g., Werner 1989). People who are resilient are not immune to bad events, but they are not broken by them. The study of resilient people shows that in addition to external support and emotional ties, some characteristics of the individuals themselves are crucial. These characteristics can also be useful for dealing with accidents and incidents. Resilient people accept the crisis or trauma. They do not assume the role of a victim, but take responsibility for themselves. They think in a solution-oriented and more optimistic way and are oriented to the future. They have networks on which they can rely and from which they get help. In medicine, resilience is mainly understood in that sense – as an attribute of an individual. Research about "resilience in the hospital" or "resilience in medicine" has focused primarily on mental health of employees, stress management, and courses for serenity.

The idea that organizations can be resilient is a very young one within safety research (e.g. Sutcliffe and Vogus 2003). That organizations deal with bad events and might even be strengthened by those is a fascinating concept, but hardly implemented in practice. Resilience in organizations could be understood as a further development of existing safety management systems and cultures. Resilience would then encompass the acceptance that accidents or crises occur but that it is possible to overcome the effects of them. This includes quickly returning to normal. We prefer the image of a tree that is buffeted and bent by a gust of wind, but straightens again. In order to do so, it must be flexible; at the same time, it needs strong roots, so that the wind does not knock it down. Roots of organizational resilience are, for example, risk management and error prevention in everyday work, a willingness to learn that is deeply rooted in the organizational culture (Chap. 16), and the willingness to make prompt decisions in a critical situation and to relinquish control to the local actors (Fig. 15.3).

To be able to return to normal after accidents or crises, organizations need characteristics (Sutcliffe and Vogus 2003) that would also be important for hospitals and other acute care facilities:

- Flexibility and the ability to improvise
- Ability to rapidly respond to an event and decide quickly
- Ability to mobilize reserves and to activate resources within the network

To respond to events or crises in such a way, organizations must be willing to adapt to change and to learn (Chap. 16), and they must know their weaknesses and

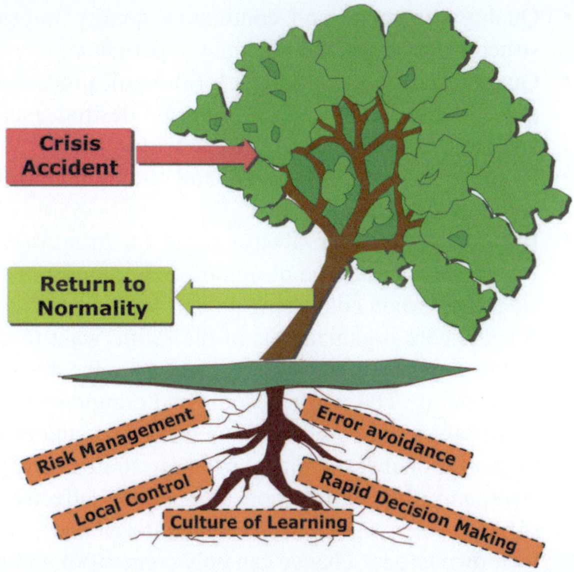

Fig. 15.3 Organizational resilience can be described with the metaphor of a tree buffeted and bent by the wind yet rising again – if it is flexible enough and the roots are strong enough to keep it from breaking

deal with them. That is where the concept of resilience meets with the notion of a high-reliability organization. Teams in an organization have a special role because they are the ones who, because of their adaptability, serve as the most likely entity to interrupt a chain of events from causing an error. This makes good team training all the more important (Chaps. 11 and 16).

In the context of patient safety, the adaptation of the concept of *resilience* is still nascent. What does it mean to be a resilient organization when a complication occurs? What does it mean when a patient has already been harmed? Currently "organizational resilience" does not seem ready for direct, operational implementation. However, the concept offers ideas and suggestions about how to effectively manage incidents and accidents – especially with flexibility, decision-making abilities, and resources based on a profound knowledge of the organization's weaknesses and strengths.

15.5 Reliable Acute Care Medicine in a Nutshell

- To increase patient safety, healthcare organizations are basically faced with two possibilities. They can try to reduce the variability of processes and the resulting complexity of the work environment, or they can strengthen their ability to cope with complexity and uncertainty. Of course it is possible to combine the two approaches.
- Clinical risk management is a prevention system intended to reduce risks in patient care and pursue the goal of continuous improvement of the quality of care and patient safety. The term is also used in a different sense, i.e., to describe a defense to counter unjust patient claims against the hospital institution.

- Quality assurance and continuous quality improvement efforts focus on the structure, process, and outcome of patient care.
- Quality management entails forming all processes in an organization in a way that the results or products have the desired quality. By quality we mean how good and also how safe the treatment is.
- Examples of methods for risk and quality management are clinical safety audits and quality circles.
- Because patients are always cared for in an organization-specific context, the system design and the design of treatment processes have to be taken into consideration when addressing patient safety.
- If acute care organizations of the future want to treat patients safely, they must follow the principles of human factors in the design of processes and technological systems. The work systems and components must be designed in a way to make safe work possible at any workplace and at any time.
- Organizational development means to strategically plan and systematically change an organization with the goal of increasing effectiveness in organizational problem solving. Since organizations are not developed from the outside, but move toward their own targets, change can only come from within hospitals themselves.
- Standardization, the deliberate strategy to maintain a high similarity in task performance, is aimed at guaranteeing the highest possible quality patient care in routine tasks.
- Standards support work and ensure quality, but they can also be seen as restricting the freedom and professionalism of caring and well-trained providers and the over-formalization of work.
- A checklist is a list of action items or criteria arranged in a systematic manner, allowing the user to record the presence or absence of the individual items listed, thereby ensuring that all have been considered or completed.
- The real challenge in introducing a checklist lies not in its creation, but in overcoming a number of sociobehavioral and technical barriers to the procedure described in the checklist.
- Patient handover at the different units is a significant and error-prone process in the context of patient care because both relevant information and responsibilities are transferred.
- Information does not equal knowledge. Only if information related to some goal is selected, sorted, processed, and finally used is it knowledge in the sense of knowledge management.
- Knowledge management refers to a range of systematic practices that capture and disseminate organizational knowledge to enhance organizational performance.
- Knowledge management faces two major challenges: First, implicit knowledge must be converted into explicit knowledge, since only explicit knowledge will be available for organizations. At the same time, processes must be designed in a way that makes explicit knowledge available when and where it is needed.
- Resilience means to accept that accidents or crises occur and to cope with them. For that, organizations need flexibility, decision-making skills, resources, and a willingness to learn.

References

AHRQ (2008) Becoming a high reliability organization: operational advice for hospital leaders. AHRQ publication no. 08-0022. Agency for Healthcare Research and Quality, Rockville

Amalberti R, Auroy Y, Berwick D, Barach P (2005) Five system barriers to achieving ultrasafe health care. Ann Intern Med 142(9):756–764

Argyris C, Schön DA (1995) Organizational learning II: theory, method, and practice. Addison-Wesley, Reading

ASHRM (American Society for Healthcare Risk Management) and Carroll R (eds) (2010) Risk management handbook, 6th edn. Jossey Bass, San Francisco

Bagnara S, Parlangeli O, Tartaglia R (2010) Are hospitals becoming high reliability organizations? Appl Ergon 41(5):713–718

Bali R, Dwivedi A (2006) Healthcare knowledge management. Issues, advances and successes. Springer, Berlin/Heidelberg/New York

Birnbach D, Nevo I, Scheinman S, Fitzpatrick M, Shekhter I, Lombard J (2010) Patient safety begins with proper planning: a quantitative method to improve hospital design. Qual Saf Health Care 19(5):462–465

Bosk CL, Dixon-Woods M, Coeschel CA, Pronovost PJ (2009) Reality check for checklists. Lancet 374:444–445

Brumby DP, Cox AL, Back J, Gould SJJ (2013) Recovering from an interruption: Investigating speed-accuracy trade-offs in task resumption behavior. J Exp Psychol Appl 19:95–107

Carayon P, Alyousef B, Xie A (2012) Human factors and ergonomics in health care. In: Salvendy G (Hrsg) Handbook of human factors and ergonomics, 4th edn. Wiley, Hoboken. pp 1574–1595

Cohen MD, Hilligoss B, Amaral ACK (2012) A handoff is not a telegram: an understanding of the patient is co-constructed. Crit Care 16:303–308

Conell L (1996) Pilot and controller issues. In: Kanki B, Prinzo VO (eds) Methods and metrics of voice communication. DOT/FAA/AM-96/10. FAA Civil Aeromedical Institute, Oklahoma City

Cooper JB, Cullen DJ, Eichhorn JH, Philip JH, Holzman RS (1993) Administrative guidelines for response to an adverse anesthesia event. J Clin Anesth 5:79–84

Dawson S, King L, Grantham H (2013) Review article: improving the hospital clinical handover between paramedics and emergency department staff in the deteriorating patient. Emerg Med Australas 25(5):393–405

Degani A, Wiener EL (1993) Cockpit checklists: concepts, design, and use. Hum Factors 35:345–359

DeVries EN, Prins HA, Crolla RM, den Outer A, van Andel G, van Helden SH, Schlack WS, van Putten MA, Gouma DJ, Dijkgraaf MG, Smorenburg SM, Boermeester MA, Surpass Collaborative Group (2010) Effect of a comprehensive surgical safety system on patient outcomes. N Engl J Med 363:1928–1937

Edwards JS, Hall MJ, Shaw D (2005) Proposing a systems vision of knowledge management in emergency care. J Oper Res Soc 56:180–192

Eichhorn S (1995) Risk management, quality assurance, and patient safety. In: Gravenstein N, Kirbi RR (eds) Complications in anesthesiology. Lippincott-Raven, Philadelphia, pp 1–15

Goldhaber-Fiebert SN, Howard SK (2013) Implementing emergency manuals: can cognitive aids help translate best practices for patient care during acute events? Anesth Analg 117(5):1149–1161

Grote G (2015) Promoting safety by increasing uncertainty – Implications for risk management. Safety Sci 71:71–79

Hales BM, Pronovost PJ (2006) The checklist – A tool for error management and performance improvement. J Crit Care 21:231–235

Handler JA, Feied CF, Coonan K, Vozenilek J, Gillam M, Peacock PR Jr, Sinert R, Smith MS (2004) Computerized physician order entry and online decision support. Acad Emerg Med 11:1135–1141

Harrison TK, Manser T, Howard SK, Gaba DM (2006) Use of cognitive aids in a simulated crisis. Anesth Analg 103(3):551–556
Hart EM, Owen H (2005) Errors and omissions in anesthesia: a pilot study using a pilot's checklist. Anesth Analg 101:246–250
Hasibeder WR (2010) Does standardization of critical care work? Curr Opin Crit Care 16:493–498
Hayashi I, Wakisaka M, Ookata N, Fujiwara M, Odashiro M (2007) Actual conditions of the check system for the anesthesia machine before anesthesia. Do you really check? Masui 56:1182–1185
Haynes AB, Weiser TG, Berry WR, Lipsitz SR, Breizat AH, Dellinger EP, Herbosa T, Joseph S, Kibatala PL, Lapitan MC, Merry AF, Moorthy K, Reznick RK, Taylor B, Gawande AA, Safe Surgery Saves Lives Study, Group (2009) A surgical safety checklist to reduce morbidity and mortality in a global population. N Engl J Med 360(5):491–499
Helmreich RL (2000) On error management. Lessons learned from aviation. BMJ 320:781–785
Hilligoss B, Moffatt-Bruce SD (2014) The limits of checklists: handoff and narrative thinking. BMJ Qual Saf 23(7):527–533. doi:10.1136/bmjqs-2013-002705
Hollnagel E, Woods DD, Leveson N (eds) (2006) Resilience engineering. Concepts and precepts. Ashgate, Aldershot
Klopfenstein CE, Van Gessel E, Forster A (1998) Checking the anaesthetic machine: self-reported assessment in a university hospital. Eur J Anaesthesiol 15:314–319
Laboutique X, Benhamou D (1997) Evaluation of a checklist for anesthetic equipment before use. Ann Fr Anesth Reanim 16:19–24
Langford R, Gale TC, Mayor AH (2007) Anesthesia machine checking guidelines: have we improved our practice? Eur J Anaesthesiol 30:1–5
Leotsakos A, Zheng H, Croteau R, Loeb JM, Sherman H, Hoffman C, Morganstein L, O'Leary D, Bruneau C, Lee P, Duguid M, Thomeczek C, van der Schrieck-De Loos E, Munier B (2014) Standardization in patient safety: the WHO High 5s project. Int J Qual Health Care 26(2):109–116
Lyons VE, Popejov LL (2014) Meta-analysis of surgical safety checklist effect on teamwork, communication, morbidity, mortality, and safety. West J Nurs Res 36(2):245–261
March MG, Crowley JJ (1991) An evaluation of anesthesiologists' present checkout methods and the validity of the FDA checklist. Anesthesiology 75:724–729
Marshall S (2013) The use of cognitive aids during emergencies in anesthesia: review of the literature. Anesth Analg 117:1162–1171
Marshall S (2015) The effect of cognitive aids on formation and functioning of teams in medical emergencies. PhD-Thesis; Dpt. of Psychology, University of Queensland, Queensland
Nonaka I, Takeuchi H (1995) The knowledge-creating company: how Japanese companies create the dynamics of innovation. Oxford University Press, Oxford
O'Connor RE, Slovis CM, Hunt RC, Pirrallo RG, Sayre MR (2002) Eliminating errors in emergency medical services: realities and recommendations. Prehosp Emerg Care 6:107–113
Pronovost P, Needham D, Berenholtz S, Sinopoli D, Chu H, Cosgrove S, Sexton B, Hyzy R, Welsh R, Roth G, Bander J, Kepros J, Goeschel C (2006) An intervention to decrease catheter-related bloodstream infections in the ICU. N Engl J Med 2006(355):2725–2732
Reason J (1990) Human error. Cambridge University Press, Cambridge
Resar RK (2006) Making noncatastrophic health care processes reliable: learning to walk before running in creating high-reliability organizations. Health Serv Res 41(4):1677–1689
Riesenberg LA, Leitzsch J, Little BW (2009) Systematic review of handoff mnemonics literature. Am J Med Qual 24:196–204
Robson M (1989) Quality circles: a practical guide. Gower, Aldershot
Runciman WB, Merry AF (2005) Crises in clinical care: an approach to management. Qual Saf Health Care 14:156–163
Russ S, Rout S, Sevdalis N, Moorthy K, Darzi A, Vincent C (2013) Do safety checklists improve teamwork and communication in the operating room? A systematic review. Ann Surg 258:856–871

Sawa T, Ohno–Machado L (2001) Generation of dynamically configured check lists for intra-operative problems using a set of covering algorithms. Proc AMIA Symp 2001:593–597

Segall N, Bonifacio A, Schroeder R, Barbeito A, Rogers D, Thornlow D, Emery J, Kellum S, Wright MC, Mark JB (2012) Can we make postoperative patient handovers safer? A systematic review of the literature. Anesth Analg 115(1):102–115

Senge PM (1990) The fifth discipline. Doubleday Business, New York

Sutcliffe KM, Vogus TJ (2003) Organizing for resilience. In: Cameron KS, Dutton JE, Quinn RE (eds) Positive organizational scholarship: foundations of a new discipline. Berett-Koehler Publishers, San Francisco, pp 94–110

Stefanelli M (2004) Knowledge and process management in health care organizations. Methods Inf Med 43:525–535

Urbach DR, Govindarajan A, Saskin R, Wilton AS, Baxter NN (2014) Introduction of surgical safety checklists in Ontario. Canada. N Engl J Med 370(11):1029–1038

Vincent C (1996) Clinical risk management. BMJ Books, London

Vincent C, Blandford A, Li Y (2014) Integration of human factors and ergonomics during medical device design and development: It's all about communication. Appl Ergon 45(3):413–419. doi:10.1016/j.apergo.2013.05.009

Weiser TG, Haynes AB, Dziekan G, Berry WR, Lipsitz SR, Gawande AA, Safe Surgery Safes Lives Investigator Study Group (2010) Effect of a 19-item surgical safety checklist during urgent operations in a global patient population. Ann Surg 251(5):976–980

Werner E (1989) Vulnerable, but Invincible. Adams, Bannister and Cox, New York

Winters BD, Gurses AP, Lehmann H, Sexton JB, Rampersad CJ, Pronovost PJ (2009) Clinical review: checklists – translating evidence into practice. Crit Care 13:210. doi:10.1186/cc7792

16 Learning for Safety

Case Study

A patient is prepared to undergo major abdominal surgery and receives a thoracic epidural catheter prior to the induction of anesthesia. Immediately after the operation, a local anesthetic is given and a patient-controlled epidural anesthesia (PCEA) pump connected in the recovery room. Following an uneventful postoperative course in the post anesthesia care unit (PACU), the patient is transferred to a general ward. He is awake and shows stable vital signs.

At 2:00 a.m., the anesthesia resident is paged by the night nurse and told that "either the catheter has become displaced or something's wrong with the pump." Further inquiry reveals the patient's complaint of increasing pain. Boluses of local anesthetic brought no relief. Upon arrival, the resident observes a fully oriented patient, with noninvasive blood pressure values of 100/50 mmHg, a heart rate of 45 bpm, and a saturation of 94 %. The anesthesiologist inspects both the insertion site and catheter and realizes that the PCEA line is connected to the central intravenous line instead of the filter. Due to the difficulty of determining when the improper connection occurred, the exact amount of local anesthetic injected intravenously is impossible to calculate. The patient is transferred to the intensive care unit. Without any additional therapeutic measures, the blood pressure and heart rate return to normal, and the patient is transferred back to the general ward during the afternoon of the same day.

The resident physician decides to enter the case into the hospital electronic critical incident reporting system. While doing so, she recognizes that this is the third case in the course of 1 year in which a PCEA pump has been inadvertently connected to a central IV line. These incidents are presented at the anesthesia department's next quality control conference. A root cause analysis prior to the presentation indicates that the contributing factors are high

M. St.Pierre et al., *Crisis Management in Acute Care Settings*,
DOI 10.1007/978-3-319-41427-0_16

staff turnover on the wards resulting in a lack of familiarity with the technique and equipment. Furthermore, many of the new nurses are unaware of the difference between patient-controlled intravenous (PCIA) and epidural (PCEA) analgesia. Also, brought to light is that the intravenous and epidural lines are similar in appearance and easy to confuse.

The members of the quality control conference suggest several solutions to the problem. First, standard operating procedures are to be developed allowing only nurses certified with appropriate training in the particular technique to operate the pump. Second, the staff of the pain clinic is to devise a plan enabling all the ward nurses to be trained on the use of the pump within the next few months. Third, a label stating "for epidural use only" is to be attached to the epidural line as a reminder to the operator. The incident is presented at the next morbidity and mortality conference and welcomed by the hospital simulation center as a new teaching case for resident physicians.

A patient receives a thoracic epidural catheter for postoperative pain relief via PCEA pump. In the course of the next hours, the line from the PCEA pump is disconnected from the epidural catheter for reasons unknown and improperly connected to the central IV line. As a result of the misconnection, the pump infuses the local anesthetic and the opioid intravenously. The incident is detected before toxic plasma levels of the local anesthetic are reached and thus has no long-term consequences for the patient. Because the hospital has established an incident reporting system (IRS), the reporting physician is able to notice that two similar incidents had occurred within the past months. Because all three incidents reveal a similar pattern, a systemic problem seems much more likely than an isolated personal failure. The physician directs the attention of the hospital's risk management to these incidents. The root cause analysis results in several practical steps to solve the problem. The knowledge gained from these incidents is fed back into the system by creating guidelines and additional teaching opportunities (e.g., morbidity and mortality conference, simulation-based training).

16.1 Learning (in the) Organization

16.1.1 What Is a Learning Organization?

The two fundamental components of risk control are changing individual and team behavior toward safer care and changing organizations toward higher reliability. These changes do not occur spontaneously. They have to be intentional, and they have to be triggered by learning, which takes place at the level of the individual health professional, at the organizational system's level.

Organizations in acute medical healthcare influence the performance of their members, the incidence of errors, and the management of errors. To move patient safety to an integrated and valued part of the organizational culture, processes and structures need to be handled thoughtfully with some degree of flexibility. And effective organizations put a premium on preserving respect for all workers and value the interaction and communication.

Organizations continuously change as they adapt to the changing environment in which healthcare is provided. If these are to occur effectively, they need a conceptual framework. Concepts of organizational development offer frameworks that have been validated in other organizations (e.g., Argyris and Schön 1996; Senge 1990).

Organizational development implies that organizations are strategically planned and systematically changed with the aim of increasing their effectiveness to solve problems. Organizational development is a long-term undertaking and requires the participation of all members and an ongoing commitment throughout the organization.

The direction of change and the determination to reach goals can only be developed and nurtured *within* a healthcare organization. Organizations are not developed from the outside. Major issues in organizational development are "knowledge," "learning," "quality," "leadership," and "flexibility." In the context of a high-stakes medical environment, patient safety, patient well-being, a transparent treatment chain, participation of members, and competition among healthcare institutions are superordinate goals. Organizations try to improve structures and processes to execute the core process, patient treatment. The most important resources for an organization wanting to achieve change are the people who work in the organization: the collective knowledge, experience, motivation, and cooperation of all staff members.

Changes to the organization include not only relevant structures and procedures but also behavioral skills and attitudes. The organization has to emphasize and value learning. This statement may sound strange at first because learning (Chap. 4) is a process generally attributed to living beings and not to an abstract entity such as an organization; however, it is the interaction between individuals and organizations that is the basis for *organizational learning* (Argyris and Schön 1996). Organizational learning is the process of transforming external information into practical, contextual knowledge that informs practices across the organization. The resulting organizational knowledge is the product of the learning process and includes internal (tacit) and external (explicit) knowledge forms. Although organizational learning begins with individual learning, it is more than the sum of its individual participants' learning. Members come and go, and leadership changes, but certain behaviors, mental models, norms, and values are preserved in an organization over time. They define a stock of acceptable behaviors that apply throughout an organization (i.e., "the way we do it") and which are frequently inherited by new generations of employees. In this respect, organizational knowledge remains long after original learners have departed because they have contributed to the organization's collective memory. In similar ways, perhaps slowly but certainly with sufficient determination and thoughtfulness, change will spread throughout an organization. Every time a problem arises (e.g., because a new regional pain therapy introduces a more complex administration process thus increasing threats to patient safety yet does not improve pain relief as hoped), several people within the organization will reflect upon the new therapy and its processes and decide how it can be improved or perhaps decide that the older, simpler therapy should be reinstated. In this way, changes in procedures, flow of information, rules, and resources will result. Because many members of the organization will experience change, it is appropriate to say that "the organization" has learned a lesson from an unsuccessful attempt.

The concept of the learning organization (Senge 1990) is that a successful organization intentionally applies learning strategies to adapt and respond to changes in the environment. A learning organization challenges its processes, instructions, assumptions, and even its basic structure, thereby redesigning itself constantly. In its totality, organizational learning is based on experiential learning: Organizations adjust their activities and mental frameworks based on experiencing successes and failures. The structure of experiential learning is simple: Actions are taken, the environment responds, and implications for future actions are formulated on the basis of feedback and the organization's ability to learn and adjust.

Organizational learning will meet resistance because humans are naturally resistant to change. Change introduces uncertainty about values and behavior. People naturally tend to avoid uncertainty (Chap. 4), so they are inclined to oppose new ideas simply because they are new.

Changes in the environment also include innovations that are put into practice based on evidence. However, despite considerable resources devoted to research, a consistent finding is that the transfer of research findings into practice is unpredictable and can be a slow and haphazard process. Research on the quality of healthcare in the United States revealed a decade ago that 30–40 % of patients do not receive care according to current scientific evidence (Schuster et al. 1998; Eccles et al. 2005). Whereas policy makers expect organizations to adapt research-based innovations in a timely manner, organizational leaders in medicine have to find ways of bridging the gap between knowing something and being inclined and able to do that something. Attempts to resolve this dilemma include the introduction of evidence-based medicine (EBM) and research on effective implementation strategies. Reviews of implementation research have consistently shown that the majority of interventions can achieve moderate improvements in care with considerable variation in the observed effects within and across interventions (Grimshaw et al. 2001).

16.1.2 Key Characteristics of a Learning Organization

Rather than responding to change and uncertainty with strict rules, learning organizations try to establish structures and processes that allow flexibility in learning and proactive behavior. These, in particular strategic learning orientations (Senge 1990; Davies and Nutley 2000), include:

16.1.2.1 Thinking in Open Systems (Systems Thinking)

Systems thinking is the cornerstone of a learning organization (Peter Senge called it the "fifth discipline"; Senge 1990). While in many organizations individual departments are considered as isolated and detached from the whole, learning organizations try to teach their members how their own activities and the activities of others are interrelated. Instead of a reductionist view (characterized by simple cause-and-effect relationships), learning organizations consider dependencies, time delays, and interactions within a system.

16.1.2.2 Personal Mastery

Organizations that strive for excellence see each individual employee as an important part of the organization's capital, and they acknowledge the need to constantly improve knowledge and skills. Since people spend a lot of their life at work and need to make sense of what they are doing, they experience the development of their own professional and interpersonal potential as meaningful. As a result, employees are personally satisfied; they commit themselves to their organization and provide professionally competent contributions. A central leadership task is to identify the strengths and talents of employees and to provide opportunities for development.

16.1.2.3 Team Learning

The exclusive focus on individual skills is insufficient and sometimes leads to wrong results. Patient care takes place in teams. Teamwork is the key factor in the development of reliable medical organizations. Learning organizations are aware of the strength of teamwork (Chap. 11). Knowledge is exchanged across department boundaries to become an efficient organization capable of joint action.

16.1.2.4 Reflections of Mental Models

This joint action is complicated by the fact that the mental models underlying the action differ from person to person and always comprise only a part of reality. In addition, the "psycho-logic" of human behavior causes people to hold on to existing perspectives and thereby makes them blind to a changed reality. To minimize this risk, learning organizations have formulated rules that help teams explore, question, and evaluate the mental models of team members (Sect. 11.3). As a result, different perceptions are not experienced as a threat, but as a learning opportunity. People do not primarily defend their points of view, but share the underlying assumptions and data. Instead of fighting about the right point of view, conceptual models are openly discussed in order to obtain a comprehensive picture of reality.

16.1.2.5 Shared Vision

In addition to encouraging personal development and open discussion of opinions, learning organizations give their members a common vision that allows the individual to understand his or her own contribution in the overall context and well-being of the organization. Ideally, visions have an appealing and strong emotional component that makes it easy for employees to identify with them.

From what has been said, it is evident that the characteristics of learning organizations – with their focus on empowered individuals, teamwork, clear communication structures, and ongoing skepticism about underlying assumptions – overlap with the characteristics of other organizational models such as high-reliability organizations (Chap. 14).

Critics point out that the concept of a learning organization is too idealistic because the real challenge lies in its implementation. A learning organization has both very high and arguably unrealistic expectations of the learning motivation and learning ability of employees and also needs charismatic leaders who can motivate employees (Chap. 13) in order to convincingly introduce and implement such a concept. To find both is probably more an exception than the norm. Despite these legitimate objections, the ideal learning organization displays features that can serve as a suitable model for healthcare (e. g., B. Davies and Nutley 2000; Garvin et al. 2008; Schüpfer et al. 2007; Stinson et al. 2006).

16.1.3 How Can an Organization Learn?

In the case study, the work-up of the incident was not limited to changing the labels of the epidural line but led to questioning previous assumptions about the appropriate timing of employee training. Learning from the event thus took various forms.

16.1.3.1 Adapting Behavior: Single-Loop Learning

Whenever something goes wrong, most people naturally respond by looking for a different strategy to address the task. In an iterative process or with the aid of external information (e.g., guidelines), procedures are changed until a new strategy leads to the desired result: "Doing things right." Like the failed strategy preceding it, the new strategy is based on established knowledge and familiar behavioral patterns. Processes and actions directed at the problem are optimized with regard to existing goals, values, plans, and rules, which all remain unchallenged. Because the characteristic feature of this kind of learning is the single loop, which exists between problem recognition and action, this learning cycle has been called *single-loop learning* by organizational theorists (Fig. 16.1; Argyris and Schön 1996). Single-loop learning can be compared to a thermostat that learns to regulate its heat according to the surrounding temperature. The thermostat can perform this task because it can receive information (the temperature of the room) and take corrective action. Single-loop learning is present each time goals, values, frameworks, and – to a significant extent – strategies are taken for granted. As a result, thinking is directed toward making a familiar strategy more effective. Single-loop learning in response to the misconnection of the PCEA line is primarily directed at the technique and making it more efficient: New labels are attached to the lines, and staff members are retrained in patient-controlled pain therapy.

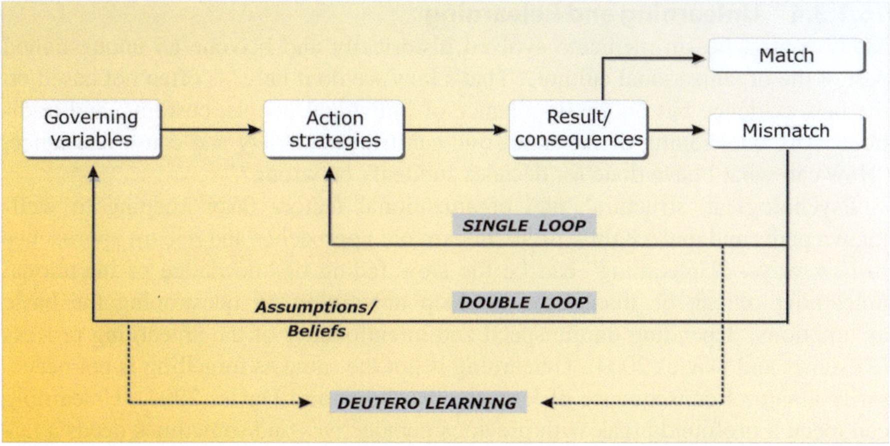

Fig. 16.1 Forms of organizational learning (Following Argyris and Schön 1999)

16.1.3.2 Changing Basic Assumptions and Norms: Double-Loop Learning

An alternative response to an error would be to question the mental models that underlie the action. In contrast to single-loop learning, *double-loop learning* corrects errors *and* changes underlying assumptions within the minds of people and the organization. Such learning may lead to a shift in the way in which strategies and consequences are framed and can lead to new goals or priorities: "Doing the right things." If an organization is able to view and modify those basic frameworks, it will be able to think previously unthought-of thoughts and develop new directions. This is necessary because often adaptive learning offers a weak or no solution at all (Fig. 16.1). Because double-loop learning implies a process of relearning basic assumptions, members of an organization often find it difficult to embrace. In view of the PCEA misconnection, double-loop learning could imply that basic assumptions about continuous education and retraining staff members have to be questioned and possibly reformulated. The consequence could be proactive training that addresses potential gaps in knowledge before insufficient experience threatens patient safety.

16.1.3.3 Change the Process of Learning: Deutero-learning

Last but not least, deutero-learning or meta learning (Bateson 1972; Schön 1975) describes how organizations make the learning process itself the focus of learning by analyzing how employees learn, under which conditions they do not learn and what strategies make positive behavioral change possible. Organizations learn how to learn. By recognizing patterns that enabled or hindered learning in similar situations, norms of behavior can be restructured. This ability is essential for a learning organization.

16.1.3.4 Unlearning and Relearning

Many approaches in medicine evolved historically and become an unquestioned part of the organizational culture. “That’s how we do it here” is often not based on the best evidence but on the dominance of individual people, customs, and traditions. Any questioning of the status quo can trigger anxiety and cause resistance, “How can what I have done for decades suddenly be wrong?.”

Psychological, structural, and organizational factors favor keeping to well-known paths and make it difficult to unlearn old approaches and relearn approaches in new ways. “Unlearning” can be the slow fading of knowledge or intentional unlearning or can be manifested as deep unlearning by questioning the basic assumptions, depending on the speed and intentionality of the unlearning process (Rushmer and Davies 2004). Unlearning is not the same as forgetting is not necessarily a natural consequence of learning (Rushmer and Davies 2004). Unlearning can mean a profound break with previous perspectives and sometimes needs a targeted approach within the organization (Sherwood 2000). Relevant examples of deep unlearning in the past were oxygen avoidance with preterm infants in neonatal intensive care units (the new approach led to great anxiety for the caregivers; Rushmer and Davies 2004), the abandonment of the Sellick maneuver to prevent aspiration as part of a “rapid-sequence” intubation, more recently the central venous insertion using ultrasound guidance, and the almost complete abandonment of hydroxyethyl starch for volume resuscitation.

Often organizations have to overcome considerable fear and resistance and need to be patient until the employees accept a new approach. These barriers to relearning can also be seen in the many years that it takes to implement amended guidelines in clinical practice. This gap between the availability of proven enhancements and the adoption into clinical practice (“translational gap”) is multifactorial and has implications for patient safety (Cosby 2013). To change successfully, organizations need the ability to identify routines, habits, and traditions that are embedded in the organizational culture, to evaluate them and unlearn them intentionally for the benefit of new approaches.

16.1.4 The Importance of Teamwork in Organizational Learning

Learning can take place at the level of the individual health professional, at the organizational systems level, and at points in between. An important in-between point that’s needed to manage risk and enhance quality is the level of teamwork (Chap. 11). Organizations have been shifting their focus from the individual to teams as a prerequisite means to improve outcomes. The emphasis is most evident in teams operating in high-reliability organizations (HROs). HROs focus on teams to learn how to balance effectiveness and safety within the complexities of the environment (Chap. 14). Encouraged by the results of other high-stakes industries, the healthcare community has begun to examine high-reliability teams (HRTs) as a model for the complex domain of acute medical care (Wilson et al. 2005; Manser 2009). Results of this research are showing that teamwork appears to *the* essential component in the pursuit of achieving high reliability in healthcare organizations.

Because improvements in patient safety and better quality of medical care are inseparably related to the process of organizational and individual learning, recent interest has emerged in teams as the primary vehicle for organizational learning and where cultural changes can most effectively be addressed. Learning occurs as an interaction within the team and extends to the team's interaction with its environment. Learning can be triggered by:

- *Problems*: Organizational learning is often rooted in problems and experience. Problems generate doubts about current strategies and lead to a search for new solutions. The case study from the beginning of the chapter illustrates this problem-based learning.
- *Opportunities*: Unforeseen events can be opportunities for learning and innovation. If team members take the time for debriefing after a critical event or an incident to collectively explore triggering conditions and to consider the role of their own expectations, perceptions, and reactions, then a variety of learning opportunities arise.
- *People*: The interaction with other members serves as a strong stimulus for learning. Reviewing the actions of team members and exploring individual mental models can challenge participants to reconsider and potentially reformulate their understanding of the issue and therefore recast their actions.

16.2 Qualification and Training

16.2.1 Training and Education: Prerequisites and Limits

The skills and knowledge of healthcare professionals are the decisive human resource for an efficient and safe delivery of patient care and the avoidance of errors. The systematic enhancement of staff qualification by providing knowledge and training opportunities is a major investment in patient safety.

Since teamwork plays a key role in ensuring highly reliable patient care, the focus of training programs should not only be medical and technical knowledge and skills but also the behavioral and teamwork skills, sometimes called "nontechnical skills" (e. g., Fletcher et al. 2002; Flin and Maran 2004; Reader et al. 2006; Yule et al. 2006). Communication, teamwork, and decision-making should be interwoven with medical-technical contents as an integral part of the professional competence of physicians, nurses, and emergency services. To meet these requirements, innovative learning approaches such as simulation training, problem-based learning, and case-based learning are suitable. Ideally, leaders are a living model of this blend of medical knowledge and behavioral skills. Nevertheless, a staff development plan for a safe hospital should include teamwork training. One of the keys to the remarkable safety record in civil aviation is that the companies have been working for over 40 years to bring about this convergence of technical and nontechnical skills.

16.2.1.1 Training as a Weak Human Factors Intervention

The discipline of human factors is wide ranging. It includes all aspects of the environment in which people work including human-computer interaction, the form and fit of devices, flow of people and equipment, comfort such as temperature, work cycles including rest, etc. A common misunderstanding in healthcare is that behavioral and teamwork training interventions, such as simulation-based training, are advertised as human factors training. This naming implies that healthcare organizations have taken human factors into account. This linguistic shorthand illustrates a narrow understanding of human factors as being comprised of only behavioral considerations.

Healthcare tends to overlook that the training of nontechnical skills in other high-risk domains (e.g., civil aviation) covers only one aspect of human factors (Russ et al. 2013).

In the true sense of the discipline, far too few human factors specialists work with hospitals. Human factors experts point out that medical organizations do not adequately consider the principle of organizational psychology, ergonomics, system design, human-machine interface, etc., when designing healthcare work environments. A saying in human factors is that "Design trumps training." That is a way of saying that when designing work environments, there are a number of highly effective considerations and solutions that potentially provide an environment that is safe and effective; i.e., design considerations should be brought to the forefront of healthcare system design, *before* training is considered. At present, the understanding of the discipline of human factors within the healthcare community is primarily shaped by misunderstanding or abbreviated understanding rather than facts (Table 16.1).

While training programs are increasingly established, overall system-related interventions such as changes in architecture, redesign of work equipment, arrangement of devices, and other measures get less attention. One reason for the preference for training intervention over changes in system design could be that the connection of developers, industry, and users in the healthcare system is not as tight as, for example, in aerospace and nuclear technology. In those high-risk areas, industry or government specifies the system that's needed and the required operational capability. They expect to purchase a fully integrated system. In healthcare, various equipments are bought from various manufacturers with a rare eye to systems integration and the humans who must use it. In addition, the intervention of training is much easier to establish, is much cheaper for the organization in the short run, and shows effects faster than the (re)design of work systems (Fig. 16.2). This does not mean that training is unnecessary! But training is a relatively weak intervention as compared to well-designed systems since its effectiveness depends on participants' memory, motivation, opportunities for using what they learned, and supportive organizational structures (Fig. 16.3).

When implementing human factors training programs, it is important to have clear expectations about the possibility or impossibility to change aspects of human memory limits and processing ability, motivation, emotion, knowledge, skills (Chap. 4), and group behavior. Some of these aspects can be changed by learning processes; other human characteristics (e.g., basic perceptual processes,

Table 16.1 Fact and fiction in the understanding of the discipline of human factors in healthcare. The comparison highlights the potential benefit for applying human factors expertise in healthcare system design

Facts about the discipline of human factors	Misunderstanding or abbreviated understanding about human factors in healthcare
Fact 1: human factors is about designing systems that are resilient to unanticipated events	Fiction 1: human factors is about eliminating human error
Fact 2: human factors addresses problems by modifying the design of the system to better aid people	Fiction 2: human factors addresses problems by teaching people to modify their behavior
Fact 3: human factors focuses on ranges from the individual to the organizational level and the interaction of humans with technology	Fiction 3: human factors work focuses on individuals
Fact 4: human factors is a scientific discipline that requires years of training; most human factors professionals hold relevant graduate degrees at the masters or doctoral level	Fiction 4: human factors consists of a limited set of principles (e.g., "15 CRM behaviors") that can be learned during simulator training. Clinicians can acquire this expertise in simulation courses and by reading journal articles
Fact 5: human factors professionals are bound together by the common goal of improving all aspects of design for human use and represent different specialty areas and methodological skills sets	Fiction 5: human factors scientists, psychologists, and engineers all have the same expertise

Modified following Russ et al. (2013)

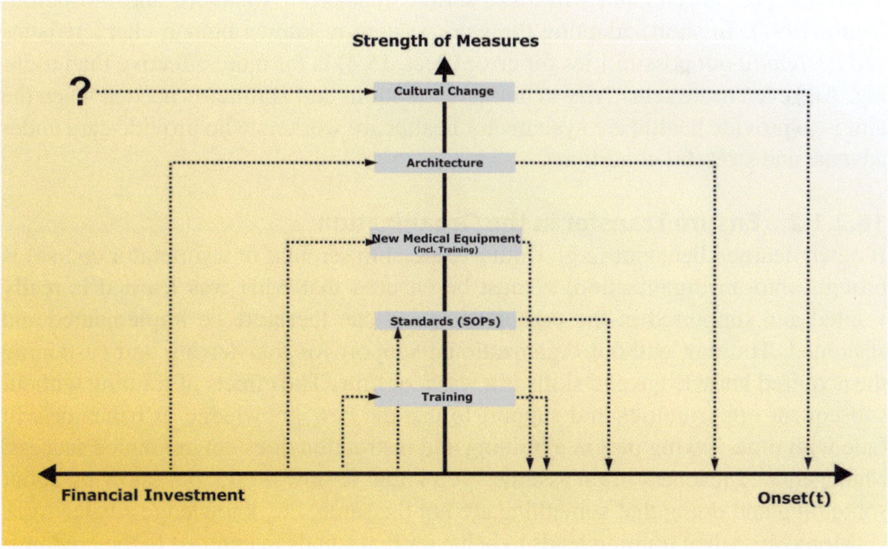

Fig. 16.2 Measures to strengthen patient safety differ in effectiveness with respect to the necessary financial resources and latency until they are effective (based on Schüpfer et al. 2007). How much investment is needed to bring about a cultural change within a medical organization is still unclear

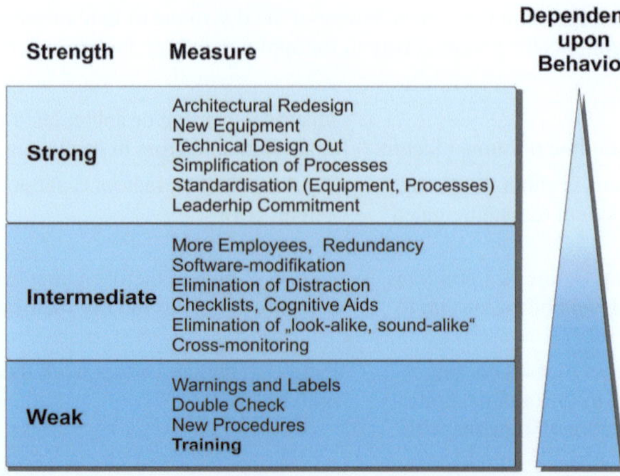

Fig. 16.3 Measures to strengthen patient safety and corresponding strength of the intervention. The more dependent a measure is on human behavior, the weaker its influence. The success of training initiatives depends on participants' memory, motivation, and opportunity to apply the learned behavior

mechanisms of visual attention, etc.) cannot be affected by training interventions. Effective attention, for example, can be maintained only for a certain time span and cannot be altered fundamentally through training and urging personnel to "pay better attention." Admonitions such as "Please try to be more careful next time!" in the aftermath of an incident are never a solution when the problem was caused by distraction, interruptions, fatigue, etc. Even well-trained, very experienced, and highly motivated persons can and will make serious mistakes (Amalberti and Mosneron-Dupin 1997). In short, adapting the work system to known human characteristics and *designing out* possibilities for error (Sect. 15.4) is far more effective than training. And even more sensitivity to human limitations and abilities is needed when the aim is to provide healthcare systems for healthcare workers who provide care under adverse and stressful conditions.

16.2.1.2 Ensure Transfer in the Organization

If newly learned behavior (e.g., from a leadership seminar or a simulator course) is brought into an organization, it must be ensured that what was learned is really wanted and supported in the organization and can therefore be implemented and sustained. Training without organizational support for transferring and sustaining the acquired knowledge and skills is a waste of time. The effects of training without subsequent opportunities and support to use the new knowledge or behavior will fade with time. Taking part in a training and instruction does not guarantee success. Managers and teachers often assume "you know it, now do it;" but knowing about something and doing that something are not the same, i.e., knowledge $\neq$ behavior.

Moreover, when training leads to behavior that stands in contrast to the predominant organizational culture, trainees probably cannot use or implement what they have learned. That can have a demotivating effect and lead to tensions within the team. For example, when after a course on hand hygiene, a physician tries to implement new guidelines in his department, he might experience negative reactions. After a few days, the old habit might then win.

When organizations implement training programs, transfer into everyday practice must be planned well in advance by answering such questions as: How is it ensured that employees are "allowed and encouraged" to use what they have learned? Are there refresher courses on order to prevent the fading of behavioral change? Will peers and supervisors also take the training?

16.2.2 Team Training and CRM

The "human factor" might be compared to Janus, the two-faced god of Roman mythology looking in opposite directions (Fig. 1.2): On the one side, it is usually involved in the error chain in some ways. On the other side, people are a key resource that helps avoid errors or recognize them and mitigate their effect. In acknowledgment of these two aspects of the human factor, civil and military aviation tried early on to use this positive side as part of an overall package of interventions and to train pilots' communication and teamwork skills (Wiener et al. 1993). In recent decades, the interest in those skills that are not linked to clinical knowledge but are essential for safe patient care has also grown steadily in healthcare. Basically, these skills belong in two broad categories:

- Interpersonal skills, such as communication, teamwork, and leadership
- Cognitive skills, such as situational awareness, planning, decision-making, and task management

The cognitive demands of pilots and anesthesiologists have similarities (e.g., dynamic decision-making under uncertainty and time pressure, the importance of monitoring, teamwork with ad hoc teams, rapid response to critical events; see Chap. 14). Therefore, the training approach of aviation (cockpit resource management, later crew resource management, or CRM) was initially adapted to the needs of anesthesiology and more specifically to the management of incidents (e.g., Gaba et al. 2006; Anesthesia Crisis Resource Management; ACRM). After positive results within anesthesiology, the concept was adopted by other acute care disciplines and implemented in training programs. The original ACRM training and related emergency management training have similar characteristics to simulator sessions in aviation. Typically, they include:

- A clinical problem that needs to be solved; often involving a high-risk low-frequency circumstance
- Teamwork and time pressure within the simulated case

- Guided debriefing of the case often assisted by video
- Considerations given to promoting lessons learned in simulation to real-world clinical care

Despite some fundamental similarities between aviation and acute care (Chap. 14), it is apparent that the knowledge, experience, and evaluation in those domains are not directly comparable in terms of safety-related behavior (Helmreich and Merrit 1998; Randell 2003; Sexton et al. 2000). Thus, various research groups began to identify and empirically validate those skills and behaviors that are important for safe patient care in the context of healthcare high-risk areas. Within these research programs, key *behavioral marker*s were identified. Behavioral markers, when articulated well, are specific for each work area and each professional group because while certain broad categories may be generalized across disciplines (e.g., situation awareness, use of resources, etc.), the behavioral descriptions within specialty (e.g., anesthesia, surgery, etc.) must include job-specific considerations (overview in Manser et al. (2012)).

According to existing data, team training is effective, depending on organizational and other conditions (e.g., Morey et al. 2002; Salas et al. 2006; Schmutz and Manser 2013). Training can be transferred into daily work (Kirkpatrick level 3), which is shown in a reduction of complications, length of hospital stay, and mortality (Kirkpatrick level 4; Boet et al. 2014) or even a return on investment (Moffatt-Bruce et al. 2015).

Despite the ever-widening evidence base that speaks for a comprehensive introduction of team training, it is still not the norm for hospitals and emergency services organizations to have physicians, nurses, and emergency medical services personnel learn to communicate, make team decisions, manage workload and resources and coordinate actions in a simulator setting, or practice and reflect on relevant team behaviors. Reasons for the hesitant acceptance could be:

- *Aspects of organizational culture*: The meaningfulness of team training is still not generally accepted, despite a plethora of data. There is a reluctance to replace authoritarian structures with more cooperative forms of work. Deep-seated habits of thought and behavior patterns need to be questioned and changed (McCulloch et al. 2009).
- *Profit-oriented environment*: Investing in safety-related training does not lead to immediate or clear causal results. Decisions made in favor of economics are often contrary to human factors and teamwork principles.
- *Personal fears*: Training in interdisciplinary teams is always a personal challenge. To overcome traditional disciplinary, specialty, and professional boundaries (and possibly cherished prejudices) is not easy.

The aviation industry had some of the same challenges. To surmount such resistance, seven factors for systematically preparing, implementing, and sustaining team training and improving performance have been identified and proposed (Salas et al. 2009):

- Align team training objectives and safety aims with organizational goals.
- Provide organizational support for the team training initiative.
- Get frontline care leaders on board.
- Prepare the environment and trainees for team training.
- Determine required resources and time commitment and ensure their availability.
- Facilitate application of trained teamwork skills on the job.
- Measure the effectiveness of the team training program.

This means that team training needs the full and long-term support of institutional leadership. The culture of acute care and lifelong habits cannot be changed in a training regimen of 1 or 2 days. It can take years of training and refresher training until effects of training programs are deeply rooted in the organizational structure. Even the best results of team training fade with time – the decision to offer team training therefore requires a long-term training plan with recurring training experiences.

16.2.3 Use of Simulation in Acute Care

Simulation is often used for team training in healthcare. The term *simulator* usually refers a device that is used to represent a patient or a part of the patient (e.g., eyes, heart, etc.). Full body (mannequin) simulators are used extensively in team or crisis management training (Fig. 16.4). A patient simulator (*full-scale simulator*) is a

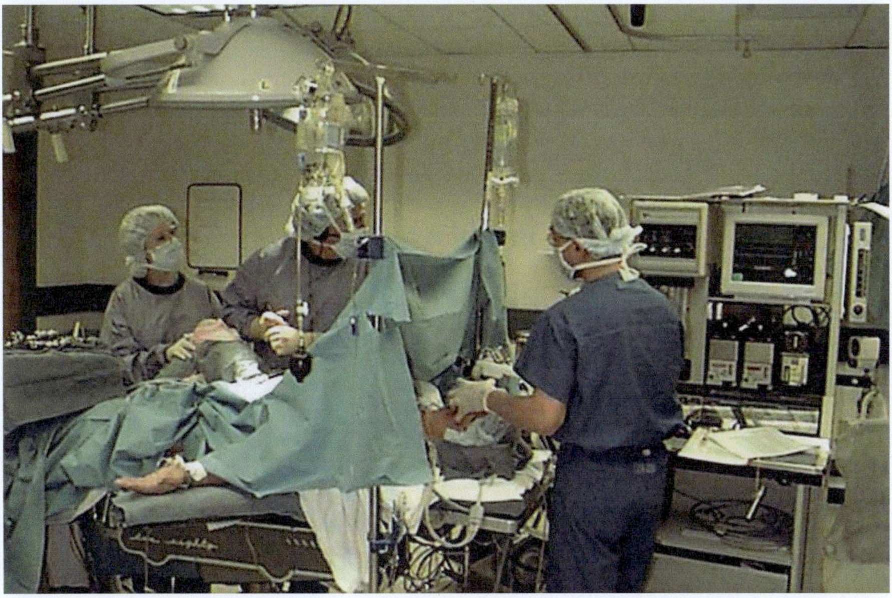

Fig. 16.4 Simulation-based training of medical emergencies. Simulation makes it possible to provide healthcare providers with realistic and challenging scenarios (Courtesy of Center for Medical Simulation in Boston)

combination of a mannequin and a control computer by which the simulation is controlled manually or based on pharmacological and physiological models (Fig. 16.4). Currently available mannequins cover all age groups (premature babies, infants, adolescents, adults) and a variety of clinical conditions (e.g., trauma, birth). Many models are self-sufficient with respect to power and gas supply and run wirelessly.

Under the headline of "simulation," however, many more methods than just the use of patient simulators can be found. On one hand, in skill-based training, technical skills like intubation, central venous catheter line insertion, umbilical venous catheter, or cricothyrotomy can be learned using simple models (*part task trainer*). On the other hand, in rule-based training, algorithms for patient care can be trained by using software (e.g., for training CPR algorithms). In decision-based simulator training, differentiated emergency diagnosis and therapy (e.g., treatment of anaphylaxis, care of trauma patients) can be practiced. The ever-advancing development of computer technology also makes it possible to simulate techniques with a surprising degree of realism: diagnostics (e.g., transesophageal echo (TEE)), interventions (e.g., cardiac catheterization), and surgery (e.g., laparoscopy). Thanks to simulation, the former teaching concept of "see one, do one" becomes "see many, train even more." In addition to scientific evidence on the effectiveness of simulator training programs, simulation as a teaching concept has thus obtained an ethical component: Any process that can be learned with a reasonably good simulation alternative should not be practiced first on a patient (Ziv et al. 2003). While the exact nature of the further development and employment of simulation is not foreseeable, in the future, patients may no longer be treated by inexperienced beginners, but by physicians who have practiced the respective examination technique, intervention, or surgical procedure extensively using simulation.

Beyond full-scale simulators or part task trainers, humans themselves can act as simulators: "Standardized patients" are actors who are trained to behave like patients with real diseases. Standardized patients are used mostly in the education of medical students where access to real patients with a specific pathophysiology may prove difficult. Here, the focus usually lies on a controlled learning process for the physician-patient (or nurse-patient) relationship. In order to improve the communication and ethical skills of their students early in their career, more and more educational institutions have established programs using standardized patients.

16.2.4 A Learning Tool: Debriefing

Organizational learning is often triggered by incidents or other unpleasant experiences. Learning after the event can be promoted by a post-experience analytic process. This process is called "debriefing." While many authors write about the debriefing process, not all use the term *debriefing* to denote the same thing. Debriefing is variously defined as (Lederman 1992):

- Appraisal and generation of knowledge from experiences in work-related tasks
- Learning through reflection on a simulation experience
- Emotional recovery from a critical incident

16.2.4.1 Debriefing of Work-Related Tasks

In the context of *work-related tasks*, debriefing provides healthcare providers with the basis for understanding why and how the new knowledge they acquired relates to what they already know. Team performance can be enhanced greatly by implementing regular debriefings at the end of every shift. A short summary of the day's tasks and problems, positive and negative experiences, and ensuing consequences for the team's future work will bond the knowledge of the team members. In aviation, this type of debriefing is normal and obligatory; in healthcare this opportunity for learning and team building is rarely employed.

16.2.4.2 Debriefing After Critical Incidents

Mass casualties or a patient's death but also severe incidents during treatment can pose an emotional strain on the caregivers resulting in a variety of stress reactions (Chap. 9). In order to avoid serious long-term consequences (e.g., post-traumatic stress disorder), many organizations now offer a multistep coping concept following a critical event (e.g., *critical incident stress debriefing*; Hammond and Brooks 2001). Debriefings help individuals to come to terms with a situation by letting them describe what happened, allowing for emotional ventilation and providing emotional support for team members. In addition, early signs of a stress response syndrome can be identified (Hoff and Adamowski 1998; James and Gilliland 2001). Depending on the situation, debriefing after a critical incident can aim at:

- Awareness of emotional strain
- Review of actions in the situation and their consequences
- Support for emotional coping
- Support for the team
- Teaching and learning

16.2.4.3 Debriefing in Simulator Training

While task-related debriefing is often skipped due to a lack of time or other adverse conditions, it is firmly established in the context of simulator training. Debriefing is regarded as the heart and soul of simulator training. Debriefing helps to facilitate learning for those who have been through the experience and those who have watched it (Dismukes et al. 2006). This process involves getting the participants to tell the story the way they experienced it, describing the feelings elicited by the experience, and reflecting on their own taken-for-granted or implicit assumptions, mental models, and professional work practices (Dieckmann et al. 2012). In an environment that feels both psychologically safe and clinically challenging, professionals improve their behavioral, communication, coordination, and decision-making skills by reflecting on their experience and considering what assumptions, rules, and practices are serving them well and which ones they might want to change.

The purpose of debriefing is not to lecture or expound but instead to facilitate self-awareness, maximize group interaction, and foster idea development (Steinwachs 1992). Leaders who debrief staff members cannot do this by keeping to conventional hierarchical patterns. In contrast, it is necessary to learn specific competencies: Debriefings demand high role flexibility, as one is obliged to be a teacher, critic, moderator, and enquirer simultaneously (McDonell et al. 1997). If possible, every team member should participate in the debriefing process. A trained debriefer can help the team by providing positive feedback on successful performance as well as surfacing topics around things gone wrong – all of which is open to discussion and consideration during the debriefing. It is important to build a "safe container" in simulation and debriefings, i.e., to create an environment of trust and openness where mistakes are not crimes to be punished, but mysteries to be solved (Rudolph et al. 2014). Often the issue of "personal failure" and inadequacy will arise; therefore, it is especially important to maintain the safe container throughout the simulation and debriefing experience to enable the required personal confidence of participants to deal with critical situations in the future. Several recent publications cover all aspects of debriefing in a post-experiential simulated setting (Dieckmann et al. 2012; Mort and Donahue 2004; Rudolf et al. 2006; Eppich and Cheng 2015).

16.3 Learning from Incidents: Reporting and Accident Analysis

Safety culture is an "informed culture" (Reason 1997) that relies on safety-relevant information from incidents, errors, or process deviations. In the event of an incident or accident, valuable information for both the organization and the individual becomes available. This information, as accurate as can be, must be collected and made accessible for the organization. One important tool for collecting safety-relevant information is the incident reporting system. Reports should be made on any event that harmed or might have harmed a patient, exposed the patient to an unnecessary risk, or could have done so. It doesn't matter if the event was preventable or not nor if it happened due to errors and mistakes or due to technical failure.

Using the nomenclature of patient safety, reports can be made on any of the following:

- *Accident:* An event that results in a patient's death or being harmed. Reporting accidents is problematic for reasons discussed in Sect. 16.3.2.
- *Incident:* An unintended event, which reduces, or could reduce, the safety margin for a patient. The improper connection of the PCEA pump is an example for such an incident. Incidents can be triggered by individual errors, the patient's pathophysiology, or organizational-process deficits.
- *Near miss:* An error or mistake that could have harmed a patient but did not.
- *Adverse event:* a harmful event caused by treatment rather than by the patient's medical condition. Adverse events can be preventable or not.
- *Critical incident:* An event that increases the likelihood of adverse events.
- *Error:* An action (or omission of action) with a deviation from plan, a wrong plan, or no plan. The result of the error is not relevant for its definition.

Considering these different definitions, the terms *error reporting system* or *incident reporting* seem inadequate as not all safety-relevant events are caused by error or have the potential for injury or death. For historic reasons, reporting systems in healthcare are called "incident reporting." We will use the term incident reporting system (IRS) here.

The technique of critical incident analysis was first introduced by Flanagan in 1954 as an outgrowth of his studies in aviation psychology (Flanagan 1954). Incident analysis was further developed by the aviation domain into a voluntary reporting system that collected, analyzed, and responded to aviation safety incidents. The incident reporting technique was first applied in the medical community to address the issue of anesthetic equipment malfunction (Blum 1971) and was adapted a few years later to uncover patterns of frequently occurring incidents in an anesthesia department (Cooper et al. 1978; Williamson et al. 1993). The first organization in healthcare to start using the critical incident technique on a national-scale plan was the Australian Patient Safety Foundation. As early as 1987, the Foundation launched the Australian Incident Monitoring Study (AIMS; Webb et al. 1993) to collect information on mishaps during and after anesthesia. The AIMS was a leading-edge project in incident reporting in high-stakes medical care and has inspired many societies and organizations to follow suit. Today, World Health Organization (WHO) guidelines for the introduction and management of incident reporting exist (WHO 2005), accompanied by a vast body of literature. Although incident reporting has been established in almost every healthcare organization, underreporting is still a problem, and reports are often not systematically prioritized and analyzed.

16.3.1 Principles for Incident Reporting Systems

Organizations can learn most from an incident or accident if the focus lies on organizational and contextual factors. Using the information collected in an incident reporting system, elements that promote "human error" can be analyzed and that analysis converted into valuable knowledge for an organization. The most worthy goal is not punishment of individuals but is the prevention of accidents and incidents.

If a reporting system is to be used in that way, the organization and especially the analysis team should be aware of following principles and limitations:

- The analysis aims only at the *prevention* of future incidents, not at legal aspects or liability. The question is never: "Who is to blame?" Incident reporting systems need solution-focused thinking as a proactive approach.
- Written reports and interviews give a *subjective account* of the person reporting on what happened, not a comprehensive overview of "what really happened." If a detailed account of events is important, other tools are needed.
- Incident reporting systems are an *employee participation* program – they work best when employees are willing to freely share their knowledge without fear or reprisal.

- Incident reporting systems alone are useless. They must be part of *clinical risk management* and quality assurance.

Incident reporting systems can only be helpful if the surrounding organizational culture supports a safety culture with a systemic approach. The basis for the collection of information about incidents and minimal events is a formalized reporting system. If it is to be successful, it has to be (e.g., WHO 2005, 2011; Leape 2002):

- *Voluntary*: In contrast to the obligation to report accidents and mandatory legal aspects of an incident, an IRS depends on the voluntary report of members. Organizations can facilitate voluntary reporting if they communicate clearly to their members that information submitted will be appreciated and not used against them.
- *Anonymous*: Incidents can be reported without any link to the sender. There are different opinions as to whether reports must be anonymous, but scholars and practitioners agree that the filing of anonymous reports must be possible.
- *Confidential*: Any information concerning people involved, events, and actions taken will be handled confidentially as the evaluation process is undertaken.
- *Non-punitive*: No report will have disciplinary consequences. Whoever reports an error or an incident must not fear punishment by the employer.
- *No cases pending in court*: In many countries, the question remains unsettled as to whether or not legal authorities can access and use data that has been entered into an IRS (e.g., in many European countries, various US states). In these countries and states, any accident pending court examination should not be reported.
- *Support by the management*: Whenever an IRS is introduced, the management has to support it strongly. The implementation is a top-down process. Leaders have to demonstrate the advantage of investigating, understanding, and taking action to ameliorate or eliminate errors and make the value of an IRS clear to all.

If a voluntary reporting system is to be successful, the organization has to take heed of the following practical steps (Billings et al. 1998; Runciman et al. 1993; Mahajan 2010; WHO 2011):

- A hospital/healthcare institution should communicate relentlessly and convincingly to their staff that a policy of "no blame" is to be pursued. Staff members must be confident that no disciplinary action will be taken in reaction to a report, except in cases of gross misconduct or criminal negligence.
- All clinical and nursing staff should receive training and periodic refresher training on risk management and incident reporting. The initial training should be followed by continuing education on the aims and importance of risk management and incident reporting and the positive differences it has made in the organization.
- Every healthcare provider, regardless of profession and rank, should be aware of the fact that safety cannot be delegated to a single person (e.g., to the risk manager). A clear statement should be made that all members are responsible for reporting

- Incident reporting forms should be "user-friendly" and readily accessible for entry. Compliance with regular reporting will decrease if staff members are forced to make unnecessary or needlessly complex efforts.
- Staff members should be encouraged, even praised, for reporting any incident they find worth communicating, irrespective of the assumed relevance or severity.
- Staff members should receive regular feedback on the consequences of their report.

16.3.2 Introduction of an Incident Reporting System

Recommendations for planning and implementing an IRS include seven steps that can be adapted to local conditions (e.g., WHO 2005):

1. Decision to implement an IRS
2. Planning
3. IRS introduction
4. Implementation of analysis and evaluation
5. Implementation of changes by risk management and units within the institution
6. Feedback about reports and changes
7. Evaluation and continuous improvement of the experience with the IRS

A report entered into the incident reporting system initiates a cyclical process (Fig. 16.5):

- Employees give information about the incident.
- The information is analyzed in terms of systemic and human factors.
- Options for actions are generated.
- From the possible options, local solutions are selected and implemented. Preventive strategies are determined.
- Employees are informed about the results.
- The effectiveness of change is monitored over time.

In addition to an observable change in processes, a report may also trigger learning within the organization: The knowledge about causes of incidents and solution strategies should remain in the organization beyond the memory of individuals (Fig. 16.5). In addition, an IRS can also help to change the organizational culture. Safety culture is strengthened when (1) the questions asked are "What happened, how, and why?" instead of "Who is to blame?" and (2) when employees experience that long-term, sustainable, and systemically effective solutions are generated.

16.3.2.1 Define the Content of Reports

The purpose of an IRS is a detailed documentation of *what* happened, *how* it happened, and *why* it presumably happened. From a technical perspective, an IRS can consist of paper-based forms or a network- or web-based system. The reporting

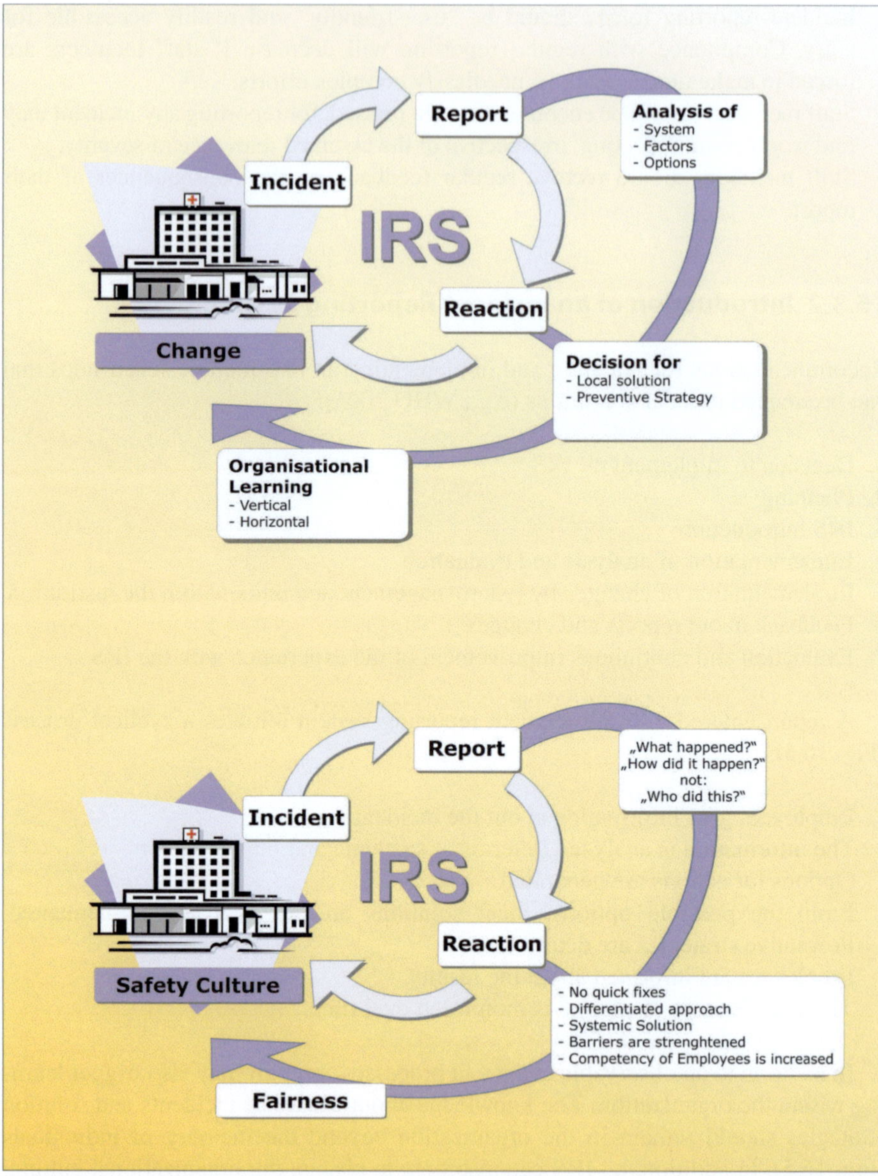

Fig. 16.5 Phases of incident reporting. A message initiates a cyclical process that results in organizational change. The information about incidents triggers organizational learning (*top of figure*). Analysis from a systemic perspective, a differentiated and systemically oriented response, strengthens the confidence of employees in the reliability and fairness of the incident reporting system. This trust is a prerequisite for the establishment of a sustainable safety culture (*lower figure*)

form should provide room for narratives rather than simple check boxes for default options.

As for the content of the report, the value of a report depends on the extent to which it is possible to elicit relevant contextual information in addition to the description of the event itself. Therefore, the documentation should cover details about situational context, function, and experience of the healthcare professionals involved, the flow of information, and actions of the healthcare provider. Information about how decisions arose, what role teamwork played in the incident, and which information was accessible are just as important as those questions concerning equipment, drugs, and diagnostic or therapeutic steps. The previous history of an incident may further help to illuminate a situation. Great care should be taken with the adequate formulation of questions and categories. This is especially true for human factor-related categories. For example, discipline unique terms such as *situational awareness* are likely to seem incomprehensible psychological jargon for the average healthcare provider; overly generalized terms such as *communication* may be too general because communication will always contribute to a critical situation in one way or another. In relation to improving those categories, it may be useful to discover "Was anyone else aware of the situation?" and, respectively, "Did anyone have relevant information who might have shared it but did not?"

In addition to providing insight into factors contributing to unsafe conditions, an IRS also presents an opportunity to look for recoveries from unwanted situations. A category "recovery" may be helpful in documenting the strategy by which the incident was managed without patient harm. In addition, reporting systems should allow for the reporter to make suggestions as to how similar incidents can be prevented in the future. Questions concerning a perceived need for change, e.g., high priority, etc., might be helpful too, because healthcare providers likely have significant insight into the system's weaknesses and strengths.

16.3.2.2 Promote Change

The documentation of incidents is only one step in the process of organizational learning. In order to be able to draw consequences from an incident, the following steps have to be clarified: which group within the organization will evaluate and investigate the reports, how will the evaluations and investigations be conducted, and how will the results be provided to the organization. It is recommended that investigations be conducted by a group of members who have a position of trust within the organization. The main tasks of this group consist of the investigating, classifying, reporting, and recommending. The IRS evaluation and investigation group should not consist of managers. Its task ends with the making of recommendations. Then, it is up to the managers to implement change and provide staff with the necessary information. It is vital for developing ongoing trust and respect that IRS reports show results visible to those who reported.

The IRS can uncover singular errors or problem constellations leading to error(s) and indicates which resources were insufficient, unavailable, or mismatched. Every case is potentially an indicator for a general structural problem. If a similar problem is encountered repeatedly, the assumption of a systematic error is probable. Solutions and recommendations generated vis-à-vis an investigation can show where and how resources can be activated or upgraded, training is needed, systems that need adjusting, etc.

The study of recovery strategies and successful management of critical situations is the second equally important aspect of IRS. "What saved the day?" is the appropriate question to ask when an organization wants to learn how a potentially dangerous situation was prevented from progressing to a bad outcome (Staender 2000). Not only the weak aspects of systems but also the innovative activities that empower humans at the "sharp end" to perform effectively provide a wealth of information that will certainly help to improve patient safety.

16.3.3 System Analysis of Accidents

If severe incidents or accidents occur, the usual approach continues to blame a clinician or clinicians and make them pay with reputation and, possibly, money and career. If the organization wants to learn from these cases, a structured approach to the analysis of incidents or accidents is needed that focuses on the multitude of contributing factors without denying responsibility.

A frequently used method, the London Protocol (Taylor-Adams and Vincent 2004), was developed based on the notion of the error chain (Reason 1990) and the system view (Chap. 3). This approach makes a lot of sense because the experience in healthcare is that institutional and task problems occur more often than individual problems. A systems view helps categorize and organize the process of incident analysis. Important steps (Fig. 16.6) are to:

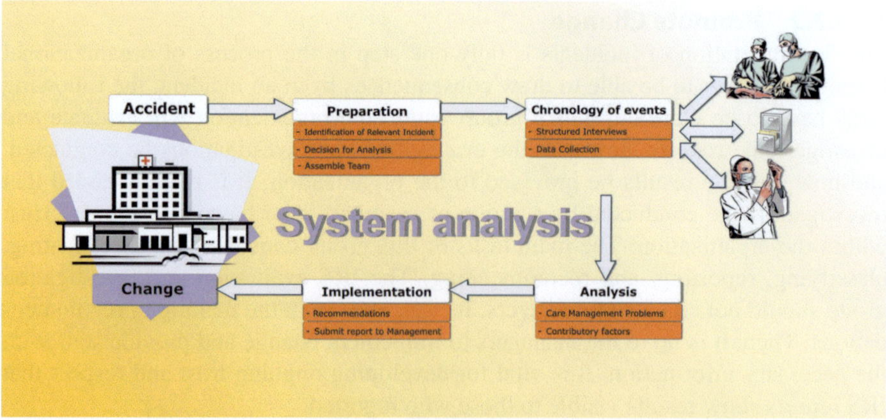

Fig. 16.6 System analysis according to the "London Protocol": in contrast to incident reporting systems, the case analysis can interact with the people involved and collect the data on site. This allows for incorporating of diverse perspectives, which in turn leads to a more nuanced analysis of accident causation

- *Identify incidents relevant for analysis*: An obvious departure from good practice will be the starting point, whether a patient was harmed or not.
- *Decide to conduct a thorough analysis*: System analysis will need time and staffing. For that a management decision is needed – either generally or for each new case. As the objective of system analysis is change, effort should only be put in when the organization is willing to implement results. The analysis of cases where the patient died or was severely injured can bring staff into conflict with their own interest in legal investigations; so here time and form of analysis should be chosen with care (and legal advice).
- *Collect all relevant data*: Patient charts, material, reports, interviews, etc., help answer the question, what exactly was done? Also collect information about clinical standards, guidelines, and standard operating procedures to answer the question "How should things be done?" The analysis team needs access to all data, and they need to be trusted by all stakeholders.
- *Assemble data in a comprehensive way*: One useful tool is a time-actor diagram. A complex event is broken down into steps of action or elements with each element comprising one entry in the time-actor diagram. The idea is to find agreement about "what happened" before trying to figure out "why." Usually it will be possible to reach consent on "what," while the answers to "why" can plausibly differ.
- *Analyze the contributing factors*: Now the actual analysis can start. Ask which factors contributed to the event or one of its elements. It is important to conduct this analysis in a systematic way and not just stop with the first factor that comes to mind. A list of contributing factors will help to consider all levels of the organization, the task, and the people involved. Identify direct factors that immediately led to the incident (active errors) and indirect or "latent" factors that contributed to it (Chap. 3). A more in-depth analysis will continue to ask "why" repeatedly, so that the answer to the first and subsequent why-questions is a potential starting point for new questions.
- *Derive actions from the analysis*: Identify solutions that prevent that kind of incident. And identify solutions that help the organization work more safely. When the team finds (and reports) processes that did not contribute to the incident but can be improved, this form of organizational learning tends to work quite well.
- *Write a report*: Usually the analysis team does not have the power to implement changes, so they need to write a short conclusive report that shares their results, consequences, and recommendations that come from the analysis. Changes, if warranted, will come from those with the ability and position to decide.

As in the analysis of incidents, the system analysis is only useful if the outlined process is followed by changes. But failure to act on recommendations is only one of the reasons why the barriers to the application of the method are high. Analyzing incidents in this way takes time – especially the collection of data, as documents and data have to be reviewed and members of staff likely have to be interviewed. The actual analysis needs a team competent with human factors and clinical issues. On the other hand, Taylor-Adams and Vincent (2004) stress that a *consistent and structured* approach to severe incidents, including interviews with staff, is less threatening to staff members involved in the incident. Furthermore, the method can promote greater openness in the organization by focusing on the system perspective.

16.4 Learning for Safety in a Nutshell

- A learning organization is an organization that considers change to be normal and has strategies for continuous development. Individual employees, teams, and the organization as a whole are in a continuous improvement process with respect to the structure of the organization and the behavior and knowledge of employees.
- Rather than responding to change and uncertainty with strict rules, learning organizations try to establish structures and processes that allow them flexibility in learning and proactive behavior. Systems thinking is the cornerstone of a learning organization.
- Learning in organizations can take the forms of single-loop learning, double-loop learning, or deutero-learning and can lead to profound changes.
- For organizations and individuals, it is easier to learn something new than to relearn.
- A well-trained and risk-aware staff is the key resource for safe work and for the prevention, detection, and mitigation of errors.
- Since teamwork plays a crucial role for highly reliable patient care, training should not be limited to medical and technical knowledge and skills but also include behavioral aspects of patient care such as team planning, organizing, communicating, decision-making, and coordinating resources and actions.
- Compared with other human factors interventions that can be done before a system is made operational, training is a weak solution. Design trumps training.
- Team training requires planning how to transfer lessons learned to the organization and management of care. The culture of medical care and lifelong habits can be changed, but it will take time and commitment.
- Simulator-based team training allows participants to exercise realistic management of medical emergencies. An essential part of this training format is skilled instructors who implement systematic debriefing of simulated cases.
- Data from incident reports can be used to find potential sources of error and uncover system vulnerabilities that have not yet been recognized.
- Incident reporting systems will only be able to fulfill all their promises when they are embedded in an organizational safety culture and are supported at all levels of the organization.
- If an organization wants to learn from serious incidents or accidents, it needs a systematic, structured approach that analyzes all factors (organizational, systems, clinical skill, resources, team, individual, documentation, etc.) that contributed to the accident.

References

Amalberti R, Mosneron-Dupin F (1997) Facteurs humains et fiabilité: quelles démarches pratiques? Octares, Toulouse

Argyris C, Schön DA (1996) Organizational learning II: theory, method, and pracitce. Addison-Wesley

Argyris C, Schön DA (1999) Die lernende organisation. Grundlagen, methode, praxis. Klett-Cotta, Stuttgart

Bateson G (1972) Steps towards an ecology of mind. Chandler, New York

Billings C, Cook RI, Woods DD, Miller C (1998) Incident reporting systems in medicine and experience with the aviation safety reporting system. National Patient Safety Foundation at the AMA, Chicago, pp 52–61

Blum LL (1971) Equipment design and "human" limitations. Anesthesiology 35:101–102

Boet S, Bould MD, Fung L, Qosa H, Perrier L, Tavares W, Reeves S, Tricco AC (2014) Transfer of learning and patient outcome in simulated crisis resource management: a systematic review. Can J Anesth 61(6):571–582

Cooper JB, Newbower RS, Long CD, McPeek B (1978) Preventable anesthesia mishaps: a study of human factors. Anesthesiology 49:399–406

Cosby E (2013) Review article: the role of practice guidelines and evidence-based medicine in perioperative patient safety. Can J Anaesth 60:143–151

Davies HTO, Nutley SM (2000) Developing learning organisations in the new NHS. BMJ 320:998–1001

Dieckmann P, Friis SM, Lippert A et al (2012) Goals, success factors, and barriers for simulation – based learning: a qualitative interview study in health care. Simula Gaming 43(5):627–647

Dismukes RK, Gaba DM, Howard SK (2006) So many roads: facilitated debriefing in healthcare. Simul Healthc 1:1–3

Eccles M, Grimshaw J, Walker A, Johnston M, Pitts N (2005) Changing the behavior of healthcare professionals: the use of theory in promoting the uptake of research findings. J Clin Epidemiol 58:107–112

Eppich W, Cheng A (2015) Promoting Excellence and Reflective Learning in Simulation (PEARLS): development and rationale for a blended approach to health care simulation debriefing. Simul Healthc 10(2):106–115

Flanagan JC (1954) The critical incident technique. Psychol Bull 51:327–358

Fletcher GC, McGeorge P, Flin R, Glavin R, Maran N (2002) The role of non-technical skills in anaesthesia: a review of current literature. Br J Anaesth 88:418–429

Flin R, Maran N (2004) Identifying and training non-technical skills for teams in acute medicine. Qual Saf Health Care 13(Suppl):i80–i84

Gaba DM, Fish KJ, Howard SK, Burden A (2006) Crisis management in anesthesiology, 2nd edn. Elsevier Ltd, Oxford

Garvin DA, Edmondson AC, Gino F (2008) Is yours a learning organization? Harv Bus Rev 86(3):109–116

Grimshaw JM, Shirran L, Thomas RE, Mowatt G, Fraser C, Bero L, Grilli R, Harvey E, Oxman A, O'Brien MA (2001) Changing provider behavior: an overview of systematic reviews of interventions. Med Care 39:II2–II45

Hammond J, Brooks J (2001) Helping the helpers: the role of critical incident stress management. Crit Care 5:315–317

Helmreich B, Merrit AC (1998) Culture at work in aviation and medicine. National, organizational and professional influences. Ashgate Publishing Ltd, Vermont

Hoff LA, Adamowski K (1998) Creating excellence in crisis care: a guide to effective training and program designs. Jossey–Bass, San Francisco

James RK, Gilliland BE (2001) Crisis intervention strategies, 4th edn. Wadsworth/Thomson Learning, Belmont

Leape L (2002) Reporting of adverse events. N Engl J Med 347(20):1633–1638

Lederman LC (1992) Debriefing: toward a systematic assessment of theory and practice. Simul Gaming 23:145–160
Mahajan RP (2010) Critical incident reporting and learning. Br J Anaesth 105(1):69–75
Manser T (2009) Teamwork and patient safety in dynamic domains of healthcare: a review of the literature. Acta Anaesthesiol Scand 53:143–151
Manser T, Perry J, Schmutz J (2012) Verhalten ist messbar: Behavioural Marker Systeme und Kompetenzentwicklung [measuring behavior: behavioral marker systems and decelopment of competencies]. In: St.Pierre M, Breuer G (eds) Simulation in der Medizin [Simulation in health care]. Springer, Heidelberg, pp 169–180
McCulloch P, Mishra A, Handa A, Dale T, Hirst G, Catchpole K (2009) The effects of aviation-style non-technical skills training on technical performance and outcome in the operating theatre. Qual Saf Health Care 18(2):109–115
McDonell LK, Kimberly KJ, Dismukes RK (1997) Facilitating LOS debriefings: a training manual. NASA technical memorandum 112192, 1997
Moffatt-Bruce SD, Hefner JL, Mekhjian H, et al. (2015) What is the return on investment for implementation of a crew resource management program at an academic medical center? Am J Med Qual. [Epub ahead of print]
Morey J, Simon R, Jay GD, Wears RL, Salisbury M, Dukes KA, Berns SD (2002) Error reduction and performance improvement in the emergency department through formal teamwork training: evaluation results of the MedTeams project. HSR Health Serv Res 37(6):1553–1581
Mort TC, Donahue SP (2004) Debriefing: the basics. In: Dunn WF (ed) Simulators in critical care and beyond. Society of critical care, Des Plaines, pp 76–83
Randell R (2003) Medicine and aviation: a review of the comparison. Methods Inf Med 42(4):433–436
Reader T, Flin R, Lauche K, Cuthbertson BH (2006) Non-technical skills in the intensive care unit. Br J Anaesth 96:551–559
Reason J (1990) Human error. Cambridge University Press, Cambridge
Reason J (1997) Managing the risks of organizational accidents. Ashgate, Aldershot
Rudolf JW, Simon R, Dufresne RL, Raemer D (2006) There's no such thing as "non-judgemental" debriefing: a theory and method for debriefing with good judgement. Simul Healthc 1:49–55
Rudolph JW, Raemer DB, Simon R (2014) Establishing a safe container for learning in simulation: the role of the presimulation briefing. Simul Healthc 9(6):339–349
Runciman WB, Sellen A, Webb RA, Williamson JA, Currie M, Morgan C, Russell WJ (1993) The Australian Incident Monitoring Study. Errors, incidents and accidents in anaesthetic practice. Anaesth Intensive Care 21:506–519
Rushmer R, Davies HTO (2004) Unlearning in health care. Qual Saf Health Care 13(SupplII):ii10–ii15
Russ S, Rout S, Sevdalis N, Moorthy K, Darzi A, Vincent C (2013) Do safety checklists improve teamwork and communication in the operating room? A systematic review. Ann Surg 258(6):856–871
Salas E, Wilson KA, Burke CS, Wightman DC (2006) Does crew resource management training work? An update, an extension, and some critical needs. Hum Factors 48(2):392–412
Salas E, Almeida SA, Salisbury M, King H, Lazzara EH, Lyons R, Wilson KA, Almeida PA, McQuillan R (2009) What are the critical success factors for team training in health care? Jt Comm J Qual Patient Saf 35(8):398–405
Schmutz J, Manser T (2013) Do team processes really have an effect on clinical performance? A systematic literature review. Br J Anaesth 110(4):529–544
Schön DA (1975) Deutero-learning in organizations: learning for increased effectiveness. Organ Dyn 4:2–16
Schüpfer G, Gförer R, Schleppers A (2007) Anästhesisten lernen – lernen Institutionen auch? [Anaesthetists learn–do institutions also learn? Importance of institutional learning and corporate culture in clinics]. Anaesthesist 56:983–991
Schuster M, McGlynn E, Brook RH (1998) How good is the quality of health care in the United States? Milbank Q 76:563

Senge PM (1990) The fifth discipline. Doubleday Business, New York

Sexton JB, Thomas EJ, Helmreich RL (2000) Error, stress, and teamwork in medicine and aviation: cross sectional surveys. BMJ 320:745–749

Sherwood D (2000) The unlearning organization. Bus Strateg Rev 11:31–40

Staender S (2000) Critical incident reporting. With a view on approaches in anaesthesiology. In: Vincent C, de Mol B (eds) Safety in medicine. Pergamon Elsevier Science, Amsterdam/New York, pp 65–82

Steinwachs B (1992) How to facilitate a debriefing. Simul Gaming 23:186–195

Stinson L, Paerson D, Lucas B (2006) Developing a learning culture: twelve tips for individuals, teams and organizations. Med Teach 28(4):309–312

Taylor-Adams S, Vincent C (2004) Systems analysis of clinical incidents: the London protocol. Clinical Safety Research Unit/University College, London. Available at: http://www.csrandorg.uk

Webb RK, Currie M, Morgan CA, Williamson JA, Mackay P, Russell WJ, Runciman WB (1993) The Australian Incident Monitoring Study: an analysis of 2000 incident reports. Anaesth Intensive Care 21:520–528

Wiener E, Kanki B, Helmreich R (1993) Cockpit resource management. Academic Press, San Diego

Williamson JA, Webb RK, Sellen A, Runciman WB (1993) Human failure: an analysis of 2000 incident reports. Anaesth Intensive Care 21:678–683

Wilson KA, Burke CS, Priest HA, Salas E (2005) Promoting health care safety through training high reliability teams. Qual Saf Health Care 14:303–309

World Health Organization (WHO) (2005) WHO draft guidelines for adverse event reporting and learning systems. From information to action. [online document] URL: http://www.who.int/patientsafety/events/05/Reporting_Guidelines.pdf. Accessed 10 Oct 2010

World Health Organization (WHO) (2011) Patient safety curriculum guide. Multi-professional Edition. http://apps.who.int/iris/bitstream/10665/44641/1/9789241501958_eng.pdf. Access 22 Nov 2015

Yule S, Flin R, Paterson-Brown S, Maran N (2006) Non-technical skills for surgeons in the operating room: a review of the literature. Surgery 139:140–149

Ziv A, Wolpe PR, Small SD, Glick S (2003) Simulation-based medical education: an ethical imperative. Acad Med 78(8):783–788

Index

M. St.Pierre et al., *Crisis Management in Acute Care Settings*,
DOI 10.1007/978-3-319-41427-0

MIX
Papier aus verantwortungsvollen Quellen
Paper from responsible sources
FSC® C105338

If you have any concerns about our products,
you can contact us on
ProductSafety@springernature.com

In case Publisher is established outside the EU,
the EU authorized representative is:
Springer Nature Customer Service Center GmbH
Europaplatz 3, 69115 Heidelberg, Germany

Printed by Libri Plureos GmbH
in Hamburg, Germany